Proud to be Flesh

Proud to be Flesh

A Mute Magazine Anthology of Cultural Politics after the Net

edited by
Josephine Berry Slater
and Pauline van Mourik Broekman

with
Michael Corris
Anthony Iles
Benedict Seymour
and Simon Worthington

Mute Publishing in association with Autonomedia

Foreword

Pauline van Mourik Broekman and Simon Worthington

The distillation of 15 years of *Mute* magazine content into one book has been a mammoth task, requiring what sometimes felt like a lifetime's worth of re-reading, re-evaluating and searching for consensus, as we pulled apart our print and web archives and put them together again in a variety of constellations. When this process started, in 2002, we were working towards a very different anthology – provisionally titled *White Cube, Blue Sky* – which covered the relationship between net art and conceptual art (a subject receiving scant analysis back then and, we felt, pregnant with potential *vis à vis* the dearth of critically historicised readings of digital art and culture on offer). That particular compilation sadly fell victim to the resource-hogging juggernaut that is day-to-day magazine production, but its legacy is woven deep into this volume and remains most evident in the chapter entitled 'From Net Art to Conceptual Art and Back'. This present incarnation of the anthology is indebted to Michael Corris who, acting as co-editor to Simon Ford, Josephine Berry Slater and Pauline on that earlier project, lent both historical insight and the all-important spur for us to re-orientate the book into a reflection of the magazine itself.

Proud to be Flesh is not a 'Best of *Mute*'. Rather, it treats the entire back catalogue of *Mute* as its critical arena, exploring how the voices and ideas to which the magazine has played host crystallised into a set of distinct themes through which 'culture and politics after the net' (the magazine's strapline since 2002) might be understood. Crudely put, this rounded on the utopian claims made for digital technologies in general and the internet in particular, subjecting them to a deepening critique, which ever more explicitly considered the socio-economic context created by capitalism. A typical example is the promise of democratic empowerment, via engagement with new media, which reverberated across a continuum from art to politics (discussed here in the chapters 'Democracy and its Demons' and 'The Open Work'). Similarly, the emancipatory figures of the cyborg and, later, the immaterial labourer were said to augur a break in historical time with far-reaching consequences for gender, creativity and work – claims which are dealt with in 'I, Cyborg' and 'Reality Check: Class and Immaterial Labour'. Concepts which emerged when internet discourse had 'matured', but which nonetheless accrued near sacred status as instances of a kind of public good – such as the information commons and, extending into the realm of social movements, horizontal organisation and openness – are tackled in the chapters 'Of Commoners and Criminals' and 'Organising Horizontally'.

All of these themes will be more or less familiar from broader discourses on digital culture. Less immediately obvious are those topics that might be attributed to *Mute*'s location in London, the global heart of the financial services sector *and* the 'creative economy', a frontier space for the aggressive pioneering of neoliberal policies, from the nation state's management of the arts to urban development and social cohesion. This necessitated an analysis of the civic assault suffered under the aegis of 'regeneration' and the antinomies of multiculturalism, and of artists' insinuation into business agendas (detailed in 'Under the Net: The City and the Camp' and 'Assuming the Position: Art and/Against Business' respectively).

By arranging the content of each chapter chronologically, we hope to convey the sense of an evolving conversation and the structural effect certain texts and authors had on the magazine's editorial (which explains some multiple appearances). And, while chapters tend to possess a germ, or concentration point, in particular periods, they also span our publication history, demonstrating the lasting import of their core questions and generating interesting parallels between 'early' and 'late' *Mute*, not all of which were conscious.

Looking back at some of the moments that defined production – at the back-end, as it were – the magazine's history can quite easily be made to fit a certain clichéd image of a '90s creative project. From the negotiations we conducted with the pre-print department at Pearson media group – to use the *Financial Times*' purpose-built plant in Docklands on a test run – to the graft we put into cleaning an old, urine-soaked telephone exchange for the magazine's launch party and the manner in which we subsidised our publishing activities with a mixture of commercial work and government aid, *Mute* looks every inch the do-it-yourself entrepreneurial venture valorised in creative economy doctrine.

And, in many respects, it has been; aside from running as an actual business (rather than a volunteer collective, for example), the magazine's foundational connection to the subjects of art and technology situated our work at the same nexus the British state sought to occupy as it amorously embraced the model of an 'immaterial' economy driven by creativity, knowledge and networks. Gradually moving eastwards from Shoreditch to Brick Lane and then Whitechapel (all of which saw local communities outpriced and displaced by a rapidly expanding 'new' economy hungry for office, retail and leisure space), even the *Mute* office resided at the juncture between the digital economy's public façade and its underside – now dramatically visible as the global economy succumbs under the weight of its own contradictions.

Acknowledgements? It is hard to know where to begin… *Mute* has taken many forms, often in the name of professionalisation, but we have spectacularly failed to terminate the intimate connection between life and work. Loves have been found and lost, passions ignited, children born, and partners and parents have stepped into the breach. To attain even the smallest degree of veracity for this story, the definitive influence of the people involved must be foregrounded. From early editors, like Suhail Malik, James Flint and Jamie King (or even before them, Tina Spear, Daniel Jackson and Paul Miller), to what must be the longest-running editorial team of the magazine's life (Hari Kunzru – with us pretty much since the beginning – plus Matthew Hyland, Demetra Kotouza, Benedict Seymour, Anthony Iles and Josephine Berry Slater, the latter three responsible for unstinting efforts in arguing the toss over the inclusions and exclusions of this book), to long-time designers Damian Jaques and Laura Oldenbourg, sales manager Lois Olmstead, and the countless individuals who either pitched to us or responded positively to pitches from us; it is these people's ideas and collective modus operandi that have functioned as the engine of development.

Mute has run treatises on the plight of student interns in its pages, but we are not above accepting their generosity and *Proud to be Flesh* has enjoyed significant contributions from Hilary Crowe, Stefano di Cecco, Lars Dittmer, Paul Graham, Kate Guarente, Caroline Heron, Charlotte Levins, Hannah Marshall, Olga Panades, Joanne Roberts and Erin Welke in everything from archive mining to proofing.

To say this book has had a chequered history is an understatement: it has travelled from pillar to post, falling foul of mergers and acquisitions, new editorial directions and mysterious silences. Support was shown by Arts Council England and the British Academy, both of whom subsidised the anthology early on and who have proven among the most patient of funders. The last two years of gestation have seen Autonomedia show equal perserverance, and faith, in helping us keep the end in sight.

On the home straight, with *Mute*'s editorial contingent intensely pre-occupied (Pauline giving birth to baby Violet and Josie working flat out on the magazine), Rebecca Gordon-Nesbitt granted this book the final bout of intensive care, attention to detail and good judgement it needed, aided and abetted by Kyle McCallum. Long-time contributor, John Barker, also offered us the unanticipated luxury of an index. We're eternally grateful for their last-minute agreements to participate. To have designers as perspicacious and text-obsessed as Sarah Newitt and Fraser Muggeridge to translate all this work into one coherent package has been the icing on the cake.

Finally, thanks to the 'constructively' critical but always serious family members who have followed – and supported – *Mute*'s winding path: Ernest, Kiddy, Ciska, Ritzo, Pam, Howard W., Raquel, Howard S. and Anthony. We know where you live.

Disgruntled Addicts – Mute Magazine and its History

Josephine Berry Slater

Mute magazine was born, somewhere between art school anomie and the thrill of the World Wide Web's appearance, in 1994. Looking back at the magazine's history on its 15th birthday, its most constant feature seems to be its wilful eclecticism and ceaseless criticality – something which, over the years, has got it into all kinds of trouble commercially, politically and with its varied readership. This concerted battle against the dominant logic of specialisation or static identity is perhaps the trace element of its founders' art school backgrounds at the Slade and Central Saint Martins.

Simon Worthington and Pauline van Mourik Broekman knew practically nothing about publishing or journalism when they set out to make *Mute.* But, as artists working in the post-conceptual era in which the requirement to master a medium was lessening, they were primed and ready for practically anything. Inspired by the broader cultural experimentation at play (from DIY culture, to nomadic 'briefcase art', to the techno-aesthetics of magazines as varied as *Mediamatic, Underground* and *Mondo 2000*), they were looking for ways to break out of the conformist pseudo-activity of gallery and institutional art. Nevertheless, the desire to explore and analyse contemporary life in all its complexity – which could involve maintaining several conflicting ideas about something simultaneously, often resulting in a position of both criticism and support – could be seen as an overwhelmingly artistic approach that remains with *Mute* to this day. This refusal to unconditionally embrace a genre, discipline or political position is not only at odds with the niched requirements of the market, but also often with political and artistic tribes.

Mute's stance of engaged criticality also seems to have characterised Pauline's attitude to art in the early-'90s. As she tells it, she was a 'disgruntled addict' of art, sickened by the UK art world's Thatcherite values in an era in the thrall of artists like Damien Hirst, but avidly following it nonetheless, scouring the scene for signs of activity at odds with the circus. Perhaps less preoccupied with the art world's schizophrenic attempts to retain critical legitimacy in its phase of high commercialism, Simon was drawn to the greener pastures of the datasphere. Soon, both began to see the web as offering the possibility to do things otherwise, to elude the stultifying structures of official culture while at the same time acting on a global stage. This techno-social revolution in the individual's ability to publish and access unfiltered information – to communicate globally without the mediating presence of elite gatekeepers – seemed to be having little impact on an art world obsessed with itself, its new found mass media appeal and Tracey Emin's dirty laundry. Accordingly, Pauline and Simon identified a new editorial genre: 'Digital Art Critique'.

From a small flat in West London, the by now paradigmatic 'home office' they shared, a marvellously hybrid bird of publishing paradise emerged. The first eight issues of *Mute* appeared somewhat quarterly, in broadsheet format and on salmon pink paper. Printed on the *Financial Times*' own press, they spliced the austere conventions of 18th century newsprint typography with vector-based computer graphics, wacky fonts and articles on digital art and post-humanism. This retro-futurist gesture of covering the 'information super-highway' and its cultures on now historical newsprint was an unexpectedly popular bit of hype deflation. *Mute*'s 'Proud to be Flesh' slogan fired another salvo at the Cartesian/Gibsonian fantasy of 'jacking into' cyberspace and leaving the 'meat' behind. The spectres of pink paper and flesh were wielded against the rising crescendo of cybermania which would climax in the dotcom bubble of the late-'90s.

Beneath the playfulness, *Mute* was advancing trenchant critiques of what these dreams of disembodiment and immateriality belied. Richard Barbrook and Andy Cameron's text, 'The Californian Ideology', made an important contribution to this endeavour, exposing the neoliberalism and neo-Darwinism which lay behind *Wired* magazine-style celebrations of cyberspace and 'bottom up' phenomena. The image by CORP on Vol 1 #5's cover proclaimed the words 'Arbeit Macht Frei' over a graphic of glass and steel office blocks and three flying computer keys – a reference to the expansion of work into daily life that digital technologies enable. Many years later, our 'Underneath the Knowledge Commons' issue, which carried a picture of a merry-go-round driven by flesh-and-blood work horses buried underneath it, would riff on a related theme – while elites experience the fruits of networked communication, the majority encounter an intensification of labour as managerial controls tighten and the ease of capital flight forces threatened workers to graft harder for less.

Focusing on the unsung, exploitative effects of new technologies, *Mute* has also consistently examined the unintended fallout from capitalism's constant development of the forces of production – and by this I mean something more than the tendency for the rate of profit to fall. The internet, of course, is a tremendous case in point. Information piracy, peer-to-peer file sharing, 'plunderphonics' and plagiarism are all ways in which capitalism's ability to create scarcity and control the commodity has been damaged by the net – that great, universal copying machine. *Mute*'s focus was increasingly the cultural practitioners and political activists – net artists and 'hacktivists' – who 'misused' the online environment to thwart attempts to own and control information and, hence, social knowledge and experience.

In 1997, some of *Mute*'s expanded editorial board – which by then included Hari Kunzru, Suhail Malik, James Flint, Jamie King and myself – took part in a presentation and workshop series at Documenta X called HybridWorkspace. This workspace, together with a net art installation elsewhere in the exhibition, were the first ever online and net art inclusions in a blue-chip, blockbuster art event. However, after the show was over, the organisers closed the Documenta site and saved the data onto discs which they then attempted to sell. But, participating net artist Vuk Ćosić had foreseen this and taken the precaution of saving the entire site to another address [www.ljudmila.org/~vuk/dx], making it publicly available as soon as the official site had closed. The ability of this new generation of web users to outwit the lumbering and proprietorial procedures of institutions and companies using digital tools created a window of opportunity and hope. The feeling that capitalism was a step behind its own state of the art technology created a rush of enthusiasm for alternative and anti-capitalist agendas.

To some degree, *Mute* attempted to manoeuvre itself within the commercial landscape of magazine publishing with comparable pragmatism and tactics. In 1997, we took the decision to come out as a quarterly glossy magazine, to situate ourselves on the news shelf (categorised, for want of any more suitable section, as 'men's lifestyle'), and to punt for some big advertising. From today's perspective, it seems astonishing that we should have ever persuaded Silk Cut to pay for a double page, full colour ad in Vol 1 #8, our first glossy. It also seems astonishing that, at that tender age, we had faith in the prospect that *Mute* could garner enough popular appeal to become part of a mainstream media diet. Surrounded by a deluge of new lifestyle titles (*Dazed & Confused, Adbusters, Wired UK*), it felt like *Mute* might ride in their slipstream, buoyed by the growing enthusiasm for digital culture and our savvy, sassy approach. This strategy would also prevent us from becoming a service journal to the new media art scene, and open the door to taking a broader view on how technology affects all of life, not just certain discrete areas.

However, this desire to hack the commercial stratum of publishing did nothing to quell the disgruntlement and intellectual ambition of the magazine. Pauline's editorial in Vol 1 #8 marked us out from the dotcom cheerleaders, by commenting on the 'epitaphs' already being laid at the 'grave of the digital revolution'. The same issue also carried a meaty section on the maturing discourse of cyberfeminism, included a rave-inspired fashion shoot, my article on outsider art, bearing the title 'How a Logic Logiced the System', and Matthew Fuller's piece on agent technology with sub-headings like 'Backzoom: From Self-absorbed to Self-dissolved'. Hardly mainstream fare then.

By the eve of the millennium, our predictions and dreams of two years earlier were proven to have been misplaced in both cases. The Silk Cut ads had tailed off sharply; but, on the other hand, the 'digital revolution' was converging with street activism to dramatic effect. While, for many, the November 1999 demonstration against the WTO in Seattle marks the consolidation of the 'anti-globalisation' movement, the Carnival Against

Capitalism in the City of London the previous June marked its spectacular beginning, at least for *Mute*'s editors. At that time, our office was located in Shoreditch, a few minutes' walk from the demo's meeting point in Liverpool St. Station and I think it's fair to say that the infamous 'starburst' of activists from multiple station exits, heading for the financial district beyond, is a force that propelled our editorial in a new direction, and one that increasingly came to dominate the focus of the magazine.

J18, N30, Genoa, 9/11; the arc of events is part of contemporary folklore. The 'movement of movements' shared many of the same organisational forms and techniques as the companies being restructured to suit the needs of capital and post-Fordist, managerial thinking. Flat networks, hollow organisations, alliances – capitalism and anti-capitalism were mirroring each other, as solid companies and once-unified political parties dematerialised into flexible, virtual and dynamic structures. 'We are everywhere' became a popular slogan for anti-capitalist groups and the title of a book dedicated to the rise of the movement edited by the Notes from Nowhere collective. Suddenly, thanks to computer networks, people could be effectively summoned from everywhere and nowhere to protest against equally diffuse elites who were dictating the terms of globalisation. Dumping the hierarchies, ideological clarity and arduous organisational means of traditional activism, large numbers of people were energised into taking part in politics on a global stage. Networks and mobility were the means, and direct action the result. But 9/11 changed all that. The declaration 'we are everywhere' was inverted into 'you (terrorists) are everywhere' and used to justify an open-ended War on Terror and on political activists.

As Jamie King asked, in his 2002 article 'Terror is the Network – and the Network is You' (Vol 1 #23), 'what happens when the "network of terror" meets the "network society"?' One answer is that this collision of networks intensifies states' control and surveillance of their populations, counteracting many of the progressive applications of those same technologies in the name of security. The superficial parallels between Al-Qa'ida and anti-globalisation activists' organisational means, not to mention their opposition to capitalism, played all too well into the hands of conservative and repressive state agendas. Jamie reports a headline from the *New York Daily News*, during the build up to scheduled protests against the World Economic Forum in the Big Apple, which declared: 'New Yorkers will not be terrorised. We already know what that's like. Chant your slogans. Carry your banners. Wear your gas masks. Just don't test our patience. Because we no longer have any.'

Although the wars in Afghanistan and Iraq gradually dispelled this American mood of 'righteous' indignation, the mainstream's post-9/11 sidelining of, and intolerance towards, summit activism seemed to deflate the confidence of the movement. The internal breakdown of its own fragile alliances, as many of its organising groups were accused of merely 'summit hopping', also contributed to the loss of momentum. Despite attempts to counter accusations of following the agendas of neoliberal elites by organising a series of alternative World and European Social Forums, once the focus had shifted away from the consensual target of free trade agreements and 'damaging globalisation' the alliances began to break down. *Mute*'s coverage of the 2004 World Social Forum in Mumbai and the European Social Forum in London was largely taken up with reports of infighting, exclusions and political censorship. Counter-counter summits began to proliferate and the Peoples' Global Action network was besieged by accusations of Eurocentrism, racism and sexism. Were these anti-globos nothing more than First World 'struggle tourists' holidaying in other people's misery?

At the same time as our writers were considering the social composition of the anti-globalisation movement, its structures and methodologies had also started to come under scrutiny. Activists' constant foregrounding of the technical and organisational forms of collaboration seemed, after a certain point, to hide an absence of political debate and the emergence of crypto-hierarchies and geographical centres. *Mute* ran several pieces – by Jamie King, Anthony Davies and Eileen Condon – exposing the fallibility of this formalist tendency amongst alliance-political groups and reminding readers that we'd been here before in the 1960s and '70s. Jamie referenced Jo Freeman's 1970 text, 'The Tyranny of Structurelessness', which had pointed to the tendency for cliques to emerge within the same radical feminist groups that had overtly rejected the patriarchal structures of leadership and hierarchy, whilst covertly or unconsciously repeating their inequalities.

Since the sacred cows had started toppling, why stop there when so many others could do with a good prodding? The Creative Commons, locative media, social networking or Web 2.0 – the default piety that surrounded these apparently social initiatives beggared belief. What they all ostensibly had in common was literally the common, and a way of organising its production, or protection, using new technologies. What was suspicious was the level of commercial and governmental support they received; 'movements' that were notionally about devolving power away from states and capital were getting hooked back into them while claiming ideological purity. The Creative Commons licence, wrote Gregor Claude in his 2002 article 'Goatherds in Pinstripes', was not an anti-property initiative but a market-orientated attempt to distribute intellectual property rights amongst small scale producers; an anti-monopolist move aimed at developing a more dynamic and inventive marketplace. In the media art world and funders' rush to embrace locative media, Armin Medosch and Saul Albert both detected a market-driven agenda, as hand-held devices and wireless networking became the cutting edge of the technological commodities market. Social networking sites or Web 2.0, argued Dmytri Kleiner, may have encouraged more people onto the net, but they drastically centralised the 'means of sharing'. Web 2.0

effectively commercialised the developments of the free software movement and peer-to-peer file sharing, imposing a homogenised format on social communication and monetising its 'long tail'.

Mute's writers and editors were certainly alert to the infinitely cunning ways in which people's communicative capacities and desires were subsumed into capitalist relations thanks, in part, to ICT. The politics of this subsumption had come to the fore with the publication of Hardt and Negri's *Empire* in 2000 – a book which argued that 'immaterial' workers comprised a new revolutionary class as a result of capital's dependence on their affective and intellectual labour. In this respect, immaterial producers could be said to 'own' the means of production, giving them a new autonomy. While critiquing the politics developing around immaterial production and the precarious conditions of its workers, *Mute* nevertheless shifted its publishing activities increasingly towards the immaterial realm. Having moved through a sequence of print formats and frequencies of publication we were, between 2002 and 2004, producing a thick, biannual coffee table edition. At this pinnacle of print luxuriousness, the high cost and labour involved in making the magazine were starting to take their toll. It was time to 'jack' our meat, and content, further into the web. We decided to go fully hybrid.

With Pauline and me going on uncannily parallel maternity leaves for the first half of 2005, this seemed as good a time as any to have a publishing holiday and completely overhaul the Metamute.org website. Simon and Raquel Perez de Eulate set to work designing and building a new site in Drupal – a free software, the bugginess of which has since earned it the reputation of a badly behaved household pet. Benedict Seymour and Anthony Iles had joined *Mute* as editors in 2004, and staffed the ghost ship *Mute* during this time, researching a cheap new form of printing called 'print on demand' (POD). This method – essentially a glorified laser print-out, prettified by the addition of full colour, perfect bound covers – allows one to print as few or as many copies as desired; you only have to pay for the number you need. This could not be more different from the newsprint process we had originally used, in which the minimum number of copies you could print was 10,000. With the show back on the road by mid 2005, our new model was to prioritise the website, publish weekly articles, solicit people to self-publish in the News and Analysis and Public Library sections, make our entire back catalogue freely available, and republish the best of each quarter's crop of articles in POD form for an affordable £5.

In commercial terms, this was a risky approach since it removed any clear incentive for people to buy the print version by giving it all up for free on the web. As an Arts Council-funded magazine, however, part of our costs was covered and the wish to participate in international debates and free intellectual exchange outweighed any commercial advantage to creating a pay-per-view website. The readership results were dramatic, with Metamute.org averaging around 25,000 page views per day – although admittedly sales of the print version did nosedive for a while.

It is tempting to try and draw some analogy between our very noughties publishing model and the increased importance of the 'virtual' financial services sector to global capitalism, in the throes of its meltdown at the time of writing. The difference, of course, is that, with the shift from material commodities to the trade in intangibles orchestrated by the proliferation of new 'financial instruments', the city temporarily managed to make loads of money from producing nothing. *Mute*, on the other hand, belongs to the legions producing largely unremunerated content for the web. This condition some understand as 'digital commoning' – a way of collectively maintaining the resources which help the precarious intellectual worker to subsist within neoliberal globalisation as living conditions, wages and job security degenerate. This notion of free production, however, belongs to the phantasm of the 'weightless economy' in which money supposedly begets money and the cognitariat produce intellectual goods for nothing – a concept that came under fierce attack in Steve Wright's article 'Reality Check: Are We Living in an Immaterial World?' (Vol 2 #1). Quoting Ursula Huws, he writes:

> Huws draws our attention back not only to the massive infrastructure that underpins 'the knowledge economy', but also to 'the fact that real people with real bodies have contributed real time to the development of these "weightless" commodities.' As for determining the contribution of human labour within the production of immaterial products, Huws argues, that, while this might 'be difficult to model', that 'does not render the task impossible'.

These 'real people', Wright concludes, are largely the 'soil tilling' majority of the Earth. The real commoner, it turns out, is capitalism whose non-reproduction of the natural resources and unpaid labour it loots is creating a tragedy of mounting proportions. As for those 'digital commoners', they are far from having transcended exchange value and returned to a pure reliance upon use values. Those commodities they continue to consume, and which sustain them in their immaterial production, are mostly produced by one hyper-exploited half of the Earth's population. It goes without saying that *Mute*'s editors and writers belong to the lucky other half.

As the analyses of immaterial production, financialisation and 'fictitious capital' intensified after 2005 – due in no small part to the editorial input of Ben and contributing editor, Matthew Hyland – the focus on digital culture and art dilated somewhat. Perhaps, with the hindsight of a 'once in a century' financial crisis, it is hardly surprising that 'fictitious capital' developed such a hypnotic hold on our attention. In September 2007, we brought out possibly the best timed issue of *Mute*'s entire career. The 'Living in a Bubble: Credit, Debt and Crisis' issue, which we'd been preparing over the Summer, intersected 'perfectly' with the US sub-prime crash's escalation into a full-blown credit crunch and the nationalisation of Northern Rock, the first in a long line of public bailouts it would later transpire.

But, despite the shift in focus, the parallels between the relational developments of art and virtual economic activity remain stark. Paul Helliwell contributed several lengthy articles on this subject, casting avant-garde art and, more latterly, 'relational aesthetics' as the vanguard of cultural commodification in its immaterial phase. Due to the commodity's demise at the hands of digital abundance, he argues, the music industry in particular, and capitalism in general, are coming increasingly to resemble relational art. For several generations, artists have critiqued and abandoned the object; after the institutional critique of the 1960s–80s, droves of artists began to abandon the 'white cube' for the real world beyond, looking to 'heal' wounded social relations by operating on them directly. Thus was born 'relational aesthetics' as Nicholas Bourriaud termed it. Whether feeding the gallery visitor noodles or creating archives of collectively produced histories in the midst of regeneration zones, the artist became ever less the detached observer and producer of objects, and ever more the provider of social and cultural services.

Mute's coverage of this cultural turn focused on how this once self-critical tendency became complicit with the forces of regeneration and social engineering. The London Particular's image/text analysis, 'Fear Death by Water', and Anthony Davies' article, 'Take Me I'm Yours', were key to this exploration. Both revealed a toxic mix of cuts in public spending and welfare, privatisation of the public sphere and the strategic deployment of culture to neutralise any resistance. This marriage of convenience between cultural producers and the neoliberal state results, they argue, in the consultative nature of community arts projects which do nothing to prevent already-decided-upon regeneration schemes, or the politically progressive programmes of institutions which nevertheless underpay their unskilled staff. This instrumentalised culture – which appears to be isomorphic with market deregulation and privatisation – is often the sad result of art's critical dematerialisation. As with the 'weightless economy', art's dematerialisation into a network of communication and relationality coincides with increased material hardship at the other end of the productive chain.

It seems that we've arrived back where we began, at the switch point between the liberating and repressive tendencies of dematerialisation. It is partly due to the overlapping concerns of these lines of enquiry that it took us over five years to assemble this book. Untangling the separate themes which now organise such a fat manual to the past 15 years of cultural politics took some doing. Art historian and *Mute* contributor, Michael Corris, gave us a great deal of help with this, moving our thinking on from the initial plan to make a book about the relationship between conceptualism and network-based art practice to a multi-themed anthology of some of our best articles. Reading over the book in its final form, I find it striking that a magazine which has continually contended with the question 'but what's it about?' has, in fact, produced such a sustained and persistent analysis. The technologically driven dematerialisation of culture, economics, social activity and control must always contend with the material world of needs, production, embodiment and desires which sustain and are sustained by these processes. We are now, as ever, and for infinitely varied reasons, Proud to be Flesh!

Chapter 1

Direct Democracy and its Demons: Web 1.0 to Web 2.0

This chapter interrogates the web's dual promise – to increase the direct democratic potential of many-to-many communication while, at the same time, perfecting the conditions for further expansion of capitalist social relations and the 'free market'. Its timeframe spans the period between the pre-dotcom '90s to the late Web 2.0-obsessed '00s – a trajectory leading from the days of the internet's initial and faltering marketisation to its mature, well-established form. As the net was popularised through Tim Berners-Lee's invention of the World Wide Web and the first commercial browsers, the 'commons' of the internet – originally developed, owned and maintained by the state – was laid open to popular usage and vulnerable to a corporate land grab. *Mute* was keen to rupture the market-orientated hype of the 'digerati' prospectors, to expose their economic bottom line, and to insist upon the continuity of social relations across real and virtual space – in this sense, we understood ourselves as the European anti-*Wired*.

Richard Barbrook and Andy Cameron's article, 'The Californian Ideology', written in 1995, describes the stakes of this struggle between commercial and radical democratic forces, and importantly exposes the economic and political underside of the seemingly hip West Coast digerati gathered around *Wired* magazine. Politically conservative neoliberalism and techno-determinism were being repackaged as the daring embrace of the new network culture, as Newt Gingrich shaded into William Gibson. The workaholism of ex-hippies developing internet start-ups in garages and their 'spare time' was revealed as anything but the slacker culture it pretended to be. As with its classical antecedents, the virtual class, performing its intellectual labour in the electronic agora, relied upon an underclass of black and immigrant workers, excluded from the networks, to perform its reproductive labour for it.

Were the digerati concerned by these exclusions and did they think the technology could help society address such inequities? In his interview with legendary techno-booster and *Wired* editor Kevin Kelly, Jamie King reveals, with comic aplomb, the self-referential nature of the Californian Ideology. Kelly – who famously argued in *Out of Control* that, like life itself, technology is a vital force that should be subject neither to ethical judgements nor to developmental interventions – is at a loss to address the question of the 'digital divide' that is developing as a result of the networks he so passionately embraces. Throughout the interview, while claiming that 'technology solves the ills of society', he continually defends its unbridled commercial development on the grounds of its naturalness. Like most neoliberals, Kelly hides his rampant free market thinking behind a barrage of unsubstantiated clichés about the natural order of things.

Pit Shultz, co-founder of the nettime mailing list (one of the hubs of 'European' media critique), is equally concerned with the growth of virtual life forms, but from a very different political standpoint. In his interview with *Mute's* Pauline van Mourik Broekman, he rejects claims that there has been a 'digital revolution' while still holding out hope for new media's ability to create channels which 'redirect the flow of power'. Without the freight of advertising, the channel produced by the mailing list itself is described as not only free but also 'silent', and, curiously, as a space that attempted to 'avoid dialogues'. Early nettime was conceived as a 'collaborative filtering' project, not the space of rhetorical theatrics it so often became.

Anustup Basu, in his piece 'Bombs and Bytes', written in the aftermath of the second invasion of Iraq, laments the role of the media in driving the shift from democratic discourses, based on knowledge and persuasion, to the mass 'psychomechanical' programming of thought made possible by informatics. Providing an example of (corporate and state media's) fascistic collaborative filtering, Basu cites the combination of the events of 9/11 with the name Saddam Hussein as a lethal instance of information's malleability. In this 'inhuman plane of massified thought', it is possible to combine two ideas which have no organic or narrative connection.

The final piece in this chapter, by Dmytri Kleiner and Brian Wyrick, brings the discussion full circle. Web 2.0, they argue, the tools and platforms which finally made 'mass participation' in the web a reality, in practice amounts to little more than 'Info-Enclosure 2.0'. Where the first round of the net's enclosure was centred on its infrastructure (its backbones, ISPs, browsers and means of governance), the second has focused on the capture of community-created content and a homogenisation of the means of sharing.

What Barbrook and Cameron dubbed the Californian Ideology has, over time, revealed itself to be none other than the informatic dimension of post-Fordism itself. As with flexibilisation in the work place, what might at first have seemed to present small gains for the working class quickly establishes itself as a more individualised, finely grained and decentralised form of control. With Web 2.0 sucking the majority of web content production into a pre-formatted and narcissistic micro-casting, the big bucks are now determining not only the shape of social reality in its massified form, but also what Deleuze calls the 'imperial-linguistic takeover of a whole social body of expressive potentialities'.

The Californian Ideology

Richard Barbrook and Andy Cameron

Vol 1 #3, Autumn 1995

Not to lie about the future is impossible and one can lie about it at will.
Naum Gabo

Hippy Capitalists

The Californian Ideology is a mix of cybernetics, free market economics and counter-culture libertarianism and is promulgated by magazines such as *Wired* and *Mondo 2000*, as well as the books of Stewart Brand, Douglas Rushkoff, Kevin Kelly and many others. The new faith has been embraced by computer nerds, slacker students, thirty-something capitalists, hip academics, futurist bureaucrats and even the President of the USA himself. As usual, Europeans have not been slow to copy the latest fashion from America. While a recent EU report recommended adopting the Californian free enterprise model to build the 'infobahn', cutting-edge artists and academics have been championing the 'post-human' philosophy developed by the West Coast's Extropian cult. With no obvious opponents, the global dominance of the Californian Ideology appears to be complete.

On superficial reading, the writings of the Californian ideologists are an amusing cocktail of Bay Area cultural wackiness and in-depth analysis of the latest developments in the high-tech arts, entertainment and media industries. Their politics appear to be impeccably libertarian – they want information technologies to be used to create a new 'Jeffersonian democracy' in cyberspace where every individual would be able to express himself or herself freely. Implacable in its certainties, the Californian Ideology offers a fatalistic vision of the natural and inevitable triumph of the high-tech free market – a vision which is blind to racism, poverty and environmental degradation, and which has no time to debate alternatives.

Saint McLuhan

Back in the '60s, Marshall McLuhan preached that the power of big business and big government would be overthrown by the intrinsically empowering effects of new technology on individuals. Many hippies were influenced by the theories of McLuhan and believed that technological progress would automatically turn their non-conformist libertarian principles into political fact. The convergence of media, computing and telecommunications, they trusted, would inevitably result in electronic direct democracy – the electronic agora – in which everyone would be able to express their opinions without fear of censorship.

Encouraged by McLuhan's predictions, West Coast radicals became involved in developing new information technologies for the alternative press, community radio stations, home-brew computer clubs and video collectives. During the '70s and '80s, many of the fundamental advances in personal computing and networking were made by people influenced by the technological optimism of the New Left and the counter-culture. By the '90s, some of these ex-hippies had even become owners and managers of high-tech corporations in their own right, and the pioneering work of the community media activists has been largely recuperated by the high-tech and media industries.

The Rise of the Virtual Class

Although companies in these sectors can mechanise and sub-contract many of their labour needs, they remain dependent on key people who can research and create original products, from software programs and computer chips to books and TV programmes. These skilled workers and entrepreneurs form the so-called 'virtual class': '[...] the techno-intelligentsia of cognitive scientists, engineers, computer scientists, video-game developers, and all the other communications specialists...' (Kroker and Weinstein). Unable to subject them to the discipline of the assembly line or replace them by machines, managers have organised such intellectual workers through fixed-term contracts.

Like the 'labour aristocracy' of the last century, core personnel in the media, computing and telecoms industries experience the rewards and insecurities of the marketplace. On the one hand, these high-tech artisans not only tend to be well-paid, but also have considerable autonomy over their pace of work and place of employment. As a result, the cultural divide between the hippy and the organisation man has now become rather fuzzy. On the other hand, these workers are tied by the terms of their contracts and have no guarantee of continued employment. Lacking the free time of the hippies, work itself has become the main route to self-fulfilment for much of the 'virtual class'. Because these core workers are both a privileged part of the labour force and heirs of the radical ideas of community media activists, the Californian Ideology, therefore, simultaneously reflects the disciplines of market economics and the freedoms of hippy artisanship.

This bizarre hybrid is only made possible through a nearly universal belief in technological determinism. Ever since the '60s, liberals – in the social sense of the word – have hoped that the new information technologies would realise their ideals. Responding to the challenge of the New Left, the New Right has resurrected an older form of liberalism: economic liberalism. In place of the collective freedom sought by hippy radicals, they have championed the liberty of individuals within the marketplace. From the '70s onward, Toffler, de Sola

Pool and other gurus attempted to prove that the advent of hypermedia would paradoxically involve a return to the economic liberalism of the past. This retro-utopia echoed the predictions of Asimov, Heinlein and other macho sci-fi novelists whose future worlds were always filled with space traders, super-slick salesmen, genius scientists, pirate captains and other rugged individualists. The path of technological progress didn't always lead to 'ecotopia' – it could instead lead back to the America of the Founding Fathers.

Agora or Exchange – Direct Democracy or Free Trade?

With McLuhan as its patron saint, the Californian Ideology has emerged from an unexpected collision of right-wing neoliberalism, counter-culture radicalism and technological determinism – a hybrid ideology with all its ambiguities and contradictions intact. These contradictions are most pronounced in the opposing visions of the future which it holds simultaneously. On the one side, the anti-corporate purity of the New Left has been preserved by the advocates of the 'virtual community'. According to their guru, Howard Rheingold, the values of the counter-culture baby boomers will continue to shape the development of new information technologies. Community activists will increasingly use hypermedia to replace corporate capitalism and big government with a high-tech 'gift economy' in which information is freely exchanged between participants. In Rheingold's view, the 'virtual class' is still at the forefront of the battle for social change. Despite the frenzied commercial and political involvement in building the 'information superhighway', direct democracy within the electronic agora will inevitably triumph over its corporate and bureaucratic enemies.

On the other hand, other West Coast ideologues have embraced the laissez-faire ideology of their erstwhile conservative enemy. For example, *Wired* – the monthly bible of the 'virtual class' – has uncritically reproduced the views of Newt Gingrich, the extreme-right Republican leader of the House of Representatives, and the Tofflers, who are his close advisors. Ignoring their policies for welfare cutbacks, the magazine is instead mesmerised by their enthusiasm for the libertarian possibilities offered by the new information technologies. Gingrich and the Tofflers claim that the convergence of media, computing and telecommunications will not create an electronic agora, but will instead lead to the apotheosis of the market – an electronic exchange within which everybody can become a free trader.

In this version of the Californian Ideology, each member of the 'virtual class' is promised the opportunity to become a successful high-tech entrepreneur. Information technologies, so the argument goes, empower the individual, enhance personal freedom and radically reduce the power of the nation-state. Existing social, political and legal power structures will wither away to be replaced by unfettered interactions between autonomous individuals and their software. Indeed, attempts to interfere with these elemental technological and economic forces, particularly by the government, merely rebound on those who are foolish enough to defy the primary laws of nature. The restyled McLuhanites vigorously argue that big government should stay off the backs of resourceful entrepreneurs who are the only people cool and courageous enough to take risks. The free market is the sole mechanism capable of building the future and ensuring a full flowering of liberty within the electronic circuits of Jeffersonian cyberspace. As in Heinlein's and Asimov's sci-fi novels, the path forward to the future seems to lie backward to the past.

The Myth of the Free Market

Yet, almost every major technological advance of the last 200 years has taken place with the aid of large amounts of public money and under a good deal of government influence. The technologies of both the computer and the net were invented with the aid of massive state subsidies. For example, the first Difference Engine project received a British Government grant of £17,470 – a small fortune in 1834. From Colossus to EDVAC, from flight simulators to virtual reality, the development of computing has depended at key moments on public research handouts or fat contracts with public agencies. The IBM corporation built the first programmable digital computer only after it was requested to do so by the US Defense Department during the Korean War. Lack of state intervention meant that Nazi Germany lost the opportunity to build the first electronic computer in the late-'30s when the Wehrmacht refused to fund Konrad Zuse, who had pioneered the use of binary code, stored programs and electronic logic gates.

One of the weirdest things about the Californian Ideology is that the West Coast itself is a creation of massive state intervention. Government dollars were used to build the irrigation systems, highways, schools, universities and other infrastructural projects which make the good life possible. On top of these public subsidies, the West Coast high-tech industrial complex has been feasting off the fattest pork barrel in history for decades. The US government has poured billions of tax dollars into buying planes, missiles, electronics and nuclear bombs from Californian companies. Americans have always had state planning, but they prefer to call it the defence budget. All of this public funding has had an enormously beneficial – albeit unacknowledged and un-costed – effect on the subsequent development of Silicon Valley and other high-tech industries. Entrepreneurs often have an inflated sense of their own 'creative act of will' in developing new ideas and give little recognition to the contributions made by either the state or their own labour force. However, all technological progress is cumulative – it depends on the results of a collective historical process and must be counted, at least in part, as a collective achievement.

Hence, as in every other industrialised country, American entrepreneurs have in fact relied on public money and state intervention to nurture and develop their industries. When Japanese companies threatened to take over the American microchip market, the libertarian computer capitalists of California had no ideological qualms about joining a state-sponsored cartel to fight off the invaders from the East!

Masters and Slaves

Despite the central role played by public intervention in developing hypermedia, the Californian Ideology is a profoundly anti-statist dogma. The ascendancy of this dogma is a result of the failure of renewal in the USA during the late-'60s and early-'70s. Although the ideologues of California celebrate the libertarian individualism of the hippies, they never discuss the political or social demands of the counter-culture. Individual freedom is no longer to be achieved by rebelling against the system, but through submission to the natural laws of technological progress and the free market. In many cyberpunk novels and films, this asocial libertarianism is expressed by the central character of the lone individual fighting for survival within the virtual world of information.

In American folklore, the nation was built out of a wilderness by free-booting individuals – the trappers, cowboys, preachers and settlers of the frontier. The American Revolution itself was fought to protect the property of the colonists against unjust taxes levied by a foreign parliament. Yet this primary myth of the USA ignores the contradiction at the centre of the American dream: some individuals can prosper only through the suffering of others. The life of Thomas Jefferson – one of the icons of the Californian ideologists – clearly demonstrates the double nature of liberal individualism. The man who wrote the inspiring and poetic call for democracy and liberty in the American Declaration of Independence was at the same time one of the largest slave-owners in the country.

Despite the eventual emancipation of the slaves and the victories of the civil rights movement, racial segregation still lies at the centre of American politics – especially in California. Behind the neoliberal rhetoric of individual freedom lies the master's fear of the rebellious slave. In the recent elections for governor in California, the Republican candidate won through a vicious anti-immigrant campaign. Nationally, the triumph of Gingrich's neoliberals in the legislative elections was based on the mobilisation of 'angry white males' against the supposed threat from black welfare scroungers, immigrants from Mexico and other uppity minorities.

The high-tech industries are an integral part of this racist Republican coalition. However, the exclusively private and corporate construction of cyberspace can only promote the fragmentation of American society into antagonistic, racially-determined classes. Already 'red-lined' by profit-hungry telcos, the inhabitants of poor inner city areas can be shut out of the new online services through lack of money. In contrast, yuppies and their children can play at being cyberpunks in a virtual world without having to meet any of their impoverished neighbours. Alongside the ever-widening social divisions, another apartheid between the 'information-rich' and the 'information-poor' is being created. Yet calls for the telcos to be forced to provide universal access to the information superstructure for all citizens are denounced in *Wired* magazine as being inimical to progress. Whose progress?

The 'Dumb Waiter'

As Hegel pointed out, the tragedy of the masters is that they cannot escape from dependence on their slaves. Rich white Californians need their darker-skinned fellow humans to work in their factories, pick their crops, look after their children and tend their gardens. Unable to surrender wealth and power, the white people of California can instead find spiritual solace in their worship of technology. If human slaves are ultimately unreliable, then mechanical ones will have to be invented. The search for the holy grail of Artificial Intelligence reveals this desire for the Golem – a strong and loyal slave whose skin is the colour of the Earth and whose innards are made of sand. The techno-utopians imagine that it is possible to obtain slave-like labour from inanimate machines. Yet, although technology can store or amplify labour, it can never remove the necessity for humans to invent, build and maintain the machines in the first place. Slave labour cannot be obtained without somebody being enslaved. At his estate at Monticello, Jefferson invented many ingenious gadgets – including a 'dumb waiter' to mediate contact with his slaves. In the late 20th century, it is not surprising that this liberal slave-owner is the hero of those who proclaim freedom while denying their brown-skinned fellow citizens those democratic rights said to be inalienable.

Foreclosing the Future

The prophets of the Californian Ideology argue that only the cybernetic flows and chaotic eddies of free markets and global communications will determine the future. Political debate, therefore, is a waste of breath. As neoliberals, they assert that the will of the people, mediated by democratic government through the political process, is a dangerous heresy which interferes with the natural and efficient freedom to accumulate property. As technological determinists, they believe that human social and emotional ties obstruct the efficient evolution of the machine. Abandoning democracy and social solidarity, the Californian Ideology dreams of a digital nirvana inhabited solely by liberal psychopaths.

There are Alternatives

Despite its claims to universality, the Californian Ideology was developed by a group of people living within one specific country following a particular choice of socio-economic and technological development. Their eclectic blend of conservative economics and hippy libertarianism reflects the history of the West Coast – and not the inevitable future of the rest of the world. The high-tech neoliberals proclaim that there is only one road forward. Yet, in reality, debate has never been more possible or more necessary. The Californian model is only one among many.

Within the European Union, the recent history of France provides practical proof that it is possible to use state intervention alongside market competition to nurture new technologies and to ensure their benefits are diffused among the population as a whole.

Following the victory of the Jacobins over their liberal opponents in 1792, the democratic republic in France became the embodiment of the 'general will'. As such, the state had to represent the interests of all citizens, rather than just protect the rights of individual property owners. The French Revolution went beyond liberalism to democracy. Emboldened by this popular legitimacy, the government is able to influence industrial development.

For instance, the Minitel network built up its critical mass of users through the nationalised telco giving away free terminals. Once the market had been created, commercial and community providers were then able to find enough customers to thrive. Learning from the French experience, it would seem obvious that European and national bodies should exercise more precisely targeted regulatory control and state direction over the development of hypermedia, rather than less.

The lesson of Minitel is that hypermedia within Europe should be developed as a hybrid of state intervention, capitalist entrepreneurship and DIY culture. No doubt the 'infobahn' will create a mass market for private companies to sell existing information commodities – films, TV programmes, music and books – across the net. Once people can distribute as well as receive hypermedia, a flourishing of community media, niche markets and special interest groups will emerge. However, for all this to happen the state must play an active part. In order to realise the interests of all citizens, the 'general will' must be realised at least partially through public institutions.

The Rebirth of the Modern

The Californian Ideology rejects notions of community and of social progress and seeks to chain humanity to the rocks of economic and technological fatalism. Once upon a time, West Coast hippies played a key role in creating our contemporary vision of social liberation. As a consequence, feminism, drug culture, gay liberation and ethnic identity have, since the 1960s, ceased to be marginal issues. Ironically, it is now California that has become the centre of the ideology which denies the relevance of these new social subjects.

It is now necessary for us to assert our own future – if not in circumstances of our own choosing. After twenty years, we need to reject once and forever the loss of nerve expressed by postmodernism. We can do more than 'play with the pieces' created by the avant-gardes of the past.

We need to debate what kind of hypermedia suits our vision of society – how do we create the interactive products and online services we want to use, the kind of computers we like and the software we find most useful? We need to find ways to think socially and politically about the machines we develop. While learning from the can-do attitude of the Californian individualists, we must also recognise that the potentiality of hypermedia can never be solely realised through market forces. We need an economy which can unleash the creative powers of high-tech artisans. Only then can we fully grasp the Promethean opportunities as humanity moves into the next stage of modernity.

The Californian Ideology: An Insider's View

Celia Pearce

Vol 1 #4, Winter/Spring 1996

I first read a draft of 'The Californian Ideology' during Andy Cameron's visit to Los Angeles last Summer for the SIGGRAPH 95 Convention. Andy stayed at a beachside motel near my house and wore sandals every day. We ate cheap Mexican food for lunch and had lively discussions. He seemed to have a lovely visit, and, if I am not very much mistaken, left Southern California with a bit of a tan.

What, Precisely, Is California?

'America and England are two nations divided by a common language,' quipped George Bernard Shaw some 60 years ago. But there's more to it than mere linguistics. Especially when you are talking about California.

It is typical of Americans to be myopically ignorant of their own history – which is how the Republican Party is able to repeatedly succeed at the polls. But a glimpse into our history, and particularly the history of California, is useful in understanding the basis for the Californian Ideology.

California has always been characterised by pioneers and gold-diggers. From the gold rush, to the movie industry, to the computer revolution, the Californian Ideology has always been one of spirited individualism and entrepreneurialism. It is also a breeding ground for greed and self-interest. By way of example, take a look at this list of just a few of the things California has brought the world:

Levi's
Movies
Charles Manson
The Grateful Dead
Ronald Reagan and Richard Nixon
Silicon Graphics
Microsoft and Apple
Industrial Light & Magic
Los Angeles and San Francisco
Scientology
Disneyland
Toy Story

A View From Inside

What is it like to live – and survive – the Californian Ideology on a daily basis? As a bona fide member of the so-called 'virtual class', I am certainly qualified to answer this. The description – independent contractor, free to come and go as they wish, well-paid, but at the same time, suffering from acute workaholism – fits me to a tee. All except the well-paid part. And that is a myth. It is true that many of us are well paid by the hour. However, we also spend 75 percent of our time trying to secure that hour of work, negotiating elaborate (and expensive) contracts, being expected to work on spec, etc. Those who are pushing the envelope the hardest, and especially those with a social conscience, must fight every step of the way. The true vanguards of the digital revolution are blazing their trail at tremendous personal risk. The condition of the virtual class cannot be blamed on the individuals within it, but must be looked at in a larger context. Artists here receive very little support from the government or, for that matter, the society-at-large. In our anti-intellectual culture, art is considered subversive and unnecessary. In America, anything that does not generate revenue – such as art and education – is viewed as gratuitous. Once you realise this fact, the Californian Ideology becomes historically inevitable.

Capitalist Cyberhippies

Why is Silicon Valley overrun with capitalist hippies? It is easy to label them revolutionaries who 'sold out' to the capitalist ethic – unless you have to live within that ethic. In the 1960s – while fighting a pointless war, and after our President, his brother, and our two most influential civil rights leaders were murdered – we learned that politics was a dangerous path to take towards revolution. The Nixon regime in the '70s further drove home the point that politics was no place for an ethical person. Furthermore, it doesn't take a genius to see that, in reality, there is no politics in America, only economics. So, it is absolutely correct to say that Americans are apolitical. In the European Community, there are countries. In America, there are corporations. Those things which are typically government-supported in social democracies – like medical insurance, education, and the arts – are provided by corporations here. We live in a modern-day feudal society consisting of corporate fiefdoms, mini-nations each with its own culture and language. And these fiefdoms are what drives politics in this country.

In the 1960s, the generation that seemed destined to revolutionise America was utterly derailed. They did ultimately change America, but not in the ways we thought they would. Those who might have excelled in politics turned instead to industry. In another time and place, it might have been Bill Gates in the White House rather than Bill Clinton. But their generation learned the hard way that politics are as treacherous in America as they are pointless. I don't think I need to tell you which of the two Bills has more power – the one who pays the bills, or the one who signs them.

Siliwood and the Military Entertainment Complex

California's two nexi of activity, Silicon Valley and Hollywood, are, ironically, connected by a common faultline. These two powerful forces have now 'gotten in bed together' (as we say in showbiz) and given birth to a new phenomenon aptly known as 'Siliwood'.

But, beneath the self-congratulatory glitter of this marriage of convenience, both regions are tied together by another bond, a bond less glamorous, but no less profitable. That bond is the military. As 'The Californian Ideology' very astutely points out, virtually every aspect of the computer industry has its roots in government-funded military technology, and California has always been a leader in military contracts. For every Apple in California, there is a Lockheed. Considering Silicon Valley is the domain of the cyberhippie-turned-capitalist culture, there is a deep irony in the fact that former peacenicks have built an empire on the shoulders of their military enemies. (Shh ... don't tell anyone.)

Nowhere has this become more evident than in Siliwood's companion movement, the 'Military Entertainment Complex'. In the wake of military downsizing, many military contractors were faced with the vexing problem: 'Who, but the military, can afford us?' There was only one conceivable answer – Hollywood! The result is a series of hybrid technologies, some of which I have helped to develop. I like the idea of turning weapons into ploughshares, especially since both of the military-cum-entertainment projects I have worked on consisted of non-violent content. In spite of my staunchly pacifistic position, I have a tremendous amount of respect for the many brilliant and innovative minds behind military technologies. In a way, the military could be looked at as the front end of the technological adoption curve. 'Adoption curve?' you may ask, 'What the hell is that?' Allow me to explain...

Adoption Curve

The authors of 'The Californian Ideology' call it elitist technological determinism. In America, we call it the 'adoption curve.' Here's how it works: Technology is developed at tremendous capital expense. It is released on the market at exorbitant prices, well beyond the means of the 'average' person. A certain demographic – affluent, young, educated, eager to impress themselves and each other – lead the market. They run out to buy 'the latest' thing, speed home in their BMWs to Marin County, and plug it in. Then, one of two things happens: either it becomes obsolete within a few months, or the 'early adopters', as they are called, build up enough market saturation that the product can then begin to be produced at a lower price and in larger quantity, thus making it accessible to the general public. This is the formula by which mass market penetration of any new product or technology is achieved in the US.

It is true that this is an elitist system. But, on the other hand, it is people at the head of the adoption curve who pay the price for making these technologies available to everyone. They buy at a premium, subsidising R&D, so that, later, others can buy at a fraction of the cost. Underlying it all is the 'bottom line': Profits, profits and more profits. In France, you give free Minitels to everyone. In America, you sell them for a lot of money to early adopters.

The Virtual Class Revisited: Social Capitalism and Autodidactic Communalism

Surviving in this complex landscape is nothing if not a challenge. You can never really separate yourself from the power structure, but, if you prefer to exist outside the corporate culture, the only alternative is to become a renegade member of 'the virtual class'. If you play your cards right, you can evolve into a consultant, which is basically just a renegade who knows how to market themselves.

Contrary to the myth, renegades do not operate in a vacuum, nor would the vast majority of us claim to. Instead, we form our own loosely structured, somewhat anarchistic communities. Because we share the common resource of the 'digisphere', we can, in fact, function in this way, without submitting completely to the protection of a feudal master. This has given rise to two systems of community. I call these 'autodidactic communalism' and 'social capitalism'.

Autodidactic communalism is our educational system. Most people in new media are autodidacts. As in all fields, education is always about twenty years behind industry, so anyone with any time in the new media business is, by definition, self-taught. The computer is, of course, the ultimate heuristic tool (and as I am speaking to a British audience, I can rest assured that you all know what this word means). But lone autodidacticism is also a myth and nowhere is this more true than in the computer field. In fact, most autodidacts work together. We learn by doing, and we learn by showing each other how to do things. We teach each other HTML, we pass around shareware, we bootleg software for each other. This is very much a part of the hacker ethic. While the corporate world takes a proprietary posture, hoarding 'intellectual property' and charging a premium for its use, and the military world is entirely shrouded in secrecy, autodidactic communalists freely share ideas and information, believing (and rightly so) that such an open architecture is to the benefit of all.

Social capitalism is an economic system characterised by the lateral, collaborative approach taken by many small companies and new media 'boutiques'. Sometimes, this work is done on contract, other times, it is taken in barter. Relationships under social capitalism are reciprocal. I may be your client one day and you may be mine the next. Or, we may be partners on a larger project. This is a sharp contrast to the hierarchical corporate system where large organisations vie for absolute power and total ownership. In this model, cooperation and a sense of community is seen to benefit all. Companies that operate this way have become the backbone of the industry, often producing content for large corporations. Unhindered by the burden of high overheads or executive bottlenecks, they are often more efficient, less expensive, and, well, just better.

Joining Forces

These two movements combine to create a community of individualists. For those of us who are trying to break new ground, we have no choice but to live on the edge. But we cannot live on the edge alone. We must of necessity join together. Many of us do share a sense of social conscience and do everything in our power to broaden the landscape to create more inclusive forms of technology. But we must always fight an uphill battle. Many young entrepreneurs are creating cybercafés, websites, and other venues that allow free and open access of technology to a much wider audience. And, although the internet does promote individual, ego-based expression, as suggested by 'The Californian Ideology', it also promotes freedom of access to information and a sense of community that transcends geographical boundaries. This disintegration of these international boundaries is precisely what makes this type of discourse possible.

As an inhabitant of the Californian Ideology, I can choose to write this article for *Mute*, rather than *Wired*. At the same time, Andy Cameron can spend his Friday nights watching American television programmes. As much as the British may regard the Californian Ideology with disdain, neither can they or its other critics deny their inextricable ties to it.

Let us consider another approach. Here we are in the midst of a number of major planet-wide transformations. Multinational corporations are changing the face of the global economy. The Earth's environment is on the brink of major disaster. While half of Europe coalesces, the other half disintegrates. Asia has become a major force in the world economy. And in and around this complex landscape is the digital 'Global Village' (to quote the oft-maligned Marshall McLuhan), simultaneously contracting and exploding, a parallel universe of which we are all the architects – whether we read *Mondo 2000* or *Mute*.

In light of all this, it seems absurd to speak at all of geographical ideologies. California has a lot to learn from Britain and vice versa. We may be divided by a common language, but we are connected by another one – HTML and the language of cyberspace. We ought to use that to form a new ideology – one which takes into account our individual political, social and economic realities, while creating a forum for change that goes beyond those limitations towards a global community consciousness that we can all work together to create.

Proliferating Futures

Franco Berardi (Bifo)

Vol 1 #4, Winter/Spring 1996

Proliferating Futures

What about the Becoming of the net? We cannot describe the net as one single process of Becoming, but as a proliferation of different coexisting processes. Therefore, we can't make a statement about the future of the net. Many different futures will coalesce within it.

Different intentions can enter the net, different processes of semiotisation can co-evolve. The net is not a territory but a multiplanary sphere. Infinite plateaux are rotating inside this sphere. What is forbidden on one level can be done on another.

The net cannot be conceptualised within the Hegelian concept of Totality. In Hegel, the Truth is the Whole. The Hegelian Whole is *Aufhebung* – the annihilation of every difference. In the net, every connection between points of enunciation creates its own level of truth. Truth is only found in singularity. In the net, the world cannot be considered as the objective reference point of a process of enunciation. The world is the projection of enunciation itself.

Networking is the method of a new social paradigm – one that goes beyond the social oppositions and conceptual contradictions inherited from the modern world. Because capitalism is still in power, acting as the general semiotic code, the old social oppositions and conceptual contradictions are not vanishing yet. This is the reason why we are still concerned with the old problem of the state versus the market. Notwithstanding the emergence of the net, the state and the market still exist.

High-Tech Deregulation

The discourse about the net (cyberculture) is still dominated by ideologies which are the legacy of the 20th century. Cyberculture is still dominated by conceptual and political alternatives coming from industrial society. A sort of high-tech neoliberalism is emerging from the American scene. In the theoretical core of this philosophical movement, I see a misunderstanding: the identification of technology with economics within the paradigm shift. Thinkers like Alvin Toffler, Kevin Kelly and Esther Dyson support the neoliberal agenda of Newt Gingrich because, they argue, the free market is the best method for expanding free communications – and free communications are the key to the future world.

Sounds good, but what does the 'free market' mean? In the social framework of capitalism, free market means power to the strongest economic groups – and the absorption or elimination of society's intellectual energies.

Kevin Kelly, in *Out of Control*, says that, thanks to the digital technologies and computer networks, mankind is evolving into a super-organism, a new biological system. The biologisation of culture and society described by Kelly is nothing but the disappearance of any alternative from the social field, the absorption of intelligence itself within the framework of capitalist semiotisation. The possibility of choice is denied, eradicated.

This is the main effect of the integration of technological development, scientific work and economic power. Michel Foucault describes the formation of modern society in terms of the imposition of discipline on the individual body and on social behaviour. What we are now witnessing is the making of what Gilles Deleuze defines as a society of control: The code of behaviour is being imprinted directly onto the mind through models of cognition, of psychic interaction. Discipline is no longer imposed on the body through the formal action of the law – it is printed in the collective brain through the dissemination of techno-linguistic interfaces, inducing a cognitive mutation.

Old Alternatives are Misleading

In their article, 'The Californian Ideology', Richard Barbrook and Andy Cameron criticise the mystification of this high-tech neoliberalism. But, with what do they oppose it? They talk of a European way – the way of the welfare state, public intervention within the economy, public control over technological innovation. Can we believe in this solution? I don't.

Barbrook and Cameron say that Minitel in France has shown the possibility of a European way of building the net. But this is pointless. This example shows exactly that public intervention cannot achieve this goal. Minitel is a rigid and centralised system, unable to face the challenges of virtualisation. And in Italy, the experience of Olivetti shows that it is impossible to innovate on the basis of state investment and control. From this point of view, the American model of development is working better. It opens the way to creative innovations. It captures these innovations through techno-social interfaces.

Barbrook and Cameron say that Europe must oppose the process of globalisation which is being led by the US. But this idea is naïve and dangerous. Stopping globalisation, preserving identities: These are the ideas which are generating nationalism and fundamentalism. These are what are called retro-fascism by Kroker and Weinstein in their book, *Data Trash*.

The war between neoliberalism and the old fashioned welfare state is not over – as shown by the strikes of the French railwaymen. The struggles of Fordist workers will probably go on for a long time, but they are doomed.

The strategic defeat of industrial labour has already happened – FIAT 1980, Peugeot, the Miners' Union, Detroit were stages in the '80s marginalisation of industrial labour.

The new composition of social labour is marked by the emergence of the cognitariat – what Kroker and Weinstein call the 'virtual class'. The social labour of collective intelligence – or general intellect as Marx calls it in the *Grundrisse* – remains dominated by capitalist social relations in spite of its formal independence. Marx distinguishes two different kinds of domination of capital over human activity: formal domination and real domination.

Formal domination is the legal imposition of discipline, the formal subordination of human time to capitalist exploitation. Real domination is the technological and material dependence of social activity on the capitalist form of social relations. Today, we are probably entering a new phase of capitalist domination, beyond the formal and real: mental domination, realised through the pervasiveness of the semiotic code of capital within the collective brain, within language, within the mind and within cognitive activity. The capitalist paradigm is imprinted on the collective intelligence, inside techno-social interfaces, in the semiotic framework of social communications.

The alternative between policies of deregulation and policies of state intervention is a false alternative. There is no way of regulating capital. Capital is a proliferating process of semiotisation, informing techno-social interfaces and producing neural pathways and frames of social interaction. Since capital is pervading all social relationships, it is the regulator, not the regulated. The problem is not the legal regulation of capitalism; the problem is capitalism itself.

The industrial world is fading, the industrial composition of labour is dissolving and a new composition of social activity is emerging, but the capitalist code is still pervading it. And, in its current virtual (dis)incarnation, capitalism seems to be a system without any alternative. The alternative cannot be found in the past.

19th Century Nostrums are not Solutions to 21st Century Problems

Louis Rossetto

Vol 1 #4, Winter/Spring 1996

Barbrook's seeming understanding of the digital revolution's crucial left-right fusion of free minds and free markets is followed by a totally out-to-lunch excursion into discussions of the role of government, racism and ecology in California, ending with a startling admission of the need to marry 'some of the entrepreneurial zeal and can-do attitude' of California to a uniquely European (but not even vaguely defined) mixed economy solution – all of it betraying an atavistic attachment to statism and an utterly dismal failure to comprehend the possibilities of a future radically different than the one we currently inhabit, one that is actually democratic, meritocratic, decentralised, libertarian.

Far from building the digital revolution, the US Defense Department sucked up 6 to 7 percent of US GNP for 40 years and utilised up to 40 percent of all engineering talent, channelling these resources not into technological growth but into tanks, bombs and military adventurism. In point of fact, it was the cutback in American defence spending following the Vietnam War and the subsequent firing of thousands of Californian engineers which resulted in the creation of Silicon Valley and the personal computer revolution.

A descent into the kind of completely stupid comments on race in America that only smug Europeans can even attempt: Any country which prohibits its own passport holders from residing within its borders, or any people who are currently allowing genocidal war to be waged in their own backyard after the stupefying genocide of World War II, shouldn't be lecturing Americans about anything having to do with race, much less events which occurred 200 years ago. The charge of technological apartheid is just plain stupid: 'Already "red-lined" by profit-hungry telcos [isn't every company, by definition, 'profit hungry?', although that description in this context is also stupid, since telcos are regulated monopolies with government-enforced rates of return], the inhabitants of poor inner city areas are prevented from accessing the new online services through lack of money.' Oh really? Red-lined? Universal telephone access is mandated in the US. And anyone with a telephone has access to online service. Lack of money? Online is cheaper than cable television, and you can get a new computer for less than $1,000, a used one for less than $500.

The utterly laughable Marxist/Fabian knee-jerk reaction – that there is such a thing as the info-haves and have-nots – is equivalent to a 1948 *Mute* whining that there were TV-haves and have-nots because television penetration had yet to become universal, the logical conclusion being that, of course, the state had to step in and create television entitlements. This whole line of thinking displays a profound ignorance of how technology actually diffuses through society. Namely, there has to be a leading edge, people who take a risk on new, unproven products – usually upper-tenish types, who pay through the nose for the privilege of being beta testers, getting inferior technology at inflated prices with the very real possibility that they have invested in technological dead ends like eight track or betamax or Atari. Yet they are the ones who pay back development costs and pave the way for the mass market, which, let me assure you, is every technology company's wet dream (the biggest market today for the fastest personal computers is not business but the home). Less haves and have-nots than have-laters.

This anal retentive attachment to failed 19th century social and economic analysis and bromides is what allows you to claim that the laughable French Minitel system is a success when, in fact, it is a huge impediment to France developing a real networked economy, since the dirigisme which mandated an instantly obsolete, closed technology for deployment into every home in France – and then conspired to stifle any alternative – has ensured that France remains resolutely outside the mainstream of the internet.

A profound ignorance of economics. The engine of development of the digital revolution was not state planning, whether you call that an industrial policy or a defence policy. It was free capital markets and venture funds which channelled savings to thousands upon thousands of companies, enabling them to start and to thrive. Contrast this with the sorry history of European technological development, where huge plutocratic organisations like Siemens and Philips conspired with bungling bureaucracies to hoover up taxes collected by local and Euro-wide state institutions and shovel them into mammoth technology projects which have proven to be, almost without exception, disasters. The true measure of failure of the European (in other words, statist) direction of technology lies in the fact that in ten years, during the biggest technology boom the planet has ever witnessed, Europe has gone from a net exporter of technology to a net importer.

Let's get real here: High European taxes have restricted spending on technology and hence retarded its development; state telco monopolies have kept prices high and service bad, again impeding networking in business and the home; state-directed technology investment has resulted in the monopolisation of risk capital, uniformly bad technology policy and the squandering of resources and opportunities; social welfare policies reward parasitical living rather than risk-taking; a truly atavistic, sick attachment to the compulsion and non-meritocratic elitism of statism as a way of life; and a knee-jerk disdain for truly radical social and political thought which falls outside Euro PC dogma (read: failed Marxist/Fabian) – have all retarded and will continue to retard Europeans. If the US and Asian countries had conspired to ensure that Europe continued to cede export markets, they could not have come up with a better strategy than the one you advocate: continued statist meddling.

Meanwhile, it's Europeans who are discussing 'Californian Ideology', not Californians who are discussing 'European Ideology'. And not because some clatch of bureaucrats in Strasbourg or Luxembourg have issued yet another directive, but because Europeans are recognising that 19th century nostrums are not solutions to 21st century problems – on the contrary, they are the problem – and it's time to encourage competition, risk taking, democracy and meritocracy, and, dare I say it, dreaming about a different, better future. Ask me again, and I'll really tell you what I think.

The Origins of the Nettime Mailing List

Pit Schultz Interviewed by Pauline van Mourik Broekman

Vol 1 #7, Summer 1997

In the wake of Timothy Druckrey's inspiring symposium on online publishing at the Dutch Electronic Arts Festival 1996 (DEAF96), Pauline van Mourik Broekman interviewed the co-moderator of nettime, a key forum for media critique at that time.

Pauline van Mourik Broekman: Could you tell me something about how nettime was started and how it has developed since then?
Pit Schultz: Nettime started as a three-day meeting in a small theatre in Venice during the Biennale '95. A meeting of media activists, theoreticians, artists, journalists from different European countries (Heath Bunting, nettime co-moderator Geert Lovink, Diana McCarty, Vuk Ćosić, David Garcia, Nils Roeller, Tomasso Tozzi, Paul Garrin and many more). We developed the main lines of a net critique along the topics of virtual urbanism, globalisation/tribalisation and the life metaphor. Also, it became obvious that it was necessary to define a different cultural (net)politics than the one *Wired* magazine represented in Europe. It was a private and intensive event, and, in a way, it defined the 'style' in which we critique and discuss issues on nettime. Nettime is somehow modelled on the table of the meeting – it was covered with texts, magazines, books, whatever we had to offer the group. It was the start of our 'gift economy' with exchanges of information. Today the list has nearly 300 subscribers, it's growing constantly with around ten subscribers a week. We do no PR and the list is semi-closed, which means new subscriptions must be approved.

PvMB: Were you intensely involved with computers?

PS: My first computer was an Atari2600 TV-game, then a ZX81, C64, Amiga1000. I switched to Mac when I began with DTP in the Botschaft group after '90, used DOS/Linux for the internet, and ended up with a DX66 under Win95, mainly to run Eudora, in an intranet. So these machines document certain phases in my life, but they don't determine them. I also studied computer science for a couple of years, but it was not what I expected, which was a more conceptual approach that reflected the development of software on a much broader, maybe cultural, level.

PvMB: ...and net culture?

PS: I was involved with THE THING BBS network from '92–94, the high time of ASCII and text-based internet like MUDs and MOOs, before the web. At the same time I was working with the group Botschaft. There were also some exhibitions of low media art, a communication performance in the TV tower in Berlin, meetings, long-term projects in the public sphere like an installation with Daniel Pflumm in a subway tunnel, a collaboration with the group handshake which later became Internationale Stadt, or Chaos Computer Club which Botschaft shared office space with. After a Bilwet event we organised, I started to work with Geert Lovink, which was a truly new phase of work.

PvMB: ...as an artist?

PS: Yes and no. I got a stipendium and did exhibitions, but always had problems accepting art as a 'closed system', and I have to emphasise here that nettime is a group project, it is not a 'piece of individual art', but a medium formed by a collective subjectivity, a sum of individuals. I'm moderating it and it has its aesthetic aspects. But you don't have to call me an artist because of that.

PvMB: I mean before you started the list, and how do you think that has affected how nettime was set up?

PS: Well, you can call it a continuation of my art practice, but it functions without naming it art. In '94, I tried to begin with projects on the web, especially the *Orgasmotron Project* (a database of recorded brain waves of human orgasms), which reflected the early euphoric times of 'first contact'. With Botschaft e.V. In '93–94, we did the 'Museum für Zukunft', a group project and database of future scenarios, ideas and views, but, during these projects, it became clear that I needed a deeper understanding of the collaborative, theoretical and discursive aspects of cyberspace to continue. During this time, I also gave up doing installations in defined art spaces. Generally, after a euphoric entry phase, I got extremely bored and disappointed with what was, and is, happening in the art field. My main interest remains what Andreas Broeckmann calls 'machinic aesthetics', a field between the social, political and cultural economy of the so called 'new media'. So I was happy to meet Geert and, through Venice and a series of other meetings, a group of people with shared interests that we're trying to bring together on the nettime list.

PvMB: It seems that nettime has gravitated more toward net-political and -philosophical discussion than that directly to do with 'art'. What role do you and Geert Lovink, as moderators, have with regard to that?

PS: Art today, especially media art, is a problematic field. When I listen to music, it may happen that I don't like it, but it comes through the radio. That's how art appears to me. You can switch it off, but there is still a lot of music around. So much for art. With the moderation – it is also a contradictory role. The less the moderator appears the better the channel flows. It is, of course, this power-through-absence thing, but we hope that we handle it carefully and in a responsible way, with the continuous group process in mind. Power flows through networks, and you cannot switch it off. From different sides, Geert and I have an interest in working with the dynamic of the aesthetic contra the political field. There are many faultlines and frontiers. One of them seems to become the art system which still has some kind of *Alleinherrschaftsanspruch* in the symbolic cultural field. This changes through new media and, even if new media will not make the term 'art' obsolete, there is something about the paradox between media and art, or media art, that I find deeply problematic.

Both have components of totalitarian systems of representation. There is the chance that new media creates channels to redirect the flow of power. That's what nettime is made for. An experimental place for (re)mixes; something I missed for a very long time. Never perfect and always 'in becoming', but not explicit, not descriptive but performative and pragmatic.

Both Geert and I have our own reasons for distancing ourselves from today's 'art discourse'. You can call nettime a political project in terms of the real effects we try to trigger, in terms of conflicting debates, reflecting and criticising the economic and social implications of the 'digital revolution'. It is a philosophical channel in terms of describing a certain 'condition', while accessing and applying traditional knowledge, including the 'postmodern' stuff. It is an aesthetic process in many aspects, while developing a collaborative writing space, experimenting with modes and styles of 'computer mediated communication'. Finally, we have the luxury of silence and don't advertise, so we don't need big investments into labels and surface – it gets spread by word of mouth – and the footer 'cultural politics of the nets' can mean many things. It's about clouds. There is this 'field of virtuality or potentiality', multiple contexts and personae, interests and intensities which, like the social aspect, the time aspect, the knowledge and news aspect, make nettime something which modulates a flow of heterogeneous subjective objects, something with an existential aesthetic of living with nettime, (including the group, events, projects which grow here) a collective and singular info-environment which exists without the need to be named art.

PvMB: At the discussion at DEAF96, I think you described nettime as a 'dirty' ASCII channel; how 'dirty' or unmoderated is it?

PS: Dirtiness is a concept here, especially for the digital realm, which produces its own clean dirtiness. Take the sound of digital distortion on a CD compared to the analogue distortion of vinyl. Take all kinds of digital effects imitating analogue dirtiness, which means, in the end, a higher resolution, a recursive, deeper, infinite structure. I used the concept because of its many aspects. It means here to affirm the noise aspect, but only to generate a more complex pattern out of it. It doesn't mean 'anything goes', or a self-sufficient ethic of productivity. It is slacker-ish in a way: slows down, speeds up, doesn't care at certain places, just to come back to the ones which are tactically more effective... there is a whole empirical science behind it, how to bring the nettime ship through dark waters... how to compress and expand, how to follow the lines of noise/pattern instead of absence/presence... (In fact, I pushed the big red button of the moderator mode only once, after a period of technical errors and an ensuing unfocused dialogue.)

The phenomenon is – and I think this is not such a rare thing – that a group of people, in a repetitive, communicative environment, begin to filter a field of possible 'communication acts' in a certain way quasi-machinically. You don't have to be professional or especially skilled in the beginning. The production of 'information' along the borderline of noise means to constantly refine a social context, maybe an artificial one, what some call immanent. I mean with rules which are self-evident and are interdependent in a dynamic way. The list-software sends a kind of basic netiquette to the new users but this affects only some formal factors. One is that we decided to avoid dialogues, without forbidding them. Nettime is not a list of dialogues of quote and re-quote, but more of a discursive flow of text, of different types, 'differentialising', contextualising each other. On the net it is called 'collaborative filtering', or earlier, it was 'social filtering'.

Dirtiness means many things here. First of all the absence of purity – you always have mixtures, *agencements*, but this becomes too trivially 'postmodern'. The constant commentary, forming a socially defined body of knowledge and, of course, a field where power is generated out of undifferentiated forces – which includes the position of the moderators or other very active participants – for defining where the scope of the flow tends to go. But, actually, anyone can post whatever she likes. This risk, which often leads to a situation of overflow and reorientation, is also the productive freedom of nettime. Another is the limited set of signs, like the Euro-English or net-pidgin, using English as a non-native speaker or the reduced character set of ASCII, or the minimal features of the perl-scripts which run the mailing list. Finally, for the authors, there is always a multiple aspect of why to write and, for the readers, why to read nettime. You definitely have to filter; I guess nobody, including me, reads every mail from start to finish. The sender has the chance to actively select texts she finds on the net and forward them. The author can pre- or republish texts, send pre-versions, test certain ideas or sample others. On the material side, there are the printouts of ZKP [Zentrum für Kunstprojekte] readers which come out in small numbers during conferences. The process of inscription, combined with a filtering process, functions a bit like a news-ticker if you want to find a comparison in the publishing world.

PvMB: Two other pertinent issues that came up at the DEAF discussion were those to do with size and finance. If online journals or lists are akin to creators of community, for example, where discussion can be catalytic due to the small size of the group and many of the contributors also knowing each other 'in real life', does their effectivity decrease beyond a certain size (I think Geert mentioned a couple of hundred)? Although nettime is still a 'closed' mailing list, its subscriber base has grown; have you adapted your methodology?

PS: As you can see, nettime is still going well. It seems there is a self-regulation process on the side of the contributors. There is the growth (which is around ten new subscribers per week, mostly on a word of mouth basis), which leads to a certain social consistency. Then, in the way texts get selected/produced and find their way to the list. The 'group' is circumscribing a network of real life relationships, a network of shared interests and a network of contextualising documents. This happens in relation to the 'outside', to the 'wideness' of the net, and to the 'deepness' of the local places where people work and live. Every document represents a vector through time in a social context, a discursive environment with many levels of reference, but a relatively concrete and simple surface: ASCII-text. The complexity and aesthetics which come out of the simple, practical rules of a mailing list are complex and dynamic enough not to feel the urge to experiment with multi-thread, hypertextual, multimedia environments, even if we think about certain extensions you find in common with infranet or groupware solutions in the corporate world. It says: 'Never touch a running system.' I think the next level will evolve through a certain economic pressure, certain cases where texts reappear somewhere without permission, or other cases where the unwritten norms are subverted by other 'content machines' running on other principles, but sharing similar fields of issues. There is a need to use the chance and experiment with new horizontal networks of producers, to respect the collaborative editorial work of a user community and, most of all, to think about financial models in terms of a sustainable quality of discussion, which includes the 'currency' of trust and credibility.

PvMB: And then, regarding finance, this obviously has enormous effects on how things can run. Nettime is a 'no budget' operation; what are the advantages and disadvantages of this, and how do you manage to keep going?

PS: First, I have to say that your question already has certain implications. It may seem natural to put anything you do into an economic model and ask, What do I get for it? What do I pay for it? But it cannot even be said that such an exchange economy runs effectively with money. There is clearly a drive to profit from new media, and, of course, money must be there for basic funding, but the goal of nettime is not financial profit. One easily comes to this point with a defensive position, or a dogmatic one, fighting against the all too present, not to say totalitarian, system of a worldwide, integrated capitalism. Even after Marx, there are social fights, and, especially within new media as in the art world, you have to face certain problems which often mean making money fast but doing bad work, or working but not getting good money. There is a certain kind of luxury today which is somehow over-coded by 'slackerdom', which is contrary to the work ethic of the yuppie or the political activist. It is a pragmatic level; we do not have to talk about just economics, but we have to develop a working model, a constant fight with risks of exploitation, burn-out, sell-out.

Finally, we would have to change nettime from its microeconomical, very basic structure if we forced its commercialisation. To make it clear, especially for mailing lists, but also many other sites with high content, it is not at all clear how to finance them in the longer term. The time of hype might be over soon, and then you have to face a shake out of centralisation that we already know from the history of radio and TV. On the other hand, I do not believe in the concept of autonomy. It leads to a sad double life. It might be that you live by state grants, or that you have to do a stupid job during the day. Between, there are many shades of grey, and among them is the possibility of alternative online economies which may reintroduce less alienated semiotics into the circulation of capitalism.

PvMB: You've talked about the importance of editors being sensitive to the exchange economies of the nets; these many economies intertwine, they are not separate are they? Highly commercial and competitive ones share technologies, content and 'participants' (for want of a better word) with ones that are more clearly like the potlatch economy you refer to. In practice, what has been your experience of keeping nettime independent within this situation?

PS: These economies intertwine, but not without friction. From the view of the poor, there is the need to disrespect certain economic barriers, for example, licences and copyright. That's what is happening in many Eastern countries. The new markets are not functioning like they promised to, at least not for all. There are still many chances to use new technology as a tool, to reach more independence, but it also gets used in the other way for a huge 'Darwinist' shake-out. And, as one can see with Microsoft, it is not at all the best who survive. So I strongly resist any logic of pre-affirming the situation. Potlatch is only a circumscription of a kind of exchange economy, which is pretty common as soon as you have the privilege to do so. I am sure that we will face models which are based on certain local exclusions of the money economy. Any family, community or friendship is based on such models. Finally, you need the friction, the potential of mixed economies, for a vivid and creative market, at least from what I understand about markets.

PvMB: This links with one of the ongoing discussions on nettime, the one to do with libertarianism or neoliberalism and social justice. It has, over time, involved posting extensive 'dialogues' on the role of *Wired* and the demonisation of the state, and has been presented as an attempt to start generating a productive, European contribution to the development of ideas on techno-cultural political organisation for the future. Is this right, and how do you feel it is going?

PS: You can describe it like that, but I don't like to make predictions here. One thing nettime does is critique. This means it reflects and constructs the present. Of course, there are strategies, and part of a strategy is that one should not talk too much about it. The important task is not to give up against the homogenising, centralising and alienating networks of a global integrated capitalism, to use these very ethical-political techniques as 'cultural' ones, to push against what is forced on us as 'economic factors' in favour of a necessary quality.

Berlin, January 1997

The Right Connections: Tea With Kevin Kelly

J.J. King

Vol 1 #8, Winter 1997

'Imagine that we live on a steel planet, and there's a hippy bus-load of things that arrive from outer space and they have these big bags of seeds – life – and they're like, "Do you want it?" and we're like, "File an EPA report" – we'd reject it. It's too risky, it's out of control, it's full of diseases. We would reject life if it was given to us right now. And that's exactly what we're doing with technology. Technology has all the same kind of qualities, and we're saying, "We can't deal with it."'

This anecdote, related to me in a recent interview with Kevin Kelly, speaks volumes about the attitude toward technology and culture promulgated by Kelly, John Perry Barlow, Nicholas Negroponte et al., whose self-promotional chutzpah has established them as the 'digerati'. The unchecked substitution of 'life' for 'technology' is a semantic sleight of hand that gives way, here, to the assertion that the same sceptics who want to refuse technology today would be the kind to have wanted to refuse life at its dawn (the implication of the gag, its utter fatuity notwithstanding, being that, since only a dumb ass would want to refuse life, only a dumb ass could want to refuse technology). Elsewhere, it's a 'switcheroo' (Kelly's word, not mine) that will lend technology the working status of a vital force that, like 'nature', operates outside the reach of social imperatives.

That, of course, leaves a nasty taste in the mouth for those comfy with a *Tomorrow's World* technology that is 'put to work' for us, achieving palpable results which can be lauded, applauded and then comfortably consumed. Connectionism, with all its zany, bottom-up, out-of-control-ness, is anathema to the prevailing picture of technology as humankind's servant. And the digerati, bless 'em, are just bursting to relieve you of such a paradigm. Fair enough, you might think.

There is a whiff, though, of something rather more pernicious here. For many of us, the invocation of the old bogey, Mother Nature, as a legitimation for any discourse raises hackles, largely because she's been made bedfellow to some particularly unscrupulous types in her time, lending dumb support to (amongst other things) radical racism and gender discrimination. But it's worse than that for the connectionists because they're not merely attempting to substantiate an ideology upon nature, but to use nature as that ideology; in the free market ecology of Kelly, Barlow and Negroponte, nature, with all its savage vicissitudes, becomes the law – a naturally occurring phenomenon beyond the dictat of culture. The middle term is expelled: no longer: 'x is right because it's natural' but 'x is natural – so talking about its rightness is pointless'.

Should the network, I ask Kelly, really be viewed as irreproachable? What happens when its emergent phenomena are violent, acrimonious, undesirable?

'I do think,' he confirms, 'of technology as a form of life. And in general, I think, the more life we have the better. Are there specific powers or disruptions that are caused by specific forms of life? Yes. What does that mean? Well, that means we have to kind of deal with it. But does it mean that we should try to stop life altogether, stop technology altogether? No.'

Well, no one was actually offering that as a serious option. We could ask, in its stead, for simple concessions; Is there, for instance, room for a social conscience in such a paradigm? A social support network? An anaemic one, at best. 'I don't think technology solves the ills of society,' Kelly says bluntly. 'Those are socio-political problems, not technological problems. Technology's not going to change those things.'

Convenient how it's possible to pull apart economics and technology after spending 600-odd pages putting them together in his somewhat infamous book. But how cool is it, I wonder, to study and promote the growth of distributed, out of control technologies when those technologies are not being put to work to help people? After all, wasn't technology, at least nominally, supposed to try to help? Vehicles to move people. Agricultural machinery to feed people. Medicine and medical technologies to save people's lives. But this network – because it's part of nature – doesn't need to help anybody.

Somehow it feels wrongheaded, or perhaps just deeply unfashionable, to pop the question. 'So what about the people who fall through the network,' I ask nonetheless, 'The homeless people, the starving, the mentally disturbed? How does the network try to extend its help to them?' Kelly doesn't falter for a moment. 'The people you're talking about have very little to do with technology and much more to do with politics and social skills. I know of no technology that is going to help the people you've just mentioned.' Well. At least we know where we stand. Nature doesn't help anybody, and why should technology?

Except that the digerati don't go this far. They don't want to be accused of cruelty, and they've developed a little fantasy that helps them to feel they're helping you. It goes like this: there're no have-nots, just 'have-lates'. Everybody will get the network in the end, even those who don't even have food right now; everybody will benefit wonderfully from it, and 'in about ten years, this question [of have-nots] is going to be perceived with great amusement. The problem is not going to be all those people who are not connected, 'cause they're just have-lates. Everybody's going to have the stuff sooner than they think, and then we're all going to be worrying about what happens when they're connected.'

But this connectionist riff about 'haves and have-lates' is another wholly unacceptable bit of semantic manoeuvring that, looked at from ground level, seems flimsy, insubstantial and more than a little crass. The question of access to knowledge is crucial, especially as such access is becoming increasingly an issue of economics, and attempting to close it with so flippant a soundbite is unforgivable. The world outside the virtual class has big problems that preclude large sections of the population from access or even thinking about access. 'We're in an era,' Kelly says to me, 'where we have tremendous stuff to gain by looking at the bottom.' Unfortunately, he wasn't talking about the rock-bottom and the very limited gains the people who reside there have to make from the connectionist project.

How many of us are going to be having this pan-capitalist global network, anyway? Is the process toward one really that clear, that inexorable? In Europe, despite isolated moves toward non-government organisations and quangos, the general political swing is manifestly toward a centralised system – which seems utterly polarised to the digerati's connectionist pronouncements about the world. How does Kelly reconcile this with his picture of a global shift to decentralisation, deregulation and bottom-up governance? By ignoring it, as far as I can tell. 'Despite backsliding in various parts of the globe, there's a very clear trend towards the decentralisation of governments. Very few would dispute that there's a general trend in that direction,' he asserts in response to my questions. I'm sorry? Backsliding? Various parts of the globe? Aren't we talking about the whole of Europe here, Kelly? He leaps over the continent in one gigantic visionary stride, hardly even taking in the point. This is typical of the quite deliberate and obstinate myopia that characterises the 'Californian Ideology' of the digerati, the same myopia that has led Negroponte to make wild assertions about the redundancy of issues of race and gender in a recent letter to *Wired US*.

I suppose I've given the game away: there's something about connectionism that I can't quite connect with. Its ideology, for reasons I hope I've pointed at, is fundamentally unsound. 'But the ideological part of it is irrelevant,' Kelly protests, 'the pervasive, ubiquitous spread of this technology will continue because it's practical.' Yeah, yeah, yeah. I'm not even convinced that any of it is going to happen, but were it to, I'd be deeply suspicious of any process founded on a purely 'natural' and 'practical' rationale, the trajectory of which sweeps straight over a whole gaggle of nasty, sticky little objections.

What happens, for instance, to privacy in a world where every dumb little thing is talking to every other dumb little thing? Isn't it all queasily resonant of some disgustingly bloated global Neighbourhood Watch scheme? 'Well, in America, the idea of privacy is a very loaded word that is actually not very clear and which means a lot of different things. A person who had true privacy was the Unabomber.' My worst fears confirmed: a network this ubiquitous, this voracious, would never tolerate absence – every silence, every unknown, would be regarded as the stirring of dissent. Mad bombers in huts in the forest; pinkos, revolutionaries and freaks hiding behind encryption codes and firewalls. It all adds up to a situation in which silence will need to be justified. 'But who wants to have no relationships?' Kelly demands incredulously. 'Who wants to have no-one know anything about you? That's inhuman, that's sick.' Who are you calling sick? I'm not saying that I necessarily want to be cut off from society, just that I'd like it to be a possibility. 'Well, if you make it easy to rebel, then there's no value in doing it,' says Kelly blithely. Great to know he has our best interests at heart.

Privacy, that's one issue. Another: protection. Have the digerati failed to notice the violent and unpalatable emergent phenomena at football matches and mob rallies? Have they ever considered that from 'natural' flux, society has doggedly organised itself into top-down and often totalitarian systems? That if you strengthen the ability of humans to communicate ideas without tempering them, you invite the spontaneous emergence of systems which may not reflect your own political intentions? A distributed system, I point out to Kelly, need not stay in motion but can reach a resting point in any one of a plethora of constellations.

For a while we skirt around each other, me arguing that his network will speed the process of tyranny and revolution into a kind of continuous repression and revolt, him arguing that it will make such tyranny 'more difficult. I'm not saying it can't be done, just that it becomes more difficult.' We manage to agree that the network, already generating conspiracy theories like Billy-o through its younger sibling, the internet, might, in future, give them an environment in which they can proliferate with even greater efficacy.

But what's the difference between conspiracy theory and religious and political movements, I ask? Kelly cuts through the question with a prophetic assertion: 'We're not going to see tyrannies, but things that are like conspiracies to the extreme.' He then comes over a bit vague and seer-ish, in an Ides of March kind of way. 'Very, very toxic, conspiratorial and rumour based things. We haven't, probably, seen that kind of thing yet.' I decide to leave it at that, and we move on swiftly to the subject of mob rule.

Suddenly we hit pay-dirt. 'I think it's impossible to have any kind of sophisticated civilisation that's run entirely from the bottom. Sure, that's a mob, and you get mob rule. So you absolutely need to have top-down control.' In a flash, I get it: even Kelly doesn't really believe any of this gab about distributed rule. 'That,' he admits, 'is just one part of the equation. You need points of control within the system. Leverage points, I'd call them.'

This, of course, is the crux of what many sceptics are trying to get across to the digerati: that the architecture of a system defines the movements of those who traverse it, and that those who design and influence that architecture should therefore pay close attention to their motivations and mind-sets. Whilst the claim was for a system that had an entirely open architecture, similar somehow to those found in 'nature', we merely wanted to point out that that didn't sound like the way 'nature' worked – or that open systems, in human society, have often led to abusive, coercive movements. Now our position as critics of this emergent Californian Ideology changes, for here is a far more dangerous admission: that the digerati, or at least some of them, are fully aware that 'leverage points' have to be hardwired into their network, and that those points will define control within that network. Now we want to know – and we have to ask – what ideology informs the placement of those points of control, what strategies govern their operation?

'Yeah,' muses Kelly, 'can we agree on a set of moral heuristics that we want to wire in?' Oh, oh. And then: 'How do we engineer consensus?'

This has all started to sound very, very worrying indeed, and I find myself considering the opinion of a couple of notable nettime writers – to whit, that the digerati are the new Mussolinis and Hitlers of our time – in a new light. Could Kelly really be an embryonic Infoführer, exhorting the virtual class to sneak leverage points and fulcrums of control into the systems they are helping to fashion? Somehow it doesn't ring true. I have to add a new criticism to the list of those he is already surrounded by: that Kelly is an intellectual naïf. By his own admission, he relies on other people to provide ideologies. 'I am very eager,' he says to me, 'to hear someone else map something out that makes sense to me.'

You really get the feeling, talking to him, that he honestly doesn't feel equipped to talk about certain issues. He's a bright guy, but I start to realise that he just isn't comfortable discussing the implications of his work when that discussion starts to touch on philosophical and socio-political theoretics. It may be that Kelly feels on safe ground in his book, therefore, with nature on his side. It's hard to go wrong with nature. It doesn't answer back, and if you describe it convincingly enough, most of your readers won't either.

Sceptics would, of course, point out to me that I bought into his disingenuity, that I'm the naïve one, and they'd probably be right. But, before I finish, let me point out that this charge of naïveté should not be taken as an attempt to mitigate Kelly's, or the digerati's, astonishing intellectual irresponsibility. 'What are your ideas?' Kelly asks me as the interview is closing. 'I'm an editor at *Wired*, I have many times asked people to prepare something that I can believe in. Give me something that makes sense in terms of what I know, and I'll try to disseminate it.' Not good enough, I'm afraid: the way to respond to the fact of your own misguided, malnourished and half-assed ideology is not to ask me, or anyone else, to come up with one; it's to start doing some thinking yourself.

'Well,' Kelly says meekly, 'I'm not much of a preacher. I'm a devout Christian, I have my own faith, my own beliefs that very few people share and very few people are actually interested in hearing about. I'm not a preacher.' Now that, I think, is interesting. But I'm going to resist giving a Christian reading of the notions of Gaia and the hive mind, and I'm going to resist setting Christianity alongside the 'natural law' argument and saying 'Look!' – both of those actions would be somewhat below the belt. I will also resist going into any detail about the incompatibility of Jesus' teachings with a system that promotes pan-capitalism and which is all but blind to those at the bottom. All this is part of a different article.

What I will say is that I, for one, would be very interested in hearing a technological discourse based not on nature, but on the Bible. Kelly, if you're truly committed to pointedly unfunny speculations about the future, you might as well jettison all this prosaic, 'natural' claptrap, put your money where your mouth is and head for the heavens. 'I am the Common Gateway Interface, the truth, and the light.' Cor, now wouldn't that be something?

Bombs and Bytes

Anustup Basu

Vol 1 #27, Winter/Spring 2004

Introduction

During the publicity drive toward building up domestic and international support for the 2003 war on Iraq, no functionary of the United States government actually made a public statement to the effect that Saddam Hussein had an active part to play in the devastation of 11 September, 2001. Nevertheless, it was subsequently noted in the opinion polls that an alarming number of American people believed that the Iraqi despot was involved in the conspiracy and its execution. Hence the two propositions – Saddam the evil one and 9/11, the horrible crime – seem to be associated in a demographic intelligence without having any narrative obligation to each other, that is, without being part of the same 'story'. The outcome, it seems, was achieved by a mathematical chain of chance by which two disparate postulates, in being publicised with adequate proximity, frequency and density, gravitate toward each other in an inhuman plane of massified thought. They, in other words, are bits and bytes of newspeak which have come to share what I will call an 'informatic' affinity with each other, without being organically conjoined by constitutive knowledge. The formation of the latter entity is, of course, something we are prone to consider a primary task of the philosophical human subject, who is also the modern citizen with rights and responsibilities. Attaining knowledge by reading the world is how we are supposed to self-consciously exercise reason, form views and partake in an enlightened project of democratic consensus and legislation. Hence, insofar as these much hallowed protocols of liberal democracy are concerned, this 9/11 opinion poll poses some disconcerting questions:

1. How does one account for the fact that what is, at face value, the most sophisticated technological assemblage for worldly communication and dissemination of 'truth', can sublimate what, in Kantian terms, must be called an unscientific belief or dogma?

2. To be mediatised literally means to lose one's rights. Hence, what happens to the idea of government by the people and for the people if the 'false' is produced as a third relation which is neither the synthetic union of two ideas in the conscious mind of the citizen, nor the general intellect of the organic community but a statistical coming together of variables?

3. If the 'false' is merely a moment in the overall control and management of an information environment and its electronic herd – that is, if it is simply a matter of manipulated distribution and saturation of facts in order to get a desired feedback in terms of public perception – what consequences does

that have in terms of human politics? How is the cynical intelligence of power that calls this into being to be configured?

4. Lastly, this distillation of the false as 'informatic' perception requires money. In other words, it requires a tremendous amount of wealth in order to not only bring the variables Saddam Hussein and 9/11 into a state of associative frequency, but also to minimise and regulate the appearance of other variables from appearing in the scenario. For instance, in this case, to reduce, for the time being, the frequency of the proper name Osama. Hence, the obvious question – what is the role of money in the purportedly postmodern, increasingly technologised, sphere of communicative action?

These are not new questions. They are a continuation of what a long line of western thinkers, from Antonio Gramsci to Giorgio Agamben, have been asking from various philosophical standpoints: how was it that modern technologies of reproduction of the artwork and electrification of the public sphere should produce European fascism as one of its first, grotesque spectacles? In a way, this anxious query seems to resonate, in a particular context, with the old Pascalian question posed at the very gestative period of a godless modern world: how does one protect the interests of abstract justice from the real, material interests of power in the world?

What is Information?

The paradox, *qua* modern publicity and communication, as it is expressed in Walter Benjamin's 'Work of Art' essay, can be outlined as follows: from the perspective of the enlightenment humanist, one could say that mechanised mass culture in the 20th century was supposed to 'de-auratise' the work of art and make it more democratically available. But, what Benjamin notices in his time is a disturbing incursion of aesthetics into politics, rather than the politicisation of art that could have been possible. This, for him, constitutes a 'violation' of the technologies of mass culture, by which the 'Führer cult' produces its ritual values of aestheticising war and destruction. Benjamin formulates the problem as belonging to a society not yet 'mature' enough to 'incorporate technology as its organ'. In Benjamin's essay, 'The Storyteller', we can see this problem being articulated as a situation in which forms of storytelling (which are at once educative and exemplary to the citizen for his cosmopolitan education, and also amenable to his freedom of critical interpretation and judgement) are replaced by a new form of communication which he calls information. The first characteristic of information is its erasure of distance – its near-at-hand-ness grants information the 'readiest hearing' and makes it appear 'understandable in itself'. The dissemination and reception of information is thus predicated on the production of the event as 'local', as 'already being shot through with explanation'. For the conscious subject, this also entails the disappearance of a temporal interval required for movement within the faculties, from cognition to understanding and then finally to knowledge. Information is that which is accompanied by the entropic violence brought about by a supersession of the commonplace, and a reduction of language into clichés. It is in the ruins of a constitutive or legislative language that the instantaneous circuit of the commonsensical comes into being. In this case, therefore, the establishment of Saddam's crimes does not remain a matter of old jurisprudence, following normative rules of argumentation, proof and deduction; it becomes an absolute movement of the commonsensical as the 'already explained'.

What is Fascism?

Fascism is the common name we accord to totalitarian power. However, we often do it irresponsibly or ahistorically, categorically identifying the concept with limited, sociologistic understandings of the German or Italian scenarios around the Great Wars, or confining it to grotesque figurations of human agency, like that of Mussolini or Hitler. If the concept is to have any critical valence whatsoever in our global, neoliberal occasion, it needs to be unpacked and re-articulated before we begin to transpose it here and there. Gilles Deleuze has re-articulated Benjamin's argument by transposing it from its organicist parabasis into a subhuman, molecular-pragmatic one. According to Deleuze, the discourses of fascism, as dominant myths in our time, establish themselves by an imperial-linguistic takeover of a whole social body of expressive potentialities. There are different forms of life and expressive energies in any situation of the historical, which are capable of generating multiple instances of thought, imaginative actions and wills to art. Fascism destroys such pre-signifying and pre-linguistic energies of the world, extinguishes pluralities and replaces them with a monologue of power that saturates space with, and only with, the immanent will of the dictator. This is the moment in which the language system sponsored by the sovereign is at its most violent; it seeks to efface historical memory by denying its constitutive or legislative relation with non-linguistic social energies; it casts itself and its unilateral doctrine as absolute and natural. For Deleuze, this is a psychomechanical production of social reality more than an organicity of community torn asunder by human alienation and the incursion of reactionary ideologies, and agents with false consciousnesses. Not that agents do not exist or are unimportant components in this matter, but that this technology of power cannot be simply seen as a neutral arrangement of tools misused by evil ones. The figure of the dictator is, therefore, not that of an aberrant individual madman, but a psychological automaton that becomes insidiously present in all – in the technology of massification itself. The images and objects that mass hallucination, somnambulism and trance produce are attributes of this immanent will to power.[1] The hypnotic, fascinating drive

1. Gilles Deleuze, *Cinema 2: The Time Image*, Minneapolis: University of Minnesota Press, 1989, pp. 263–9.

of fascism is thus seen to paradoxically operate below the radar of a moral and voluntaristic consciousness of the human subject; fascism becomes a political reality when knowledge-based exchanges between entities of intelligence give way to a technologism of informatics.

Thinking, knowledge or communicability (which is different from this or that technologism of communication) becomes foreclosed in such an order of power because one cannot really say anything that the social habit does not designate as something already thought of and pre-judged by the dictator. The publicity of fascism is one where friend and foe alike are seen to be engaged in tauto-talk, repeating what the dictator has already said or warned about. Benjamin calls this an eclipse of the order of cosmological mystery and secular miracles that the European humanist sciences of self and nature, and an enlightened novelisation of the arts, sought to delineate and solve. There can be neither secrecies in fascism, nor anything unknown. Conspiracies, in that sense, can only be manifestations of what is already foretold and waiting to be confessed. The SS can, of course, procure and store 'classified information', but it can never say anything that the Führer does not know better. Information, therefore, becomes an incessant and emphatic localisation of the global will of the dictator; in its seriality and movement, it can only keep repeating, illustrating and reporting the self-evident truth of the dictatorial monologue.[2] For Deleuze, it is in this immanence of dictatorial will that Hitler becomes information itself. Also, it is precisely because of this that one cannot wage a battle against Hitlerism by embarking on a battle of truth and falsehood without questioning, and taking for granted, the very parabasis of information and its social relations of production. 'No information, whatever it might be, is sufficient to defeat Hitler.'

Hence, like any other individual, Adolf the Aryan anti-Semite does not exhaust the figure of Hitler. Informatics has not ceased after the death of Adolf and his propaganda machine, or the passing away of the particular discourse of the Adolphic oracle and its immediate historical context. As a figural diagram, as a special shorthand for a particular technology of power, Hitler subsequently must have only become stronger; that is, if indeed we are to still account for him as an immanent will to information that invests modern societies. But how can one conceptualise him without the formalist baggage, in other words, without the grotesque, arborescent institutions of repression, like the secret police or the concentration camps, which constitute an historicist definition of fascism? If one were to put the question differently, that is, occasion it in terms of a present global order of neoliberalism marked by American style individualism, consumer choices, democracy and free markets that supposedly come to us after the agonistic struggles of liberation in the modern era are already settled, how

2. In this context, see Hannah Arendt's useful elaborations in *The Origins of Totalitarianism*, Fort Washington: Harvest Books, 1973.

can one enfigure the dead and buried tyrant in our midst in such an 'untimely' manner? How is Hitler possible in a liberal constitution? The question is a complicated one because, if we go back to the example we began our essay with, we will see that it actually satisfies the conditions of democratic accountability in terms of the human lie (the President never said this). Besides, it is also not the result of the state, as collective capitalist, monopolising the public sphere for propaganda purposes.

Perhaps one has to begin by not trying to enfigure Hitler in the contours of the human, as the irrational apex of the suicidal state or the pathological Goebbelsian liar who perverted the tools of human communication into mass propaganda machines. Hitler, in that sense, would not simply be the mediocre and grotesque madman who uses or abuses technology. He would still be a proper name for technologism itself; but, in his latest neoliberal incarnation, he would not be one who simply imprisons the human in enclosed spaces like the death camp or exercises a Faustian domination over him through arborescent structures like the Nazi war/propaganda machine. The 'postmodern' technology of information that we are talking about *qua* Hitler is neither external nor internal to the human; it is one that is a part of the latter's self-making, as well as that of the bio-anthropological environment in which he lives. Hitler enters us through a socialisation of life itself, through a technology of habituation that involves our willingness to be informed. It is a diffuse modality of power that perpetually communicates between the inside and the outside, erasing distance between the home and the world. It is in this context that Deleuze's statement, that there is a Hitler inside us, modern abjects of capital, becomes particularly significant. Hitler, as per this formulation, becomes an immanent form of sovereignty that is biopolitically present, percolating individuals and communities in an osmotic manner. Hitler as information, as socially immanent micro-fascisms, is not the addresser who speaks to us while we listen. It was only Adolf who did that in the old days, as the anachronistic caricature of the sovereign who had not yet had his head cut off but had simply 'lost it'. Information, on the other hand, is a metropolitan habit of instant signification; it is an administered social automaton that does not presume a contract between the speaker and the hearer. Since it has no point of origin other than the person informed, the instance of information is thus always one where the self listens to the commonsensical within the self itself, to the point where the two become indistinguishable. Hence, it is neither a lying President who says that Saddam Hussein had something to do with 9/11, nor was such a sublimation the result of unilateral state propaganda in the style of old Adolf or old Stalin. Information, in this sense, is indeed a commodified effect – a compact of words and images that is called into being by a non-linear and inhuman intelligence that, amongst other things, produces the human caricature or the icon of the Dictator himself. Informatisation, therefore, evades the legal question altogether by creating a situation where the commonsensical relation between Saddam Hussein and Al-Qa'ida is established not by the word of the sovereign (which can always be produced as evidence and contested in tribunals of justice) but by a manifest immanence of an inhuman sovereign will.

It is only when we understand the cult of information as a social mode of production that we can understand that the problem of mediatisation that we have been talking about does not concern the agency of the individual human at all. To put it blandly, this is not about a conspiracy of a cabal of capitalists and money mongers who manufacture truth in a determined manner; that is, Hitler in an anthropomorphic form who arbitrates what should be said and what should not. We are also not simply talking about representational intentions (what Karl Rove really wanted us to believe) or prejudices about representational capabilities (Americans, as a people, need to mature in order to be able to separate the wheat from the chaff). The effort, on the other hand, is to understand a situation where screen time is money time, where one has to have money or be sponsored by corporate interests of money, in order to be able to exercise one's right to 'self representation'. The fact that we are mediatised, hence bereft of rights, thus applies only differentially – all of us are Hitlers who command attention or nigger-infants (the Greek etymology of the word infant, as in *in-fans*, refers to the being without language) who listen without speaking, but only in differential degrees of hierarchised mediation. Without Adolf's old dividing walls, everyone can speak, blessed with the freedom of speech. Nominally, everyone can play the game of representations, since everyone has money. It is a different matter altogether, one that has not much to do with the language games of neoliberal economics and ideology, that some have a lot more of it than others.

Conclusion

A new form of political thinking has to begin by taking into account vast amounts of energies in the world that are antagonistic to capital. This has to be done in terms other than those pertaining to the figure of the human citizen and his charter of rights. It is part of the transcendental stupidity of the cult of information to impart such energies with a catalogue of profiles: the criminal, the delinquent, the madman, the negro, the woman, the child, the African AIDS victim, the poor, the unemployed, the illegal immigrant or the terrorist. Informatics is about the reporting of the state's pharmacopic action on these bodies, as objects of charity, aid, medication, schooling or military action. This is why the unspeakable antagonism of living labour in the world is never 'visible' on CNN, Fox or any other corporate, geo-televisual schema of metropolitan representation. The latter can discern only the ontology of money and its coalitionary interests – that which perpetually makes screen time money time. Humans, who are merely refugees great and small, can only climb into one or many of the designated profiles of massification. The centralising, perspectivist drive of CNN – as commentary of the world, as a repetitive human psychodrama of development (birth pangs of modernity in the frontier, subjugated and freed consumer desires) – overlooks the energy from the margins of the frame in trying to fit entire crowds into the telegenic face. This is why populations can be categorically divided into simple binaries like 'with us' or 'against us'. Labour and its multiple wills to antagonism (of which various narratives of resistance are only partial but undeniably important molar expressions) are thus un-representable precisely because they lack a 'human' face, or rather the face of the future American consumer. Global antagonisms to capital are at once utopic (as in 'non-place' since the logic of globalisation cannot posit an 'outside') and pantopic; they are, in multiple forms and in different degrees of sublimation, nowhere and everywhere. It is a complex, political understanding of such matters – like linking insurrectionary violence in different corners of the world to unfair and imbalanced trade practices like agricultural subsidiaries, dumping and tariff walls by first world countries – that spectacular informatisation removes or minimises from the public sphere. Politics therefore is replaced by symbiotic exchanges between peace and terror, and fear and security. Communication, likewise, is overwritten by a great monologue of global managerial-elite interests in which power speaks to itself.

A judgement of the panorama of expressions of this global antagonistic will on the lines of good and bad can take place only as an afterthought; political thinking in our occasion can begin only with the acknowledgement of these energies as eventful, and not subject to essential categories of a state language that has become global. In other words, thinking has to proceed acutely, from an awareness of that very point of danger, where the state fails to 'translate' such affective hostilities into repetitive instances of its own already explained story. It must be remembered that informatics, as a form of social production of consent, is able to attain a normative power precisely because it is accompanied by an epistemic presumption of the end of the historical process altogether.[3] Stories therefore cannot be seen to be teaching us anything new in terms of constitutive politics because in the new world order of a globally rampant neoliberalism, there can be nothing new to narrate at all, in terms of alternative destinies and potentials of the world. They can only be local instances of crisis and management in a grand chronicle of financialisation of the globe that is already foretold. It is this dire poverty of political language that the neoliberal state tries to cover up with violence dictated in a situation of 'emergency' that is legitimised by an emotionalist, folksy rhetoric of 'good' and 'evil'. Here I must strongly clarify that I am not registering support for

3. I am, of course, alluding to Francis Fukuyama's Kojèvian-Hegelian thesis in *The End of History and the Last Man*, New York: Avon Books, 1992.

either the undeniably tyrannical Saddam Hussein, or a statist ideology of violence like that of Al-Qa'ida. These two totalitarian entities, like some of their Western counterparts, merely capture and mobilise some of these antagonistic energies. As far as the latter is concerned, it is not difficult to see how informatics peddles the worst clichés of neoliberalism in trying to enframe antagonism through a host of good and evil profile doublets – the model minority contra the inner city delinquent, the healthy contra the mad, the peaceful Arab contra the Islamic bigot – according to which a population is invented and managed, or policed and fed. In terms of spectacle and violence, it thus falls perfectly within the logic of war/information to have the yellow cluster bomb be interspersed with the yellow food packet during the recent war in Afghanistan. The global state of surveillance and security today violently tries to foreclose the political by informatising complex insurrectionary potentialities in terms of a simplistic, self-evident and bipolar logic of peace and terror. The latter thus becomes a generic term to reductively describe a multiplicity of forces – from Latin American guerrilla movements, to African tribal formations, to Islamic militancy in the Middle-East to Maoist rebellion in Nepal. The freedom of choice offered by the globally rampant North Atlantic machine of war and informatics is no longer between dwelling as a poet or as an assassin, but between a statistic or a terrorist.

Info-Enclosure 2.0

Dmytri Kleiner and Brian Wyrick

Vol 2 #4, Winter 2006/Spring 2007

Wikipedia says that:

> Web 2.0, a phrase coined by O'Reilly Media in 2004, refers to a supposed second generation of internet-based services – such as social networking sites, wikis, communication tools and folksonomies – that emphasise online collaboration and sharing among users.

The use of the word 'supposed' is noteworthy. As probably the largest collaboratively authored work in history, and one of the current darlings of the internet community, Wikipedia ought to know. Unlike most of the members of the Web 2.0 generation, Wikipedia is controlled by a non-profit foundation, earns income only by donation and releases its content under the copyleft GNU Free Documentation Licence. It is telling that Wikipedia goes on to say '[Web 2.0] has become a popular (though ill-defined and often criticised) buzzword among certain technical and marketing communities'.

The free software community has tended to be suspicious, if not outright dismissive, of the Web 2.0 moniker. Tim Berners-Lee dismissed the term, saying 'Web 2.0 is of course a piece of jargon, nobody even knows what it means'. He goes on to note that 'it means using the standards which have been produced by all these people working on Web 1.0'. In reality there is neither a Web 1.0 nor a Web 2.0; there is an ongoing development of online applications that cannot be cleanly divided.

In trying to define what Web 2.0 is, it is safe to say that most of the important developments have been aimed at enabling a given community to create, modify and share content in a way that was previously only available to centralised organisations which bought expensive software packages and paid staff to handle the technical aspects of the site and to create content which was generally published only on that organisation's site.

A Web 2.0 company fundamentally changes the mode of production of internet content. Web applications and services have become cheaper and easier to implement, and, by allowing the end users access to these applications, a company can effectively outsource the creation and the organisation of their content to the end users themselves. Instead of the traditional model of a content provider publishing its own content and the end user consuming it, the new model allows the company's site to act as the centralised portal between the users who are both creators and consumers.

For the user, access to these applications empowers them to create and publish content that previously would have required them to purchase desktop software and possess a greater technological skill set. For example, two of the primary means of text-based content production in Web 2.0 are blogs and wikis which allow the user to create and publish content directly from their browser without any real need for knowledge of markup language, file transfer or syndication protocols, and all without the need to purchase any software.

The use of the web application to replace desktop software is even more significant for the user when it comes to content that is not merely textual. Not only can web pages be created and edited in the browser without purchasing HTML editing software, photographs can be uploaded and manipulated online through the browser without the need for expensive desktop image manipulation applications. A video shot on a consumer camcorder can be submitted to a video hosting site, uploaded, encoded, embedded into an HTML page, published, tagged and syndicated across the web all through the user's browser.

Paul Graham's article on Web 2.0, 'What Business Can Learn From Open Source', breaks down the different roles of the community/user into more specific roles, those being the Professional, the Amateur and the User (more specifically, the end user). The roles of the Professional and the User were, according to Graham, well understood in Web 1.0, but the Amateur didn't have a very well defined place. As Graham describes it, the Amateur just loves to work, with no concern for compensation or ownership of that work; in development, the Amateur contributes to open source software whereas the Professional gets paid for their proprietary work.

Graham's characterisation of the Amateur reminds one of *If I Ran The Circus* by Dr. Seuss, where young Morris McGurk says of the staff of his imaginary Circus McGurkus, 'My workers *love* work. They say, 'Work us! Please work us! We'll work and we'll work up so many surprises You'd never see half if you had forty eyses!' And, while 'Web 2.0' may mean nothing to Berners-Lee – who sees recent innovations as no more than the continued development of the web – to venture capitalists, who, like Morris McGurk, daydream of tireless workers producing endless content and not demanding a pay cheque for it, it sounds stupendous. And indeed, from YouTube to Flickr to Wikipedia, you'd truly never see half if you had forty eyses.

Berners-Lee is correct. There is nothing from a technical or user point of view in Web 2.0 which does not have its roots in, and is not a natural development from, Web 1.0. The technology associated with the Web 2.0 banner was possible, and in some cases readily available, before; but the hype surrounding this usage has certainly affected the growth of Web 2.0 internet sites.

The internet (which is more than the web, actually) has always been about sharing between users. In fact, Usenet, a distributed messaging system, has been operating since 1979! Since long before even Web 1.0, Usenet has been hosting discussions, 'amateur' journalism, and enabling photo and file sharing. Like the internet, it is a distributed system not owned or controlled by anyone. It is this quality, a lack of central ownership and control, which differentiates services such as Usenet from Web 2.0.

If Web 2.0 means anything at all, its meaning lies in the rationale of venture capital. Web 2.0 represents the return of investment in internet startups. After the dotcom bust (the real end of Web 1.0), those wooing investment dollars needed a new rationale for investing in online ventures. 'Build it and they will come', the dominant attitude of the '90s dotcom boom, along with the delusional 'new economy', was no longer attractive after so many online ventures failed. Investors were no longer interested in building infrastructure or financing real capitalisation; capturing value created by others, however, proved to be a more attractive proposition.

Web 2.0 is Internet Investment Boom 2.0. Web 2.0 is a business model; it means private capture of community-created value. No one denies that the technology of sites like YouTube, for instance, is trivial. This is more than evidenced by the large number of identical services, such as DailyMotion. The real value of YouTube is not created by the developers of the site, but rather it is created by the people who upload videos to the site. Yet, when YouTube was bought for over a billion dollars worth of Google stock, how much of this stock was acquired by those that made all those videos? Zero. Zilch. Nada. Great deal if you are an owner of a Web 2.0 company.

The value produced by users of Web 2.0 services such as YouTube is captured by capitalist investors. In some cases, the actual content they contribute winds up the property of site owners. Private appropriation of community-created value is a betrayal of the promise of sharing technology and free cooperation.

Unlike Web 1.0, where investors often financed expensive capital acquisition, software development and content creation, a Web 2.0 investor mainly needs to finance hype-generation, marketing and buzz. The infrastructure is widely available and cheap, the content is free and the cost of the software is either free or negligible. Basically, by providing some bandwidth and disk space, you are able to become a successful internet site if you can market yourself effectively.

The principal success of a Web 2.0 company comes from its relationship to the community; more specifically, the ability of the company to 'harness collective intelligence', as O'Reilly puts it. Web 1.0 companies were too monolithic and unilateral in their approach to content. Success stories of the transition from Web 1.0 to Web 2.0 were based on the ability for a company to remain monolithic in its brand of content or, better yet, its outright ownership of that content, while opening up the method of that content's creation to the community: Yahoo! created a portal to community content while it remained the centralised location for finding that content; eBay allows the community to sell its goods while owning the marketplace for those goods; and Amazon, selling the same products as many other sites, succeeded by allowing the community to participate in the 'flow' around their products.

Because the capitalists who invest in Web 2.0 startups do not often fund early capitalisation, their behaviour is markedly more parasitic as well. They often arrive late in the game, when value creation already has good momentum, swoop in to take ownership and use their financial power to promote the service, often within the context of a hegemonic network of major, well financed partners. This means that companies that are not acquired by venture capital end up cash-starved and squeezed out of the club.

In all these cases, the value of the internet site is created not by the paid staff of the company that runs it, but by the users who use it. With all of the emphasis on community-created content and sharing, it's easy to overlook the other side of the Web 2.0 experience: ownership of all this content and the ability to monetise its value. To the user, this doesn't come up that often – it's only part of the fine print in their MySpace Terms of Service agreement, or it's the Flickr.com in the URL of their photos. It doesn't usually seem like an issue to the community; it's a small price to pay for the use of these wonderful applications and for the impressive effect on search engines when one queries one's own name. Since most users do not have access to alternative means to produce and publish their own content, they are attracted to sites like MySpace and Flickr.

Meanwhile, the corporate world has been pushing a whole different idea of the Information Superhighway, producing monolithic, centralised 'online services' like CompuServe, Prodigy and AOL. What separated these from the internet is that these were centralised systems that all users connect to directly, while the internet is a peer-to-peer (P2P) network; every device with a public internet address can communicate directly to any other device. This is what makes P2P technology possible. This is also what makes independent internet service providers possible.

It should be added that many open source projects can be cited as the key innovations in the development of Web 2.0: free software like Linux, Apache, PHP, MySQL, Python, etc. are the backbone of Web 2.0 and the web itself. But there is a fundamental flaw with all of these projects in terms of what O'Reilly refers to as the Core Competencies of Web 2.0 companies – namely control over unique, hard-to-recreate data sources that get richer as more people use them; the harnessing of the collective intelligence they attract. Allowing the community to contribute openly and to utilise that contribution within the context of a proprietary system where the proprietor owns the content is a characteristic of a successful Web 2.0 company. Allowing the community to own what it creates, though, is not. Thus, to be successful and create profits for investors, a Web 2.0 company needs to create mechanisms for sharing and collaboration that are centrally controlled. The lack of central control possessed by Usenet and other peer-controlled technologies is the fundamental flaw; they only benefit their users – they do not benefit absentee investors, as they are not 'owned'.

Thus, because Web 2.0 is funded by Capitalism 2006, Usenet is mostly forgotten. While everybody uses Digg and Flickr and YouTube is worth a billion dollars, PeerCast, an innovative P2P live video streaming network that has been in existence for several years longer than YouTube, is virtually unknown.

From a technological standpoint, distributed and peer-to-peer technologies are far more efficient than Web 2.0 systems. Making better use of network resources by using the computers and network connections of users, P2P avoids the kind of bottlenecks created by centralised systems and allows content to be published with less infrastructure, often with no more than a computer and a consumer internet connection. P2P systems do not require the massive data centres of sites such as YouTube. The lack of central infrastructure also comes with a lack of central control, meaning less censorship – often a problem with privately-owned 'communities' that frequently bend to private and public pressure groups and enforce limitations on the kinds of content they allow. Also, the lack of large, central cross-referencing databases of user information has a strong advantage in terms of privacy.

From this perspective, it can be said that Web 2.0 is capitalism's pre-emptive attack against P2P systems. Despite its many comparative disadvantages, Web 2.0 is more attractive to investors, and thus has more money to fund and promote centralised solutions. The end result of this is that capitalist investment flowed into centralised solutions, making them easy and cheap or free for non-technical information producers to adopt. Thus, this ease of access compared to the more technically challenging and expensive undertaking of owning your own means of information production created a 'landless' information proletariat ready to provide alienated content-creating labour for the new info-landlords of Web 2.0.

It is often said that the internet took the corporate world by surprise, coming as it did out of publicly funded university and military research. It was promoted by way of a cottage industry of small independent internet service providers who were able to squeeze a buck out of providing access to the state-built and -financed network.

The internet seemed anathema to the capitalist imagination. Web 1.0, the original dotcom boom, was characterised by a rush to own the infrastructure, to consolidate the independent internet service providers. While money was thrown around quite randomly as investors struggled to understand what this medium would actually be used for, the overall mission was largely successful. If you had an internet account in 1996, it was likely provided by some small local company. Ten years later, while some of the smaller companies have survived, most people get their internet access from gigantic telecommunications corporations. The mission of Internet Investment Boom 1.0 was to destroy the independent service provider and put large, well-financed corporations back in the driving seat.

The mission of Web 2.0 is to destroy the P2P aspect of the internet. To make you, your computer and your internet connection dependent on connecting to a centralised service that controls your ability to communicate. Web 2.0 is the ruin of free, P2P systems and the return of monolithic 'online services'. A telling detail here is that most home or office internet connections in the '90s, modem and ISDN connections, were synchronous – equal in their ability to send and receive data. By design, your connection enabled you to be equally a producer and a consumer of information. On the other hand, modern DSL and cable-modem connections are asynchronous, allowing you to download information quickly, but upload slowly. Not to mention the fact that many user agreements for internet service forbid you to run servers on your consumer circuit, and may cut off your service if you do.

Capitalism, rooted in the idea of earning income by way of idle share ownership, requires centralised control, without which peer producers have no reason to share their income with outside shareholders. Capitalism, therefore, is incompatible with free P2P networks, and, thus, so long as the financing of internet development comes from private shareholders looking to capture value by owning internet resources, the network will only become more restricted and centralised.

It should be noted that, even in the case of commons-based peer production, so long as the commons and membership in the peer group is limited, and inputs such as food for the producers and the computers that they use are acquired from outside the commons-based peer group, then the peer producers themselves may be complicit in the exploitative capturing of this labour value. Thus, in order to really address the unjust capture of alienated labour value, access to the commons and membership in the peer group must be extended as far as possible toward the inclusion of a total system of goods and services. Only when all productive goods are available from commons-based producers can all producers retain the value of the product of their labour.

And, while the information commons may have the possibility of playing a role in moving society toward more inclusive modes of production, any real hope for a genuine, community-enriching, next generation of internet-based services is not rooted in creating privately owned, centralised resources, but rather in creating cooperative, P2P and commons-based systems, owned by everybody and nobody. Although small and obscure by today's standards, with its focus on P2P applications such as Usenet and email, the early internet was very much a common, shared resource. Along with the commercialisation of the internet and the emergence of capitalist financing comes the enclosure of this information commons, translating public wealth into private profit. Thus, Web 2.0 is not to be thought of as a second generation of either the technical or social development of the internet, but rather as the second wave of capitalist enclosure of the information commons.

Virtually all of the most used internet resources could be replaced by P2P alternatives. Google could be replaced by a P2P search system, where every browser and every web server were active nodes in the search process; Flickr and YouTube could also be replaced by PeerCast and eDonkey-type applications, which allow users to use their own computers and internet connections to collaboratively share their pictures and videos. However, developing internet resources requires the application of wealth, and, so long as the source of this wealth is finance capital, the great P2P potential of the internet will remain unrealised.

Chapter 2

From Net Art to Conceptual Art and Back

For those introduced to new media art in the 1990s, the discovery of an earlier history of conceptual, computer art was often quite a startling revelation. Although the stand-alone, hard-drive based new media art of the late-'80s and early-'90s was often put into the same lineage as art made in the commercial computer labs of the past, there was a whole streak of more autonomous and socially critical technology-orientated work that was being sidelined by the new media art circuit. It was to these artists that *Mute*'s coverage increasingly turned, as their historically and politically grounded approach provided tools with which to critique some of the worst excesses of new media art naïveté. As the heady euphoria surrounding the www 'revolution' subsided, and its promise of delivering communicative equality and social autonomy revealed itself to be a cyber-fantasy, the desire to bring the force of avant-garde critique to bear on the market-complicit gadgetry of so much new media art became an almost compulsive desire for the *Mute* editors.

The chronological arrangement of this chapter charts the intensification of such looping-back into the themes of earlier, technologically-orientated conceptual art, which departs from the contemporary altogether. Rather than intending to suggest any dying off of contemporary art coverage in the magazine per se, this trajectory is dictated by the decision to remain faithful to the chapter's main theme. This could loosely be defined as art's engagement with the potentials of techno-scientific development in the wake of modernity's failed narrative of (science- and technology-driven) progress.

In the temporal span of the chapter, it is interesting to see how certain concerns regarding the relationship between art and technology persist. Far from celebrating the ICA's 1968 show, Cybernetic Serendipity, as the first exhibition in the UK dedicated to 'the computer and the arts', Gustav Metzger, dismissed it for obscuring computing's principal deployment in modern warfare and social control, claiming that, 'whilst more and more scientists are investigating the threats that science and technology pose for society, artists are being led into a technological kindergarten.'

Writing some 30 years later, about another ICA show – Imaginaria, dedicated to art and digital technology – Ewan Morrison claims, 'The inherent technological utopianism of Digital Art is irresponsible, naïve and dangerous.' He goes on to argue that technology always serves the interests of power, and that so-called digital artists fall prey to an agenda not their own. A similar concern is expressed by '90s net artist, Vuk Ćosić, as he discusses artists who are 'following high-tech and trying to be posh', when actually 'they are only selling equipment'. 'As an artist', he concludes, 'you're only falling within the boundaries of the imagination of an engineer if you're working with an off-the-shelf product.'

But, while there is a perennial return of certain themes, there is also a total amnesia regarding others – according to Morrison at least. Crucial to his argument against digital art is the apparent failure of these artists to deal with the postmodern crisis of human progress. Technology hasn't been used as a tool for social emancipation but for mass annihilation, and the associated modernist projects of communism and humanism have similarly failed. Intimately related to this is a loss of faith in art – therefore, says Morrison, any idea that the computer is giving rise to a *new* art form fails not only to recognise this epistemological crisis but to adequately respond to it. Art's only respectable path, he asserts, is to revisit the conditions of its impossibility and those of society.

Although such critiques of techno-utopian art are well grounded, they don't recognise the attempt by certain artists to find, in the very techniques and logic of the military-industrial complex, a way of mirroring, and thereby exposing/ subverting, this system of power. As Matthew Fuller puts it: 'We live in an era in which the dominant mode of politics is systems analysis. Power has been handed over to a series of badly animated, white-shirted technicians who deliver fault reports and problem-fixes that can only be answered with an 'Okay' [...] In this context, it is essential for artists and others to synthesise an un-format-able world.'

Josephine Bosma in her piece, 'Is It a Commercial? Nooo... Is It Spam?... Nooo – It's Net Art!' – one of the earliest published overviews of the emerging genre of net art – takes another tack. In essence she argues, albeit in 1998, that the speed with which artists have taken to the web has succeeded in outstripping the art world's ability to keep pace. Accordingly, commodification of the artwork was proving difficult, abetted by the rate of browser development, which meant that artworks designed to run on older browser softwares quickly became obsolete. The ephemerality of the medium was actively embraced by artists, many of whom also refused to 'sign' their works or to locate them in a permanent place. Rather than promoting a utopian view of the technology, then, these artists could be said to have exploited the faults in a specific technical system to advance a materialist critique of art's own system.

However, Bosma also discusses the attempt by an early 'experimental net-based company' called ada'web to develop new ways of funding art by offering net art as a form of 'creative research' to the corporate sector, rather than asking for '"charity" money'. Founder, Benjamin Weil, is quoted as explaining that this 'could make them understand better the medium they were investing in, and draw attention to their corporation as being innovative'. Not only does this strike one as a classic piece of knowledge economy rationale, it also reminds us of how commercially intoxicating the relationship between high-tech and art continues to be. One quickly sees the risks faced by artists working with technology in an avowedly experimental way – making medium-specific work which both critiques *and* advances those means – rather than deploying familiar technologies to draw attention to existing modes of life.

Michael Corris' piece, 'Systems Upgrade', gives a crucial overview of the 'white hot' technological and scientific environment of the 1960s, and artists' responses to it. In the wake of the accelerated technological development of war-time production – and the advancements in the productive base this had achieved – scientific and technological R&D were seen as central to the economy, and funded as never before. The significance of systems theory, cybernetics and information theory at this time – which artist, Stephen Willats, affirms in the interview *Mute* undertook with him in 2000 – took hold of the '1960s imagination', expressed in a general enthusiasm for logic, order and systems. Corris discusses how these technocratic theories, hatched from 'the objectives of military or corporate management', were integrated into art both optimistically and critically. Impacting on conceptual art's generalised bureaucratic and informatic aesthetic, the likes of Roy Ascott took matters further, seeking to transform art through the adoption of 'homeostatic, self-regulating, self-assessing systems'. At the other end of the scale, argues Corris, systems theory provoked artists like Hans Haacke to deconstruct the entire social system in which the artwork participates. In other words, and in contradistinction to Morrison's argument, the neo-avant-garde was able to rehearse the dystopian aftermath of modernity using its own techno-scientific tools. However, a distinction needs to be made between using a systems-based analysis to demystify the apparently neutral context of art, and using digital technology's tendency to become obsolete – its glitches and failures – within the postmodern context of art's endgame.

Any residual positivism in Haacke's method had well and truly vanished from the net art of the '90s – as it has from the general culture. And, as the Cold War – which provided the backdrop to artistic engagements with technology in the '60s and '70s – threatens to reignite itself (with Russia's invasion of Georgia and the construction of a US missile shield at the former superpower's borders), technology's destructive power once again comes to the fore. With the social acculturation to computer technology virtually complete – thanks, in part, to the user-friendliness of Web 2.0 – the return of its repressed military uses in the form of Cold War II will no doubt challenge the hegemony of touchy-feely, 'socially engaged' varieties of media art. Conversely, however, the aura of warfare in the age of embedded reporting and incessant blogging has waned. The extent to which the civil application of computing will come to haunt its military matrix, or to which its military origins will crack the upbeat veneer lent to it by social networking, remains to be seen. Artists' engagements with bleeding-edge tech will always have the potential to critique its destructive civil and military applications, as well as the potential to be co-opted by them – as propaganda or R&D – as the rise of the so-called knowledge economy has amply demonstrated. This chapter hopefully conveys how delicate the equilibrium between art and technology remains.

THE THING: A Sysop Describes his Art Bulletin Board and the Network of which it is a Part

Andreas Rüthi

Vol 1 #1, Spring 1995

THE THING is an independent computer network, initiated in 1992 in New York by artists, art critics and curators. The following European cities are now connected: London (since 1994), Cologne, Berlin, Düsseldorf, Frankfurt, Hamburg, Munich, Vienna, Basel and Copenhagen. Future points of connection will be in Paris and Amsterdam.

Since the early-1990s, art discourse and the discussion of its social context have begun to have the equivalent standing in the actual realisations of artworks. This can be seen in the plethora of workshops, lectures and discussion events that more often than not follow institutional and curatorial frameworks, but hardly ever actively reflect the form of the discourse itself. Rather than following the classical mode of disseminating information, i.e. the lecturer (as transmitter) and the audience (as receiver), THE THING was conceived as a tool for artists, art critics and curators, to allow a multi-relationary communication and intervention, rather than being an end in itself. This choice of format is influenced by the dematerialisation of art's parameters which began in the '60s. The distribution of information in the art context takes certain discrete forms (whereby discrete knowledge = capital); the ability to be anonymous as a network user allows similar strategies. This fact makes one sceptical if, in the end, the hidden subtext is more significant to the art discourse than the 'open' discourse which is coded by other interests.

Up to now, public presentation of THE THING has primarily been indicated by the presence of a workstation in public galleries (Dagegen-Dabei: Production and Strategy in Art Projects since 1969 at Kunstverein Munich, and Interface at Kunstverein Hamburg). This signifies the activity but doesn't encourage audience participation. Therefore, the importance is placed on the evidence that such an activity is currently taking place, rather than what is actually happening. If you consider that, in the paradigms of the '90s, lots of artistic positions are contextual and/or intervention-based, then, as a result, every form of cultural activism can use electronic communication as a vital tool. This would mean that THE THING functions at the line between real artistic presence (exhibitions, workshops, discussions) and the 'invisible' forms of discourse, which have initiated the former or have been derived from them. Owing to the regularity and speed of the contact, this creates a social texture which printed media cannot develop as quickly. It is important to recognise that there can't be editorial control of THE THING. Passive use is discouraged, since each user is intended to be both reader and writer. The result could be seen as a network of secret agents which represents a small part of the contemporary art scene. The linking up with the internet, in April 1995, is compatible with the structure and aims of THE THING. Assuming that we will see a further contextualisation of post-conceptual art, then we need to ask ourselves whether non-art areas will profit from the impulses of art or the other way round. In relation to THE THING, this could mean that, if we continue discussing art exclusively, the discussion could ultimately refer only to itself and go round and round in circles. The discourse between contextual art positions and those of external disciplines – such as biotechnology, media sciences, biology, ecology etc. – will create a perspective that is indispensable to the art of the '90s. The merit of THE THING has been to locate the possibilities of technological communication within contemporary art. The border character of THE THING provides the possibility to create such a constructively mixed culture.

Is It a Commercial? Nooo… Is It Spam?… Nooo – It's Net Art!

Josephine Bosma

Vol 1 #10, Summer 1998

The most annoying discussion surrounding net art is the one that asks whether or not net art is truly a new art form. While some critics continue to deny the existence of this new art form within the communication networks, net art should be given some definition and positioned in relation to offline culture.

Place, History, Time

The term 'net.art' was first used in 1996 when Vuk Ćosić organised the small gathering, net.art per se, in Trieste. The dot in it made the term a sexy and humorous one. The people who got involved with net.art were mostly connected through 'nettime' – the mailing list for net.criticism [www.desk.nl/~nettime]. Nettime also saw the first criticism of the term, which soon provoked a broader discussion about art on the net. From the outset, this discussion was complex and it had many layers. The discourse around net.art and its many relatives (net art/netart/web art/art on the net) is confusing in the extreme.

In essence, this complexity is caused by net art's embeddedness within networks, a characteristic that also makes it so hard to describe. Building theory around art on the net, and, more specifically, doing this in constant discourse with others on the net, exposes one very directly to a mass of conflicting opinions, levels of perception and layers of communication. Add to this the unavoidable connection to the offline world and you have an explosive mixture of interests, cultures, schools and markets.

While the art world (a complex of the art market, academies, theorists and journalists) tries to get its expansionist grip on the development of new media art, the old electronic arts scene keeps to itself, sceptical of this newfound interest in electronic media. With the development of new media art, the art market is, quite literally, losing sight of the matter, and, with it, the self-evident creation of a product to sell. Whereas the electronic art scene (I am thinking of the circuit including Ars Electronica, V2, ZKM and ISEA) has based seminars and thematic exhibitions around online arts for years, the art world has suddenly been forced to deal with a shift away from commerce and postmodern capitalism by a medium with which it is hardly familiar. The art world is now desperately trying to find ways to encapsulate the electronic arts, and professionals are repositioning themselves on all fronts in this process. The development of electronic media has redistributed the tools of production and shifted the understanding of the value of art: What will become of the artist and the artwork? How will art be funded, and for what will artists be rewarded?

Ada'web

The recent discussion around ada'web [www2.awa.com/artnetweb/ia/] – an art site which recently lost its corporate funding and had to close down – is only one example of how delicate the new forms of collaboration are within communication networks. Ada'web was an experimental net-based company, and its story shows why the strategies of 'net.experiments' require constant re-examination. What seem like good tactics during one period can become obsolete, or downright dangerous, during another. Benjamin Weil of ada'web explained on nettime:

> Part of ada'web's founding mission was to explore possible alternatives as far as funding for art online was concerned [...] It was my belief that the development of the web would be an extraordinary opportunity for art to desegregate itself, and (re)gain a central position in ambient cultural discourse and practice [...] Rather than knocking at the corporate door asking for 'charity' money, we thought we could convince them that art could be a valuable asset, [...] it could be understood as a form of creative research which could make them understand better the medium they were investing in, and draw attention to their corporation as being innovative.

Ada'web tried to sell creativity and innovation, as a necessary commodity, to companies. It is questionable whether this is art's main strength, though, and, arguably a subtle misjudgement was made on the part of ada'web in positing art's 'functionality' in this way. Perhaps ada'web would have been more credible in the eyes of both the corporations and the net artists if it had tried to convince its benefactors of art's intrinsic value before entering the 'art as innovative inspirer' chapter. On the other hand, ada'web made many important steps, one of which was to present artworks by their names and not those of the artists. In this way, value was assigned more to the work than to its provenance. Detaching work from its 'brand' could be a dominant strategy in the near future, and the experience of ada'web urges caution. For one thing, we will need to pay attention to the inability of small enterprises and individuals to protect authorship of their work, as big corporations are as protectionist as ever.

What is Net Art?

Art on the internet is more than just a continuation of 20th century art, and the notion that net.art/net art is just another step in art history is, however, presently used derisively. The experiments being carried out on the internet are, in a certain sense, without precedent. Furthermore, art on the net is catalysing a resumption of discourses centred more on art's intrinsic value than on the mechanisms of the art market.

Very early net art could mostly be defined as performative – it was temporary and left almost no trace within the networks. What distinguishes net art from earlier electronic art is its expanded connection to the internet (or the net's predecessors). One could say that the more complex these connections become, the more we are able to talk about net art. This complexity is not necessarily found in literal hardware connections. Some more recent works achieve complexity through their poetic use of the whole network space. Artists have become so much more at home in the communications networks that an emotive but subtle use of those features is now possible.

Early net art mostly worked with data transmissions that were reassembled at creative will, on all ends of the 'line', and comprised sound, text and performance, simultaneously taking place in cyberspace, the mass media (mostly radio) and in physical spaces. An example would be *The World in Twenty Four Hours* by Robert Adrian, presented at Ars Electronica in 1982.[1]

In the recent work of 'young' art groups like Fakeshop or Re-lab (Xchange), one can find complexity in various forms. The poetic complexity I referred to earlier is found in, for instance, 'subtle' uses of the locality of servers, like in the Refresh project initiated by Alexei Shulgin, Vuk Ćosić and Andreas Broeckmann. It can also be found in Olia Lialina's work, *Agatha Appears*, in which a ghost-like female figure appears in the same position on the pages of different servers. Lialina has published part of her diary on the net, in which she shows her subjective experiences of a 'culty' secret net.art meeting. She has also published her will online, which contains only her online works, to be inherited almost exclusively by people with a similar obsession for net.art. To Lialina, the network environment is almost sacred, and she wants to pronounce its features strongly in a sensitive, sometimes romantic, way.

An example that stands out because of its unique style is Jodi (the collective name of artists Joan Heemskerk and Dirk Paesmans). Jodi's work is both deeply poetic and complex, although they rarely work within decentralised art projects, preferring to concentrate on their site, Jodi.org. Jodi.org dates back to the grey Browser Netscape 1.0. Yet, Yahoo! refused to list it under *any* category. Now the Jodi site is, without doubt, the most interesting and most discussed art website.

So, is it relevant to make a distinction between net art and other art? On the whole, the question is irrelevant. Names for new art forms are just tools; they should be helpful in understanding what we are dealing with on a very basic, practical level. In essence, there is nothing wrong with the categorisation of different art forms. Equally, artists who do not describe their work as art can avoid limiting discussions about the relevance and value of their work within an art market.

Temporal Theory

To place net art in the right perspective, art history must be partly rewritten. Too much emphasis has been placed on the commodity status of artworks during this

1. Tilman Baumgaertel, journalist for both off- and on-line publications, wrote a long article on *Telepolis*, which is a brave attempt to put the entire history of net art into sequence. The article is available, in German only, at www.heise.de/tp/deutsch/special/ku/6151/1.html

century. Inevitably, this tendency has excluded certain art and artists who do not satisfy related criteria. Perhaps net art offers us the opportunity to rethink the criteria by which art is valued. For instance, one can already distinguish between those artists using, or making work about, technology and electronic media who indulge in utopian fantasies (like the Futurists with their fascist tendencies) – and those whose experiments demystified the media (for example, in the '60s and '70s), and the playful approach of present-day artists who handle media with great ease and humour and with less reverence.

Of course, net art is not an easily perceivable object. A lot of art on the net appears very scattered due to its transience and use of multiple media. In order to experience it, one has to be an avid follower of net.culture. Nowadays, there is already a tendency amongst net artists to make their work more lasting, which is possibly a consequence of the increased interest in net art. Artists act and react within an environment. Some net artworks are more or less lost today, like early Jodi works that need to be viewed on older, virtually extinct browsers.[2] Some net artists try to be invisible and dissolve into fake identities and ephemeral works.[3]

Not recognising its uniqueness is obstructing the development of discourse around art on the net, and good opportunities for deeper understanding are missed because the theoretical framework around net art does not keep pace with the artworks. Perhaps art only profits from this obscurity.

Related URLs:

Vuk Ćosić, net.art per se: www.ljudmila.org/naps/
ada'web: adaweb.com
nettime archive for 'funding for the arts' discussion: www.factory.org/nettime
The homework project: jupiter.ucsd.edu/~bookchin/finalProject.html
Mr. Net.Art: www.irational.org/tm/mr/
Robert Adrian: www.aec.at/freelance/rax/24_HOURS/
Norman White: www.bmts.com/~normill/artpage.html
Fakeshop: www.fakeshop.com/
Re-lab/Xchange: xchange.re-lab.net
Olia Lialina, *Agatha Appears*: www.c3.hu/collection/agatha
net.art diary: www.design.ru/olialia/diary.htm
Will: will.teleportacia.org/
Refresh: sunsite.cs.msu.su/wwwart/refresh.htm
Recycling The Future: thing.at/orfkunstradio/FUTURE/RTF/index.html
Strange but good site full of net art links (on a Peruvian server):
ekeko.rcp.net.pe/lagaleria/

2. *Digital Rain* is an example of an early Jodi work that has suffered from the new generation web browers jodi.org/beta/rain/digi.html
3. For example, Rachel Baker or 'Trina Mould'.

Ten Reasons Why the Art World Hates Digital Art

Ewan Morrison

Vol 1 #11, Autumn 1998

The art world hates digital art. The ICA's show, Imaginaria, which sets out to showcase the best of digital art from 1997–8, has helped to clarify the reasons why digital art is shunned by the art world, and why it will never be accepted into the canon of high art. The following is a list of reasons why 'digital art' will not be accepted as fine art.

1. A new art form – give it up! Art is dead. There is nothing more futile than aspiring to the condition of art at a time when giving up art is the only legitimate art form.

Since Jean Baudrillard claimed that art is dead and continues to exist only as a simulation of its former self, the only way to make art has been to endlessly replay the death of art – to take 'the authentic' and show that it is a simulation. Digital art seems to start from a misreading of Baudrillard: it attempts to make art out of simulacra and then claim authenticity for its own products.

Within Imaginaria, there is one work which seems to stand as a metaphor for the status of digital art within the art world: *Anabiosis*, by Simon Tegala, monitors the heart rate of the artist through a screen display. 'Anabiosis' is the medical term for 'revival after apparent death'. Could it be that digital art sees itself as a new lease on life within an art world obsessed with death, obsolescence and redundancy? Perhaps suicide could be suggested as a way for this artist to be accepted into the canon of contemporary art.

2. 'Digital art' does not exist. In proclaiming itself as a new medium, digital art has failed to recognise that art is no longer medium-specific. Artists now operate across disciplines – text, image, moving image, event – and use whatever tools are at their disposal.

Digital artists are mistaken in thinking that a medium can have inherent properties and that the realisation of such can be called art. As such, it shares a common history with photography. Photography struggled throughout the century to become realised as an art form in its own right. It experienced a period of fine art credibility in the mid-'80s with Jeff Wall, Cindy Sherman and Sherrie Levine, all of whom were 'artists who used photography', but none of whom could call themselves 'photographers'. The recent retreat of photography into 'specialist' galleries is a testament to its failure to become an art form 'in itself'.

Digital technology exists. Art exists. Art which uses technology exists. Digital art does not exist 'in its own right'.

3. Deconstruction. Ever since Jacques Derrida pronounced that the frame (and possibly even the wall) were part of the artwork, art has been emptied of content and been transformed into a self-conscious deconstruction of the history and context of art.

Artists no longer make statements; instead, they 'critique the medium of representation itself'. To actually communicate, without deconstructing the mode of communication that one uses, shows a failure to understand the importance of the deconstructive method in contemporary art.

So-called digital artists are just too damned excited by the medium's infinite potential for new representation to engage in any meaningful discourse on the subject of its own limits. Digital art does not start from the premise that language has to be taken apart; instead it is at the relatively unsophisticated stage of 'inventing' its own language. Digital art has got to reach the limits of its own potential, roll over and die before the post-mortem can begin.

4. Anti-teleology. The future is not a better place, as Hegel, Marx and Darwin claimed. There is a strong anti-Hegelian thrust in postmodern art, which manifests itself as a distrust of the idea of 'progress' and a belief that 'the new' has positive value in itself. The notion that the future is leading us somewhere, and that technology is the tool for the emancipation of society, has been abandoned due to the failure of the modernist technological utopia and its inversion in the Holocaust, to colonialism and to the failure of teleological projects such as communism, humanism and feminism. This is why digital artists are often accused of 'techno-fascism' by their critics. The inherent technological utopianism of digital art is irresponsible, naïve and dangerous. Contemporary art, in contrast, is going nowhere – and proud of it. It is, after all, safer to mull over the shadows of the past than to be blinded by the brightness of a new future.

5. Foucault's critique of technology. The myth that technology is a 'tool'. Technology always serves the interests of power. Artists get used by technology. Not the other way around.

The horror of the artist/reviewer meeting, Imaginaria, is that it is technology and science that sets the agenda. Thus, artists fall prey to an agenda which is not theirs, to a set of concerns that they cannot control or limit and to a set of outcomes (since many works are set up as 'experiments') which are predetermined and not as 'open ended' as the artists would like to think.

6. Heidegger's opposition between art and technology. The debate on art and technology is always prefaced by some reference to Heidegger. For Heidegger, technology keeps humanity from recognising 'being': we deny ourselves when we see the world 'technologically' – that is, as a tool for our own use. Against the evils of technology, Heidegger set the virtues of art, through which 'being' expresses itself to us. Heidegger's views on art were dominant in the '50s and have had a lasting impact.

Although very few contemporary artists would support Heidegger's philosophy and its endorsement of the notion of the autonomous individual, the ethically existing subject and the expression of inner truth, the art world continues to distrust technology.

The postmodern rejection of Heidegger should have seen an abandonment of the old opposition between art and technology and paved the way for a reconciliation of the old opposites. However, the result has not been a new belief in the compatibility of art and technology, but, instead, the belief that both art and technology are equally lacking in an ultimate justification. In this way, Heidegger's split is reconciled – through mutual failure.

7. Post-Duchampian hatred of technique. Since the revival of Duchamp and the death of painting, art which requires any form of technical skill has been devalued to the lowly status of mere craft. The ready-made has taken the place of the well-designed or expressive object. Anything can be a ready-made: a feature film by someone else or an ashtray teaming with cigarette butts. The intention behind the ready-made is not just to reject technical skills but to insult the notion of committed endeavour, purposeful action or virtuosity.

Thus, a work like *Technosphere V2* by Jane Prophet – in which a graphically designed world is undoubtedly the product of immense technical mastery and several years of committed hard graft – can, to a follower of Duchamp, seem like a complete waste of time.

8. The cult of failure. Once the future has been abandoned and belief in the expressive function of art has been rejected, once artists have come to hate the market which supports them, there is one last petty act of rebellion which can keep the artist going: making art which is deliberately banal.

Thus, we have seen, over the last ten years, the growth of the cult of contemporary artist as heroic failure. Technical inadequacy has been elevated to a virtue. This is not technical naïveté but deliberate and self-conscious faux naïveté.

The justification for this is clear and has a history dating back from performance art to Dada. Against the mantle of artist as genius, the heroically failing artist says quite simply: 'No I will not stand up as a spokesman for humanity – I will, instead, be deliberately pathetic and banal.'

The complexity of these spiralling circles of self-loathing nihilism seems lost on digital artists, who somehow want to aspire to technical virtuosity, style and belief in their own work.

9. Gimmickry. Nothing offends the sensibilities of those who have been raised on a diet of conceptualism and minimalism more than gimmicks and theatricality. There is a good reason for this. Gimmickry always hides something, usually a lack of content or an inability on behalf of the artist to deal with the meaning of their work. Digital art seems to present the artist

with an infinite variety of technical gimmicks. As such, it should be viewed with suspicion.

Take, for example, Simon Robertshaw's *The Order of Things*. Eliminate the reference to Foucault, the spooky theatrical lighting and the trip switch, which activates the video signal when you get close to the viewing surface, and look what you are left with: archival footage of a patient receiving ECT. In its original context, the footage was viewed for medical reasons. In a gallery, we are being asked to deal with it in terms of visual pleasure – the thrill of the peep show. Such treatment of this type of material is in poor taste and is an example of an artist becoming seduced by technical gimmicks and being inevitably unaware of the other meanings they are putting out.

10. Distance. Interactive art destroys the objective distance that, since Kant, has been the basic premise for the contemplation of aesthetic experience. In more contemporary terms, Baudrillard has repeatedly discussed the diminishing of objective distance through digital technology and described the horror that this presents to the Western philosophical tradition – the terrible immediacy, the obscene reciprocity of the virtual experience, the closing down of the gap between observer and object. This, he claims, in Kantian style, is the death of aesthetics.

Without objective distance, there is no contemplation; without contemplation, there is no metaphysics. Virtuality and interactivity are the death not only of art but also of culture itself. Interactivity is a vacuum, a self-perpetuating, self-referring closed circle that coils in on itself. We do not need 'digital interactivity' to see this; it is displayed well enough in 'live TV'. The messages of 'interactive art' and live TV are the same: each is itself. In Imaginaria, Sera Ferneaux's work, *Kissing*, is an example of the vacuousness of instantaneous interactive experience.

Ironically, such a work claims to be social – and sociable – but only further opens up the vacuum that exists in social experience. This is the perverse state that Baudrillard predicted: when we are no longer alienated by technology but share our alienation as a form of pleasure. As Baudrillard pointed out, the *horror vacui* of this death of the social is invariably presented to us in the guise of a smiling face. In this instance, the face is not smiling but kissing, and it is your own face staring back at you. The artwork is no more than an image of the viewer. You are being invited to participate in the collapse of your own culture.

Ten Reasons Why the Art World Loves Digital Art

Matthew Fuller

Vol 1 #11, Autumn 1998

1. We live in an era in which the dominant mode of politics is systems analysis. Power has been handed over to a series of badly animated, white-shirted technicians who deliver fault reports and problem-fixes that can only be answered with an 'Okay'. All the control and trustworthiness of Norton Utilities is delegated to a bunch of frightened, useless pilots, gibbering out of control at the keyboard of a system they no longer understand. In this context, it is essential for artists and others to synthesise an un-format-able world.

2. The art world loves digital art because there is a large, submerged part of the latter – as of the former – that is invisible to the viewing public and only ever read by interpretative machines. Digital art is an autonomous field with its own opportunities, norms and institutions. It understands that the distinction between the fields is necessary in order to maintain the integrity and thoroughness of both fields. For all artists, it is imperative that they maintain the field in which they work as an autonomous sphere. The strength of a specific field can be measured precisely by the degree to which participants recognise the contributions of their peers and therefore develop each other's richness in specific capital. The collapse of a discipline can be measured precisely by the degree to which heterogeneous elements are able to exert force within or upon it.

3. Jeff Koons recently described the patterns produced by the interrelations of basic, repeated units, motifs, forms, colours, in his sculptures constructed of variegated patterns of boxed basketballs, as a basic form of artificial intelligence. Mainstream art has already begun to incorporate the terminology and methodologies of digital cultures as a way of talking about itself and finding sympathetic refrains within a wider culture.

4. The art world loves digital art because it reminds the art world of the limits of its knowledge and the wisdom to be found in the open, non-prejudicial contemplation of the unknown. Likewise, it is always useful to have a relatively large amount of the unknown to call upon in the event of a vague legitimation crisis. In the past, it has proven good insurance to have a few unknown things knocking about in the rear. Graffiti, macramé, female artists and other minor genres have all played their part in the past.

5. Large, prestigious art museums, with marble foyers, love web-based art because it implicitly solves some of the problems of distribution for

non-gallery-orientated works that were faced by video art. Because the web guarantees at least some kind of circulation, this frees them from the embarrassment of undergoing similar rituals to those undertaken on behalf of artists thoughtless enough to produce painting, sculpture or installation.

Given the medium's self-sufficiency, widely promoted, attentively curated exhibitions – with all their background manoeuvring, public attention, critical discussion, historicisation machinery, high artists' fees and other negative influences on the pure essence of artistic creation – can all be avoided, leaving the work to be safely ignored.

6. For similar reasons, those who are interested in reading Marx without illusions believe that the 'Fragment On Machines' in the *Grundrisse* has important implications for technology and art. Here, Marx suggests that what he terms 'general intelligence' – the general, social knowledge, or collective intelligence, of a society in a given historical period, particularly that embodied in 'intelligent' machines – reaches a decisive point of contradiction when actual value is created more on the basis of the knowledge and procedures embedded into these machines than in simple human labour. This frees digital artists from having to exist, or at least frees them from being any less cheap and infinitely reproducible than their work or equipment.

7. The art world loves digital art because someone other than the Royal Society of Portrait Painters has to take the conventions of pictorial representation into the future. Whilst virtual worlds might still be to the mid-'90s what Roger Dean album covers were to the mid-'70s, the onward march of technology will one day surely permit an upgrade-obedient artist to produce a final form of perfection: an utter conformity to perceptual mechanisms, the perspectival instructions of which permit viewing only by the most perfected of subjects. At this sublime moment, being empties in entirety onto a computer and thus, perhaps, allows isolation on a hard drive to be stored or destroyed.

8. Artists wait in ambush for the unique moments at which an unrecognisable world reveals itself to them. They pounce on these little grains of nothingness like beasts of prey. It is the moment of full awakening, of union and of absorption, and it can never be forced. Artists never formulate a plan; instead they balance and weigh opposing forces, flexions, marks, events, distribute them in a sort of heavenly layout, always with plenty of space between, always alternating between the heat of integration and the coolness of critical distance, always with the certitude that there is no end, only worlds within worlds, ad infinitum, and that, wherever one left off, one had created a world.

The sublimation of technique to the advantage of a separate category known as creation is consistent between all sections of art. Programmers, technicians and other people are glad to work hard to make the realisation of the vision of the artist possible. Providing such freedom for the artist is essential because, in this way, providence always triumphs over ego.

9. Because art that is not solely about content but that is multiply reflexive – concerned with materials, that is, about the lustres and qualities of light, about the tonality of certain gestures, about modes and theatres of enunciation – refuses to make a strict separation between creation and technique. Concept and execution fold in and out of each other, blurring the categorical imperatives of rule by the head or by the dead. The most powerful art, digital art, art which is digital in spite of itself, is, regardless of the context which codes it and from which it escapes, derived in this way precisely from hooking into an expanded compositional synthesis.

A multitude of currents of heterogeneity destabilise digital art's status as an autonomous field. Most prosaically, this occurs in the production of art that takes the needs of sponsors to heart, so much that it is indissociable from them. Heterogeneity can also disrupt the autonomy of a field and, thus, its internal self-evolving richness, when it comes in the form of interpretation: in lazy journalistic work, the primary concern of which is the humorous gratification of what it presumes are its audiences' prejudices, in works that are diagrammatically pre-formatted by pre-existing critical criteria or, most importantly, in works whose relationship with certain flows of words amplifies both.

10. Both fields, art and digital art, attempt to control what art and artists should do and what they should be called. This is simply as a necessity for their maintenance and development. At the same time, even their own historical emergence is, or was, dependent upon the eventual impossibility of such control. Those moments at which that impossibility is made concrete are what produce artists worthy of the name, as well as those to whom the word means nothing. Paradoxically, this very impossibility is what art and digital art claim as grounding their ability to speak, to be paid attention. It is only when they lividly and completely fail to betray that claim that art becomes worthy of anything but indifference.

Artware

Saul Albert

Vol 1 #14, Autumn 1999

The idea becomes a machine that makes the art.
Sol LeWitt[1]

The rise of conceptual art, which occurred around the time that Sol LeWitt wrote 'Paragraphs on Conceptual Art', coincided neatly with the birth of hacker culture – between the transformation of MIT's Tech Model Railway Club into the AI lab in 1963–4, and 1969, the year that ARPANET was set up. Although it is not possible to chart the links between these events in a linear fashion, it is interesting to note their more recent convergence. Artist-programmers have been hunched over computer screens in bedroom-studios (and, now, in trendy new media labs), bearing much resemblance to the stereotypical teenage hacker of the '80s. Many of the theories in LeWitt's text draw a strong analogy between the conceptualist use of the 'idea-becoming-machine' and contemporary uses of software in art.

It is one of the defining characteristics of computer programs that they blur the boundaries between user and author. The move towards software engineering – from a more commonplace 'click here' approach to computer-based art – can be seen as an attempt by artists to engage the user as a co-author of their experience. This relates clearly to the conceptualist strategy of relying on the viewer to make (or imagine the making of) the artwork, whereby 'To work with a plan that is pre-set is one way of avoiding subjectivity [...] The plan would design the work.'

LeWitt regarded the execution of the conceptual plan as a tactic for avoiding the 'expressive', or self-consciously authored, art object, and the conceptualists developed the form of 'instructions for the making of art'. This represented a shift in authorial hegemony, from a centralised model (centred on the body of the artist) to a distributed one. However, although by following the instructions anyone could make the artwork, the instructions themselves retained the authorial privilege. The 'original' idea remained sacrosanct. This highlights a contradiction in the stated intention – to de-subjectify the artwork – and the final result, in which the user/viewer is still subjected to the didactic stance of the artist.[2]

Writing in 1998 about artistic developments since the '60s, Jon C. Ippolito described how 'an emphasis on specific objects gave way to an investigation of instructions as an art form and the role of the artist as communicator to the public

1. Sol LeWitt, 'Paragraphs on Conceptual Art', *Artforum*, Vol. 5, no. 10, Summer 1967, pp. 79–83.
2. I am not criticising LeWitt's work with this observation. I am simply pointing out a link between his work, and the issues surrounding the work of artists using software.

gave way to the artist as instigator of public events.'[3] In a recent interview with Tilman Baumgärtel, John F. Simon Jr. describes the workings of his homemade paint program: 'Using the artwork to create more artwork [...] When you run the program you are demonstrating the writing of the program.' The use of the program generates artwork, and Simon invests equal artistic value in the program itself. It seems that Simon's programmed artwork retains LeWitt's contradiction; on the one hand, enabling the user to direct the making of artworks, while at the same time preventing them from directing the way in which the artworks are made, a fact he acknowledges in interview, 'I have to say that I am not very interested in defining my work through the actions of other people.'

This limitation on authorship can be attributed to other factors besides Simon's conceptualist artistic heritage. The limitations placed on the user of the artwork are framed by the artist's limited authorial privilege in writing and running the program. For example, the program is written in a language that has a given structure and syntax, to which the artist must adhere in order for it to function. Aside from this and countless other dependencies, the artwork/software runs within an operating system that has a given visual feel and a given functional structure, not to mention the political, cultural, economic and legal intricacies of IT infrastructure. Of course, all of these limitations have their analogous limitations in the physical world of canvas, plaster, dealer and gallery, but it is the nature of these limitations which make the artist-programmer a distinctive figure.

The structures that surround the work of the artist-programmer can be examined by looking at the various ways in which artists approach software. Without pretence at exhaustive analysis, I will present the work of a few artists who represent diverse approaches to the artistic use of software.

Keith Tyson wrote his Art Machine program using Prolog, a language well suited to AI applications. He feeds the program with a variety of sculptural ingredients, the Art Machine then translates these into instructions on how to make a sculpture. Tyson makes the sculptures, exhibits them and sells them on the art market. The relationship Tyson has with this program is mutually controlling. He programs the Art Machine with possible sculptural ingredients and a framework for configuring them, then the Art Machine programs him with conceptualist-style 'instructions' for making artwork. The sculptural product of the process can then be introduced into the art market, which has its own means of distributing, evaluating and promoting sculptural forms.[4] Tyson subjects himself to programming, in much the same way that John F. Simon Jr. does when he – rather than another subjected user – is running his homemade software. The products of these interactions are manifestations of the artist's

3. On nettime, 4 September 1998.
4. Tyson has drawn up Jackson structure diagrams (family-tree-like hierarchical arrangements) of the way money flows through the art market. His use of the Art Machine to interface with these money flows is extremely well calculated.

ideas, displayed in a compatible format (sculpture and drawing), for assimilation by the art market. Viewers are placed in an art gallery context, yet have no direct interaction with the Art Machine other than by seeking its rationale through its many bizarre products. They are invited to examine how Tyson's relationship with the Art Machine affects his status as the artist, and theirs as viewers.[5]

Paul Garinn's name.space (NS) project is realised and distributed in an entirely different arena. NS is an alternative, autonomous Domain Name System (DNS) with which Garrin hopes to establish a 'Permanent Autonomous Net'. He speaks about the existing DNS being a dominating and semantically territorial regime nefariously controlled by ex-CIA officials, whereby: 'In the meme of the "DOMAIN NAME SYSTEM" the message is "CONTROL", "DOMINATION", "TERRITORY".'[6]

Whether or not this is the case, Garrin's creative use of software is masterful. With only a couple of servers, he has created an alternative DNS. His system does not rely on geographical referents, such as .uk, .au or .jp. Instead, name.space is open to user-directed suggestion as to how the name syntax is defined, for example http://timothy.leary. The art world is sidelined here; Garrin is playing to a potentially mass market, and for potentially high financial stakes. Other companies with similar ideas, such as Alternic, started up at around the same time as NS, so he even had commercial competition, and his right to incorporate his system into the mainstream DNS is being contested in the courts.

This artistic use of software attempts to throw off some of the strictures of the technology to which internet users are subjected. Both of the applications Garrin uses – Apache and WebStar – are available free (or as shareware) over the internet, and are not necessarily intended for use as independent Domain Name Servers – the end to which Garrin cunningly exploits their functionalities. His idea is to facilitate a use of the internet which is less mediated by commercial and governmental interests, allowing a user's internet presence to be nominally self-directed. By playing with the server software that makes up the infrastructure of the net, he is attempting to bolster the authorial rights of its inhabitants. In this struggle for (signified) territory, Garrin takes his cue from Situationist tactics of *détournement*, using the technology of the dominators to undermine and subvert their aims.[7]

The art collective, Mongrel, has also taken this Situationist approach to software, by hacking into a popular commercial image editing application and giving it a political charge. The user is invited to edit their heritage using this software tool and, with commands such as 'Purge' and 'Invert', to alter the image

5. Tyson's under-used Replicators project for ada'web works along similar lines and is worth a try at: http://adaweb.walkerart.org/influx/tyson/
6. Paul Garrin interviewed by Pit Schultz, nettime, 13 June 1997.
7. 'Retired' artist and 'aspiring revolutionary', Heath Bunting, relates to this territorial struggle in a recent interview at London's Expo Destructo. Although he has shifted ground to biotech, his intentions and methods are very similar to those of Garrin.

of a skin-masked face using a racially charged visual language. This method of software intervention derives from a hacking tradition of game patching – writing software agents or altering image resources to change the look, or function, of pre-existing software. Mongrel breaks the smooth, simulated surface of the program and gives the user insight into the politically dubious and racialised norms of routinely used software. The cropped language of the commands ('Purge', 'Execute') reveals the software's own military heritage, and the shocking imagery, combined with the 'user-friendly' interface, is very unsettling. By altering the program in these ways, Mongrel shows how mainstream programs direct what is produced and even limit the imagination and capabilities of users.

In early 1999, the panel of judges for the Prix Ars Electronica chose Linux, the Open Source Operating System[8] as the winner in the '.net' category. If just the name Linux sends you into a boredom-induced coma, skip the next paragraph, in which I will try to outline some of the reasons Linux won. The legalities at the basis of Linux's usage are dealt with under the General Public Licence (GPL), which free it from the grasp of commercial software corporations. The central ethos of its development policy has been to make available all the information, tools and code necessary for users to alter the program; accordingly, the operating system does not constitute a visual or functional 'given' for any artwork/software made or shown using Linux. The ability of Linux to gather a community of users/authors was acknowledged as a contributing factor to it winning the Golden Nica. The distribution, evaluation and promotion of Linux is done within this open source community, ensuring its continuity and growth. It is this combination of features which allowed the Linux development community to grow so large that Linux's efficiency, quality and speed of reaction to user demand far outclass those of the commercial competition. As a result of this and the tumult of media hype now surrounding Linux, it has become the only real challenger to Microsoft's market dominance.

When Linux is examined using artistic criteria, it reveals a very high degree of critical rigour in its execution and conception (this rigorous approach was necessary to the legality of the project). Most of all, Linux is a beautifully clear realisation of the idea of open source. As to how the judges came to choose Linux for the Ars Electronica prize, LeWitt's words are resonant: 'The idea becomes a machine that makes the art.' By awarding the prize to Linux, the judges were revealing the connection between LeWitt's conceptualism and the hacker/hobbyist dreams of the last forty years.

It is the idea of open source, which became a machine (Linux), which both constitutes and facilitates the artwork.

8. For those of you who don't know what open source is, try Eric S. Raymond, 'The Cathedral and the Bazaar', http://www.catb.org/~esr/writings/cathedral-bazaar/

Art is Useless

Vuk Ćosić Interviewed by Josephine Berry

Vol 1 #17, Summer 2000

Vuk Ćosić believes in essences – the originality of the avant-garde, the possibility of narrative, the lessons of history, the area of art's jurisdiction, the right way to make coffee or to prepare a California roll. In one of his best known net artworks, *The History of Art for Airports*, Ćosić compresses thousands of years of art history, from the caves of Lascaux to the net art of Jodi, into a few images of recombinant toilet people interacting with cocktail glasses and other airport fare (eat your heart out Ernst Gombrich!). Stripped of its aura, art history is clad in the uniform of utility, its canonical works whittled down to one-liners. But, if representing thousands of years of art history using airport signs seems like a consummately postmodern gesture, you only have to consider the substance with which these minimal icons endow their referents.

Unlike postmodernism's typically de-historicising language of pastiche, this account of aesthetics roots each developmental moment within a lifeworld. The lifeworld is primarily constructed through an elaboration of art's functionality: art in the service of religion, art in the service of the state, art attempting to elude power. These spare images provide dense ideological and temporal diagrams in the manner of a user's manual of art history. However, this is the kind of manual that shows you how to take something apart and put it back together again without telling you what the thing is intended for in the first place. Ćosić paradoxically combines a positivist modernism of means with a postmodern ambivalence of ends, a strategy which finds its natural home in the economically and ideologically contested space of the internet.

Given the conventional framing of net art in terms of political resistance – an account which almost naturalises its radicalism by associating its virtuality with a resistance to commodification and its existence within the global specular and financial network with a default media activism – it is interesting to piece together Ćosić's art histories and his attitude to the politics of art: 'I like to believe that art is useless. It liberates me from all these worries.' The conjunction of *The History of Art for Airports* and this comment beg the question: Can art be understood as both utilitarian and useless?

But, let's start at the beginning, and in Ćosić's own words:

> I was born in '66 so that makes me 32 now… I studied archaeology, graduated, used to teach methodology a bit in Belgrade and then I left the country in '91. At that time I was already writing and editing magazines, and doing political satire and also regular literature… I was doing various art stuff too: texts, collages, land art, some shows. I started working creatively with HTML in '95 and making net.art in '96 because that's when we invented the term.

Ćosić draws a direct line between his archaeological training and his acute historical consciousness: 'For me, it was always important to be fully conscious of the era you live in, it was very important – like in archaeology – to be able to date things, be aware of when, and in what kind of context, objects were made, or used.' And, despite what is said about the loss of historical consciousness being the hallmark of postmodernity, the coincidence of the internet and the break-up of former Yugoslavia must have provided two quite awesome historical developments for someone of Ćosić's archaeological persuasion.

The Yugoslav experience, of passing from dictatorship to civil war, may not be an explicit concern in Ćosić's art, but it should certainly be borne in mind when considering his stance on the relationship between aesthetics and politics. Talking about a radio play he wrote at the age of 19 which was pulled on air by a 'telephone intervention' from the party headquarters, it is possible to see how an early belief in political art has turned into a purer form of aesthetics:

> And, as a young person, of course you went for the toughest points, but I like to compare it to today's situation because everyone who was active in the political process claimed, even today, that it was a necessary step because it was impossible to live before. But, if you look at the reality today, ten years after, there's not a single place, except for Slovenia maybe, where life is in any way comparable. So that's weird, and I like to insist on that. It's terrible, it's just a redistribution of money and power. Look at Serbia and Croatia – that's the best example – and Bosnia, no comment, Macedonia doesn't exist really, and so on. But hey, come on, this is politics.

Growing up in Yugoslavia and feeling that he was at the periphery of cultural production also cultivated Ćosić's strong sense of authentic and derivative artistic styles:

> I was always pissed off when they were selling new books and translating literature which was actually written 30 years earlier. Somehow, in our country, there was always this massive delay, and it was reflected in the actual local cultural production… I was never interested in the best Albanian pop art, I was interested in the best pop art… Isn't it better, I thought as a kid, to actually be at the source and possibly influence the birth or the way that work in this new area is going on.

In discussing this point, I couldn't help but contrast Ćosić's unequivocal belief in the continued originality of art with Fredric Jameson's sentencing of art production to the imitation of dead styles lifted from the 'imaginary museum' of global culture. Turning the mic back on Ćosić: 'Maybe aesthetic appropriation does give some kind of a valid output, and I'm not arguing that this should be banned. I'm simply noticing that, according to my temperament, the juiciest work happens the first time around.'

Enter the internet – a medium within which art had no history, the meta-medium, the vehicle of accelerated cultural and informational cross-pollination, the embodiment of contemporaneity par excellence. Art practice on the net is, ipso facto, 'juicy', and it is happening within what has well nigh become a signifier not only of the new but of the future too. Given the historicity of 'the new', however, it is small wonder that Ćosić's work is concerned with looking back at cultural history and carving out its own position within it. Having no desire to go vitrine shopping in the 'imaginary museum' of culture, Ćosić processes history through computer-specific languages and codes, such as ASCII, HTML and Java, thereby creating history and style as a referent within the contemporary symbolics of the computer medium. History and future collapse into each other within the computer's symbolic matrix. Having said that, it is important to note the degree to which ASCII has already accrued a retro appeal, and science fiction has become a language of nostalgia. Post-modernism's refusal of 'the new' is what riles Ćosić most about this account of cultural logic:

> It's too complicated to in any way criticise or analyse postmodernism because it's totally unclear what it is. Are we talking about a practice or a group of people or what? But, here we are, I'm looking at the positive effects of the introduction of this ideology. What it did was it levelled the unsustainable pluralism of before, unsustainable for the lazy… I think that absolute freedom of expression or appropriation got institutionalised and canonised and all possible meanderings, all possible developments in a linear history of development, somehow got sanctioned and a priori incorporated into the postmodern point of view. But, because, of course, this point of view says 'anything goes' – and I'm not trying to make a caricature out of it – and by saying that anything that will ever be invented falls into the category of 'everything', then, of course, you've appropriated all future creativity. Just at the level of rhetoric, I think, you have sort of made a bad friend of posterity. I think the term 'net art' is one of those problems in which postmodernism already includes it a priori. Before me or Alexei [Shulgin] moved a single tag in HTML, we were already part of that movement, or group or era. Just because it's so loosely defined, and it says 'everything'.

Here, we stumble upon the enigma of Ćosić's relationship to the internet. The internet is at once a perfect reification of the velocity, specularity and virtuality of postmodernity and the place where something 'happens for the first time'. It offers an opportunity for originality within the site of optimum reproducibility and the site of resurgent history in the flattened space of historical amnesia. But, if Ćosić is undeterred by what has come to be seen as the historical constructedness of the concept of originality, his historical sense of how to market originality is acute:

> I think it is very logical that the old guys who were doing early video art insisted that they were video artists, and not just artists who were interested in a new toy. They insisted really seriously, and because of that there was a whole ecosystem around them and their work. And maybe in a similar way, we are slowly developing an ecosystem around net art. People are writing their PhDs about net art, and we have net art critics – an ecosystem.

And, in almost complete contradiction to the early utopian accounts of net art, in which it was claimed – perhaps more by the critics than by the artists themselves – to transcend the commodifying and etiolating processes of the market, Ćosić states:

> I think simply that it's not the massive desire of museums to maintain prestige that's going to draw net art into the collections successfully. It's more the conformism on the side of the artists, who are going to create technically commodifiable pieces or a model for the accommodation of net art within the museum situation. So it is interesting to observe net artists' ambitions as the driving force behind this process of commodification. Simply, some of us have no problem with this. What can we do? I myself look at this as the only thing that I do, and, interestingly enough, my mother's capital knows limits.
>
> There is some type of illusion of virginity that used to exist, earlier on, in what I call the 'heroic period' – a term that Olia [Lialina] is using also – that was a time when what we did was known almost only to us, and that was a time when whoever you encountered that had anything to do with net art was usually also a practitioner because nobody else was interested. So, those were the good old days, two years ago, who remembers when? But, in the process, all these very nice offers you can't refuse started popping up, and it's not easy, but it's not a world premiere either – it's biblical. There's a school of thought – and the nettime mailing list is one of the places in this world where you can often encounter people who believe in it – that money shouldn't exist, that all human labour should be done for free and exchanged for services; err I do your website and you give me a bucket of beer. But somehow it's a problem that it's impossible to imagine a human being, or a net artist, who doesn't interface with any of the networks and infrastructures that surround you, like economy, streets, public space, private space. Every instance of interaction with those systems is a loss of this same virginity that is being defended with the claims like 'net art should not be sold', which, of course, makes it very ugly. But how do you think you got your first Sex Pistols record? Because they didn't want to sell it to you? Still, it worked, most of the aesthetics and qualities remained – I repeat most, because, of course, something does happen. Unfortunately, it's a necessity, but what can I do?

Does Ćosić regard the potential of the internet for artists to take distribution and sales into their own hands as an attractive option?

> What I like to think is that it's simply helping artists by giving them a much better negotiation position than, say, video artists. This, again, is a pragmatic, strategic viewpoint that should, perhaps, never be uttered. A video artist could blackmail his gallerist, maybe, by saying that he has full control over the production, but the gallerist could also tell him to fuck off because the gallerist still owned the means of distribution. Nowadays, if you are an online artist, you control all of it and in a way, put the guy in a tight corner, because really he's not empowering you or in any way giving your work exposure that it doesn't already have... And, yes, I would like to have a show at Stedelijk because, when Stedelijk moves their machine of promotion, it will do miracles to distribution, and that shows on the log of my server.

At last we arrive at the crunch question: So, what is politically radical about net art? 'Some artists use up the medium very well,' says Ćosić, 'I consider my copy of the Documenta website a very political act, but of course within the art system. This is a relatively clear example of a political gesture, but, nevertheless, I still haven't seen a really political-political net artwork.'

Ćosić's definition of political art effectively turns it into an oxymoron: 'Political art is art about politics, it's not politics,' and he further states that net art is in no way 'changing reality'. Ćosić is also unromantic about the power structure of the internet:

> It is easy to identify US involvement with the internet simply as an imperialistic gesture and as a prelude to internet 2.0, which will be all about commerce, and somehow the US already is the hub of all communication. What's it called? The Theory of Information, you know Roman Jakobson and all those old guys? It's folklore, basically; whoever owns the channel owns the content, period. It was applied to some earlier communication systems, because the anecdote is from the '30s, and it is applicable now because the internet is working on broadcast principles, especially with this shift which everyone is predicting to cable systems, which are broadcast systems. And the many-to-many model, even now, isn't really working because you are connected, or your server is connected, to only one upstream server, not to many many points. This upstream system makes you very vulnerable because that nuclear bomb from the old story about how the internet was made kills you very well.

As with the condensation of art history into terse airport signs, Ćosić is also able to reduce the elaborate relations between the internet, power and net artist into a comically potent image: 'To put it simply, I think that Bill Gates has a button under his pillow on which it says "internet on/internet off". That's where my work has anything to do with that power.'

For Ćosić, then, the internet would seem to provide the opportunity for art to extend its internal discourse on the basis of its formal and technical qualities. In this space of media, economic, political and artistic convergence, art remains as it ever was – a developmental process whose moments of originality are intimately linked to, and yet independent from, the wheel of social change. Politics and society are the block upon which the form of art is hammered out, but the two remain unalloyed.

I ask whether he believes that art's autonomy is essential to the maintenance of its 'artness':

> It's a beautiful thing to try. For instance, that would be nice. I prefer to do that than to change society. You can see me doing that in my use of, say, low-tech, which I can misuse properly, and that, for me, is a sign of 'artness' because something is being used in a way that the engineer didn't intend it to be used. Whereas you have all these artists following high-tech and trying to be posh, but actually it's only selling equipment. As an artist, you're only falling within the boundaries of the imagination of an engineer if you're working with an off-the-shelf product. So this is where I'm looking at 'artness' as freedom.

London, 2000

King of Code

Stephen Willats Interviewed by Josephine Berry and Pauline van Mourik Broekman

Vol 1 #17, Summer 2000

Since the early-1960s, Stephen Willats has repurposed system-based theories in the social context – initiating multimedia art and design projects everywhere from suburban tennis clubs and public galleries to inner city housing estates. Fusing cybernetic models, an authorial death-wish and an enduring commitment to participatory politics, his work is poles apart from the media-friendly individualism of the yBa (young British artist) era. But, tempting as it is to attribute the renewed interest in his work to the rise of socially responsible product on the modern art taste-index, its context and implications are far wider; in a world in which horizontal communication structures are being hardwired on global proportions and social problems increasingly tend to beget technological solutions, his experiments with self-organising systems are instructive.

The scientific inspiration, apparent rationalism and political contradictions of Willats' work make his investigations, in terms of classic net debates, irresistible. So, surrounded by the steady ticking of his studio's many clocks, the conversation between Willats and *Mute* opened up some of the following questions: To what extent can models lifted from the 'hard' sciences work their magic in the social sphere? Can socio-structural open-endedness be engineered? Are there forces controlling so-called 'open systems' and, if so, is resistance futile? Betraying a long love-hate relationship with art, his answers turned on the mutable question of the cultural model and – in contrast to its scientific and technological equivalents – what it might achieve.

Pauline van Mourik Broekman: Can we begin by talking about the Drian Gallery, where you worked in the late-'50s? You have described this as a formative experience in terms of wanting to generate a different model of how art could work.

Stephen Willats: Well, it was a strange situation because I came to work in this art gallery from the world outside and it was an unimaginable leap of reality, really. I found myself working in what was, at that time, a very avant-garde gallery environment, and I hadn't come with any kind of lumber or been to art school or anything like that.

It quickly became apparent to me that no one ever went to the gallery except those who were already involved. It was a kind of capsule, really. This enabled me to have plenty of time to dream about different speculative models of how things could be. We have these moments of insight, and, in my case, I remember we were showing this artist called Agam – an Israeli constructivist whose work incorporated slats of colour that, as you moved across them, changed. They stimulated me to imagine that there could be quite another relationship of an artist to a work of art, because implicit in the work was the audience.

This led me to set up a lot of diagrammatic models in '58/'59, which postulated that, instead of the audience coming along and finding objects of certainty – icons of emulation – in a sort of passive, almost awe-inspired way, they came into what I described at the time as a 'random variable'. It was task-orientated; they were part of the creation of the work, of the meaning of the experience. The word I think I used at the time was 'relativity' – the relativity of perception and meaning. Another artist, Kosice, a Marxist Argentinean constructivist who made constructions with water which you could move and turn around, stimulated in me the idea of task orientation and tactile involvement.

Josephine Berry: What about other kinds of post-studio art? Anything from Andy Warhol's factory to Robert Smithson's land art which tried, with very different means, to create something that exceeds that oppressive model of the artist, and which often used industrial technology to transform the mode of production to break with this older regime of meaning?

SW: London in the late-'50s was quite provincial, and I remember quite clearly the first exhibition of big American painting at the American Embassy – these were devastating injections of culture from remote places and had a completely fundamental effect on many artists. Casting off the shackles of the '50s was a rebellious experience and, indeed, there was this term, 'Angry Young Man', which seemed to sum up that general feeling. By the '60s, another kind of feeling had come about which was much more optimistic and which could see the possibility of another social realm altogether, another sort of ideological-political existence. An important aspect was the idea that nothing was the preserve of any one person. The idea that some scientist was involved in a discipline that he could keep hegemony over was anachronistic. People felt that they were in a free flow of information, and this was very fertile. Other people felt that they could be artists, as well. The models we are talking about didn't really become influential – in my opinion – until about '63.

PvMB: Did you feel an affinity with these models when you encountered them?

SW: I found, and continue to find, myself at odds with most American political thought. I wasn't overwhelmed by the vast resources available to American practice, and the kinds of cultural domination that it seemed to want and, in fact, got. I saw most of these models which were being represented in a highly verified and supported manner for what they were – a kind of determinism. They wanted emulation, what I was talking about was contextualism. I certainly fell out with artists – especially American ones – who thought that great art was universal. It was complete bullshit – all art is contextually dependent on social relations and agreement.

JB: So, if there were any artists that you looked to at that time, who were they?

SW: Although people knew about my practice, it was seen as quite marginal. I found people like Gordon Pask and the people around Systems Research, as well as Roy Ascott and his Ground Course, really stimulating. In '65, I stopped calling myself an artist and called myself a 'conceptual designer', with the specific purpose of terminating what I saw as the history of art and moving on. My idea was to infiltrate the infrastructure of society, to deal with accepted behaviours and norms and to transform them. So I thought that what I could do with clothing, for instance, was to develop the idea of self-organising clothing – you could alter your relationship to other people in a process of exchange.

JB: So, why did you go back to calling yourself an artist?

SW: Because nobody understood what I was talking about, basically (laughs). It was quite lonely.

JB: But, why work with art at all? Were you harnessing art as an agent of transformation – something that operates interstitially, between disciplines, for example – and non-instrumentally?

SW: Well, we wanted to take the fundamentals of what we felt an artist might be and relate this to what we thought was relevant to the social landscape. In '65, for example, I was working at Ipswich with Roy Ascott on his course, and had a group of 20 students for a whole year for whom I had to develop my own programme. The students came from Ipswich and Suffolk and hadn't been, shall we say, conditioned in the history of art – the same way I hadn't. We had the idea that we would develop collaborative practice, that the artist as sole author would not exist, and that all art would be social expression. The students operated as a collective and we decided we'd look at what would happen if we started from zero as artists: How would we develop a practice in relationship to the social situation? We had to look at basic ideas about audience, context, language, meaning, procedures of intervention, things like that. The group divided itself into four and each group developed a different strategy for a different audience group. The idea was that theory had to precede practice.

We took a housing estate on the outskirts of Ipswich and attempted to start from fundamentals – what language we were going to use. We'd have to start with their language, and we thought that the context should be their context. Instead of trying to vary their behaviour so that they came to the art gallery, why not place the work within their existing behaviours?

The students set up a means of retrieving this information from the audience group, through a doorstep questionnaire looking at restricted language codes, restricted visual codes, speech and so on. Another group was looking at priorities and behaviours. Out of this, they formulated a strategy that turned out to be a set of signposts for the neighbourhood, telling people where things were.

PvMB: How was this project related to the cybernetic systems of feedback that you were interested in at the time? And notions like consensus, collaboration and competition that figured in computer-based research, for instance in war games?

SW: Well, it wasn't just cybernetic models. It was a whole host of different disciplines which seemed to be parallel – information theory, communication theory, learning theory. They were interesting to me because they provided models which were conceptual but which also stimulated practice. I didn't see that they were to be copied slavishly or that their goals were necessarily my goals, but they could be appropriated.

JB: Do you think that the methods you use to create this kind of communication and interaction are neutral? You often use that word in association with the idea that you want to create a 'neutral interface', or something which doesn't over-determine the process which then unfolds. But, do you think that neutrality can be achieved in any method? You're using, as you mentioned, information theory, cybernetics and so on, and those are coming out of a scientific practice which has been critiqued, at least latterly, as existing within the Enlightenment project – not a relativist project, but as something that deals in empirical truths.

SW: No, I think that, certainly in the case of Ipswich, the outcome was sort of unknown at the beginning – it was open-ended. The construction of response is so dependent on experience. When I say that the thing is or isn't neutral, it really depends on intention. You could say that everything is neutral and nothing is neutral, depending on the position you wish to take. In a way, one means the same as the other philosophically; you can find yourself in a sort of circuit. But, the intention was that it was an open frame, so, in that sense, it was neutral. When I say a system or a work is 'neutral', I actually mean that the outcome is not determined – that it doesn't have a preferred view. But, of course, the work itself is not neutral because it actually is its own message. When you engage with the work, it brings you into a kind of model of social relationships which are built around exchange and self-organisation – this is what I meant by being neutral. It isn't meant in any kind of scientific manner – you're getting confused between the way I'm operating as an artist and the foundation of science and cybernetics.

PvMB: Can we go back to the agreement and consensus issue? When manifested on a larger scale, consensus is often associated with conservative or oppressive social paradigms. Are there glass ceilings for consensus acting productively, and how can we differentiate consensus from agreement here?

SW: I think you have to be careful about the way that you perceive these models operating. The notion of agreement implies, within it, a recognition of the complexity of the other person, whereas consensus doesn't necessarily do that.

PvMB: Maybe we should look at this through an example of your work, say, the project you initiated in Holland during 1993, *Democratic Model,* in which people tried to picture an ideal space.

SW: Well, this particular work was actually about the formation of society. I saw that the basic element, a sort of building block, within society was the small group. If you look at the dynamics within the small group, you can infer larger structures – there is a tendency toward agreement; within a small group, there's the psychological possibility of the recognition of complexity within others – and a process of exchange.

We invited 32 people who had never met each other before and who represented different roles in Dutch society to come together to this community room in Den Haag on Saturday morning. I didn't know the people in advance – my friends assembled them. They were given a task, which was to externalise an implicit representation of themselves within an ideal space. By answering a question, you externalise what is implicit. You encode it. I see the act of ordering something on a sheet of paper as reinforcing the process of externalisation to then feed it back to the self. It is a fundamental element of the creative process, which is why I've used the question so often in my work.

People spent half an hour or so drawing. At the end of it, I blew a whistle and we threw a die which paired people together. It seemed that two people were the basis of a cooperative structure. They were then given a larger piece of paper on which they had to try to make a joint space. They could do this in various ways, but it meant that they entered into a period of negotiation. At this point, everything was fine. I threw the die again and we had four people – two groups of two coming together.

If we look at conformity and compliance, there's a tendency to want to reduce the complexity of your own role by compliance. But, within a group of four people, they were all really willing to open themselves up to a group because that group was based on a sort of agreement, not consensus per se. This principle seemed OK to eight, but when it got to 16 it became impossible. At that point, all kinds of complex situations came to the forefront. Some people sought to try to exert influence, which they hadn't done before; some tried to organise the group; some people tried to break away from the group; different things started to happen. But the basic thing was that the group became unstable and upset with itself. And the reason they became upset with themselves was because they'd lost the feeling of society that they had before.

JB: But don't you think that most radical social transformation does need to entail friction? I'm thinking about historical revolutions and the moments at which transformation is most dramatically figured or realised – albeit only temporarily, I would also argue.

SW: Well, no I don't agree. I'd say that you were involved in very radical transformations of the infrastructure of society and of cognition of the self, but that this has happened in a totally implicit way – evolution. It is interesting to note that, in the late-'50s and early-'60s, we had a situation in which the development of philosophical models had got beyond the technology. It led to a point, in the late-'60s, at which science and art became so engaged with each other that science became political. People started to want to take responsibility for the ramifications of their own actions. So, by the 1980s, we have a revolution taking place in the infrastructure without anybody knowing. The implications of what was being thought about in the late-'50s is really beginning to affect the world we live in now. But it's not a revolution based on conflict – it's come about through evolution in the infrastructure. And, when we talk about technology, it's just a vehicle, a medium of exchange. It embodies different possibilities to which you can open yourself up.

JB: But the technological capacity of a society has huge ramifications in its culture and politics wouldn't you say? McLuhan, for example, talks about how the book was indispensable to colonialism because it meant that an identical message could be duplicated infinitely and could propagate national culture within a colonial setting.

PvMB: And, if we take the technology of the net, its multi-nodal, 'interactive' architecture is viewed as having a democratising potential. Has its development played out in as empowering or democratising a way as you'd once hoped, or do you see the flipside?

SW: Well, I think you mustn't get confused between agreement and democracy. I mean, democratic processes aren't necessarily based on agreement, they're based on acquiescence. We go along with the majority verdict. Agreement is not that; agreement is about agreement.

PvMB: But, in the same way that you saw engineering culture build something evolutionarily, do you see a process of empowerment going on, now that that something is reaching a serious level of massification?

SW: Of the individual? No, I don't think it's got anywhere near that point. If you're talking about the relationship of the person to the terminal and the representation of reality on the screen, it's so encoded as to represent within itself a realm of meaning. I think the point is that the person is psychologically detached in referring that realm of meaning to the reality surrounding them. This means that people can make decisions within the interface that they can distance themselves from in reality, and that's an extremely interesting effect. In my work in the 1970s, I developed a thing called a Symbolic World. The idea was to encode reality and create a psychological distance so the viewer could engage more freely in a kind of remodelling. It's not dissimilar to the representation of reality through the screen.

PvMB: Could you tell us a bit about your recent show at the Laure Genillard Gallery, Macro to Micro?

SW: Macro to Micro came out of a similar desire as the work in Ipswich from 1965. It seems necessary, at the moment, to set up models of practice that can be discussed. When I say discussed, I mean in a way that is useful to the development of the way we think about art practice. I wanted to represent something about the complexity of the language of the contemporary world, and show that we construct order from what we almost randomly experience. This also comes into the idea of exchange and that of the work of art not being the product of any one person – whether we like it or not.

To start, I invited a group of actors who sort of specialised in disturbing normality. I told them my thinking turned around constructing four events, with one leading on to the other in time. Touring around West London, I had come across a shopping parade in Hayes with a very wide pavement which formed a natural kind of stage. The actors went along there and I left them to it, really, saying I didn't really want to know what they were going to do, but that they would be recorded. With the documentary group, we set up the idea of a concept frame – a purely artificial device to break down this multi-channelled picture of reality – and made various boxes, of which each person elected one to document. We used Super 8 cameras, primarily, because they're informal devices and provide an interesting way of recording reality.

The event itself was quite interesting: At 12:15 on a Saturday, the documentary group crossed the road in Hayes and started filming all kinds of people, but they soon found out who the actors were and they followed them along these four events. Then there was a series of workshops over three months in which the whole group edited the material collectively. The selected frames were then made into one still and printed up on a laser printer.

The 'macro to micro', in this sense, is that there's no ending and no beginning to it. It's presented in the gallery space as a sort of multi-frame piece of information from which the viewer constructs their own order. So, it was meant to illustrate certain kinds of ideas about divestment, which, I think, is a very important model for the future of culture, and, in a way, is very ideological because it goes completely against the idea of the sole authorship and the elevation of the individual in terms of culture.

JB: Why did you decide to start using your name again in 1973? Was it just a practical means of survival?

SW: Yes, just practical. I felt that the idea had to dominate over the culture of the personality. And in that respect, I always felt that I was at completely the opposite end of practice from someone like Daniel Buren, whose name you'd hear and then each work was like a variation on the same thing. There were works developed by large numbers of people; it was just the idea of the work. So, you had the *Social Resource Project for Tennis Clubs*, and that was it. Even with *Metafilter*, it's only known as 'Metafilter'. But, when I started to try to intervene in the institutional process, it wasn't possible to maintain that. I always retained the name of the idea above the name of the artist. So, instead of the name of the artist being big, it's the idea that's big – there's no particular fetish about the authorship of the work.

JB: But it's remembered as a Stephen Willats, or goes down in archives under Stephen Willats.

SW: So it might do, but that's not the point. The point is the practical way in which it operated as a tool to work with, rather than as an emulative icon. So, this is the difference in the paradigm of the work itself. These works were initiated by myself and that's their actuality. They wouldn't exist otherwise; you're in a tautology there.

JB: From the way I observe your work, I can't see a totalistic political critique – say, Marxist. Your work is definitely very left-wing, but it doesn't employ a pre-existing political language. I'm interested in knowing whether your work advances something like a Grand Unifying Theory or whether it's opposed to that idea.

SW: Well, I don't think it's either. You can't approach it that way. I think that the work is ideological in the way that it has an idea of the future. It proclaims a notion of what the future could be. And, if you think of the future implied in the works from the early-'60s, for instance, we can say that the ramifications of these works have been taken up by what's happening around us at the moment. The problem I had with a lot of the artists from the '70s was that they became deterministic in their political outlook and this actually constrained them.

The reality of the situation we're in is that it's fluid, but that doesn't mean to say that you lose track of your ideological position. I'm thinking, with my work, about the notion of transformation, the transformation of reality into self-organising structures which actually empower the notion of the individual. Now, this is not a sort of dogma, but, in my practice, it's a way of externalising my view into the reality of the culture around me. But, I don't want to take on the harness of any particular political dogma. Going back to your interest in engineering and cybernetics, one thing that was interesting about that period was the notion of being able to set up radical models of society without political dogma. I think that that was the interesting outcome of those debates. So, I've always maintained a position of being independent of any particular dogma.

JB: Would you say that, in comparison with other kinds of subcultural groups, artists aspire to a greater reception, to making transformations far beyond their own context? Unlike, perhaps, subcultural groups looking to exclude, or operating on the basis of an exclusion from, 'normal society'?

SW: What I mean by 'normal society' is how society is projected by itself. So, there's a sort of bandwidth of behaviour that is perceived as being normal. But we all know that there's no such thing as normality. I want to address a bigger audience than just the primary people I work with. My motive for inviting the art world is to open up the nature of art practice. I think it's very important that artists get beyond the idea of sole authorship.

JB: So, in a way, that's your subcultural group – other artists.

SW: I'm in the business of trying to influence the cultural direction and transforming the future of culture. And, certainly, moving towards the idea of more complex and interactive structures within relationships which are ultimately self-organising. These are ideas which I think are very relevant to the current moment.

London, 2000

Systems Upgrade: Conceptual Art and the Recoding of Information, Knowledge and Technology

Michael Corris

Vol 1 #22, Winter 2001

This article examines how some conceptual art recoded the scientistic theories that helped drive the technological revolution of the 1960s as an aesthetic ideology. At the outset, we should note the intense interaction, during the 1950s and '60s, between technology and all forms of culture and visual art. The emergence of conceptual art during the 1960s coincided with a tremendous surge in economic activity in North America and Western Europe that 'seemed powered by technological revolution'.[1] John F. Kennedy's 'new frontier' and Harold Wilson's 'white heat of technology' were both images intended to denote and exploit the appeal of technological innovation in the mind of the electorate.[2]

Writing on the period of post-war prosperity that originated in 1945 and reached its peak around 1970, historian, Eric Hobsbawm, offers three observations on the distinctive social and economic effects of this technological leap: firstly, the utter transformation of everyday life in the industrialised nations and, to a lesser extent, in the developing world; secondly, the new centrality of 'Research and Development' (R&D) to the economic growth of the industrialised nations; and, thirdly, the structural effect on the labour market of the new, capital-intensive technologies. It is this latter feature that prompted the period's technocrats to dream of 'production, or even service, without humans' and to speculate on the prospect of human beings as 'essential to such an economy only in one respect: as buyers of goods and services'.[3] Even though the 'restructuring of capitalism and the advance in economic internationalisation' are probably more central to our understanding of this broad period of economic expansion, the image and promise of technology undoubtedly captured the intellectual, popular and artistic imagination of the West, as well as guaranteeing its continued economic superiority.

In the United States, the development of technology and the dissemination of the technocratic dream was fuelled, on the one hand, by the growing power and influence of corporations and, on the other, by the 'military-industrial complex'. The marriage of Cold War policy and private sector enterprise

1. Eric Hobsbawm, *Age of Extremes: The Short Twentieth Century, 1914–1991*, London: Michael Joseph, Ltd, 1994, p. 264.
2. Arthur Marwick, *The Sixties: Cultural Revolution in Britain, France, Italy, and the United States, c. 1958 – c. 1974*, Oxford: Oxford University Press, 1998, p. 248.
3. Hobsbawm, op. cit., pp. 265–7.

sustained America's military advantage and guaranteed a steady flow of resources to support appropriate technological developments. Alongside the many programs initiated to develop weaponry and communications systems, there arose a parallel stream of research funding that was made available to disciplines such as linguistic theory and pure mathematics. These fields of theoretical research were the targets of strategic state funding, which aimed to steer the production of knowledge into avenues that might yield results applicable to the future development and production of high-speed electronic computing machines, electronic communications systems, exotic new weapons, powerful information processing programs and encryption devices. Many of the innovators in the field of game theory, information retrieval, modal logic and transformational grammar pursued initial research under the aegis of this rich stream of state- and NATO-sponsored funding.

During the 1960s, such theories dominated the intellectual landscape and quickly became the object of social and political controversy. Systems theory, in particular, maintained a strong hold on the 1960s imagination. Typically associated with the aims and objectives of the military, or corporate management, systems theory was first promoted in a generalised form 'capable of addressing patterns of human life' by the mathematician and inventor of cybernetics, Norbert Wiener. Cybernetics – conceived during the 1940s, in the context of military research on improved radar systems – is essentially a theory of control, based on the concept of the feedback loop, whereby a system is in a state of dynamic monitoring and adjustment of its performance with respect to a specified goal. The biological analogue to cybernetics is homeostasis, the processes through which an organism is able to maintain itself in a state of dynamic equilibrium with its environment. According to Wiener, 'the physical functioning of the living individual and the operation of some of the newer communication machines are precisely parallel in their analogous attempts to control entropy through feedback'.[4]

The concept of a 'system', which became part of the *lingua franca* of the 1960s, was not destined to remain the exclusive property of a technologically-minded elite of engineers, scientists and mathematicians. In the hands of intellectuals, artists and political activists, it would become a key ideological component of the 'cultural revolution'. It is generally agreed, for example, that Robert Smithson's obsession with inorganic molecular structures (crystals), geological processes, time, and entropy – the latter being a concept derived from classical thermodynamics, but also performing a central role in communication theory – represented a strong cultural challenge to technology's progressive self-image. British art critic, Lawrence Alloway, likened the production, distribution and consumption of art to a non-hierarchical network, 'a shifting multiple goal coalition', and supported his claim by citing the work

4. Norbert Wiener, *The Human Uses of Human Beings*, New York: Avon Books, 1954, p. 38.

of industrial psychologists and sociologists.[5] Systems theory also figured prominently in the student revolt of the 1960s, prompting historian, Howard Brick, to declare that 'by the late 1960s students in American universities and colleges easily grasped the concept of a "system"'.[6] In the volatile atmosphere of confrontation with the Establishment, the term itself – which simply denotes the 'orderly processes at work in any complex array of multiple, interacting variables, be it a living organism, an environmental milieu or a computing machine' – was to be demonised. The meaning of the term 'system' was highly politically inflected and its application to the flux of human affairs or the natural environment was strongly contested. Despite its origins in the field of weapons research, social activists, environmentalists, student radicals and artists appropriated the term and used it effectively to polarise social discourse. Oppositional or counter-cultural uses of systems theory typically emphasised a consciousness of '"connections" among diverse social problems' indicating that 'the flaws in society were fundamental, endemic – not incidental'.[7]

What was art's response to a set of technocratic theories, ideologies and new structures of intellectual production (such as the 'think tank') that seemed to be collectively committed to the transformation of people into objects of 'technical and administrative measures'?[8] Not all artists believed that such knowledge and technology was indelibly tainted. In the visual arts, some practitioners were more inclined to celebrate technology and to read the growing influence of the social sciences as a sign of society's rapid modernisation, a future imagined as 'a technologically utopian structure of feeling, positivistic and "scientistic"'.[9] These artists sought to emphasise how the enlightened application of these new social and scientific theories – particularly semiotic theory, the dream of which 'had been the quest for inter-disciplinary forms, which would cross different types of human forms of expressions'[10] – could achieve socially progressive ends. Roy Ascott established his innovative 'Ground Course' at Ealing College in 1961, in the hope that a reorientation of art education – informed by cybernetics, semiotics and other theories of communication – could form the basis for a new visual sensibility. The enthusiasm displayed by Ascott for graphic notations as diagrams of a 'new space' had its counterpart in the American field of conceptual art, which Robert C. Hobbs characterises as the aestheticisation of knowledge and the fetishisation of 'quasi-scientific' (objective) modes

5. Lawrence Alloway, 'Network: The Art World Described as a System', *Artforum*, XI, Vol. 1, no. 29, September 1972.
6. Howard Brick, *Age of Contradiction: American Thought and Culture in the 1960s*, Ithaca: Cornell University Press, 2000, p. 124.
7. Ibid, pp. 124–5.
8. Theodor Adorno, *Minima Moralia*, London: Verso, 1985, p. 56.
9. David Mellor, *The Sixties Art Scene in London*, London: Phaidon Press, 1993, p. 107.
10. Ibid., p. 112.

of display.[11] In 1967, the British artist, Stephen Willats, argued that intellectual resources drawn from 'modern information areas', such as psychology and communication theory, would enable the artist to 'look at such important issues as audience composition' and the relation between the concerns of art and those of its audience. Willats envisaged a practice of art that 'structured function as an integral part of the environment'.[12] In 1971, he wrote that 'the development of homeostatic, self-regulating, self-assessing systems has been one of the most important conceptual developments in respect of behavioural structures, for it is in the nature of these systems that they are capable of determining their own structural relationship between input and output'.[13] A more radical example of the adoption by artists of strategies and intellectual resources usually found in the cultural space of corporations and government policy institutes is the reconfiguration of the 'think tank' and the modern corporate figure of the management consultant by British artists, John Latham and Barbara Steveni, co-founders in 1966 of the Artist Placement Group.[14]

Others took a more benign approach to the concept of the system, using it to denote a set of parameters, or rules, that can impart the image of structure and motive to artistic practices that are invariably performative and contingent. Such work was constituted through moments of social encounter and interaction, rather than through the disposition of materials. The concept of a template or schema – already familiar to conceptual art, as the work of Dan Graham, Sol LeWitt, Hanne Darboven, Douglas Huebler and On Kawara attests – provided an armature on which to organise a variety of social scenarios, as in Lee Lozano's *Dialogue Piece*, initiated in 1969, or some of the early projects of Vito Acconci. Acconci, not ordinarily associated with systems theory as such, was interested, in the late-1960s, in organising performances that would place himself into a pre-existing situation or social circuit, 'something that already existed'.[15] Acconci's contribution to the Museum of Modern Art's 1970 exhibition, Information, was a structured performance, which the artist described as a 'mail system-museum-exhibition-system'. Other works by Acconci, such as his solitary physical self-improvement performances, display an absurdist caste which links him with those artists who were far more interested in undermining the social authority of systems

11. Robert C. Hobbs, 'Affluence, Taste, and the Brokering of Knowledge: Notes on the Social Context of Early Conceptual Art', Michael Corris (Ed.), *Conceptual Art: Theory, Myth, and Practice*, Cambridge: Cambridge University Press, 2003.
12. Stephen Willats, 'Statement', 1967, reprinted in Clive Phillpot and Andrea Tarsia (Eds.), *Live in Your Head: Concept and Experiment in Britain 1965–75*, London: Whitechapel Art Gallery, 2000, p. 161.
13. Stephen Willats, 'Behavioural Nets and Life Structures', *The Paper*, no. 1, 1971.
14. Michael Corris, 'From Black Holes to Boardrooms: John Latham, Barbara Steveni and the Order of Undivided Wholeness', *Art+Text*, 49, September 1994.
15. Martin Kunz, 'Interview with Vito Acconci About the Development of his Work Since 1966', Marianne Eigenheer (Ed.), *Vito Acconci*, Luzern: Kunstmuseum Luzern, 1978, unpaginated.

theory through parody, by pushing the application of a system to the point of absurdity. Systems theory, cybernetics and game theory were misrepresented and diminished by a strategy of over-generalisation, whereby the most banal situations of everyday life would be subjected to isolation, rationalisation and analysis in a travesty of corporate efficiency or military control. One example is the early work of David Askevold – *Three Spot Game* (1968), *Shoot Don't Shoot (A Sum Zero Game Matrix)* (1970) and *Taming Expansion* (1971) – which is consciously modelled after a simple game theory decision matrix.

The holistic insight that all systems, regardless of size or complexity, are interconnected, lurks at the heart of systems theory and was mercilessly exaggerated, to the point of paranoia, in the novels of Thomas Pynchon, such as *The Crying of Lot 49* and *V.* Earlier, Len Deighton's *The Ipcress File* – the 1962 literary debut of an ex-Royal College of Art student turned novelist – anticipated 'the synthesised environment of technological fantasy only so far as the severely bureaucratic, hierarchical and class-ridden aspects of British culture would permit'.[16] Even the influential work, in America, of George Brecht and John Cage – which Robert Morris characterised in the late-1960s as the 'final secularisation' of art and systems of chance[17] – may be read as an indictment of technocratic and bureaucratic modalities of control. It was a defiant statement of the poverty of such a world view, a warning about the hubris of all attempts to overcome indeterminacy and an encouraging sign that led to the innovation, by some conceptual artists, of more explicitly 'democratically' structured artworks and situations.

The engagement of conceptual artists with systems theory, information theory, cybernetics and electronic technology had a real basis in ideological and social conflict, though, at times, it seemed to be the result of contingency. Jack Burnham argues that Hans Haacke 'wanted to reveal the way the world functions on its most essential levels'.[18] Haacke took as his subject matter the totality of all systems, regardless of their nature as physical, biological or social, although his work before around 1968 concentrated on the first two categories. Haacke's central artistic strategy has been defined as the 'production of systems, the interference with and the exposure of existing systems'.[19] He is concerned with the 'operational structure of organisations, in which transfer of information, energy, and/or material occurs'.[20] Fredric Jameson has likened Haacke's methodology to that of homeopathy. Jameson writes that 'Haacke poses the political dilemma of a new cultural politics: how to struggle within the world of the simulacrum by using the arms and weapons specific

16. Mellor, op. cit., p. 110.
17. Robert Morris, 'Some Notes on the Phenomenology of Making', *Artforum*, VIII, no. 8, April 1970.
18. Jack Burnham, 'Hans Haacke's Cancelled Show at the Guggenheim', *Artforum*, IX, no. 10, June 1971.
19. Ibid.
20. Ibid.

to that world which are themselves very precisely simulacra.'[21] Provoked by the assassination of Martin Luther King in 1968 and referring to the utility of so-called 'political art', Haacke expressed the belief that 'the production and the talk about sculpture has nothing to do with the urgent problems of our society [...] We must face the fact that art is unsuited as a political tool.'[22] The artist stressed that 'any work done with and in a given social situation cannot remain detached from its cultural and ideological context'.[23]

The challenge launched by Haacke against the ethical constraints imposed on art by a particularly narrow sense of professionalism is enabled, in large measure, by the artist's embrace of systems theory and systems 'thinking'. In particular, it is the notion of an ecosystem that is most relevant to Haacke's projects of the early-1970s, imparting a sense of structure and coherence on works such as *10 Turtles Set Free* (1970) and *Goat Feeding in Woods, Thus Changing It* (1970). *Beach Pollution* (1970) – a pile of driftwood and other rubbish that had been collected on a Spanish seafront – not only signals Haacke's concern with environmental issues, but also initiates a dialogue with the anti-formalism of the late-1960s. Visually, *Beach Pollution* is a work that seems to invite an experience of 'unmediated physical encounter with matter, an encounter unfettered by language and *a priori* assumptions'[24] similar to that intended by Robert Morris in his work *Threadwaste* (1968). Yet, what distinguishes Haacke's work is not its physical composition as a pile of scavenged rubbish but its conceptual relationship to the exogenous cultural space of the emerging environmental movement. That such a difference is not available to visual inspection but is constituted through language marks a significant shift away from the phenomenological claims of minimalism.

One of the lessons to be drawn from a study of the art of the 1960s and '70s is that systems analysis, information theory and the like cannot be applied unproblematically to the practice of art. In fact, the contemporary application of systems theory to art, in one instance at least, yields a dramatically different conclusion. I am referring to the work of the sociologist, Niklas Luhmann, who describes the domain of art as an operationally closed and self-referential communicative system.[25] According to Luhmann, art's purpose, like that of other social-symbolic systems, is communication. But, where Luhmann and the 1960s enthusiasts for systems theory in art part company, is in their respective

21. Fredric Jameson, 'Hans Haacke and the Cultural Logic of Postmodernism', *Hans Haacke: Unfinished Business*, New York: The New Museum of Contemporary Art, 1986, pp. 42–3. Jameson notes that 'such a strategy – even conceived provisionally – has little of the vigorous self-confidence and affirmation of older political and even proto-political aesthetics, which aimed at opening and developing some radically new and distinct revolutionary cultural space within the fallen space of capitalism. Yet as modest and as frustrating as it may sometimes seem, a homeopathic cultural politics seems to be all we can currently think or imagine' (p. 43).
22. Hans Haacke to Jack Burnham, correspondence 10 April 1968.
23. Ibid.
24. James Meyer, *Minimalism: Art and Polemics in the Sixties*, New Haven: Yale University Press, 2001, p. 267.
25. Thanks to Michael Baldwin and Mel Ramsden for bringing Luhmann's *Art as a Social System* to my attention.

understanding of the nature of communication in and through art. The artists and critics of the 1960s and '70s used systems theory pragmatically, to facilitate the integration of art and the world; in doing so, they risked the disintegration of art. Luhmann uses systems theory analytically, to stress the difference between art and the world, a move that risks being mistaken for an attempt to rehabilitate the modernist practice of resistance through negation.

Technological Kindergarten: Gustav Metzger and Early Computer Art

Simon Ford

Vol 1 #26, Summer / Autumn 2003

On 21 January 2003, a crowd of onlookers watched as the 77-year-old artist, Gustav Metzger, scurried through 100,000 newspapers piled up in the dark basement of T1&2 Artspace, a squatted building in Spitalfields, London. With the newspapers filled with reports on the coming war in Iraq, Metzger's actions appeared especially charged. Here was a man who, in his own words, had dedicated his life 'to the task of eliminating war and other social injustices'.[1]

Metzger was born on 10 April 1926 in Nuremberg. His Polish-Jewish parents had immigrated to Germany just eight years before. In January 1939, they sent the 12-year-old Gustav, along with a brother, to England as part of the Refugee Children movement. It was just in time. Those members of his family that remained in Germany were subsequently murdered in the Nazi concentration camps. After a brief period living in a commune in Bristol, Metzger decided to become an artist. His studies took him to Cambridge, London, Antwerp and then back to London, where he studied at Borough Polytechnic School under David Bomberg. By this time, his experience of fascism in Germany and the nuclear destruction of Hiroshima and Nagasaki had already provided the foundations for his life-long political commitment:

> The atomic bomb is really the starting point of my own work. This is the point when I was an art student and I was very conscious that from now on everything was different, including art. From that point, I started to probe the limits of art, of what one could do and what one had to do in relation to society, in relation to helping society so that this couldn't happen again.[2]

Metzger's commitment to the anti-nuclear movement soon became the most obvious manifestation of his opposition to Cold War nuclear proliferation, but it also informed his development of auto-destructive art. Announcing a new form of 'public art for industrial societies', Metzger's first auto-destructive art manifesto appeared in November 1959.[3] His second manifesto, 'Manifesto Auto-Destructive Art', appeared in 1960. In it, he described 'man in Regent Street' and 'rockets' and 'nuclear weapons' as auto-destructive, along with

1. Gustav Metzger, 'The Artist in the Face of Social Collapse', Melanie Keen (Ed.), *Frequencies: Investigations into Culture, History and Technology*, London: inIVA, 1998, p. 8.
2. Gustav Metzger in Kristine Stiles, 'The Destruction In Art Symposium (DIAS): The Radical Cultural Project of Event-Structured Live Art', unpublished PhD thesis, Berkeley: University of California, 1987, p. 74.
3. Gustav Metzger, 'Auto-Destructive Art', London, 4 November 1959. The manifesto accompanied an exhibition, at 14 Monmouth Street, of discarded cardboard packaging that Metzger discovered on Fulham Road.

materials and processes such as acid, ballistics, cybernetics, electricity, explosives, feed-back, human energy, mass-production, nuclear energy and radiation. Auto-destructive art transformed technology into public art and mirrored 'the compulsive perfectionism of arms manufacture – polishing to destruction point'.[4]

Fittingly, Pat Arrowsmith, Field Secretary for the Direct Action Committee Against Nuclear War, wrote one of the earliest reviews of Metzger's work for *Peace News*: 'I myself walked into London beside him at the end of last year's Aldermaston March. [... He also] stood up on a soap box to address the stall-holders of Watton market.'[5] Metzger's activism led him to become a founding member of the Committee of 100, a group dedicated to non-violent civil disobedience. In September 1961 at Bow Street Magistrates Court, Metzger, along with other members of the Committee, refused to be bound over to keep the peace for a year. For this, Metzger was imprisoned for a month along with other Committee members including Alex Comfort, Bertrand Russell, Arnold Wesker and Christopher Logue. At his trial, he read out a prepared statement:

> I came to this country from Germany when 12 years old, my parents being Polish Jews, and I am grateful to the Government for bringing me over. My parents disappeared in 1943 and I would have shared their fate. But the situation is now far more barbarous than Buchenwald, for there can be absolute obliteration at any moment. I have no other choice than to assert my right to live, and we have chosen, in this committee, a method of fighting which is the exact opposite of war – the principle of total non-violence.[6]

In July 1961, just before his trial, Metzger organised a key auto-destructive event: an open-air demonstration at the South Bank in London. Armed with a spray-gun filled with acid and dressed in combat clothing and a gasmask, he attacked three large sheets of nylon attached to a metal frame. The accompanying manifesto contained Metzger's first mention of computers as a possible ingredient of auto-destructive art:

> Auto-destructive art and auto-creative art aim at the integration of art with the advances of science and technology. The immediate objective is the creation, with the aid of computers, of works of art whose movements are programmed and include 'self-regulation'. The spectator, by means of electronic devices can have a direct bearing on the action of these works. Auto-destructive art is an attack on capitalist values and the drive to nuclear annihilation.[7]

4. Gustav Metzger, 'Manifesto of Auto-Destructive Art', London, 10 March 1960.
5. Pat Arrowsmith, 'Auto-Destructive Art', *Peace News*, 22 July 1960, p. 11. The review was of a demonstration that took place at the Temple Gallery, London, on 22 June 1960.
6. Gustav Metzger in 'Quotes from Bow Street', *Peace News*, 15 September 1961, p. 7.
7. Gustav Metzger, 'Auto-Destructive Art, Machine Art, Auto-Creative Art', London, 23 June 1961.

It took another four years before Metzger provided a more detailed proposal to create an artwork that included a computer as an integral element.[8] *Five Screens with Computer*, he wrote, would consist of five walls, or screens, made of stainless steel, each 30 feet high, 40 feet long and two feet deep. They would be arranged about 25 feet apart in a central area between three high-rise tower blocks. Each wall would be composed of 10,000 uniform elements made of stainless steel, glass or plastic and be square, rectangular or hexagonal in shape. Each element would be individually ejected from the screen over a period of ten years until the screens literally fell to pieces.

Metzger still had to work out how the elements would be ejected, but, at this point, he proposed the use of magnets and compressed air. The computer's job was to control – according to a program devised by the artist – the sequence of these ejections. This program would take into account the quality of light and shade, the revolution of the Earth, the various seasons, the weather and spectator participation via photo-electronic switches. Metzger claimed that the computer would link art, technology and society and only through its use could the artist 'achieve forms and rhythms that correspond[ed] to his aims'. Through the work, Metzger aimed to re-channel the destructive potential of the computer: 'Today, death is fed into, processed and administered by the computers'. Unlike his acid-on-nylon paintings, the computer also provided an escape from connotations of expressionism and the fetishisation of the mark left by the artist's hand. This huge sculpture, in such a prominent public space, would make a spectacle of destruction and, in the process, Metzger hoped, would 'initiate a series of controversies that can become a kind of mass-therapy as well as educational programme'.[9] Equally, you could imagine some viewers, especially those living in the nearby tower blocks, reading the random ejections of the units as analogous to the lack of autonomy and control in their own lives. And, of course, the irony now is that it is the tower blocks themselves that are regularly demolished in celebratory and public spectacles of destruction and regeneration.

Metzger's interest in computer art in 1965 coincided with a number of key events in its early history, most significantly the first computer art exhibitions at the Technische Hochschule in Stuttgart and the Howard Wise Gallery in New York. A year later, IBM recruited its first artist-in-residence, John Whitney, Sr, and the Museum of Modern Art purchased Charles Csuri's computer-generated image, *Hummingbird*.[10]

8. Gustav Metzger, *Auto-destructive Art: A Talk at the Architectural Association*, London: Destruction/Creation, 1965. In the text, Metzger acknowledged the assistance of Beverly Rowe, then chief applications programmer at the University of London Computer Centre, who became a founding member of the Computer Arts Society.
9. Ibid.
10. See Charlie Gere, *Digital Culture*, London: Reaktion Books, 2002, p. 100. Metzger was also well aware of the work of Roy Ascott and shared his interest in cybernetics. In December, 1962, Ascott invited Metzger to give a lecture on auto-destructive art at Ealing College of Art. In the audience was Pete Townshend, who later took some of Metzger's ideas into the realm of rock music with his spectacular auto-destructive performances with The Who.

Metzger spent much of 1966 organising the Destruction In Art Symposium (DIAS) and much of 1967 dealing with its consequences,[11] but he returned to the problematic of working with computers in 1968 for the exhibition Cybernetic Serendipity: The Computer and the Arts.[12] Curated by Jasia Reichardt, it was the first exhibition in Britain to demonstrate the creative potential of computers. Metzger's participation, however, did not prevent him from severely criticising the exhibition. His focus remained on issues of social responsibility, for both the artists and scientists involved in the new technology, and he countered those who advocated the utopian possibilities of the coming computer age with sobering details of its origins in military research. 'Cybernetic Serendipity', he complained, provided

> a perfectly adequate demonstration of the reactionary potential of art and technology. No end of information on computers composing haiku – no hint that computers dominate modern war; that they are becoming the most totalitarian tools ever used on society. We are faced by this prospect – whilst more and more scientists are investigating the threats that science and technology pose for society, artists are being led into a technological kindergarten.[13]

Metzger's contribution to the exhibition took the form of a description of his latest version of *Five Screens with Computer*. Slight modifications included increasing the distance between the screens from 25 feet to 30 feet and also the introduction of a festive element when suggesting that the 'frequency of ejections on holidays may reach 600 a day'.[14]

The work's most developed description came a year later, during Event One at the Royal College of Art (29–30 March 1969). The most significant modification saw the number of elements in each screen reduced from 10,000 down to 1,200. Metzger also provided more details on how the individual elements would operate: 'These elements can be moved forwards or backwards within a frame at controlled speeds, and will finally be ejected at various controlled speeds, reaching a maximum distance of 30ft.' Metzger utilised the computer in three key areas: design, operation and recording.

> Design
> Since all the decisions on the activity of the screens will be made before production begins it is necessary to have the most complete understanding of the work's potential at the design stage. A computer allied to graphic

11. DIAS ran from 31 August – 30 September 1966. After the performance by Hermann Nitsch at St. Bride Institute on Fleet Street, on 15 September 1966, Metzger and fellow organiser, John Sharkey, were charged with 'having unlawfully caused to be shown a lewd and indecent exhibition'. On 19 July 1967, the court found Metzger guilty and he accepted a £100 fine rather than spend four months in jail.
12. The exhibition was held at the Institute of Contemporary Arts, London, 2 August – 20 October 1968. See also: Jasia Reichardt, (Ed.), *Cybernetics, Art and Ideas*, London: Studio Vista, 1971.
13. Gustav Metzger, 'Automata in History: Part 1', *Studio International*, March 1969, pp. 107–9.
14. Gustav Metzger, 'Five Screens with Computer', Jasia Reichardt (Ed.), *Cybernetic Serendipity: The Computer and The Arts*, London: Studio International, 1968, p. 31.

output will be used to plot the numerous possibilities for moving and ejecting elements, and for visualising the possible shapes of the screenis in transformation. 55 percent of the elements will be ejected on a pre-determined program. The rest (including one entire screen) will be ejected in a random manner. These random ejections will be sparked off by intense sun or electric light, or by the assembly of people above a certain number in the vicinity of a screen. Random ejections are subject to a variety of controls such as structural considerations, and will be co-ordinated with the overall program.

Operation
A computer will be in general control of the electro/mechanical activity of the sculpture – continuous adjustments (online) will be necessary. The computer will also direct peripheral activity such as the raising of the glass wall surrounding the site before ejections can take place.

Recording
The computer will be used to print out and draw the day-by-day development of the screens. This will be necessary to check on operational, structural, and safety factors, and will be an aid to maintenance activities. This graphic output, along with photographs and films, will be preserved as part of the documentation on the work.[15]

In another text from this period, Metzger stated that, when not being employed by the ejections, the computer could be used by the inhabitants of the flats: 'By means of telephone lines it can serve as a local convenient library for the inhabitants'.[16]

Metzger's description of the project offered little explanation of how the artwork's immediate audience might be consulted or invited to interact with the sculpture. As Metzger clearly stated in the Event One text, 'all the decisions on the activity of the screens would be made before production begins'. This point is significant because, if realised, such a sculpture would almost certainly have attracted great resentment from its local audience. Not only would there have been extensive and expensive construction and maintenance work, there would also have been considerable noise from the explosive ejection of the units, which, in themselves, would have posed a serious health risk (only belatedly allayed by Metzger's suggestion that a retractable glass wall should

15. Gustav Metzger, 'Five Screens with Computer (1963–69)', *Event One*, London: Computer Art Society, 1969, unpaginated. Metzger accompanied the text with a schematic drawing of 'the development of one screen (no. 3) in the first three years of its activity'. The drawing is credited to Mr. D.E. Evans, of the Computer Unit, Imperial College, London, and was produced on an 'IBM 7094 11 (32K memory) with CALCOMP plotter'.
16. Gustav Metzger, speech at the conference Computers and Visual Research, Zagreb, 1969, transcript in *Bit International*, no. 7, 1971. As a further sign of Metzger's commitment to computer art at this time, he was also working on the translation into English of Herbert Werner Franke's seminal work, *Computer Graphics, Computer Art*, published by Phaidon in 1971.

surround the site, protecting both the public from the sculpture and the sculpture from the public).

It was probably these and many other pragmatic concerns that stopped Metzger from taking his proposals any further. After Event One, his engagement with computers and art became increasingly bound up with a new organisation, the Computer Arts Society (CAS), set up 'to encourage the creative use of computers in the arts and allow the exchange of information in this area'. The idea for the Society was first mooted on the afternoon of 7 August 1968, at an informal session on Computers and Music at the IFIP Congress in Edinburgh.[17] Alan Sutcliffe, then head of the Programme Research Unit at Imperial College, London, became its chairman, R.J. Lansdown, Architectural Partner of Ian Fraser and Associates, became its secretary and Metzger volunteered to be the founding editor of its newsletter, *PAGE: Bulletin of the Computer Arts Society*. The Society initially held its meetings in rooms donated by the British Computer Society at 29 Portland Place, London, but, by June 1971, it had moved into its own permanent space, two rooms on the second floor of The Dairy in Camden, a large complex of artists' studios run by SPACE.

In 1971, the membership of CAS consisted of 500 enthusiasts worldwide. At this time access to computers was severely limited, with most being owned by scientific and military institutions. Artistic projects formed only a small, and often informal, element of their operation, so as part of the Society's brief to publicise and lobby for artistic projects, it hosted events such as the Computer Art session at Computer Graphics 70.[18] Advertised as 'More than a symposium – more than an exhibition – an international meeting of minds', the conference boasted key representatives from the military-industrial complex: General Motors, Lockheed Georgia, Mobil Oil Corporation, Royal Navy, Ford Motor Company, Space Flight Center, Boeing, Sperry Rand and Unilever. At the conference, Metzger presented a paper on 'New Ideas in Plotter Design Construction and Output' and two months later, on 24 June, he gave another paper, this time at the British Computer Society, entitled 'Computers and Sculpture'.

Such activities formed part of Metzger's plan to 'seek an alliance with the most advanced research in natural and artificial intelligence'.[19] It also complemented his active membership to the British Society for Social Responsibility in Science[20] and culminated in a two-page essay for *PAGE*, in which he listed every article that had appeared in the main professional journals of the day (*Computers and Automation* and *Communications of the Association for*

17. Mission statement and information from *PAGE: Bulletin of the Computer Arts Society*, no. 3, June 1969.
18. Hosted by Brunel University, Uxbridge, Middlesex, 14–16 April 1970. Information from conference programme: *Computer Graphics 70*, Uxbridge, 1970.
19. Gordon Hyde, Jonathan Benthall and Gustav Metzger, 'Zagreb Manifesto', *Studio International*, June 1969, p. 259.
20. Formed in April 1969.

Computing Machinery) that exposed links between computers and weapons of mass destruction. For Metzger, these references and selected quotations also provided ample proof that the development of computers and armaments were both closely integrated with the capitalist economy.[21]

Metzger's involvement with *PAGE* ended with issue 26, in November 1972, when the bulletin announced he was 'too busy' with other projects to continue.[22] These projects included his participation in 3 Life Situations at Gallery House, his assistance in founding the Artists' Union and his preparations for the Art Strike, 1977–1980.[23] He published no further plans for *Five Screens with Computer* and, for most of the 1980s, kept an extremely low profile, only returning to public life in the 1990s with proposals for artworks that focused increasingly on environmental issues. More recently, curators have included his work in important historical group shows, such as Life/Live, Out of Actions and Live in Your Head,[24] and a major retrospective of his work took place in 1998 at Oxford's Museum of Modern Art.[25] To date, though, most attention has continued to focus on Metzger's spectacular acts of destruction with little attention being paid to his brief engagement with computer science.

In retrospect, *Five Screens with Computer* appeared at the height of what became the first false dawn of computer arts. It would take at least another two decades, the development of personal computers and the growth of the internet before digital art once again achieved even nominal art world status. Thirty-odd years on, however, Metzger's critique of the dubious techno-utopianism of some computer artists and his inconvenient pointing at the origin of much computer technology in the military and state security sectors still hold true. Also sadly prescient is his non-ironic assertion, in 1971, that, in terms of computer art, at least, 'the real avant-garde was the army'.[26]

21. Gustav Metzger, 'Social Responsibility and the Computer Professional, Part 1', *PAGE: Bulletin of the Computer Arts Society*, no. 11, October 1970. There was no part two.
22. Anon, *PAGE: Bulletin of the Computer Arts Society*, no. 26, November 1972.
23. Gustav Metzger's announcement can be found in *Art into Society – Society into Art*, London: ICA, 1974, p. 74.
24. Life/Live, Musée d'Art Moderne de la Ville de Paris, 5 October–5 January 1997; Out of Actions: Between Performance and the Object 1949–1979, The Geffen Contemporary at the Museum of Contemporary Art, Los Angeles, 8 February–10 May 1998; and Live in Your Head: Concept and Experiment in Britain, 1965–75, Whitechapel Art Gallery, 4 February–2 April 2000.
25. See the catalogue Gustav Metzger, Kerry Brougher and Astrid Bowron (Eds.), Oxford: Museum of Modern Art, 1998.
26. Citing as evidence the success – in the first computer art competition organised by Computers and Automation in 1963 – of the US Army Ballistic Missile Research Laboratory. See Metzger, op. cit., *Bit International*, no. 7, 1971. According to Charlie Gere, the US Army also won second place. See Gere, op. cit., 2002, p. 100.

Chapter 3

I, Cyborg: Reinventing the Human

Donna Haraway's unforgettable 'Cyborg Manifesto', written in 1986, provides the catalyst for the 'post-human' politics discussed in this chapter. This might be where the resemblance ends, however, since you will soon notice that the politics of post-humanism turn out to be extremely varied. When *Mute* launched in 1994, the Manifesto had recently been published in Haraway's *Simians, Cyborgs and Women: The Reinvention of Nature* (1991). In the same way that digital networks were breathing new life into neoliberal economics at one pole, they were also reinvigorating a feminism mired in 'identity politics' at the other.

Inspired by French writers such as Luce Irigaray and Monique Wittig, Haraway was interested in building a politics based on the non-essence of identity, on affinities built between partial and contingent identities – 'affinity politics' rather than 'identity politics'. Part of her challenge to the patriarchy which coded women as nature and men as culture was to create a feminist figure that lived in the breach between all categories of identity (nature/culture, machine/animal, animate/inanimate). But Haraway's cyborg probably excited feminists as much for her embrace of information technology as for her love of the alien. As biotechnology, computing, life sciences and military hardware, transformed by IT, grew increasingly to resemble one another, code and networks were grasped by Haraway as primary agents of social transformation within late capitalism.

For Suhail Malik, in an article appearing on the front page of the pilot issue of *Mute*, Michael Jackson served as the mass-cultural embodiment of Haraway's cyborg. Neither black nor white, adult nor child, fact nor fiction, human nor animal – this medially enhanced pop chimera was also a tragic victim. After his child abuse scandal, writes Malik, Jackson lost his already-fictional innocence. By wanting to live outside the law, 'by becoming child (woman, animal, satellite, white, whatever)', his very elusiveness precipitated his re-inscription in the law. If Michael Jackson serves as a failed image of identity mutation, one that was both propelled and ultimately destroyed by the delusional sovereignty of mega-stardom, what would be a positive one?

Caroline Bassett's critique of the cyberfeminist politics popularised by Sadie Plant was *Mute*'s next serious attempt to deal with the question. In what, at the time, felt like a refreshingly sober assessment of cyberfeminism's rabid computer love, Bassett argued that Plant effectively replaces one form of essence with another: woman-as-nature becomes new-technology-as-woman. Far from throwing off the constraints of identity à la Irigaray – for whom 'any theory of the subject will always have been appropriated by the masculine' – Plant places her hope for female emancipation in self-organising technologies and computer networks. Unlike Haraway, who is deliberately using 'her master's tools' to revolutionary ends, Plant sees in computers and code the quintessence of the female condition (simulation, connectivity, patchworking). For Bassett, therefore, Plant's is less a politics than an eschatology, the (mere) *hope* for future things.

When, in 2001, we returned to the question of the 'Cyborg Manifesto' and the politics it had spawned, ten years after its initial publication, it was in the form of a 'head-to-head' debate. María Fernández's response echoes some of Bassett's earlier criticisms – where Haraway pursues boundary transgression as a feminist, socialist and anti-racist strategy, cyberfeminists eschew all definitions, including political goals, and even fail to build alliances across identities. Suhail Malik's return to the cyborg theory that had been his defining contribution as an early member of *Mute*'s editorial board, yielded surprising results. Arguing that the universal celebration of boundary transgression is simplistic and inattentive to the precise difficulties involved, he concludes that Haraway's engagement with techno-rationality is undialectical and superficial since it leaves intact a left-liberal, 'proto-hippy' critique of technology.

The debate on post-humanism gains a profoundly materialist orientation in two of the closing articles of this chapter. Andrew Goffey and Luciana Parisi both highlight unorthodox biological research to critique the anthropocentric and (bio-)political orientation of the life sciences. Goffey is interested in how classical immunology has reinforced the metaphysical split between self and other by focusing on the 'defensive' activity of antibodies apparently able to differentiate between 'friend' and 'enemy'. Instead, he draws attention to alternative theories of the immune system, which focus on its 'non-negligible' activity in the absence of germs, as well as its continuous attempt to assimilate, not reject, foreign bodies, attacking only what it can't assimilate. Consequently, the self is understood as a constantly mutating historical construct, not a pre-existing one fighting to defend its boundaries.

A similarly non-anthropocentric view of evolution is taken by Parisi in her article, 'Abstract Sex'. Rejecting the Darwinian paradigm of evolution – based on copulatory sex and nucleic DNA transmission – she uses the case of non-nucleic DNA transmission in mitochondrial (parasite) bacteria – which participate in the 'host' bacteria's DNA transfer – to argue for a radically arbitrary account of nature's organisation. With myriad channels existing for information transmission beyond copulation, she argues that transgenesis and, indeed, 'biotech [were, in fact] invented 3,900 million years ago by bacteria'. Add digital technology into the mix and the opportunities for non-linear DNA transmission ramify. 'Abstract Sex', then, 'opens up the bio-physical and bio-cultural organisation of sex to radical destratification' and, with it, jettisons all human teleologies, whether Darwinian, neoliberal or, interestingly, post-autonomous.

Parisi's argument for bio-cultural turbulence mounts a stinging attack on the pseudo-embrace of non-linearity, whether in the form of the market's 'invisible hand' or the post-autonomous concept of the multitude's innate creativity. For her, these models posit repetition without difference and fear mutations. But Parisi's thinking also opens the door to the total indifference of life's organisation. If this borderline nihilism represents one pole of post-humanist discourse, Haraway's – with its overt politics and stowed-away humanism – represents the other. One thing is for certain, the post-human leviathan will not, in the words of cyberfeminist Sandy Stone, 'stand up', even if we say please.

The Immateriality of the Signifier: The Flesh and the Innocence of Michael Jackson

Suhail Malik

Vol 1 pilot issue, Winter 1994

This article abandons at least one of the questions that this issue of *Mute* tries to address – namely whether art can survive the 20th century – in favour of another question which is perhaps less secure, perhaps not so quickly available to a polemic whose positions could be distributed according to what 'art', or the '20th century', or even 'survival' are said to be and what sense any of these terms are said to have here, today; a question which perhaps attempts only to invoke whatever instability may be possible in just these terms (and some others, not least 'technique' and 'world' and 'today') thereby remaining useless to any position in the dispute over art's 'survival', a question as to whether the 20th century – whatever that is – can survive (the) art(s).

Such survival – of (a) time – matters 'today', matters now, precisely because the notion of a continuation or a change or even an end to art 'today', indicating an art or arts or an anti-art out of or beyond the 20th century, seems inextricably tied to a technology – of the image and of sound – that is itself 'new'. But this is itself nothing new: in just this way it could be asked whether the 19th century could survive the inventions of photography and sound recording on the one hand, and Cézanne and jazz on the other (and is any one invention less a matter of 'technique' than another?), and – to short-circuit an enormous argument – that the word that the Ancient Greeks had for art (where the 'West' is sometimes said to have been born) was only just *techn.* Which century, which time, then, is art, are the arts, and the anti-arts (there are no non-arts) in today? And where? Especially if 'today', 'now' that where and when cannot be removed from the time of technique, 'our' time, the end of the 20th century (at least). Does that mean an exacerbating materialisation or immaterialistion of fabrication and of figure, of silences and of blanks? Which is why...

...I want to talk to you about Michael Jackson. Because Michael Jackson is innocent.

I'm not making any claims here about Michael Jackson's legal status (though, since the allegations you'll all be familiar with have yet – if ever – to be heard in court, he remains innocent as far as that's concerned). And I'm not making any claims about what Michael Jackson may or may not have done or continues to do, whether or not he caressed, fondled or 'orally copulated' and masturbated Jordan Chandler,[1] the 13-year-old around whom the allegations

1. See *The Independent,* 15 September 1994.

centre. What I hope to talk about is what's up for grabs in all of these allegations, defences and anxieties around Michael Jackson: namely, innocence. Michael Jackson is innocent – because what Michael Jackson wants and wanted, and had, more than anything else, even now, in the company of children (boys, but what does this matter?) is innocence itself. And, just that far, Michael Jackson is more innocent than ever before, more innocent than any child.

In her essay, 'A Cyborg Manifesto',[2] Donna Haraway introduces and lays out many of the themes that have come to dominate the central concerns of, and discussion around, what is now known as 'Cyberpunk'. I'm going to adopt Haraway's quasi-definition of what's at stake here: 'A cyborg', she says, 'is a cybernetic organism, a hybrid of machine and organism, a creature of social reality as well as a creature of fiction. Social reality is lived social relations, our most important political construction, a world-changing fiction.'[3] I'll carry on with the rest of this paragraph, but with a greater hesitance. Some of what Haraway goes on to say here I'll be taking issue with implicitly. She continues:

> The international women's movements have constructed 'women's experience', as well as uncovered or discovered this crucial collective object. [That is without doubt.] This experience is a fiction and fact of the most crucial, political kind. Liberation rests on the construction of the consciousness [...] The cyborg is a matter of fiction and lived experience that changes what counts as women's experience in the late 20th century. This is a struggle over life and death, but the boundary between science fiction and social reality is an optical illusion.[4]

I'll quickly outline Haraway's argument about the 'processes' of 'social reality' in the 'informatics of domination' that is the 'integrated circuit' of society today, 'coded', she says, 'by C3I command-control-communication-intelligence' – the planning strategy centre of the US military. The model of domination and control Haraway is talking about above is one aspect of the 'technological apparatus'. Let's move on and pick out a second strand from Haraway's essay which will allow a return to this apparatus and its dispersion (if, that is, that apparatus isn't just that dispersion), and Michael Jackson, namely the 'three boundary breakdowns' that are, for her, the logic of the cyborg, if it is a logic.

What are these three 'boundary breakdowns'? Firstly, 'the boundary between the human and the animal is thoroughly breached'. The second 'leaky distinction' is 'between animal-human (organism) and machine'. Thirdly, the 'boundary between physical and non-physical is very imprecise for us'.[5]

2. Donna Haraway, 'A Cyborg Manifesto', *Body/Politics: Women and the Discourses of Science*, New York: Routledge, 1990.
3. Ibid, p. 149.
4. Loc. cit.
5. Ibid, pp. 150–3.

Everything here is to do with borders, boundaries and their establishment. And this, as Haraway recognises very well, is because the cyborg is just a border that is not yet properly in place, and what happens there? You, me, politics.

Let me pass quickly over these border skirmishes. Of the border between the animal and the human she says:

> Biology and evolutionary theory over the last two centuries have simultaneously produced modern organisms as objects of knowledge re-etched in ideological struggle or professional disputes between life and social science [...] Biological-determinist ideology is only one position opened up in the scientific culture for arguing the meanings of human animality.[6]

What does this mean? Simply that the person – man – is studied, in the life sciences at least, alongside every other animal and in much the same way. (This has usually meant the cutting to bits, incarceration or close-up study of both, either microscopically or environmentally, a recurring theme in the work of Sterling and Gibson.) But the 'much the same way' is important here. There are still marked and important distinctions between the study and use of animals and persons (not least when it comes to consumption, eating and what, on humans, would pass for torture).

But there's also another side of this argument which Haraway points to when she argues that:

> [M]any people no longer feel the need for [the] separation [between human and animal]; indeed, many branches of feminist culture affirm the pleasure of connection of human and other living creatures. Movements for animal rights are not irrational denials of human uniqueness; they are a clear sighted recognition of connection across the discredited breach of nature and culture... There is much room for radical political people to contest the meanings of the breached boundary. The cyborg appears in myth precisely where the boundary between human and animal is transgressed.[7]

(Haraway goes on to comment that [b]estiality has a new status in this cycle of marriage exchange'.)

Who, then, in our public culture, in our mediatised and cultural currency, could or would be a more 'radical person' than Michael Jackson in his most intimate relation or connection with Bubbles, his chimp and good friend? And it is not just one animal that Michael Jackson spends his time with; the stories and reports of his menagerie – true or not – are well known enough to confirm the point. I'll cite a report from about ten days after the Michael Jackson child molestation story first broke, when Jackson could no longer afford to be seen

6. Ibid, p. 152.
7. Loc. cit.

as he always had been with an accompanying child, just after he had been brain scanned following his cancelled concerts in Singapore: 'Two adult and four young orang-utans were brought to Michael Jackson's Singapore hotel room yesterday where the singer entertained them at the poolside'.[8]

Who, then, in this new and breached relation between human and animal, could be more 'transgress-lively' cyborg in turning his back on the company and companionship of his fellow humans for animals? Grizzly Adams, perhaps, and the rest of the 'Return to Nature' brigade (you'd want to include here the anti-culturist 'crusty', together with the dominant primitivistic, liberatory aspects of rave – rather than clubbing – codes). But these are precisely the most naïve and inept responses to the boundary as boundary (they simply confirm that boundary, simply or merely changing sides and consequently always failing to work it at all). And these responses (or Donna Haraway) cannot even begin to touch the actual transformation of Michael Jackson into animal form (panther) at the end of one of his videos. Things are more complicated with Michael Jackson. Not least because he occupies and breaches the other two 'leaky boundaries' as well (and not only them), defying all stabilisation; defying, that is, all desire for it. Recall that the second unstable and disordered boundary was that between organism and machine. Haraway states that 'the certainty of what counts as nature – a source of insight and promise of innocence – is undermined, probably fatally'.[9]

Let's extend the boundary to that between the organic and the non-organic, and intersect it with the border between the natural and the non-natural, as Michael Jackson does, for example, in the multiple transmogrifications during many of his videos; transmogrifications that are again the actualisation of the breaching of this border – but that this is possible and, in some sense at least, acceptable is what is of interest here (be it taken as deranged).

And, even if Michael Jackson is the most public and contemporary manifestation of this troubled border, he is not alone. On the one hand, the entire Cyberpunk genre, from *Blade Runner* on, has written, filmed and discussed little else; from Gibson's fetishistic *Mona Lisa* to Arnie as half-humanoid, half-machine (but which half?), the constant stress has been on the compatibility and encroachment of the prosthetic device on the body, on the brain, on memory and so on. They are the anxieties in the face of a cyborg future, Michael Jackson.

The massive transfiguring of Michael Jackson is not merely restricted to these two borders, it also steps around Haraway's third 'imprecision', that of the material and the immaterial. A leaching of visibility and tactility is most explicitly shown in the video for 'Do You Remember' from the *Dangerous* album, where Michael Jackson constantly appears and disappears in several different guises, but also appears and disappears *tout court*.

8. See *The Independent*, 3 September 1993.
9. Haraway, op. cit., pp. 152–3.

Again, I want to suggest that there is also another level at which Michael Jackson's materiality/immateriality allows for the phenomenon that he has become and will continue to be. This level of immateriality is that which, in fact, allows Michael Jackson to be quite the star he is – because, as Haraway points out, in effect he is cyborg:

> Our best machines are made of sunshine; they are all light and clean because they are nothing but signals, electromagnetic waves, a section of spectrum, and these machines are eminently portable, mobile [a matter of immense human pain in Detroit and Singapore – with Michael Jackson, no less, a matter of some pleasure]. People are nowhere so fluid, being both material and opaque. Cyborgs are ether. Quintessence.

It's this last point I want to stick with and which, I think, presents the greatest difficulty in talking about Michael Jackson because it allows us to ask this question: What is the consistency of Michael Jackson? That is, if Michael Jackson is not simply a person because he is also the infraction of the border between the human and the animal, between the organic and the non-organic (which is also to say between the living and the dead – see the 'Thriller' video), between the material and the purely communicative ethereal manifestation that takes place in no one place as such and, because of this, takes place everywhere; if, that is, Michael Jackson is neither merely animal nor merely human, merely living nor merely dead, merely material nor merely signal and both animal and human, living and dead, material and signal; if Michael Jackson is a configuration of a stew which is, or wanted so badly to be, also neither merely male nor female, man nor woman and both male and female, and, similarly, for the separations between black/white, child/adult, victim/aggressor, innocent/profane, public/private, real/fictional, human/nonhuman (whatever it may be to be human) and so on; what then does Michael Jackson consist of? What consistency and manifestation can he have (or not have, in so far as he makes sense)? It seems that it isn't a matter here of a clearly demarcated cyborg manifesto, but a much messier and depthless cyborg manifest-stew.

Michael Jackson's own articulation of this business (if it matters) is straightforward: He wants to be like a child. Which is why he resorts to the company of animals ('They're just like children,' he says to Oprah), why his sexuality has yet to be fathomed out; why his gender had to be determined (his speaking voice indeterminable); his race unimportant (and it's certain that he's the last person to whom it matters if you're black or white). He becomes the person that straddles all these divisions and categories that the world and its politics are made up of, that lead to wars and conflict, laws and legislation, violence and states, desire and disorder.

In short, Michael Jackson is the humanist end-point, the freest of all restrictions specified by the markings of the political body (in both senses), and he achieves this by the most advanced technological apparatus available.

And this basic human freedom is, for him and for what are called 'our times', supposed to be childhood: the dispersion of a body that, to be the body it tries to be, cannot be held together as such, that takes place everywhere and nowhere (which is why there is not even one Michael Jackson). A humanist end-point, that is, that seems to be the complete evacuation of the human (into the machinic, the animalistic, the immaterial). This is why the police examination of Michael Jackson's genitals and lower body parts, a search made to confirm Jordan Chandler's description of Michael Jackson's penis (which could be taken, publicly, as a police examination to see if Michael Jackson has a penis – that he has a body to be examined) was said by Michael Jackson himself to be 'dehumanising'.[10]

Nothing can touch Michael Jackson, it's certain, for he does not exist for real. If he exists (for himself, above all) and if his global, political and ideological success, the anxiety and fascination that surrounds him, can be indicated, it might be through what he offers (to us, for himself): an escape to an innocence in childhood that has been lost, a childhood that, as he tells Oprah, 'he never had' and, now, has no more. For, what was lost in the Michael Jackson 'affair', was Michael Jackson's already fictional innocence. The child he befriended, innocently, corrupted him by mistaking his affection sexually. The child, if a 13-year-old is a child, corrupted Michael Jackson. The child was sexualised and sexualised Michael Jackson (he has a penis: the police have, the polis has, seen it, confirmed it for us). The child, in all innocence, in therapy, was more adult than Michael Jackson. The innocence Michael Jackson wanted (and not only in his bed, 'like a slumber party',[11] kissing, the boys report,[12] 'like you kiss your mother'), corrupted Michael Jackson, deprived Michael Jackson of his innocence; innocence depriving itself of its fiction. And that is the law, its fiction. Michael Jackson, in short, was and remains guilty of his innocence, guilty – innocent – of his fiction.[13]

In other words, Michael Jackson's escape from the world, from the bind of the law and its poisoning corruption, is always and only a fiction, an idea of a childhood and innocence that he wishes for and which has yet to come. And now more than ever. How will he ever 'Heal the World' now?

It looks, then, like Michael Jackson's cyborg manifest-stew wants to escape politics and violence, be outside of the law, by becoming child (woman, animal, satellite, white, whatever), a return to a childhood that has never happened (but, recreated, is now) and which will leave him inarticulate, apart from the shouts of sheer pleasure and delight of his music, the pleasure and satisfaction of desire that he gets and gives – in fans. I'll finish, then, with two quotes: a long citation from the recent essay 'Prescriptions' by Lyotard (about Kafka's 'In the Penal

10. See *The Independent*, 23 December 1993.
11. See *The Independent*, 27 August 1993.
12. Ibid.
13. Ibid.

Colony'), drawing together the threads of materiality, infancy and why Michael Jackson in fact – as with every attempt to escape law, binding and politics – only ever re-inscribes that which it attempts to escape; in Michael Jackson's case, a total and totalitarian re-inscription of the law as an aesthetics; his corruption (why his body had to fall apart once the allegations were made; his dehydration, his painkiller addiction confession, related to his hair catching fire, his corporeality catching up with him in his dehumanisation); and a second citation from the four minute confession (on 22 December 1993, on global TV) in which Jackson admitted all of this. Lyotard:

> To be aesthetically is to be there, here and now, exposed in space-time and to the space-time of something that touches before any concept and even any representation. This before is not known, obviously, because it is there before we are. It is something like birth and infancy (Latin in-fans) – there before we are. The there in question is called the law comes, with my self and language, it is too late. Things will have already taken a turn, this first touch. Aesthetics has to do with this first touch, which touched me when I was not there [. . .] This touch is necessarily a fault as concerns the law [. . .] If the law must not only announce itself, but also make itself obeyed, it must vanquish the resistance of this fault or this offending potentiality constituted at birth. By which I mean: deriving from the fact that one is born before being born to the law. For the law, the body is in excess [. . .] But the law must be concerned with this excess of the body. If the law is to execute (itself), it will have to inscribe itself on the body, also like a touch.

Jackson proclaims, just as well, 'that if he was guilty of anything, it was of giving all he had to children'[14] and, quoting directly, 'of believing what God said about children: "Suffer little children to come unto me and forbid them not, for such is the Kingdom of Heaven." It is not,' Jackson continues, well aware of his media, 'that I think I am God, but I try to be God-like in my heart.'

14. See *The Independent*, 23 December 1993.

With a Little Help from Our (New) Friends

Caroline Bassett

Vol 1 #8, Winter 1997

What is cyberfeminism? Sadie Plant claims it is an absolutely post-human insurrection – the revolt of an emerging system which includes women and computers against the worldview, and material reality, of a patriarchy which still seeks to subdue them.[1] This is an alliance of 'the goods' against their masters, an alliance of women and machines. It is a revolt of the chattels.

It also claims to be a revolt on a certain – rather grand – scale. At the opening to *On the Matrix: Cyberfeminist Simulations*, Plant says that cyberfeminism – and/or the complex systems and virtual worlds upon which it is based – has the capacity to undermine the 'world view and material reality of two thousand years of patriarchal control'. Later in the same article, she suggests this is already happening. 'Tomorrow came' – we are, she says, already downloaded.

Cutting across the absolute certainty of this rhetoric of transformation, though, is a surprising admission of uncertainty. Plant freely admits that she is talking about an 'irresponsible feminism'; more than that, she wonders if what she is talking of 'is a feminism at all'.

This uncertainty opens up certain questions about cyberfeminism. Crucially, this one: Does it amount to a politics, or a technology? Is Plant talking about a possible feminist response to computerisation? Or is she, rather, documenting/predicting a technologically determined alteration in the condition of woman, an alteration which women should embrace because it is a change in their favour, but about which they can do very little.

Two themes in particular emerge as keys to unravelling the claims of cyberfeminism. It is useful to consider how, first, Plant locates cyberfeminism within debates around the subject, and, second, the arguments she makes around the nature of self-organising machines.

Plant + Irigary = One + Zero

Cyberfeminism is only a new twist in a long love/hate relationship between modern feminisms and technologies. From Mary Shelley's *Frankenstein* onwards, feminism has found an edge point in technology. It is regarded as desirable, treacherous and despised, while always revealing of the condition of women, and being implicated in it.

1. Sadie Plant, 'On the Matrix: Cyberfeminist Simulations', Rob Shields (Ed.), *Cultures of the Internet: Virtual Spaces, Real Histories, Living Bodies*, London: Sage, 1996, pp. 170–83.

In this sense, cyberfeminism is part of the feminist tradition, but it also repudiates it. Plant's cyberfeminism emerges, in fact, out of what she understands as the failures of earlier feminism – more broadly, out of the failure of the Enlightenment – she doesn't want a re-enchantment of the world.

Cyberfeminism, then, begins at the point at which humanism is abandoned. Plant's analysis focuses on the French philosopher Luce Irigaray's contention that, for women, a sense of identity is impossible to achieve, since women cannot escape the 'specular economy' of the male – an economy in which, through the controlling phallus and eye (the member and the gaze), woman is always comprehended as 'deficient'. Woman is always 'the sex which is not one', the sex which always lacks the equipment to have one.

Given this analysis, the goals of earlier feminisms – those which have demanded for woman her place as the also-subject of history, her share of human domination over nature – are the wrong goals. Pursuing the 'masculine dream of self control, self-identification, self-knowledge, and self-determination', as Plant puts it, will always be futile, since 'any theory of the subject will always have been appropriated by the masculine' (Irigaray). Rather, the only possible politics for the sex which is not one, and can never be one, is a politics which takes as its starting point the destruction of the subject. The question, then, is how this work of destruction might be carried out. Irigaray's answers have always been tentative. Plant is not so diffident. She has an answer and it is, of course, self-organising technology: the femaleness of the new species, which is not a species but an emergence, and one that is dangerous to men.

Plant's contention is that self-organising technology – 'a dispersed and distributed emergence composed of links between women, between women and computers, computers and communications links, connections and connectionist nets' – can perform Irigaray's work of destruction (which is the grounds of possibility for new works of assembly) because it provides space for woman to assemble herself – with a little help from her (new) friends. Cut loose from patriarchy, woman is now 'turned on with the machines'. (Do we want this?)

Man, meanwhile, despite his Cartesian disdain for being 'earthed', is also enmeshed in cybernetic space, becoming simply a 'cyborg component of a self organizing process beyond his perception or control'. From where Plant begins – with the necessity for destruction, infiltration and corruption – there is some joy to be had in finding Man caught in the nets he spread precisely to consolidate his own position. (Perhaps we do want this.)

Essential Female Machines

This turn of events depends, of course, not only on a particular analysis of the position of woman. It also requires a particular understanding of technology.

And here, I think, cyberfeminism falters. While eco-feminism holds technology as hostile to woman, precisely because it understands that technological 'advances' represent a further encroachment by 'man' upon 'nature' and 'woman', cyberfeminism, by contrast, asserts that complex systems and virtuality work the opposite way around.

How so? For cyberfeminism, the new nature of new machines might be encapsulated in the notion of self-organisation; as Plant puts it, 'tools mutate into complex machines which begin to think and act for themselves'. These machines, being emergent, do not have origins to which they must be faithful. They twist beyond the specular economy, and the particular twist they take is toward the 'female'. Computers do not represent an encroachment of logic, but its confusion. Crucially then, the valence of technology has changed.

But What Does it Mean to Say that Computers are Female?

Three claims Plant makes for technology as female are these:

1. Like women, computers are simulators, having no fixed identity, but, rather, performing. Computers and women are, therefore, using Irigaray's formulation, 'not one' but always multiple, being both nothing (zero) and everything/everywhere at once. The nature of the computer and the nature of women converge.

2. A second way in which the female is invoked is via a return to weaving, understood in *On the Matrix* as an authentic, 'feminine craft' (certified female by Freud). Weaving, undeniably processual, comes to symbolise elements of technology which cannot be explained in terms of domination and control (i.e. of man putting nature on the carpet). Plant suggests that this technology, always technically demanding, has sewn its cross-stitches into the new: '[F]emale programmers were to find connections between knitting, patchwork, and software engineering and find weaving secreted into the pixellated windows which open on to cyberspace.' Weaving is invoked as a celebration of that which is/always has been female about a certain kind of technology. Plant's alliance between 'the goods' – females and female technologies – suddenly looks remarkably similar to the old 'cobwebs against bombs' tactics of the weaving women of Greenham Common.

3. Finally, Plant claims that only those at 'odds' with the masculine can access the plane of the new machines. If new technology is not masculine, it is because some of its inventors were not either. She invokes Alan Turing, the inventor of the Turing machine, the forerunner to the modern computer, who was forced to take oestrogen as 'therapy' after being convicted of homosexuality by the British courts. Turing's brain she says, 'newly engineered and feminised', produced the Turing machine.

As a matter of fact, it didn't. Turing invented his machine before he was prosecuted and certainly before his 'therapy' took hold (at least according to Andrew Hodges' biography). But the factual error is less significant, perhaps, than the rather brutal essentialism evident here. (Is a hormone really all it takes to 'be' a woman?)

Cyberfeminism claims to ride the new edge of technology, but it also rides a very old edge of feminism. Plant is essentially essentialist; there is little in her account which suggests ways in which the category of the female might itself be subject to mutation.

The When Question

In another way, too, cyberfeminism's conception of emergent/self-organising technology is to be questioned. Technology changed, says Plant, but is this not equally true of computers, neural networks, telecoms networks, nanotechnology (the latter of which could very easily read as an attempt at absolute, molecule by molecule control of nature), biotechnologies, AI? *On the Matrix* glances across an array of technologies, each one produced as 'proof' of 'the change', but never precisely described. As a rhetorical strategy, blinding with science (or in this case technology) has surely been (over)done. In addition, there is always a tension between contention and tense; 'tomorrow came', says Plant, but she admits that many of these technologies are still under development.

There is a problem, then, with cyberfeminism's understanding of technology. Plant's assertions about the long list of technologies she invokes are, often, simply assertions. More than that, they might be understood to reduce technology insofar as they characterise it as 'female'. Surely it will never be enough to understand emergent technology 'as feminine', just as other technologies can never be understood purely and simply 'as masculine'? This, paradoxically, is to deny the complexity of technology.

This conflict, between gender essentialism and technological transformation, is a faultline that runs through cyberfeminism. It means that, although cyberfeminism understands that everything has changed, in the end it also suggests very little has changed. Despite the rhetoric, cyberfeminism is not ambitious enough.

Conclusion

To return, finally, to the question of a feminism, following the threads of Plant's arguments through *On the Matrix*, it becomes clear that Plant never provides a definitive answer to the question: 'Technology or politics?' There is always, in her work, a slippage – from what might be effected through a politics practised by women to what will be effected by virtue of virtual (and complex) systems. This slippage is the point for Plant, who courts and develops ambiguity in her writing, consistently con-fusing and re-fusing distinctions between woman – who is 'turned on by the machines' – and self-organising machines themselves.

Women and machines, gathered under the same unvarying sign (the sign of the female – the always multiple zero set against the one – in non binary opposition) are, as Plant sees it, elements of the same networks. In this proliferating confusion, distinctions about who or what is doing what to whom – distinctions, that is, about what might amount to 'doing politics' and what might amount to celebrating a technology – might seem difficult to draw. More than that, they might even seem irrelevant. 'As technology changes, woman changes,' says Plant. Shouldn't that be enough for us? I don't think it is, because it lets cyberfeminism off the hook. It makes certain claims to being an active, radical form of politics, one adapted to post-humanism, but it also comes close to suggesting that the position of woman is simply intrinsic to a certain form of technology.

In the moments at which cyberfeminism relies not on humans (women) but on the emerging force of machines (presumed to be 'female'), Plant seems to deliver us less to a politics than an eschatology: a hope and desire for future things. In this way, despite the sound and the fury of cyberfeminism's (effective) rhetoric, and, despite the power and precision of its destructive moment (the destruction of the desire for a re-tooled Enlightenment), it often comes close to a politics of quietism.

The Cyborg: Sweet Sixteen (and Never Been Cloned)

María Fernández

Vol 1 #20, Summer 2001

In an era in which nearly everything, from small seeds to large computer networks, entails practical or metaphorical organic and machinic fusions, the 'cyborg' – that product of early Cold War cybernetic theory, *détourned* by Haraway a generation later – has lost its political clout. Haraway's cyborg, 'not of woman born', the illegitimate offspring of militarism and patriarchal capitalism, was modelled upon the *meztisaje* (racial mixing) of Mexican Americans. Given that she wrote her central thesis at a particular historical moment and primarily for women, Haraway's cyborg was an inconstant figure able to incorporate spiral dancers, electronics factory workers, poets and engineers – a figure that allied diverse oppositional strategies, from writing to biotechnology. Given this radical theoretical openness, what did the Cyborg Manifesto (CM) really manage to achieve?

1. CM was an early recognition of the fundamental and irreversible changes brought about by digital technologies. Predating Dolly, the Visible Man, the Visible Woman and the (purported) completion of the Human Genome Project, Haraway discerned both society's transformation into a 'polymorphous information system' and 'the translation of the world into a problem of coding', as phenomena with specific resonance for women worldwide. In the 1980s, Haraway was one of a handful of cultural critics to write about the double-edged possibilities of biotechnology, which has become a major focus of cultural work today. Her prediction – that control strategies applied to women to give birth to new human beings would be developed using the language 'of goal achievement for individual decision-makers' – had, by the 1990s, been all too fully borne out.

2. CM urged feminists to embrace new technologies as tools for feminist ends. This was a pressing antidote to the pernicious notion, popular at the time, that women belonged exclusively to 'nature'. The manifesto proposed that feminists definitely could and should use the master's tools to destroy (or at least disrupt) the master's house.

3. CM contributed to the growth of a pan-global labour consciousness, acknowledging the key role of women as workers in the global economy. It also inspired the development of 'cyberfeminism' in various parts of the world. But, in contrast to Haraway's feminist, socialist and antiracist politics, cyberfeminism eschewed definitions, political affiliations (including feminism) and even goals. The political effectiveness of such an undirected movement

is still to be determined. Issues of race and racism, primary in Haraway's formulation of the cyborg, have been avoided in cyberfeminism. This silence could prove as destructive here as it was to second wave US feminism. One can only hope that cyberfeminism is still open to transformations.

4. CM proposed feminist associations based on affinities rather than identity. Haraway wrote the manifesto in response to the endless fragmentation of the US second wave feminist movement along lines of ethnic, racial and sexual identity. The manifesto called for the crossing of boundaries and for a reorganisation of women on the basis of political kinship. Cyberfeminists followed Haraway's lead to associate on the basis of affinities; but, at present and with some exceptions, these affinities tend to be career-orientated rather than political.

5. CM reinforced and popularised earlier utopian feminist imaginings of a world rendered gender-free by technology. Effectively, what this really meant was that those who could afford medical services and technology would be able to 're-generate' themselves at will. For a small segment of the world's population, this has indeed been liberating and empowering; previously 'monstrous' prostheses became beautiful.

If the original radicality of Haraway's cyborg lay in its illegitimacy, the ubiquity of digital, ex-military, and genetic technologies suggest that the cyborg is now a recognised legal citizen, much more a creature of social reality than of fiction. The utilisation of the cyborg as an image of edgy radicalism was, and still is, the territory of electronics and the fashion industry. Yet, because cyberfeminism emphasises the cyber element of the formulation at the expense of the feminism, the most radical politics of the manifesto have largely been ignored.

The Cyborg: Fifteen Years On, Five Complaints

Suhail Malik

Vol 1 #20, Summer 2001

We know what a cyborg is: the hybrid transfiguration of the human and the machine into one continuous, prosthetically extended, techno-organically enhanced whole. The hope of this integration is for a trans-organic or trans-human future, something like an entirely new evolutionary stage of life which will surpass the organic limitations of brain and body in favour of new, unlimited potentialities. A new sort of future, undermining the divisions and boundaries between the human and its others, a cross-disciplinary movement that, as Donna Haraway asserts in her foundational 'Cyborg Manifesto', has characterised liberal societies in postmodernity.

The cyborg is yet another manifestation of the collapse of the traditional, bounded stability of the human and its anthropocentric beliefs, but this notion of the cyborg is a lazy reconfiguration of already well-established political and moral sensibilities. Why?

1. It duplicitously welcomes the techno-scientific hybridisation of the organic and the technical while maintaining and perpetuating the critique of techno-logical rationality which has characterised left-liberal activism and humanities. Neither aspect is transformed by what is, in fact, a confrontation but comes to exist side-by-side in a typically vague optimism in which all transgressions of boundaries are welcomed, without adequate consideration of content or the difficulties involved. In this way, the theory of the cyborg perpetuates the standard assumptions of leftist (and proto-hippy) critique.

2. This hypocritical determination serves only to reinforce equally naïve notions of an extended freedom and responsibility of which, rather, the cyborg is in the service. There is something disgustingly, liberally 'communitarian' about the cyborg in its current appreciation, which could readily be taken as a covert, if naïvely assumed, parochialism or, better, Americanism. No surprise that this should come from those on the Nice Left, where 'contestation' always involves 'respect' and 'creativity' rather than war and destruction (see Hardt and Negri's approbation of Haraway in *Empire*).

3. Cyborg theory is mostly a self-serving, sexing-up of critical liberalism through great gadgetry and concept-busting movements in the techno-scientific organisation of living material and extended systems. Tie-dyed T-shirts are swapped for leather deathpants, and ethnic beads for prosthetic hardware in a desperate bid for contemporaneity.

4. But the errors and dogmatism of the now common notion of the cyborg also extend to the understanding of what is actually happening in the techno-sciences. The cyborg is a theoretical fiction, since how the machinic and the organic in fact materially interact and combine is not, and cannot be, accounted for by a theory ultimately based on abstractions.

5. This tendentious, primarily phantasmic appropriation of techno-scientific development as 'cyborgian' precludes a technically precise and fully inventive understanding of organico-machinic integration in favour of asserting what has been going on in well-meaning, left-liberal circles for some time anyway. It is a complacent reduction of the actuality of the organico-machinic nexus, dulling it into politically comprehensible and polite terms.

The Future is Female

Irina Aristarkhova

Vol 1 #23, Spring 2002

The 'Very Cyberfeminist International' conference in Hamburg was the culmination of several cyberfeminist events organised by the Old Boys Network (OBN) – a network of feminist artists, activists and theorists whose members include Verena Kuni, Helene von Oldenburg, Claudia Reiche and Cornelia Sollfrank. Following on from the 'First Cyberfeminist International' (Kassel, Documenta IX, 1996) and the 'Next Cyberfeminist International' (Rotterdam, 1999) – participants eagerly anticipated evidence of the cross-national and cross-cultural networks that had been built over the intervening five years. And, of course, it was interesting to speculate over what the word 'very' implied – was the event planned to be 'Very Cyberfeminist', 'Very International', or 'Very' something else?

By the time the event finally came around, apparently due to disagreements and personal conflicts within OBN, the conference deserved the title 'Very Emotional'. But, rather than treating it simply as a symptom of OBN development (or the end/transformation of the group), it might be more productive to review this emotional uproar in the light of issues, listed in the programme, which were never adequately discussed at the conference, namely: 'Resumption of New Border Concepts', 'Media and War Techniques' and, especially, the network and networking in general.

The conference started with a presentation of posters. They were big, bright and numerous and dealt, rather predictably, with themes such as: 'network', 'machine', 'sexuality', 'cyborg' and 'biotechnology'. The most exciting, in my opinion, was the presentation by SubRosa from the US, who made a multi-functional poster that you could wear, recycle, use as a kitchen towel, curtains, etc. – a complete departure from the ordinary, 2D still images being presented by others.

On several occasions, I heard that this, the third Cyberfeminist International conference, would distinguish itself from others by welcoming diversity among feminists engaging with new media. Sadly, though, while some of the white women participants shared the illusion of diversity, women of colour at the conference all expressed their dissatisfaction with the lack of discussion and concrete engagement with the topics of race, ethnicity and cultural difference in relation to new media. According to María Fernández:

> As with other OBN events, the Very Cyberfeminist International was successful in bringing white women together, especially those from Europe and the United States. As with previous OBN events, the Very Cyberfeminist 'International' did little to foster communication between white women and

> the rest of the world. Rather than helping to bridge differences, it exacerbated them. Racial difference seemed to be extremely divisive as points raised by women of colour were met with antagonism. When the same points were raised by white women, the speaker was invariably met with encouragement or at least respectfulness. Even superficial familiarity with post-colonial theory might have helped to prevent the common stereotypes into which the few women of colour at the conference were pushed: oppressed, ignorant of technology, bound by the body, political, not intellectual etc.

Apparently the issue of racial and ethnic difference remains the hardest to address at any new media event – whether academic or activist. Just like last year's Third International Cultural Studies Conference in Birmingham (where I organised two sessions on cyberfeminist strategies), the majority of discussions on cyberfeminist theory, gender, new communication and biotechnologies were nearly all 'totally white'. These discussions dealt with post-human and postmodern conditions, woman-machine hybrids, entailed a critical re-evaluation of disembodied cybertheory and touched on differences *among* women whilst, at the same time, silencing and repressing many of them. It feels like we have to start all over again – first Western feminism was blind to difference, then we started paying more attention to differences among women. Now, after being swept along by uncritical, universalising cybertheory and practice for the past decade, we have to learn again that race has not disappeared in the age of the internet and human-machine interactions, never mind its potential for gender bending and 'identity tourism' (as Lisa Nakamura termed such 'race swapping'). At the same time, I feel that a careful outline should be made of the earlier use of terms such as 'race' and 'ethnicity' in postcolonial and feminist theory, to prevent us from bypassing the ethical and political complexities of such notions and their use altogether.

The discomfort shared by many over the concept of 'post-humanity' also met with an inadequate response from those who cautioned that, once again, we are being lured by the illusion of oneness – which sounded like old wine in new cyber-tech bottles. Such tensions were accompanied by a constant chorus of questions raised by OBN members: 'How do YOU do this or that?', 'What can we do?', 'How can we welcome other women?', 'We had very good intentions and an open-door policy – why does it seem to have failed?' Of course, nothing has failed – I think that this crisis within OBN represents the impossibility of 'discussing difference', but the strong desire and will to actually start practising diversity.

Apparently, the main European players of cyberfeminism are still struggling to find ways to create more heterogeneous communities, especially with the 'other' women in their own countries, who are conspicuously absent from conferences like this (which was especially apparent during the poster session).

Let us not naïvely fool ourselves that 'there have been no great black women cyberfeminists', or that 'the door is open, but they are not coming to our meetings'.

The question remains: What, if not feminism, could survive its own deconstruction and flourish? Feminism has always been attentive to, and hyper-critical of, every gesture it makes, every action it takes, every statement it formulates on difference among women – why should cyberfeminism, which claims to be so sophisticated and complex, be running scared? Many of the presentations gave us hope. They pointed to a different kind of work going on in critical and political circles: in France (Isabelle Massu, Nathalie Magnan), in Belgium (Laurence Rassel) and the US (SubRosa). That was the strength of this conference and of OBN; despite internal disagreements between the organisers, they managed to bring a group of interesting and diverse women together.

We also witnessed a RAWA (Revolutionary Association of Women of Afghanistan) presentation at the end of the conference, which seemed like it had practically nothing to do with the 'cyberfeminist agenda' as such, but was an informative fundraising event (I was told that this presentation had travelled through the US and Europe in almost identical form). Of course, this leads us to the questions about the 'framing' of such presentations, and whether organisations like RAWA should be included like a trophy (and token) in any and every feminist event wishing to claim diversity and 'cutting-edge political credentials'. Apparently, a great deal of effort and resources were spent on bringing them to the conference. Their presentation was an important event in itself, but one was left wondering how this one-off show could save us from the necessity of engaging in day-to-day interactions with racial/ethnic others, online and offline (*corps-a-corps avec l'Autre,* to paraphrase Irigaray).

So, what about cyberfeminism – its network, tactics, theories, art and politics? All of this was part of conference life too, though these subjects might not have been discussed by the conference speakers during the main sessions. What seems to have changed within cyberfeminism is that it is no longer desperately seeking to distinguish or distance itself from feminism or anything else ('What is it? Where is it? Are you a cyberfeminist or a feminist? Please identify yourself…'). This points to its maturity and proliferation, to its increasing depth. When a movement evolves without guarding its borders and membership too closely, as was the case in Hamburg, we might start to anticipate a future 'Any Cyberfeminist International' that would focus on the issues of everyday cyberfeminist theory and practice. That is what I consider to be the main success of the conference, and, of course, of its organisers. Old Girls Network?

Mens Sana in Corpore Sano (or Keep Taking the Tablets)

Andrew Goffey

Vol 1 #24, Summer 2002

A recent report, in a broadsheet newspaper, that a favourite holiday destination in Thailand promises eager tourists a week of colonic irrigation, offers a potent image for the fate of the ethics of self-governance under multinational capitalism. The *caput mortuum* of decades spent as an avid consumer in the West is sluiced into a Southeast Asian bucket, leaving you and your intestines free to jet back West to accumulate another year of crap. Beneficiaries of this process report – after an initial feeling of faintness – an enormous sense of well being. This is hardly surprising, given that the fat which can clog the intestine from decades of consumption sometimes gets so thick that the weight of one's bowels has been known to shoot up to around 40 lbs.

I mention this vignette not to shock or to condemn – although there is something a little perverse about the geopolitics of it all – but to make a point about the almost neurotic medicalisation to which current techniques for the care of the self testify. It is not so much the curiously solid links between the anally retentive dynamics of capital accumulation and the bourgeois concern with the clean and proper which needs emphasis. A technique of the self which involves washing out your insides – in much the same way that you might wash a car on a Sunday morning (if you had one) or unblock a sink – while not an entirely surprising development, provides us with a strangely empty concept of the body. Other examples suggest that this is not an isolated phenomenon: the pill popping antics of vitamin munchers anxious to boost 'their' immune system; Michael Jackson, or Montgomery Burns from *The Simpsons*, with their Howard Hughes-type phobias about germs; and the national socialist regime in 1930s–40s Germany and its obsession with the health of its people all point toward the pervasive medicalisation of identity. The British media and political elite's recent willingness to focus public energies on the state of the National Health Service only confirms the issue. In fact, technologies of government here might suggest that being ascribed a medically informed identity (being 'normal' is a reputedly positive clinical condition) and being constantly enjoined to manage your own health are functional weapons in capitalist crisis management.

I would not, of course, claim to be the first to have noticed this phenomenon, or wish to be interpreted as saying that the odd bit of internal hygiene or reform of the NHS is necessarily a bad thing. For starters, Michel Foucault's identification of biopower as the primary form in which power exercises itself in contemporary society has already led a generation of researchers in the natural sciences down the path I have been trying to signpost here. And, that certain social actions can have unintended consequences or occur within a framework unknown to the actors themselves, will surprise few social scientists – this is the main lesson of Max Weber's work on the protestant ethic and the spirit of capitalism. More pointedly, the spread of AIDS and the consequent highlighting of a supposed norm of health, of which it would be an apparently monstrous contravention, shows quite clearly what an 'epidemic of signification' we have been subjected to, which almost certainly had some role to play in the current intensification of medical policing.

Not so much has been said, though, about the sciences that play such a key role in defining the substrate of the clean and healthy body and determine the operations that can be performed on it. Foucault himself – his early work *The Birth of the Clinic: The Order of Things* and his identification of 'bios' as a focal point for the exercise of power notwithstanding – had little to say about the life sciences and preferred to confine his attention to the social sciences.

However, in an exemplary work, the Italian philosopher, Giorgio Agamben, has explored some of the ramifications of the development of modern biopower, and given us food for thought when it comes to assessing the state of play in the life sciences (Giorgio Agamben, *Homo Sacer: Sovereign Power and Bare Life*). Agamben's argument is that 'We are not only animals, in whose politics our life as living beings is at stake, according to Foucault's expression, but also, inversely, citizens in whose natural body our very political being is at stake.' It is, he further contends, impossible to undo the strict interlacing of the naked biological life (or *zoe*) and the cultural form of life (or *bios*) once and for all. Instead, he says, we would do better to 'make of the biopolitical body, bare life itself, the place where a form of life which is entirely transposed into bare life, is constituted, where a bios which is nothing but its zoe is instituted'. Agamben believes that, in so doing, a new field of research will open up, one beyond the limitations to be found at work in the disciplines which have hitherto attempted to think something like a bare life. It is an open question as to how this new field of research will eventually look. However, the convergence of the biological and the political in modern immunology might give us some suggestions towards an answer.

The link between the self and the political is not an affair of simple 'discursive articulation', as some people would profess to believe, any more than it is a particularly new one. Whilst the self is certainly something defined in language, it is also something produced physiologically. In the 19th century, Nietzsche, for one, was not only disinclined to think of the self as peaceful coexistence – witness the prevalence of the themes of war and combat in his writings – but was also very much inclined to emphasise the physiological dimensions of European culture's morbid disorders. Freud, as is well known, took a keen interest in the defensive approach of the ego to forces beyond its control. In his 1895 *Project for a Scientific Psychology*, Freud's approach is based

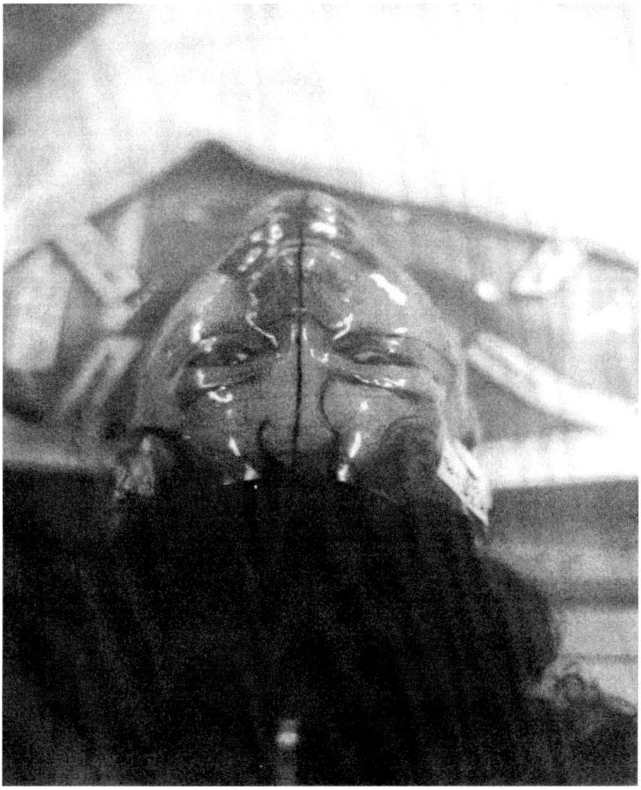

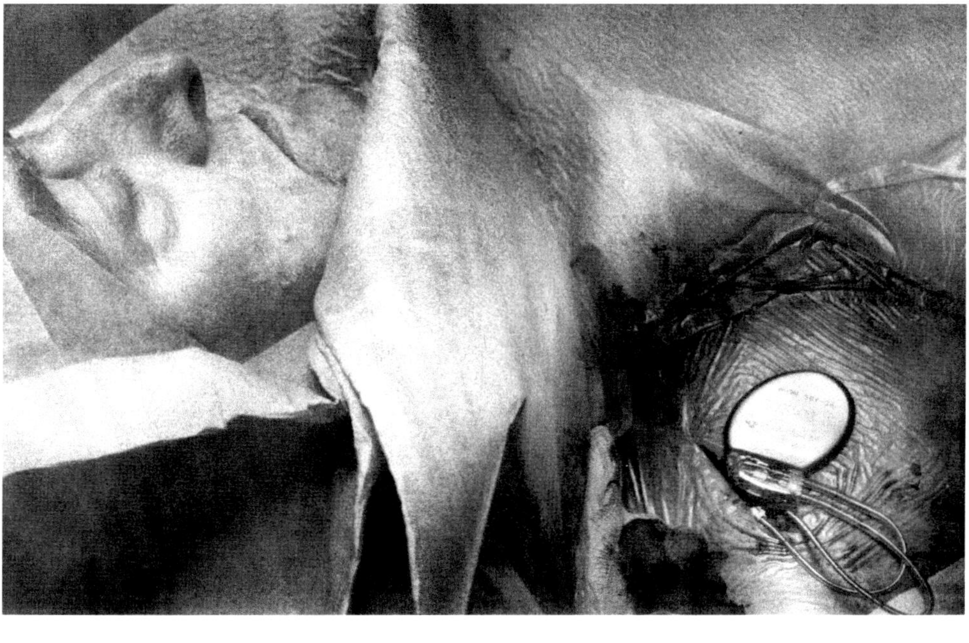

Lubna Hammoud, *Half Machine* and *Radiotherapy*, 1995, artist's project, Vol 1 #2, Summer 1995

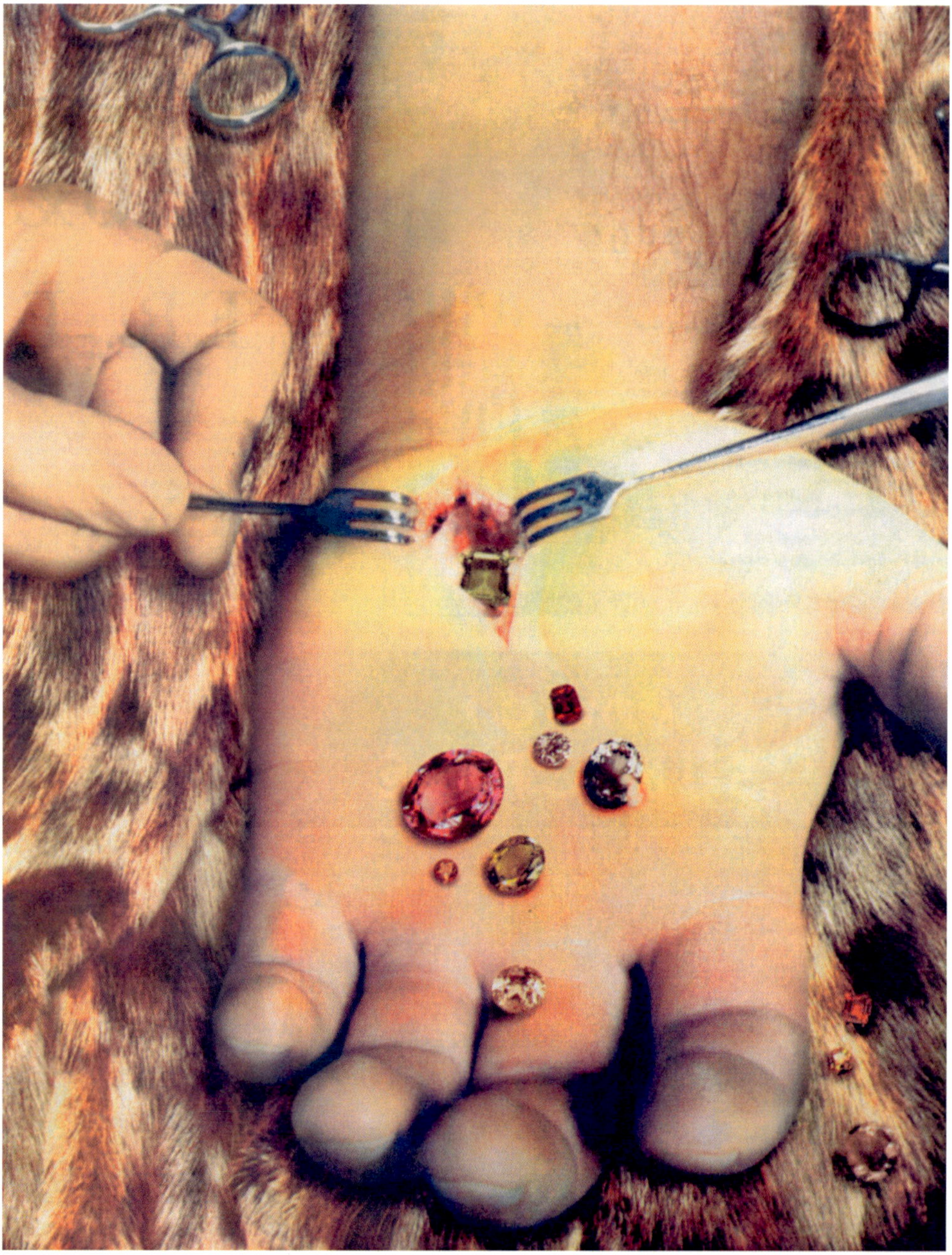

above: Alexa Wright, *Precious II*, used to illustrate Margot Leith Butler's review of Wright's work, Vol 1 #4, Winter/Spring 1996
opposite: Pauline van Mourik Broekman's Piet Mondriaan-inspired layout for the Online Publishing special feature, Vol 1 #7, 1997

NETTIME

Could you tell me something about how *nettime* was started, and how it has developed since then?

...e started as a 3-day-meeting in a small ...e in Venice during the Biennale 95. A ...ng of Media-activists, theoreticians, artists, ...alists from different European countries. ...n Burting, Geert Lovink, Diana McCarty, ...osic, David Garcia, Nils Roeller, Tamasso ... Paul Garrin, and many more.) We devel... the main lines of a net-critique along the ... of virtual urbanism, globalisation/tribali... and the life metaphor. Also, it became ...s that it was necessary to define a dif... cultural (net)politics than the one *Wired* ...ine represented in Europe. It was a pri... ...nd intensive event, and in a way, it defined ...yle' that we critique and discuss issues on ...e, *nettime* is somehow modelled on the ...f the meeting – it was covered with texts, ...nes, books, whatever we had to offer the ... It was the start of our 'gift economy' with ...ges of information. Today the list has ... 300 subscribers, it's growing constantly ...round 10 subscribers a week. We do no... ...the list is semi-closed, which means new ...ptions must be approved.

...you intensely involved with computers?

...t computer was an Atari2600 TV-game, ... ZX81, C64, Amiga1000, I switched to Mac ... began with DTP in the Botschaft group ...0, used Dos/Linux for the Internet, and ...up with a DX66 under Win95, mainly to ...dora, is an Intranet. So these machines ...ent certain phases in my life, but they ...determine them. I also studied computer ... for a couple of years, but it was not ... expected, which was a more conceptual ...ch that reflected the development of soft... ...n a much broader, maybe cultural, level.

...net culture

...nvolved with The Thing bbs network from ...the high time of ascii and text based ...t like MUDs and MOOs, before the Web. ...same time I was working with the group ...aft. There were also some exhibitions of ...dia art, a communication performance in ...tower in Berlin, meetings, long term pro... ...n the public sphere like an installation ...aniel Pflumm in a subway tunnel, a col... ...ion with the group handshake which later ... Internationale Stadt, or Chaos Computer ...hich Botschaft shared office space with. ... Bilwet event we organised, I started to ...th Geert Lovink, which was a truly new ...f work.

...artist

...no, I got a stipendium and did exhibi... ...ut always had problems accepting art as ...d system', and I have to emphasise here ...*ttime* is a group project, it is not a 'piece ...vidual art,' but a medium formed by a ...ve subjectivity, a sum of individuals. I'm ...ing it and it has its aesthetic aspects, ...don't have to call me an artist because

...you started the list and how do you ...hat has affected how *nettime* was set

...ou can call it a continuation of my art ... But, it functions without naming it art. ... tried to begin with projects on the Web, ...ly the Orgasmotron Project (a database ...rded brain waves of human Orgasms) ...eflected the early euphoric times of 'first ... With Botschaft e.V. in 93-4, we did the 'Museum fuer Zukunft', a group project and database of future scenarios, ideas, and views, but during these projects it became clear that I needed a deeper understanding of the collaborative, theoretical, and discursive aspects of cyberspace to continue. During this time I also gave up doing installations in defined art spaces. Generally, after a euphoric entry phase I got extremely bored and disappointed with what was and is happening in the art field. My main interest remains what Andreas Broeckmann calls 'machinic aesthetics', a field between the social, political, and cultural economy of the so called 'new media'. So I was happy to meet Geert, and through Venice and a series of other meetings, a group of people with shared interests that we're trying to bring together on the *nettime* list.

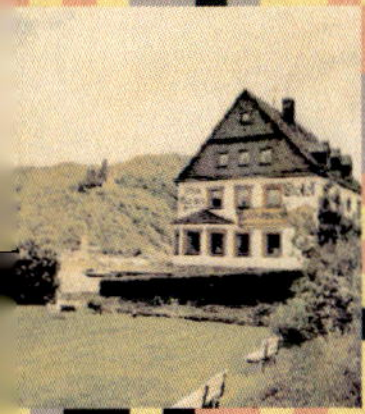

It seems that *nettime* has gravitated more towards net-political and -philosophical discussion than that directly to do with 'art'. What role do you (and Geert Lovink?), as (a) moderator(s), have with regard to that?

Art today, especially media art, is a problematic field. When I listen to music, it may happen that I don't like it, but it comes through the radio. That's how art appears to me. You can switch it off, but there is still a lot of music around. So much for art. With the moderation – it is also a contradictory role. The less the moderator appears the better the channel flows. It is, of course, this power-through-absence thing, but we hope that we handle it carefully and in a responsible way, with the continuous group process in mind. Power flows through networks, and you cannot switch it off. From different sides, Geert and I have an interest in working with the dynamic of the aesthetic contra the political field. There are many fault lines and frontiers. One of them seems to become the art system which still has some kind of Alleinherrschaftsanspruch in the symbolic cultural field. This changes through new media and even if new media will not make the term 'art' obsolete, there is something about the paradox between media and art or media art that I find deeply problematic. Both have components of totalatarian systems of representation. There is the chance that new media creates channels to redirect the flow of power. That's what *nettime* is made for. An experimental place for (re)mixes; something I missed for a very long time. Never

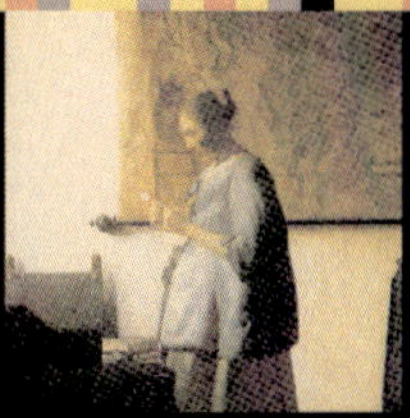

perfect and always 'in becoming,' but not explicit, not descriptive but performative, and pragmatic.

Both Geert and I have our own reasons to distance ourselves from today's 'art discourse'. You can call *nettime* a political project in terms of the real effects we try to trigger, in terms of conflicting debates reflecting and criticising economic and social implications of the 'digital revolution'. It is a philosophical channel in terms of describing a certain 'condition', while accessing and applying the traditional knowledge including the 'postmodern' stuff. It is an aesthetic process in many aspects, while developing a collaborative writing space, experimenting with modes and styles of 'computer mediated communication'. Finally, we have the luxury of silence

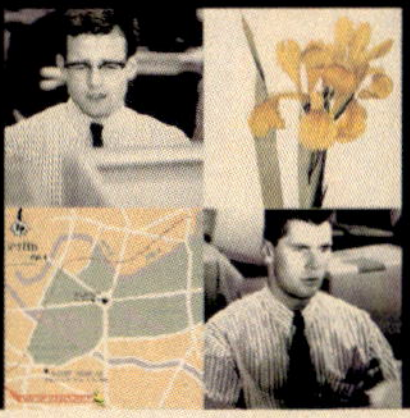

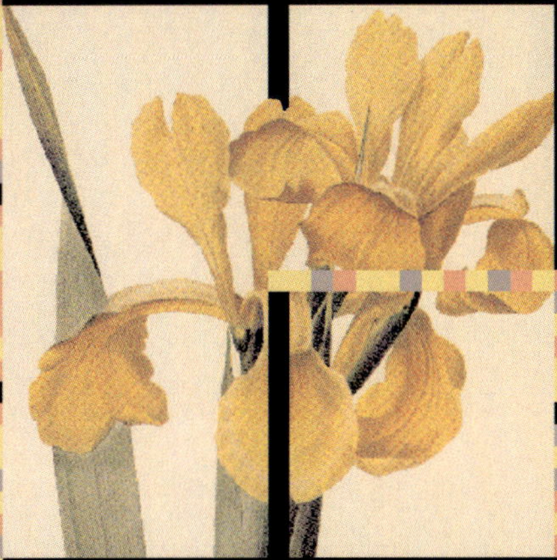

and don't advertise, so we don't need big investments into labels and surface, it gets spread by word of mouth, and the footer 'cultural politics of the nets' can mean many things. It's about clouds. There is this 'field of virtuality or potentiality,' multiple contexts and personas, interests and intensities which, like the social aspect, the time aspect, the knowledge and news aspect, make *nettime* something which modulates a flow of heterogeneous subjective objects, something with an existential aesthetic of living with *nettime*, (including the group, events, projects which grow here) a collective and singular info-environment which exists without the need to be named art.

At the discussion at DEAF96, I think you described *nettime* as a 'dirty' ascii channel; how 'dirty' or unmoderated is it?

Dirtyness is a concept here, especially for the digital realm, which produces its own clean dirtyness, take the sound of digital distortion of a CD compared to analogue distortion of Vinyl. Take all kinds of digital effects imitating the analogue dirtyness, which means in the end, a higher resolution, a recursive, deeper, infinite structure. I used the concept because of its many aspects. It means here to affirm the noise aspect, but only to generate a more complex pattern out of it. It does not mean 'anything goes', or a self-sufficient ethic of productivity. It is slackerish in a way, slows down, speeds up, doesn't care at certain places, just to come back to the ones which are tactically more effective... there is a whole empirical science behind it, how to bring the *nettime* ship through dark waters... how to compress and expand, how to follow the lines of noise/pattern instead of absence/presence...

(In fact I pushed the big red button of the moderator mode only once, after a period of technical errors and a following unfocused dialogue.) The phenomenon is – and I think this is not such a rare thing – that a group of people, in a repetitive, communicative environment, begin to filter a field of possible 'communication acts' in a certain way quasi machinically. You don't have to be professional or especially skilled in the beginning. The production of 'information' along the borderline of noise means to constantly refine a social context, maybe an artificial one, what some call immanent. I mean with rules which are self-evident, and are interdependent in a dynamic way. The list-software sends a kind of basic netiquette to the new users but this affects only some formal factors. One is that we decided to avoid dialogues, without forbidding them. Netttime is not a list of dialogues of quote and requote, but more of a discursive flow of text, of different types, 'differentialising', contextualising each other. On the net it is called 'collaborative filtering' or earlier, it was 'social filtering'.

Dirtyness means many things here. First of all the absence of purity, you always have mixtures, 'agencements' .. but this becomes too trivially 'postmodern'. The constant commentary, forming a socially defined body of knowledge, and of course, a field where power is generated out of undifferentiated forces, which includes the position of the moderators or other very active participants for defining where the scope of the flow tends to go. But actually anyone can post whatever she likes. This risk, which often leads to a situation of overflow and re-orientation, is also the productive freedom of *nettime*. Another is the limited set of signs, like the Euro-English or net-pigeon, using English as a non-native speaker or the reduced character set of ascii, or the minimal features of the perl-scripts which run the mailinglist. Finally, for the authors, there is always a multiple aspect of why to write, and for the readers, why to read *nettime*. You definitely have to filter. I guess nobody, including me, reads every mail from start to finish. The sender has the chance to actively select texts she finds on the net and forward them. The author can pre- or republish texts, send pre-versions, test certain ideas, or sample others. On the material side, there are the print cuts of ZKP, readers which come out in small numbers during conferences. The process of inscription combined with a filtering process functions a bit like a news-ticker, if you want to find a comparison in the publishing world.

Two other pertinent issues that came up at the DEAF discussion were those to do with size and finance. If online journals or lists are akin to creators of community, for example, where discussion can be catalytic due to the small size of the group and many of the contributors also knowing each other 'in real life', does their effectivity decrease beyond a certain size (I think Geert mentioned a couple of hundred). Although *nettime* is still a 'closed' mailing list, its subscriber base has grown; have you adapted your methodology?

As you can see, *nettime* is still going well. It seems there is a self-regulation process on the side of the contributors. There is the growth, (which is around 10 new subscribers per week, mostly on a word of mouth basis) which leads to a certain social consistency. Then, in the way texts get selected/produced and find their way to the list. The 'group' is circumscribing a network of real life relationships, a network of shared interests, and a network of contextualising documents. This happens in relation to the 'outside', to the 'wideness' of the net, and to the 'deepness' of the local places where people work and live. Every document represents a vector

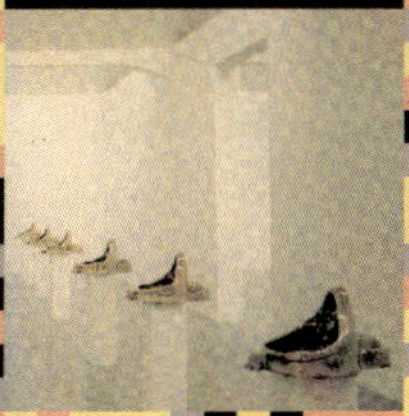

through time in a social context, a discursive environment with many levels of reference, but a relatively concrete and simple surface: ascii-text. The complexity and aesthetics which come out of the simple practical rules of a mailinglist are complex and dynamic enough not to feel the urge to experiment with multithread hypertextual, multimedia environments, even if we think about certain extensions you find in common with intranet or groupware solutions in the corperate world. It says: never touch a running system. I think the next level will evolve through a certain economic pressure, certain cases where texts reappear somewhere without permission, or other cases where the unwritten norms are subverted by other 'content machines' running on other principles, but sharing similar fields of issues. There is a need to use the chance and experiment with new horizontal networks of producers, to respect the collaborative editorial work of a user community and most of all, to think about financial models in terms of a sustainable quality of discussion, which includes the 'currency' of trust and credibility.

And then regarding finance. This obviously has enormous effects on how things can run. *nettime* is a 'no budget' operation; what are the advantages and disadvantages of this and how do you manage to keep going?

First I have to say that your question already has certain implications. It may seem natural to put anything you do into an economic model and ask: what do I get for it? What do I pay for it? But it cannot ever be said that such an exchange economy runs effectively with money. There is clearly a drive to profit from new media, and, of course, money must be there, for a basic funding, but the goal of *nettime* is not financial profit. One easily comes to this point with a defensive position, or a dogmatic one, fighting against the all too present, not to say, totalitarian system of a world wide integrated capitalism. Even after Marx, there are social fights, and especially within the new media, you have to face, like in the art world, certain problems, which often mean, make money fast, but do bad work; work, but don't get good money. There is a certain kind of luxury today, which is somehow overcoded by 'slackerdom' which is contrary to the work ethic of the yuppie or the political activist. It is a pragmatic level, we do not have to talk about just economics, but we have to develop a working model, a constant fight with risks of exploitation, burn out, sell out.

Finally, we would have to change *nettime* from its microeconomical, very basic structure if we would force its commercialisation. To make it clear – especially for mailinglists, but also many other sites with ai content – that it is not at all clear how to finance them for the long term. The time of the hype might be over soon, and then you have to face a shake out of centralisation that we already know from the history of radio and TV. On the other hand, I do not believe in the concept of autonomy. It leads to a sad double life. It might be that you live by state grants, or that you have to do a stupid job during the day. Between, there are many shades of grey, and among them is the possibility of alternative online economies which may reintroduce less alienated semiotics into the circulation of capitalism.

You've talked about the importance of editors being sensitive to the exchange economies of the nets; these many economies intertwine, they are not separate are they? Highly commercial and competitive ones share technologies, content and 'participants' (for want of a better word) with ones that are more clearly like the potlach economy you refer to. In practice, what has your experience been of keeping *nettime* independent within this situation?

These economies intertwine, but not without friction. From the view of the poor, there is the need to disrespect certain economic barriers, for example, licenses and copyright. That's what is happening in many Eastern countries. The new markets are not functioning like they promised to, at least not for all. There are still many chances to use new technology as a tool to reach more independence, but it also gets used in the other way for a huge 'Darwinist' shakeout. And as one can see with Microsoft, it is not at all the best who survive. So I strongly resist any logic of preaffirming the situation. Potlatch is only a circumscription of a kind of exchange economy which is pretty common, as soon as you have the privilege to do so. I am sure that we will face models which are based on a certain local exclusion of money economy. Any family, community, or friendship is based on such models. Finally, you need the friction, the potential of mixed economies, for a vivid and creative market, at least from what I understand about markets.

This links with one of the ongoing discussions on *nettime*, the one to do with libertarianism or neoliberalism and social justice. It has, over time, involved posting extensive 'dialogues' on the role of *Wired*, the demonisation of the State and been presented as an attempt to start generating a productive, European contribution to the development of ideas on techno-cultural political organisation for the future. Is this right and how do you feel it is going?

You can describe it like that. But I don't like to make predictions here. One thing nettime does is critique, this means it reflects and constructs the present. Of course there are strategies, and part of a strategy is that one should not talk too much about it. The important task is not to give up against the homogenising, centralising, and alienating networks of a global integrated capitalism, to use these very ethical-political techniques as 'cultural' ones. To push against what is forced on us as 'economic factors' in favour of a necessary quality.

Berlin, Jan 1997

contact: pit@contrib.de, geert@xs4all.nl
reading: news://alt.nettime or news://news.thing.at/alt.nettime
zkps+archive: www.desk.nl/~nettime

Just like one of its most notorious representatives, the cyborg, cyberfeminism is many things to many people. Arguing its coherence as a movement would do it little justice as it is by nature and intent diverse, mutable and eternally incomplete. Its most defining characteristic is a willingness to unthink traditional dualisms; between man and woman, nature and culture, and technology and the human so as to try and formulate a radically new ontology for both humans and nonhumans. Since they both exacerbate and challenge oppressive systems, accelerating technological, economic and biological changes are both its friend and foe.

Preferring construction to deconstruction, cyberfeminism moves constantly between the 'reading' of popular culture and the 'writing' of it. Subversive offshoots of science fiction have provided inspiration through their daring reformulations of identity, reproduction and social organisation – the cultural operating systems cyberfeminists seek to recode. Aggressively playful, wilfully ironic, cyberfeminism takes its inspiration and material from wherever it can – with the rich, contradictory and often hateful pickings of popular culture occupying a special place in its heart.

In an era where the loss of traditional humanist values is being lamented by the mainstream, cyberfeminism asks what they meant in the first place. To coincide with our review of Donna Haraway's Modest_Witness@Second_Millennium, we make one of many possible inroads in which Josephine Bosma, Faith Wilding, Sue Thomas, Caroline Bassett and Josephine Berry ask: "Where does she want to go today?"

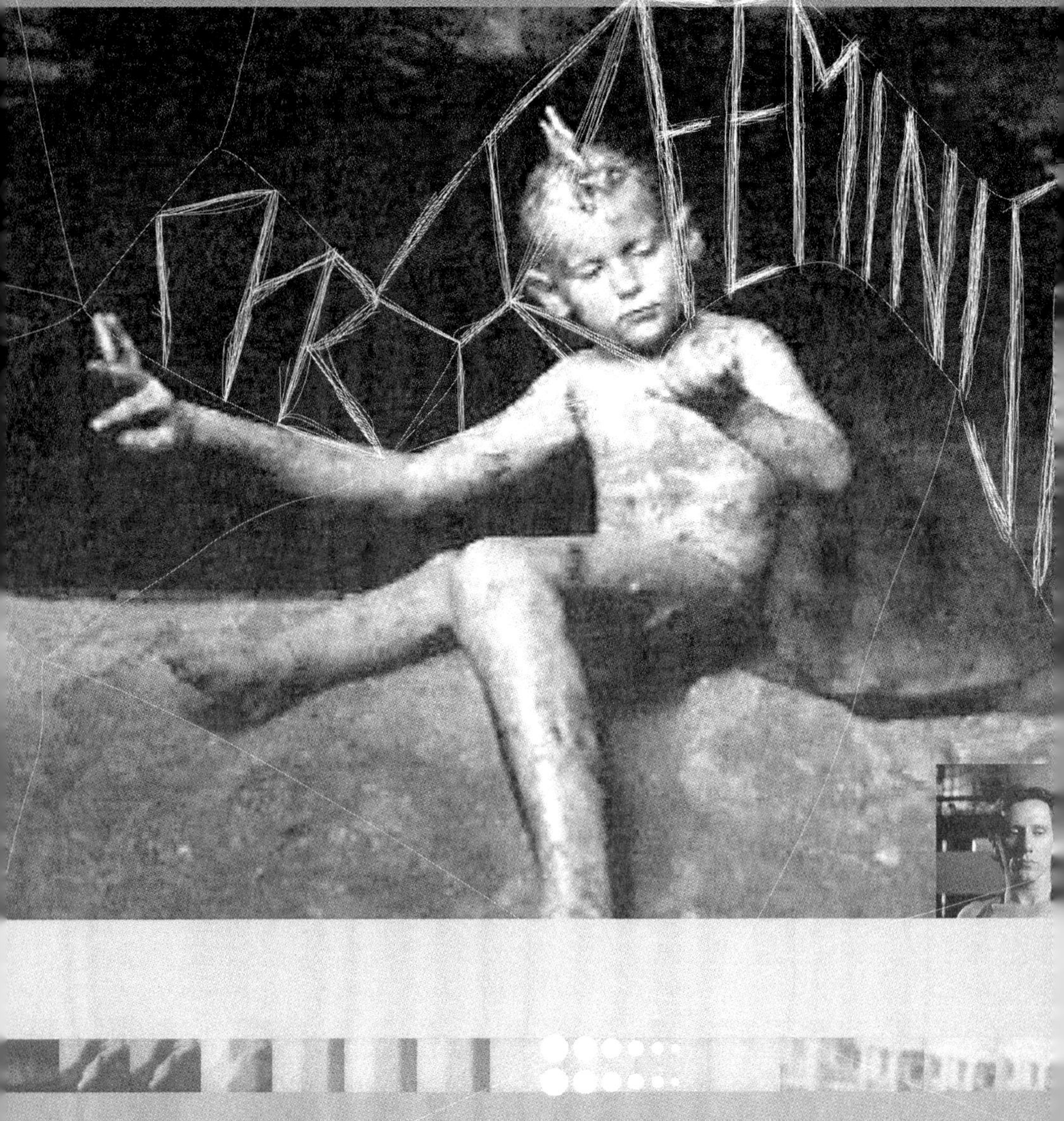

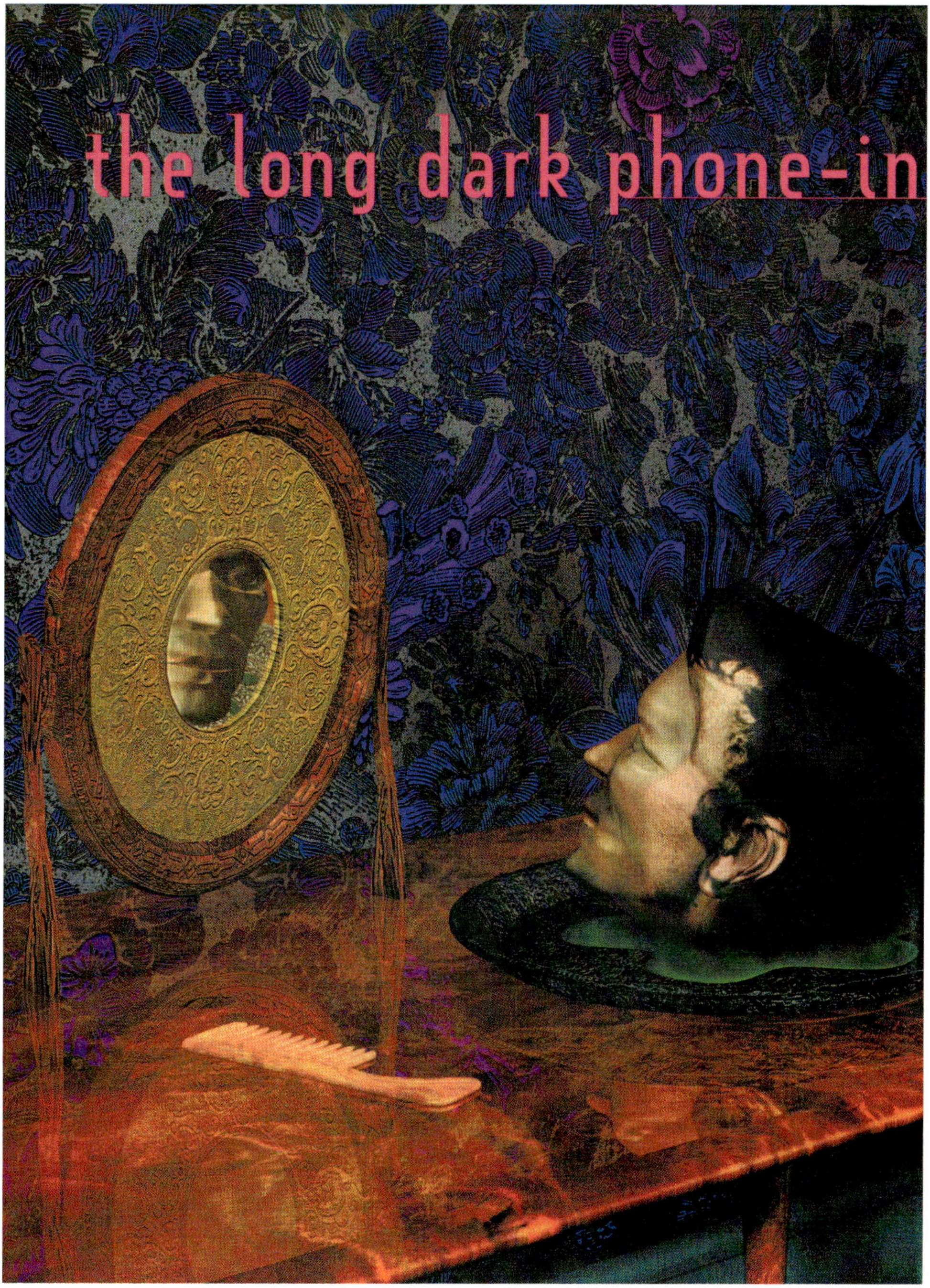

opposite: Simon Worthington and Pauline van Mourik Broekman, composite image, incorporating a still from *Alien Resurrection*, used to illustrate the Cyberfeminism special section, Vol 1 #8, Winter 1997
above: 50% Gray, used to illustrate Matthew Fuller's 'The Long Dark Phone-In of the Soul', Vol 1 #8, Winter 1997

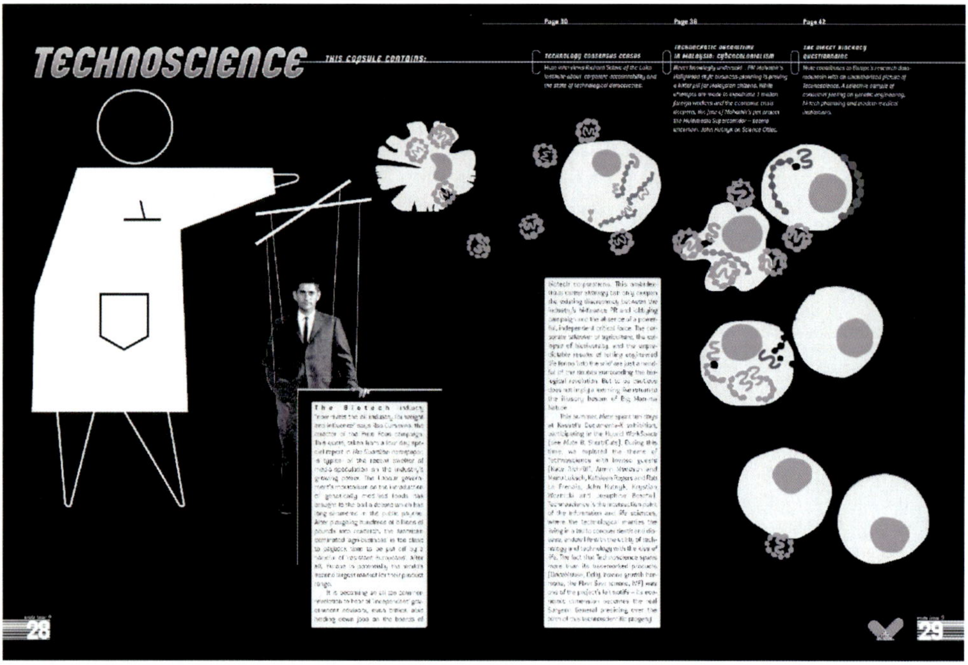

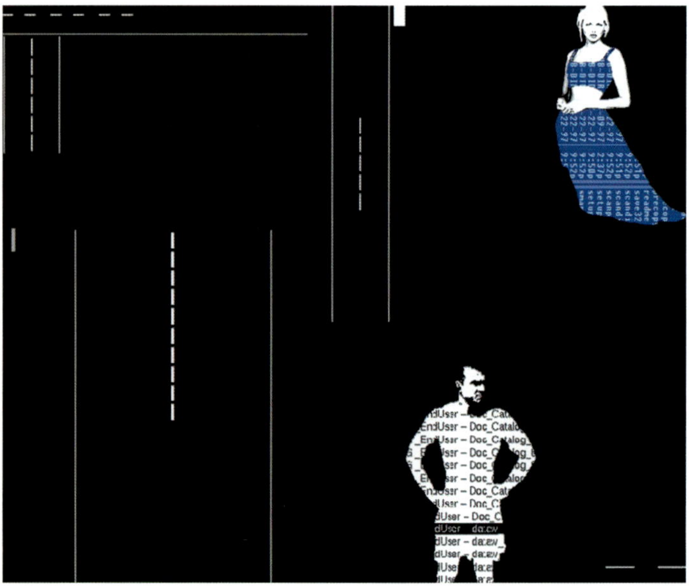

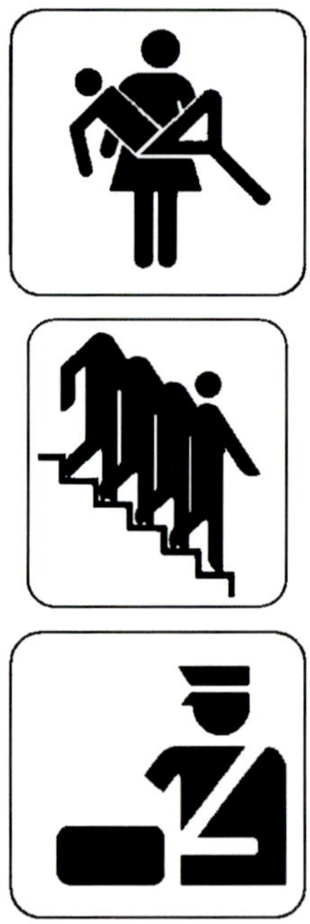

top: Damian Jaques and Simon Worthington, used to illustrate the Technoscience special section, Vol 1 #9, Spring 1998
bottom left: Olia Lialina, screenshot from *Agatha Appears*, used to illustrate Josephine Bosma's survey piece 'Is It a Commercial? Nooo… Is It Spam?… Nooo – It's Net Art!', 1997, Vol 1 #10, Summer 1998
bottom right: Vuk Ćosić, from the series *The History of Art for Airports*, 1998, used to illustrate Josephine Berry's interview with Ćosić, 'Art is Useless', Vol 1 #13, Summer 1999

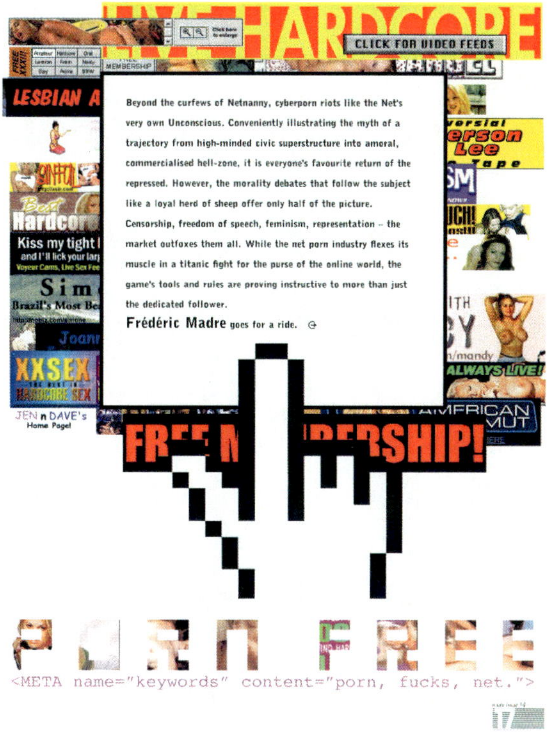

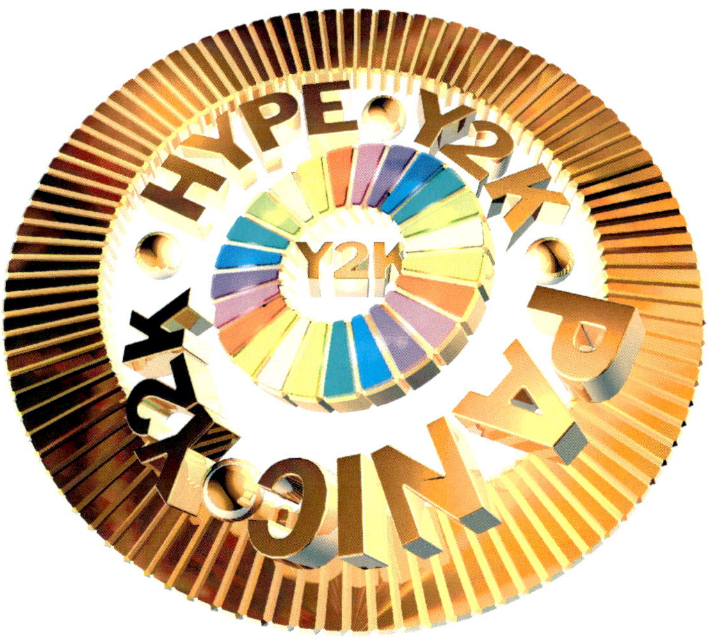

top: Simon Worthington, used to illustrate Frédéric Madre's 'Porn Free', Vol 1 #14, Autumn 1999
bottom: Laura Bangert, *Hype – Y2K – Panic*, used to illustrate Mark Fisher's 'Y2K-Positive', Vol 1 #15, Winter 1999

Multiple Clothing

Modern Dream

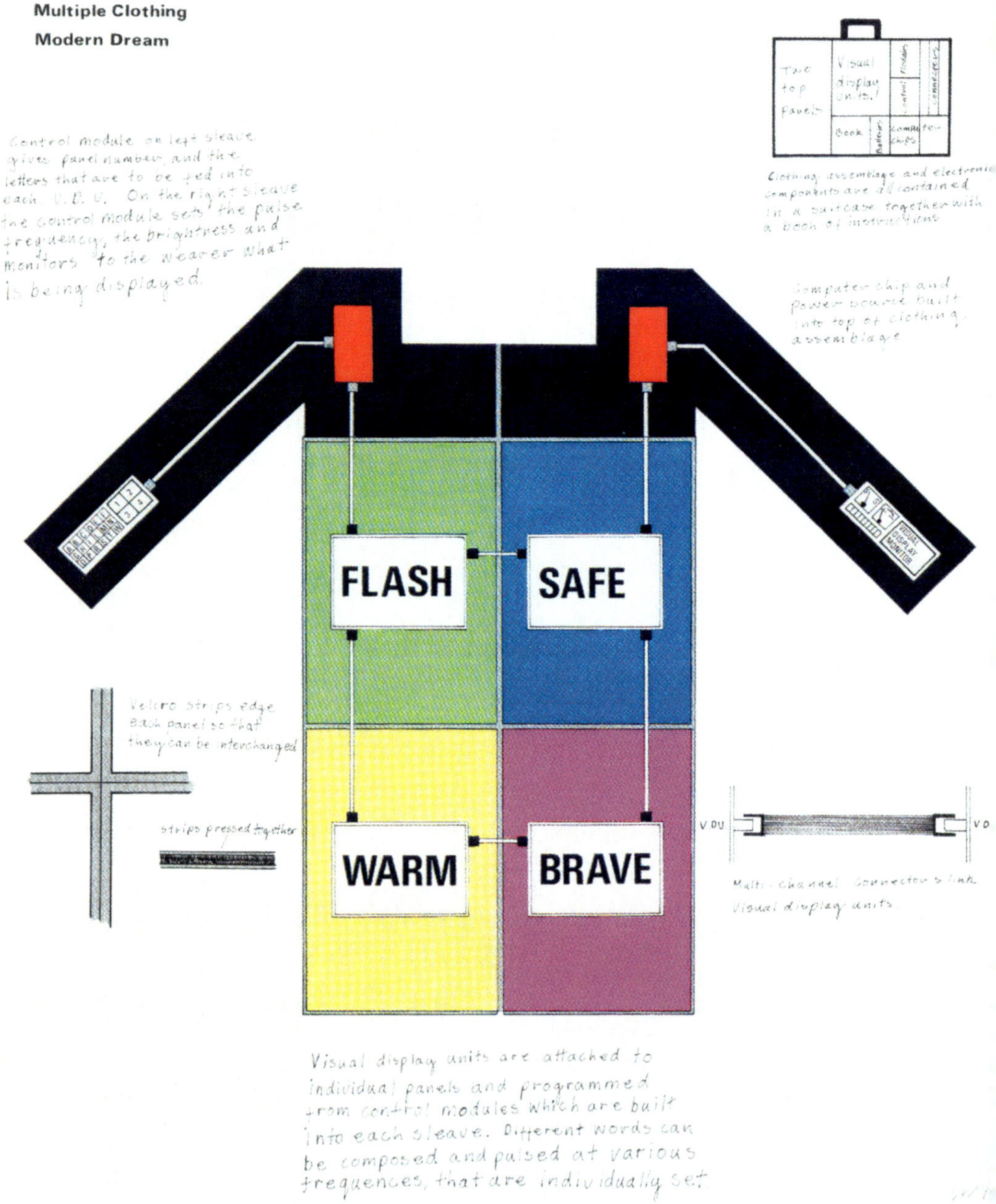

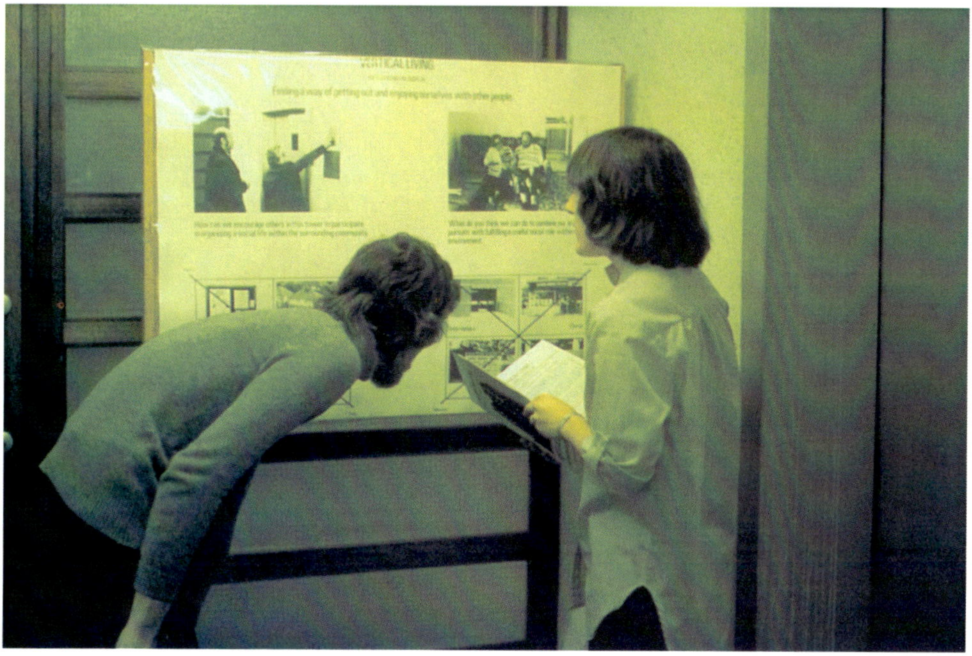

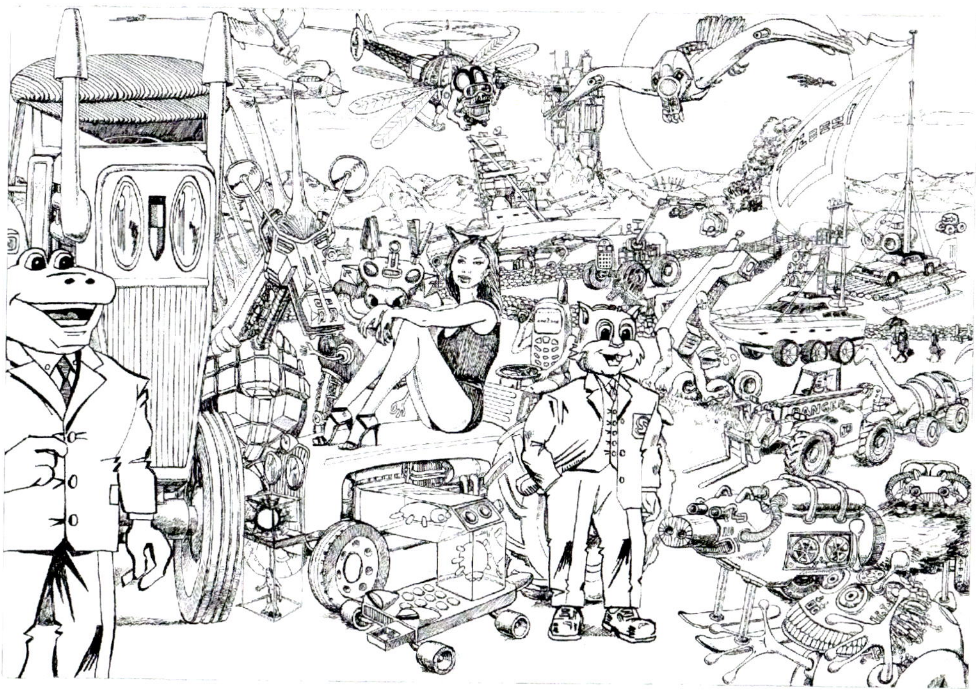

opposite: Stephen Willats, *Modern Dream*, 1991, used to illustrate Josephine Berry and Pauline van Mourik Broekman's interview with Stephen Willats, 'King of Code', Vol 1 #17, Summer 2000
top: Stephen Willats, *Vertical Living*, Hayes, 1976, one of the public display boards positioned in the landings of Skeffingdon Court, used to illustrate 'King of Code', Vol 1 #17, Summer 2000
bottom: Merlin Carpenter, *A Colloquium of Traktors*, 2000, used to illustrate María Fernández and Suhail Malik's 'Whatever Happened to the Cyborg Manifesto?', Vol 1 #20, Summer 2001

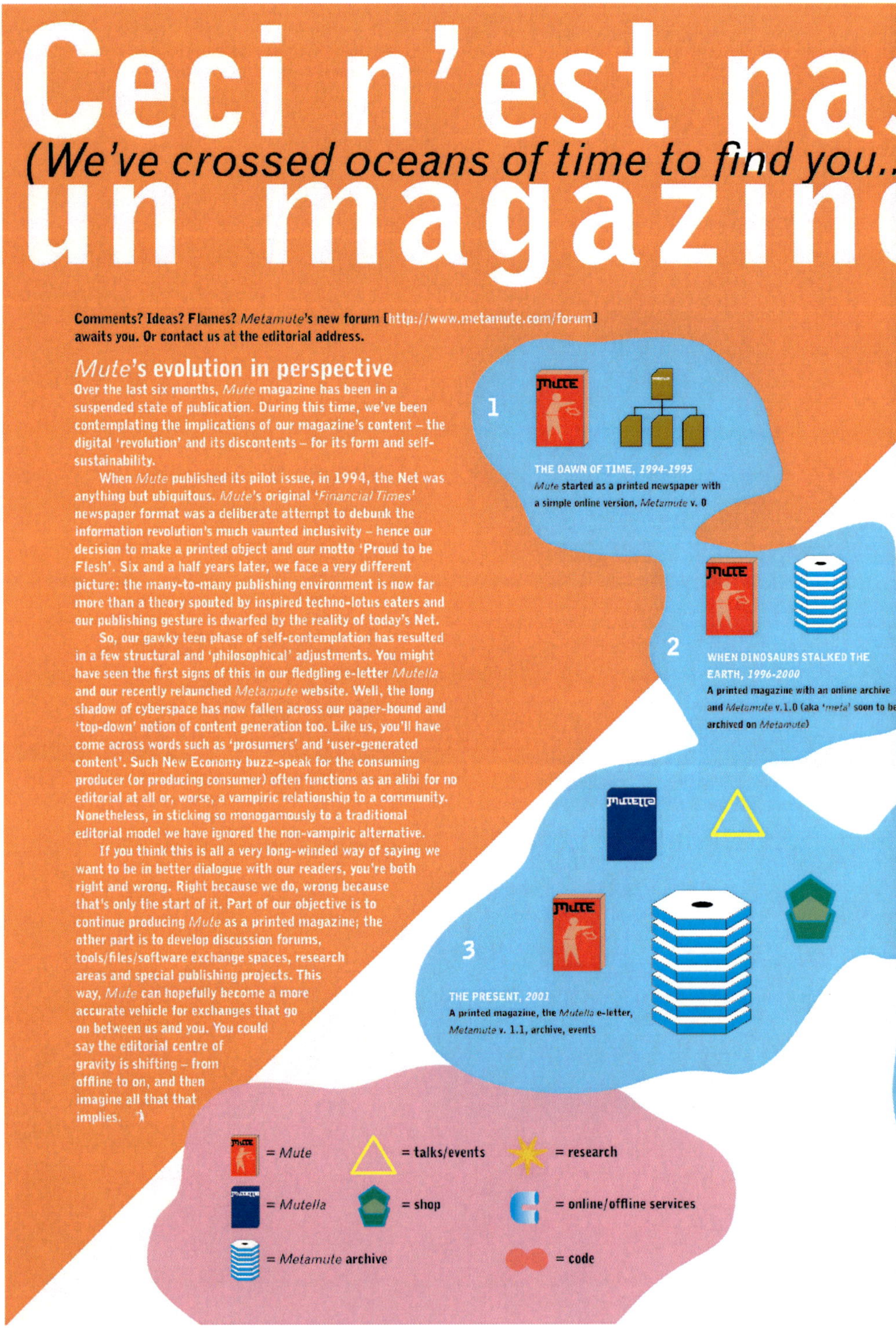

Ceci n'est pas un magazine

(We've crossed oceans of time to find you...

Comments? Ideas? Flames? *Metamute*'s new forum [http://www.metamute.com/forum] awaits you. Or contact us at the editorial address.

Mute's evolution in perspective

Over the last six months, *Mute* magazine has been in a suspended state of publication. During this time, we've been contemplating the implications of our magazine's content – the digital 'revolution' and its discontents – for its form and self-sustainability.

When *Mute* published its pilot issue, in 1994, the Net was anything but ubiquitous. *Mute*'s original '*Financial Times*' newspaper format was a deliberate attempt to debunk the information revolution's much vaunted inclusivity – hence our decision to make a printed object and our motto 'Proud to be Flesh'. Six and a half years later, we face a very different picture: the many-to-many publishing environment is now far more than a theory spouted by inspired techno-lotus eaters and our publishing gesture is dwarfed by the reality of today's Net.

So, our gawky teen phase of self-contemplation has resulted in a few structural and 'philosophical' adjustments. You might have seen the first signs of this in our fledgling e-letter *Mutella* and our recently relaunched *Metamute* website. Well, the long shadow of cyberspace has now fallen across our paper-bound and 'top-down' notion of content generation too. Like us, you'll have come across words such as 'prosumers' and 'user-generated content'. Such New Economy buzz-speak for the consuming producer (or producing consumer) often functions as an alibi for no editorial at all or, worse, a vampiric relationship to a community. Nonetheless, in sticking so monogamously to a traditional editorial model we have ignored the non-vampiric alternative.

If you think this is all a very long-winded way of saying we want to be in better dialogue with our readers, you're both right and wrong. Right because we do, wrong because that's only the start of it. Part of our objective is to continue producing *Mute* as a printed magazine; the other part is to develop discussion forums, tools/files/software exchange spaces, research areas and special publishing projects. This way, *Mute* can hopefully become a more accurate vehicle for exchanges that go on between us and you. You could say the editorial centre of gravity is shifting – from offline to on, and then imagine all that that implies.

Ceci N'est Pas un Magazine, *Mute*'s manifesto for user-driven publishing, artwork concept by Quim Gil, drawn by Damian Jaques, Vol 1 #19, Spring 2001

WHO IS WHO?

In the classical editor-reader relationship the roles are simple: editors edit and publish, readers read and pay. What we are more interested in is a variant of the slogan '**Stop spending money, generate your own value!**' In effect, can that badly maligned entity known as a 'community' generate an economy of its own.

Illustration: originated by Quim Gil <qgil@metamute.com>
Executed at dawn by the fine hand of young Damian Jaques
NB you are approaching a simplification of Reality!

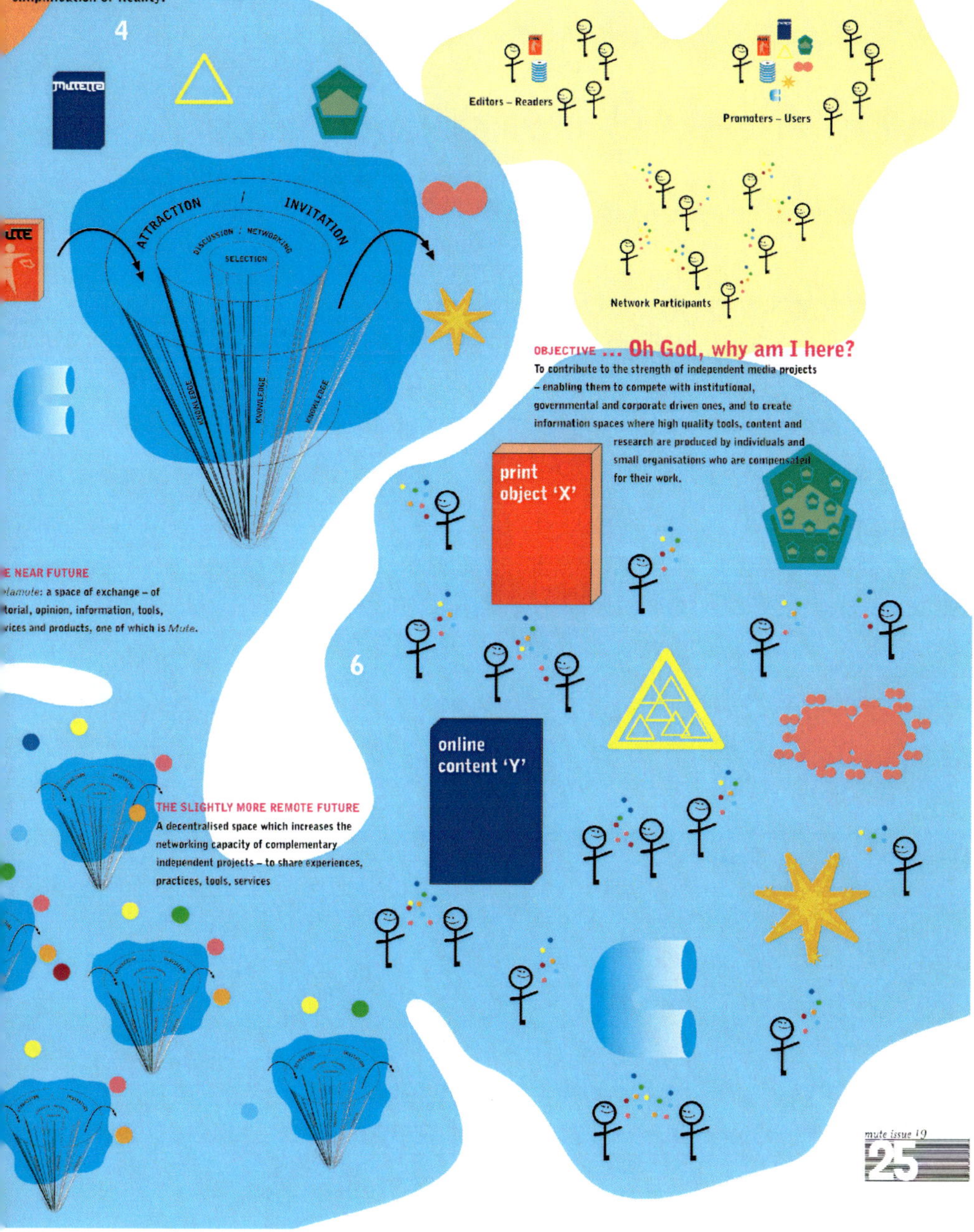

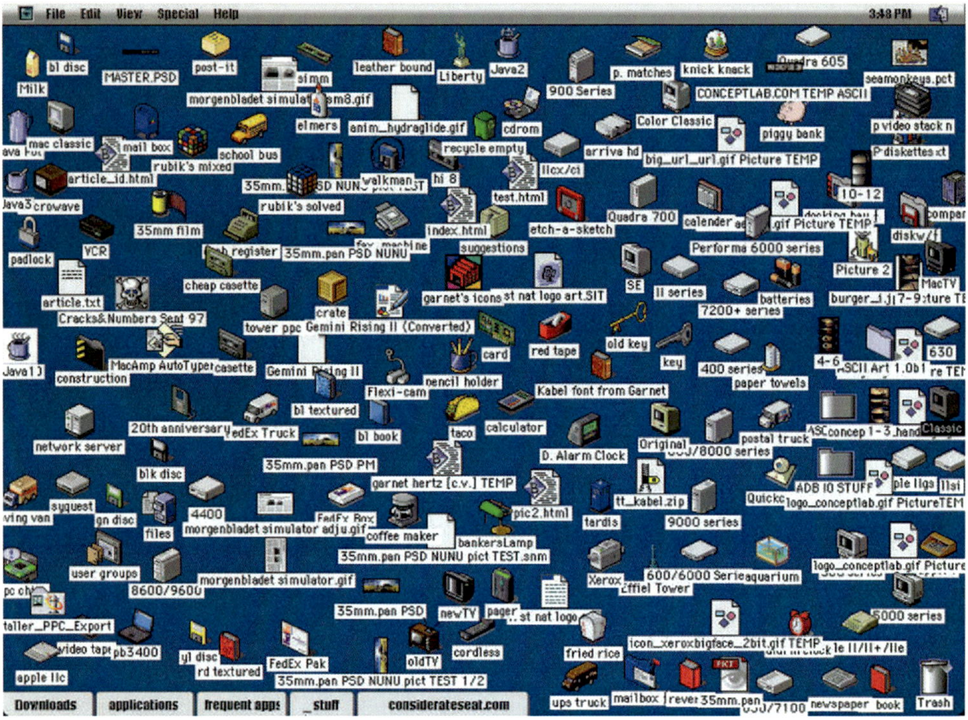

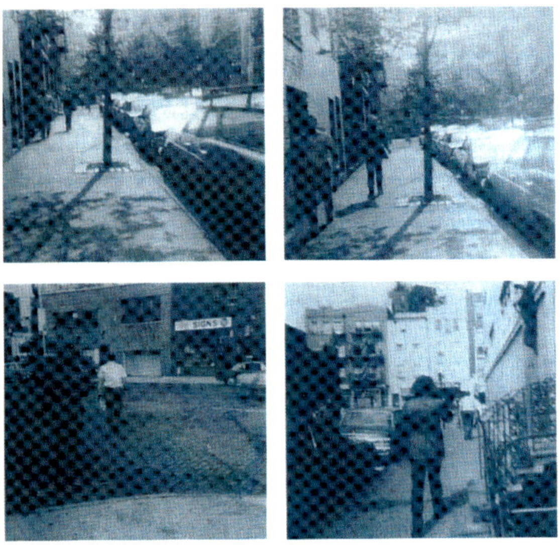

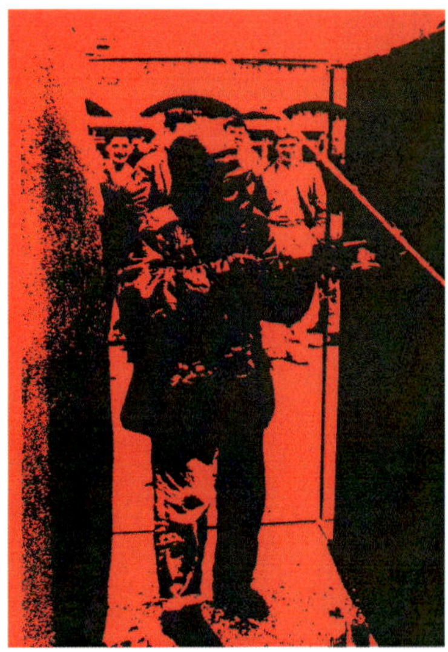

top: Alexei Shulgin, *Desktop Is*, 1997, used to illustrate Josephine Berry's brief history of net art, 'Repeat and Win', Vol 1 #22, Winter 2001
bottom left: Vito Acconci, *Following Piece*, New York City, 1969, used to illustrate Michael Corris' 'Systems Upgrade', Vol 1 #22, Winter 2001
bottom right: Gustav Metzger, *South Bank Demonstration*, July 1961, photo courtesy of Hulton Getty Picture Collection, used to illustrate Simon Ford's feature on the artist, 'Technological Kindergarten', Vol 1 #26, Summer/Autumn 2003

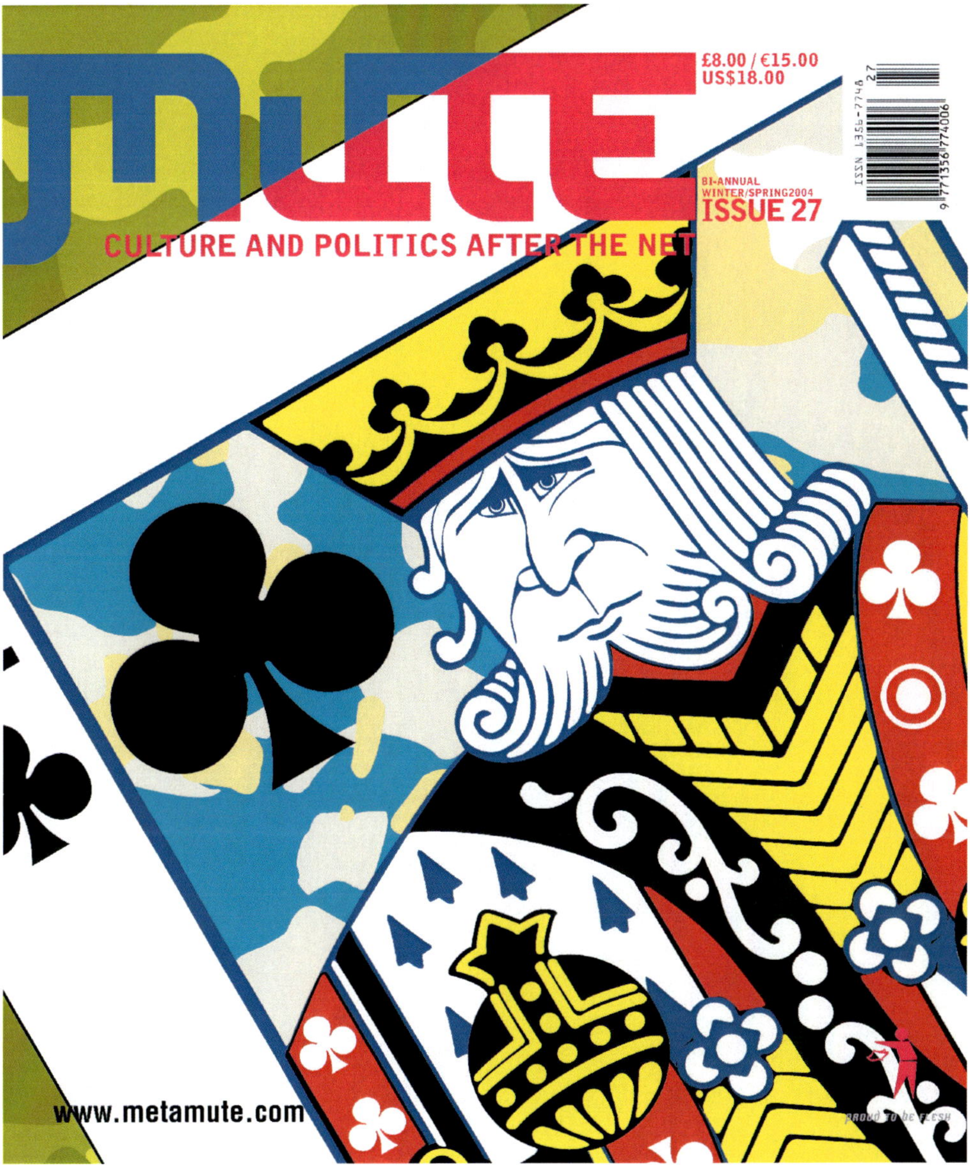

Simon Worthington and Damian Jaques' George W. Bush playing card, used to illustrate Anustup Basu's 'Bombs and Bytes' and used as the cover image, Vol 1 #27, Winter/Spring 2004

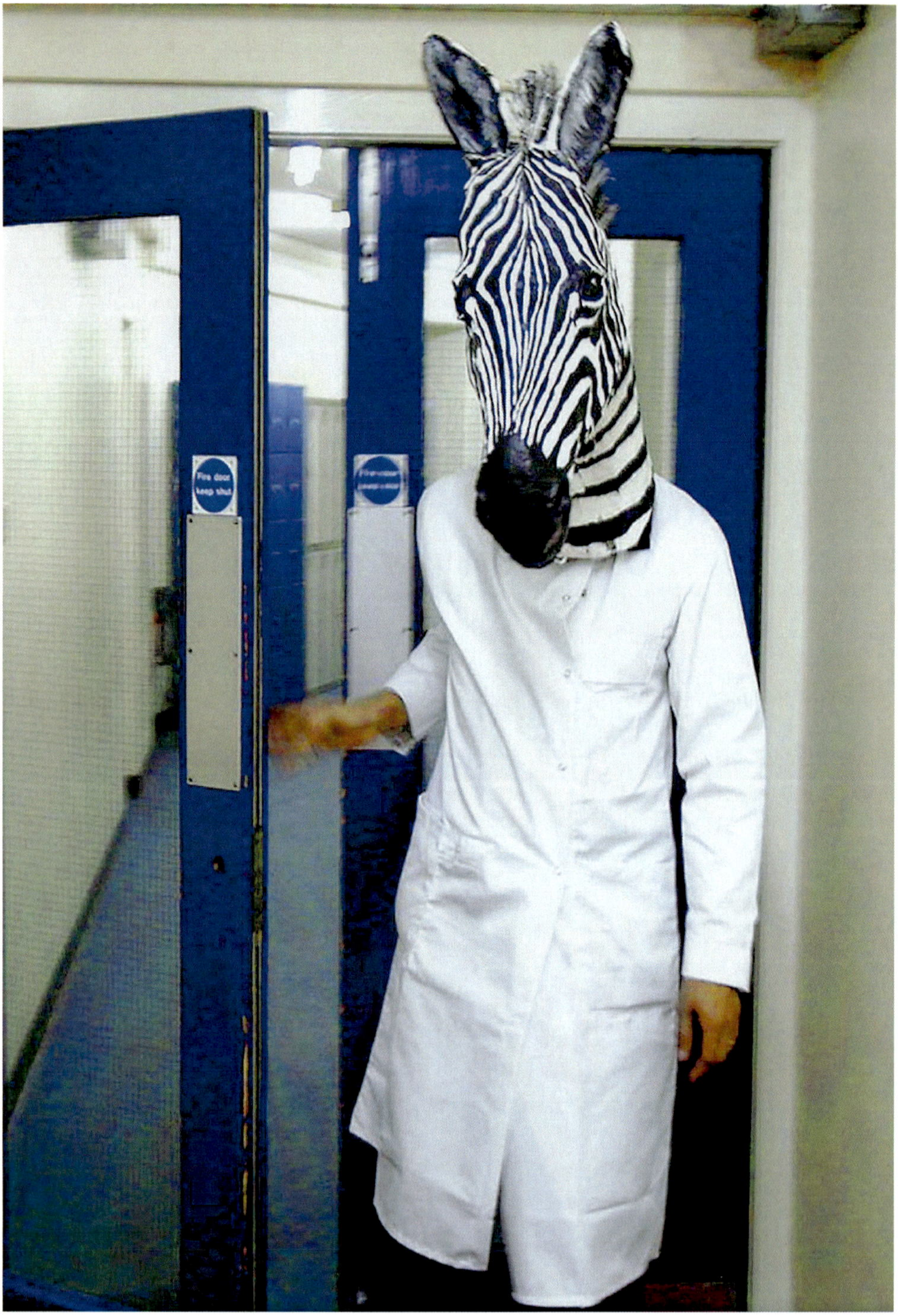

above: Ansuman Biswas, *Zebra*, 2003, courtesy of the National Institute for Medical Research, London, used to illustrate Betti Marenko's 'Museum Epidemiology', Vol 1 #27, Winter/Spring 2004
opposite: Pauline van Mourik Broekman, cover image for the Web 2.0: Man's Best Friendster? issue, Vol 2 #4, Winter/Spring 2007

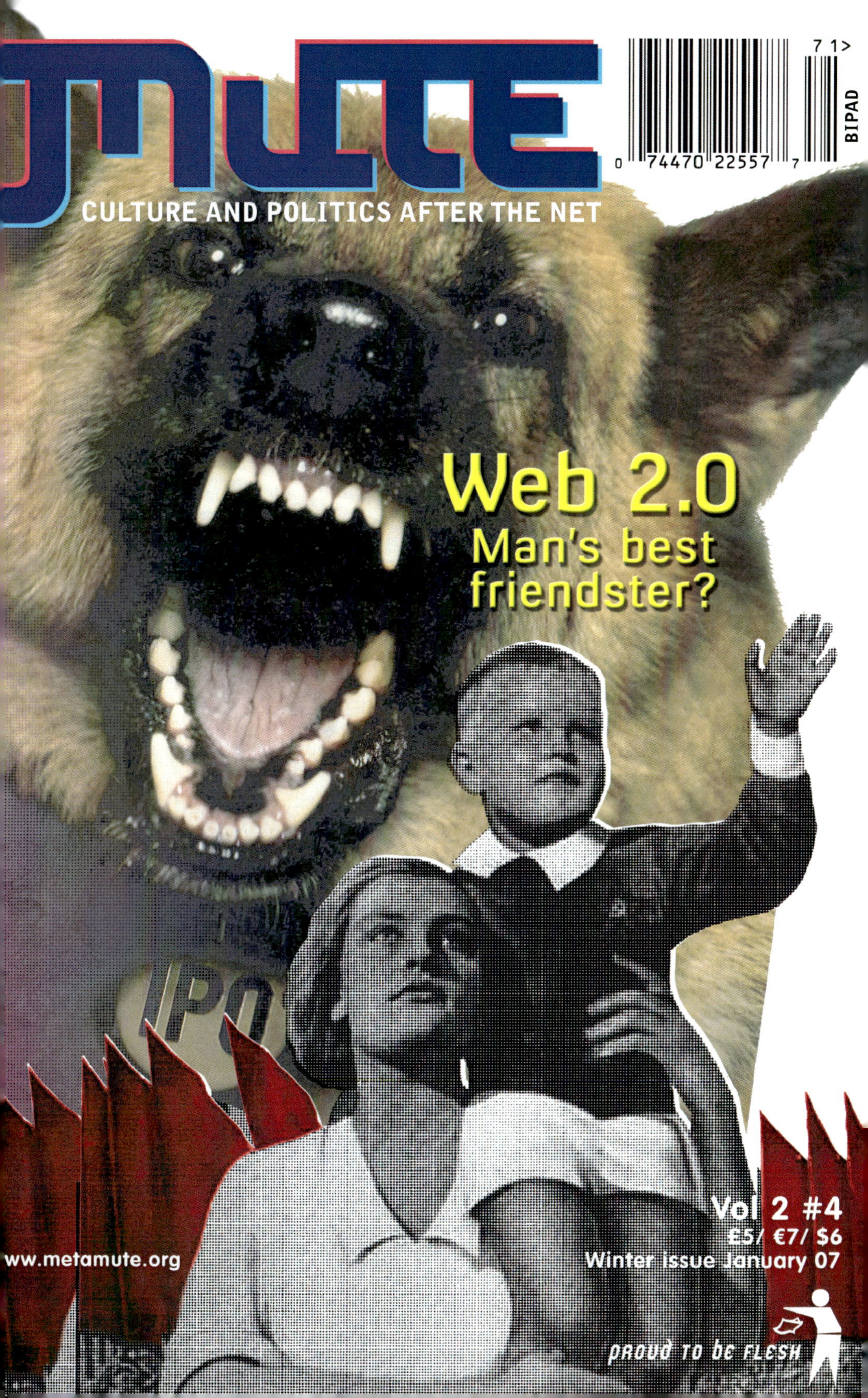
MUTE
CULTURE AND POLITICS AFTER THE NET
Web 2.0
Man's best friendster?
IPO
Vol 2 #4
£5/ €7/ $6
Winter issue January 07
www.metamute.org
proud to be flesh

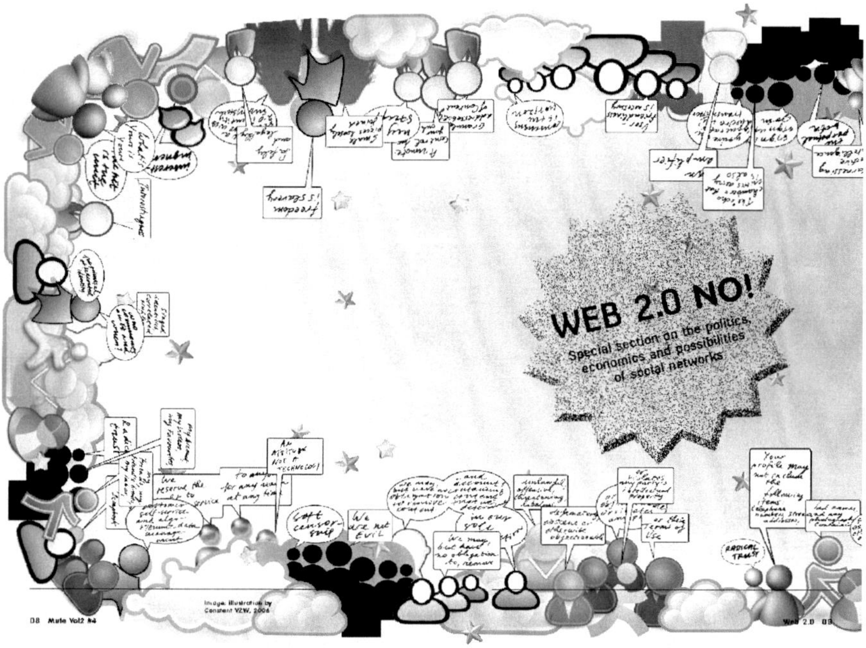

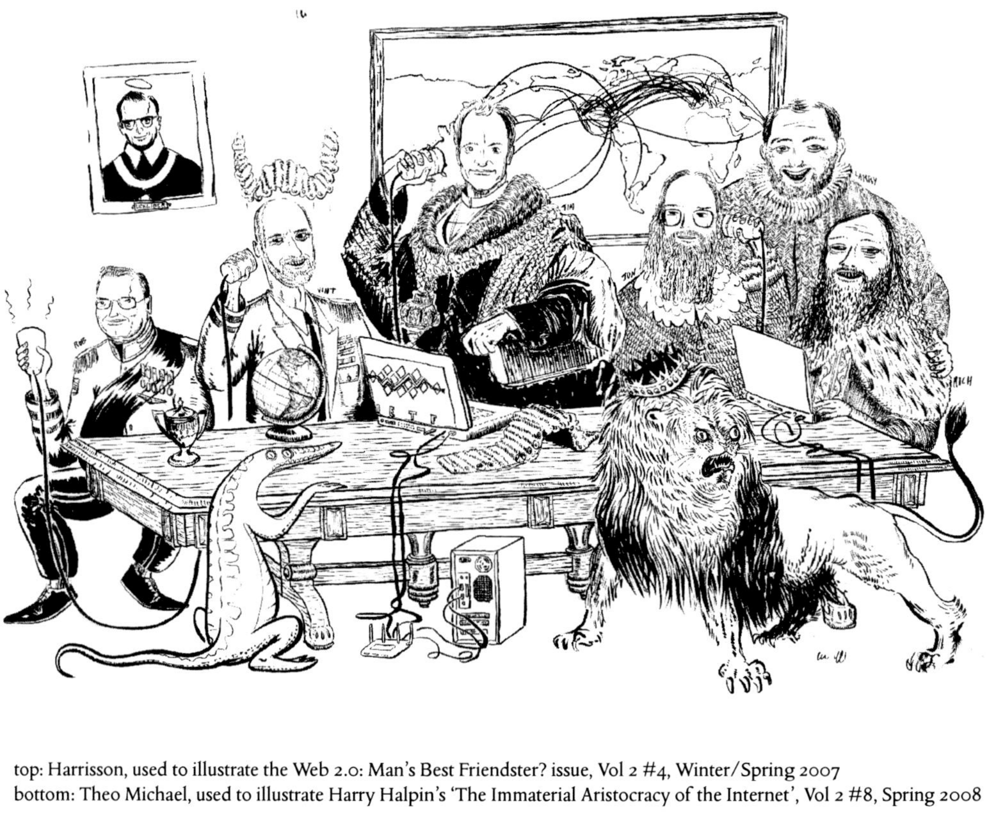

top: Harrisson, used to illustrate the Web 2.0: Man's Best Friendster? issue, Vol 2 #4, Winter/Spring 2007
bottom: Theo Michael, used to illustrate Harry Halpin's 'The Immaterial Aristocracy of the Internet', Vol 2 #8, Spring 2008

on the quantification of energy flows, rather than the interminable hermeneutic question of 'what it all means'. Immunology has a background curiously congruous with Nietzsche's physiological accounts of strength and weakness. Although the development, by Edward Jennings in 1798, of the smallpox vaccine had been suggestive of the mechanics of the immune system, it was not until the 19th century, with the growth of public health reforms, that modern immunology really came into being. The astonishing efficacy of the practice of vaccination was strong evidence for the existence of a remarkable 'system' for protecting organisms from infection. The immune system seemed somehow to 'know' what was not good for the organism, and thence to destroy it. Quickly, a paradigm for research developed around the work of Paul Ehrlich, which adopted a 'humoral' (read: biochemical) explanation for how the system functioned. Later, in the 20th century, research drawing on the findings of biologists into genetics conferred on immunology the privilege of being the 'science of self-nonself distinction'.

The remarkable successes of immunology should not obscure its less palatable inscription within the modern apparatus of biopower, which makes it a *prima facie* candidate for critical analysis. It is not simply because of its background in the very public health reforms of the late 19th century, which Foucault has flagged as evidence of the paradigmatic shift in the exercise of power. Nor is it the fact that its innocently scientific status – bolstered by its phenomenal success in treating the most publicly worrying of illnesses – has contributed to a sense of its benevolent neutrality as science (and hence also, in the Foucauldian optic, to its efficacy for power). We cannot ignore the fact that, like many other subfields of the life sciences, immunology benefited enormously from advances in genetics in the late-1950s (although it wasn't until the 1980s that some of the fundamental genetic mechanisms of immunological functioning were experimentally confirmed). An innocent enough fact, perhaps, but of great importance to the economy of the science's explanations – explanations which demonstrate a remarkable congruence with 'scientific' developments elsewhere.

According to Agamben, one of the noteworthy facts about national socialism is that its politics developed through a decisive mobilisation of science in a synthesis of biology and economy. One Otto von Verschuer, Professor of Genetics and Anthropology at Frankfurt University, argued, in a semi-official publication called *State and Health*, that doctors should see 'in the state of health of the population, the condition for economic profit' and that the 'oscillations of biological substance and those of material equilibrium generally go hand in hand'. Arguing against the view that the biopolitics of the Third Reich should be seen uniquely under the epithet of 'racism', Agamben suggests that the extermination of the Jews must be seen in a perspective whereby the 'protection of health and [the] struggle against the enemy have become absolutely indiscernible'.

If Agamben is correct, it is somewhat disquieting to find a parallel convergence between immunology, politics and metaphysics. In its routine arguments about the fundamental function of the immune system, immunology uses a language which is loaded with political and metaphysical connotations. The immune system is primarily a system of defence against attack; immunology seeks to explain how it is that the self can differentiate between friend and enemy, or between molecular compounds which are non-lethal and those foreign pathogens which are lethal. Of course, no one is saying that this isn't what the immune system does. But it is curious to see how the immune system is immediately inscribed within the political and the metaphysical. Since there is no intrinsic property to mark out biochemical elements as belonging to this organism rather than another, to talk of the self at a chemical level is clearly a wishful metaphysical fiction. And to make sense of what is going on at the molecular level by using the language of the political – friend and enemy, the foreign body – raises questions about what it is, exactly, that immunology is doing.

Pointing out these parallels is not to claim that immunology is a racist discourse. But we shouldn't see in its language the innocent play of metaphor. The political aspects of a science are to be sought in terms of its dominant structures of explanation. In combination with the excess of meaning supplied by the language of defence and attack, foreign bodies and so on, these structures produce a set of resonances between immunology and explicitly political discourses which makes their affinity more than a matter of mere chance – to think otherwise is to ignore the disturbing evidence Agamben has collated about national socialism.

The dominant modality of immunological discourse was effectively fixed by the Nobel Prize-winning research of British immunologist, Sir Macfarlane Burnet. Whilst antibodies were discovered in Germany in the 1890s, it was Burnet who came up with the idea that the immune system 'discriminates' between self and nonself, and, in so doing, he perpetuated the already well established notion that the immune system defended the pre-existing identity of an organism. Immunology was, in his view, founded on an 'intolerance of living matter for foreign matter'. His solution to the problem of explaining how it is that lymphocytes and the antibodies they produce, while being capable of recognising and destroying any molecular compound, don't routinely destroy the elements which compose the organism in which they reside, became known as 'clonal selection theory'. In its typical reactive operation, when the immune system detects a pathogen, it responds by the mass production of clones of an antibody which can bind with, and hence neutralise, the invader. The efficiency of this process is improved firstly by extensive somatic mutation of the DNA coding for antibody production. Rearrangements of the inherited (germ line) genes, which account for the production of antibodies, enables an organism to generate an enormous variety of different antibodies (a sort of selection mechanism within the organism itself). It is also improved 'second time around', i.e. if the system has previously been exposed to a pathogen, it effectively maintains a memory trace of that pathogen and can respond more quickly. This was a fact understood from the inception of immunology, and it contributes to the popularity of those strands of research which consist in isolating the response of the system to specific, precisely defined pathogens.

Burnet's clonal selection theory argued that clones, produced by the immune system, which would recognise and attack the self were simply eliminated during the organism's development, through a learning process. Subsequent to his claim, all sorts of peculiar experiments were devised as a way of confirming this theory; because the system learned to discriminate between self and nonself, you could, in theory, fool it. More importantly, the theory seemed to drive a wedge between a self – understood as pre-existing the immune system, presumably defined on a genetic basis – and the nonself. Because the role of the immune system was that of defending a given identity, through a process of learning, the identity of the self somehow fell outside of history and became a *tabula rasa*, an immunological bare life, protected by a set of unconnected 'individual' defence responses.

In effect, Burnet's theory prescribed, or rather sanctioned, the dominant trend in immunological research, which is the investigation of an unconnected set of discretely causal mechanisms. Just as some take metaphysical comfort in locating the gene for genius, for aging, for schizophrenia or for homosexuality (the implication – oh praise eugenics – being that you might then simply turn it on or off), so too research which promises to locate the cell, or cells, responsible for combating a particular illness imparts ontological security. Your identity is safe with us, say the pharmaceutical companies, thoroughly caught up in this process of reification.

It is not difficult to see why this conception of the immune system has been so successful. Recall that immunology really took off as a result of public health reforms, and that it was bolstered by the practice of vaccination. Vaccination exemplifies the 'discrete' logic of explanation, and provides a miraculously dramatic confirmation of the powers of the system. Some historians have suggested, though, that, prior to vaccination programmes, the immune system showed itself to be far less effective as a defence mechanism; without the artificial stimulation of antibody production by vaccines, the immune system was relatively powerless against the kinds of epidemics which have ravaged the world throughout the centuries. In the late 20th century, the example of AIDS has shown that it is infections with low degrees of 'pathogenicity' which can be most lethal. In any case, it is difficult to maintain an unequivocal role for the immune system. It has been known since the early-1970s, for example, that, whilst the immune system can destroy tumours, it can also, under certain circumstances, promote their growth.

Perhaps immunology has been asking the wrong kinds of questions. The absence of any cure for AIDS, for example, suggests that the dominant framework is ill-adapted to the kinds of immune problems accompanying HIV. Over recent decades, there has been a growing realisation amongst a minority of immunologists that the inconsistencies of clonal selection theory *vis-à-vis* the available evidence, coupled with a tendency to do the wrong kind of research, might indeed be leading immunology in the wrong direction.

In the first instance, there is evidence to suggest that the existence of auto-antibodies (ones that will react to self) are not quite as exceptional as had been previously thought. Such autoantibodies can be found in both the maternal immune repertoire, which is inherited from the child organism's mother, and in its 'induced' repertoire, which develops in ontogeny. The existence of these autoantibodies has often been downplayed, and we can now see why – they are inconsistent with the predominant explanation of how the immune system works and what its purpose is.

Secondly, if the immune self is a uniquely genetic inheritance, how is one to explain that a neonatal immune system can recognise as 'foreign' antigens derived from its parents? And how is one to explain the existence of non-negligible levels of immune activity in organisms isolated in a germ-free environment?

Since around the middle of the 1970s, there has been an alternative view of the immune system, one which explores its role in a very different way. In 1974, Niels Jerne published a paper which proposed a theory of 'idiotypic networks' as a way of explaining the anomalies. Idiotypic network theory suggested, in direct opposition to clonal selection theory, that not only does the immune system interact with itself but that this is its primary activity. Whilst the defensive struggle against the enemy displays the remarkable power of the immune system (presumably delegated by the sovereign self), it misunderstands the peculiar organisation of the immune system's capacities.

Idiotypic network theory can be glossed as follows: some cell type is recognised by a specific variety of lymphocyte or clone-producing antibody (a B-cell, in the jargon. Call it A). This stimulates the production of more clones to attack the initial cell type. These clones themselves are then recognised by another B-cell (call it B), which produces its own clones. The clones of B down-regulate the activity of the clones of A, but themselves stimulate the production of C clones by yet another B-cell. This chain, or 'cascade' of events eventually closes on itself (say, when the clones of A recognise and down-regulate clones produced by lymphocyte Z). In this scenario, the immune system does not primarily defend a pre-existing self but actually constitutes that self as the ongoing product of a series of interactions in a complex molecular environment, an idiotypic network in other words. Further, the defensive efficacy of the system becomes easier to explain. The system doesn't need to be able to specifically recognise nonself in order to launch an attack.

Because the network primarily recognises itself, it only attacks what it cannot assimilate. To put it another way, the defensive function is a consequence of the system's weakness and not its strength.

The differences between these two positions may seem slight, but Jerne's theory forces us to acknowledge the processes by which the immune self is constituted. Available evidence suggests that the gap between the genetically hardwired and the learned is not as clear or as large as clonal selection theory had suggested, and that autoantibodies can function both as part of an idiotypic network as well as against non-network elements. The 'self' is, in this view, an historical product, and not some essence which might delegate its powers to the immune system. More interestingly, the immune system is no longer seen as being essentially bound up with the 'fight against the enemy'. Whilst it still clearly has a role to play in combating infection and so on, this is not its primary role, and we should understand it on the basis of a different logic. But, then, what is the immune system's purpose? If it didn't arise in evolution to fight bacteria and to protect the pre-constituted individual, for what purpose did it evolve?

Controversial research, based on a speculative reconstruction of the evolutionary steps leading from organisms without an immune system (invertebrates) to those with, has suggested that the immune system might have had a role in actually constituting the individual as a unit of biological selection. In this respect, it served to unify a set of different cell types into a coherent unit. This theory is controversial and, it is true to say, has not gained the assent of the immunological community at large, yet it does provide an interesting explanation for a fundamental problem in evolutionary theory – that of explaining how the individual organism actually came to be. And, if the individual vertebrate organism came to be, it can of course come not to be.

Contemporary language centred on the care of the self undoubtedly has many sources, and the self as such has components from all over. But it is difficult not to notice how often the language of private property appears. Your sexuality, your politics, your immune system (which of course you regulate by regular boosting, don't you ?). Poor proles that we all are nowadays, poor subjects of a biopolitical constitution, being commanded to exercise proprietorial control over an immune system (or a sexuality, set of political options and so on), which in fact defines us, is not just a grammatical error. If the parallels I have suggested between the dominant understanding of the immune system and Agamben's theorisation of bare life are accurate, there is much more than a linguistic sop to a lack of power at stake. To forget that 'you' are a complex chemical ecology, in which what can't kill you can only make you stronger, might give you a limited stake in a restricted biological-economic exchange, but it won't make you immune from the fascist life. Think about that the next time you are in the chemist.

Abstract Sex

Luciana Parisi

Vol 1 #27, Winter/Spring 2004

> [...W]e have seen [...] that it is most closely-allied forms, – varieties of the same species, and species of the same genus or of related genera, – which, from having nearly the same structure, constitution, and habits, generally come into the severest competition with each other; consequently each new variety or species, during the progress of its formation, will generally press hardest on its nearest kindred, and tend to exterminate them. We see the same process of extermination amongst our domesticated productions, through the selection of improved forms by man. Many curious instances could be given showing how quickly new breeds of cattle, sheep, and other animals, and varieties of flowers, take the place of older and inferior kinds.
>
> Charles Darwin, *On the Origin of Species*, 1859

> Whether it be in the development of the Earth, in the development of Life, upon its surface, the development of Society, of Government, of Manufactures, of Commerce, of Language, Literature, Science, Art, this same evolution of the simple into the complex, through a process of continuous differentiation, holds throughout. From the earliest traceable cosmical changes down to the latest results of civilisation, we shall find that the transformation of the homogeneous into the heterogeneous, is that in which Progress essentially consists...
>
> Herbert Spencer, 'Progress: Its Law and Cause', 1891

The Bacterial Assembly

In 1981, Lynn Margulis' research into bacterial mitochondrial transmission called into question the foundations of Darwinism and neo-Darwinism. Margulis argued that mitochondria, organelles residing in the body of nucleated animal and plant cells, are in fact descendents of free-living bacteria. Enclosed in their mitochondrial membranes, these ancient bacteria have an independent genetic apparatus of their own, but were at some stage – possibly the moment in which oxygen entered the atmosphere 200 million years ago – captured within the cell body, outside the nucleus.

However they found their way into the cell body originally, the presence of mitochondrial messenger material outside the nucleus of the host cell constitutes a parallel process of transmission long unknown to science and unaccounted for within the Darwinian paradigm. Like all bacteria, these mitochondria reproduce, but their genetic transfer is non-linear and takes place only by way of the mother. It would seem that nucleic transmission is not the exclusive determinant of the evolution of the organism after all; indeed, nucleic DNA is itself altered by the mitochondrial material that surrounds it. In other words, there are not one but two parallel and mutually infecting channels of genetic communication that determine the organism's development. Indeed, within the same species, the nucleic germline and the bacterial somaline exhibit differential rates of mutation. From these findings, Margulis has revolutionised the classical evolutionary understanding of the development of life.

Margulis' work draws on that of Russian scholar-biologist, Konstantin S. Mereschovsky, who, in the first quarter of the 20th century, had already rejected the Darwinian theory of natural selection and invented the term 'symbiogenesis' to describe the prolonged symbiotic, parasitic associations that precede the appearance of a new organism[1] – 'guest' bacterium, entering the cell, takes part in a transfer of DNA information with those 'host' bacteria already present. Bacteria move across phyla without regard, altering the genetic material of each lineage as they go.

Dismissed for a long time, symbiogenesis is acquiring a constitutive scientific importance, supported by biochemistry and molecular biology's questioning of the classical division between the plant and animal kingdoms and the classifications based on this division. Symbiotic processes now, in fact, seem to explain the emergence of the cellular and genetic modifications of sex and reproduction, disrupting the 'zoo-centrism' of the theory of evolution (the priority of *Homo sapiens*) in demonstrating that 'each animal cell is, in fact, an uncanny assembly, the evolutionary merger of distinct bacterial metabolisms'.[2]

Biotechnology: The Oldest Science

In this sense, not only are genetic engineering and cloning not new, but they are not even particularly innovative complexifications of life. Instead, they strongly resemble the trading of genes invented by bacteria 3.9 billion years ago – non-nucleated cells transmitting information without copulation. Perhaps all that is marked by 'biotech' – the human recombination of genetic material between independent cellular bodies – is the re-emergence of the most ancient sex: bacterial sex.

But biotechnologies such as transgenics and cloning – insofar as they entail the horizontal transfer of genetic material, the re-engineering of cells across species barriers – do expose new levels of symbiotic mixture. For bacteria and endosymbiotic parasitism, they mark a new threshold – a new channel for a bacterial trading that will not remain constricted to the intentions of the

1. Jan Sapp, *Evolution by Association: A History of Symbiosis*, Oxford: Oxford University Press, 1994; Dorion Sagan, 'Metametazoa: Biology and Multiplicity', *Incorporation*, New York: Zone Books, 1992, pp. 362–85; Lynn Margulis, *Symbiosis in Cell Evolution*, San Francisco: W.H. Freeman, 1981, pp. 1–14.
2. Sagan, 1992, op. cit., p. 363.

scientists who opened it. Transgenesis accelerates differential mutations in patterns of evolution so that biotechnologies – used, for example, to improve organs and cell transplants, make insulin or produce new cells and tissues for 'cell therapies' – are in fact promoting parallel, unknowable, non-filial recombinations of genetic sequences and cellular compounds that favour the emergence and re-emergence of new viruses alongside new generations of mutant vegetables, insects, fish, reptiles, sheep and humans. No longer species or individuals, forms or functions, transgenesis highlights evolution's underlying pattern: packs of relations between bodies that engineer new bodies. It is simply not accurate to say that genetic engineering is technology's colonisation of the biological; at the same time, the biological is abducting the transmission layer that biotechnology produces.

What is produced in this cross-colonisation of the biological and the technological layers of organisation is a bio-digital assemblage, a symbiotic modification of matter that is not part of any natural 'design'. The bio-digital assemblage of bodies – a mouse and a microchip, a virus and a human organism – propagates the tendencies of symbiotic matter and accelerates the turbulent and unexpected swerves of non-linear DNA transmission. Micro-mutations within and across species are enabled and accelerated. The tendencies of the bio-digital assemblage of matter are non-linear, and the transactions between various chronological moments – the biological, the technological, the biotechnological – take place via the nexus of symbiotic contagion. At this nexus, bio-digital sex catalyses the emergence and re-emergence of unprecedented life forms.

Re-Mapping DNA

According to the central belief of evolutionary dynamics and embryology, nucleic DNA – the germline – is the true organiser of life, that which decides the destiny of parts. Cloning, on the contrary, suggests that somatic substances themselves have specific abilities and potentials of individuation unknown to nucleic DNA, and that it is not nucleic DNA that determines variation. Via the movement of bacterial DNA in and through physical space – through the membranes of phyla and species, through time, folded into layers of sedimentation or re-emerging into the atmosphere in one of Earth's eruptions – DNA's linear transmission and progressive evolution are, in fact, thoroughly and constantly disrupted through intensive bacterial trades.

According to neo-Darwinists, sexual reproduction has been directly selected to accelerate the evolution of the most varied traits across generations by driving sexed organisms to adapt faster to changing conditions. But the parallel transmissions of endosymbiosis, bacterial sex and parthenogenesis (the reproduction of an unfertilised egg into offspring) present as many genetic variations as two-parent sex. The primacy of sexual reproduction in increasing complexity is, then, undermined. Indeed, sexual reproduction itself can be expected to have arisen from previous symbiotic associations, from parasitisms and transgenic trades between distinct bacteria under certain pressures, and bacterial symbiosis is thoroughly folded into the process of nucleic transmission.

This leads to a conception of life as a 'dissipative dynamics', a non-teleological account of nature's organisation. Margulis' work on microbial sex suggests that unprecedented reorganisations of life occur through symbiotic trade, a non-cumulative mixing giving rise to new compositions that do not resemble the parts from which they were generated. In endosymbiosis, novelty does not imply the enrichment of matter; the rule of symbiotic life is chance encounter – unforeseeable responses to unknowable conditions.

Abstract Sex

> Your people will change. Your young will be more like us and ours more like you. Your hierarchical tendencies will be modified and if we learn to regenerate limbs and reshape our bodies, we'll share that ability with you. That's part of the trade. We're overdue for it.
> Octavia E. Butler[3]

The distance between the macro and the micro no longer applies to this world of bacterial trade, proliferating through symbiotic contagion rather than nucleic filiation. There are as many sexes as there are terms in symbiosis, generating an ecosystem of micro-mutations which intersect at different speeds. This symbiosis, catalysed by chance encounters between molecular bodies, maps a dynamics of evolution that resonates with the metaphysics of Deleuze, Guattari and Spinoza.

For them, nature is machinic, an engineering process of paths never becoming a whole. Life forms do not result from a forced, or spontaneous, cooperation between individuated bodies struggling to reach a shared goal or to survive in a hostile environment. They are defined neither by a harmonious nor a conflictual state of nature driven by group collaboration or by individual competition. Altruism and egoism are both rooted in a humanisation of evolution that is undermined by symbiotic trade.

Instead, symbiotic assemblages make use of chance encounters that include reverse abductions, viral transmission, nuclearisation and multiparasitism. These processes of becoming are machinic involutions on a nature-culture continuum. Unknowable mutations are entailed in all of the parts caught up in their composition. I call these mutations abstract sex.

Abstract sex designates the potentials of intensive mutant matter – potentials that require no teleological aim towards novelty. Abstract sex

3. Octavia Butler, *Dawn*, New York: Warner Books, 1987, p. 40.

names neither a progressive nor a regressive state of materiality. Rather, it is a conception of nature defined by continuous mutations across all layers and stratifications. It is a non-deterministic process, a phylum of immanent relations traversing traditional strata in a parallel, anti-genealogical dynamic. Abstract sex opens up bio-physical and bio-cultural organisation of nucleic sex to radical de-stratification.

Bacterial Micropolitics

It is the singular moment of Darwinism and social Darwinism, initially triggered by the combination of social urbanisation and technological industrialisation, that must today give way to abstract sex. Together with this pairing goes the entire theory of evolution that has become central at the biological, social and economic layers, dominating, for example, psychology, sociology, anthropology and political theory. The function of adaptation, the 'survival of the fittest', can finally be disentangled from the social field, and the conspiracy of culture to 'make' nature is ended.

In the Darwinian logic, the blind force of natural selection regulates variations by ensuring common descent. This explains the driving force of capitalist development: capitalism is the invisible hand of order that selects the most successful mode of reproduction originating from the individual struggle for survival. In neo-Darwinist Kevin Kelly's famous analogy, the self-organisation of natural systems mirrors the increasing development of the free market: self-organisation takes the place of natural selection, regulating and channelling the world's randomness into a working whole. This is 'control without control' – an operation of selection that, for Kelly, does not involve a hierarchical chain of command. Rather, the 'invisible hand of selection' controls, without authority, the networked architecture of natural and economic systems. Biological networks match a democratic model of the market, defying the transcendence of centralised control.

The determinism of evolutionary complexity, in which self-organising networks add simple units to constitute complex systems, maintains a finality for nature. Capitalism as Darwinian evolution requires repetition without mutation, the passage from actuals to actuals, the preservation of the same variation, the selection of an always already individuated difference. This logic of 'control without control' only recentralises humanism in nature, a dynamic process of teleological evolution that dismisses the vaster, more aimless processes that, in fact, constitute them.

Of course, the continuous folding-in of indeterminate populations and mutant bodies must ultimately confound the supposed primacy of 'self-organisation'. Not only does abstract sex radically call into question the biological determinism that takes determinate forms and functions as examples for all organisations, but the fact of continuous symbiotic trade destroys Kelly's naturalist logic of economic systems and the unitary logic it imposes on the population of genetic material. In abstract sex, potential mutations accompany the most diverse stages of organisation on a nature-culture continuum, refuting the use of biology as a model for laissez-faire, liberal economics.

The aimlessness of abstract sex also calls into question the 'creative power of the multitude', theorised by Hardt and Negri in the book *Empire*.[4] For them, the multitude constitutes 'the networked real productive force of our social world, whereas Empire is a mere apparatus of capture that lives off the vitality of the multitude'.[5] The multitude is defined by creative, communicative, networked relations of virtualised production (i.e. immaterial labour), based on the decentralised, innovative and 'abstract cooperation' of bodies that constitutes global capitalism. By considering Empire as a parasitical web of bodies living off the creative vitality of a multitude, characterised by the networked intelligence of humans and machines, Hardt and Negri still presume a formal distinction between the self-enclosing or self-organising structure of capitalism, on the one hand, and the cooperative, creative forces of the multitude on the other. And, although they argue for the primary potentials of the multitude over apparatuses of capture – state capitalism – their model recentralises human agency in the material dynamics of evolution with creativity as the organic force that will always resist parasitic capture.

Rather than engaging with molecular mutations, Hardt and Negri characterise capitalism through the negative qualities of parasitism as opposed to the striving, living qualities of the multitude. This reinstates vitalist creativity and re-installs the human at the centre of matter's dynamics. *Empire* misses the dynamics of transmission visible in the endosymbiotic coexistence of bacterial and nucleic, informational trading through markets and anti-markets. Abstract sex demands a radically ambivalent picture of the relation between the host and the guest, the abductor and the abductee, the parasite and that upon which it is parasitic. If each symbiotic assemblage involves the modification of all parts participating in its composition, unleashing the emergence of unpredictable mutations, then apparatuses of capture can never be external to the multitude. On the contrary, there is a constant, interdependent relationship between these distinct modes of organisation. Hence, not only can the most rigid monopoly feed on the sparsest grassroots, but counter-power can also hijack and grow through power's channels.

This open-ended trading entails no aim, interest or finality. It is a non-given micropolitics of de-stratification and mutation: a pragmatics under construction on the nature-culture plane. It concerns bodies defined by relations and potentials rather than the macropolitical determination of differences in position by kind and degree. This micropolitics of bodies resonates with the ethics (or

4. Michael Hardt and Antonio Negri, *Empire*, Cambridge: Harvard University Press, 2000.
5. Ibid, p. 62.

ethology) of Spinoza, subtracting the body's field of action from the humanist logic of self-interest, whereby political activity requires the identification of groups occupying visible social categories (e.g. class, race and gender).

Abstract sex instead offers a pragmatics of encounters, abductions and contagions between bodies, laying out a dynamics of sociability that emerges in situ rather than being determined by social positions. It entails a bodily participation in pulling out potential threads of mutation from actual conditions and distributing turbulent variations. Sex becomes an indeterminate quantum of thought and extension, proliferating through the contagious trading of matter, affecting – acting upon – the socio-cultural determination of identity positions.

This practice of intensifying bodily potentials to act and become is an affirmation of desire without lack which signals the non-climactic, aimless circulation of bodies in a symbiotic assemblage. This desire is not to be equated with something natural or given, spontaneous or induced. It is not primarily intentional. It has no final peak. It exists in symbiotic compositions giving rise to novel mutations. As a micropolitics, this continuous construction of non-climactic assemblages entails indeterminate fields of action in which each local activity modulates a global state. Very small interventions resonate unknowably across the plane. These assemblages of bodies are as biological and cultural as they are collective and political. It is the body that bears the potentials of action and mutation, and abstract sex mobilises them, spinning off new symbionts across the evolutionary logic of nature, economics and desire.

Post-Humanism = Post-Animality

Tim Savage

Vol 1 #29, Winter/Spring 2005

Donna Haraway's 100-page pamphlet, *The Companion Species Manifesto: Dogs, People, and Significant Otherness* (2003), deserves a central place at the table of a newly emerging conversation exploring 'the question of the animal'.[1] Yet, since what we know as 'the human' has always been defined against a seemingly endless taxonomy of putative others – be they 'dehumanised peoples', 'plants', inanimate 'objects' or 'animals' – what 'humanity' is conceptualised as finds itself fundamentally at stake with this question, too. Recent contributions to this topic include Giorgio Agamben's new book *The Open: Man and Animal* (2004), two recent anthologies entitled *Zoontologies: The Question of the Animal* and *Animal Rites: American Culture, the Discourse of Species, and Post-humanist Theory*, as well as a number of Jacques Derrida's recent musings. Deleuze and Guattari's earlier work about 'becoming-animal' finds pride of place at this human/animal/table interface, too.

Haraway opens the first pages of this new manifesto in characteristic fashion by immediately historicising her earlier work:

> I appropriated cyborgs to do feminist work in Reagan's Star Wars Times of the mid-1980s. By the end of the millennium, cyborgs could no longer do the work of a proper herding dog to gather up the threads needed for critical inquiry. So I go happily to the dogs to explore the birth of the kennel to help craft tools for science studies and feminist inquiry in the present time, when secondary Bushes threaten to replace the old growth of more liveable naturecultures in the carbon budget policies of all water-based life on earth.

She then proffers the 'Companion Species' as a heuristic figure to replace her earlier 'cyborg' and for the political tasks which lie so urgently at hand. 'Companion Species' are the hybrid beings co-constituted by humans and any other species that have symbiogenetically given birth to and co-evolved each other. Symbiogenesis, albeit reductively, refers to how various beings (i.e. bacteria, genes, larger organisms, etc.) can in fact only come into living existence through utter co-dependence on other quite different beings. Haraway asserts that particular populations of humans and dogs have, in fact, co-evolved each other throughout most of humanity's history, and that there can be no way in which humans can accurately understand not only what 'canines' are but what 'humans' are without accounting historiographically for this complex mongrel fact.

1. Donna Haraway, *The Companion Species Manifesto: Dogs, People, and Significant Otherness*, Chicago: Prickly Paradigm Press, 2003.

Thus, 'human' and 'canine' species are not ontologically distinct identities, and any narration of history which pretends that humans are the central historiographical agents is not only historically incorrect but also politically reactionary. In line with Theodor Adorno's proviso against all identity thinking after Auschwitz, Haraway asserts that 'relation' is the minimal unit of analysis and being. Here, then, the bourgeois borders of all 'individual identities' are smashed open, and even biology's conventional species taxonomies are no longer held to be sacrosanct.

This 'question of the animal' then also poses a huge problem for conventional humanist forms of historiography – or, how we tell historical stories. For Haraway, both the historical content and historical form known as 'Modernity' can mockingly be characterised as 'The Greatest Story Ever Told'. Nietzsche long ago observed that, with Modernity, God is declared dead and humans jettison themselves into his mythic historiographical position – that of magically possessing almost exclusive world-making powers and historiographical agency. Here, humans become 'subjects' and pretty much everything else is relegated to the role of 'objects' for instrumentalisation. Haraway's work is certainly far from unique in revealing the violent power relationships inherent in this humanist historiographical picture, and yet she is peculiar in the way in which she attempts to engender, decolonialise, queer and animalise it. This, she believes, will result in a telling of historical tales that are not only more historically accurate, but that will also constitute a better resource for our collective future.

The Companion Species explores the human-canine hybrid and symbiogenetic being in a non-systematic variety of different ways. Rigorously materialistic, Haraway opens the manifesto with a queasy admission that her dog's tongue has, upon occasion, caressed the back of her own throat. She speculates that viral vectors and non-filial genetic exchanges have actually made the two species up, in the flesh. The manifesto concludes with a scene of sexual voyeurism which, due to the anticipated sensitivities of *Mute* readers, I will not attempt to describe here.

In between, Haraway explores dog-human relationships. She critiques the dangerous fiction of unconditionally loving dogs, and relationships whereby humans treat dogs as furry surrogates for children. Haraway would prefer to have dogs than children, and, if she ever did give birth, she would prefer the offspring to be an alien. While, occasionally, a working relationship may grant specific canines a greater chance of surviving in this far from perfect world. The human-pet relationship is challenged as too difficult a feat for most animals to perform. Haraway also narrates her own dog-training experiences and glosses some of the theories surrounding appropriate human-canine relationships.

What the reader will not find in these pages, however, is any celebration of animal rights or any abstracted notion of equality alleged to exist between dogs and people. And, lest the reader expects a love story with soppy, romantic undertones, Haraway reminds us of dogs' historical role in the genocide of

Native Americans, in the maintenance of African-American slavery and in assisting US soldiers in carrying out war crimes in Vietnam. *The Companion Species* was written sometime before Abu Ghraib.

The manifesto also rewrites the history of two registered breeds of dogs – the Great Pyrenees and the Australian Shepherd. Yet Haraway knows the importance of the undocumented, be they human or canine, and so she also turns to the Satos (Puerto Rican street dogs whose presence in cyberspace facilitates their adoption into Northern US homes with all the attendant colonialist baggage such adoption practices customarily portend). Haraway's historicising resolutely shows that biological notions of 'pure breeds' are as fictitious as their racist counterparts in the human world. Everywhere, though, the question of who these various and quite different populations of non-human others are, what they might need and how we can enter into a more mutually beneficial relationship with them is foregrounded.

A few comments remain. I wonder what this new attempt at historiography would have turned into if the symbiogenetic figures chosen had been other than humans and dogs. A wide universe of complex relationship is figured, but the story is partially skewed toward these two initial, however complexly constituted, non-identitarian historiographical agents. Yet, in fairness, no one can escape partial, selective and biased accounts of history. Haraway always admits this, which is what her earlier essay, 'Situated Knowledges', is all about. However, perhaps with the inappropriate quibbling of the vegetarian, after reading her declaration that she fed her dog liver biscuits and that she ate hamburgers at Burger King, I found myself asking what this story would have looked like if it had been written from the vantage points of those deadened meaty beings. Is there not a truly subaltern form of historiography potentially creatable here? Specific dogs are creatures Haraway loves. I'm not sure that this in itself is a sufficient recipe for constructing the type of historiography that we so desperately need.

It may also be that conflictual relationships are overly sidelined, although being far from absent here. Haraway is rightly loathe to provide grist to the mill of the neoliberal social Darwinists who overpopulate this planet, but real history consists in huge amounts of conflict that are absolutely central to what we have all become. Telling new (her)stories wields the potential power to produce better worlds, but I am unconvinced that her text inhabits the historical violence that generates it well enough.

What if the existence of something akin to class difference, not just between humans but between humans and dogs and between different animals themselves, were figured into the story? Absurd to some perhaps, but as I write this review in a Manhattan where there are restaurants for pampered dogs, maybe not. It is not only issues of co-constitutive loving but issues of complex insurgency that I hope this emergent conversation about the 'question of the animal' will begin to consider in the times ahead.

Chapter 4

Of Commoners and Criminals

What do the themes of this chapter – the Great Enclosures of the 18th century, free/libre open source software, climate change, slavery and development – have to do with each other? You may well ask! The answer entails the ongoing battle to defend people's right to access the means of survival (the commons) from capitalism's ongoing looting of natural and human resources. This chapter draws a zigzag line between various historical eruptions of this battle, while tracing *Mute*'s shifting interest in the stakes of the commons as they are presently conceived and struggled for.

Mute's interest in the commons was initially piqued by the movement to preserve a 'public domain' during an era of aggressive intellectual property (IP) enforcement, provoked by the increased ease of digital copying. With the hardwiring of IP protection into the international trading system in 1994, by way of a piece of WTO-orchestrated legislation called Trade Related Aspects of International Property (TRIPS), the difficulty of enforcing IP rights across borders was substantially resolved. Dreams of a free culture, underpinned by the internet, in which information could be freely circulated and shared across borders and beyond the reach of the law, was seriously imperilled.

In Summer 2001, we first addressed this area in an issue entitled 'The Digital Commons', which contained an interview with Duke University law professor, James Boyle, who had recently helped to initiate a campaign to protect the public domain called Creative Commons (CC). Following the example of the GNU General Public Licence (written by Richard Stallman in 1989, and adopted by Linus Torvalds to protect the Linux operating system as a free resource in '92), Boyle, together with law professor and author Lawrence Lessig and other liberal lawyers, had developed a series of CC licences to protect creative production in general from the threat of enclosure. Copyleft turns copyright law inside out, inverting its power to enforce restrictions on use to defend the work *against* the *misuse* of restriction. Creative Commons licences, however, adulterate this pure concept of copyleft by reserving certain rights and adding caveats.

Ted Byfield's interview with James Boyle in *Mute* was one of the earliest pieces to expose CC's underlying free market politics. Boyle explains quite matter-of-factly how the intention of CC is to counteract IP's ability to 'mess [...] up processes of beneficial competition.' The commons, here, is understood as a necessary adjunct to the market, not as a proto-communist phase of development. However, Boyle's willingness to entertain the idea that the Great Enclosures saved lives and helped to build contemporary democracy, by freeing people from feudal ties and vastly increasing the productivity of the land, is not entirely divorced from Marx's own position. For Marx, the dissolution of the commons was an important step in the transition to capitalism (hence, ultimately, to communism, for which it serves as the precondition), by freeing people from subsistence production and allowing them to produce socially, i.e. as part of a totality of producers. But, Boyle's admission does put clear blue water between CC and the autonomist politics of another notorious commons enthusiast, Peter Linebaugh, who is also included in this chapter.

Paying no heed to the digerati's latter-day romance with the commons, social historian Linebaugh is interested here in the crisis of the enclosures of the 1720s, and their contravention of Magna Carta and the Charter of the Forest – medieval laws which had prevailed since the 13th century. These charters formed the basis of English law, not only by setting out the principles of justice, but also by defining 'subsistence commoning' – the use rights of the commons; rights that would be overturned as the medieval means of subsistence were swept away in the storm of finance capital known as the South Sea Bubble. As Linebaugh relates, new forms of financial liquidity in this period made possible the distributed investment of surplus value which had arisen largely from slaving. The 'capitalist commoning' of the slave trade was partly responsible for the increased pressure on other freely abundant resources; commoners were thrown off the land to enable the felling of trees for ship building and the supply of labour to the colonies. In the process, commoners were criminalised and racialised, described as 'Arabs' and 'banditti'; and so, argues Linebaugh, was born a common global and multi-racial struggle.

The notion that contemporary digital commoners are really indulging a 'post-materialist luxury limited to those on the sunny side of the digital divide' while having nothing in common with their historical namesakes, is addressed by Soenke Zehle in his article on free software and Africa. The availability of a free software resource is more than a lifestyle choice for the creative workers of the developed world. While acknowledging the strong arguments for the adoption of *pirated* proprietary software over Free/Libre Open Source Software (FLOSS), he also emphasises the barrier to development presented by IP for countries in Africa. Where the Asian Tigers in the Cold War period were able to 'disembed the technology from its capital base', by simply copying other people's ideas or reverse engineering, TRIPS has now kicked away this particular ladder to development. FLOSS, however, does offer some possibility for African countries to gain the IT base required to compete in the global economy. So, as Zehle is keen to point out, FLOSS should not necessarily be understood as an anti-capitalist philosophy, but as anti-monopolistic practice equally attractive to capitalists and states.

In this chapter's concluding article, on climate change, Will Barnes argues that, by confronting the Earth's natural resources as raw material, capitalism is destroying the very basis of life on which it so obviously depends. The 'tragedy of the commons' – the scenario in which freely given resources are destroyed by those who selfishly profit from them – appears, then, to be a better description of capitalism's appropriation of free inputs than ancient commoning, whose use rights are clearly defined and whose culture is one of life's sustenance. The danger with contemporary, digital varieties of commoning (especially those reliant on the logic of property) is that they end up sustaining the life of capitalists, often providing them with free inputs. Equally, it is impossible to envisage an anti-capitalist culture that can flourish in the absence of free and shared resources, resources that are needed to fight the continual erection of new enclosures.

Control_Shift_Commons

James Boyle Interviewed by Ted Byfield

Vol 1 #20, Summer 2001

Law as an Activist Framework

Ted Byfield: I have two general lines of enquiry. The first has to do with your ideas about ecology and the environment as an analogy for informatic politics, the second with your practice within the framework of US law, a field that many people view as itself a hegemonic threat. Does it offer the best overarching forms of analysis for what's going on?

James Boyle: Well, no claim there – it's not the best. Important battles are being fought through there, but, sadly, much of what we're doing is slowing down train wrecks. Still, the US legal framework has more resources than people give it credit for: it's a complicated, multifaceted, philosophical-political tradition with lots of abandoned pathways to be explored. But the best? That would be silly.

TB: Is that why you adopt, in some cases, an explicitly Marxist or Marxian analytical framework? It does come as a bit of a shock to see a US legal theorist doing that.

JB: Certainly, there are a lot of ideas from Marxist, neo-Marxist or post-structuralist work that are incredibly useful. How could anyone who thinks about social theory and property systems, or the relationship of ideology to social structure, not be influenced by these ideas? They're some of the richest traditions we have in social theory. And a lot of mainstream work is simply a version of Marxist or neo-Marxist ideas with normative indicators turned from plus to minus – or from minus to neutral!

TB: Well, I agree, as would lots of others. But isn't the role these sorts of ideas play within the practice of US law limited at best?

JB: Well, if I was working on an Amicus brief, I certainly wouldn't be citing the *Grundrisse* or *An Analysis of Alienated Labour*, so, yes, there are limitations on what kinds of political theory you can overtly bring into work directed towards a court. But American legal academia is surprisingly broad and open to a variety of viewpoints; if it has a problem, it's not one of simple exclusion but of omnivorousness – everything is grist for its mill.

As to American legal practice, there's the legal system in the sense that people outside of law think of it: rules, courts, expectations about how officials behave and so forth. But, even there, there are very explicit arguments which appeal to different visions of the ways that societies can malfunction: 'We need to worry about majorities tyrannising minorities', or 'No, we need to worry about powerful elites pursuing factional ideals', and so forth. These ideas form a large portion of American law, which tends to be much more explicitly policy-orientated and politically regarding than other common law systems. And people do fairly quickly appeal to them.

But I won't romanticise it; there are lots of ideas that don't get discussed, and, overall, it does tend to focus more on the dangers of rampant populist majorities than on the dangers of disenfranchised, alienated and passive majorities. It's not a completely open field.

TB: How has that field changed, in your experience?

JB: During the 1980s and 1990s there was a revival of a republican – with a small 'r' – tradition, which no longer spoke of a constitutional tradition devoted to a liberal image of a state envisioned simply as a neutral and transparent framework in which atomistic individuals pursue their own individual value preferences without any possible rational assessment. Rather, this other tradition holds that the goal is to build a well-functioning republic, which depends on democratically active citizens; and that, in turn, implies many other things – for example, state intervention to shape the media and responsibilities to fund education.

Now, that's a different rhetorical tradition to the democratic socialist tradition in Europe, although it shares themes with it: the belief that well-functioning citizens are not completely cut off from their economic circumstances, that the republic does not function very well with massive wealth disparities, that there are certain material requirements for things to work, and that the state sometimes needs to intervene to produce something which is affirmatively seen as good – in this case, a democracy-enhancing, participation-enhancing politics.

That's a theme, or a strand, in American law: you can see cases here, lines of thought there. When you make an argument, both academically and to a court, which plucks on those themes, it's not alien; you won't hear, 'What on earth are you talking about?!' It may not win the day, but it's not seen as completely beyond the pale. So my own view of law is that there's a lot of room for making arguments like that, even narrowly, to decision-makers – that is, to courts or legislatures – while always acknowledging the massive constraints there!

More broadly, though, legal ideas have so permeated political space in the United States. Often this is not a good thing. For example, the idea of viewing politics as 'rights' – there are real problems with this. But one works from where one is; and, in a political sphere which has been 'legalised', so to speak, legal arguments can have influence far beyond their actual domain of applicability.

As an example of that is you'll often hear people complain, 'That company can't tell me what to say when I work there because I have a First Amendment right!' Well, of course, you have no First Amendment right against a private actor. Nevertheless, the idea has floated free of its narrow legal incarnation and become a more general notion that speech ought not to be regulated by powerful entities – which is far from the actual legal rule.

TB: OK, so legal practice is very heterogeneous: legislatures that craft laws, various courts in different kinds of jurisdictions, and all manner of relations within a broadly based legal community. But isn't theoretical work influential only at the highest levels? How does one go about presenting a provocative idea – for example, 'ecology' or 'environmentalism' – as an analogue, or homologue, for the digitalisation of culture? Where does the rubber meet the road?

JB: At every level. It would be a huge mistake to concentrate one's energies merely on making clever arguments to Appeals Court judges or to court clerks. One of American liberalism's dead ends has been the notion that, if we just come up with a really great rights theory, all we have to do is convince five out of nine people in a building in Washington DC and we win automatically, we win 'everywhere'.

The Environment: A Powerful Parallel

JB: This is why I think the environmental movement is a good analogy. If you look at the kinds of ideas produced by the environmental movement, you'll find people arguing at quite high levels of discourse: discussing the extent to which ecology, or our understandings of ecology, shows how limited our ability is to map changes onto a physical system which rapidly becomes quite chaotic – and how this prevents us from predicting consequences very far down the road.

Say you start by clearing out a harbour, and it causes a parasite population to explode, which in turn destroys shellfish, which in turn undermines otters... fairly quickly, the whole thing spins out of control. Now, these are arguments made at one level, a very 'fancy' level, to people in the [US] Environmental Protection Agency. But the argument also functions on a very common sense level. People who are considering whether, for example, a new power plant should be constructed may say, 'Well, they claim such-and-such, but they don't really know, do they?' That's hardly an elitist argument.

One of the many things to learn from the environmental movement – not just the environment but the environmental movement – and one of the reasons I picked it as an analogy is that it didn't locate itself at any one level. But nor did it fantasise some set of powerful policy-makers and make highly idealised arguments to them in the belief that one day someone would read an article and translate it into state policy. Both of those approaches strike me as dead ends.

And, after all, there's a lot of stuff between those extremes: mid-level policy analysis, or purely technocratic economic arguments, to mention only two examples. I'm making the latter kind of argument for a reason, namely, that the economic discourse doesn't capture it all; you can point out that, even on its own terms, this makes no sense.

TB: What's a good example of an environmental idea that's undergone such a development?

JB: Take Pigouvian externalities – the notion that, unless you're forced to internalise the cost of your actions, you won't make optimal use of resources, and frequently will exploit them in ways that will despoil your environment. Sixty or 70 years later, we hear this on talk shows: somebody will say, 'Well, shouldn't gun manufacturers, or tobacco manufacturers, or producers of acid rain be forced to pay for the related costs? If they don't, they'll just get away with doing it for free!' Well, that's the Pigouvian idea brought to a level where it makes sense to many people. If you'd said in 1920 or 1930 that this idea, then being presented in a highly abstract economic argument, would one day be a sort of commonplace in popular culture, people would have said that was ridiculous.

However, it's not just a question of producing accessible versions of fancy ideas; there's movement both ways. Popular fights over Love Canal, over burning rivers and so forth, produce the policy discourse needed to articulate these ideas.

Environment and the Commons – Compatible Concepts?

TB: You've written about the commons on the one hand, and environmentalism on the other. Historically, these two ideas are quite distinct: they arose in different regions with dramatically different social and political conditions. Do you see any contradictions between the notion of an ecology and a commons?

JB: Contradictions? Well, one of the most exciting things about these analogies are the multiple parallels.

Take the enclosure movement and viewing our current circumstances as a kind of second enclosure movement. In both cases, private groups appeal to the state, saying, 'Help us to fence this off, and change the property rules to allow us to do it – only thus can we move to higher, more efficient forms of production'. So many dimensions of the enclosure movement have been written about: what it did in terms of social structure, of future politics, of concentrations of wealth, how it disrupted our relationship to the land, with attendant changes in meaning and semiotics. All these dimensions seem to be applicable to our current condition: questions about our relationship to our own genes, to cultural changes as culture becomes commodified...

Some contemporary economic historians have argued – and it's a very important point – that the enclosure movement saved lives and helped to build contemporary democracy by producing groups no longer tied in a feudal way to the land. And it did, by vastly improving the productive power of inefficiently run land systems. Now, this is the kind of claim being made by big pharma: private property saves lives. It's extremely important to take that argument seriously; what's more, it may actually be right in some cases. If one could grant a monopoly right to someone for 20 years on a drug which cures a disease affecting millions, there are worse things than having to pay through the nose for it – if, after 20 years, it will be available for pennies. It doesn't quite work that way, of course: we end up with more stuff for obesity and male pattern baldness than we do for sleeping sickness or malaria – and then the drugs get evergreened. But, still, we must at least take claims of this kind seriously.

We tend to think about the commons mainly in terms of the tragedy of the commons – the claim that it fosters inefficient resource use. That notion has driven a lot of remarkable environmental scholarship; but there's a counterweight of scholarship arguing that commons can run quite well. For example, Carol Rose at Yale has written a great article called 'The Comedy of the Commons', arguing that, in some cases, a commons may in fact be more efficient. However, that speaks only in efficiency terms; it leaves aside many other values. Another example is Elinor Ostrom, who has written about management of the commons, examining whether it's true that we must move to a neoliberal model in which everything is commodified. Neoliberals say that the problem is there aren't enough property rights, that we've only gone halfway, and that once we go all the way the market will clear. Ostrom and others like her have argued that it's not true that all commons are tragedies: they develop interesting, complicated mechanisms, both informal and formal, for governing themselves, and sometimes they work better than formalised, top-down control systems marked by a single controller of the resource in question.

Now, Ostrom isn't writing about the free software movement; she's writing about the management of traditional water systems, air rights and so forth. But it's a very interesting notion that, in the free software movement, we effectively have a management of a kind of commons. Clearly, it has lots of rules: some are legal – the GPL [General Public Licence] – some purely contractual, some are customary, like prestige or shame-based economies.

So, to return your question, if there is a line between the enclosure movement and the commons and the fights of the 14th century through the 19th century on the one hand, and the environmental movement on the other, it's not a straight line.

The story of the enclosure movement is retold by economists as the story of the tragedy of the commons, and the tragedy of the commons, in turn, is at the heart of many environmental problems that have produced all kinds of possible solutions.

TB: So it sounds as though 'importing' ideas – the commons – into American law as 'alien objects' is a fairly powerful way of generalising US law. At the same time, though, that kind of generalisation is happening anyway for other reasons: say, absurd situations in which the proverbial Inner Mongolia is concerned about 'First Amendment rights' because ideas like that have become so predominant on the net.

JB: Oh, and in other ways, too. There's been some remarkable historical research that breaks these ideas down inside the United States, as well. For example, Betty Mensch at the State University of New York at Buffalo has written about colonial property regimes in New York. As it turns out, the colonists assumed that we all own the land, and they divided it into private parcels; but, contrary to what we may have thought, when new arrivals came, it was re-subdivided to account for the new arrivals, lest they be excluded. So, as is always true, when you step up the power of the microscope, apparently homogeneous things aren't so homogeneous.

Another example – with a very different normative valence – is the open range, and the fights between ranchers and farmers. There are a few different notions at work here: one holds that the land is infinite, so it doesn't matter how big a claim someone stakes; the other is that it's not owned by anyone. Each reflects a different kind of romanticism. And these romanticisms aren't the same as that associated with the lovely commons, where we all play around the maypole – though it does have similar features. So, it's certainly good to import ideas in order to shake things up a bit, but you also need to look closely at indigenous traditions.

Out of Control or Too Much Control?

TB: These constellations of issues are largely drawn (or forced) together by 'technology', or at least by theories of technological determinism, which are very hard to evaluate. Several years ago, there was a spate of books about how things are 'out of control' – Kevin Kelly, Manuel DeLanda and so on – which presented the condition as extremely fruitful and creative; but now we seem to be more retrospective, or at least willing to consider whether it's a dangerous condition instead. In part, these evaluations are defined by how we periodise our circumstances. When and how does one 'stop' a system in order to assess its dominant dynamics? And don't those initial choices determine the outcome of one's analysis?

JB: Well, funnily enough, at least half of the libertarian-anarchist types I'm aware of – Kevin Kelly, the Cato Institute, the Progress and Freedom Foundation and so forth – totally agree with my work. In their view, a wonderfully chaotic, spontaneous, decentralised system was forming until the state came along and mucked things up by imposing regulations like copyright, patent, etc. These, in their view, were just the same old things the state's been doing badly – massive rents being handed over to moneyed interests – messing up processes of beneficial competition. Yet we gave these expansive property rights, along with many others – for example, to polluters – without forcing them to pay for the costs of their pollution. This could be seen as the result of control rather than the result of lack of control. It's up for grabs whether things like copyright and intellectual property are seen as sacred property, as the foundation for a spontaneously operating decentralised market or, rather, whether the danger is that the absence of any regulation tends to push things out of control.

TB: So, perhaps the question of periodisation as such has become a battleground and we've ended up in a systemic situation where there's no consensus about 'when' we are.

JB: If so, I see that as a good thing. A lot of the bad things going on now rely on triumphalist neoliberalism, with its beliefs that we're at the end of history, that market democracy has won, and so forth. It irritates me immensely that not only do a lot of people accept this story blindly but that they haven't even looked back to the extremely good arguments made about market triumphalism the first time it appeared: the response to the Gilded Age, the contributions of welfare economics and so forth. These responses still make a lot of sense; it's amazing how they've dropped out of popular consciousness. Part of my work, then, is simply a rediscovery of the work of people like the legal realists and the institutional economists of the 1930s.

It's easy to see doom and gloom in intellectual property and the march of commodification; there are certainly lots of negative things going on, and yet there's also an amazing openness in these debates. People are actually asking if it's better to have property or not. And 17-year-olds are saying, 'No, you probably end up with better stuff in the absence of property rights' – and not because they've been reading Kropotkin. They've been reading Richard Stallman or Linus Torvalds. That's important, and not because free software is important, although it is; rather, it suggests that there isn't any inexorable historical logic to this particular moment – and that our particular ideas about property are very much up for grabs. The internet, the Ensemble Project, the Human Genome Project may represent a story in which we end up better off with less centralised control, one in which strong property rights might actually be bad.

TB: These shifts sound as though they'll present some serious predicaments for the left or political liberals, or progressives, or whatever one wants to call them.

JB: Well, it's pushing the left if not exactly toward a libertarian position then toward a position which is more sceptical of these technologies of control, whether imposed by governments or by private parties. How often do you find yourself agreeing with libertarian ideas? I find myself agreeing with libertarians more often in terms of the net than in terms of other communications media. And why is that? It could be that I've been completely taken over by the power of the discourse – in fact, that probably is part of it. But another reason is that arguments about regulation often take the form of a normative, conceptually driven, slippery slope argument: 'If we start by doing this, then that will inevitably lead to doing other things.' Technology doesn't change everything in the way the techno-fantasists believe it does, but Larry Lessig's work is absolutely right with regard to the net and the universalising power of code. With the internet, the slippery slope isn't so much a normative slippery slope anymore: A is conceptually like B, so if you do it to A you must do it to B.

Rather, it's a technical slippery slope. The technology that would give us the power to enforce, for example, municipal ordinances related to what some regard as 'pornography' would also allow the Taliban to filter extremely effectively for women's education. And that tends to make you wonder if the game's worth the candle.

However, we also need to ask what this does to traditional libertarianism. Libertarians argue, 'Well, we'll hand over to you an absolute property right, and whatever you want to do within that property right is your thing and we can't interfere'. But intellectual property rights are the problem case for that view because they make it very clear that these rights are not 'natural' and that they have powerful impacts on what others can do – in all kinds of contentious ways. And there are no clear lines demarcating harm.

TB: How else is this affecting the political landscape?

JB: Well, for example, through most of the 1980s and 1990s, I agreed that the US Federal Communications Commission (FCC) should be able to exercise some pathetic little fragment of control over broadcasting in the United States – to impose, for example, requirements that some kind of non-commercial children's television should be available. Their justification, both practical and constitutional, was that broadcast was based on scarcity: spectra are scarce, and they have to be allocated on the basis of scarcity. But with new techniques like frequency-hopping, that argument becomes problematic: What scarcity are we talking about?

Yochai Benkler has pointed out that now liberals and conservatives are both lining up to support privatising and propertising – selling, not just issuing temporary licences for the airwaves – liberals because they like the prospect of the government getting the money, conservatives because they like the idea of everything being turned into private property. The FCC agrees that they can sell it off, but they still maintain their belief in scarcity and insist on acting as the boundary police. Well, should we support that, or should we instead acknowledge all the new possibilities for building something like the internet in the wireless spectrum? Such a system would probably include smart terminals acting as senders and receivers, using packet switching and allocating spectrum dynamically. In effect, we'd all have our own little radio station: no one entity would have 93.5 on the radio dial.

Now, that's going to lead to a lot of Rush Limbaughs. But is this a vision which might lead us to say we need less control? Or should we maintain the last pathetic gasp of a role for the interventionist state in seeking to regulate this allegedly scarce resource? Now, suddenly we're sounding rather libertarian, which is not the position that the left has always taken. It's not that the state has no role; the state has a very important role – but it's a different role than it had in the static, finite-spectrum, one-to-many communications. These questions pose challenges to the ideologies of both left and right. I have no easy answer, but we cannot just go on finding arguments to support the positions we took last year.

Goatherds in Pinstripes

Gregor Claude

Vol 1 #23, Spring 2002

Digitopia seems to have died. A couple of years ago, received wisdom had it that the internet was a new realm of freedom, unbound by the regulations and restrictions that controlled life offline. The internet seemed to exist in the absence of law, outside of any particular state's jurisdiction. It was as if law had been transcended through information technology. But, more recently, we have seen a string of copyright-related lawsuits, legal intimidation and legislation. Napster was shut down by a judge and then bought by one of the plaintiffs; Princeton computer science academic, Edward Felten, was threatened with legal action by the Recording Industry Association of America if he published his research into encryption; Russian programmer, Dmitri Sklyarov, was arrested under the US Digital Millennium Copyright Act because he wrote software allowing people to read Adobe Software's encrypted version of *Alice in Wonderland*, a text already in the public domain and legally available for free. These events have made it abundantly clear that the law had been there all along.

The latest project to come out of Washington, that legislative workshop of the world, is the Security Systems Standards and Certification Act (SSSCA), a proposed bill that would mandate built-in hardware copy-control protection in all new PCs and consumer digital media devices, from your walkman to your computer. According to *Wired*, which has obtained a draft of the SSSCA, the law would create new federal felonies, punishable by five years in prison and fines of up to $500,000, for 'anyone who distributes copyrighted material with "security measures" disabled or has a network-attached server configured to disable copy protection'. It would be illegal to create, sell or distribute any device capable of 'storing, retrieving, processing, performing, transmitting, receiving or copying information in digital form' unless it contained certified copy protection technology. Hang on to your old computer because it just might be more functional than next year's model.

The law was drafted in close consultation with none other than global culture industry giant, the Walt Disney Corporation. Disney's Executive Vice President, Preston Padden, claimed that the law was an 'exceedingly moderate and reasonable approach'. Padden's idea of moderate and reasonable is chilling; at an event in December 2001, he dismissed criticism of the SSSCA, saying 'There is no right to fair use. Fair use is a defence against infringement'. In copyright law, fair use means the right to use copyright material, regardless of the wishes or intentions of the copyright owner. This means that when you buy a book, you can quote it elsewhere, criticise it or cut it into bits and make a work of art out of it if you are that way inclined. For Disney's Padden, the fair use provisions of copyright law amount to an unfair tax on the copyright holder, as if public access to copyrighted knowledge or culture is some kind of pinko perversion. It's as if montage was a criminal act. Next time you feel that cut and paste urge coming on, make sure you look over your shoulder and check if Big Mickey is watching you.

When this is what passes for reasonable in Washington and beyond, it comes as no surprise that the nucleus of an attempt to counter this copy protectionism is emerging. Increasingly, arguments against stronger intellectual property rights deploy the concept of the 'digital commons' (*Mute*, Vol 1 #20). November 2001 saw two key moments in this emergence. The first was the release of Lawrence Lessig's *The Future of Ideas: The Fate of the Commons in a Connected World.* Following on from his 1999 book, *Code and Other Laws of Cyberspace*, Lessig's new book reads like a manifesto; it doesn't pretend to hide its goal of doing for the digital commons what Rachel Carson's *Silent Spring* did for the natural environment in the 1960s. The second key moment, the Conference on the Public Domain held at Duke University, was co-organised by the Center for the Public Domain and Duke's James Boyle. The conference brought together the leading figures of the digital commons debate, focussing on Boyle's keynote paper, 'The Second Enclosure Movement and the Construction of the Public Domain'.

These two events bring into sharp focus the critique of intellectual property and defence of the public domain, or commons, and could come to be seen as the founding moments of an important new campaign. Whatever their future, they have set the tone, established the language and introduced the concepts of a challenge to the privatisation of culture online. Yet, both Lessig's and Boyle's approaches have significant weaknesses. But, before discussing where they're coming from, what are they talking about?

The Commons: From Goatherds to Server Farms

So, what is the digital commons? First, an important clarification: we are not talking about commons as in the Parliamentary House of Commons, but commons as in the village commons, a resource held in common. Even without peculiarly British confusions, Boyle acknowledges that the commons can be a 'distressingly messy' concept, subject to many different interpretations. Here is Lessig's description:

> It is commonplace to think about the Internet as a kind of commons. It is less commonplace to actually have an idea what a commons is. By a commons I mean a resource that is free. Not necessarily zero cost, but if there is a cost, it is a neutrally imposed, or equally imposed cost. [...] No permission is necessary; no authorisation may be required. These are commons because they are within the reach of members of the relevant community without the permission of anyone else. [...] The point is not that no control is present; but rather that the kind of control is different from the control we grant to property.

Lessig goes on to give examples of commons: Central Park, public streets, Fermat's last theorem, Linux source code. These resources exist outside the normal rules of property. It's not that commons are the opposite of property, but they lack property's key feature: the *exclusive* right to use or access the object owned.

In a world based on the production, circulation and exchange of privately owned commodities, the commons have always proven a bit of a headache for mainstream economists. Today's discussion of the commons is informed by an influential paper, published in *Science* in 1968 by Garrett Hardin, called 'The Tragedy of the Commons'. In it, Hardin argues that resources held in common are doomed to inefficient misuse. 'Picture a pasture open to all,' begins Hardin. As the story goes, each herdsman will try to keep as many cattle as possible on the commons. Adding one more animal to his herd imposes a shared cost (goats gotta eat) on all the herdsmen, but the gain of the one extra animal belongs exclusively to its owner. Alas, all the herdsmen come to the same conclusion. As Hardin continues with the literary flair of a modern Ezekiel, 'Each man is locked into a system that compels him to increase his herd without limit – in a world that is limited. Ruin is the destination toward which all men rush, each pursuing his own best interest in a society that believes in the freedom of the commons. Freedom in a commons brings ruin to all.'

Now, you might think this is a misanthropic and ahistorical Malthusian argument for restraint whose assumption that ancient goatherds can stand in for the modern, rational individual acting as a self-maximising subject could be dispelled by a look at some elementary anthropology, but never mind that now because the essay has been hugely influential in both the environmental movement and in economics. It is important here because it sheds light on why the digital commons is different.

Lessig spends the first hundred pages of his book detailing the 'building blocks' of the digital commons, providing an exhaustive account of why and how the internet functions as a commons. If you don't know how the internet works and want to find out, start here. This is a fascinating tour of what makes the net a unique medium that will, in places, leave you awestruck at the untapped potential of this technology, and even more awestruck at the genius of the scientists and engineers who put it together. If you know this already, prepare to skim read. But, for Lessig, the main point of going through this technological detail is to demonstrate how the physical network of the internet, as well as the open source software it runs on, is a common resource that all can access without discrimination.

This is not to say that everything on the net is free and uncontrolled. Servers and cables and so on are always owned by some entity; access to many files is restricted. Of course there are private roads, Lessig would argue, but the road network is still a common resource. Or, take another example: the routers that send data packets across the internet don't discriminate based on the content of the data packet; they treat all packets equally. This is a 'dumb' or 'end to end' network; all data processing takes place at the network nodes rather than in the network. It would be conceivable to run a more centralised network, in which, for example, different data types would be routed according to different priorities. But with the internet today, all the network does is transmit data; it is a *neutral* network and, so, while the routers are not your property, you use them as a common resource when you connect to the network.

So, the internet is a commons, but how can it escape the fate of Hardin's greedy goatherds? The internet is what economists call a 'nonrivalrous resource'. You can have your cake, eat it and distribute a round for all your friends at the same time; a nonrivalrous resource is undepletable. Digital media on the internet is in a permanent glut; this is an economy not of scarcity but superfluity. Bottlenecks might occur in bandwidth or storage space, but not in content.

There is one final aspect to the digital commons, and one that provides the strongest argument in favour of maintaining the internet as a commons. As Lessig puts it, 'all the stuff protected by copyright law [...] depends fundamentally upon a rich and diverse public domain. Free content, in other words, is crucial to building and supporting new content'. The case can be made even more strongly: the raw material of culture is culture. Creativity always appropriates the results of past creativity. New culture continually re-purposes already existing culture, making it into something new. Digital media, in addition to allowing more perfect control, also allows more perfect appropriation.

This capacity for appropriation opens up new possibilities for culture. It also points to the internet as more than just a nonrivalrous common resource, but as a resource that actually *increases* in both quality and quantity the more it is used. The ability to exploit, repurpose, consume and appropriate digital content as a commons creates a virtuous cycle, acting as a cultural accelerator.

The Chicago School and the Case for Maximum IP Control

Disney's Padden and the SSSCA also use the language of innovation. But instead of seeing the locus of innovation at the level of a dispersed network, drawing on and contributing to a common digital resource, they see large culture corporations as the incubators of creativity. For them, tight copy protection is necessary to allow these creative corporations to flourish.

This view is informed by 'Chicago School' economics, the tradition of free market economics associated with Milton Friedman and others that emerged in the 1960s, shaped the Reagan-Thatcher years and remains influential today. For the Chicago School, resources are always more efficiently used when distributed by the market. The legal wing of the Chicago School, initiated by judge and scholar Richard Posner, is known as the 'law and economics' approach and is today the most widely accepted doctrine among the US Judiciary. For law and economics, law is seen not as an instrument of justice or of social order, but, above all, as a tool to help markets run smoothly and to promote social wealth. Accordingly, all social phenomena could be understood as the result of rational choices based on costs and benefits, and law was no different. Ascendant in the 1970s and effectively institutionalised under Reagan in the 1980s, law and economics transformed the application of anti-trust law. What was once a populist measure to check the power of big business became a means of smoothing the path for US corporations.

Preston Padden really does think that his approach and that of the SSSCA is 'exceedingly moderate and reasonable'. From their point of view, the internet is an enormous risk. For 'content companies' like Disney, it is imperative to maintain exclusive control over their copyright material. They look at the internet and see an unstable and uncertain market they cannot trust. They cannot guarantee the integrity of their goods. The cost of this uncertainty, and of any potential losses, must be taken into account, and the consequence (which threatens Disney) is that they will not be able to support the same levels of investment in developing new content.

From this perspective, the internet has created an imbalance in the market, and legislation is needed to restore market equilibrium. If the cost of copying has plummeted, then the strength of copy control should be increased in equal and opposite measure. The justification for this control is the free market assumptions of law and economics (though Judge Posner, infamous as a contrarian, has argued against such a conclusion). The logic of control today is not alien to the market but rather emerges from it.

Lessig, the Free Market and the Internet Anomaly

It seems peculiar, at first, that there are so many similarities between this argument and Lessig's. As it turns out, he is something of a Chicago School prodigal son: Lessig was Posner's clerk from 1989 to 1990. Though they evidently have plenty of disagreements, Lessig has conceded Posner's influence: 'We are all law-and-economists now'.

Lessig's free market proclivities periodically pop up through his book like awkward, spotty teenagers. 'Though most distinguish innovation from creativity,' he writes, 'or creativity from commerce, I do not.' And there I was thinking that always casting culture and experimentation in terms of commerce was part of the problem. In a later example of failing to distinguish between markets and innovation, he writes, 'coders learn what free markets have taught since Smith called them free: that innovation is best when ideas flow freely'.

So how does Lessig square his passion for the market with the digital commons? In one of his important differences from the traditional Chicago School, he is strongly anti-monopoly. Lessig echoes the concerns articulated by free market theory of the late-1980s and early-'90s. At that time, fashionable economic theory sought to re-emphasise the role of the entrepreneur in contrast to the situation J.K. Galbraith had described in *The New Industrial State*. Galbraith's analysis of the post-war 'industrial system' sketched a bureaucracy in which businesses, governments and unions had all ceded control to a quasi-autonomous technostructure resistant to nearly all attempts to alter it. After the first wave of the Chicago School sought to deregulate corporations and cut them loose from this technostructure, later Chicagoans became frustrated with the notion that businessmen were paralysed by structure and fell on the idea of celebrating the innovation of the entrepreneur. Lessig echoes this repeatedly in discussions on the role of the digital commons in 'lowering the barriers to entry' into a market. It is as if he aspires to an internet agora in which intellectual and cultural producers are not held down at the neck by giant copyright corporations, but are, rather, cultural entrepreneurs or knowledge entrepreneurs who enter the marketplace of ideas or the marketplace of culture, whose barriers to entry are minimised by state regulation.

But most importantly for Lessig, the internet is the great exception to market rule. He writes:

> to the extent a resource is physical – to the extent it is rivalrous – then organising that resource within a system of control makes good sense. This is the nature of real-space economics; it explains our deep intuition that shifting more to the market always makes sense. And following this practice for real-space resources has produced the extraordinary progress that modern economic society has realised [...] But perfect control is not necessary in the world of ideas. Nor is it wise.

He continues, 'The digital world is closer to the world of ideas than to the world of things'. In the end, then, the digital commons is a technical issue: it is only because digital media frees information from the 'real world' printed page that it becomes inefficient to organise ideas as tightly controlled property like books.

Of course, it's not that this diminishes Lessig's campaign particularly, but it certainly gives us a better idea of what it is about. It is striking that, underneath it all, Lessig's digital commons is nothing more than a well functioning market. If the right laws are passed and the right code implemented, a harmonious free market will deliver innovation. At a time of severe 'market creep', when market relations persistently encroach upon life, the case for its extension through cyberspace is less than convincing.

Boyle's Rhetorical Lobby

James Boyle is less hung up on the market; he is more likely to talk about market failure than about market efficiency. He comes from the 'critical legal theory' tradition, drawing on postmodernists like Michel Foucault and Stanley Fish to understand law as a 'discourse of power'. But, for all Boyle's postmodernist references, his approach is much more like the traditional single-issue lobby with which Washington knows how to work.

His reference point and role model is the environmental movement. As he describes it, it is a loose coalition of groups and interests. Their aims, strategies and tactics diverge, but they share a unifying concept of 'the environment'. It is a concept that is, in many ways, a fiction, notes Boyle, but it is a rhetorical strategy that alone can bring a large group of varied interests under one umbrella. Accordingly, the campaign for the digital commons, for Boyle, begins with its rhetorical invention: 'the language of the public domain will be used to counter the language of sacred property.'

But the problem with the linguistic approach of the postmodernists that Boyle adopts is particularly stark when applied to the idea of a public domain. Can a public domain, or common resource, really be built on nothing more than a structure of belief and a rhetorical strategy? Conspicuously absent from this proposal is… the public. Public spaces, whether real or digital, are so easily enclosed, or privatised, because the public claim on them is so weak. The privatisation of public life began as a political process long before the internet hit the shelves, and it is no surprise that this privatisation is reflected online. A linguistic postmodernism, which reads all the world as text, enables a rewriting of the problem of a diminished public, and political, sphere rather than addressing the problem and attempting to resolve it. For Lessig, the digital commons can exist because it is a technological anomaly not subject to market organisation. This allows him to ignore the thorny issue of the public. The danger is that Boyle's linguistic first step may, in the end, be just as empty as Lessig's technological one.

The environmental impulse could too easily echo the problem by creating a coalition to provide an interface between government and a minority lobby, perhaps with a broad base of passive, public moral and financial support. The politics of the environment is too often that of self-appointed guardians of a resource that the general public and big business combine in ignorance and avarice to despoil and pollute. Again, this is a model dangerously conducive to building on public passivity rather than challenging it.

Boyle's use of environmentalism reflects the limits of political possibility that exist today. Recognising the need for an information politics, he takes a prefabricated contemporary political form and seeks to pour information politics into it. But to have real substance, the public domain can't do without the public.

Information Politics – Information for What?

The digital commons debate opens up a field of possibilities, my criticism notwithstanding. Boyle and Lessig are two of the great pioneers of that opening.

Many others have now begun to think about how these issues can be used politically. Most ambitiously perhaps, Michael Hardt of *Empire* notoriety, has recently been working on intellectual property and other forms of what he calls 'immaterial property', arguing that they present the opportunity for making a new communist case against private property as a whole.

Whether or not any of this work leads anywhere, there is still an important unanswered question that the issue of information control runs up against: information for what? Why should anyone care who controls knowledge if there is no perception of a particular need for it? Programmers need the software source codes that the free software movement is fighting to make freely available because they are the tools of their trade. People get upset about the file-sharing issue, exemplified by the Napster case, because the lawsuits and legislation pushed by industry lobbies are a barrier to the steady, cheap flow of their cultural consumption. The concern for control over biotech patents is rooted in either a precautionary fear of the possibilities of science, or, from a different angle, a concern with the supply of medicine to, and the exploitation of, 'underdeveloped' countries. These are issues of concern, but nevertheless are a narrow focus. The missing question is: Knowledge for what?

Commercial Commons

Researchers at the Economic Observatory of the University of Openess

Metamute.org, November 2004

The Creative Commons (CC) licences have become a kind of default orthodoxy in non-commercial licensing. Every unpunctuated half-sentence spilled into a weblog, every petulant rant published by 'Free Culture' pundits, every square millimetre of Lawrence Lessig's abundant intellectual property is immediately and righteously staked out as part of the great wealth of man's Creative Commons.

First off, this proposal still holds the basic assumption that everything I make and say is property which in most areas of 'creative' work is both ridiculous and reactionary, as well as generally objectionable. The logic that more politically aware CC pundits use, that you can't ignore the reality of the market and you have to use copyright to fight copyright, is fine in theory, but makes the assumption that every maker and sayer has equal recourse to legal process. Putting aside, for a moment, this little problem of economic and legal inequality, I am still suspicious of anything advocated strongly by clever, sleek, young lawyers. Are they really 'streamlining' the legal process, cutting out the armies of jabbering middlemen in their patronising promotional movie? Or, are they waxing lyrical about a supposed 'commons' while making the convoluted mess of intellectual property ownership even more complex and impossible for lay people to negotiate? Imagine the process of making a new work with copyleft material: Hmm... let me see, I can reproduce this part of that lyric, but I have to credit it, and this bassline allows me to sell the piece, but means my tune has to have the same share-alike-non-commercial licence on the whole track, and using this guitar riff means I have to make sure anyone who uses my tune abides by the Geneva Convention on Human Rights.

Yes, some of these 'pick and choose' licences even have such moralistic overtones. The 'Common Good' public licence insists that anything licensed by it must not be used in a way that contravenes the Geneva Convention. Everyone is in favour of the Geneva Convention, but this is so unimplementable as to be purely symbolic. Although the prospect of AC/DC suing the US military for blasting 'insurgents' in Fallujah with 'Hell's Bells' is appealing, there are many far more effective ways, both symbolic and material, to contribute to human rights causes. If I want other people to use my work and have already made the conceptual leap of contributing to a public domain, why would I want to impose arbitrary, untested restrictions on them? I certainly don't want their arbitrary restrictions imposed on me.

The public domain is about non-ownership, not more accurate descriptions and granularity of ownership. Licensing structures like the Creative Commons help copyright owners and their lawyer lackeys catch up with today's faster moving, smaller-scale and more intricate network of information exchange between 'prosumers' not by 'freeing' it but by describing it as intellectual property more efficiently.

The clue as to whose interest is served by that efficiency is in the cringe-makingly patronising spiel about 'human readable', 'lawyer readable' and 'machine readable' licences. The solution to incomprehensible legalese is not to say, 'Oh, you poor little human, you shouldn't have to take responsibility for your own labour, let us take care of that'. The solution is to reform arcane legal language and customs so that everyone can understand them. If half the Creative Commons licence-using bloggers donated half the money and time they spend on trendy haircuts to initiatives such as the Plain English Campaign, the 'lawyer readable' section could be obsolete within a year.

And the machine readable part? I can already see the software these shysters are going to build. You'll no longer need to call your lawyer when someone plagiarises you (or weaponises your music). There will be automated systems that will discover licensing inconsistencies, call the appropriate lawyers who (as part of the Creative Commons service) will simply bill your credit card for their micro-legal fee and credit your account with an out-of-court micro-settlement. You might find out about the whole ordeal when checking your credit card bills at the end of the month, wondering why you're getting poorer and poorer while the solicitor next door has just installed a jacuzzi in his back garden.

There are some fights worth fighting – like the fight for someone to be able to make something that does not become intellectual property by default, the fight for an accessible and fair legal system and the fight for someone's right to make a living from their work without having to sue anyone. That is what copyright is for. It works; it has been tried and tested in the courts for hundreds of years. The enemies in this fight are the greedy, powerful people and corporations that have bullied copyright law into an absurdity, and will continue to abuse any other system that anyone comes up with until we make them stop existing.

Discussion Among University of Openess Wiki Users

To a point interesting but I think you have a fundamental misunderstanding of copyright law and the aim of Creative Commons licences (I am one of those lawyers).

CC aims to make explicit what pre-existing rights the author (well OK… not *just* authors, but it's a shortcut word) has chosen to waive, in a way that is easily accessible and understandable. The 'machine readable' part is simply trying to make those waivers explicit to search engines in order to increase the accessibility of work under the CC licence. It's more about making life easier for people who might want to use Anita's work (cartoon above, which, of course, you wouldn't have been able to use without the waiving of rights) than about making life easy for Anita. There are of course people who take issue with copyright law, but that's not a reason to generalise the complaint to a licensing system designed to address some of the problems that result from the law.

Some thoughts:

- CC is not about tying up creative work in legal jargon. It doesn't introduce arbitrary restrictions – it can only introduce conditions to the relaxing of rights which already exist.
- You are *more* free to use a CC licensed work than if no such licence was used.
- The author does not have to use a CC licence, but they have every right to choose to.
- You do not have to use CC licensed work, but you are bound by copyright law.
- The average author may not have the knowledge to structure their own licence from scratch and might well not want to waste their time doing so. Like it or not, 'lawyer readable licences' are what courts look at.
- Even if authors did have the knowledge and inclination, the likely result would be a mess of different licences, each with its own separate conditions. That would be less accessible to you than the CC standardised forms.

I'm *very* surprised to see a rant against CC here [on the Wiki of the University of Openess]. I'd actually been thinking of pointing out the related Science Commons project as something Uo might be interested in looking into.

Some responses:

> I'm *very* surprised to see a rant against CC here.

I would just like to point to the UoClaimer [http://twenteenthcentury.com/uo/index.php/UoClaimer] here. I'm sure many in the Uo are very interested in pursuing Creative Commons and Science Commons approaches.

I fully understand the rhetoric surrounding the Creative Commons; it does what it says on the tin. Having heard the arguments, I am not convinced. Like many liberal reformist movements, the 'good' intentions of the Creative Commons are easily hijacked by the people who are currently exploiting existing copyright law and the original 'good' intentions for that. As soon as the dinosaur copyright holders and collecting organisations wise up to the world of micro-payments and infinitesimally divisible rights and waivers, the bureaucracy and compensation situation of compound licensed works will become far more Byzantine than it already is.

> It doesn't introduce arbitrary restrictions – it can only introduce conditions to the relaxing of rights which already exist.

That may be true of the Creative Commons, but other attempts to map very successful free software licences onto non-technical fields have often decided to impose arbitrary and sometimes absurd restrictions. Actually, I think you may be wrong about this anyway. Surely the 'share-alike' insistence that derivative works be licensed under the same agreement can be seen as an arbitrary restriction.

> You are *more* free to use a CC licensed work than if no such licence was used.

But less free than if the work is in the public domain. If you want to play, contribute to the public domain. If you want to reserve your rights, do. Also, If I buy the right to use your work using existing copyright law, I can use it for anything I want and adopt whatever licence I like for my derivative work. In this sense, freedom, as in 'libre', for my derivative work is more attainable under default copyright law than if you impose a perpetual Creative Commons licence, it just costs me some money. If you use a Creative Commons licence, I can't use your 'non-commercial-share-alike' component for my commercial venture at all, ever, even if I want to buy that right.

> Like it or not, 'lawyer readable licences' are what courts look at.

Then concentrate efforts on cleaning out the legal language, reform the *application* of copyright law and the legal processes in general – which most people are currently too scared to get involved with unless under duress.

Lazy orthodoxy and co-opted reform is what's under attack here, and you haven't answered the meat of the questions raised. The implicit proposal of this attack on the CC is:

- Concentrate efforts on reforming abuse of existing tested systems.
- Concentrate on making existing processes and infrastructures accessible to everyone.
- Concentrate on expanding the public domain through education and campaign against default copyright.

In my opinion the CC hype is just a distraction from these older, harder and more important battles.

> In my opinion the CC hype is just a distraction from these older, harder and more important battles.

I think you both make good points, but would the logic of the above argument mean that Stallman should not have bothered with the GPL? Also, I thought the CC approach was in part a response to the IP gold rush rather than its cause.

> Also, I thought the CC approach was in part a response to the IP gold rush rather than its cause.

I'm certainly not arguing that CC is the cause, but that its motivations and parameters do not depart from the market logic that results in abuse of IP law.

> Would the logic of the above argument mean that Stallman should not have bothered with the GPL?

There is a distinction to be made between the GPL and the CC. The GPL was just good engineering methodology for years before Eric Raymond and others evangelised Free Software into venture-capital friendly 'Open Source'. The CC and the GPL are nothing more than efficient methods of regulating property and labour in an information economy. There's nothing wrong with that, but using the word 'commons', and associating this engineering/labour methodology with a pre-enclosure, J.S. Mill-esque political 'freedom' is misleading. The GPL may have been evangelised, but at least it is honest about what it is: 'a licence'. The whole 'commons' crowd – Bollier, Lessig et al. – scare me because they do not wear their colours as clearly as the Free Software people, whose radical libertarian politics are very openly progressive one minute, and openly disturbing (see Eric S. Raymond's Gun Nut page) the next.

Eric S. Raymond is not among the Free Software people. He's an Open Source guy.

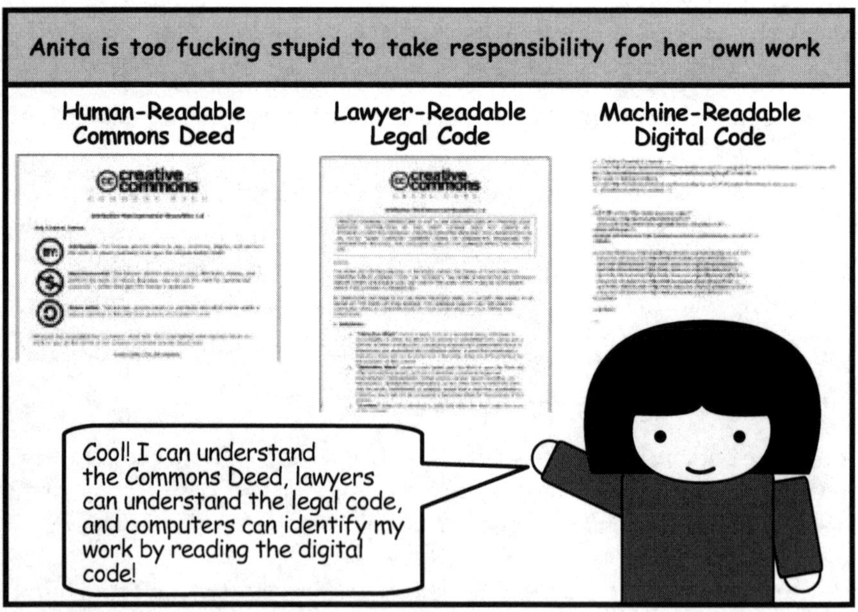

Original cartoon concept and design for above illustration by Neeru Paharia, original illustration by Ryan Junell, photos by Matt Haughey, licensed under Creative Commons

CopyCan and CopyCan't

The first point about unequal recourse to litigation makes the rest of this discussion a moot point. The legal mediation of intellectual property as a mass market service product is a horrifying prospect. In the case of the Creative Commons, the rhetoric simply ignores the material reality that most people cannot afford to, and would probably never want to, engage in litigation of any sort, certainly not against powerful, rich companies with armies of lawyers.

At the same time, given current distribution media and formats, copyright is practically unenforcible. Punitive enforcement of copyright law in a few highly publicised 'example' cases, in which individuals are persecuted for downloading copyright material, is deeply irresponsible on the part of the rights holders. Irresponsible because they must bear some responsibility for the ease with which their material is duplicated and distributed, which is an intentional strategy on their part.

Take the example of commercial software. It is in the interests of the software company for their software to be easily pirated. Many specialist software titles are hard to 'crack', but in many cases 'industry standard' applications are easily pirated. If, for example, it were impossible to pirate Adobe Photoshop, this software would not occupy the position of market leader for photo manipulation. Students, learners, tiny companies that currently find it easy to download and use pirate versions of these warez, grow up to found established companies and businesses that are no longer 'under the radar' of the copyright holders, and so buy licences. If it were impossible to do so, they would use something else and buy licences for that product if and when it became necessary and profitable for them to do so. Knowing this, Adobe maintains a relatively relaxed copyright enforcement and security implementation policy. They do not seem to prosecute individuals, although presumably they have the right to do so.

The same logic applies on another level to music distribution. Music becomes popular in some markets because it is easily distributable. If the only way for Bulgarians to listen to Britney was for them to spend 10–12 leva, or €5–6, on a CD, they would not listen to Britney. Piracy created this market and many others.

There is a harsh duplicity in the way large, multinational IP owners use copyability as a publicity strategy on one hand, and then, on the other, bully the public into paying extortionate prices for dead media by singling out individuals and persecuting them as examples for taking the bait of copying the 'property' they have made intentionally copyable.

If, as is constantly threatened, Digital Rights Management becomes a reality and it is then impossible to buy hardware, software and media that allow the reproduction and distribution of copyrighted information, punitive enforcement of redundant copyright law on individuals will no longer be necessary because it will simply be impossible for them to copy and redistribute this property.

Thinking again about how to articulate copyright and copyleft, there seems to be a need for a functional articulation of the reality of how this law is applied, rather than the legalistic, utopian fantasy of an IP 'commons'. For this purpose, I suggest the principles of 'CopyCan and CopyCan't'. Simply, it is possible to copy CopyCan material, and impossible to copy CopyCan't. No lawyers necessary. It becomes the responsibility of the producer to prevent the copying of their material. If this entails the implementation of DRM, fine. If it requires cyborgs to register a serial number keyed to an iris print and a cochlear implant for every piece of commercial music that they buy, which prevents others from hearing the uniquely signed, secure transmission of this audio unless they also buy it, fine. See how many people buy Britney's albums on these terms.

Charters of Liberty in Black Face and White Face: Race, Slavery and the Commons

Peter Linebaugh

Vol 2 #1, Winter/Spring 2005

I am thinking about revolution and constitution, where the former means the overthrow of capitalism and the latter means the ways in which we re-constitute our governance. Capitalism is the accumulation of commodities and the production of surplus value by means of unpaid labour. Government concerns the rule of the Many by the Few, a task solved by *divide et impere* and named the Constitution.

The legal cliché is that America has a written constitution, while the English one is unwritten. Yet, strictly speaking, this is untrue inasmuch as both have stemmed from Magna Carta of 1215.

The Norman and Angevin kings afforested as much as a quarter of England, making game reserves and monopolising hydrocarbon energy resources, in zones where the only law was the King's pleasure. They were crusaders, in world competition with Jews and Arabs for the commerce of the Mediterranean, and to launch such crusades they forced marriages among the barony and took children hostage, pulled the teeth of Jewish money lenders, as well as squeezing the serfs and villeins dry. Civil war was the result, but ceasefire was obtained with Magna Carta. It revealed the contradictions between state and church, between monarchs and barons, between them and merchants, between all those three and the commoners who were dependent on forest resources.

Magna Carta has 63 chapters. It is accompanied by a smaller charter, the Charter of the Forest, with seventeen chapters. They belong together. They are the two documents printed first in the book of English law for over five centuries. The most esteemed commentators, Edward Coke – who influenced the 17th century English Revolution – and William Blackstone – who influenced the 18th century American Revolution – always treated the two charters as one: the English charters of liberty. We can follow their precedent.

A word about each: Magna Carta used to be well known and what was most well known in it was Chapter 39 because four principles of justice are sometimes derived from it, *viz.* habeas corpus, trial by jury, prohibition of torture and due process of law. All of these have been curtailed by the USA Patriot Act. The Charter of the Forest assumes a notion of the 'commons' or a practice of subsistence commoning in the hydrocarbon energy resources of the time. This important presupposition is indicated by technical terms, *viz.* herbage, assarts, pannage, chiminage and estovers. Herbage means grazing for cattle; assarts means clearing trees and grubbing stumps for gardening or growing grains;

pannage means letting pigs into the woods for mast and nuts; chiminage means no tolls on the roads and paths; estovers means getting wood for fuel, for housing, and for tools and implements.

Now, to express these theoretically we might say that they refer to use rights rather than exchange value, and thus they refer to particular, concrete labours rather than abstract labour with its universal equivalent in money. From this formulation, we might then say that they refer to a pre-capitalist mode of production, or we might say that they refer to those classes of people whose goal in economic life is the consumption of uses rather than the accumulation of money. In short, they refer to the Many, not the Few.

Considering the two charters, some of their provisions concern subsistence and some concern government. Some are negative; they prevent or prohibit arbitrary behaviour by armed forces of the King, such as bailiffs, sheriffs, knights and so forth. Others are positive; they provide fuel, travel, food, milk and clothing for commoners. So, like two baskets of law, panniers on the back of a mule, they have trudged down the centuries, sometimes hidden from view or apparently stuck in a slough, at other times requiring a goad to get going again.

There is a third point: The mule can turn around and go the other way. Both charters were committed to disafforestation, or the removal of the King's sole law and the return to conditions prior to the afforestation of the Norman Conquest. Energy resources were to be returned or restored, and reparations made for harm done. The King took what did not belong to him; two centuries later he was made to return it. Thus, they reversed 200 years of history making it, so to speak, go backwards. So much for the self-serving bourgeois doctrine of progress!

The important difference between English and American constitutional development is not that one is unwritten and the other is written. The difference is Africa. American constitutional and revolutionary history depended, first, on taking Indian lands, and, second, on maintenance and expansion of unwaged labour on the plantation where slaves produced surplus value. This is an 18th century problem, as references to the Declaration of Independence and the American Revolution make clear, and as the references to the US constitution of 1787, as amended subsequently, also make clear.

In England, the protracted struggle to maintain subsistence by access to the commons, or (to express this dynamically) by *making* commons, or commoning, had the unintended consequence of closing England through the repressive response of the Parliamentary Enclosure Acts passed between 1760 and 1830. What was the relationship between, on the one hand, the expropriation from Africans by the slave trade and the resistance to enclosures and, on the other hand, the formation of the working class? This was the problem some of us of the 'Warwick School' set ourselves in the early-1970s. We saw it, at first, as a problem of 'crime'. Then we saw it as a problem of 'custom'. We did not see it as a problem of 'colour', nor did we treat it as a problem of 'capitalism'. Certainly, we failed to see it constitutionally.

To see it as crime was easy enough. George Rudé taught us that revolutionary crowds were criminalised by counter-revolutionaries and their historians. E.J. Hobsbawm taught us that the romanticised criminal, Robin Hood, appears in the transition into capitalism, but not during the transition *out* of capitalism. Plus, were not the great revolutionaries imprisoned, and did not the prisons – Siberia, Kilmainham, Devil's Island, Soledad, Robbin's Island – become seminaries of truth?

We were conscious of colour, because unpaid labour in America depended on it. In 1963, James Baldwin published 'The Fire Next Time', an essay whose wrath anticipated the municipal rebellions of the future, but with a title alluding to the rainbow sign.[1] In the same year, the English translation appeared of Frantz Fanon's *The Wretched of the Earth*, which expressed the hurricane-like energy of the Third World in general and North Africa in particular. It warned against black capitalism. That was also the year of E.P. Thompson's *The Making of the English Working Class*, whose version of the working class saved it from Cold War dismissals and whose call to human agency seemed to revive the nerve of change, as it showed the autonomous self-activity of workers in the past in strike, riot, mutiny and commotion. These American, African and English voices were anti-capitalist and anti-imperialist.

Between 1963 and 1968 occurred the great municipal rebellions in American ghettoes under the slogan of 'Black Power'. How was a revolutionary class analysis to be made? Though we understood black, we were not yet aware of white. We did not yet understand the DuBois principle of 'the wages of whiteness'.[2]

In 1968, after 'the summer of love', I drove across the country from Columbia University anti-war sit-ins to the Berkeley commune and the bulldozing of People's Park. We stopped in Bloomington, Indiana, in whose rare books library I found a scholarly key to the contradictions besetting the world. It was yet another book by 'anonymous' who in my naïveté I thought was the most frequently mentioned 'author' in the library card catalogue. 'Anonymous' seems to have understood the problem, and here was the answer, called *The History of the Blacks of Waltham in Hampshire* (1723). I had it photocopied and then protected by some cardboard covers I made and hinged with band-aid tape and I took it with me to England where 'criminality', black history and the English working class were going to join, I thought, in a grand revolutionary project. Edward Thompson soon had us formed into a research

1. Editor's Note: The title alludes to a slave song: 'God gave Noah the rainbow sign, No more water, the fire next time'.
2. David Roediger, *The Wages of Whiteness: Race and the Making of the American Working Class*, New York: Verso, 1991. In the preparation of this essay, I thank David Roediger and his colleagues at the University of Illinois, Champaign-Urbana.

collective and I gave him my treasured copy of *The History of the Blacks*, which surely would introduce to England the Black Power discussions which were rocking the US. Some years later, he returned it, with his marginalia, after it had helped him get started with *Whigs and Hunters* (1975), which was published with *Albion's Fatal Tree* (1975).

He wrote a brilliant book about law and the ruling class, but it was not the book I had dreamed of. It did not lay the axe to the root. I wanted a book about Africans and commoners. I would put forward the fact that the poachers defended commoning, not just by disguising themselves but by disguising themselves as Negroes, and they did so at Farnham, near the heart of what became the quintessence of England as Jane Austen so gently wrote about it, or Gilbert White, the ornithologist, so carefully observed it, or William Cobbett, the radical journalist, so persistently fulminated about it.

Around Farnham, timber was wanted for the construction of men-of-war and East Indiamen which stopped in Portsmouth for repairs or were built there from scratch for the purpose of the globalisation of commodity trade characteristic of the time. Here's how a flashpoint in the episodes of the Waltham Blacks began:

> Mr. Wingfield who has a fine Parcel of growing Timber on his Estate near Farnham fell'd Part of it: The poor People were admitted (as is customary) to pick up the small Wood; but some abusing the Liberty given, carry'd off what was not allow'd, which that Gentleman resented; and, as an Example to others, made several pay for it. Upon which, the Blacks summon'd the Myrmidons, stripp'd the Bark off several of the standing Trees, and notch'd the Bodies of others, thereby to prevent their Growth; and left a Note on one of the maim'd Trees, to inform the Gentleman, that this was their first Visit; and that if he did not return the Money receiv'd for Damage, he must expect a second from [...] the Blacks.

This is not exactly tree-hugging or Indian *chipko*, though it did have warrant among local antiquarians in the 19th century who searched for a charter of such commoning. The leader of the Blacks and '15 of his Sooty Tribe appear'd, some in Coats made of Deer-Skins, others with Fur Caps, &c. all well armed and mounted: There were likewise at least 300 People assembled to see the Black Chief and his Sham Negroes [...]'.

Charles Withers, Surveyor-General of Woods, observed in 1729 'that the country people everywhere think they have a sort of right to the wood & timber in the forests, and whether the notion may have been delivered down to them by tradition, from the times these forests were declared to be such by the Crown, when there were great struggles and contests about them, he is not able to determine'. The Waltham Blacks, they said, 'had no other design but to do justice, and to see that the Rich did not insult or oppress the poor'. They were assured that the chase was 'originally design'd to feed Cattle, and not to fatten deer for the clergy, &c'. The central common right was pasture, 'common of herbage' as the Forest Charter says. Keeping a cow was possible on two acres, and less in a forest or fen. Half the villagers of England were entitled to common grazing. As late as the 18th century, 'all or most householders in forest, fen, and some heathland parishes enjoyed the right to pasture cows or sheep'.[3] So, the Waltham Blacks were class conscious. There was also an awareness at the time that the keeping of a cow, essential to the material constitution of the country, was backed up by charter.

Timothy Nourse denounced commoners at the beginning of the century. They were 'rough and savage in their Dispositions'. They held 'levelling Principles'. They were 'insolent and tumultuous' and 'refractory to Government'.[4] In September 1723, Richard Norton, the Warden of the Forest of Bere, wished to 'put an end to these arabs and banditti'. The commoner belonged to a 'sordid race'. The commoner was compared to the Indian, to the savage, to the buccaneer and to the Arab.

The 'Blacks' defended the customs of the commoners; the commoners were both criminalised and racialised in the discourse of the enclosers, the privatisers and the big wigs. There was even the suggestion that attacking them was a sort of crusade. The Waltham Black Act of 1722 thus became, among other things, a means of drawing a colour line and criminalising common right.[5]

We can put forward as evidence what was neglected in Thompson, the fact of the African slave trade. Blacking, wrote the anonymous historian in that treasured pamphlet history, commenced 'about the times of general confusion, when the late pernicious schemes of the South Sea Company boure all things down before them, and laid waste what the industry and good husbandry of families had gather'd together'.[6] The South Sea Company was a slave trading company formed a few years earlier to take advantage of the *asiento*, or licence, to trade to Spanish America. On 11 September 1713, Royal African Company congratulated itself on obtaining 'such advantageous terms, as never were before granted to the people who undertook the furnishing of negroes to the Spanish West Indies'. The crisis of the commons began as a financial crisis which itself arose from slaving.

The South Sea Bubble was the wreck of a kind of capitalist commoning. Thirty years earlier, this new form of commoning had been produced through developments within English constitutional governance. During the 1690s, sovereign legal authority (King-in-Parliament) united with the financial form

3. J.M. Neeson, *Commoners: Common Right, Enclosure, and Social Change in England, 1700–1820*, Cambridge: Cambridge University Press, 1993, p. 317.
4. Timothy Nourse, *Campania Foelix, Or a Discourse of the Benefits and Improvements of Husbandry*, London, 1700, pp. 15–6.
5. 'The Black Act was instituted in 1723 [...] in response to the Waltham deer poachers. It made it a felony (that is, a hanging offence) to appear armed in a park or warren, or to hunt or steal deer, with the face blackened or disguised [...]', http://en.wikipedia.org/wiki/Black_Act
6. Anonymous, *The History of the Blacks of Waltham in Hampshire*, 1723.

of value resulting in the Bank of England, Lloyd's Insurance Company and the Coinage Act. Money, and other financial instruments, liquefied the clumsy, cumbersome form of wealth as private property which was presented as use values in warehouses, docks, ships, shops, etc. and, moreover, placed it directly under fiscal state command. The creation of monetary liquidity permitted the distribution of surplus value as investment in various commercial and industrial enterprises according to the needs of capital as a whole without regard to rates of exploitation in individual enterprises. Investment and speculation appeared insubstantial, disembodied, atmospheric or gaseous. The South Sea 'bubble' burst, owing to cupidity which seemed infinite and to anonymous Atlantic obstacles, namely resistance, recalcitrance and revolt.

The decade between 1716 and 1726 was the golden age of piracy, Marcus Rediker informs us.[7] The significance of piracy during these years was twofold – it was multiracial and it was against the slave trade. They blockaded ports, disrupted the sea lanes. The pirate ship 'might be considered a multiracial maroon community'. Hundreds were African. Sixty of Blackbeard's crew of 100 were black. Rediker quotes the Negro of Deptford who, in 1721, led 'a Mutiny that we had too many Officers, and that work was too hard, and what not'. They also prevented the slave trade from growing. This was the complaint of Humphrey Morice, MP, Governor of the Bank of England, owner of a small fleet of slavers, who led the petitioning to Parliament and who suffered severe losses in 1719, the year that serious blacking commenced. A naval squadron was sent to West Africa. Four hundred and eighteen pirates were hanged. The conjuncture of apparently very distant forces, struggle for common rights and the Atlantic slave trade, in fact met in intimate proximity.

Daniel Defoe, the most prolific prose writer in the English language, was preoccupied with the issues of Atlantic labour power. Coincidentally, his writing transpired during the privatisation of the printed word by means of Queen Anne's Copyright Act. He precisely combined the intimate conjunction of opposites with a trans-Atlantic background. *Robinson Crusoe, Mariner* was published in 1719. The book dramatises the labour theory of value, glories in the intricacies of the division of labour and puts the European foot (Crusoe) on the African neck (Friday). Alexander Selkirk, the real life prototype of *Robinson Crusoe*, died in February 1721 as a sailor in a naval squadron that was sent to West Africa to extirpate the piracy interrupting the slave trade. *The Adventures and Misadventures of Moll Flanders*, published in 1722, treats the issues of criminalisation of the commons and large scale cooperative labour. Upward social mobility was not accomplished by 'affirmative action' but by negative criminality, as Moll Flanders hooked up with highwaymen on the first step of the ladder to success, whose final rung she at last attained – a Virginia tobacco plantation – so that she too could put the boot to the African enslaved.

7. Marcus Rediker, *Villains of All Nations: Atlantic Pirates in the Golden Age*, Boston: Beacon Press, 2004.

These are the classic fictional disquisitions on subsistence, survival and surplus in that era of off-shore and homeland plunder; they also present heroic prototypes of the 'white' worker. Indeed, these novels coincided almost to the year with 'the invention of the white race', to give the title of Ted Allen's compelling thesis.[8]

A buffer stratum was to be created by offering material advantages to white proletarians to the lasting detriment of black proletarians. When and how did the 'wages of whiteness' originate? The first date DuBois gives in the protracted process is 1723, when laws were passed in Virginia making Africans and Anglo-Africans slaves forever. In 1723, the bonded people objected to the Bishop of London and the King 'and the rest of the Rullers'. 'Releese us out of this Cruell Bondegg' they cried. In the same year, Richard West, the Attorney General, objected to the same law: 'I cannot see why one freeman should be used worse than another, merely upon account of his complexion [...]' But the Governor of Virginia understood the necessity of 'a perpetual Brand' – skin colour, or the phenotype, which marked the person as surely as the burnt flesh caused by the golden brands used by the South Sea Company. In this way, Ted Allen tells us, a 'monstrous social mutation' occurred, namely that stratum within the American class structure which derives its hopes, security and welfare from white skin privilege. It has been essential to the constitution of American class relations ever since.

This was not known to Thompson. The experience within England (though not Ireland) was different, where the policing of the wage relationship, or the exploitation of the Many by the Few, did not depend upon the colour line, and where, therefore, it was unnecessary to constitute that structure of white supremacy. Thompson wrote the famous 'rule of law' coda to *Whigs and Hunters*. 'As the last imperial illusions of the twentieth century fade, so preoccupation with the history and culture of a small island off the coast of Europe becomes open to the charge of narcissism. The culture of constitutionalism which flowered here, under favoured conditions, is an episode too exceptional to carry any universal significance'. Yet, even smaller than Britain was the island where Robinson Crusoe met Friday, and that story spread worldwide.

The colonists of the North American mainland, even at the time of Robinson Crusoe (1719), the Waltham Black Act (1722) and the South Sea Bubble (1722), had begun to graft some of that English constitutionalism to their own purposes. For example, *The New England Courant* in its Summer issue of 1722 sought to rectify the stupidity of the colonists by quoting Chapter 39 of Magna Carta and commented, 'No Freeman shall be taken, &c. These words deserve to be written in letters of gold, and I have often wondred that they are not inscribed in Capitals in all our Courts of Judicature, Town-halls, and most

8. Ted Allen, *The Invention of the White Race, Volume Two: The Origin of Racial Oppression in Anglo-America*, New York: Verso, 1997.

publick edifices; they being essential to our English Freedom and Liberties [...]' 'No man ought to be put from his Livelyhood without answer' rings hollow to the unemployed, or to the Indians who were proclaimed rebels in the same newspaper for attacking 15 commercial vessels intruding on their fishing grounds and whose women and children were taken in captivity to Dunstable. 'No man can be exiled or banished out of his native country' is hypocrisy to the men and women and children from the West coast of Africa enslaved in America. *The New England Courant's* sole advertisement reads 'A likely Negro Woman to be sold by *Mr. Thomas Selby* at the Crown Coffee-House, the lower end of Kingstreet.'

Thompson, however, did not accept a South Sea or Atlantic perspective, much less a planetary one in his references to constitutionalism. He reversed himself, moving from a mood of postcolonial narcissism to one of praise for the English ruling class as a whole: '[...] the inhibitions upon power imposed by laws seem to me a legacy as substantial as any handed down from the struggles of the 17th century to the 18th, and a true and important cultural achievement of the agrarian and mercantile bourgeoisie, and of their supporting yeomen and artisans.' And when Thompson writes of the culture of constitutionalism, why does he exclude the charters of liberty?

Dorothy Thompson, many years later, attributed this coda to heated arguments with her husband and co-worker, Edward, arguing that 'he was leaning too far in the direction taken by some of the contributors to *Albion's Fatal Tree* in dismissing the law simply as an instrument of class power'.[9] The discussions about these books took place in 1970 and 1971, when, for instance, Howard Zinn in November 1970 said, 'the problem is civil disobedience,' and he ran down the law, how the Bill of Rights is publicised but not enforced, how the property laws are enforced but not publicised. He showed how decorum and propriety fool us and cause us to revere the law. He reminded us that we often have to go outside the legal framework – the Civil War, the Union drives, the American Revolution. He said, 'people in all countries need the spirit of disobedience to the state [...]'. The American and the English experiences were different. The Attica revolt was in September 1971, and the trial of the Mangrove Nine finished in 1971. Internment without trial was introduced in 1971, and 'Bloody Sunday' was in January 1972. These events of state terrorism had not yet been answered by similar violence from those taking an anti-imperialist stand. Furthermore, they still seemed to be part of an ancient constitution in which 'race' played trumps.

Our books were not published until 1975; during the interval the world changed direction. The PLO assassinated Israeli athletes at the Munich Olympics. The IRA brought the war to England. The Guildford pub bombing

9. Daniel H. Cole, '"An Unqualified Human Good": E.P. Thompson and the Rule of Law', http://papers.ssrn.com/sol3/papers.cfm?abstract_id=169264

of October 1974 left five dead; a month later, the Birmingham pub bombing killed 21. While the political climate became more violent, the intellectual climate became more academic, more legalistic, more obscure. Critical Legal Studies (formed in 1977) stuck to the high theory of Frankfurt School, and French post-structuralism was obtusely reluctant to engage English social history or to raise the constitutional issues of race or the commons.

There is a vast amount of English social history since 1975 (and before) recording the importance of customary rights to common forest resources. Moreover, that story is now clearly understood to have happened all over the world. J.M. Neeson produced a great book about the commons from earlier discussions concerning custom. Called *Commoners*, it showed that subsistence use rights remained a material basis of many English agrarian workers. Meanwhile, others of us adduced the evidence that the wage relation arose from the process of criminalisation and the process of criminalisation arose from custom. The irrationality of the wage concealed the unpaid labour, but could these *aperçus* attain constitutional importance, or were they destined to dismissal as untheorised ditty?

> The law locks up the man or woman,
> Who steals the goose from off the common,
> But lets the greater villain loose,
> Who steals the common from the goose.

The violence and the terror, 'the military option' as the Italian Red Brigades put it, made it harder to see the Charters, or the commons, as anything other than a wild goose chase. Looking back now, we can see that the issue was not the rule of law vs. terrorism; the issue was the preservation of commoning vs. new enclosures.

We could use some theory of the kind that transformed Magna Carta for the Levellers, of the kind that transformed Magna Carta for the abolitionists. In 1774, former African American slave, Olaudah Equiano, put on white face in London in order to obtain a warrant of habeas corpus. This is among the first actions by which Magna Carta was appropriated for the trans-Atlantic movement to abolish slavery. In the same year, Granville Sharp wrote:

> The wisdom of ages has made [Magna Carta] venerable, and stamped it with an authority equal to the Constitution itself, of which it is, in reality, a most essential and fundamental part; so that any attempt to repeal it would be treason to the State! This glorious Charter must, therefore, ever continue unrepealed: and even the articles which seem at present useless, must ever remain in force.[10]

10. Granville Sharp, *A Declaration of the People's Natural Right to a Share in the Legislature*, Philadelphia: John Dunlap, 1774, pp. 202–3.

Granville Sharp used the charters against slavery, racial and otherwise; but, despite an obsession with the gothic frankpledge, he did not take his stand with the commons, unlike Thomas Spence or Gracchus Babeuf. Similarly with Frederick Douglass, who, in 1854, said, 'Let the engine of the Magna Carta beat against the Jericho walls of Slavery, and no seven days blowing of rams' horns would be necessary' – a reference to the jubilee which, while emancipating slaves, also restored the commons.

Edward Thompson failed to mention Magna Carta and, more strategically, he omitted the Charter of the Forest. There was an opportunity to link the constitution to the commons at that point in time, Walpole 1720–3, when some English and African commoners could be found together on the seven seas and in the wild wood. The moment passed; privatisation and slavery advanced together. We hear Blackstone crow as he defines private property as 'that sole and despotic common which one man claims and exercises over the external things of the world, in total exclusion of the right of any other individual in the universe'. (He admitted in his *Commentaries* that there are elements such as light, air and water which 'must still unavoidably remain in common'.)

Today, the commons comes back to us from the South! Subcommandante Marcos provided the voice of the Zapatistas and the indigenous people of Chiapas by calling for the return of Article 27 and the *ejidos*, or common land, while reminding us of Magna Carta. As the Many demand water, energy and wherewithal against the surplus value hogged by the Few, we must reprise those moments when the act of constitution showed not racist *divide et impere* but that old, old friend of all, the commons. This enterprise calls for our contemporary appropriations of *both* of the Charters of Liberty.

Copy that Floppy!

Palle Torsson Interviewed by Anthony Iles

Vol 2 #1, Winter 2005

Anthony Iles: The Pirate Bay is one of the most popular BitTorrent trackers. Could you tell us about how The Pirate Bay and Pirat Byran came about?

Palle Torsson: Pirat Byran (PB) was born in 2003 from an integrated internet radio broadcast community and IRC channel populated by the Swedish hacker community and demo scene. PB was initiated to support the free copying of culture and launched the BitTorrent tracker and website, The Pirate Bay (TPB). When TPB expanded to become the biggest BitTorrent tracker in the world, it was natural for them to split up into two different entities. PB has evolved into a community and an information site in Swedish with news, forums, articles, resources and a shop and has, to date, over 50,000 members. PB organises events, appears in debates, writes and answers questions about IP and filesharing. TPB has recently gone through a major internationalisation and can now be browsed in many languages, from Mandarin to Icelandic.

AI: Some time ago, I read a report on interactivist [http://linkme2.net/50] about filesharing protests in Sweden. I understand you spoke at the demo?

PT: Yes, but the speech I made took most of my energy. It was the second year that internet lovers, filesharers and pirates gathered in Stockholm to express their fight for internet freedom. There was music and three speakers talking about the transgression of IP law and creativity. A hand to hand copyswap was extended to a coffin where you could place and share CDs. A big crowd of something like 800 people assembled with banners declaring things like: 'No Software Patents', 'Sharing is Caring' and 'All Your Base [Stations] Belong to Us'. This aggressively humorous attitude is something that characterises the movement in Sweden. One beautiful example is the letter written by TPB in response to legal threats and the request by big companies like Microsoft, DreamWorks and Warner Bros. to remove copyrighted material: [http://thepiratebay.org/legal.php]

Last year, the transgression of IP law spurred a copy riot in Sweden; people from right to left have woken up and spoken out on the subject. This escalated further when Sweden's anti-piracy lobby organisation, Antipiratbyran (APB), raided a Swedish ISP, claiming they hosted unlicensed material. The raid was conducted in an unlawful manner and it was discovered that, for several months, APB had paid an infiltrator to upload copyright-protected material and place hardware at the ISP.

This spawned a public outcry and the lawyer and spokesperson for APB, Henrik Pontén, received hate-SMS, including death threats, from a lot of angry kids. The homepage of APB was hacked by a group calling themselves Angry

Young Hackers, and mails between people from APB were published showing that APB was also infiltrated. In response, PB has pressed charges against APB for their different unlawful actions, and APB was told by the Swedish authorities to withdraw the most aggressive of these threats to protect their own integrity.

The demonstration was mostly a great celebration, with a lot of different people sharing and also making connections. The slogans at the demonstration were: 'Copy me – we will continue to copy everything', 'Don't touch our internet' and 'Welfare begins at 100 Mbit'. The counter-allegations against the anti-pirate organisation, APB, for the action and the raid at the Swedish ISP, Bahnhof, was ready at that time and was handed to the police.

AI: As I understand it, Sweden has yet to sign European agreements on copyright law. Does this make it a 'zone of exception' as far as the increasingly aggressive policing of IP is concerned?

PT: No, but for a long time it was legal to download for personal use. Now the EU [Copyright] Directive is implemented and in force in Sweden (as of 1 July), even though there have not yet been any cases resulting from the new law. This 'zone of exception' comes rather from the fact that people accept and live with filesharing; the police don't have the will, priorities or resources to criminalise kids. TPB and PB is a concrete, factual and living example of this, among other things. This 'zone of exception' is important and natural for this generation, and is not something that will change any time soon.

AI: What is the bigger picture behind these protests? Was this the first public act of disobedience in opposition to the new laws, or are there events that have prefigured this one?

PT: PB has a broad political base, from high-tech autonomists to free libertarians. A group based in Malmö, called The Street Action, looks upon filesharing as digital class struggle and organises public copyswaps inside shopping malls in order to desecrate the commodity. And there are several other interesting projects based on disobedience in Sweden, of which my favourites are Planka.nu and Snatta.nu. Planka.nu is a site for free subway riding and runs a fund to which you can subscribe and get your money back in case you get caught and fined. Snatta.nu is a site for shoplifting culture.

AI: You spoke of finding the 'power to strike again'; at what forms of power are you directing these attacks and through what means?

PT: I always appropriate, borrow or steal other people's work to make something new. I live in, distribute and take from the circulation of information. The configurations of the medial structures in which this information exists is the pipeline in which I work. The motivation for my work is to try to intervene in this structure and to create an alternative work space, basically to make my Becoming, a place where I am free to appropriate again.

There is an endless amount of targets to strike that oppose our way of living, but right now it feels important to build the alternative playground of sharing and gift culture. The confrontation comes naturally in the process of exploring these grounds. The primary means for this is collaboration and exchange of knowledge. I think hacking that involves hardware modification will become more important because the industry understands they have lost the information battle and are moving towards the protection of hardware. This means that it will be important to realise real infrastructures of communication, like Wi-Fi and meshed networks and self-made entities for IP broadcast.

AI: What, then, are the implications of a 'post-scarcity' system in which the cultural products of immaterial labour are available for free exchange, whilst the cost of living and reproducing oneself rises?

PT: The flow of money and information are immanent to each other. When information is transformed into commodities, they become potential allocators of the money with which you could buy food. If you are a student, you'd rather spend your money on beer, and, as a parent, you spend your money on food rather than paying for CDs or books. If you use alternative circulations like the library, sharing or downloads, your economy becomes richer.

The hacker, the artist, or the housewife for that matter, do not live independent from the economic structure of society; on the contrary, they are parasites upon existing structures within welfare systems, companies and universities. Like all people, they are attached to a grey zone in which they produce an important surplus value for society that we find more important than most are willing to openly admit.

AI: Trackers (and other P2P technologies) are playing a powerful role in the 'economy of attention'. They are becoming important producers of opinion, hype and desire around new releases from multinationals, as well as facilitating their distribution. Are there ways that Pirate Byran can radicalise this process?

PT: Yes, by bringing in new groups to filesharing. For instance, as in the project 'small pirates' run by PB where the focus is on filesharing for parents and kids, or bringing new content to the trackers, as in the project Vidensdeling.nu run by the Danish Pirat Gruppen. I think there is a radical process inherent in the movement, so what is needed is to deepen the understanding of the redistribution of culture. One recent attempt was the book produced by PB about filesharing culture, *Copy Me*. A lot of projects have evolved from the forums at PB. I think it is important to always branch out into different projects so that the process becomes independent from singularities of any kind.

There are always different levels of involvement in a community, some rising and some falling. I think filesharing and open source has a radicalising process attached to it right now because it points to the structural division of information in society. I would say that these links you talk about already exist; the important thing is to make them visible. The best way to do so is to get important files and projects online for filesharing. One of the more recent examples initiated by the sister organisation of the PB in Denmark, Pirat

Gruppen, is a project called Vidensdeling.nu. Students are encouraged to digitise and share the expensive books on their reading lists and in this way use filesharing to create a digital library resource for fellow students, circumventing the costs and control of large publishers. So far, the campaign has resulted in books being shared on The Pirate Bay, while the publishing companies have joined the entertainment industry in their desperate hunt for filesharers. The Pirate Bay can be used by anyone who wants to share files or come up with new models for distribution.

AI: The asymmetry of access to ownership of communications media is a major factor provoking their seizure and redistribution. Historically, piracy has arisen at times of enormous economic hegemony (empire), and, though formed in opposition to dominant culture, frequently plays an economic and geopolitical role in reproducing it. How can the new forms of data piracy support and nourish alternatives and even opposition to dominant economic imperatives?

PT: Overcoming lack of access is not a very important notion in our approach. Not even opposition to dominant forms of culture. Internet piracy is all about desire production, and, in the long run, its deepest effects may well not have so much to do with access, or may go far beyond that notion – just as Walter Benjamin talked about art as the production of desires that cannot yet be satisfied, but will inevitably reach far beyond goals originally impossible to imagine.

Maybe what is most important now is to bypass the urge for solutions, for victory in battles or for compromise and stability. For example, talking bout how to 'compensate' copyright holders obscures the truth about the social production of culture, replacing it with the myth of copyright as some kind of 'wage' for artists. On the contrary, trying to keep the 'grey zone' as open and wide as possible will almost automatically produce better conditions for going beyond prevalent economic imperatives. If nothing else, it will do this by simply curing some of the neurotic sickness of copying control. But making general statements about different political implications and alternative economic models when talking about piracy and free copying would almost be like accepting copyright's claim to universality.

I think the shift to alternative ways of organising, in more of a rhizomatic manner, is driven by desires and the possibilities of connection. The drive to think, invent and discover alternative processes of production is the affirmative power of life as an experiment in complexity.

FLOSS Redux: Notes on African Software Politics

Soenke Zehle

Vol 2 #1, Winter 2005

With a host of corporations, foundations and organisations active in the fields of advocacy and assistance, free and open source software (FLOSS) has become a dynamic area of info-developmental cooperation. In the eminently pragmatic approach adopted by many of these efforts, the intense controversy over free vs. open source software and the extent to which advocacy should stress freedom over commercial applicability somehow seems a thing of the past. At the same time, the focus on FLOSS as an economic strategy of autonomous development within global network capitalism, rather than as a post-capitalist practice of collaborative creation, recalls some of the general ambivalences at the heart of software-political struggles.[1]

FOSSFA

In many African countries where computer users are not necessarily owners, important choices are often made by those in charge of establishing public Information and Communication Technology (ICT) infrastructures. While many companies and organisations have chosen to adopt FLOSS on their own, the status of governments as the largest procurers of ICT means that government action is bound to stimulate industry in various ways, including the provision of FLOSS training and support. The recently founded Free Software and Open Source Foundation for Africa (FOSSFA), currently headquartered in Nairobi, Kenya, has therefore identified national ICT policy and procurement procedures as major advocacy targets.[2] For Bildad Kagai, co-founder and one of its secretaries, the licensing, localisation and local skill-building advantages of FLOSS, coupled with 'leapfrogging' technologies like wireless that help skip an entire generation of expensive infrastructural investments, offer an alternative to the technological dependency and resource drain associated with an exclusive reliance on mainstream proprietary software.

Given the many problems that beset the ICT sector in Africa, FLOSS advocacy is inevitably tied to political reforms in contracting, public services and competition policy, as well as the creation of FLOSS-related employment and business opportunities. Taking advantage of the organisational dynamic

1. For an account of free software vs. open source software in terms of the struggle over discursive hegemony, see David Berry, 'The Contestation of Code: A Preliminary Investigation into the Discourse of the Free/Libre and Open Source Movements', *Critical Discourse Studies*, April 2004, Vol. 71, no. 1, pp. 65–89, http://opensource.mit.edu/papers/berry1.pdf
2. http://FOSSFA.net

of WSIS [The World Summit on the Information Society] and working closely with civil society organisations, corporations and international donors, FOSSFA has created an effective advocacy coalition: Kenya's ICT policy now gives preference to open source (and open standards) over proprietary solutions, and FOSSFA also convinced the Committee on Development Information of the Economic Commission for Africa (CODI) to adopt a policy that prioritises FLOSS.

This is no small feat, given that many African states have yet to articulate any ICT policy whatsoever, and FOSSFA is also educating policy makers across the continent about FLOSS.[3] The 2004 Idlelo meeting in Cape Town, co-organised by FOSSFA and the African Virtual Open Initiatives and Resources Project (AVOIR) at Western Cape University, was the 'First African Conference on the Digital Commons'.[4] Bringing some 200 FLOSS activists and developers from across the continent together with international researchers, Idlelo emphasised the need to shift from the mere adoption of FLOSS to the local development of FLOSS applications, the use of FLOSS in education and the development of non-proprietary open content alternatives. Hoping to be able to recruit government representatives from all 53 African states, Idlelo 2 has already been scheduled for 2006.[5]

South Africa Goes Open Source

The breakdown of Idlelo participants by country reveals the uneven geography of ICT development in Africa: by far the largest contingent came from South Africa, followed by Nigeria and Kenya.[6] South Africa's influence in the African FLOSS movement is related to its dominance of the African IXT sector at large. But there are other reasons, one of which is the impact of projects sponsored by Mark Shuttleworth.[7] A South African celebrity entrepreneur known for his space travel – he was the first 'afronaut' – as well as his philanthropic ambition, Shuttleworth has overseen the development of Ubuntu (an already popular Debian-and-GNOME-based Linux distribution updated in regular release cycles), and his Shuttleworth Foundation has co-launched a nationwide 'Go Open Source' campaign.[8]

3. Bildad Kagai and Nicolas Kimolo, 'FOSSFA in Africa: Opening the Door to State ICT Development Agendas – A Kenya Case Study', *SSRC The Politics of Open Source Adoption*, 2005, http://www.ssrc.org/wiki/POSA CODI, 'Resolutions of the Fourth Meeting of the Committee on Development Information (CODI-IV)', UNECA Commission on Development Information, 23–28 April 2005, http://www.uneca.org/codi/codi4/codi_iv_report.pdf. See the country policy tables at http://www.bridges.org/FLOSS/index.html
4. http://avoir.uwc.ac.za
5. http://www.FOSSFA.net/idlelo2
6. Derek Keats, 'Idlelo: First African Conference on the Digital Commons', *Final Report to Department of Science & Technology*, South Africa, 2004, http://www.catia.ws/Documents/Indexpage/IdleloFinalReport.pdf
7. http://www.markshuttleworth.com
8. http://www.ubuntulinux.org, http://www.go-opensource.org

Supported by the Meraka Institute of the South African Council for Scientific and Industrial Research (CSIR) as well as HP and Canonical, the campaign has included the production of the first ever television series on open source – broadcast on public television and available for download – and the installation of 'Freedom Toasters', stand alone CD/DVD burners loaded with the latest FLOSS operating systems and applications, across South Africa.[9] In addition to working on an 'edubuntu' classroom version of its Linux distribution, the Shuttleworth Foundation also works with South African schools to set up FLOSS-based thin client networks through its 'tuXlabs' initiative.[10] And, following the 2005 'Go Open Source Task Team' conference, South Africa's national policy on free/open source software and open content is now being turned into an ambitious action plan.[11]

But is South Africa 'really' Africa? FOSSFA's Kagai notes that ICT developments in South Africa are not representative of Africa at large, and some see in the ideas of an 'African Renaissance' less a new pan-Africanism than a mere culturalisation of South Africa's own economic and geopolitical ambition.[12] Yet it would be a mistake to associate less well off areas of the continent with a lack of interest in digital and network technologies – a point made years ago by none other than John Perry Barlow (ex-Grateful Dead and Electronic Frontier co-founder).[13] From his own experience of country life, Barlow had concluded that Africans might have preserved a pre-industrial sense of connectedness and would want to bypass the crippling effects of an individualist industrialism to embrace the digital technologies of the network society. Even after the dotcom crash, his occasionally, albeit ironically, exoticist travelogue is still worth a read, in part because much of his 'let's wire Africa' enthusiasm was shared by the initial wave of international ICT task forces that were to turn the new economy experience into a fully fledged paradigm of info-development. And it encouraged Russell Southwood, a former UK management consultant, to start Balancing Act Africa, already one of the most important information services on ICT-related developments across Africa, including the failures and successes of FLOSS advocacy.[14]

9. http://www.freedomtoaster.org, http://www.go-opensource.org/go_open
10. http://www.edubuntu.org, http://www.tuxlab.org.za. A thin client is a computer (client) in client-server architecture networks which have very few resources, so it has to depend primarily on the central server for processing activities. A thin client network centralises maintenance tasks to a (remote) server.
11. http://wiki.go-opensource.org/taskforce
12. For a middle of the road assessment of the African Renaissance, see Elias K. Bongmba, 'Reflections on Thabo Mbeki's African Renaissance', *Journal of Southern African Studies*, June 2004, Vol. 30, no. 2. For more critical views, see Neil Lazarus, 'The South African Ideology: The Myth of Exceptionalism, the Idea of Renaissance', *South Atlantic Quarterly*, Fall 2004, Vol. 103, no. 4, pp. 607–28, and Neville Alexander, 'South Africa – Example or Illusion?' *An Ordinary Country: Issues in the Transition from Apartheid to Democracy in South Africa*, New York: Berghahn Books, 2003, pp. 137–73, 188–90.
13. John Perry Barlow, 'Africa Rising', *Wired*, 1998, Vol. 6, no. 1, http://www.wired.com/wired/archive/6.01/barlow_pr.html
14. http://www.balancingact-africa.com

Perhaps somewhat surprisingly, FLOSS has not been an easy sell. One reason, suggests Ethan Zukerman, might be the overemphasis on free beer at the expense of free speech – a reference to Richard Stallmann's famous definition of free software.[15] Zukerman, a co-founder of GeekCorps – 'an international non-profit organisation that transfers tech skills from geeks in developed nations to geeks in emerging nations' – and initiator of 'BlogAfrica', believes that many African users continue to associate 'inexpensive' with 'inferior', legacy of technology transfer and appropriate technology projects that sometimes amounted to little more than the dumping of obsolete technology.[16] And, in areas where non-licensed copies of proprietary software are widely available as well as a great deal of corresponding 'street' expertise, comparatively expensive manuals and a lack of bandwidth for accessing online support can easily increase the total cost of ownership of non-proprietary alternatives generally assumed to be 'free'. FLOSS advocates should stress the expandability, transparency and resulting high performance of their software instead.

While a growing number of studies make an empirically based case for FLOSS in general, less is known about the experiences of FLOSS adoption across Africa.[17] One such report has been published by Bridges.org, an international NGO with offices in South Africa and the US.[18] According to Bridges.org, the availability of the source code is actually an advantage rarely exploited at the computer lab level, whereas the cost of software licences – the 'free beer' argument – remains a key concern, especially evident when these costs are expressed in terms of GDP share. Among the factors that reduce software costs, piracy is the most important, followed by donations and so-called thin client configurations that bring back to life hardware generally considered obsolete. FLOSS, concludes the report, has become a mainstream alternative. Yet, because of the level of expertise required to establish and maintain a FLOSS-based computer lab, it tends to work better in large projects that have the resources to address the practical problems of migration, training and support, in contrast to individual labs that can simply take advantage of proprietary solutions already in place.

Info-Political Visions

Beyond the issue of appropriate means, how do the local politics of software relate to competing visions of what 'info-development' is, and should be,

15. Ethan Zukerman, 'Free Beer Doesn't Sell', *Linux Journal*, July 2003, no. 111, http://www.linuxjournal.com/article/6785
16. http://www.geekcorps.org/ http://www.ethanzuckerman.com/blog
17. David Wheeler, 'Why Open Source Software/Free Software (OSS/FS, FLOSS, or FLOSS)? Look at the Numbers!', May 2005, http://www.dwheeler.com/oss_fs_why.html
18. Bridges.org, 'Comparison study of Free/Open Source and Proprietary Software in an African context: Implementation and policy-making to optimise community access to ICT', May 2005, http://www.bridges.org/software_comparison/index.html

about? In the larger info-political vision that frames local decisions over software and standards, questions of autonomy are central, frequently articulated in response to the hegemonic presence of corporate software and IT giants. FLOSS advocates have criticised the most recent wave of international public-private partnerships in this area, for example, because they only involve the usual transnational suspects. Microsoft, HP and Cisco are all well represented in the activities of major development agencies, advertising themselves as 'partners in development' to promote ICTs as the vehicles for 'good governance' and 'effective service delivery', but also to stake out their own commercial claims, crowd out grassroots or public sector alternatives and subvert South-South cooperation.

Take SchoolNet Namibia.[19] Having to work with substantially fewer resources than the Shuttleworth Foundation, SchoolNet has nevertheless set up FLOSS-based thin client networks in over 100 schools, launched an ISP to offer subsidised internet services and is exploring the set up of wireless access in rural areas. Once they found that students were a lot more likely to embrace FLOSS than their teachers, and standard advocacy tools were not doing much to change that, SchoolNet launched Hai Ti ('Listen Up!'), a comic strip that features real life FLOSS users.[20] Its contractual agreement with schools specifies that the teams who manage the local computer lab include students as well as teachers. Yet, occasionally, SchoolNet finds that their FLOSS LANs remain unmaintained, while students use equipment donated by Microsoft and administered with support from MS certified engineers. Executive Director, Joris Komen, is convinced that Microsoft has targeted Namibian schools specifically because SchoolNet Namibia has become an outspoken critic of the company and its philosophy.[21] Commenting on recent agreements between Microsoft and the New Partnership for African Development (NEPAD), the United Nations Development Programme (UNDP) and the United Nations High Commissioner for Refugees (UNHCR), Bildad Kaigai of FOSSFA agrees that such deals work to confine the software choices these agencies can make and effectively transfer wealth away from an emergent local software industry.

Kagai calls on African leaders to emulate the successful development strategies of Asian countries instead.[22] Other ICT analysts note, however, that African countries will have to do so under dramatically different circumstances. Yash Tandon of SEATINI stresses that 'most of the so-called "technology transfers" [...] are essentially excuses for transnational corporations (TNCs) to take over local companies, or to carve out a share of the domestic markets'.[23]

19. http://www.schoolnet.na
20. http://www.schoolnet.na/haiti
21. http://tatejoris.blogspot.com
22. Bildad Kagai, 'FOSSFA Responds to Microsoft-UNDP Deal', February 2004, http://FOSSFA.net
23. Yash Tandon, 'An Alternative View on Technology', SEATINI, September 2004, http://www.seatini.org/publications/factsheets/technology.htm

Rather than 'stripping naked' to attract foreign direct investment (FDI) from the North, Tandon also makes the case for the 'creation of a home-based Domestic Scientific and Technology Capacity (DSTC), including capacity to undertake relevant research and development, the actual purchase (as opposed to transfer) of appropriate technology from the open market, and a transfer of technology, preferably between South-South, only under certain conditions'. But Tandon also notes that options exploited by the 'Asian Tigers' are no longer available to Africa:

> Countries such as Korea and Taiwan, as all other now advanced economies in history, were able to do it because they disembedded the technology from its capital base (by, for example, copying intellectual property, and through reverse engineering), and by creating a 'national' base for capital. Some countries were able to do this during the cold war years when the West needed them to fight against the Communist threat coming from China and Vietnam. [. . .] Since the end of the cold war, this option is no longer available. [. . .] Now, with intellectual property rights embedded in the World Trade Organisation (WTO) under the Trade Related Aspects of Intellectual Property Rights (TRIPS), scientific knowledge has become monopolised in the hands of a few thousand multinational corporations that use this knowledge to control the economies of the third world.

For Tandon, Africa has only so many options: 'It is in this context that Africa must develop its own DSTC, including a policy on relevant research and development. The R&D policy must be based on the production conditions in the region, the need first to produce for the domestic/regional market (only secondarily for the export market), and Africa's location within the global value chain.'

It seems that Third Worldist strategies, sustained by a generalised critique of neo-colonialism, have been replaced by the exhausting creation of advocacy networks that hold local governments just as accountable as transnational corporations.[24] Yet, while visions of Africa's future have sobered significantly, the emergent dynamic of South-South cooperation still echoes a tricontinentalist spirit. Brazil's official commitment to what its minister of culture, Gilberto Gil, has referred to as a 'tropicalisation' of open source has been a major push for FLOSS advocacy in Africa. One such example of a South-South technology transfer was Brazil's support for the adoption and implementation of open source software for the management of Top Level Domain (TLD) registries in a number of African countries, a process that will eventually automate TLD registries.[25]

24. Thandika Mkandawire, 'Good Governance: The Itinerary of an Idea', *D + C Development and Cooperation*, 1 October 2004, Vol. 31, no. 10, http://www.inwent.org/E+Z/content/archive-eng/10-2004/tribune_art1.html
25. Rebecca Wanjiku, 'Brazil Opens Its Arms to Africa', *Highway Africa News Agency*, 5 April 2005, http://www.highwayafrica.ru.ac.za/hana/textviewer.asp?item_id=339

Increasing 'post-Third Worldist' cooperation is visible in other international info-political fora, as well. One example is the campaign for a World Intellectual Property Organisation (WIPO) 'Development Agenda' and a Treaty for Access to Knowledge, supported by a broad coalition of southern governments as well as grassroots organisations.[26] WIPO is a UN agency whose current mandate is 'the maintenance and further development of the respect for intellectual property throughout the world'. In the eyes of its critics, this mandate limits WIPO to the role of an enforcer of Euro-American positions on intellectual property, by supporting the WTO's Agreement on TRIPS as well as at least condoning the aggressive 'TRIPS-Plus' bilateralism both the US and the EU have engaged in to effectively bypass the ongoing review process of key TRIPS provisions.[27] The Access to Knowledge campaign puts the question of FLOSS and the struggle over open standards in a much broader context. WIPO defines creativity in relation to the prospect of proprietisation, as culture is defined as the creation of private property. The FLOSS controversy, on the other hand, is not only about reducing the cost of running a computer lab but also about the implications of its approach to 'commons-based peer production' (Yochai Benkler), i.e. processes of collaborative creation and an information and knowledge commons actively enlarged in opposition to the 'second enclosure' (James Boyle) associated with an ever-expanding IPR regime.[28]

Take the role of FLOSS developers. Rishab Ghosh, FLOSS Programme Leader at the Maastricht Economic Research Institute on Innovation and Technology (MERIT), stresses that licensing costs do matter, especially when GDP is taken into account.[29] But another key emphasis in his studies on FLOSS in developing countries is the building of skills in FLOSS networks. In addition to standard developer skills, open source communities address, almost by default, questions of copyright law and licensing, and introduce users to new forms of collaborative creation. Ghosh calls these 'informal apprenticeships', the social cost of which is, of course, borne by individual users, but it is done so voluntarily, and he even considers the free sharing of developer expertise (often based on expensive degrees) a form of technology transfer. Most definitely exploited by employers who often encourage their employees to participate in FLOSS fora on the job, this voluntarist dynamic is also the basis of networks

26. http://www.cptech.org/a2k, http://www.eff.org/IP/WIPO/dev_agenda and http://www.access2knowledge.org/cs
27. Peter Drahos and John Brathwaite, 'Who Owns the Knowledge Economy? Political Organising Behind TRIPS', *Corner House Briefings*, September 2004, http://www.thecornerhouse.org.uk/pdf/briefing/32trips.pdf also see http://www.bilaterals.org
28. Yochai Benkler, 'Coase's Penguin, or Linux and the Nature of the Firm', 2002, http://www.benkler.org/CoasesPenguin.html, James Boyle, 'A Politics of Intellectual Property: Environmentalism For the Net?', 1997, http://www.law.duke.edu/boylesite/intprop.htm
29. Rishab Ghosh, 'Free/Libre/Open Source Software for Developing Countries: Skills, Employment and Costs', 2nd National Congress on Software Libre, Buenos Aires, Argentina, 7 June 2005, http://www.flossproject.org/papers.htm

of 'roving technology consultants' like GeekCorps or E-Riders, as well as the collaborative practices of the FLOSS community at large.[30]

Info-Political Pragmatism

Rhishab Ghosh has been a major global FLOSS advocate, and his projects specifically address the use of FLOSS outside Europe. Yet, some of his economic arguments are based on the assumption that proprietary alternatives are not locally produced. What Ghosh describes as the benefits of 'deep access' offered by locally developed FLOSS applications – customisation, quick bug fixing, as well as the re-use of code in other applications – is exactly how Herman Chinery-Hesse, CEO of Ghana's successful Soft Tribe, describes his own approach.[31] All of Soft Tribe's software is based on 'tropically relevant' code, Chinery-Hesse's reference to the full spectrum of constraints he associates with local computer use: frequent savings to disk help deal with power failures, and work offline lowers costs for online access. In the case of Soft Tribe's document management software for the Ghana Human Rights Commission, storage on remote servers addresses possible interruptions caused by a change in government. And, unlike Ubuntu, Soft's applications are optimised for the low-end hardware that dominates Ghana's offices and cybercafés.

Soft trains the majority of Ghana's programmers, often left to their own devices in poorly equipped computer science departments. Yet Chinery-Hesse thinks that FLOSS would impede the development of a local software industry, as developers would, he worries, be reduced to installers of pre-existing applications. His main concern, however, seems to be possible tampering with the code, both by users and competitors – Chinery-Hesse fears internal mismanagement and has no interest in interoperability that could threaten Soft's pole position in the local software market. Soft rarely releases beta versions, software does not have an autoinstall function and bug fixes are not generally released. As evidence of Chinery-Hesse's entrepreneurial pragmatism, he has entered into a cooperation agreement with Microsoft, hoping to take advantage of its global distribution channels to bring an add-on from Ghana to desktops around the world.

For Guido Sohne, a former Soft employee and vocal FLOSS advocate, Soft's deal with Microsoft is a form of technology transfer rather than a simple sell-out, prompted by the departure of some of its key developers without whom their previous portfolio of applications could no longer be maintained.[32] Sohne left in part because Soft did not want to explore FLOSS-based alternatives to address this development impasse. Microsoft is there to stay

30. http://www.eriders.net
31. G. Pascal Zachary, 'The African Hacker', *IEEE Spectrum Online*, August 2005, http://www.spectrum.ieee.org/WEBONLY/publicfeature/aug05/0805ahac.html
32. My assessment of Soft is based on an email exchange with Guido Sohne, September 2005. Also see http://sohne.net

(the new Kofi Annan International Peacekeeping Centre in Ghana also entered into a deal with Microsoft), but it looks like Soft Tribe's emergent competitors are already relying on FLOSS. So, while Ghana's developer community as a whole has not yet embraced FLOSS, this is likely to change.

In the current 'Africanisation' of the politics of software, the proprietary/non-proprietary divide is but one of several vectors. Perhaps this should not come as a surprise, given the hybrid dynamic of FLOSS itself. In her analyses of the cooperation between corporations and the FLOSS community, techno-feminist Yuwei Lin describes this process as 'hybrid innovation', marked as much by a sense of interdependence and mutuality as by unease over the irresolvable tension between commercial and community-orientated practices.[33]

The dependence on corporate support illustrates the paradoxes of immaterial labour, and suggests that common assumptions regarding the relationship between FLOSS and visions of a post-capitalist future be revisited. Often understood in terms of an anti-monopolistic practice, FLOSS is not, as such, anti-capitalist (GPL founder, Richard Stallman, describes himself as anti-fascist instead). One of the reasons for the popularity of the FLOSS paradigm is that it appears to be able to accommodate a wide range of visions of cultural, economic and social transformation, from cyberlibertarian views of natural capitalism to the post-autonomist vision of a coming communism, actively anticipated by way of multitudinal self-organisation. Counter-cultural cachet notwithstanding, the high visibility of FLOSS as a mainstream alternative to proprietary software is due in large part to the support from corporations like IBM or Sun Microsystems, and the commitment to openness reverberates with an info-capitalism attempting to reinvent itself around concepts of trust and transparency.

And, while the controversies over software licences are so intense because their clauses redefine what property means in the network society, not all of FLOSS is geared toward an enlargement of the information commons. Following the popularity of user-defined licence provisions like Creative Commons, Sun Microsystems has announced its own 'Open Media Commons' initiative to develop FLOSS-based Digital Rights Management tools.[34] FLOSS, already adopted by cost cutting governments across the world, is also easily aligned with state power – South Africa's FLOSS and open content strategy includes, after all, the migration to FLOSS of its prison management systems.[35]

33. Yuwei Lin, 'Hybrid Innovation: How Does the Collaboration Between the FLOSS Community and Corporations Happen?', *Knowledge, Technology and Policy*, Summer 2005, Vol. 18, no. 2, http://opensource.mit.edu/papers/lin4_hybrid.pdf

34. http://www.openmediacommons.org. As the history of commons-based resource management systems shows, 'commons' doesn't necessarily imply the free-for-all often associated with it, and it is not necessarily obvious – a point frequently made by advocates of indigenous and traditional knowledge databases – that 'commons' and 'access restrictions' are mutually exclusive; what emerges instead are 'hybridised' commons that take the information needs of specific communities into account.

35. http://wiki.go-opensource.org/taskforce/CorrectProj

This makes one-size-fits-all approaches to the politics of software almost impossible, even more so in the context of African ICT controversies.

Yet, what is certain is that an African info-politics is already emerging along key faultlines of network-economical conflict, challenging images of an Africa forever mired in 'tribal rampages' and natural disasters. And, while it is too soon to say what transformative impact FLOSS efforts may already have had, examples like FOSSFA or SchoolNet show that FLOSS is not reducible to an imperial voluntarism out of sync with the 'real' Africa. FLOSS' collaborative ethic is not a post-materialist luxury limited to those on the sunny side of the digital divide. Instead, the Africanisation of FLOSS in terms of an 'ubuntu' philosophy of sharing may soon connect to other collective efforts in a larger pan-African vision of renewal. This project, driven mainly from below, is rarely included in the sovereign perspective of Afro-pessimist prophecies accompanying the current wave of imperial nostalgia.[36] In his documentary, *afro@digital*, Congolese director, Balufu Bakupa-Kanyinda, retrieves the story of the Ishango Bone, the oldest known table of prime numbers, to suggest that mathematics, and by implication the network society as a whole, needs to be given a new, Afro-centric genealogy. FLOSS advocacy may not have to go that far. Yet perhaps a discussion of software politics in Africa should not begin with the question of software but with the contradictory images of Africa that linger in the collective post-colonial imagination.

36. Martin Meredith, *The State of Africa: A History of Fifty Years of Independence*, London: Free Press, 2005. Seumas Milne, 'Britain: Imperial Nostalgia', *Le Monde Diplomatique*, May 2005. Also see Chris Landsberg and Shaun Mckay, 'Engaging the new Pan-Africanism', Centre for Policy Studies, September 2005, http://www.sarpn.org.za/documents/d0001537/CSO-Guide_pan-africanism_2005.pdf

Climate Change and Capital

Will Barnes

Vol 2 #5, Spring/Summer 2007

Capitalist Criminality

With invaluable assistance from modern science and technology, capital is perpetrating a crime for which there is no name, the enormity of which has hitherto been and, apart from the literary holocausts of anti-utopian science fiction, largely remains unimagined.

Capitalist development, whether expanding or contracting and crisis-ridden, merely intensifies and exacerbates ecological degradation. The mindless and extraordinarily destructive disregard for the ecological consequences of the profitable pursuit of exploitable 'natural resources' has led, for example, to the consumption of hydrocarbon-based fossil fuels that are producing a warming of the Earth that is melting the ice caps and raising sea levels, thus threatening the vast seaboard populations of the world. It has produced, specifically, the denuding of tropical forests which, in the end, will deprive humanity of incalculable medicinal wealth. This pursuit has produced the strip mining and clear cutting of vast tracts of land, which has, in turn, created desertification, rendering potentially agriculturally productive lands depleted. It has created a biotechnology centred on genetic engineering that has introduced transgenes, transmitted through natural interspecies crosses, which, in turn, have allowed emergence of resistant superweeds and superpests, which, in their turn, demand the application of further chemical poisons, i.e. herbicides and pesticides, which end up in groundwater, waterways and oceans and poison the food chain. The profitable pursuit of exploitable 'resources' of nature has further led to industrialisation of poultry and livestock production that, in the interests of a greatly enlarged worldwide markets for meat consumption (chicken, beef, pork), has generated life threatening strains of antibiotic-resistant bacteria (E. coli, Campylobacter, etc.) and highly pathogenic, potentially pandemic viruses. It has led to the massive and criminal termination of animal species and microbiotic life forms, an extraordinary contraction in the very basis of life itself. More precisely, the pursuit of exploitable 'natural resources' for capitalist production on a world scale has created a geological and biological regression, reversing thousands and millions of years of natural evolution.

Indeed, species, new ones, come into being and they disappear; Human beings, abrupt climatic changes and even the occasional (by geological standards) natural calamity originating from beyond the Earth, in the solar system, bring about extinctions, even the rare mass extinction. Yet, if the Arctic polar bear dies out (as a consequence of its inability to gain access to food sources, as global warming melts the ice fields it uses to traverse distances, and as a result of the early death of its young, as PCBs [Polychlorinated biphenyls], the product of industrial emissions that fall in their greatest concentration to Earth in the Arctic, lodge in the milk of lactating mother bears), it is an unnecessary loss of a majestic creature, one that is final. Extinct species do not make evolutionary reappearances. Nonetheless, this loss, unintended and undesired, is not of the same order or magnitude as that at which bourgeois civilisation unknowingly takes aim. The problem is that specifically capitalist social transformations are borne along by an objective logic, the outcome of which is necessarily the very destruction of the natural world in its autonomy, cohesion and otherness, that is, in its abiotic coherence as living, and as a presupposition of human life. It is the natural world, as the totality of earthly nature (earthly nature as a totality and in its totality), that capitalist social transformation takes as its object.

The grand sweep of capital's movement at the beginning of the 21st century can only portend a future in which nature, because for capital nature is raw material for commodity production, at the very least undergoes continuous and ever greater homogenisation. Homogenisation means, in the most minimalistic sense, the ongoing destruction of ecological diversity, of species-specific ecological niches and, accordingly, species destruction. It entails, first, the loss of nature as an aesthetically beautiful setting and context in which human and other life forms live. Second, homogenisation of nature is characterised by the emergence and proliferation of a limited number of dominant species (e.g. coyotes, rats, starlings, cockroaches), highly adaptable to the disrupted habitats which will increasingly be unsettling to life practices of other species. Third, it means the gradual disappearance of real, organic foundations of human (and generally animal) health and medicine as centres of biodiversity (such as the Amazon forests) disappear or collapse. Fourth, produced in and through the movement of capital, homogenisation of the Earth will tend toward the creation of nature existing at two poles: uglified raw material basins (denuded forests, open mines, desertified grasslands, etc.) at the start of a cycle of commodity production, and toxic wastelands and garbage cesspools (wetlands turned into landfills, decaying urban centres, vast stretches of ocean densely littered with plastic refuse, etc.) at the end of that cycle, i.e. with commodity consumption. Human beings acting and interacting in nature in this form will tend over several generations to become organically, physiologically and perhaps even anatomically and morphologically a degenerating species.

The precondition for homoeostatic, biospheric nature (i.e. nature as a self-regulating totality capable of internally modifying and adjusting its moments to maintain stability and equilibrium in the face of external changes, e.g. increases in ultraviolet radiation) is sufficient internal diversity. This diversity includes, among other things and relations, a variety of different climatic regimes and zones, a multitude of regional landscapes and, centrally, a huge assortment of different life forms. Thus, it is precisely this internal diversity that the movement of capital is destroying and destroying independently of climate change, and, accordingly, it is the self-regulating character of nature – and life as it has developed over tens of thousands of millennia – that is disappearing.

Climate Change

What is important to recognise here is that the criminality of capital goes beyond the vast and potentially catastrophic problems that climate change has introduced. Even if societies of capital at the level of the world come to grips with ongoing climate change in a manner that allows them to maintain the 'achievements' of capitalism (densely populated reserve industrial armies and objective substance, i.e. built environment, means of production and the mass of circulating commodities) on capitalist terms, generalised ecological collapse as described above is encompassed by capitalist development itself, that is, by the practical reduction of surrounding nature to raw materials for capitalist production.

Let us here and now, though, consider climate change. The Earth as we immediately apprehend it, what we call the biosphere, is a unitary phenomenon; its various partial systems (weather, oceans, atmosphere, abiogenic matter, organic life including 'man') are fully integrated and mutually dependent. It is a self-regulating 'system', the internal diversity of which (precisely that which capital is destroying without regard to climate change) provides its own coherence and guarantees the preservation of life on Earth. As the 'external envelope' of Earth, it orders the constant energy inflow from space (solar energy) on which it is dependent. The constitution of Earth's biosphere has qualitatively changed over geological time, meaning its composition, hence its structure (or the 'laws' governing its 'behaviour'), has also changed. For any evolving, real totality, such would have to be the case. What is basic for the Earth as self-regularity is comprehended physically; the Earth, from this perspective, is grasped as an energy system that makes 'self'-adjustments to maintain an energy equilibrium (inflow of solar heat equals its outflow over time). Climate change is the mechanism of this adjustment, and climate is the immediate expression of this constitution of Earth's biosphere.

To understand climate, and climate change, we must consider reconstructions of the Earth's geography on a geological time scale. While the Earth, at some 3.8 billion years of age, is estimated to be nearly as old as the solar system, geological dating begins in earnest 570 million years ago with the emergence of truly complex, highly developed life forms (fish, insects, reptiles). For the entirety of this vast sweep of geological time down to the present, we can designate 'cool' and 'warm' climate modes on Earth. A simple determination of a climate mode is offered, namely, the presence of ice ranging from periods of intense glaciation (emanating from the poles covered with permanent ice caps) to phases in which the high altitudes have been seasonally cold. Tectonic activity, because it is capable of shifting continental-sized landmasses, has played the largest role in making possible intense cold, especially glaciation. The latter only occurs when there are landmasses very near or over the poles. It should be obvious that, over this simply enormous stretch of geological time, there were periods when landmasses were near or at the poles, and periods when they were not.

Antarctica split off from the ancient, gigantic continent known as Gondwana (encompassing present day Australia, Antarctica, South America, Africa, Asia Minor and Arabia) and arrived at its current locale over 30 million years ago. But, by the time it reached what we identify as the southern pole, it had already begun to glaciate (in response to tectonic changes, to plate uplifting and volcanism). The formation of the Southern Ocean, as an open waterway (with accompanying winds) sweeping round the Earth, isolated Antarctica, creating an atmospheric barrier against weather systems beyond this continent. Until recently, Antarctica has largely made its own climate – a very cold and dry one – which, in turn, has helped to cool an Earth that was hitherto (prior to its separation and drift) warm and wet, with Gondwana remaining largely a temperate rainforest. Some 20 million years ago, tectonic activity entered a period, still ongoing, of considerable diminution (after the continents as we know them today formed), lessening, for the geological time being, its determination in the formation of climate. (Continental drift has brought large landmasses near to the poles, thus allowing the Earth's orbital eccentricity to cyclically create ice ages.) These cooler, drier conditions were particularly noticeable in Africa. And, under these newly forming climatic conditions, species, especially some of the truly large species (ancestors to many of today's large mammals who to them stand only as dwarf instances), died off and new ones appeared. Among the latter group were hominid lines, including the larger brained hominids who appear to be *our* ancestors.

Beginning about 2.5 million years ago, the dynamic climatic structure ('laws') characterising the most recent geological epoch stabilised. So what does our geologically 'contemporary' climatic structure look like?

For an answer to this question, we must consider physical theory aimed at solving the problems of recurrent ice ages (glaciation). Today, our understanding of glaciation in the geological time frame we live in (it began, more or less slowly, 15 million years ago) has largely been resolved into three great cycles that drive the Earth's climatic variability. The Earth's orbit around the sun is elliptical, completing a cycle every 100,000 years. At its greatest, as opposed to its smallest, distance from the sun, a determination of the Earth's eccentricity, there is a 20–30 percent reduction in the amount of radiation (heat) that reaches the Earth. At that eccentricity, it is this relation (of sun to Earth) that has produced ice ages at regular intervals over the past 2,000 millennia. The second cycle concerns the tilt of the Earth on its axis, its obliquity. Tilt determines where the most radiation from the sun will fall on the Earth. A full cycle occurs every 42,000 years. As the Earth revolves around the sun, tilt produces seasons. The last, shortest cycling, periods of 19,000 and 23,000 years, turns, so to speak, on the Earth's wobble (called precession). Created by the magnetic mass distributed unevenly and off-centre between the Earth's inner core and mesosphere, wobble creates a shift, on average, every 21,700 years in its 'true (celestial) North' (North determined along its axis in contradistinction from the Geographical North Pole) from Polaris to Vega. This shift affects seasonal intensity (e.g. hot summers, frigidly cold winters). In the case of all orbital cycles, the changes in radiation that reach the Earth are amplified by the amount present (more or less) of those gases, especially carbon dioxide, which traps solar radiation in the atmosphere.

We note that once the current warming synonymous with the last interglacial (the end of the last ice age was roughly 11,600 years ago) was under way, 'archaic', stateless communities first began to form. Early on during this interglacial (effectively extended by the greenhouse gas emissions warming of the last century and a half), the rudiments of agricultural, sedentary social life, the state and civilisation emerged for the first time. Relative to over two million years of 'contemporary' geological time, historically constituted patterns of weather, such as the regularity of seasons, each with its own predictable structure, are today disappearing. Instead, weather patterns that have existed over millennia are vanishing, and, based on these vanishing patterns, 'the weather' itself is losing its predictability. Similarly, climatic 'regimes' characteristic of specific geographical regions (e.g. a temperate region with mild summers and cold winters) are losing their defining features as these regimes become much more 'elastic'. Destabilised, under conditions of global-warming-induced climate change, the occurrence of weather at its extremes becomes more and more frequent (increased intensity of hurricanes in the Gulf and El Niño effects) because warming radically increases the moisture content in the atmosphere and thus produces extreme weather. The unpredictability and extremism of global warming is perfectly consistent with instances of 'normality' by historical standards, e.g. frigid cold such as in Moscow last Winter. It should be added that those extremes are not fixed. What is an extreme today may be 'normal' five years from now, and what is extreme then might very well hardly be conceivable today. In an abstract way, the only requirement for such warming is that, over time, the average annual temperature rapidly rises for the planet as a whole.

Consequences – A 'New Nature'?

Climate change, and in particular warming as we now understand it, can be abrupt, occurring over years or decades, and not over millennia (or hundreds or maybe thousands of millennia). Abrupt climate change has certain tipping points that 'force' change. Under geologically current conditions, there are three components of the self-regulatory system of the Earth that are crucial for the constitution, if you will, of a 'new nature'; that is, a different regime of climate, seasonality and weather. They are a shut-down of thermohaline circulation in the North Atlantic (the Gulf Stream as it warms Europe, which would be disastrous for Britain and North Europe), the destruction of the Amazonian rain forests, and the release of gas hydrates (clathrates, ice crystal-trapped methane, a carbon-based gas) from the ocean floors. All three are threatened by warming as it is generated by capitalist activity on the scale of the world. For example, sufficient warming (say, by no later than 2080) would melt enough of the Greenland ice sheet to shut down the Gulf Stream in the North Atlantic (the melting of which pushes fresh water into the Stream's current – a vast conveyor of hot water from the Gulf – diluting the heavier saline Gulf water, thus preventing it from dropping toward the ocean floor in the area of Iceland, further preventing it from pulling more warm water in behind it, i.e. effectively shutting it down). The shutdown would induce cooling which, in turn, would bring a halt to ice sheet melting that, in turn, would eventually restart the current and a re-warming, all of which could go on for centuries until the ice reserve had reached a reduced threshold, at which point it could no longer add enough fresh water to stop the circulation. Climatic see-sawing of this sort is one possible, under current conditions likely, outcome of warming. Climatic see-sawing is not, however, a lawful creation of a 'new nature', for example a 'warm' or 'cold' mode; or better, as long as see-sawing continued, a new mode would not be firmly established as climate, at least in some parts of the world, alternated between the two. On the other hand, a massive release of clathrates premised on sufficient warming of the oceans, leading to species extinctions on the order of the Permo-Triassic extinction event, is another, this time abrupt, shift that could usher in a new climatic regime in just decades.

Suspending consideration of the shape of a 'new nature', let us briefly reflect on some of the features of warming as it is now occurring. These include, among others things, increasing frequency and intensity of extreme weather (ice storms, hurricanes or cyclones, tornadoes spun from hurricanes, etc.), rising sea levels and, possibly, the cooling of Northern Europe (not to mention elsewhere the shift northward of subtropical seasonality and temperature into temperate zones).

To even the casual observer here in the United States, the incidence of extreme weather has qualitatively been on the upswing since the 1980s. For example, in 2005, the North West experienced a severe Winter drought; Western states had a record heat wave in July; in the South West, a marked increase in Winter storms included record rain and snow; the central states had a major drought worsening throughout the Summer; the South and South East experienced a record number of hurricanes, 14, seven of which were major; and the North East had flooding in April and record precipitation in October. In two decades, rising sea levels will flood as much as a quarter of the land mass of

Bangladesh; Dhaka, now on average 221 km from the sea, will reach the Bay of Bengal at 97 km; and 30 million people will be displaced, countless others will be dead. Today, the freshwater wells immediately south of Dhaka have become increasingly saline, the water nearly undrinkable. Or, again, in two decades, parts of Sydney, Australia, beginning from its harbour, will be under water. At the time of writing (28 February 2007), the temperature in London (latitude 51.52°N) reached 47°F (8°C); in the region of Moosonee (latitude 51.31°N) in eastern Ontario at the southern tip of James Bay, temperatures ranged from 9 to 14°F (-13 to -10°C). Both are roughly seasonal averages. And, while London may generate 10°F (6°C) of its temperature as a consequence of its concentration of built environment, Moosonee is London's fate under conditions of a shutdown of the thermohaline circulation in the North Atlantic.

'Man-Made' Climate Change?

The overwhelming consensus among scientists and spokespeople of capitalist states in the world today (and even in the US, Australia and Bangladesh, among the most recalcitrant of states, there is grudging acceptance) is that, in terms of causation, 'man' is responsible for warming-induced climate change.

While the evidence is straightforward, the attribution both of culpability *and* the liable agent are effectively ideological, masking real agency and responsibility. Consider, first, the evidence.

From the outset of the current interglacial, some 11,600 years ago, to the end of the 18th century, average global surface temperatures have risen slowly, very slowly, but steadily. This increase, it should be noted, is relative. Plot the average from the peak of the last ice age (last glacial maximum) 22,000 years ago, and that incremental increase (circa 9600 BC to 1760 AD) is not noticeable. But plot average global surface temperature from 1760 to 1870 and the line of temperate approaches a positive 15° angle of incline. Plot it from there to the present and the angle of incline rises to roughly 45°. Back up and plot it from 8000 BC to the present, and those last 235 years present a nearly straight vertical rise.

Note the dates: As suggested earlier, circa 8000 BC is the point at which we mark the beginnings of sedentary agriculture, social division and the rise of the state. And 1760 marks that point at which we can date the commencement of the mechanisation of industry in the West (i.e. in capitalist England). In the former case, initial sedentary life and, with it, rising population began to generate a human input, methane (CH_4) and carbon dioxide (CO_2), into the atmosphere, nothing that, before 1760, might delay a glaciation, but incrementally, in the short view, noticeable. The development of capitalist industrial production after 1760, however, has indeed transformed the chemical make-up of the atmosphere. How?

On a geological time scale, atmospheric CO_2 has ranged from lows of 200 parts per million (ppm) during major glaciations to highs of 280–300 ppm during warm interglacials. Today, atmospheric CO_2 concentration stands at marginally more than 380 ppm and is rising, in geological terms, at an extraordinary and unprecedented rate with, at this moment, no end in sight. Best estimates put a tipping point (qualitatively hastening ice cap melting) as low as 480 ppm, reachable with even modern emissions reductions before 2080. This, then, is the major piece of evidence for anthropocentric-based warming.

Second, consider the attribution of agency and, accordingly, responsibility for climate change. The Intergovernmental Panel on Climate Change (IPCC) tells us that 'man', 'his' activity, is altering climate. In one sense, a very crude argument can and has been made (though not explicitly by the IPCC) that sheer human numbers, a global population of 6 billion, and the outputs that result from the volume of activity of so many people bear direct responsibility. While the quality of human (animal and plant) life may well be grounds for limiting population growth, global warming does not result merely from the activity of masses of humans at any level of development: Today, an Indian child (the Indian subcontinent being one of the most densely populated regions on Earth, India having the second largest population in the world) consumes 1/90 of the annual energy that his or her American counterpart does. The problem is forms of consumption, energy inefficient consumption, not to mention profligate consumption, and the type of development that underpins that consumption.

If we have raised ourselves to the level of understanding at which it is intuitively obvious that human population, either in the contemporary sense or the historical sense (going back some 10,000 years) or both, is neither the agent nor, accordingly, responsible for climate change, we have dissolved one mystification. 'Man' (here, human population generally) as such is a merely formal concept without a determinately real referent. Perhaps, then, the 'industrial system' is at issue. Or, perhaps, it is a question of 'man' in the 'industrial system'. In either case, we are dealing with empty abstractions. The issue is the historically specific configuration of groups of living men and women working within that 'industrial system', i.e. capitalist production. More precisely, the issue is the group which dominates that production. We refer, here, to those personifications of economic categories, capitalists (as well as the bloc of

classes they have in tow). Capitalists (and states that unify otherwise disparate or competing capitals) make decisions concerning the allocation of monies and capital, concerning what and the manner in which 'natural resources' are exploited and utilised and concerning the technologies on the basis of which those activities are carried out. Still, it is not just those decisions but the entire system of social relations that is at issue in climate change. In this sense, it is the subject of society (a part of nature, yet confronting it as raw material for the production of commodities) that is the agent responsible for climate change. It is not 'man' that is remaking, as it were, the biosphere; that remaking is a product of 'his' own objectified and alienated power. This power is capital: Capital is the real subject of human society under conditions of capitalist production (real domination).

At the 'price' of cataclysmic human and social costs, abrupt climate change could transform the geography and sociology of social life. Over the period of decades, a qualitative increase in regimentation and repression of domestic populations to ensure compliance with Draconian restrictions on energy consumption; drought and starvation, massive, unnecessary death; depopulation of coastal areas around the world, forced dislocation, creation of huge frontier zones and camps of displaced persons along national borders, refugees in the tens of millions living in squalor without hope, resource wars between states, ethnic cleansing and genocides as a regular feature of daily life. Nonetheless, while capital *cannot* stem the ecological collapse which its very movement is engendering and within which climate change is situated, it can and, in the view of this author, will meet the warming-induced climate crisis. Whatever else, the social relations of capitalist production will neither disintegrate nor disappear in the maelstrom of climate change.[1] The real question is whether capital, at unimaginable human cost, will set the terms on which this change is confronted, or whether we shall.

1. It has been nearly two years since this article was first penned and, in the intervening time, the climate change catastrophe has become impossible to ignore. Today, the author no longer thinks that capital can meet this crisis on its own terms. Lacking a revolutionary working class transformation at the global level, the outcomes of this catastrophe will, most likely, include (beyond the climate change itself, which will be unpalatable to most forms of life as we know them, entailing massive species extinction): human demographic collapse; attempted, and far more repressive, statist-totalitarian political and economic solutions, culminating in renewed imperialist world war; and the destruction of capitalist civilisation, with a reversion of humanity to a level below that at the origins of agriculture, stratified societies and the state ten to twelve thousand years ago.

Chapter 5

Organising Horizontally

The internet's structure as a distributed network was seen by many as providing the tools with which to run mass experiments in direct democracy, perhaps for the first time. The appearance of the World Wide Web in the early-'90s was accompanied by new forms of political activity, coordinated across the internet, which took on analogously distributed and networked forms, and helped to grow the anti-globalisation movement which culminated at the end of the decade. The aim of many of these emergent political organisations and platforms was to supersede the outdated vanguardism of the party form and to forge alliances across diverse groups, without the need for a controlling centre, a clearly defined ideology or a set of goals. While this revitalisation of political energies by the net was doubtless also felt on the right, *Mute* was concerned with its anti-capitalist manifestations. As the decade wore on, and open publishing sites like Indymedia and alliance-political experiments came of age, we found our pages increasingly filled with debates around the viability of so-called horizontality.

The first sustained analysis of the new political shoots of many-to-many media in *Mute* was Richard Barbrook's article, 'Holy Fools'. In it, he traced the left's disillusionment with party politics post-May '68, through the 'schizo-politics' of Deleuze and Guattari and its latter-day, and purportedly de-politicised, re-adoption by the digerati. For Barbrook, the professed rejection of vanguardism by the New Left – alongside the project of modernity *tout court*, in the name of psychologised 'molecular revolution' – nevertheless gave rise to a kind of covert elitism and snobbery within the political and artistic avant-gardes. According to Barbrook, writing in 1998, the digerati were adopting D&G and their 'poetry of flows' as a way of feigning progressiveness while abandoning revolutionary politics in the aftermath of the Soviet Union's collapse. Unnoticed by these 'techno-nomads', however, capitalism was quietly withering away in the net, as the gift economy was normalised and mass participation in media gave rise to a far more experimental culture than that of the official avant-garde.

The year following Barbrook's text saw an explosion of anti-capitalist activity and civil disobedience, with London's financial district sustaining millions of pounds worth of damage during the Carnival Against Capitalism (J18), and, later, the mass boycotting of the WTO meeting in Seattle (N30). These events triggered a wave of protest that finally broke with the events of 9/11 – or so left mythology would have it. But, reading across the articles we published on the question of organising and alliance-based politics at the time, it seems that the seeds of dissolution were sown from the start in highly festishised, but broadly under-examined, forms – horizontality and openness. As Eileen Condon describes in her text on London's May Day, 2000, the 'confoundingly atomised' protests of J18, in which a clear anti-capitalist message was given, had degenerated into a 'locatable, better containable core' whose message was easily hijacked. The Guerrilla Gardening escapades in Parliament Square and the Cenotaph's defacement were interpreted as an attack on the nation, with Reclaim the Streets acting as spokesperson.

Writing in 2002, Horacio Tarcus touches on similar experiments with leaderless organising in the context of Argentina's economic crisis. As the country's economic meltdown led to the widespread rejection of parliamentary politics and the state's loss of legitimacy, *Assemblias*, or neighbourhood assemblies, sprang up across the country. Here, people debated and decided upon local issues, often for the first time. Of course, despite the revolutionary hopes vested in these direct democratic structures, Tarcus describes the power struggles which took place within them between independents (in which 'a good deal of libertarian mettle exists') and party members. The complexity of this particular situation, and, indeed, the problematic in general, lies in the simultaneous attempts at 'rejecting politics' and 'politicising society'.

It is this complexity which J.J. King picks up on in his careful study of the so-called 'open organisations' of the anti-globalisation movement. Using the tools of the web and adopting the collaborative working methods of Free/Libre Open Source Software (FLOSS), many groups ran, and continue to run, experiments in dismantling the 'formal hierarchical membrane of groups'. Despite making declarations of organisational openness and a general faith in the progressiveness of these structures, closer analysis revealed that 'tacit control structures' tended to emerge. The tearing away of hierarchical structures seemed to allow for the self-reinforcement of the inequities which structure society in general.

Hydrarchist – in his autopsy of the Italian extra-parliamentary group, the *Disobbedienti* (Disobedients) – homes in on the other problematic inherent in horizontality's rejection of representative politics: how to 'have an effect'. Despite the relative failure of these experiments, there has been no mass defection to older structures such as the party form. Even if only as a kind of negative critique of mainstream or failed revolutionary politics, openness and horizontality still maintain a progressive allure. And, while a religiose devotion to collaborative structures persists in many quarters (*pace* relational aesthetics, FLOSS and 'consultative' politics), the idea that they might, in themselves, provide a panacea to society's ills appears to be on the wane. How we de-programme our capitalist selves, however, still seems as relevant a question today as it did in '68.

The Holy Fools

Richard Barbrook

Vol 1 #11, Autumn 1998

> 'But I don't want to go among mad people,' Alice remarked. 'Oh, you can't help that,' said the Cat: 'We're all mad here. I'm mad. You're mad.' 'How do you know I'm mad?' said Alice. 'You must be,' said the Cat, 'or you wouldn't have come here.'
>
> Lewis Carroll, *Alice in Wonderland*

The Lost Utopia

The net is haunted by the disappointed hopes of the 1960s. Because this new technology symbolises another period of rapid change, many contemporary commentators look back to the stalled revolution of thirty years ago to explain what is happening now. Most famously, the founders of *Wired* appropriated New Left rhetoric to promote their New Right policies for the net.[1] Within Europe, a long history of class-based politics and compulsive theorising makes such ideological chicanery seem much more implausible. However, this does not mean that Europeans are immune to embracing digital elitism in the name of 1960s libertarianism. Ironically, this bizarre union of opposites is most evident in writings inspired by Gilles Deleuze and Félix Guattari.

Although these two philosophers were overt leftists during their lifetimes, many of their contemporary followers support a form of aristocratic anarchism which is eerily similar to Californian neoliberalism.[2] By doing so, the Deleuzo-guattarians have unwittingly exposed the fatal weaknesses within what appears to be an impeccably emancipatory analysis of the net. Trapped within the precepts of their sacred creed, the disciples of Deleuze and Guattari can't even begin to grasp why the spread of the net is really such a subversive phenomenon.

At the end of the 20th century, the superficiality of postmodernism is no longer fashionable among radical intellectuals. But, because the Soviet Union has collapsed, the European avant-garde cannot return to its old obsession with Leninism so, instead, theory jockeys (TJs)[3] look back to the libertarian spontaneity epitomised by May '68. Even after decades of reactionary rule, the folk memory of the 1960s still remains an inspiration in the present. The democratic ways of working, cultural experimentation and emancipatory lifestyles initiated in this period survive – and even flourish – within the DIY culture of the 1990s.[4]

1. See Richard Barbrook and Andy Cameron, 'The Californian Ideology', *Mute*, Vol 1 #3, Autumn 1995.
2. See Hari Kunzru, 'Rewiring Technoculture', *Mute*, Vol 1 #7, Winter 1997 and James Flint, 'Harvesting the Tubers: the Planting of Deleuze and Guattari', *Mute*, Vol 1 #7, Winter 1997.
3. Amsterdam slang for intellectuals who cut'n'mix philosophies like DJs in a club.
4. See Elaine Brass and Sophie Poklewski Koziell with Denise Searle (Eds.), *Gathering Force: DIY Culture – Radical Action for Those Tired of Waiting*, London: *The Big Issue*, 1997.

However, as belief in the overthrow of capitalism is no longer credible, contemporary European intellectuals have turned social transformation into theoretical poetry: a revolutionary dreamtime for the imagination.

The cult of Deleuze and Guattari is a prime example of this aesthetisation of 1960s radicalism. Above all, their most famous book, *A Thousand Plateaus*, now provides the buzzwords and concepts for a specifically European understanding of the net. In contrast with the US, when it emerged in Europe, the net was initially seen as a place for social and cultural experimentation rather than as a business opportunity, and the writings of Deleuze and Guattari seemed to describe its non-commercial aspects. For instance, the rhizome metaphor captures how cyberspace is organised as an open-ended, spontaneous and horizontal network, and their Body-without-Organs formulation can be used to romanticise cybersex. Deleuze and Guattari's nomad myth reflects the mobility of contemporary net users as workers and tourists.

Within the rhizomes of the net, the Deleuzoguattarians form their own subculture: the techno-nomads. These adepts are united by specific 'signifying practices': computer technologies, techno music, bizarre science, esoteric beliefs, illegal chemicals and cyberpunk novels. Above all, these techno-nomads possess a radical optimism about the future of the net. While all that remains of hippy ideals in *Wired* is its psychedelic layout, the European avant-garde and its imitators still champion the lost utopia of May '68 through the theoretical poetry of Deleuze and Guattari. The revolution will be digitised.

The Politics of May '68

Far from deterring an audience educated in structuralism, the hermetic language and tortured syntax of *A Thousand Plateaus* is seen as proof of its analytical brilliance. However, this idiosyncratic Deleuzoguattarian discourse is causing as much confusion as elucidation among their followers. For instance, the Rhizome website blandly announces that 'rhizome is [...] a figurative term [...] to describe non-hierarchical networks of all kinds'.[5] At no point does this website explain either the political meaning of this peculiar concept or how its principles might be applied within the net. On the contrary, rhizome is simply a hip European phrase, borrowed to celebrate the disorganised nature of the New York cyberarts scene. Yet, Deleuze and Guattari were not simply avant-garde art critics; as *soixante-huitards*,[6] they championed the most radical expression of 1960s politics: anarcho-communism. As its name suggests, this stood for the destruction of both state power and market capitalism; society would be reorganised as a direct democracy and as a gift economy. Its appeal derived not only from abstract theory but also from concrete practice.

5. See the FAQ section on Rhizome (was www.rhizome.com, now www.rhizome.org)
6. See Gilles Deleuze, 'Control and Becoming', *Negotiations: 1972–1990*, New York: Columbia University Press, 1995: 'May '68 was a demonstration, an irruption, of a becoming in its pure state [...] Men's only hope lies in a revolutionary becoming: the only way of casting off their shame or responding to what is intolerable'.

During the 1960s, anarcho-communists led the search for radical solutions to the historically novel problems facing young people. Above all, many people now wanted a say in the decisions which affected them. They were no longer willing to accept leadership from above without some form of dialogue. Responding to these circumstances, young militants rediscovered and updated anarcho-communism, not only as a theory but also as a practice. Unlike their parents' parliamentary parties and trade unions, the New Left could articulate their contemporaries' demands for greater participation. Instead of others deciding their lives for them, young people wanted to do things for themselves.

> '[Anarcho-]communism is not a new mode of production; it is the affirmation of a new community.'[7]

The Romance of 'Schizo-Politics'

Like many other gurus of the New Left, Deleuze and Guattari believed that the state was the source of all oppression, using top-down, tree-like structures to subjugate people since the dawn of agrarian civilisation, through a process of 'territorialisation'. In contrast with Marxist analyses, Deleuze and Guattari believed that economics was only one manifestation of the state's primordial will to dominate all human activity.

Deleuze and Guattari thought the traditional style of left-wing politics obsolete. As part of the 'guaranteed' sector of the economy, private and public sector workers had not only been bought off by the system, but had also had their desires manipulated by the family, the media, the dominant language and psychoanalysis. Facing the transhistorical enemy of the state was a new opponent: the social movements. Like much of the post-'68 New Left, the two philosophers looked instead to youth, feminists, ecologists, homosexuals and immigrants to 'deterritorialise' the power of the state. As part of the 'non-guaranteed' sector, people in these movements were excluded from the system and were, therefore, supposedly eager to fight for the revolution.[8]

In *A Thousand Plateaus*, the nomads poetically symbolise the 'molecular' social movements making the anarcho-communist revolution against the 'molar' tyranny of political power. Far from trying to seize political power, nomads used their mobility to avoid the 'territorialised' control of the authoritarian state. These members of the social movements constituted a multiplicity of hippy tribes, which were autonomous from all centralising and hierarchical tendencies, especially those supported by the mainstream left. Along the 'lines of flight' mapped out by the New Left, the oppressed would escape the control of the authoritarian state into autonomous rhizomes formed by the social movements; the rhizome became the poetic metaphor for this nomadic vision of direct democracy.

7. Jacques Camatte, *The Wandering of Humanity*, Detroit: Black & Red, 1975.
8. See Félix Guattari, *Molecular Revolution: Psychiatry and Politics*, London: Penguin, 1994.

For Deleuze and Guattari, the overthrow of political power was only the beginning of the anarcho-communist revolution. They believed that political domination was made possible only through personal repression. The anarcho-communist revolution, therefore, had to liberate the libidinal energies of people from all forms of social control. The individual 'delirium' of schizophrenics prefigured the chaotic spirit of collective revolution. This meant that radicals not only had to detonate a social uprising but also to personally live out the cultural revolution. The New Left revolutionary was symbolised as the Body-without-Organs – a person who was no longer 'organised, signified, subjected' by the rationality of the state'.[9] Such individuals were forerunners of the new type of human being who would emerge after the anarcho-communist revolution: a hippy equivalent of Nietzsche's *Übermensch*: '[…] The possibility […] to rear a master race, the future "masters of the earth"; a new tremendous aristocracy […] in which […] philosophical men of power and artist-tyrants will […] work as artists on "man" himself.'[10]

For Deleuze and Guattari, therefore, anarcho-communism was not just the realisation of direct democracy and the gift economy. In their 'schizo-politics', the revolution would destroy bourgeois rationality so that each individual could become a holy fool: '[The Fool…] is the vagabond who exists on the fringe of organised society, going his own way, ignoring the rules and taboos with which men seek to contain him. He is the madman who carries within him the seeds of genius, the one who is despised by society yet who is the catalyst who will transform that society'.[11]

The Moment of Community Radio

Within the exuberant writings of the Deleuzoguattarians, there is a curious – and revealing – omission. They almost never mention Guattari's claim, in the 1980s, that the Minitel system – the French proto-net – was about to replace top-down mass media with bottom-up 'post-media'.[12] The reason for this absence must be found in the close similarity between Guattari's Minitel utopia and his earlier dreams about the revolutionary potential of community radio. Paradoxically, it is Guattari's anarcho-communist adventure within radio that provides the answer to why his disciples have developed such a curious affinity to the aristocratic ideology of *Wired*.

After May '68, many members of the New Left believed that producing alternative media was the most effective and fun way of putting their

9. Gilles Deleuze and Félix Guattari, *A Thousand Plateaus: Capitalism and Schizophrenia*, London: Athlone Press, 1988.
10. Friedrich Nietzsche, *The Will to Power*, New York: Vintage, 1968. Deleuze commended Nietzsche for the 'positive task' of inventing the reactionary concept of the *Übermensch*.
11. Alfred Douglas, *The Tarot*. This Gnostic vision of human freedom is remarkably close to the liberating role of insanity championed by the two philosophers.
12. See Félix Guattari, 'Three Ecologies', *New Formations*, no. 8.

revolutionary theory into practice. In both Italy and France, nationalised radio and television corporations had been disseminating propaganda from the ruling conservative parties for decades. During the 1970s, New Left activists challenged this monopoly by setting up pirate radio stations. As the regulations against unlicensed broadcasting collapsed, thousands of 'free radios' emerged, first in Italy and later in France. Although most were commercial, a minority were run by New Left activists.

According to Guattari, community radio stations were the only alternative to the domination of the airwaves by mindless 'disco radios'. He wanted radio broadcasting to be used to create an electronic form of direct democracy that could replace the corrupt system of representative democracy; instead of listening to elected politicians, people would directly express their own opinions on the programmes of community radio stations. The ultimate aim of 'free radio' was the subversion of bourgeois rationality and repressive sexuality within everyday life. When people were able to express their own views over the airwaves, Guattari hoped that the 'delirium' of desire would be released within the population.[13]

In the early-1980s, Guattari was the leader of Fréquence Libre, a community radio station licensed to broadcast across Paris. However, it soon became obvious that turning Deleuzoguattarian theory into practice was impossible. Far from encouraging audience participation, the sectarian politics of the two philosophers actually discouraged people – including many on the left – from getting involved in their community radio station. Guattari and his colleagues were more interested in lecturing the audience than in engaging in discussions with them. This revolutionary elitism even extended to the musical policies of the station. When some rappers approached Fréquence Libre about the possibility of making some programmes, the station refused to let any hip-hop crews on air until their lyrics had been politically vetted! After they'd alienated most of their potential activists and audience, Guattari's 'free radio' encountered growing difficulties in raising sufficient cash and recruiting enough volunteers to operate the station. Eventually, Fréquence Libre went bankrupt and its frequency was sold to pay its debts. Guattari's attempts to turn theory into practice within the 'free radio' movement had ended in tragedy.[14]

From Stalin to Pol Pot

Techno-nomad TJs are attracted by the uncompromising theoretical radicalism expressed by Deleuze and Guattari. Unwilling to connect abstract theory with its practical application, the techno-nomads cannot see how Deleuze and

13. See Félix Guattari, 'Les Radios Libres Populaires', *De la Necessité Socio-culturelles de l'Existence de Radios Libres Indépendantes*; and his introduction to Collectif A/Traverso, *Radio Alice, Radio Libre* (translated in *Molecular Revolution: Psychiatry and Politics*).
14. Interview with Fréquence Libre contributor, Jean-Paul Simard, April 1985. Annick Cojean and Frank Eskenazi, *FM: la folle histoire des radios libres*, Paris: Grasset, 1986.

Guattari's celebration of direct democracy simultaneously became a justification for intellectual elitism. But this elitism was no accident; many young people in the 1960s experienced a pronounced 'generation gap' between themselves and their parents and believed that society could only be changed by a revolutionary vanguard composed of themselves and their comrades. This is why many young radicals believed in two contradictory concepts. First, the revolution would create mass participation in running society. Second, the revolution could only be organised by a committed minority.[15]

The New Left militants were reliving an old problem in a new form. Back in the 1790s, Robespierre had argued that the democratic republic could only be created by a revolutionary dictatorship. During the 1917 Russian Revolution, Lenin had advocated direct democracy while simultaneously instituting the totalitarian rule of the Bolsheviks. As their 'free radio' experience showed, Deleuze and Guattari never escaped from this fundamental contradiction of revolutionary politics. Far from being a participatory democracy, Fréquence Libre was dominated by a few charismatic individuals: the holy prophets of the anarcho-communist revolution.[16]

In Deleuze and Guattari's writings, this deep authoritarianism found its theoretical expression in their methodology: semiotic structuralism. Despite rejecting its 'wooden language', the two philosophers never really abandoned Stalinism in theory. Above all, they retained its most fundamental premise – that the minds of the majority of the population were controlled by bourgeois ideologies.[17] During the 1960s, this elitist theory was updated through the addition of Lacanian structuralism by Louis Althusser, the chief philosopher of the French Communist Party.[18] For Deleuze and Guattari, Althusser explained why only a revolutionary minority supported the New Left. Brainwashed by the semiotic 'machinic assemblages' of the family, media, language and psychoanalysis, most people desired fascism rather than anarcho-communism. This authoritarian methodology clearly contradicted the libertarian rhetoric within Deleuze and Guattari's writings. By adopting an Althusserian analysis, Deleuze and Guattari were tacitly privileging their own role as intellectuals, the producers of semiotic systems. Just like their Stalinist elders, the two philosophers believed that only a vanguard of intellectuals had the right to lead the masses – without any formal consent from them – in the fight against capitalism.

For young militants, the problem was how this committed minority could make a revolution without ending up with totalitarianism. Some of the New Left

15. The vanguard was a military term used for the advance guard who opened up the path for the main army. Applied to politics, this phrase emphasised the leadership role of radical intellectuals within revolutionary organisations.
16. For a critique of New Left vanguardism, see Jo Freeman, 'The Tyranny of Structurelessness', *Untying the Knot: Feminism, Anarchism and Organisation*, London: Dark Star/Rebel Press, 1984.
17. See V.I. Lenin, *What Is To Be Done?: Burning Questions of Our Movement*, Beijing: Foreign Language Press, 1975. Georg Lukács, *History and Class Consciousness*, London: Merlin, 1968.
18. See Louis Althusser, *Lenin and Philosophy and Other Essays*, London: New Left Books, 1971.

thought that anarcho-communism expressed their desire to overthrow both political and economic oppression.[19] However, even this revolutionary form of politics appeared to many as tainted by the bloody failure of the Russian Revolution. Had not the experience of Stalinism proved that any compromise with the process of modernity would inevitably lead to the reimposition of tyranny? Consequently, anarcho-communist thinkers increasingly decided that just opposing the oppressive features of economic development was not radical enough. Desiring a complete transformation of society, they rejected the transcendent 'grand narrative' of modernity altogether, especially those left-wing versions inspired by Hegel and Marx. The whole concept of progress was a fraud designed to win acquiescence for the intensification of capitalist domination; while the mainstream left still wanted to complete the process of modernisation, the New Left should instead be leading a revolution against modernity.[20]

Following May '68, support for rural guerrillas resisting American imperialism quickly became mixed up with hippy tribalism, concerns about environmental degradation and nostalgia for a lost peasant past. Disillusioned with the economic progress championed by the parliamentary left, many on the New Left synthesised these different ideas into hatred of the mass urban society created by modernity. For them, a truly libertarian revolution could only have one goal: the destruction of the city.[21]

Deleuze and Guattari enthusiastically joined this attack against the concept of historical progress. For them, the 'deterritorialisation' of urban society was the solution to the contradiction between participatory democracy and revolutionary elitism haunting the New Left. If the centralised city could be broken down into 'molecular rhizomes', direct democracy and the gift economy would reappear as people formed themselves into small nomadic bands. According to Deleuze and Guattari, anarcho-communism was not the 'end of history'; on the contrary, the liberation of desire from semiotic oppression was a perpetual promise: an ethical stance which could equally be lived by nomads in ancient times or social movements in the present. With enough intensity of effort, anyone could overcome their hierarchical brainwashing to become a fully liberated individual: the holy fool.[22]

Yet, as the experience of Fréquence Libre proved, this rhetoric of unlimited freedom contained a deep desire for ideological control by the New Left

19. Above all, anarcho-communism was seen as the heir of those left Communists who had fought for direct democracy organised through the Soviets against the dictatorship of the Leninist party. See Maurice Brinton, *The Bolsheviks and Workers' Control: 1917–1921*, London: Solidarity, 1970. Ida Mett, *The Kronstadt Uprising 1921*, London: Solidarity, 1967.

20. See Camatte, op. cit. Of course, a much diluted variant of this attack on oppressive 'grand narratives' later formed the ideological basis for the self-styled postmodernists.

21. In classic New Left films like *Weekend* and *Themroc*, rebellion against a repressive and alienating urban society was symbolically represented through a return to primitive simplicity. Curiously, both films portrayed cannibalism as the ultimate expression of liberation from bourgeois morality!

22. See Deleuze and Guattari, 1988, op. cit.

vanguard. While the nomadic fantasies of *A Thousand Plateaus* were being composed, one revolutionary movement did actually carry out Deleuze and Guattari's dream of destroying the city. Led by a vanguard of Paris-educated intellectuals, the Khmer Rouge overthrew an oppressive regime installed by the Americans in Cambodia. Rejecting the 'grand narrative' of economic progress, Pol Pot and his organisation instead tried to construct a rural utopia. However, when the economy subsequently imploded, the regime embarked on ever more ferocious purges until the country was rescued by an invasion from neighbouring Vietnam. Deleuze and Guattari had claimed that the destruction of the city would create direct democracy and libidinal ecstasy. In practice, the application of such anti-modernism resulted in tyranny and genocide. The 'line of flight' from Stalin had led to Pol Pot.[23]

The Antinomies of the Avant-Garde

Ironically, the current popularity of Deleuze and Guattari comes from their stubborn refusal to recognise the failure of the anti-modernist revolution. Even when Fréquence Libre went bankrupt, Deleuze and Guattari never questioned their 'schizo-politics'. Instead, they transformed the historically specific politics of the New Left into a theoretical poetry which existed outside history.[24] For 'cutting edge' TJs, it is now almost compulsory to sample from Deleuze and Guattari and their political irrelevance does not seem to discredit their theoretical poetry among radical intellectuals. On the contrary, the defeat of the New Left has enabled their disciples to complete the transformation of anarcho-communism from the hope of social revolution into the symbol of personal authenticity: an ethical-aesthetic rejection of bourgeois society.

The aestheticisation of revolutionary politics is a revered tradition of the European avant-garde. Back in the 1920s, the Surrealists perfected the fusion of artistic creativity with social rebellion. Inspired by Lenin, this avant-garde movement claimed that the consciousness of the majority of the population was controlled by cultural mediocrity and puritan morality. Therefore, radical intellectuals had the heroic task of freeing the people from ideological domination. Their innovative art would undermine the repressive cultural norms of bourgeois society; their bohemian way of living would challenge the dull conformity of everyday life under capitalism. In this interpretation of Leninism, cultural experimentation became the privileged expression of revolutionary

23. Apart from its emphasis on peasants rather than nomads, Khmer Rouge ideology was very similar to the anti-modernism espoused by Deleuze and Guattari. See Michael Vickery, *Cambodia: 1975–1982*, Hemel Hempstead: Allen and Unwin, 1984.
24. In contrast, most of their contemporaries gravitated towards either electoral politics or postmodern nihilism. See Jean-Pierre Garnier and Roland Lew, 'From The Wretched of the Earth to the Defence of the West: An Essay on Left Disenchantment in France', *Socialist Register 1984: The Uses of Anti-Communism*, London: Merlin, 1984.

politics. Innovative paintings, sculptures, photography, films and literature would be made '[...] in the service of the revolution'. [25]

The cult of Deleuze and Guattari is the latest manifestation of this European avant-garde tradition. The change in language disguises a continuity in practice. Just like its Surrealist predecessors, the contemporary avant-garde equates experimental art and bohemian lifestyles with social rebellion. Despite their involvement with radio and Minitel, Deleuze and Guattari hoped that the 'line of flight' from modernity would lead back to the tribal past. By contrast, their contemporary followers have no ambiguity about their relationship with modern technologies. Far from desiring the destruction of the city, radical intellectuals hope that the Deleuzoguattarian utopia will emerge from the high-tech net. Using intellectual alchemy, they transmute their gurus' anti-modernist scriptures into a philosophy of hyper-modernism.

This aestheticisation of May '68 is made much easier by the poetic style of Deleuze and Guattari. As in modernist painting, the 'realism' of the text has been superseded by a fascination with the formal techniques of theoretical production. For Deleuze and Guattari, theory was a piece of literature expressing authentic emotion rather than a tool for understanding social reality. Following this example, techno-nomad TJs sample Deleuzoguattarian discourse to produce leftfield philosophy. Yet, as with Britpop bands, something is lost in these respectful homages to the past. The European avant-garde is now discarding the few remaining connections with practical politics. Using Deleuzoguattarian discourse, avant-garde intellectuals recreate May '68 as a theory-art project for the net.

Yet, like the Leninist vanguard, the European avant-garde is haunted by the fatal contradiction between popular participation and intellectual elitism. For decades, radical intellectuals have adopted dissident politics, aesthetics and morals to separate themselves from the majority of 'herd animals' whose minds were controlled by bourgeois ideologies.[26] Despite their revolutionary rhetoric, avant-garde intellectuals fantasised about themselves as an artistic aristocracy ruling the philistine masses. Following this elitist custom, Deleuzoguattarians champion nomadic minorities from the 'non-guaranteed' social movements rather than the supposedly stupefied majority from the 'guaranteed' sector. Once again, the revolution is the ethical-aesthetic illumination of a minority, rather than the social liberation of all people.

Earlier in this century, this dream of an artistic aristocracy sometimes evolved into fascism. More often, the avant-garde supported totalitarian tendencies within the left. Nowadays, cultural elitism can easily turn into implicit sympathy with neoliberalism. The European avant-garde and its imitators could never

25. From 1930 to 1933, the Surrealists' journal was called *Le Surréalisme au Service de la Révolution.* See Helena Lewis, *Dada Turns Red: The Politics of Surrealism*, Edinburgh: Edinburgh University Press, 1990.
26. According to Nietzsche, the culturally impoverished masses were 'herd animals' compared to the 'eagles' of the artistic world.

openly support the free market fundamentalism of the Californian Ideology. Yet, as TJs cut'n'mix, the distinctions between right and left libertarianism are blurring. On the one hand, the Californian ideologues claim that a heroic minority of cyber-entrepreneurs is emerging from the fierce competition of the electronic marketplace. On the other hand, the Deleuzoguattarians believe that this new elite consists of cool TJs and hip artists who release subversive 'assemblages of enunciation' into the net. In both the Californian Ideology and Deleuzoguattarian discourse, primitivism and futurism are combined to produce the apotheosis of individualism: the cyborg *Übermensch*.

The High-Tech Gift Economy

Following the collapse of the Soviet Union, the contemporary avant-garde must substitute itself for the missing political vanguard. The techno-nomads, therefore, remix Lenin with Nietzsche into Deleuzoguattarian discourse. In the late-1990s, revolutionary elitism can only be expressed in the words of May '68. Yet, important pioneers of the New Left were highly critical of this tradition of cultural elitism. For instance, the Situationists advocated transforming the social context of cultural production rather than the aesthetics of art; instead of following the avant-garde elite, everyone should have the opportunity of expressing themselves.[27]

Above all, the Situationists looked for ways of living free from the corruptions of consumer capitalism. Despite their Hegelian modernism, they claimed that anarcho-communism had been prefigured by the potlatch – the gift economy of Polynesian tribes. Within these primitive societies, the circulation of gifts bound people together into tribes and encouraged cooperation between different tribes. This tribal gift economy demonstrated that individuals could successfully live together without needing either the state or the market. Moreover, the Situationists believed that there could be no compromise between tribal authenticity and bourgeois alienation. After the social revolution, the potlatch would completely supplant the commodity.[28]

Following May '68, this purist vision of anarcho-communism inspired a generation of cultural activists. Emancipatory media could only be produced within the gift economy. During the late-1970s, pro-Situ attitudes were further popularised by the punk movement. From then to the present day, the 'cutting edge' of music has remained participatory. Crucially, every user of the net is now also participating within a gift economy. Although funded by the Pentagon, the net could only be successfully developed by letting its users build the system for themselves. From scientists through hobbyists to

27. See Ken Knabb (Ed.), *Situationist International Anthology*, California: Bureau of Public Secrets, 1981.
28. See Raoul Vaneigem, *The Revolution of Everyday Life*, London: Practical Paradise, 1972. The Situationists discovered the tribal gift economy in Marcel Mauss, *The Gift*.

the general public, the charmed circle of users was slowly built up through the adhesion of many localised networks to an agreed set of protocols. Crucially, the common standards of the net include social conventions as well as technical rules. Without even thinking about it, people continually circulate information among each other for free. They cooperate without the direct mediation of either politics or money. Far from being the privilege of intellectuals, anarcho-communism is the mundane activity of ordinary people within cyberspace.

Above all, the founders of the net never bothered to protect intellectual property within computer-mediated communications. Far from wanting to enforce copyright, they tried to eliminate all barriers to the distribution of information. Within the commercial creative industries, advances in digital reproduction are regarded with suspicion for their ability to make the 'piracy' of copyrighted material ever easier. In contrast, the academic gift economy welcomes technologies which improve the availability of data, on the basis that users should always be able to obtain and manipulate information with the minimum of impediments. [29] The design of the net, therefore, assumes that intellectual property is technically and socially obsolete.

Despite the commercialisation of cyberspace, self interest ensures that the high-tech gift economy continues to flourish. The giving and receiving of information without payment is almost never questioned, encouraging people to become anarcho-communists within cyberspace. By adding their own presence, every user contributes to the collective knowledge accessible to those already online. In return, each individual has potential access to all the information made available by others within the net; everyone takes far more out than they can ever give as an individual.[30] In the absence of states or markets to mediate these social bonds, network communities are formed instead through the mutual obligations created by gifts of time and ideas.

The high-tech gift economy is even at the forefront of software development. For instance, Bill Gates admits that Microsoft's biggest competitor in the provision of web servers comes from the Apache program.[31] Instead of being marketed by a commercial company, this program is a communal product. Because its source code is not protected by copyright, Apache servers can be modified, amended and improved by anyone with the appropriate programming skills. Shareware programs are now beginning to threaten the core product of the Microsoft empire: the Windows operating system. Starting from the original software by Linus Torvalds, a community of user-developers are building their

29. See Warren O. Hagstrom, 'Gift Giving as an Organisational Principle in Science', *Science in Context: Readings in the Sociology of Science*, Milton Keynes: The Open University, 1982.
30. See Rishab Aiyer Ghosh, 'Cooking Pot Markets: An Economic Model for the Trade in Free Goods and Services on the Internet', http://www.firstmonday.org/issues/issue3_3/ghosh/index.html
31. See Keith W. Porterfield, 'Information Wants to be Valuable: A Report form the First O'Reilly Perl Conference', http://www.netaction.org/articles/freesoft.html

own non-proprietary operating system: Linux. For the first time, Windows has a real competitor.[32] But the ideological passion of anarcho-communism is dulled by the banality of giving gifts within cyberspace.

Beyond the Avant-Garde

The New Left anticipated the emergence of the high-tech gift economy, whereby people could collaborate with each other without needing either markets or states. However, the New Left had a purist vision of DIY culture, and there could be no compromise between the authenticity of the potlatch and the alienation of the market. Bored by the emotional emptiness of postmodernism, the techno-nomads are entranced by the uncompromising fervour of Deleuze and Guattari. However, as shown by Fréquence Libre, the rhetoric of mass participation often hides the rule of the enlightened few. The ethical-aesthetic commitment of anarcho-communism can only be lived by the artistic aristocracy. Yet the antinomies of the avant-garde can no longer be avoided.

Anarcho-communism exists in a compromised form on the net, with the gift economy and the commercial sector expanding through mutual collaboration within cyberspace. The free circulation of information between users relies upon the capitalist production of computers, software and telecommunications. The profits of net companies depend upon increasing numbers of people participating in the high-tech gift economy. Under threat from Microsoft, Netscape is now trying to realise the opportunities opened up by such interdependence. Lacking the resources to beat its monopolistic rival, the development of products for the Linux operating system has become a top priority. Anarcho-communism is now sponsored by corporate capital.[33]

The purity of digital DIY culture is also compromised by the political system. Because the dogmatic communism of Deleuze and Guattari has dated badly, their disciples instead emphasise their uncompromising anarchism; however, the state isn't only the potential censor and regulator of the net, it is also its funder and promoter. The cult of Deleuze and Guattari is threatened by the miscegenation of the high-tech gift economy with the private and public sectors.

Anarcho-communism symbolised moral integrity: the romance of artistic 'delirium' undermining the 'machinic assemblages' of bourgeois conformity. However, as net access grows, more and more ordinary people are circulating free information across the net. Far from having any belief in the revolutionary ideals of May '68, the overwhelming majority of people participate within the high-tech gift economy for entirely pragmatic reasons. In the late-1990s,

32. See Eric S. Raymond, 'The Cathedral and the Bazaar', http://www.firstmonday.org/issues/issue3_3/raymond/index.html
33. See Netscape Communications Corporation, 'Netscape Announces Plans to Make Next-Generation Communicator Source Code Available Free on the Net'.

digital anarcho-communism is being built by hackers like Eric Raymond, 'a self-described neo-pagan [right-wing] libertarian who enjoys shooting semi-automatic weapons [...]'.[34]

Threatened by the banalisation of the high-tech gift economy, the European avant-garde is surreptiously embracing the capitalist fundamentalism of the Californian Ideology. For this convergence to take place, Deleuze and Guattari's anathema to market competition must be skilfully abandoned. First, their adepts deny the wealth-creating powers of human labour; then, the work of living beings is subsumed within the mobility of dead matter. Finally, far from being condemned as a 'machinic assemblage' imposed from above, market competition is sanctified as the apotheosis of self-organising systems. As in the Californian Ideology, this Deleuzoguattarian heresy believes that the market is a chaotic force of nature which cannot be controlled by state intervention. Abandoning any residual connections with the left, TJs instead celebrate the new aristocracy of nomadic artists and entrepreneurs who surf the 'schiz-flows' of the information society. In this bizarre remix, anarcho-communism becomes interchangeable with neoliberalism.

Denying the ability of people to determine their own destinies, techno-nomads believe that information technologies are the semiotic forces determining culture, consciousness and even the conception of existence. However, there is nothing inherently emancipatory in computer-mediated communications; these technologies can also serve the state and the market. In the future, electronic commerce will play a significant economic role and public services will increasingly be made available online. The 'new economy' of the net is an advanced form of social democracy.[35]

The techno-nomads cannot comprehend the subversive impact of the everyday activities of net users. For them, there can be nothing particularly special about the mundane activities of net users who aren't producing fashionable theory-art. Yet, at this particular historical moment, market competition is disappearing for entirely pragmatic reasons. While commodified information is closed and fixed, digital gifts are open and changeable. Instead of fixed divisions between producers and consumers, users are simultaneously creators on the net. Obsessed with immanence of semiotic flows, the Deleuzoguattarians cannot appreciate the deep irony of this contingent moment in human history. While the old faith in the inevitable triumph of communism has lost all credibility, market competition is quietly 'withering away' within cyberspace.

Over the past few centuries, people in the industrialised countries have slowly improved their incomes and reduced their working hours. While still having little autonomy in their money-earning jobs, workers can now

34. Andrew Leonard, 'Let My Software Go!'
35. *Wired* uses 'The New Economy' as a synonym for its neoliberal fantasies about the digital future.

experience non-alienated labour within the high-tech gift economy. From writing emails through making websites to developing software, people do things for themselves without the direct mediation of the market and the state. As net access spreads, the majority of the population is beginning to participate within cultural production. Unlike Fréquence Libre, the avant-garde can no longer decide who can – and cannot – join the high-tech gift economy. The net is too large for Microsoft to monopolise, let alone a small elite of radical intellectuals. Art can therefore cease being the symbol of moral superiority. When working people finally have enough time and resources, they can then concentrate upon '[...] art, love, play, etc, etc; in short, everything which makes Man [and Woman] *happy*.'[36]

At such an historical moment, the European avant-garde is being made obsolete through the realisation of its own supposed principles. The techno-nomads celebrate digital DIY culture to distinguish themselves from the rest of society. Yet, far from being confined to a revolutionary minority, increasing numbers of ordinary people are now participating within the high-tech gift economy. Rather than symbolising ethical-aesthetic purity, the circulation of gifts is a pragmatic way of working within cyberspace. Although it is impossible to predict the future of the high-tech gift economy, one thing is almost certain. The intellectual elitism of Deleuzoguattarian discourse is being superseded by the emancipatory 'grand narrative' of modernity. As more and more 'herd animals' go online, radical intellectuals can no longer fantasise about becoming cyborg *Übermensch*. As digital anarcho-communism becomes an everyday activity, there is no longer any need for the leadership of the cultural avant-garde.

The time for the revolution of holy fools has passed. As has already happened within popular music, the most innovative and experimental culture will be created by people doing things for themselves. By participating within the high-tech gift economy, everyone can potentially become a wise citizen and a creative worker: '[...] The word 'creation' will no longer be restricted to works of art but will signify a self-conscious activity, self-conceiving, reproducing for its own terms [...] and its own reality (body, desire, time, space), being its own creation'.[37]

This is an edited version of a text which appears in full at: www.imaginaryfutures.net

36. Alexandre Kojève, *Introduction to the Reading of Hegel: Lectures on the 'Phenomenology of Spirit'*, Ithaca: Cornell University Press, 1969.
37. Henri Lefebvre, *Everyday Life in the Modern World*, New Brunswick: Transaction Publishers, 1984.

A Response to Richard Barbrook's Holy Fools

Florian Cramer

Vol 1 #12, Winter 1998

To: mute@metamute.com
From: Florian Cramer <paragram@gmx.net>
Subject: The Net as really existing anarcho-communism
X-Attachments:

Dear Editors,
When Richard Barbrook ('The Holy Fools', *Mute*, Vol 1 #11), refers to 'the net as really existing anarcho-communism', he echoes a popular view of the internet in the early-1990s which I think needs to be revised. It might be trivial to note, in the first place, that the internet is not free. It's wrong to assume that its content is free only because users don't pay content providers, because they contribute to a multi-billion dollar industry of ISPs, telephone companies and computer equipment manufacturers. Arguing that 'the design of the net' implies that 'intellectual property is technically and socially obsolete', Richard Barbrook seems to overlook that the same design is equally perfect for exchanging encrypted information and that, with the help of digital signatures, it provides a very secure protection of copyrights and intellectual ownership.

But, even in the case of the 'gift economy' Barbrook observes in Free or Open Source Software (which he mistakenly calls 'shareware'), such binary oppositions as copyright vs. anti-copyright or capitalism vs. anarcho-communism don't seem to fit the case. Open source licences – like the GNU, BSD and Mozilla 'copylefts' – permit, and even encourage, commercial distribution. Companies like Red Hat, Caldera and Cygnus make several million dollars a year selling 'free software'. Aside from that, the political backgrounds of Free/Open Source software development are diverse and can't be pinned down to left-wing politics, let alone 'anarcho-communism'. Leading open source developers are motivated by technological pragmatism (Linus Torvalds), Christian belief (Larry Wall) and even – to refer to the prominent open source advocate, Eric S. Raymond – right-wing libertarianism. The only clear leftist in the movement, GNU founder Richard M. Stallman, is constantly being criticised, or even flamed, for his politics from within the open source community.

Several arguments could also be made against Barbrook's claim that the gift economy of free software contradicts 'market competition'. Free software structurally relies upon competition between projects which attempt to attract developers and outside advocates. The currency in this market is not money, but fame. This fame also helps developers to get highly paid jobs in the computer industry after they leave university. As in any capitalism, the mechanism of this market of fame often leads to compromised solutions. The success of the Linux kernel, for example, has marginalised the better designed GNU Hurd kernel, and the popularity of the KDE and Gnome desktop environments, with their Windows-like interface paradigms, is currently marginalising the older, and technically more ambitious, GNUstep project.

There are a number of other points against juxtaposing free software and capitalism:

- Free software tools – like Linux, the Apache Web server or the Perl scripting language – are typically being written by system programmers and network administrators to speed up and simplify their daily wage work. This, after all, is also a capitalist incentive.
- Even if free software should replace commercial software entirely, it would create a huge support industry of distributors, consultants, journals and book publishers. The more software is freely available, the more software will be used and the more support will be needed. This idea has proven a successful business model for, among others, RedHat software and O'Reilly publishers.
- Free software will sell more hardware. Consumer PCs could be $100–$200 cheaper – or gain their manufacturers respectively more profit – without licenses for bundled commercial software. If free software revises the paradigm that 'computers always crash' by being less bug-ridden than commercial software, even more people will buy PCs and increase the profits of their manufacturers and the free software support industry. Free software could, therefore, be seen as a self-sanitising measure by the capitalist market that puts software where it belonged in the first place, which is in the service industry.
- Open source operating systems will increase competition, i.e. 'sane capitalism', in the hardware market. Since they can be quickly ported to, and recompiled on, new hardware platforms, binary compatibility and chip architecture legacy (like x86) become marginal issues, as Corel Inc.'s non-Intel, Linux-based Netwinder computer demonstrates.

After all, the computer industry itself has understood the capitalist potential of free software. Big players like Intel, Compaq/Digital, HP, Apple, Corel and Sun actively invest in the development of Linux. I would be surprised if their motives were 'anarcho-communist'.

J18 and All That

Anthony Davies

Vol 1 #14, Autumn 1999

The Carnival Against Capitalism – 'J18' – was a day of protest that took place in 43 countries to coincide with the G8 summit in Cologne on 18 June. The coordinates of this event can be traced back to 1997/8 when a coalition of innovative social movements – Peoples' Global Action (PGA) – outlined a new protest movement with a series of bulletins and four organisational principles or 'hallmarks'. As Dr Simon L. Lewis recently pointed out in the Spring issue of *Corporate Watch*, 'PGA is not an organisation, as such, it is a network and a tool [...] PGA is all of us who take on the hallmarks and the act.' The impact of these hallmarks on business clusters is a key to understanding the global success of J18 and, in particular, the protest in the City of London.

To encourage relocation and maintain its position in the global economy, the City of London has, throughout the '90s, based its promotional pitch on the high concentration of related businesses, customers and competitors (a feature of the financial services industry). J18 momentarily transformed the perception of the City, confirming for the first time the vulnerability of geographical business clusters to 'network based' protest.

The combination of a new confrontational attitude and an 'organisational philosophy based on decentralisation and autonomy' (PGA hallmarks) resulted in a networked coalition converging on the square mile – each unit with its own agenda. This form of protest is virtually impossible to gather adequate prior intelligence on – there was no central chain of command and many of the groups were not in direct communication. The resultant impact on the command and control structure of the City of London Police was unprecedented; in a recent report, Commissioner Perry Nove refers to a 'starburst' occurring at Liverpool Street Station (where the main body of protesters split into groups and moved on the City in different directions), as the pivotal moment at which tactical control of the event collapsed. Whether or not this form of dispersal was highly organised is unclear. It certainly enabled a well informed, loosely coordinated assault to take place that fully exploited the geographical proximity of targets and, for a day, turned the City on its head. The level and sophistication of planning of J18 paradoxically mirrors the operational logic of corporate capitalism – in which resistance can now be 'as transnational as capital' and, more tellingly, networks replace normal rules and forms of organisation with informal ones. An innovative feature was the scope of the protest and the absence of a centre or core group. The focus on London's Reclaim the Streets (the West European convenors of PGA), Earth First and Movement Against the Monarchy has been a predictable attempt to hit a centre that doesn't exist. The shift to a decentralised, network based protest movement represents a serious threat to sectors (financial/corporate) where flat or networked organisations are in the process of replacing centralised, hierarchical bureaucracies (like the City of London Police). It's early days and the debate now cuts across all sectors with network strategies, opening up sites of protest and resistance unimaginable a decade ago. The process of decentralisation and autonomy that has transformed the global protest movement has been offset by a range of corporate 'partnership' and collaboration initiatives right across the board (social/cultural/political). The impact of this activity on sections of the 'creative industries' has produced an increasingly compliant and economically dependent resource for governmental and corporate strategies (Cool Britannia). These are now potential flashpoints.

Mayday, Mayday

Eileen Condon

Vol 1 #17, Summer 2000

In what must seem like an unbelievable resurrection to those in the West who declared it defunct, street protest has resurfaced as a widespread and regular phenomenon. After a period of systematic marginalisation, new forms of protest are gaining serious currency in mainstream politics and media under the recurring theme of a 'carnival' against global capitalism. Harnessing all niches of modern media and full wardrobe facilities for their symbolic resonance, the protest movement has rediscovered the power of performance.

Despite the 'need for dialogue' pleas of multinationals (epitomised by recent statements from Monsanto, Shell and McDonald's, calling for constructive exchange with their critics), this political influence is not testament to a new sensitivity on the part of the establishment. The underlying success of recent protests is attributable mainly to the manner in which a roster of loosely-knit, but broadly sympathetic, political groups have forged a new type of alliance. Under the aegis of a networked protest 'against global capitalism', they have targeted the institutions viewed as its most pernicious instruments – the IMF, World Bank, WTO, etc. The global remit of these organisations, and the reach of the corporations cast as their only real beneficiaries, has ensured the formation of a broad oppositional coalition that can link groups as diverse as US Teamsters and Earth First, students, anti-road protestors and anarchist groups. As the shareware manifesto of 'J18', last June's large-scale networked protest, stated, 'Resistance is as transnational as capital'.

As the frequency of these events increases, a rush to homogenise and historicise has occurred: 'J18' (occasion: G8 summit, Cologne, 18 June 1999), 'N30' (occasion: WTO meeting, Seattle, 30 November 1999) and 'A16' (occasion: World Bank and IMF meetings, Washington, DC, 16 April 2000) are now routinely placed in a sort of analytical string of pearls. As a closely connected series, they can be effectively employed – by both protest organisers and police – as models with which to think through issues of organisation, mediation and security. The meaning of these 'pearls' is as pliant to the strategies deployed by the various police forces as it is to the historical abstractions and political posturing of the protesters ('Luddites – Reclaim the Streets').

London's recent May Day celebration is a case in point. To all intents and purposes, the Reclaim the Streets performance held on Parliament Square conformed to the non-programme and non-ideology of J18, N30 and A16. However, 'Guerrilla Gardening' (an RTS slogan erroneously used by the media to name the 'mass action') lacked a singular contemporary catalyst symbolic of the 'Washington Consensus' (free market determinism). Instead of protesting against capitalism's crude stand-ins, RTS, the self-styled front '(dis)organisation', chose to celebrate holistic, non-alienated lifestyles of the urban realm under the new banner 'Resistance is Fertile'. In equal measure, this was to be a 21st century homage to a pre-modern mythos (May Day) and a modern collectivism (International Labour Day), paid in the bright colours of a Situationist carnivalesque.

But the events in Parliament Square can also be seen within the broader counter coordinates of a resurgent and politically reductive form of nationalism. In the face of the socio-economic fallout of globalisation, the British government and its 'opposition' are reaching for some tried and tested political formulae.

'Guerrilla Gardening' occurred at a watershed moment for New Labour. The first day of May was the third anniversary of Labour's landslide victory in 1997; the debacle of an unwanted mayoral candidate being elected in London loomed (4 May), as did disappointing results in the regional elections and Romsey by-election, and a disastrous end to the BMW/Rover negotiations in Longbridge, which threatened thousands of jobs and Labour's questionable reputation as a staunch supporter of industry. Adding insult to injury in a show of Conservative opportunism, Anne Widdecombe and William Hague were making vociferous, xenophobic attacks on Labour's 'soft touch' asylum and immigration policies.

It is an understatement to say that New Labour is sensitive to public opinion: it is focus-group- and opinion-poll-obsessed. This tsunami of negativity – itself not extraordinary for a government near the end of its first term – called for a firm stance and a reiteration of its core values. May Day provided the occasion: an event ideologically and structurally malleable enough to represent a win-win opportunity. Showcasing the tolerance in Jack Straw's 'zero tolerance' (digging up Parliament Square was permitted and graffiti was allowed on Whitehall) – as well as the subsequent police clampdown when the so-called single radical element violated its predictable target (McDonald's) – the government deftly choreographed pro-free-speech postures with those defending British national identity and security. Neither the liberal nor conservative ends of the political spectrum were to be left wanting. Tony's catch-all outrage was widely quoted the next day: 'The people responsible [...] are an absolute disgrace. Their actions have nothing to do with convictions or beliefs [...]. To deface the Cenotaph [...] is simply beneath contempt. It is only because of the bravery and courage of our war dead that these idiots can live in a free country at all.' The formula is clear: free market values = freedom = Britain.

Cultural war veteran Reclaim the Streets did little to avert this as organiser or disorganiser; by making the seat of government the main theatre of operations, it allowed Labour's nervous nationalism, disguised as a defence of Western democracy, to eclipse its anti-capitalist cause. In anticipation of May Day, financial institutions had criticised the Metropolitan Police's handling of J18 – which led to 101 arrests and millions of pounds of damage in the Square Mile – and forewarned of further dangers to London's reputation as a financial centre. By their own admission, the police had been wrong-footed by J18's 'starburst' tactics. Determined not to allow a repeat performance on May Day, they staged their biggest security operation for 30 years.

In the aftermath of J18, large sections of the media managed to build RTS into a quasi-official front organisation. On this occasion, it performed that role enthusiastically from the outset. It's a curious stance for a self-declared Situationist entity. Naturally, the media and hordes of observers ignored the RTS call for a 'no spectators' event. As self-styled performance group and front organisation with easy access to the press, it missed a critical opportunity to juxtapose conflicting paradigms of freedom and 'rights'.

In abiding by free market determinism – even the 'soft' type that Labour has – national governments protect the illusion of democracy, but waive their power to legislate against the excesses of global capitalism. While they wag their fingers at Haider's Freedom Party's xenophobia and racism, British 'social democrats' make full concessions to, and even use of, it on their home turf. While they negotiate easier entry for high-skilled tech workers, they rely on thousands of Eastern European labourers to toil on their farms illegally and draft Draconian Asylum and Immigration Bill. RTS does not believe in speeches, leaders or representative politics. But, on May Day, its oddly centralised carnival triggered a paradoxical slide – away from a confounding, atomised protest under one banner, toward a locatable, better containable core under none.

Together Forever

Tiziana Terranova

Vol 1 #20, Summer 2000

Douglas Engelbart's oNLine System (NLS) appeared to have died in 1975, when federal funding into networked, intellectual team work dwindled and XEROX PARC's computer scientists shifted the paradigm to a 'one user one computer' model. NLS was an advanced file-sharing multimedia system which allowed users to communicate by means of shared, visual displays of information. Conceived as a working tool for intellectual collaborations, Engelbart's NLS was based on a fundamental, cybernetic intuition, namely that the nature of intelligence does not exclusively depend on, or originate from, the individual capacities of the human brain. Rather, intelligence was conceived of as a cybernetic system that Engelbart named the 'H-LAM/T system' or 'Human using Language, Artefacts and Methodology in which he is Trained'. Engelbart dreamed of a total system 'of a human plus his augmentation devices and techniques [...] This field constitutes a very important system in our society: like most systems, its performance can be best improved by considering the whole as a set of interacting elements rather than a number of isolated elements.'[1]

Engelbart understood from very early on that the process of thinking could no longer be modelled on that of the isolated genius, and that computers could be much more than simple number crunchers or static memory banks. The increasing amount of information available and the increasingly complex nature of the problems faced by intellectual work demanded an internal reconfiguration of the H-LAM/T system. For Engelbart, any intervention at any level of the system would automatically engender, through a system of feedback loops, a resonance which would propagate and challenge the whole structure. Even the simple introduction of a low-level capability like text editing and word processing was bound to alter the overall structure of thinking, freeing up a surplus of labour which could be qualitatively reinvested in the process.

NLS was eventually funded by the Information Processing Techniques Office (IPTO), which implicitly tied up research into augmentation with existing research on time sharing (Engelbart Augmentation Research Centre, ARC, was one of the first original nodes of ARPANET, another key project funded by the IPTO). In 1964, the IPTO provided Engelbart with a million dollars a year to run a time-sharing system and half a million dollars a year for his augmentation research. With time-sharing, and following Engelbart's

1. Douglas C. Engelbart, 'A Conceptual Framework for the Augmentation of Man's Intellect', *Vistas in Information Handling, Volume 1: The Augmentation of Man's Intellect By Machine*, Washington DC: Spartan Books and London: Cleaver Hume Press, 1963, p. 5.

encounter with Peter Drucker's work, the emphasis shifted to intellectual team work, which the ARC team identified with the future of knowledge work. The ARC was an infinitely hot and dense 'dot' comprising all the components that would later disperse into the disparate, but connected, galaxies of the digital economy: an 'engine room', where the new time-sharing computers were located; a hardware workshop, where the constantly upgraded computer system and experimental input-output devices were built and maintained; and, as Howard Rheingold states in his book *Tools for Thought*, a model 'intellectual workshop that consisted of an amphitheatre-like space in which a dozen people sat in front of large display terminals, creating the system's software, communicating with each other, and navigating through dimensions of information'.

An intensive open source workshop, NLS conceived of its users as the 'designer-subjects' of the experiment. Using the system meant being involved in its evolution, a machinic enslavement which was also a new mode of subjectification based on higher-than-ever levels of positive, transformative feedback. Pioneers of open source and burn-out syndrome, the ARC team would be tested to the limits by the creative destruction of proliferating positive feedback loops. *Tools for Thought* describes how, at the end of the project, a psychologist had to be brought in to consult on 'those parts of the system that weren't to be found in the circuitry or software, but in the thoughts and relationships of the people who were building and using the system'.

Get Rid of the Lot of Them! Argentinean Society Stands Against Politics

Horacio Tarcus, translation by Adolfo Olaechea

Vol 1 #25, Winter 2002

The Collapse of an Economic Model

The extraordinary social protests that erupted in Argentina last December were a reaction to the *corralito* regulations. *Corralito* literally means fencing and refers to the restrictions imposed by the government on the withdrawal of bank deposits at the beginning of that month. This measure was the last impotent throw of the dice by a bankrupt economic model. This model, blessed by the IMF, was established by the neoliberal economist, Domingo Cavallo, in 1993, under the neo-Peronist regime of Carlos S. Menem. It remained in place during the two years of the Radical government of Fernando de la Rúa, when Cavallo was also the Minister of Finance.

One of the pillars of this model was the so-called 'convertibility', which pegged the Argentinean Peso to the US Dollar and established a parity rate of 'one peso to one dollar'. Following the traumatic hyper-inflationary experiences of the 1989–1991 period, the monetary stability afforded by convertibility conferred long years of legitimacy to the Menem government and his super-minister Cavallo. For the salaried, retired workers and pensioners, incomes (fixed and in pesos) would not continuously erode. For the middle classes, it meant a chance of keeping their savings in dollars, buying imported products at artificially low prices and travelling abroad. For the local bourgeoisie, it signalled an opportunity to undertake spectacular business deals.

Some sectors, however, were driven to the wall: for example, local producers such as the textile manufacturers unable to compete against imported products while the dollar was artificially undervalued, or the traditional farming industries, which saw the value of their exports decline for the same reason. However, a new 'export/finance' bourgeoisie did grow at breakneck speed under the wing of political power. The apparent success of stability, the consumer boom and the emergence of the newly rich pushed issues such as the Menem government's absurd levels of corruption, and the scandalous submission of the judiciary and parliament to the executive, into the background. Even though these were the main political themes for the opposition, they only confronted the government from a democratic institutional and ethical stance, and the Menemists were therefore able to respond with the legitimacy of efficiency. That was sufficient for Menem to get re-elected in 1994, following constitutional reform.

Nevertheless, another hidden iceberg was the asset stripping by the state deemed necessary to pay for its economic model. The Menem/Cavallo regime began an extraordinary process of privatising the patrimony of the state. Thousands of millions of pesos – received from the sale of oil and gas fields, railways, airlines, telephone networks and the metropolitan underground transport systems – silently financed the model, supplying the dollars needed to keep up the 'one to one' convertibility. Within the framework of monetary stability and convertibility, Menem's offer of the state's industrial and service companies was more than tempting for international investors who did their billing in overvalued pesos and then returned their profits abroad, having exchanged them into dollars. It was a fabulous business indeed. But, at the end of the day, the model was financed by the creation of chronic indebtedness.

Of course, the model had its winners and its losers, the latter consisting mainly of the low-paid and the unemployed. However, it did work for the first five years with the support of the middle classes. Finally, after several years of recession, the system broke down in December 2001, causing the most serious social cost imaginable. Given that it was inevitable, the escape from convertibility to a clearer system could have been achieved in a negotiated, gradual and less traumatic fashion. Also, convertibility could have lasted many more years. This would have required the government to shift the economy from a deficit into a substantial surplus by collecting outstanding taxes, investing productively and promoting exports.

The collapse of convertibility occurred because it became impossible for the state and private sector to obtain any more credit to paper over the ongoing monetary deficit. In permanent expansion, this deficit had three causes: firstly, the public deficit generated by gigantic tax evasion and a state pension system covered by external loans; secondly, the private deficit generated by the incapacity of local industry to compete in the global market; lastly, the accumulation of interest on contracted loans feeding back into the public deficit.

The prohibition on withdrawal of cash from the banks was a side effect of the wave of speculation which started when the masses of depositors realised (several months after the banks that had taught them not to think beyond the parameters of convertibility) that the rate of exchange was unsustainable and that dollar funds were at risk. Efforts to avoid the collapse of the banks led the government to embargo the savings of hundreds of thousands of depositors and caused the collapse of both internal savings and external credit. The collapse of economic activity resulted in a spiral of bankruptcies, wholesale layoffs among the work force, as well as a new drop in salary levels.

Given all this, the collapse of convertibility is a by-product of a type of profit generation and a form of relationship between the state and the private sector, based upon the most parasitic and primal tendencies of capitalism. Companies harvested monopolist rents from the internal market, totally unsupervised by any form of user, or consumer, organisation. These companies subsequently exchanged these profits into dollars sold to them by the state at bargain basement rates. This was an ultra-inefficient role for the state, incapable of planning or using resources to fulfil socially valuable criteria and subjected to the individual demands of companies and economic blocs.[1]

Crisis of the State

In parallel with the economic crisis, an unprecedented crisis of the state has developed. Without doubt, this is also the result of 25 years of persistent neoliberal policies aimed at reducing the state's capacity to regulate, so as to 'liberate', market forces. Left to its own dynamics, the 'invisible hand' of the market led to something slightly different from the 'productive revolution' promised by Menem in 1989; it led to a truly unproductive revolution. If any doubt remained, today it is clear that there is no place for Argentina in capitalist globalisation. In the space of a few years, one of Latin America's most prosperous countries had gone from role model to basket case.

The fragility of the state is such that it hardly seems to exist at all; it lacks all substantive attributes and does not perform any of its essential functions. For instance: In the matter of guaranteeing compliance with the law, the De la Rúa government fell when the population challenged the state of siege. In maintaining public security and issuing and supporting its currency, not only the public, but also certain state institutions keep their reserves in dollars abroad. In collecting taxes, the Argentinean system is completely regressive; the Argentinean bourgeoisie does not pay and has never paid their taxes. In safeguarding property, consider the way the property of the bank depositors has been dealt with. In defending the unity of the country, the former Governor of San Luis Province, who was president of the country for a few brief days after the fall of De la Rúa last December, recently began to speak about 'secession'.

A Rebellion of the Middle Classes?

Having said all this, I would suggest that the classical system of analysis, which holds that 'an economic crisis gives rise to a sequel of political crisis', does not address all the nuances of the current scene in Argentina. Moreover, the equation – economic model in crisis + seizure of depositors' savings = sudden mobilisation of the 'middle class' – not only devalues any analysis but, in fact, distorts it.

During the events of 19–20 December, a new social protest movement was born in Argentina. The direct trigger was the run on the banks of 30 November and the economic measures that followed the fencing of bank accounts and

1. See Ricardo Aronskind, 2002.

fixed-term deposits. This led many observers to point out that it was the middle class that propelled the social protest of December, and hence it was dubbed a 'French Revolution' in the mass media and other quarters.

There is no question that the fencing of bank accounts directly affected and maddened the small and medium sized depositors, and that the lack of ready funds did the same to shopkeepers and other traders. However, it also affected, directly or indirectly, all workers as well as the retired and other recipients of state or private pensions. A special characteristic of the social protest was that very diverse types were swept along with it: unemployed workers and youths who had never been employed, ordinary workers and retired workers, small depositors, shopkeepers and other traders.

Did the working class stay away? It was not visible in its classic trade union guise of marching columns. One should say, then, that it was the trade unions that were not present in December. This was particularly true of the two factions into which the Peronist CGT (Confederación General del Trabajo) is divided: the hard-liners and those in favour of the government. The more militant CTA (Central de Trabajadores Argentinos) was also slow to come on board.

The massive demonstrations in the Plaza de Mayo or in the Plaza del Congreso (Parliament Square) lacked the characteristics of traditional mass actions accompanying general strikes, with each worker marching under the banner of his own union, political party or union tendency. There is no doubt that the workers took part in these events, but they did not come out into the streets and squares in organised columns. They came alone, or at most in small groups, and were then amassed by way of some sort of molecular dynamics.

The spontaneous character of the mobilisation and the deliberative role adopted by the groups that swarmed the street corners and squares in the various neighbourhoods were – in that sense – reminiscent of the mass mobilisations of Holy Week, 1987. However, those were mass actions either to support or to put pressure on – according to the different tendencies – the democratic government in the face of a military rebellion. Today, 15 years later, the scene is different. In a country in ruins, a popular uprising has overthrown a government impotent in the face of national and global economic power. Cavallo was the symbol of that economic power, De la Rúa the embodiment of an impotent government.

Social Dynamics of a Political Crisis

On 19 December, within a few hours, the masses that began by demanding the resignation of Cavallo, the Minister, were demanding the resignation of De la Rúa, the President. And, along with the ghostly round of presidential musical chairs that occurred between the end of December and the first days of January, the cry 'Get rid of the lot of them' increasingly became the slogan of the different sections involved in the social protest.

According to a Buenos Aires newspaper from early December,[2] the government believed that, by somehow relaxing the bank fencing regulations and by granting a measure of 'social welfare', the protest would start to die down. This suggests that the so-called political class believes that, even if a revival of social enthusiasm for politicians cannot be effected, society can at least return to its passive, sceptical state.

The problem is that, while the present political crisis blew up days after the introduction of the bank fencing regulations, it results from a social process with much deeper roots. For example, the elections of 14 October 2001 – with their towering levels of absenteeism and invalid and spoiled ballot papers – had already given expression to a very serious political crisis blowing across the whole of Argentina. These (non)voters were once believers. Aware, now, that they had been defrauded, they had lost faith in politics. Up until the events of Argentina's 'hot summer', their protest was almost individualistic, an impotent expression of political discontent.

Taken together with the secession of a younger generation, brought up in a world in which politics was devalued, these elections could have been used by politicians to give collective and political meaning to individualised discontent, but the political class and the mass media had, for many years, glossed over these phenomena. On polling day, its impact could no longer be ignored. Barely two months later, and ever since, the so-called protest vote has ceased to be something passive and has turned into mass action; it has moved beyond the polling booth and into the streets.

The aspirations of different sectors within this movement converge, with aspirations being partially modified and adopting new meanings in the process. Horizontally, the crisis is cutting across diverse social and political strata. Men and women, old and young, employed and unemployed, pensioners and people in active service, wage earners and bank depositors, union members and non-union workers are all converging into a movement in which the only common denominator appears to be the desire to 'Get rid of the lot of them!'

The demand has spread like wild fire and is chanted at all public demonstrations. There is no doubt that it is less naïve and more complex than it appears at first sight. It expresses the libertarian protest of society against the state and all its institutions, from parliament to the police, as well as the entire official mass media. It is the protest of the little people, the common men and women, against a political class they now perceive as a parasite preying on society.

Antonio Gramsci defined a political crisis in terms that may be useful today: 'At a certain moment in their historical development, social groupings divorce themselves from their traditional parties. This means that traditional parties, given the organisational form they embody, with those specific persons who

2. 'Talks between Duhaldeism and the UCR seek to avoid attacks on politicians', *Clarín*, 3 December 2002.

constitute, represent and lead them, are no longer recognised as the appropriate expression of their class or of a section of a class.' For the Italian thinker, in 'these situations of contrast between the represented and their representatives', the political crisis 'is transmitted to the entire organism of the state'. Gramsci held that such situations could arise 'when the leading class had failed in some political enterprise for which it had demanded or compelled by force the consent of the wide masses'. He pointed out that these situations could also arise 'alternatively, because a broad mass of people [...] went suddenly from political passivity into a certain activity and proceeded to make demands that in their chaotic whole amounted to a revolution'.[3]

Gramsci's ideas seem to offer useful angles from which to consider the crisis in Argentina, where the evacuation of content from the political parties was extended to the entire organism of the state. From 1984 to the present, the ruling class of Argentina has repeatedly failed to create its hegemony – a social order that the masses would at least accept. The masses, in turn, moving beyond the protest vote, have extracted themselves from political passivity and gone on to win the streets and the public spaces.

However, we are far from what Gramsci understood by the term 'revolution'. We are a little bit closer than we were on 18 December 2001, but a protracted process of collective building lies ahead of us. If, as Rosa Luxemburg believed, the crisis is the expression of the fact that the old is dying but not yet dead, and the new is being born but not yet out of the womb, we have crisis ahead for a long time to come.

Today, the state is waiting for a certain erosion to occur from so much social mobilisation, so that it can try to punish all those who violate Article 22 of the National Constitution, which states that 'The people do not rule or deliberate except by means of their representative'. This is precisely how Senator Raúl Alfonsín (a Radical Party leader, President of Argentina between 1983 and 1989) put it in his speech of 21 February last year in the Senate.

It is a fact that Peronists and Radicals are holding consultations, seeking a legal framework to curtail mobilisations and *escarches* (impromptu mass protest meetings) so as to return the masses to their jobs and homes. They aim, by means of depoliticising society, to put politics back in the hands of the state. However, President Eduardo Duhalde warned them that, 'If this ever gets interpreted as a self-serving corporate law, or as a barrier to the democratic freedom to demonstrate, we will be throwing petrol on the flames.'[4]

In other words, it is currently impossible to repress society by declaring it to be in rebellion just because people are holding public discussions and articulating a wish for self-government, while patently repudiating their so-called representatives ('Get rid of the lot of them!'). Nevertheless, a latent threat to the

3. Gramsci, 1962, pp. 76–7.
4. *Clarín*, 3 March 2001.

movimientos piqueteros (picket movement) and the neighbourhood assemblies exists. On 26 June this year, during ferocious police repression of a picket in Avellaneda on the outskirts of Buenos Aires City, two unemployed youths, Darío Santillán and Maximiliano Kosteki, were gunned down.

Picket Movements and Neighbourhood Assemblies

The *villas miseria* offer a postcard image from the Menem decade; these are the cardboard shacks of the homeless, hardly noticeable when one is driving fast along the highways. However, this view changes when the unemployed climb onto the tarmac to form a 'picket', burning tyres and blocking traffic while bellowing out their battle cry of '*Piqueteros, carajo*!' (The Pickets are here, damn it!)

While it is true that pickets interrupting traffic is something that goes back a long way in the history of Argentina's workers' strikes, the characteristic feature of the new pickets is that they are made up of the unemployed. The movement was born in 1996 in Neuquén province, when Menem was still president. There, the sacked workers of YPF, the state oil company, erected a blockade on a key highway. It was born of dire necessity, a desperate measure to directly force the government – bypassing the patronising structures of church or political parties – to give the strikers access to *planes trabajar* (the state's monthly unemployment allowance of 150 pesos, around 40 dollars today). Once the *planes* were granted, the picket was lifted and, from then on, 'misery became socialised'.

Five years on, the movement has spread like wild fire all over the country, gaining momentum with the tempo of the crisis. The picket movement is not limited to blockading highways; a remarkable solidarity network has grown up alongside it. It is a network that runs communal kitchens, allotments, school supplies, health centres, libraries, etc. Each 'picket-man', collecting his 150 pesos, must survive for the whole month on that money, less the three pesos he pays to the movement. That money goes into a common fund for the organisation's expenses. Moreover, they are obliged to help at the Picket Action Centres for four hours a day from Monday to Friday. The pickets run a horizontal organisation, but, nevertheless, some leading figures do arise. The leaders are members or former members of the leftist movements, but the rank and file has no political formation of any kind. They come to the pickets driven by unemployment and hunger. The most militant and hardline sections are the least inclined to negotiations and the most anti-politics in outlook.

There are three tendencies in the picket movement: The first one is affiliated to the CTA, and one of its leaders, Luis D'Elía, who comes from the militant wing of Peronism and currently leads the Federación Tierra y Vivienda (Land and Housing Federation). Its other leader, Juan Carlos Alderete, is close to the CCC (Corriente Clasista y Combativa) which is linked to the Maoist Party (PCR). A second tendency, the Bloque Piquetero, is an umbrella for the picket groups linked to the left-wing political parties, such as the Polo Obrero, run by the Workers Party (Trotskyist), and the Movimiento Territorial de Liberación, run by the CP. However, the most important current in this bloc, the Movimiento Teresa Rodríguez, led by Roberto Martino, is independent. The third tendency, and perhaps the one most independent and remote from the world of political parties, is the Coordinadora Aníbal Verón. The two picketing youths assassinated by the police on 26 June belonged to this organisation.

While this movement was born prior to the mobilisation of December 2001 and in its aftermath, it began to garner more popular support and to grow spectacularly. At that time, two new movements were also born: firstly, the movement of the bank depositors demanding the return of their funds, and, secondly, the movement of neighbourhood assemblies. The former, while basically limited to the middle classes, has not lowered its banners during nine months of mobilisations. But the latter, without any doubt, is the most novel because of its organisational form and its collective discussions on street corners and in public squares. In this movement, citizens of all ages, walks of life, professions and social extractions, hitherto uninterested in public affairs and hardly ever bothering to vote, are now debating what is to be done about the serious crisis in the neighbourhood hospital or school. They also discuss how to tackle the problems of security – without giving more power to the police. Each assembly, in turn, sends its delegates to an assembly of assemblies, the *Interbarrial* (Inter-Neighbourhood Assembly).

Just as they do within the picket movement, strong tensions exist between the independents – non-party members who generally have no previous political experience and who are much more 'horizontal', more libertarian and more averse to political/institutional ways – and the old left-wing movements seeking to seduce those social strata. A programme of ideas and action for a left that is open to criticism, for a left that is in tune with the era, should, among other things, try to help strengthen pickets and neighbourhood assemblies. It should try to ensure their democratic operation and to enrich their political culture. The left-wing currents that take part in these movements would benefit from this, too, because this type of participation would rebound upon them, raising their own political culture and their internal democracy. There are left-wing groups that dream of the neighbourhood assemblies playing the role of 'Soviets in embryo'. Many attempt to sneak in their slogans or boast about how much they exert control over these assemblies. Maybe there are sections of this militant left who are overlooking the libertarian mettle the social protest is demonstrating. The political crisis is affecting left-wing organisations, too, in good measure, along with their leaders, their apparatuses and their instrumental approach to politics.

It is not simply his own weakness in directing the transitional period that has dictated the President's call for early elections in March 2003. Eduardo Duhalde, who was invested by Congress as President, is precariously supported by a makeshift federation of Peronist governors who, in turn, are involved in serious wrangling amongst themselves. The decision to bring the elections forward was also dictated by a need to diffuse the mobilisations and social protests.

The electoral calendar and the tempo of the social movement are not in tune. The left vacillates between taking part in a process – where it sees the prospect of increasing its vote – and marching alongside the most militant sections of the social movement, those who are rejecting the government's call for elections.

So what is to be done? 'Get rid of the lot of them!' say some. Others respond: And then, what happens? Take part in official politics? Reject all politics? Create a different type of politics? These are the issues being debated today by the social movements and the left-wing groups in Argentina. At the same time, there is talk of rejecting politics and politicising society. The state is rejected, but at the same time there are demands for education, health, security, social policies. There is rejection of paternalism and of the substitution of the self-led actions of the masses by a political leadership, all within a vacuum of political leadership in general. Argentinean society has transformed itself into a great Assembly. There is a willingness to talk and also to listen, to learn and to build. There is no better moment than the present for the birth of a new collective will. A new left.

The Packet Gang: Openness and its Discontents

J.J. King

Vol 1 #27, Winter/Spring 2004

The Idea of Openness

Since the founding of the Free Software Foundation by Richard Stallman in 1985 and the Open Source Initiative by Eric Raymond in 1998, the idea of openness has enjoyed some considerable celebrity. Simply understood, open source software is that which is published along with its source code, allowing developers to collaborate, improve upon each other's work and use the code in their own projects. The cachet of this open model of development has been greatly increased by the high-profile success of GNU-Linux, a piece of 'free-as-in-libre and open source software' (FLOSS). But, taken together with the distributed co-composition offered, for example, by the wiki architecture[1] and the potential of peer-to-peer networks like BitTorrent and Gnutella,[2] a looser and more nuanced idea of openness has suggested itself as a possible model for other kinds of organisation. Felix Stalder of Openflows identifies its key elements as '[...] communal management and open access to the informational resources for production, openness to contributions from a diverse range of users/producers, flat hierarchies, and a fluid organisational structure'.[3]

This idea of openness is now frequently deployed not only with reference to composing software communities but also to political and cultural groupings. For many, this is easily explained: FLOSS' 'self-evident' realisation of a 'voluntary global community empowered and explicitly authorised to reverse-engineer, learn from, improve and use-validate its own tools and products' indicates that 'it has to be taken seriously as a potential source of organising for other realms of human endeavour'.[4] In these circles, openness is now seen as 'paradigmatic'. Computer book publisher and guru Tim O'Reilly's presentation at the Reboot conference in 2003, entitled 'The Open Source Paradigm Shift', placed FLOSS at the vanguard of a social phenomenon whose time, he said, 'had come', its methods of ad hoc, distributed collaboration constituting a 'new paradigm' at a level consistent with, for example, the advent of the printing press and movable type.[5]

1. See 'What is Wiki?', http://wiki.org/wiki.cgi?WhatIsWiki
2. See http://www.zeropaid.com for a review of current peer-to-peer and fileshare services.
3. Felix Stalder, 'One-size-doesn't-fit-all: Particulars of the Volunteer Open Source Development Methodology', http://openflows.org/article.pl?sid=03/10/25/1722242
4. Adam Greenfield, 'The Minimal Compact: Preliminary Notes on an "Open Source" Constitution for Post-National Entities', http://www.v-2.org/displayArticle.php?article_num=339
5. Tim O'Reilly, 'The Open Source Paradigm Shift', Keynote at Reboot 2003, http://www.reboot.dk/reboot6/video

Such accounts of the socio-political pertinence of the FLOSS model are increasingly common. A recent essay by activist, Florian Schneider, and writer, Geert Lovink, for example, exhibits the premature desire to collapse FLOSS-style open organisation into a series of other political phenomena: 'freedom of movement and freedom of communication [...] the everyday struggles of millions of people crossing borders as well as pirating brands, producing generics, writing open source code or using P2P software'.[6]

More soberly, Douglas Rushkoff has argued recently, in a report for the Demos think tank, that 'the emergence of the interactive mediaspace may offer a new model for cooperation':

> The values engendered by our fledgling networked culture may [...] prove quite applicable to the broader challenges of our time and help a world struggling with the impact of globalism, the lure of fundamentalism and the clash of conflicting value systems [...] One model for the open-ended and participatory process through which legislation might occur in a networked democracy can be found in the open source software movement.[7]

Rushkoff does not try to draw direct parallels between FLOSS and other forms of activity in the manner of Schneider and Lovink, but argues equally problematically that the model used in open source software-composing communities could be usefully applied to democratic political organisation. 'A growing willingness to engage with the underlying code of the democratic process,' he contends, 'could eventually manifest in a widespread call for revisions to our legal, economic and political structures.'[8] Clearly, then, the idea of openness has appeal across rather different constituencies – here we already have both the liberal-reformist and the radical activists claiming openness as their ally. Indeed, as ICT theorist, Biella Coleman, suggests, the widespread adoption and use of the idea of openness and its 'profound political impact' may precisely be contingent on its peculiarly transpolitical appeal. 'FLOSS,' she writes, resists 'political delineation into the traditional political categories of left, right or centre [...but] has been embraced by a wide range of people [...] This has enabled FLOSS to explode from a niche and academic endeavour into a creative sphere of socio-political and technical influence bolstered by the internet.'[9]

But the broad-church appeal of the idea of openness suggested by FLOSS need not necessarily be a cause for celebration, especially since many of the

6. Florian Schneider, 'Re: <nettime> Reverse Engineering Freedom', Nettime, Tuesday 14 October 2003, http://www.mail-archive.com/nettime-l@bbs.thing.net/msg01248.html. See also Florian Schneider and Geert Lovink, 'Reverse Engineering Freedom', *Make Worlds*, 2003, http://www.makeworlds.org/?q=book/view/20
7. Douglas Rushkoff, 'Open Source Democracy: How Online Communication Is Changing Offline Politics', Demos, 2003, http://www.demos.co.uk/opensourcedemocracy_pdf_media_public.aspx
8. Ibid.
9. Biella Coleman, 'Free and Open Source Software', *Survival Kit, Part one*, proceedings of RAM4.

constituencies making use of it conceive of themselves as fundamentally opposed. Can the idea of openness embraced by these divergent constituencies really be the same? And how can it be that they consider it sufficient to their very different aims?

The chief purpose of this article is not to answer these questions by examining the 'self-evident' truths of open source production. Such studies are already being carried out in forums like Oekunux [www.oekonux.de]; indeed, in this issue of *Mute*, Gilberto Camara, Director for Earth Observation at Brazil's National Institute for Space Research, publishes research that challenges some key tenets of the FLOSS model. His research exposes the possibility that, in many cases, FLOSS does not innovate significantly original software or sustain projects outside of corporate or large scale academic involvement. Instead, this article seeks to address the intense political expectation around open organisation among diverse elements of the diffuse activist organisations which, post-Seattle, have been loosely referred to as 'the social movement' or 'social movements'. In referring to the social movement, this article concerns itself primarily with groups such as Peoples' Global Action, Indymedia, Euraction Hub and other such non-hierarchical collectives; it does not have in mind more traditionally structured organisations like the Social Forums, Globalise Resistance or so-called 'civil society' NGOs.

In the social movement thus defined, openness is clearly becoming a constitutive organising principle, as it connects with the hopes and desires circulating around the idea of the 'multitude', a term whose post-Spinozan renaissance has been secured by Michael Hardt and Antonio Negri's book, *Empire.* The multitude is a defiantly heterogeneous figure, a collective noun intended to counter the homogenising violence of terms such as 'the people' or 'the mass'. For many thinkers in the post-autonomist tradition, this multitude is a way of conceiving the revolutionary potential of a new 'post-Fordist proletariat' of networked immaterial labourers. In certain circuits within the social movement, in which *pace* Schneider and Lovink, FLOSS organisation is seen as the techno-social precondition of a radical democracy in becoming. However tenuous this assemblage may be, it goes some way to explaining how FLOSS and openness have become quite central rhetorical terms in the struggle to produce an identity for the networked, anti-capitalist movement. But it is also true that certain characteristics of the idea of openness have genuine organisational influence within the movement. A study of openness in this context is useful in three degrees: first, to the social movement itself 'internally'; second, to 'outsiders' wanting to gain an understanding of 'what it is'; third, as a critique of those who would seek to represent the movement with, or attempt to manipulate it through, a particular deployment of the idea of openness.

'The Revolution will be Open Source'

It is too easy to make sweeping generalisations about the ways in which the social movement realises the idea of openness. Instead, we need to look at the ways in which the kind of openness identified in FLOSS may practically correspond to specific moments of organisation in the social movement. Based on my direct involvement in the social movement in contexts such as the anti-G8, No Border Camps, PGA meetings and various actions, I think it is possible to see correspondences in five key areas:

Meetings and Discussions

The time and location of physical meetings are published in a variety of places, online and off. The meetings themselves are most often open to all comers, sometimes with the exception of 'traditional' media. Although often no recordings or photography are allowed at meetings, there is rarely any other vetting of those who attend. Anyone is allowed to speak, although there is often a convenor or moderator whose role is to keep order and ensure progress. Summaries of discussions are often posted on the web (see Documentation) where they can be read by those unable to attend a physical meeting or those otherwise interested parties.

The same is true of IRC [Internet Relay Chat] meetings, which anyone may attend, and for which the 'logs' are usually published (again, see Documentation).

Net-based mailing lists, through which much discussion is carried out, are usually open subscription and, as with physical meetings, those joining are not vetted.

Decision-Making

Most often, anyone present at a meeting may take part in the decisions made there, although these conditions may occasionally be altered. Currently, the majority of decision making is done using the 'consensus' method, in which any person present not agreeing with a decision can either choose to abstain or veto ('block'). A block causes an action or decision to be stopped.

Documentation

In general, documents that form organisational materials within the movement are published online, usually using a content management system such as a wiki. In most cases, it is possible even for casual visitors to edit and alter these documents, although it is possible to 'roll back' to earlier versions, for example, in the case of defacements.

Demonstrations

The majority of demonstrations are organised using the above methods. Not only is their organisation 'open' but, within a certain range of political persuasions, anyone may attend. Self-policing is not 'hard' but 'soft'.

Actions

Even some 'actions' – concentrated interventions usually involving smaller numbers – are 'open', using the above methods to organise themselves and, if the action is ongoing, even allowing new people to participate.

Thus some key moments within the social movement share certain characteristics with the FLOSS model of openness. Indeed, the movement deploys many of the same tools as FLOSS communities (i.e. wiki, IRC and mailing lists) to organise itself and carry out its projects, but its characteristic uses of openness are not enshrined in any formal document. Rather, they have developed as a way of organising that is tacitly understood by those involved in the social movement: an idea of openness that, to differing degrees, inflects its organisation throughout. Although the principles are not rigidly followed, there is often peer criticism of groups who do not declare their agendas or who act in a closed, partisan fashion, and, generally speaking, any group or project wanting to keep itself closed has an obligation to explain its rationale to other groups.

Some of these attitudes and principles derive from the Peoples' Global Action (PGA), an influential 'instrument' constituting a visible attempt to organise around networked openness. The organisational philosophy of PGA,[10] which was formed after a movement gathering in South America in August 1997, is based on 'decentralisation'. With 'minimal central structures', the PGA 'has no membership' or 'juridical personality'; 'no organisation or person represents' it, nor does it 'represent any organisation or person'; it is a 'tool':

> [A] fluid network for communication and coordination between diverse social movements who share a loose set of principles or 'hallmarks' [...] Since February 1998 [...] PGA has evolved as an interconnected and often chaotic web of very diverse groups, with a powerful common thread of struggle and solidarity at the grassroots level. These gatherings have played a vital role in face-to-face communication and exchange of experience, strategies and ideas [...][11]

The PGA has attempted to structure itself around a set of 'hallmarks' which have been updated at each key meeting. These are currently as follows:

1. A very clear rejection of capitalism, imperialism and feudalism; all trade agreements, institutions and governments that promote destructive globalisation.

2. [... A rejection of] all forms and systems of domination and discrimination including, but not limited to, patriarchy, racism and religious fundamentalism of all creeds [...An embracing of] the full dignity of all human beings.

10. See http://www.apg.org

11. 'Sophie', ChiapasLink UK, 'We are everywhere! Peoples' Global Action meeting in Cochabamba, Bolivia', posted to A-infos list, 8 December 2001, http://www.ainfos.ca/01/dec/ainfos00120.html

3. A confrontational attitude, since we do not think that lobbying can have a major impact in such biased and undemocratic organisations, in which transnational capital is the only real policy-maker.
4. A call to direct action and civil disobedience, support for social movements' struggles, advocating forms of resistance which maximise respect for life and oppressed peoples' rights, as well as the construction of local alternatives to global capitalism.
5. An organisational philosophy based on decentralisation and autonomy.[12]

These hallmarks function to structure participation in the PGA process. In theory, they allow the network to remain 'open' while designating the kinds of activities that don't fall within its field. PGA meetings, for example, do not exclude those who don't subscribe to its hallmarks, but neither would discussions explicitly contrary to them be given much attention. Certain kinds of discussion are openly privileged over others on pragmatic grounds.

Structures like PGA and those being experimented with more widely are part of the social movement's general rejection of organisational models based on representation, verticality and hierarchy. In their stead comes 'non-hierarchical decentralisation' and 'horizontal coordination'. 'From this movement', writes Massimo De Angelis, 'emerges [...] the concept and practice of network, horizontality, democracy, of the exercise of power from below.' For this 'radical political economist', this form of 'social-cooperation' is 'ours'. It is 'our' horizontality and these are 'our' networks, part of a set of:

> modes of coordination of human activity that go beyond the capitalist market and beyond the state [...] we are talking about another world [...] the slogan on T-shirts in Genoa was entirely correct: another world is not only possible. Rather, we are already patiently and with effort building another world – with all its contradictions, limitations and ambiguities – through the form of our networks..[14]

In other words, it is the open, networked, horizontal form of the movement that produces its radical potential for social change; the message, yet again, is the medium. In the case of the self-described 'open publishing' project Indymedia, for example, the open submission structure is said to collapse the distinction between media producer and consumer, allowing us to 'become the media'. The Indymedia newswire, write the collective, works on the principle of Open Publishing, an essential element of the Indymedia project that allows anyone to instantaneously self-publish their work on a globally

12. PGA hallmarks, http://www.nadir.org/nadir/initiativ/agp/free/pga/hallm.htm
13. Massimo De Angelis, 'From Movement to Society', *The Commoner*, August 2001, http://www.commoner.org.uk/01-3groundzero.htm
14. Ibid.

accessible website. The Indymedia newswire encourages people to 'become the media'. While Indymedia reserves the right to develop sections of the site that provide edited articles, there is no designated Indymedia editorial collective that edits articles posted to the Indymedia.org newswire.

Here, the idea of openness presents itself as absolutely inimical to the 'dominant multinational global news system', where 'news is not free, news is not open'. With open publishing:

> the process of creating news is transparent to the readers. They can contribute a story and see it instantly appear in the pool of stories publicly available. Those stories are filtered as little as possible to help the readers find the stories they want. Readers can see editorial decisions being made by others. They can see how to get involved and help make editorial decisions. If they can think of a better way for the software to help shape editorial decisions, they can copy the software, because it is free, and change it and start their own site. If they want to redistribute the news, they can, preferably on an open publishing site.
>
> The working parts of journalism are exposed. Open publishing assumes the reader is smart and creative and might want to be a writer and an editor and a distributor and even a software programmer [...] Open publishing is free software. It's freedom of information, freedom for creativity.[15]

Accounts such as this and De Angelis' bear out my argument that an extreme amount of expectation is being focused on openness as an agent for change. Not only is openness central to the organisation of the social movement, but, in many cases, it is taken as read that the organisational quality of openness is inherently radical and will be productive of positive change in whichever part of the socio-political field it is deployed. This is seen, for example, in the work of the group Open Organisations, comprised of three individuals – Toni Prug, Richard Malter and Benjamin Geer – who were previously closely involved with UK Indymedia and who have, until relatively recently, been united in their belief in the radically liberatory potentials of openness. For them, it is simply an as-yet insufficiently theorised and elaborated form, and thus they have been working on what might be characterised as a 'strong' or 'robust' openness model, which recommends a set of working processes or practices intended to foster it. 'Open Organisations' are entities that anyone can join, that function with complete transparency and flexible and fair decision-making structures, ownership patterns and exchange mechanisms that are designed, defined and refined by members as part of a continual transformative and learning process.[16]

15. Matthew Arnison, 'Open Publishing is the Same as Free Software', March 2001, http://www.cat.org.au/maffew/cat/openpub.html
16. Statement taken from http://wiki.uniteddiversity.com/open_organisations

Crypto-Hierarchies and Problems with Openness

In effect, by creating 'structured processes', Open Organisations try to provide for a consistent openness. In doing so, they implicitly recognise that there are inconsistencies between the rhetoric and behaviour of contemporary political organisations. But what are these problems and who, indeed where, are openness' discontents? In fact, they may be found everywhere. In the case of Inydmedia's 'open publishing' project, for example, openness has been failing under the pressures of scale. Initially small 'cottage-industry' IMCs [Independent Media Centres] were able to manage the open publishing process very well. But, in many IMCs, when the number of site visitors has risen past a certain level, problems have started to occur. Popular IMC sites have become targets for interventions by political opponents, often from the fascist right, seeking opportunities to disrupt what they regard as an IMC's 'counter-cultural' potential and a platform from which to spread their own rhetoric. Of course, there is nothing to prevent this in the IMC manifesto, but it has impelled the understandable decision to edit out fascist viewpoints and other 'noise', using the ad hoc teams whose function was previously to develop and maintain the IMC's open publishing system. Some IMCs have ultimately been seen to take on a rather traditional, closed and censorial function that is all too often undeclared and in contradiction with the official IMC 'become the media' line. In other words, Indymedia channels are often politically censored by a small group of more or less anonymous individuals to quite a high degree.

This emergence of soft control within organisations emphatically declared open is becoming a common and tacitly acknowledged problem across the social movement. As with Indymedia, practical issues with open development and organisation too often give the lie to the enthusiastic promotion of openness as an effective alternative to representation. After one PGA meeting, the group Sans Titre had this to say:

> Whenever we have been involved in PGA-inspired action, we have been unable to identify decision making bodies. Moreover, there has been no collective assessment of the effectiveness of PGA-inspired actions [...] If the PGA process includes decision making and assessment bodies, where are they to be found? How can we take part?[17]

This problem runs through the temporary constitutions and dissolutions of 'open' organisations that make up the social movement. The avowed 'absence' of decision making bodies and points of centralisation can too easily segue into a concealment of control per se. In fact, in both the FLOSS model and the social movement, the idea that no single group or person controls development and decision making is often quite far from the truth. In both cases, it is formally

17. Sans Titre, 'Open Letter to the Peoples' Global Action', 5 September 2002, http://www.pgaconference.org/_postconference_/pp_sanstitre.htm

true that anyone may alter, or intervene into, processes according to their needs, views or projects; but, practically speaking, few people can assume the necessary social position from which to make effective 'interventions'. Open source software is generally tightly controlled by a small group of people. The Apache Group, for example, very open-handedly controls the development of the Apache web server, and Linus Torvalds has the final say on the Linux kernel's development.[18] Likewise, in the social movement, decision-making often devolves to a surprisingly small number of individuals and groups who make a lot of the running in deciding what happens, where and when. Though they never officially 'speak for' others, much unofficial doctrine nonetheless emanates from them. Within political networks, such groups and individuals can be seen as 'supernodes', not only routing more than their 'fair share' of traffic but actively determining the 'content' that traverses them. Such supernodes do not (necessarily) constitute themselves out of a malicious will to power; rather, power defaults to them through personal qualities like energy, commitment, charisma and the ability to synthesise politically important social moments into identifiable ideas and forms.

This soft control by crypto-hierarchies is tacit knowledge for many who have had first hand experience with 'open' organisations. Statements such as the following by a political activist introduced to what he calls 'the chaos of open community' at a Washington State forest blockade camp in 1994 and then later the Carters Road Community, are typical:

> The core group, by virtue of being around longer as individuals, and also working together longest as a sub group, formed unintentional elites. These elite groups were covert structures in open consensus based communities which said loudly and clearly that everyone's influence and power was equal [...] We all joined in with a vigorous explanation that [...] there were no leaders... The conspiracy to hide this fact among ourselves and from ourselves was remarkably successful. It was as though the situation where no leaders existed was known, deep down by everyone, to be impossible, outsiders were able to say so, but communards were hoping so much that it was not true that they were able to pretend [...][19]

To examine how much this 'pretence' is the rule within the social movement is beyond the scope of this piece. But what is clear is that each of the five characteristics of 'openness' described above, when subjected to scrutiny, reveal themselves as extremely compromised. The details, for example, of meetings and discussions are published and circulated, but this information is primarily received by those who are able (and often privileged to be able) to connect to

18. See, for example, Paula Roone, 'Is Linus Killing Linux?', *TechWeb*, 28 January 2001, http://www.techweb.com/wire/story/TWB20010126S0013
19. Chris Lee, 'An Article Concerning the Issue of Covert Power Elites in Open Communities', 4 December 2001, http://cartersrd.org.au/covert_elites.html

certain (technological/social) networks. Likewise, the language of a 'call' or equivalent can determine whether a party will feel comfortable or suitable to respond to it. Like PGA's 'hallmarks', language and phraseology is a point of 'soft control', but not one that is openly discussed and studied. Furthermore, meetings may be 'open to all', but they can quickly become hostile environments for parties who do not, or cannot, observe the 'basic' consensus that is often tacitly agreed between long-term actors in a particular scene. This peer consensus can indeed, on occasion, so determine the movement's 'open' decision-making process as to turn it into a war of attrition on difference, with divergent points of view gradually giving themselves up to peer opinion as the 'debate' wears on and on. The block, or veto, is in fact rarely used because of the peer pressure placed on those who would use it ('Aw, come on, you're not going to block, are you?' – a common enough plaint at movement meetings). In some cases, the apparently neutral 'moderator' role can also become bizarrely instrumentalised, giving rise to the sensation that 'something has already been decided' and that the meeting is just for performative purposes.

Likewise, documentation of meetings and decisions usually only tells half the story. Points of serious contention are frequently left out on grounds that the parties involved in the disagreement might not want them to be published. This 'smoothing over' of serious difference is quite normal. In fact participants in IRC discussions habitually inflect what they say because of the future publication of the logs, using private channels to discuss key points and only holding 'official' discussions and 'lines' in the open. Too often the open channel only 'hears' what it is supposed to hear, and important exchanges are not published.

All of this explains why some activist-theorists are beginning to interrogate the experiment with openness as it is taking shape in the social movement. History has put significant resources at their disposal. Jo Freeman's 'The Tyranny of Structurelessness' is a key document, originating from the experiences of the '60s feminist liberation movement, and provides a critique of the laissez-faire ideal for group structures still absolutely relevant today. As Freeman argues, such structures can become

> [A] smoke screen for the strong or the lucky to establish unquestioned hegemony over others. Thus, structurelessness becomes a way of masking power. As long as the structure of the group is informal, the rules of how decisions are made are known only to a few, and awareness of power is limited to those who know the rules.[20]

Freeman's insight is fundamental. The idea of openness does not in itself prevent the formation of the informal structures that I have described here as

20. Jo Freeman, 'The Tyranny of Structurelessness', first printed in *The Women's Liberation Movement*, USA, 1970 http://www.anarres.org.au/essays/amtos.htm

crypto-hierarchies; on the contrary, it is possible that it fosters them to a greater degree than structured organisations. Underneath its rhetoric of openness, the non-hierarchical organisation can thus take on the qualities of a 'gang'. As Jacques Camatte and Gianna Collu realised in 1969, such organisations tend to hide the existence of their informal ruling cliques to appear more attractive to outsiders, feeding on the creative abilities of individual members whilst suppressing their individual contributions, and producing layers of authority contingent on individuals' intellectual or social dominance. 'Even in those groups that want to escape [it]', writes Camatte, 'the [...] gang mechanism nevertheless tends to prevail [...] The inability to pose theoretical questions independently leads the individual to take refuge behind the authority of another member who becomes, objectively, a leader, or behind the group entity, which becomes a gang.'[21]

Openness: Open to All Constituencies

What this initial investigation has indicated is that the idea of openness, which is receiving such a promotion on the heels of the free-libre and open source software movement, is not, in and of itself, an immediately sufficient alternative to the bankrupt structures of representation. There seem to be good reasons for the discontent with open organisation felt by many activists, much of it based on evidence that must remain, by nature, anecdotal. But, what is clear is that, if we are going to promote open organisation within the social movement, we must also take care to scrutinise the tacit flows of power that underlie and undercut it. The accounts here suggest that once the formal hierarchical membrane of group organisation is dismantled – in which, for example, software composition or political decision making might have previously taken place – what remains are tacit control structures. In FLOSS, limitations to those who can access and alter source code are formally removed. But, what then defines access, and the software that is produced, are underlying determinants such as education, social opportunity, social connections and affiliations. The most open system theoretically imaginable, this is to say, reveals perfectly the predicating inequities of the wider environment in which it is situated. What the idea of openness must tackle first and most critically is that a really open organisation cannot be realised without a prior radicalisation of the socio-political field in which it operates. And that, of course, is to beg the oldest of questions.

21. Jacques Camatte, 'On Organisation', in *Invariance*, Anee V, Serie II, no. 2, reprinted in *This World We Must Leave and Other Essays*, New York: Autonomedia, 1995, p. 30.

Disobbedienti, Ciao

Hydrarchist

Vol 1 #29, Winter/Spring 2005

No formal announcement certified the end of the *Disobbedienti* (Disobedients) in Italy, but the once-dominant extraparliamentary network's demise scarcely seems in dispute. What originated as the *tute bianche* (White Overalls or WO) alliance between groups in the Veneto, Rome and Milan in 1998, encompassing satellite groups in other cities, is now in full decomposition as its constituent elements abandon the logo and reassume identities related to their everyday, territorial reality. The consequences are manifested both in a reshuffling of the relationships between the movements and the political parties and a plurality of campaigns as the focus of struggle. But first some background and explanation.

The widespread riots and fierce police repression that accompanied the G8 in Genoa dealt a mortal blow to the model of controlled conflict and hybridisation with other political forces that had constituted the WO project since 1998. A language of heightened confrontation was adopted prior to the G8, but the scale of state reprisals found them unprepared. Afterwards, there was a failure to assess what had really happened, as each group attempted to distance itself from responsibility. But repression can also produce unity, and transregional ties were galvanised between some of the fractious inheritors of Autonomia Operaia (where a strong Rome-Padua axis can be traced to the late-'60s), the youth section of Rifondazione Comunista (RC – an offshoot of the old Communist Party and still a major force on the reformist left) and the Greens around a platform of 'social disobedience'. Thus occurred an apparently seamless transition from White Overalls to Disobedients, presented as a laboratory for experimentation with new political forms rather than a proposition for any type of unitary organisation. Nonetheless, the new network suffered numerous defections due to exhaustion and unhappiness with the way in which Genoa had been managed and from a sense that the open and experimental spirit which fuelled the WO had now disappeared. From this point onward, the Disobedients would be perceived as a force threatening to hegemonise and erode the autonomy of other groups. Their national nature, media presence and involvement with political parties made them easy to cast as imperialist and overbearing.

Apart from a shared hostility towards the suffocating and disciplinary pressures of the Communist Party, there have always been radical differences within the autonomist left as to the attitude to assume towards elections. From 1976, some 'extraparliamentary' groups ran candidates on the list of Democrazia Proletaria (absorbed by RC in 1992). Participation was justified as a means to construct counter-power and extend the dynamic of conflictuality to these institutions. Others assumed an abstentionist position, rejected mediation and advocated social autonomy – the daily unfolding of material conflict in perpetual antagonism to politics, understood as an institutionalised management of social conflict.

Relations with the parties vary according to local factors, which in Italy can never be underestimated. In the Veneto (Padua, Venice), acute hostility towards the Communist Party tradition, combined with the evisceration of concentrations of labour in the factories – the Veneto's restructured economic form based on small-scale networked production has made it a textbook example of post-Fordism – and the importance of environmentalism, have made the Greens the post-autonomists' political vehicle of choice. Being a 'salon' party with neither tradition nor consolidated grassroots, the Greens are less resistant to new ideas, more malleable to internal reconfiguration. This relationship has allowed the translation of the autonomists' strong territorial presence into an increased political visibility and thus provided a greater margin for action. There are concrete benefits as well: the stability of occupied spaces, the ability to create structures within which its militants can survive materially, and legitimation through a role in local government.

Meanwhile, in Rome, the chaotic urgency of the metropolis produces self-organised re-appropriation for the resolution of basic needs, especially housing. RC remains an important force in the city and contains significant pro-movement elements. Here, the Disobedients have reformed around ACTION (Agency for Social Rights), driven by activists from the social centre, Corto Circuito, which, through a series of occupations, has won accommodation for more than a thousand people and earned considerable respect. Since 1997, they have also elected city and district councillors as independents on the list of RC, a relationship which extends their capacity to negotiate over housing and provides protection from otherwise certain police prosecution. In both Rome and the Veneto, work with migrants, for housing and papers, has been central in recent years; this extends to libertarians and activists of all stripes, and has been an area in which intervention at an institutional level is both useful and inevitable.

Fracture

Tensions over the relationship with political parties came to a head in the Disobedients during the European elections in June. Whilst the Veneto section supported the candidacy of the Greens' Bettin, the Romans ran a popular candidate on the list of RC, Nunzio D'Erme, famous for having dumped several bags of manure in front of Berlusconi's Roman residence. Polling better than expected, he was their fifth highest vote winner nationally. RC's share of the vote gave them five seats to distribute, but D'Erme was passed over in favour of Niki Vendola from the South, where the RC are currently enjoying considerable growth. Given that a candidate from the Northeast was given a seat with a far smaller number of votes, this was understandably viewed as betrayal, and evidence of a cynicism toward the movements to which it had professed an openness since the mid-'90s. This crisis polarised existing divisions within the Disobedients, and political bloodletting on a local level led to a reversion to local identities and a retreat from hybridisation. RC are now openly in cahoots with the government-in-waiting of Romano Prodi, whose Grand Democratic Alliance will challenge and probably defeat Berlusconi at the next election. Consequently, the radical left needs to reposition itself with respect to the future power structure, both to get what they need and to retain a clear oppositional profile.

Nonetheless, some type of relationship with the political system remains unavoidable, even if unformalised or unwitting. How one conceives the purpose of representation will fashion the terms on which it occurs. One vision explicitly legitimises local politics as a space in which to establish a counterweight to the deterritorialising tendency of globalised production and a stage for practical demonstrations of counter-government. Here, parallels are made with Zapatista autonomous communities, which, transposed to Italy, has meant involvement at a municipal level and the election of councillors. Elsewhere, Antonio Negri recently set out criteria for the relationship with party politics in general, insisting on the absolute primacy of the social movement over political parties whose legitimation resides solely in their capacity to serve, resource and open up political space for extra-political activity.[1] Accordingly, party alliances are justified, provided that the relationship is not one of subalternity (whereby parties exploit social movements so as to rebuild their diminishing base), but one of 'navigational' authority, in which party direction derives from demands expressed externally. Handily enough, this functions as both a justification for the past as well as a programme for the future, and an argument for keeping RC at arm's length.

In the meantime, the rapid rise to prominence of social precarity as a political flashpoint has seen an influx of former Disobedients (now re-branded as 'Invisibles' and 'Global') into the organisation of the May Day parade in Milan.[2] A derivative network named PreCog – precarious and cognitive workers – has taken shape in the last year, popularising the cult of San Precario – the mythopoetical patron saint of dispossessed, but combative, subjects – with the intention of rejuvenating the popular imagination in a fight for new social rights. As a network, PreCog contains many sensibilities external to the former Disobedients, including a 'Neurogreen' tendency (environmentalist and libertarian with a focus on imposing pressure at local and European level) which sees in the Green Party a vehicle for more flexible political opposition and a global environmentalist sensibility proper to the problems of advanced capitalism. Meanwhile, the social autonomy perspective within PreCog and

1. Antonio Negri, 'Contro il pensiero molle dell'organizzazione', *Posse, Nuovoi Animali Politici*, Manifesto Libri, April 2004.
2. http://www.globalproject.info, http://www.euromayday.org

'National Network for a Guaranteed Income' – which continues to prioritise the diffuse conflictuality of the 'precariat' and its ability to configure the social balance of forces – is also in a process of growth and re-composition.[3] In spite of these heterogeneous approaches, the outline of a shared trajectory emerged around the question of income, encompassing the national demonstration for a guaranteed income on 6 November 2004 and next year's May Day parades.

The Precariat Strikes Back!

The simmering tension between parties and movements came to a head during the November demonstration. Under the playful acronym GAP – Grand Alliance of the Precarious, a parody of Prodi's Grand Democratic Alliance – workplace committees, from Alitalia to care workers, grassroots trade unions and social centres of every hue converged for direct actions of re-appropriation to protest the increasing cost of living, and demand access to wealth via a street parade through the city centre. 'Autoreduction' is an Italian term for imposing a discount 'from below', and it was planned to perform one in a suburban supermarket. Having neutralised police attention through cunning use of the subway system, the protestors eventually arrived in Pietralata, immortalised in Pasolini's films *Theorem* and *Accatone*, where a shopping centre owned by Berlusconi is handily located by the train station. Once inside, 700 participants filled their trolleys with goods and blocked the cash registers, chanting 'Everything costs too much!' Negotiation began with management for a discount of 70 percent for everyone in the store, but, in the meantime, many people simply walked out with their trolleys and began distributing goods to families and pensioners, drinking wine and sharing sweets. This gesture was initially met with incredulity, but soon the party was in full swing. Meanwhile, the electronics and clothing departments upstairs were by now in the grip of frenzy; computers, phones, DVD players and flat screen monitors made their way out of the door. At this point, many 'ordinary shoppers' had succumbed to repressed desire and started to help themselves. Faced with a plainly uncontrollable situation, the small number of police present were powerless. Later that day, it had been planned to distribute copied DVDs inside the Feltrinelli book and entertainment chain as a symbolic rejection of the copyright laws that limit access to culture and knowledge. Echoes of the morning, however, were too strong; as the demonstration passed by, 200 people entered, filled their arms with books and charged back out into the street into the parade of 25,000 people made up of workers' committees, migrants, grassroots trade unionists, house occupants and students, and a hundred other shades of precarity.

Predictably, the media and political class have embarked on a hysterical condemnation of these actions, and have attempted to impute responsibility to the Disobedients, who, as recounted above, scarcely exist. Arrests and

3. See http://www.incontrotempo.info

a 'zero tolerance' policy have been promised. Notwithstanding the brouhaha, commentators have had to acknowledge both a widespread sympathy for what happened and the emergence of the precariat as a problem henceforth at the centre, rather than the margins, of society.[4] Individual MPs from both the Greens and the RC have even expressed support, but the parties have officially distanced themselves from the acts, widening the schism between the movement and orthodox forms of representation. RC's current fixation with consensus, and its terror at any taint of illegality which could be depicted as being violent, makes constructive cooperation nigh on impossible. But, no violence was involved and the action was performed without any attempt to conceal participants' identities, a fact for which participants will pay a heavy legal price.

Amidst all this, however, GAP has maintained a tortured silence, torn between the need to respond whilst in the public eye and the unresolved distrust of collective representation. Journalists have filled this void by nominating former Disobedients as the voice of the precarious. This unhelpful personalisation derives from their use of 'spokespeople' – in fact leaders – that monopolised media coverage of the 'no global' period. Such distorted representations allow the action to be pigeonholed as belonging to prefabricated media constructions – 'autonomists', 'Disobedients', 'inheritors of '77' – cast as alien to people's everyday experience of contradiction within their living conditions, inhibiting any broader social identification.[5]

A renewed realism as to the acute difficulties faced in everyday life underlies the emphasis on precarity. Spiralling rents, an increased cost of living and poor social/labour mobility – not to mention the apocalyptic turmoil worldwide – are generating a pervasive sense of uncertainty about the future. In the absence of a substantial social welfare buffer, this focus enables a narration of needs and desires in the first person and facilitates a rupture with discourses of the 'no global' period which often lapsed into a jaded Third Worldism, in which the 'serious' problems were often exoticised or abstracted as somebody else's, somewhere else.

Social movements in Italy function best when external factors oblige cooperation and marginalise intra-movement rivalry, yet an inability to coldly appraise the efficiency of discarded strategies threatens to nullify the benefits of experience. The Gordian knots of representation, relations with the institutions and internal and network democracy are not going away. With a centre-left government on the horizon, and the fertile ground for reactionary demagogy this promises, the challenge will be to maintain abrasive contestation, autonomous from the party system, without being relegated to the margins, where the only dividend is unceasing police attention.

4. For a good introduction to the politics and cartography of precarity, see *Green Pepper*'s issue devoted to the theme at http://www.greenpeppermagazine.org
5. Hierarchical political action remains prevalent in Italy, a fact that is often missed.

Chapter 6

Assuming the Position: Art and/Against Business

> I want to burn down all your factories!
> Gustav Metzger

> The last thing we should be doing is embracing our miserable marginality.
> Bifo

The title of this chapter hopefully conveys a sense of the dangers involved in mirroring the corporate 'other' by self-understood radicals. As the slogan on a badge produced by the artists' collective, Inventory, has it: 'Ironic mimesis is not critique, it is the mentality of a slave!' This formula's vitriol no doubt derives from over-exposure to at least a decade's worth of 'adbusting' and 'culture jamming'. Such strategies, argues Neil Mulholland in his article on the cultural logic of Ambient, amount to little more than an attempt at ethical capitalism. But, if adbusting is now widely understood to be a kind of 'anti-corporate corporatism', are all mimetic strategies deployed by the postmodern and post-web generation to be so summarily dismissed? *Mute*'s coverage of 'political net.art' and electronic civil disobedience, especially during the latter half of the '90s, reveals a thinking around the mimicry of capitalism's modalities that goes beyond mere liberal reformism or radical chic. This chapter deals with the self-mirroring transformations of business and culture within digitally networked globalisation, and compiles the arguments for and against imitating the veneer, if not logic, of corporate activity within networked capitalism.

The interview with Artist Placement Group co-founders, Barbara Steveni and John Latham, by myself and Pauline van Mourik Broekman, uncovers some of the early moves in the courtship between art and business in the mid-1960s. In step with a contemporary desire to spin the modes and materials of industrial capitalism in new directions, this UK-based group of conceptual artists, negotiated industrial placements for artists. This project, the aim of which was to throw a creative catalyst into the heart of commercial production, created some very divergent results. Gustav Metzger drove a captain of industry out of the APG-convened Industrial Negative conference by declaring, 'I want to burn down all your factories!' Meanwhile, in the 2002 interview, Steveni reveals her more conciliatory position by describing companies as 'conglomerates of individuals' open to influence. Capitalism, this suggests, could be reformed by converting key players at the top of the tree, not by violent proletarian struggle from beneath. While some of its members engaged in class-based politics,

APG could certainly be accused of pre-empting today's neoliberal 'culture industry' and alliance culture.

Neil Mulholland's above-mentioned critique traces the trajectory of culture's assimilation into commerce to its suffocating terminus. Amongst a wide array of things ambient, he discusses the work of Glasgow-based artists David Shrigley, Ross Sinclair and Jonathan Monk. These artists, working in the cash strapped, post-recession '90s, used nonchalant, witty and minimal strategies for 'interrupting the equilibrium and continuity of temporal space'. These low-budget means of 're-narrating' the city were 'gradually disassociated' from art and academia to become, by the end of the decade, the tools of viral advertising and 'ambicommerce'.

Reviewing the ICA's CRASH! Corporatism and Complicity show of 1999, however, Benedict Seymour questions the implied obligation for art to perform a critical function. While the show's curators and many of its artists struggled to thwart the paradigm of ironic mimesis, or complexify it beyond the point of simple co-optability, Seymour suggests that less self-flagellation and more 'being in uncertainty', even luxuriant escapism, may be what's required.

While Seymour speculates that the solution to the riddle of contemporary cultural politics is, perhaps, a rejection of art's ethical responsibility, interviews with Critical Art Ensemble (CAE) and Electronic Disturbance Theatre's (EDT) Ricardo Dominguez strike a very different note. Rejecting the efficacy of representative democracy and, in CAE's case, the attendant forms of street-based protest bar highly localised ones, they advocate a proliferation of anarchist-style cells working across the internet to thwart the smooth functioning of power. This electronic civil disobedience should be as nomadic and distributed as its state-corporate target. Rather than accepting the 'voyeuristic' and 'narcissistic' relationship to virtual space prescribed by the military-industrial complex, EDT advocate that participants in net culture assume an ethical stance *vis-à-vis* a 'distant other'. Both groups have pursued a 'marriage of convenience' between activists and hackers to disrupt techno-capitalism and hit it where it hurts – its databases.

In their 'Culture Clubs' article, Anthony Davies and Simon Ford formulate a similar response to the flattened networks and hollowed-out companies that characterised the commercial landscape of the '90s, and continue to do so. As outsourcing and flexibilisation become the order of the day for business, cultural organisations followed suit, and these hollowed out institutions, part-funded through corporate sponsorship (rather than patronage), were increasingly made available to commercial agendas. As faith in the culture industry peaked with New Labour and the newly desirable arts were understood as the 'secret weapon of business', any residual idea of art's autonomy beyond the sphere of commerce perished.

But if, in response, adopting the virtual and nomadic forms of capital seemed to be justified by the successes of the anti-globalisation movement of the late-'90s and early-'00s, its cultural variant was arguably less successful. In his text, 'Learning the Right Lessons', which revisits the politics of 'tactical media' ten years on, David Garcia quotes Bifo's denunciation of the Telestreets movement at a 2004 meeting in Senigallia. While representatives from the micro-broadcasting movement met in an obscure Italian seaside town, Berlusconi's government passed the Gasparri law, consolidating his grip on the Italian mediascape. Bifo and others berated the Telestreets producers for embracing their 'miserable marginality' and consequently missing the opportunity to attack the legislation head-on. The diffusion of efforts and effects, amidst loosely allied producers, despite being a celebrated tactic for subverting networked capitalism, risks evaporating altogether. As with the alliance culture of the business sector, such loose ties of commitment and intention can produce as much instability as contingent support. The mimesis of capital's modus operandi by radical groups and artists, though not necessarily displaying the mentality of the slave, is liable to the same turbulence and collapse that its markets are currently experiencing. In the multimedia age, if a return to the politics of what Baudrillard called 'the system of meaning and representation' is no longer an option, what forms of collaboration will develop within, and against, capitalism's nomadic networks? And, whatever happened to the strategy of burning down its factories?

BIT on BIT

The Bureau of Inverse Technology (BIT)

Vol 1 #3, Autumn 1995

Significant Unmanned Event

Extracted from an interview (19/20 August, 1995) by blindterminal CU-SeeMe conference (tenuously) connecting bureau members in Melbourne, Berlin and San Francisco with London (me). Some degree of appropriate mordant futility in doing walkie talkie on a Pentium. Depress your mouse now. Reset the VideoSpigot.

The bureau members are difficult to assess, their number officially shifts between 11 and three – and they refuse to be represented in impromptu conversation. They insist on responding to the questions in a kind of database tele-grammar, statement packets assembling on conflicting sides of the international Dateline delivered deadpan as a set of formal announcements. This insistence on the high-tech convulsive is characteristic.

It makes for a disconcerting interview habitat. However…

Since inception three years ago, the bureau has maintained a noncommittal presence, hovering at the edges of academic-art-world-faux-fashion-real-scientific conversation. BIT, formed as a self-described bureaucracy in Melbourne, Australia (1992), operates now in global distribution between Australia, Europe and the United States.

The bureau pursues an active engagement with the technologically given, deploying a variety of domestic and high-end technologies to emit an erratic supply of highly packaged artefacts.

BIT activity is enacted from within an immaculate collective anonymity – a denial of identity reducing their availability to a numbered email address in Finland.

BIT Frames a Rabid Techno-science

So, I question, across oceans in 80-millisecond network packages, VAT-generated audio: What brought this on?

BIT: (eventually) The bureau formed spontaneously in 1992. It originated as a form of civic industrial discourse, our first coherent engagement, Body vs. Architecture in Melbourne, 1992, involved the introduction of the body into architecture. BIT bodies were demonstrated on skyscraper precipices, freeway edges, bridge suspensions, in wrongful escalator interpretations and violatory parking situations: a wilful misuse of public scale.

From there, the development into other forms of advanced technological occupation was obvious.

k®: Regarding the anonymity thing – a guerrilla girl comparison must be obligatory here…

BIT: So what?

BIT anonymity is critical. We believe, no identification, no security. BIT opposes the name-manship of known art-culture production. Anonymity keeps us honest.

We have always seized on marked artists and other public figures as helper applications, correctly deployed they form a kind of decoy identity set around core BIT impersonality.

(People in general acknowledgement of BIT affiliation include Stelarc, Bruce Sterling, Marina Gržinić, Orlan, Kathy Acker, Jeremijenko, Andrea Juno, Mark Pauline, Rosie X...) Not having a specific identity gives you a certain edge.

k®: You maintain a discernible female presence though: you've been classed in with the 'cyberbabe' effect – people like Jaime Levy, VNS Matrix, gashgirl – is gender hacking an inevitable issue of your work?

BIT: This is an assumption. Some of us may be very important men.

k®: OK, next question. Some, if not most, of you are working for large corporations and institutions – would you say that being in an atmosphere of power, money and unlimited resources has its advantages?

BIT: Give us power tools. Don't divulge secrets, learn during work. A certain amount of hardware osmosis goes on, we get access to a lot of high-end things... airbags, electricians, SGIs, photocopiers, 3D-glasses, tunnelling electron microscopes, docuprint, hallmark cards, laser diodes, plastic project boxes, CD-Rom writers, solid state power inverters – the list goes on.

Observe the parasitic process by which the bureau becomes proximate to a legitimate corporation.

Conversely, contact with the corporate other has made us alert to the seamless enslavement imperative of present technological production, code-named interactivity.

The designed cultivation of obedient icons userfriends, office-bred devices, the rote inert... Prototype hologram folk to play submissive in high-ender games of Simon says... serfware interactives, BOBtype personality applications consumed by their own tedious life code... Intuitive interfaces shamelessly integrate with your existing system in one seamlessly integrated application... (Guy Debord, PDA Voice Cognition Lackeys Make Tearless Secretaries, 1994).

BIT signals a concern for the safety of the corporate imagination and its designs on our technological futures. BIT reprotocols for human/machine interactions. We reengineer and reconstruct product. Disengage office-bored and civil devices from their directed labours and transfer them to fields of greater resonance and disorientation. Intimate with public circuitry, office furnitures, domestic instruments amplifying the natural a-systemic determination of international business machines and re-orientating rational technologies to an impetuous/non-specific precision.

k®: Well, can you give me some specifics: What exactly are you working on at the moment?

BIT: Expanding the boundaries of technological decency.

BIT seeks to complicate the commodification of the product, Bureau market research returns indications that products sell. The bureau proposes to invert this to sell products. We are manufacturing identity solutions. Motoring accessories. Military documentation. BIT products report a tendency to degrade. Information follows.
[FILE TRANSFER: ftp://ftp.lobe.upn.pit/file//CATALOG—BIT]

ITEMBIT 0023
Product Suicidebox. The Bureau of Inverse Technology is pleased to announce the installation of a security substation under the Golden Gate Bridge, San Francisco. Vertical motion-triggered camera device is designed to capture a digital videorecord of all falls from the bridge. The resulting footage will record as a continuous sequence the trickle of people who jump off the bridge. There are approximately four to eight bodies retrieved per month by the coastguard. Some lives are lost in low visibility. BIT believes that this action will need to be done without the knowledge of the bridge authorities. The bureau records nonspecific suicide and other data margins. Certain images derived from these tapes have transcended the mundane. Untold Domestic Potential. Contact us for more information.

ITEMBIT 00747
BITPLANE (product pending). The two-protagonist BITvideogame in which video images are fed live to the players from two radio-controlled sail-plane gliders, operated by the players and instrumented with onboard b&w video camera transmitters, 2000 image range. Stated BITgame aim is to shoot down the opponent plane. No artillery equipment supplied: winner must destroy own plane in order to destroy opponent. Game finish in assured devastation: GAMEOVER FATAL ERROR ABORT. Each BITplane comes with unique text on the upper wing surface. Plane text to be deciphered in flight by opponent camera before both planes are reduced to debris. The only reward for destruction is the satisfaction of knowing.

Includes: instructional drills, default pilot commands, video training, black box, joy stick, head set, mouth piece, cock pit. This BITgame collapses the mirage of screen-imagined heroics into nonvirtual system-crash. It asks urgent questions of the substitute reality market and its attraction to the sights of renewable disaster.

Buy into the techno-political. Price on application.

ITEM 0032
BIT PHONE: This is a telephone interpretation of the hypermedia experience, available to the casual phone user from home or in public.

The user navigates through the audio architecture of the BIT digital touch tone telephony system. A single phone call will initiate an immediate response. THANKYOU FOR DIALLING. Branching submenus of retractable choices make available a highly rendered information superstructure, along with a voice-order catalogue for BITremote accessories: 3D sound devices, the BITplane videogame, personal satellite units and other teleobjects. TO REGRET YOUR CHOICES PRESS # NOW.

System currently operational in San Francisco, Montreal, duplicate systems due to be installed in Melbourne and Berlin (*deutsche fassung*) Oct–Nov 1995.

> Relocates the frontiers of space hallucination in the electronic not-space.
> Wired 3.07

> Indeed.
> Bruce Sterling

k®: Captivating... Could you name some future or brewing projects...?

BIT: BIT Rom. We have observed a recent tendency to make CD Roms. The bureau constructs an imitative investigation into this techno-redundant activity.

BIT looks into cyberspace at a clinical imagery, estranged from its inherent life and engaged in unnatural digital acts. BIT feeds back in to the multi media moment. Catering to the alienation sidemarket reaction to hi-gleam, quick-jack consumption industries. Currently under construction in Silicon Valley California, contact us for more information.

Other future interests include icons. BIT plans the reinstatement of the icon as a resonant autonomous object of multiple or intangible purpose. The expression of a being projected beyond itself. Do not print or click.

Also: personal satellite availability. Microminiature accelerometers. Interactive sex. Contact us for more.

Vector Block on Telecom Avenue

Critical Art Ensemble Interviewed by Mark Dery

Vol 1 #10, Summer 1998

Call them Legion, for they are many; though small in number, Critical Art Ensemble contains multitudes, philosophically speaking. An artistic collective whose inventive blend of multimedia performance and philosophy in the mosh pit explores the intersection of radical politics, postmodern theory and vanguard art, CAE is a philosophical terrorist cell – a splinter group of mutant free radicals from the post-everything left. Founded in Tallahassee, Florida, in 1987, by Steve Kurtz and Steve Barnes, Critical Art Ensemble began as an avant-garde video/theory collective. From the outset, the group's screenings and lectures incorporated slide shows, film projected on paintings and live performance, and were staged in unconventional venues such as nightclubs and bars. Dedicated to the proposition, 'Give the audience one quick "riot of semiosis" and then move on', CAE's performances were hit-and-run events inspired by guerrilla art forms such as street theatre – swift, tactical insertions into a public mind that was unprepared, to say the least.

Currently comprised of Barnes, Kurtz and his wife, Hope [now deceased], Dorian Burr and Beverly Schlee, CAE has evolved into an alt.theory think tank. Its performance-lectures have become must-see events at European symposia on the politics of cyberculture. Cloned from the cultural DNA that yielded William S. Burroughs's *Electronic Revolution*, Guy Debord's *Society of the Spectacle*, Hakim Bey's *Temporary Autonomous Zone* and other primers of 'nomadic resistance', CAE's essays (many of them archived at [www.critical-art.net]) have become instant classics of what the media theorist, Geert Lovink, calls 'net criticism'.

In *The Electronic Disturbance* and *Electronic Civil Disobedience* (1994 and '96 respectively, both published by Semiotext(e)'s Autonomedia imprint), the group downloads intellectual shareware from Marx, Foucault, Deleuze, Bataille, Kristeva, Debord, anarchism, the 'zero work' polemics of Bob Black and the pro-plagiarism rhetoric of anti-copyright advocates, customising it with CAE's own idiosyncratic theories. The result is a quick-and-dirty but robust hack – the philosophical equivalent of the 'sloppy corrective programming' extolled by Marvin Minsky in Stewart Brand's *The Media Lab.*

Re-calibrating leftism to the cultural torque of post-industrial capitalism, CAE targets the political ground zero of the late 20th century. *Electronic Civil Disobedience* (ECD) asks, 'What are the strategies and tactics needed to fight a decentralised power that is constantly in a state of flux?' The argument begins in the key of Marxist historical materialism, but soon modulates into a postmodern leftism familiar from Jean Baudrillard. 'Before computerised information management, the heart of institutional command and control was easy to locate', the group writes. 'Castles, palaces, government bureaucracies, corporate home offices and other architectural structures stood looming in city centres, daring malcontents and underground forces to challenge their fortifications.' But in a digital age based on the manipulation of symbols of one sort or another, 'power is neither visible nor stable'; the imposing edifices that once housed it are now monuments to its absence. With the virtually unchallenged global dominance of a 'post-national' capitalism, for which the regulatory meddlings of nations are comic relief, power has 'retreated into cyberspace where it can nomadically wander the globe, always absent to counter-forces, always present whenever and wherever opportunity knocks'.

Unaccountably, the left, whose ideology is supposedly built on historical bedrock and whose recent critiques stress the significance of our shift from an industrial to an information economy, remains doggedly wedded to the tactics of '60s-style civil disobedience – a tactical misstep CAE attributes to 'the continued presence of the remnants of the '60s New Left within the ranks of activist groups'. According to CAE, 'nostalgia for '60s activism endlessly replays the past as the present, and, unfortunately, this nostalgia has infected a new generation of activists who have no living memory of the '60s. Out of this sentimentality the belief has arisen that the "take to the streets" strategy worked then, and will work now on current issues'.

This magical history tour suffered serious collateral damage during the Gulf War, when the Pentagon's stage management of media reality, coupled with the war's made-for-TV brevity and its Nintendo bloodlessness (from the American perspective, at least), presented the anti-war movement with a frustratingly stealthy target, seemingly designed to evade or outmanoeuvre the tactics of traditional activism.

Conceding the historical gains of street protests at a local level, CAE maintains that such tactics have had little effect on 'military/corporate policy': 'CAE has said it before, and we will say it again: as far as power is concerned, the streets are dead capital! Nothing of value to the power elite can be found on the streets [...]' Since transnational capital – and, by extension, global power – resides increasingly in the immaterial elsewhere of the internet, CAE advocates *electronic* civil disobedience – 'nomadic resistance' for an age of decentralised, dematerialised power. 'As in civil disobedience, the primary tactics in electronic civil disobedience are trespass and blockage', the group writes. Political pressure is brought to bear on corporate, governmental or military wrongdoers by activist hackers who block offenders' access to their own databanks.

The group proposes an unlikely alliance between 'anti-authoritarian' hackers and to-the-ramparts activists, a marriage of convenience that would presumably politicise the hacker class, even as it dragged the left, kicking and screaming, into the terminal reality of the late 20th century. (Precisely how this shotgun wedding would be arranged is never explained.) Weary of Marxism's faith in the assertion of a 'collective will' by a radicalised global proletariat (a utopian fiction whose epitaph is written in the internecine bloodletting of identity politics), CAE pins its hopes to a 'technocratic avant-garde' of politicised hackers and jacked-in activists, organised into small cells on the model of anarchist terrorists (and, ironically, the right-wing militia movement and eco-guerrillas such as Earth First!). 'Collective democratic action may be weakly effective on the local (micro) level,' argues CAE, 'but it becomes next to useless on a macro scale'; the individual interests of nations often trip each other up, 'the complexity of the division of labour prevents consensus, and there is no apparent apparatus through which to organise... To fight a decentralised enemy requires decentralised means... If the cells are working in double-blind activities in a large enough number, and are effective in and of themselves, authority can be challenged.'

Not that CAE's theories of nomadic resistance to peripatetic power spring full-blown from the group's brow: In 'Striking at the Heart of the State' (1978), his acid-bath critique of a gang of Marxist terrorists called the Red Brigades, Umberto Eco synopsises the intellectual framework that undergirds modern terrorism, anticipating CAE's argument that the social and economic dominance of multinational capitalism 'rests on the ability of an institution to move where resistance is absent'. Eco notes that multinationals, in the eyes of terrorists like the Red Brigades, can only be thwarted 'through acts of harassment, exploiting their own logic: if there exists a completely automated factory, it will not be upset by the death of the owner but rather by erroneous bits of information inserted here and there, making work hard for the computers that run the place'.

But CAE goes further, enacting the cultural trajectory tracked by its argument, moving from the hard-headed rationalism of Marxist historical materialism to a Deleuzean 'schizo-analysis' (or its political equivalent), better suited to an age of chaos capitalism, in which commodity futurists such as George Gilder inform *Forbes* readers that 'equilibrium is death' and managerial gurus such as Tom Peters proclaim 'the limits of rationality' and exhort corporate culture to 'lighten our attachment to logic'.

CAE's amok politics is loosely rendered at best, but its fuzzy outlines bear at least a passing resemblance to the surrealist liberation of the unconscious; to the Dionysian psycho-politics of radical Freudians like Norman O. Brown; to Deleuze and Guattari's embrace of the free-floating, fragmentary psychology of the schizophrenic as a wrench in the repressive, Oedipal machinery of capitalism; and to Hakim Bey's ontological anarchism.

As always, CAE's arguments sew the seeds of their own rebuttals. Taking as its cornerstone the premise – inherited from post-structuralism and identity politics – that the democratic notion of consensus is merely a user-friendly term for the dictatorship of the majority, CAE stakes its faith in an 'emergent' resistance borne of the disparate, decentralised activities of innumerable activists, all waging covert actions against an 'authoritarianism' that's equal parts Darth Vader and Scrooge McDuck. It's a leftist leap of faith that begs the obvious question: How do we agree, in the absence of democratic consensus, on what constitutes 'authoritarianism'? 'Let each group resist from the coordinates that it perceives to be the most fruitful', CAE hedges. All well and good, but how, then, do we avoid the absurdist nightmare of undercover agents, unknown to each other, working at cross-purposes? Then, too, what happens when CAE's massively parallel, unknowing co-conspirators hack the pan-capitalist mainframe? 'While we may not extract tactical possibilities for political and cultural resistance from these observations', the group writes in *ECD*, 'we do hope to contribute to the production of the ideational conditions for such possibilities to emerge in the realms of appearance and action.' As with the workers' paradise of Marxist theory and the rapture of Christian eschatology, CAE's morning after, like the liberatory *dénouements* of so many theoretical utopias, is forever forestalled.

Even so, Critical Art Ensemble is one of very few voices on the techno-literate left, ready to take the fire fight to the enemy's doorstep. Eschewing the technophilia of the libertarian digerati and the neo-Luddism of centrist liberals like Bill McKibben and Sven Birkerts, the group foregrounds issues of social justice and economic equity in a wired world. Tinkered together from radical politics, pirated theory and postmodern sci-fi, CAE's broadsides are a welcome corrective to the DOS-for-Dummies futurism of Nicholas Negroponte and the tie-dyed cyberbole of John Perry Barlow – logic bombs for those of us in the Empire of the Wired who dream of Striking Back.

Mark Dery: *The Electronic Disturbance* includes scorched-earth critiques of traditional theatre and performance art, with its Me Generation exaltation of the solipsistic self. You call for a 'postmodern theatre of resistance' that incorporates acts of poetic terrorism in the real world and information warfare in virtual realms. I was surprised to stumble, in the thick of your argument, on an approving reference to the Living Theatre's attempts to demolish the proscenium arch and take its psycho-politics into that mythical site of all '60s resistance, the streets. 'It collapsed the art and life distinction, which has been of tremendous help by establishing one of the first recombinant stages', you write, the other being the virtual world of the net.

I couldn't help wondering: To what extent does CAE draw inspiration from the radical theatre of the '60s – from the Living Theatre and the San Francisco Mime Troupe to Yippie pranks such as the celebrated attempt to levitate the Pentagon, and the media manipulation of proto-postmodernists such as Abbie Hoffman and the New York-based anarcho-Situationist group, the Motherfuckers?

Critical Art Ensemble: Radical American theatre of the '60s certainly contributes to our identification with street action, but no more than the many other manifestations of resistant performance. Berlin Dada, Theatre of the

Oppressed, feminist performance of the '70s, Guerrilla Art Action Group or the Situationists proper were just as inspiring.

Street action is a strange project because there's no more progress to be made. The tactics have been thoroughly researched and tested, its spatial limits are understood – it's really only useful at a local level, and its primary function is to create pedagogical situations for consciousness-raising. Certainly, guerrilla art activity continues ever onward, reintroducing itself with each new situation that calls for shifting political perception; however, the research and experimental phase of the genre seems finished – the early-'70s was the last time it had an experimental form.

CAE's interest in the Living Theatre stems from our belief that it offered a proto-postmodern model of cultural production. The group quite consciously located itself in the liminal position between the real and the simulated. Various behaviours were appropriated and redeployed so perfectly that, regardless of their ontological status, they had the material impact of the real. The Living Theatre performed the crisis of the real before it had been adequately theorised, and contributed to the conceptual foundation now used to understand and create virtual theatre. It helped make it clear that for virtual theatre to have any contestational value, it must loop back into the materiality of everyday life.

In the case of electronic resistance, the prank has become the dominant model. Unfortunately, it's the one with the least political impact. While we can take personal delight in pranks, they're not tactically viable in any political sense. CAE wrote *Electronic Civil Disturbance* in an attempt to create a narrative to show what was at stake, to present the contestational opportunity that is currently available, and to hurry the research process into more sophisticated forms of resistance.

MD: I'm disheartened to hear that CAE feels pranks aren't 'tactically viable in any political sense', since the best ones would seem to incorporate the postmodern tactics you advocate, striking at the heart of the spectacle, to update the battle cry of the Red Brigade. I'm thinking of the infamous phone hack that re-routed calls to the Palm Beach County Probation Department to a phone-sex hotline, free of charge, or the covert addition of kissing men to SimCopter by a gay employee who wanted to call attention to the absence of gay characters in computer games, or the Barbie Liberation Organisation's (BLO) corrective surgery on Barbies and 'Talking Duke' G.I. Joes, transplanting sound chips so that Barbie bellowed, 'Vengeance is mine!', while Joe chirped, 'Will we ever have enough clothes?' Then, too, such pranks display a sense of humour sorely lacking on both the old left, with its flatfootedly earnest agit-prop, and the postmodern left, with its hectoring identity politics and its poured-concrete jargon.

CAE: First, we need to make some distinctions. There is a very big difference between a piece like Igor Vamos' BLO action, and rerouting calls to a phone sex hotline. The latter is exemplary of what CAE means by the term 'prank'. The call reroute gag is unquestionably funny, but it's a lot like putting a tack on the teacher's chair. The teacher sits on it, the class gleefully exclaims 'ha-ha', and then it's business as usual. Other than demonstrating a brief moment of defiance, there's no real purpose. CAE looks at the BLO action as interventionist art. What makes the BLO action different from the re-route prank is that it creates a pedagogical situation in which people are given the opportunity to escape the taken-for-granted authority of stereotypical gender codes. In this moment of liberation, they can think about alternative possibilities for gender identities and roles. This kind of work is extremely important, and CAE gives it full respect and support. However, such action is pedagogical, not political. It prepares the consciousness of individuals for new possibilities, and in the best of cases moves them to political action. The activity inspired by the piece is the political action. (In this context, by political action, CAE means the temporary or permanent redistribution or reconfiguration of power relationships.)

MD: Could you recap on a few of the examples given in *ECD*, for the benefit of our readers?

CAE: What CAE suggests in *ECD* is moving the tactic of civil disobedience (CD) into cyberspace. CD has lost most of its power as tactical leverage in political struggle (except on a local level) because the use of electronic equipment allows those under pressure to simply move their operations to another location. This is the major advantage that the nomadic corporate state currently has over traditional street activism. This leaves the question: What is of value to the corporate state and how can it be appropriated? The answer, of course, is its data and/or means of communication. Without it, the velocity of information capital slows, and the system collapses into its own inertia. Relentless strikes of this kind would cause such financial disruption that it would be cheaper for capitalist agencies to offer tangible concessions to the activists than to continue the battle with them.

As for examples of this activity, how could we know of any? No activist would publicly speak about it since such activity is currently placed under the sign of high criminality bordering on treason. This framing occurs in spite of the fact that *ECD* does not destroy or vandalise data, it only blocks it. Any institution which was struck by this action would never go public about it for reasons I'm sure you can deduce. And, if CAE did know of any examples, we certainly wouldn't speak about them! This kind of activism is real political action, and not the politics of spectacle, so it has no public forum. Only the theory can appear; the activity is underground.

MD: In *The Electronic Disturbance*, you exhort 'resistant cultural producers' to use consumer media technologies to parry the relentless assault of corporate media – a call to arms that reminds me of Andrew Ross and Constance Penley's vision, in the introduction to their *Technoculture* anthology, of everyday cyberproles 'turn[ing] technocommodities into resources for waging a communications revolution from below'.

I'm as much of a sucker as anyone when it comes to romantic myths of political resistance, but isn't it time we dissected some of these stories in the unforgiving light of the 'materiality of everyday life' CAE ritually invokes? In *The Temporary Autonomous Zone*, Hakim Bey writes, 'Many anarchists and libertarians have deep faith in the PC as a weapon of liberation and self-liberation – but no real gains to show, no palpable liberty.' At the end of the day, isn't symbolic disturbance just that – symbolic? Obviously, classic Marxism's hardheaded materialism blinds it to the significance of cultural politics – the subcultural acts of subversion and perversion that Stuart Hall calls 'resistance through rituals'. But, just as obviously, Michel de Certeau's argument that consumption can be a form of production has its limits, and we slam headlong into them in cultural studies essays that place our last, best hopes for micropolitical resistance in the Dionysian promise of the rave, the Bakhtinian carnival of the Burning Man festival, pornographic *Star Trek* fanzines or (not again!) online gender-bending. Even Hal Foster, whose critical anthology, *The Anti-Aesthetic*, helped secure the art world beachhead for postmodernism, has heralded the 'return of the real' in his book of the same name, proclaiming the resurrection of art and theory grounded in – heaven forefend! – 'actual bodies and social sites'.

How do we (and CAE) wriggle out of the philosophical Catch-22 implicit in the fact that any analysis of the flux and flow of power in the late 20th century has to reconcile the material effects of power with the increasingly *immaterial* nature of power in the Information Age? CAE argues, on one hand, for an engaged activism grounded in 'the materiality of everyday life', and on the other for an ontological anarchism whose brief-lived pirate utopias recall Deleuze and Guattari's 'deterritorialised' social spaces or Hakim Bey's temporary autonomous zones. Can you (and we) really have your politics both ways – materialist and surrealist?

CAE: Let's begin with 'symbolic disturbance'. The impact it's going to have depends upon what symbols are disturbed. If the disturbance is aimed at cultural representations, such as gender codes, then you're correct; all that's being disturbed is the symbolic plane, although it can be for a very good purpose and have very good results. Pedagogical action is not political action, but it's still an essential part of the resistant political process. However, other symbols have a material impact when disturbed. If Baudrillard taught us anything, it's that simulated activities and the disruption of simulations can have direct and dramatic material results. An obvious example is information. If a lab can't access its research data, can that lab function? If a wholesaler can't access his/her shipping data, can that business function? In both cases, symbolic disturbance causes deep disruption on the material plane because the representational and the material are interdependent, so much so that there are times when it's difficult to tell which is which. This kind of appropriation of representation can be used as a point of political leverage that can, in turn, be used to reconfigure the material arenas that you just listed.

So, to answer your question about whether we're 'Surrealists' or 'materialists', CAE is both – not by choice but because we have to be. As cultural activists, we have to be prepared to continuously produce new cultural possibilities in the minds of others – or, to put it negatively, to help people escape from dominant cultural codes – and we have to be able to create environments that thwart separation and allow people to come together in a situation where social activity is not predetermined. As political activists, we must aggressively confront vectors of domination with the goal of reducing their velocity. These are two different, but equally important, tasks, and they both require action on the symbolic, as well as the material, planes.

MD: To my mind, CAE's synthesis, in the late-'80s, of politics, postmodern philosophy and performance art forms part of the now voguish genre of performance theory typified by Arthur Kroker, who declaims Baudrillardian one-liners over Wagnerian techno, or Allucquère Rosanne Stone, whose lectures are a sort of avant-vaudeville, incorporating props, slides and audience participation. What does this trend say about the academy's relationship to pop culture in general, and performance art in particular? Are we witnessing the 'voguing' of theory by the academic hip-oisie here, or something more substantive?

CAE: Perhaps we're back to the Living Theatre again: appropriate and redeploy in accordance with what the situation calls for. The ivory tower has done all it can (as an institution of information managers) to remove itself from those not in information management. In fact, it's even worse than that. The differing specialisations within the academy no longer have a common language with which to speak with one another. I think the more progressive to radical elements in the academy recognise the need to reconnect with the public. To reach those outside the institution, popular techniques, performative or otherwise, become a viable option. Whether this research project will be fruitful or not remains to be seen. Academics are just beginning to toddle into new territories of process and presentation. The situation is at least cause for some optimism.

MD: Some would argue that the Ivory Tower of Babel is not only unable to converse with itself, but incomprehensible to a larger world that doesn't speak academese – a serious challenge to the populist dream of 'reconnecting with the public'. To be sure, carping about academic jargon is often just anti-intellectualism in drag. Still, there's no denying the obvious irony of a professoriat that purports to speak for, and to, the proletariat in a language unintelligible to it.

I find CAE's texts exciting but uneven – the inevitable result of so many cooks stirring the broth. At best, they're as pithy and plainspoken as IWW pamphlets; at worst, they descend into Arthur Krokerian cybaroque. How does such arguably arcane pomo critspeak advance CAE's vision of an engaged academy that 'reconnects with the public'?

CAE: We may have an example of the Tower of Babel right here. When speaking of academia as an information management system separated from those not of that profession, what was meant is that its members have a very difficult time speaking to the 'public'. But let's take some time to share the blame. The problem isn't theory-speak; theory-speak is a small symptom of a larger tendency. As the division of labour becomes increasingly complex, each segment is forced to develop its own specialised language. This language is designed primarily for internal discussion among specialists. It's rare to find a social segment that doesn't have a specialised language. If you're not a part of the profession in question, who can understand the specialised language of a computer maintenance person, a mechanic or a doctor? Now, some professions that must regularly interact with non-specialists ('the public') have researched other methods of communicating, and this is what more progressive elements of the university are beginning to do. Talking to the public is a pretty new and contested concept in the university. With any luck, academics will get better at it.

As for the discussion of radical politics among intellectuals using a specialised language, CAE has no problem with that any more than we would with any other social segment using one. Admittedly, CAE uses specialised languages. We use a recombinant style that drifts in and out of different rhetorical possibilities. When CAE wants to communicate with social segments that find no significance in books, we use other methods. Writing is just another weapon in our arsenal, and we like to think we efficiently deploy it in appropriate contexts.

MD: There's a tart critique, in *The Electronic Disturbance*, of leftist political documentaries, a time-honoured form of agit-prop which you argue is no less manipulative than the mainstream media it decries: 'Anywhere along the political continuum the electronic consumer turns, s/he is treated like media sheep'. Do you really believe that independent media voices such as Paper Tiger and Deep Dish TV are as pernicious as mainstream Murdochian media simply because they're 'monologic', as you put it, employing coercive techniques familiar from network news? This strikes me as a textbook example of the long-standing habit in academic theory (taken to Laputan heights by postmodernists) of exaggerating the effects of epistemological assumptions on everyday reality. I mean, does raw power really work this way, in our daily lives? Would CAE honestly argue that *Manufacturing Consent*, an undeniably polemical documentary about Noam Chomsky, is no less Orwellian than Leni Riefenstahl's *Triumph of the Will*, simply because of a mutual reliance on persuasive cinematic rhetoric and positivist assumptions about truth?

And, as long as I'm emptying my ammo clip here, I'm also worried by the whiff of vanguardist contempt for progressive populism that lingers over CAE's argument. For example, in *ECD* you dismiss community-based art projects as 'a sanctioned bureaucratic category' in which 'very little work pertaining to the "community" is done'. There's at least a hint, here, of the elitism that makes strange bedfellows of radical voices on the far left and right.

CAE: When documentaries replicate the status quo of power relationships in terms of cultural consumption, CAE is immediately sceptical, regardless of the message the work presents. The use of such methods and forms indicates the dangerous duplicity of 'do as I say, not as I do'. This is a behaviour that I, for one, find very elitist. Using a top-down method of presentation – the enlightened attempt to illuminate the unenlightened – is not a smart thing to do when other options are available.

Your choice of Paper Tiger is a smart example of a viable documentary style. Their tapes are presented as editorials, not truth; they always call attention to the fact that the speaker is a specific voice and not a universal one; and they always call attention to the means of production and to the fact that their tapes are manufactured products. CAE believes that better, and more visually exciting, models of production have been developed, but this die-hard, New Left, Brechtian theatre style is still useful.

As for your charges of elitism, we can't agree. Kept within our social context, we're only promoting and defending our minority location on the political continuum. How can we be elitist? CAE has no power to separate itself from 'the rabble', let alone enforce our opinions as universals. Charging us with elitism is like saying that a black person who speaks against white popular culture is elitist and racist.

Admittedly, CAE isn't fond of progressives primarily because they still believe the state will save them. The Law/the Logos/the Patriarchy is not going to help anyone, and empowering it further only serves to increase the gravity of power bearing down upon us. But, because of faith in democracy (or at least its simulation), they are always ready to be the dupes of various power vectors. You mentioned community art – a perfect example of this problem. All of a sudden, and out of nowhere, planning and institutional grants have an outreach component. That's where the bulk of cultural development money in the US is right now. Why? Because managed cultural practice is a great way to buy some time in regard to the problem of collapsing urban infrastructure. Instead of doing what needs to be done to rejuvenate dying urban areas, you send in the artists to do projects with the 'community' (a horrid concept of the same ilk as 'family values'), run the documentation through the spectacle engines and show how things are improving.

Finally, this bedfellow thing. To reduce CAE's position to a distorted simplicity, we are admittedly anti-state and committed to liberationist practices. The radical right would probably say the same thing about itself. However, CAE is not dedicated to racism, sexism, militarism, Christian (or any other) fundamentalism, patriotic revolution, laissez-faire capitalism or blind obedience to authority. Given these characteristics, one has to question how committed this movement is to principles of anti-state or liberationist practice. In fact, CAE would go so far as to say that the radical right and left have nothing in common at all. This bedfellow accusation lives only in the minds of liberals, conservatives and other centrists.

MD: Fighting words. With all due respect, I think you've misunderstood my use of the admittedly hot-button term, 'elitism'. I was referring to the classist contempt, among radical-chic cultural vanguardists, for the allegedly 'centrist', 'middlebrow' (read: 'bourgeois liberal') political values championed by populist progressives – the virtues of compromise, of working within the system (via grassroots coalitions) as well as outside it (via civil disobedience, electronic and otherwise). What, for example, is wrong with a faith in the radical promise of democracy? Although it would undoubtedly shrink from the term, CAE inarguably shares cultural DNA with a century's worth of avant-gardism, whose common thread – from the proto-fascist Futurists to the (sometimes) Marxist Surrealists – is a romanticising of *The Most Radical Gesture* and a thinly veiled contempt for the dull, dirty business of political change on the ground.

CAE: Before you go on, a couple of quick comments. I don't think you're talking about elitism as a socio-economic situation, but about political snobbery and political purity – the last refuge of the disempowered – where the catatonia of a café alcoholic is the only untainted activity. That's hardly worth speaking about. But identifying with centrist bourgeois liberal values must be addressed. (CAE was actually thinking you meant the liberal fringe, so we were going to be sympathetic, but not now.) To be overly simplistic for a moment, there are two types of authoritarian states. The first is retro-authoritarianism – this one CAE can at least respect, because at least it doesn't pretend to be other than it is. The second is friendly authoritarianism, and this is the domain of the liberal. This political camp, like the conservatives, is always willing to give their sovereignty (and everyone else's!) to the state in exchange for security. The difference is that they try to hide the sell-out under the banner of social progress: 'We need more police, more laws, more jails, more state social workers, more therapists and psychiatrists, more institutions that discipline and punish to stop violence against women, gay bashing and protect abused children.' The liberals are empowering the system that caused the problems they say they are against. Do you throw yourself on the mercy of the patriarchy to stop violence against women? Do you throw yourself on the institutions of racism to stop racism? To do so is galactically stupid. Centrists rarely do any dirty work; they let cops and lawyers do it for them.

Now, for those who are in independent organisations that function out there on the front lines, feeding and sheltering the homeless, working with addicts, and doing all the other everyday life work necessary to bring some glimmer of hope into oppressed, desperate people's lives, CAE wishes them the best – more power to participation in those processes. Such activity will never change the system that created those situations, but at least it makes a tangible difference in the lives of some individuals.

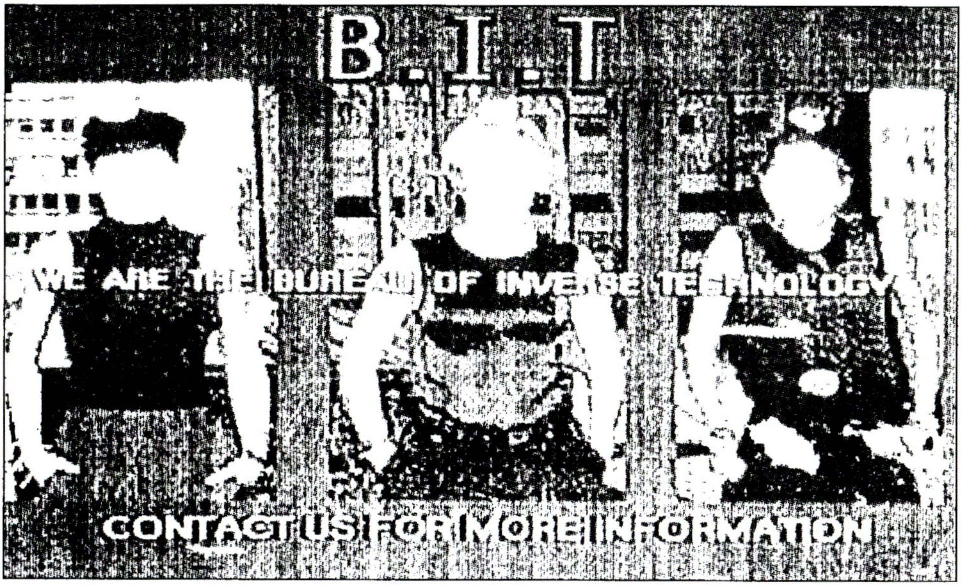

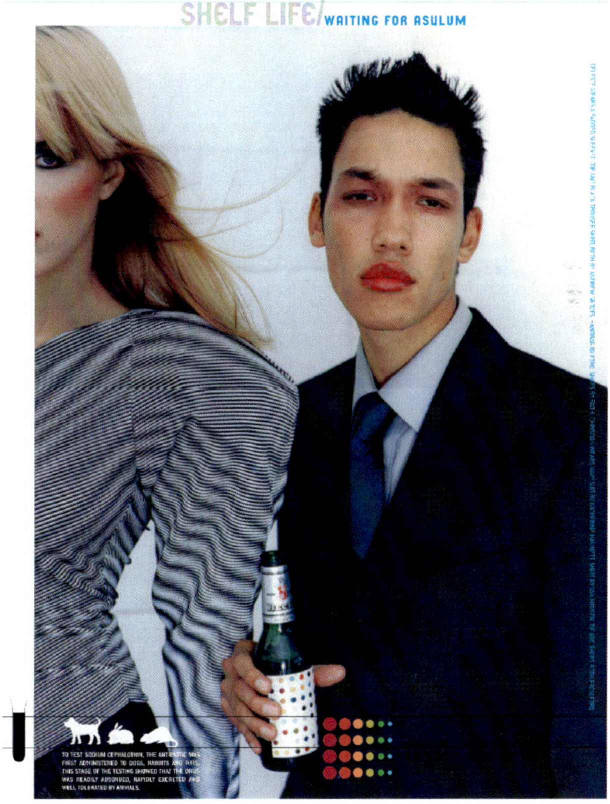

top: Bureau of Inverse Technology, *Self-Portrait*, used to illustrate 'BIT on BIT', Vol 1 #3, Autumn 1995
bottom: William Shoebridge and Richard Dawson's 'Waiting for Asylum' shoot for *Mute*'s fashion section, Vol 1 #9, Spring 1998

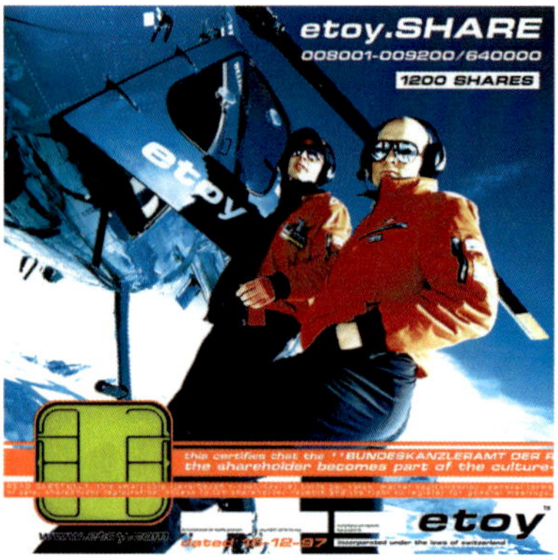

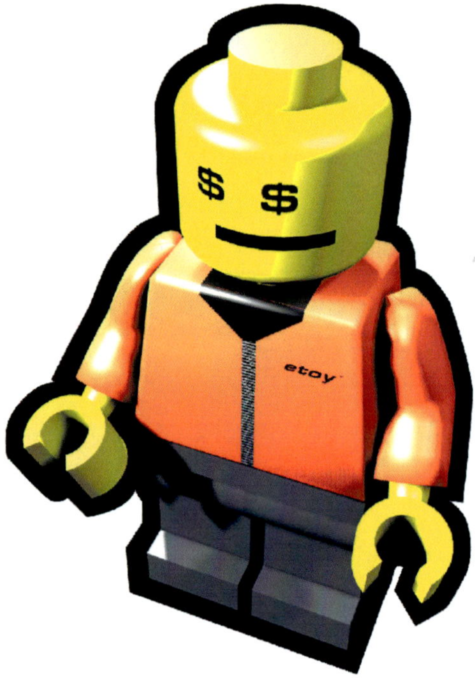

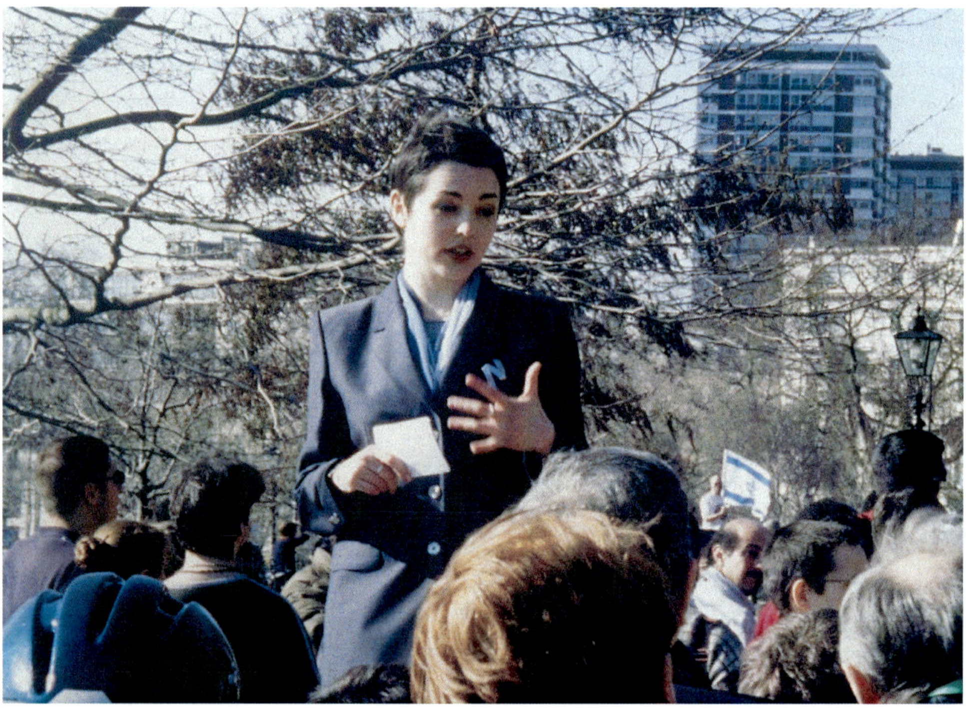

top: etoy, an etoy.SHARE and a TOYWAR.soldier, 1999, used to illustrate Josephine Berry's review, 'Do As They Do, Not As They Do', Vol 1 #16, Spring 2000
bottom: Carey Young, still from *Everything You've Heard is Wrong*, 1999, used to illustrate Benedict Seymour's review of the CRASH! exhibition, 'Everything Must Go', Vol 1 #16, Spring 2000

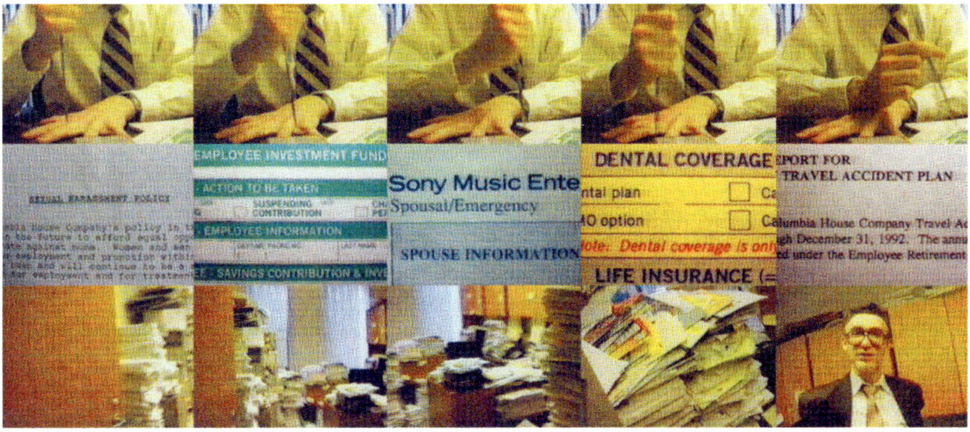

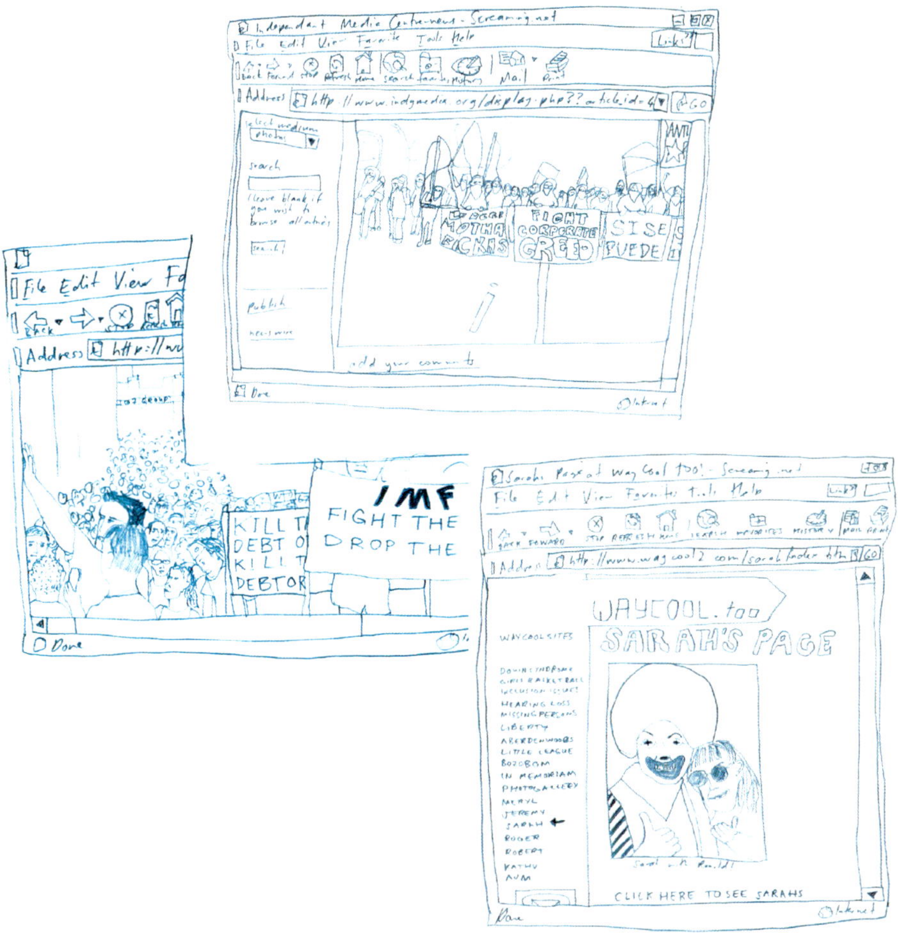

top: Chris Wilcha, stills from *The Target Shoots First*, 2000 (official release 2002), used to illustrate Chris Darke's 'Branded to the Bone', Vol 1 #17, Summer 2000
bottom: Francis Upritchard, used to illustrate Benedict Seymour's review of Michael Hardt and Antonio Negri's *Empire*, 'Rabble Rousers', Vol 1 #18, Autumn 2000

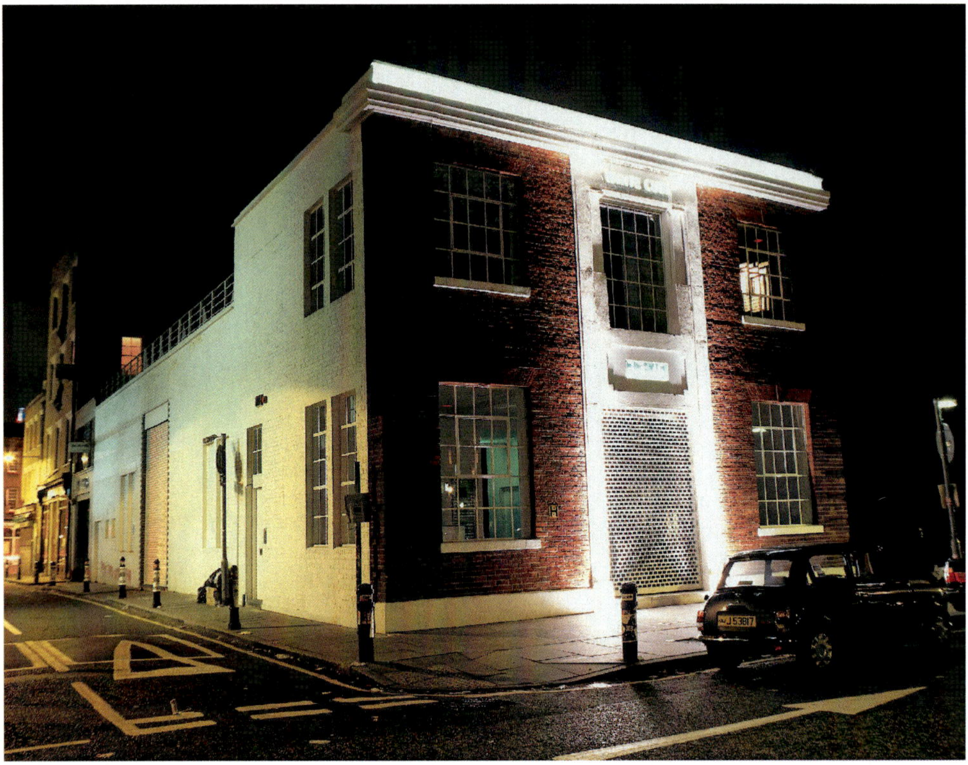

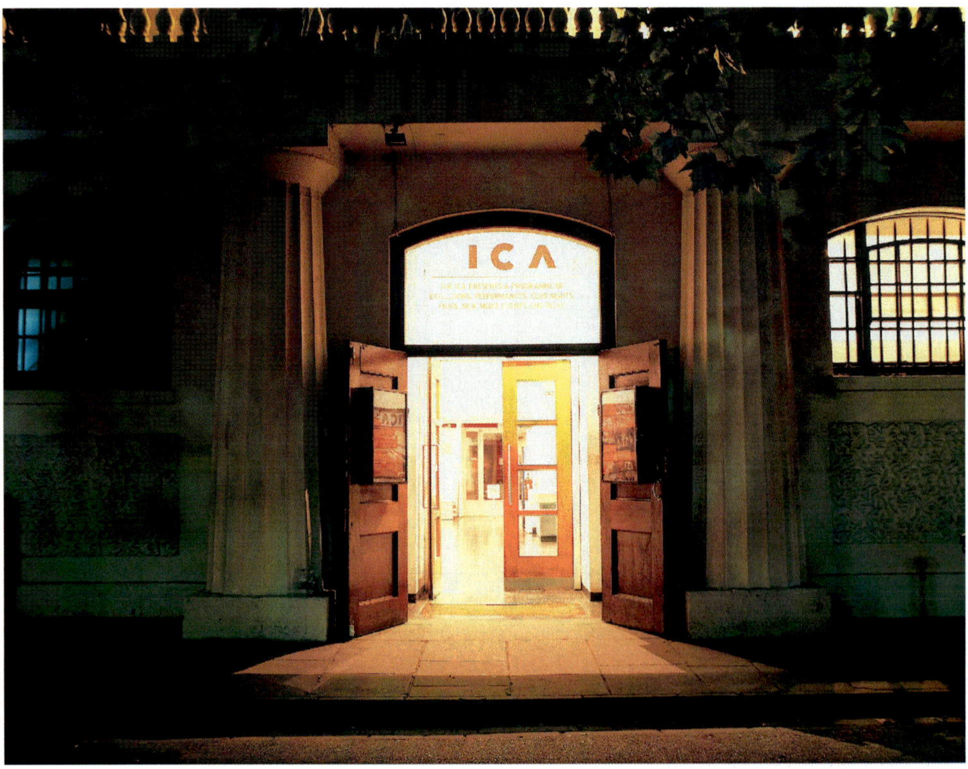
ICA

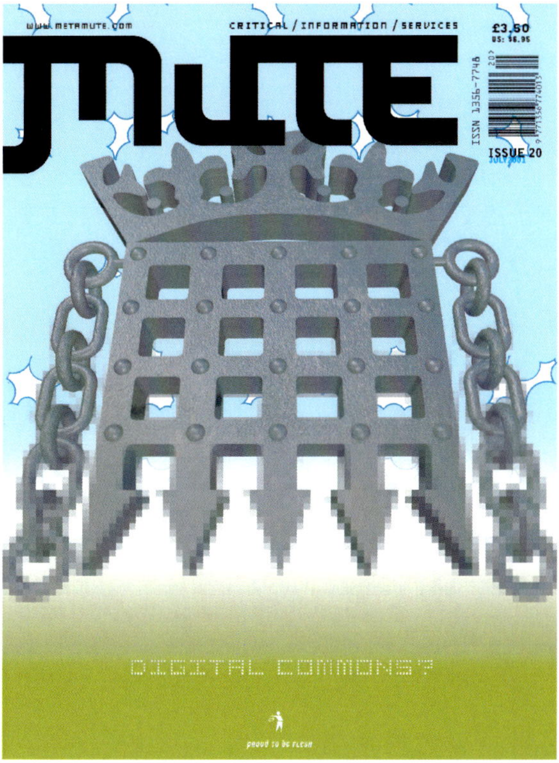

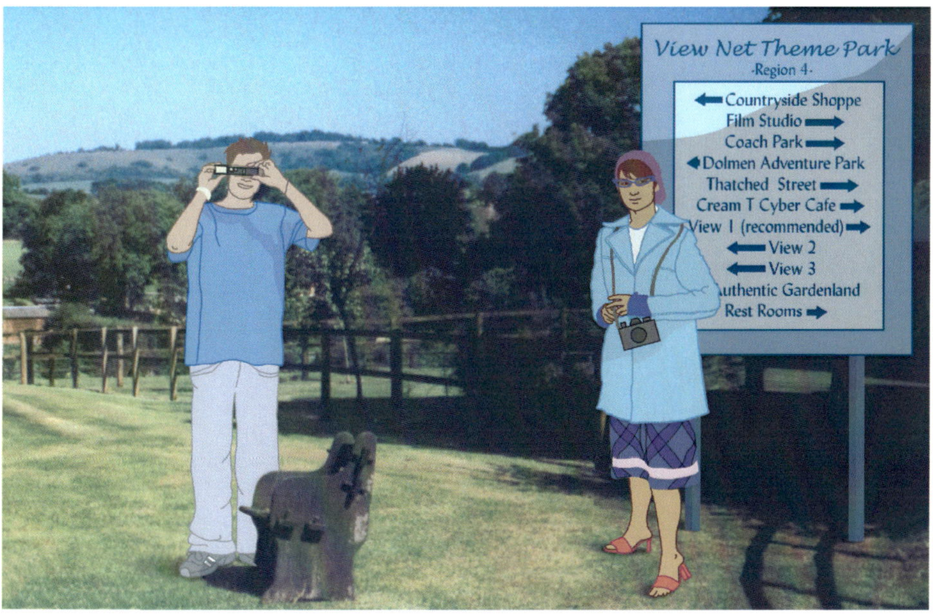

opposite: Daniel Jackson and Simon Worthington, White Cube and the ICA, used to illustrate Anthony Davies and Simon Ford's 'Culture Clubs', Vol 1 #18, Autumn 2000
top: Max Mlinaric, cover image for the Digital Commons issue, Vol 1 #20, Summer/Autumn 2001
bottom: Catherine Story, used to illustrate James Flint and Hari Kunzru's futurecast of the British countryside, 'A Greenish Brown and Unpleasant Land', Vol 1 #20, Summer/Autumn 2001

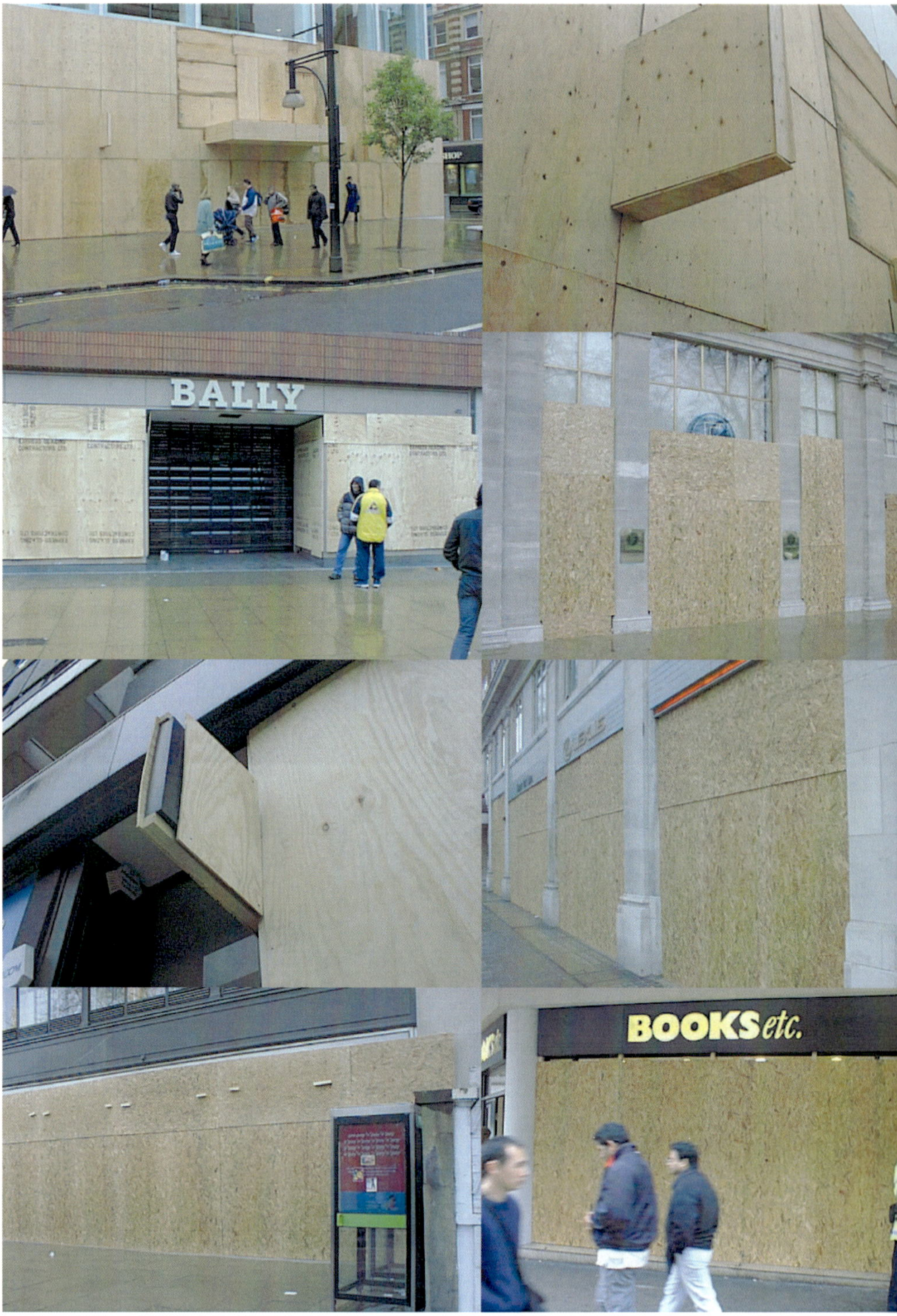

Jakob Jakobsen, *They Don't Want Our Desires Today*, Oxford Street/Park Lane, Mayday 2001, artist's project, Vol 1 #20, Summer 2001

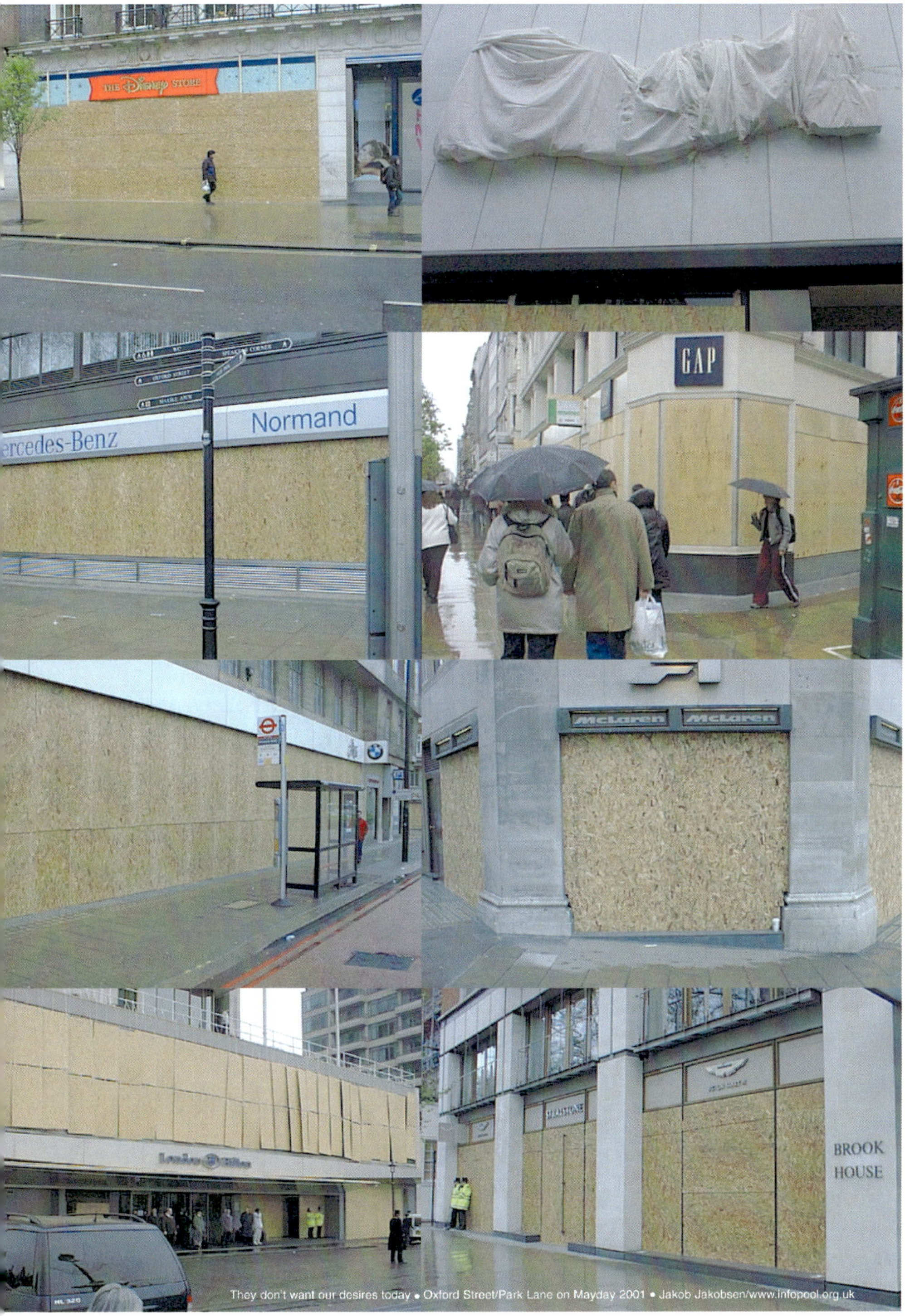

They don't want our desires today • Oxford Street/Park Lane on Mayday 2001 • Jakob Jakobsen/www.infopool.org.uk

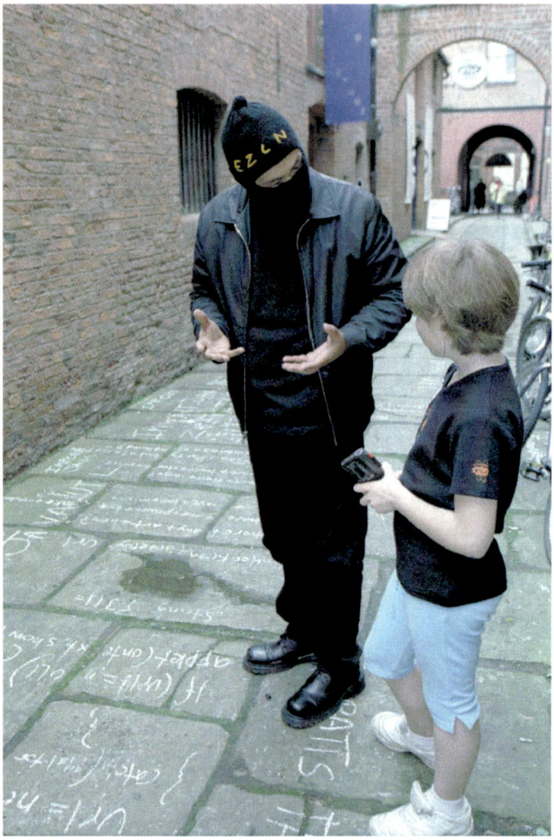

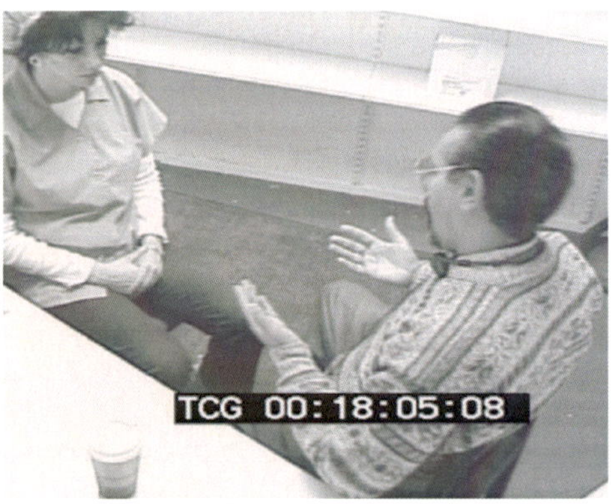

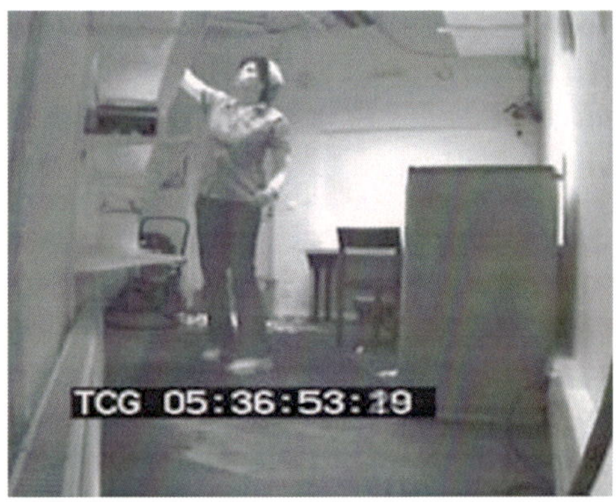

top: Ricardo Dominguez, *Mayan Technology*, 2000, used to illustrate 'Wide Area Disturbance', a conversation between Dominguez and Coco Fusco, Vol 1 #23, Spring 2002
bottom: Coco Fusco and Ricardo Dominguez, *Dolores from 10 to 22 hrs*, a net performance, November 2001, used to illustrate 'Wide Area Disturbance', Vol 1 #23, Spring 2002
opposite: Simon Worthington and Damian Jaques, used to illustrate J.J. King's 'Terror is a Network and the Network is You', Vol 1 #23, Winter/Spring 2002

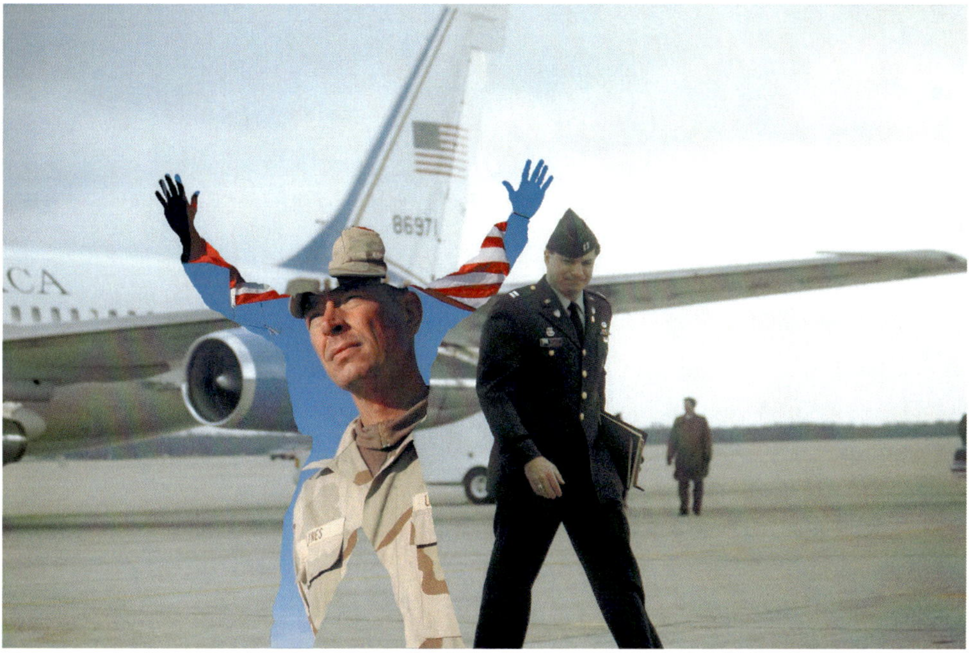
86971

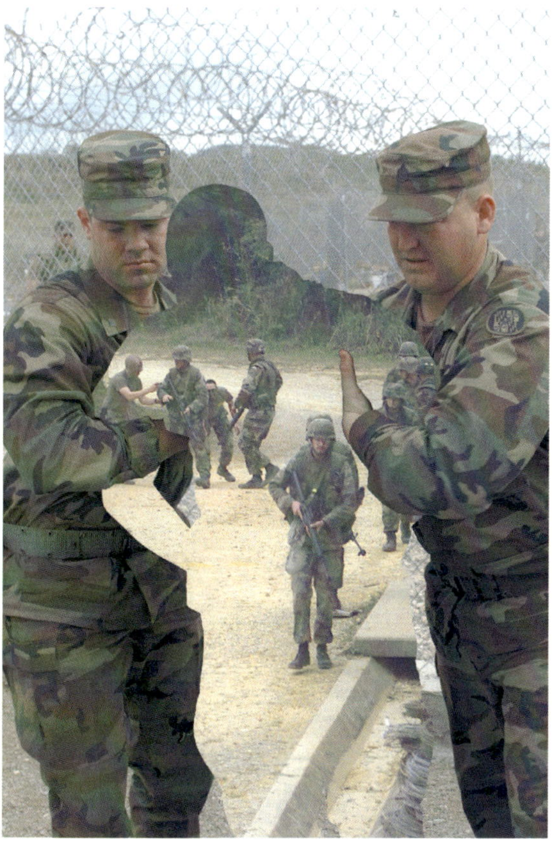

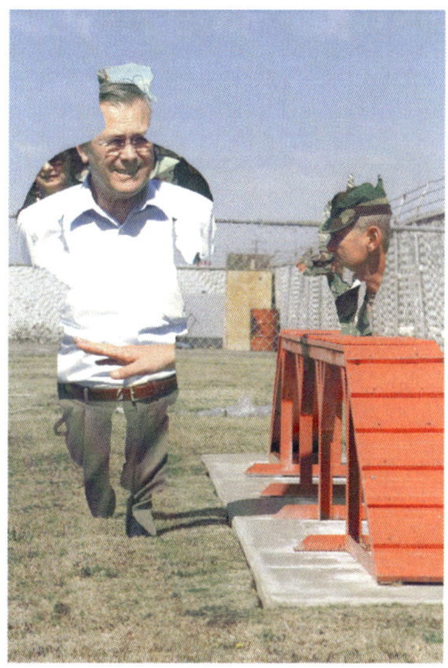

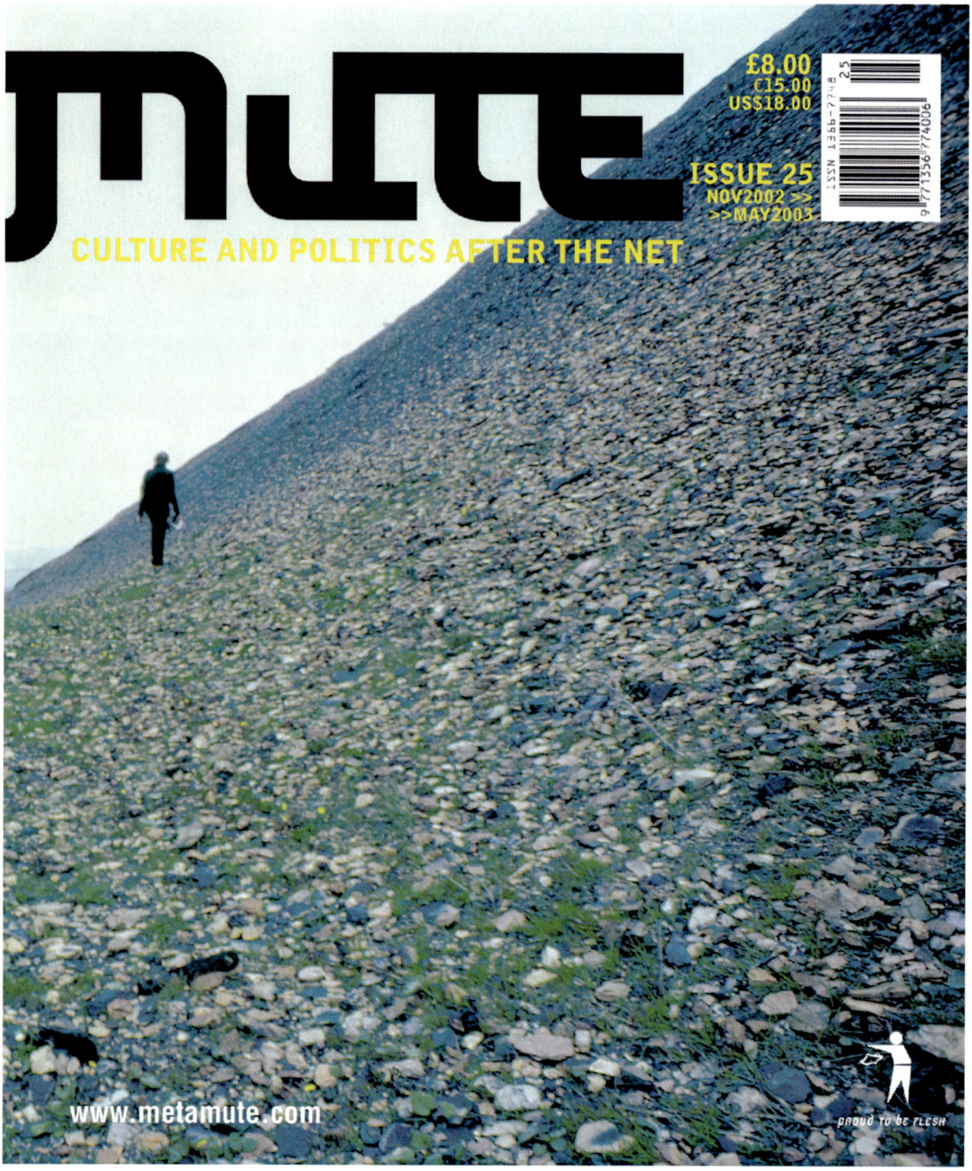

above: John Latham, *Scottish Office Placement*, detail of shale deposit, West Lothian, 1975, used to illustrate Josephine Berry and Pauline van Mourik Broekman's APG interview 'Countdown to Zero, Count up to Now' and used as the cover image, Vol 1 #25, Winter 2002

opposite from top:

Andre Dipper, *Esso Petroleum Ltd.*, 1970, from his APG Placement, used to illustrate 'Countdown to Zero, Count up to Now', Vol 1 #25, Winter 2002

David Shrigley, *Lost*, 1996, used to illustrate Neil Mulholland's 'Bill Posters is Guilty', Vol 1 #25, Winter 2002

Wall art, Grimsby Street, London 2001, courtesy of http://sublimephotography.co.uk, used to illustrate 'Bill Posters is Guilty', Vol 1 #25, Winter 2002

The Migrants' March in Genoa, July 2001, used to illustrate the Glocal Research Centre's 'The Invisible Network', Vol 1 #28, Summer/Autumn 2004

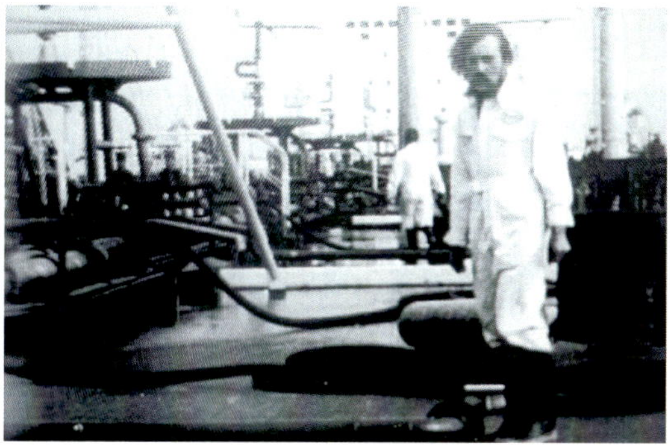

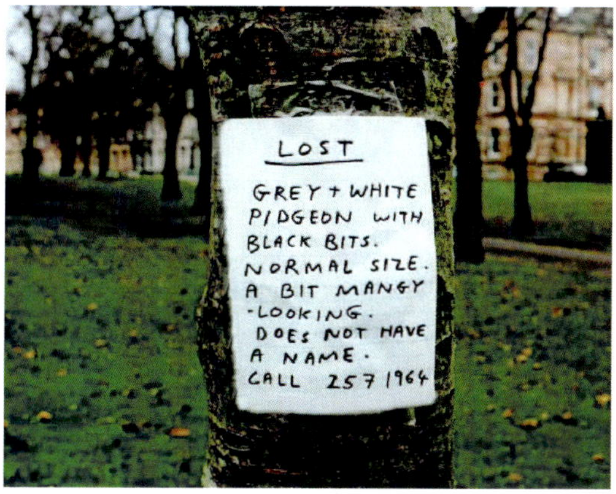
LOST
GREY + WHITE
PIDGEON WITH
BLACK BITS.
NORMAL SIZE.
A BIT MANGY
-LOOKING.
DOES NOT HAVE
A NAME.
CALL 257 1964

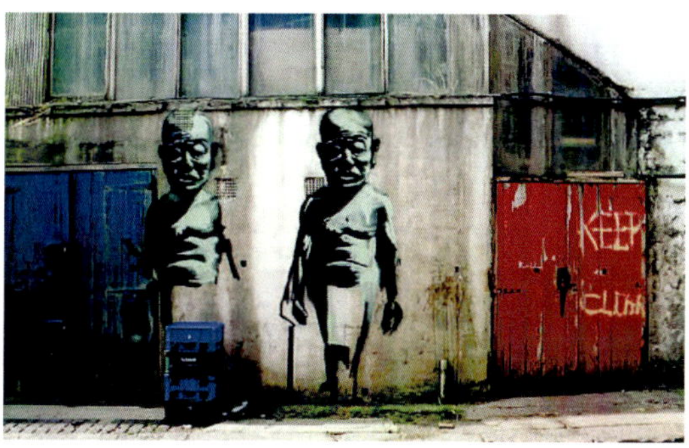

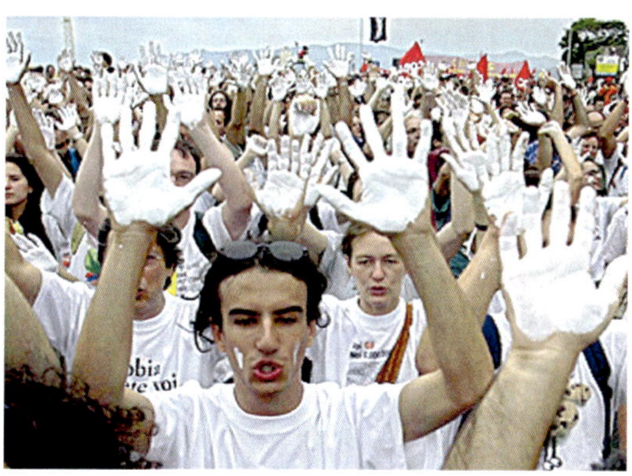

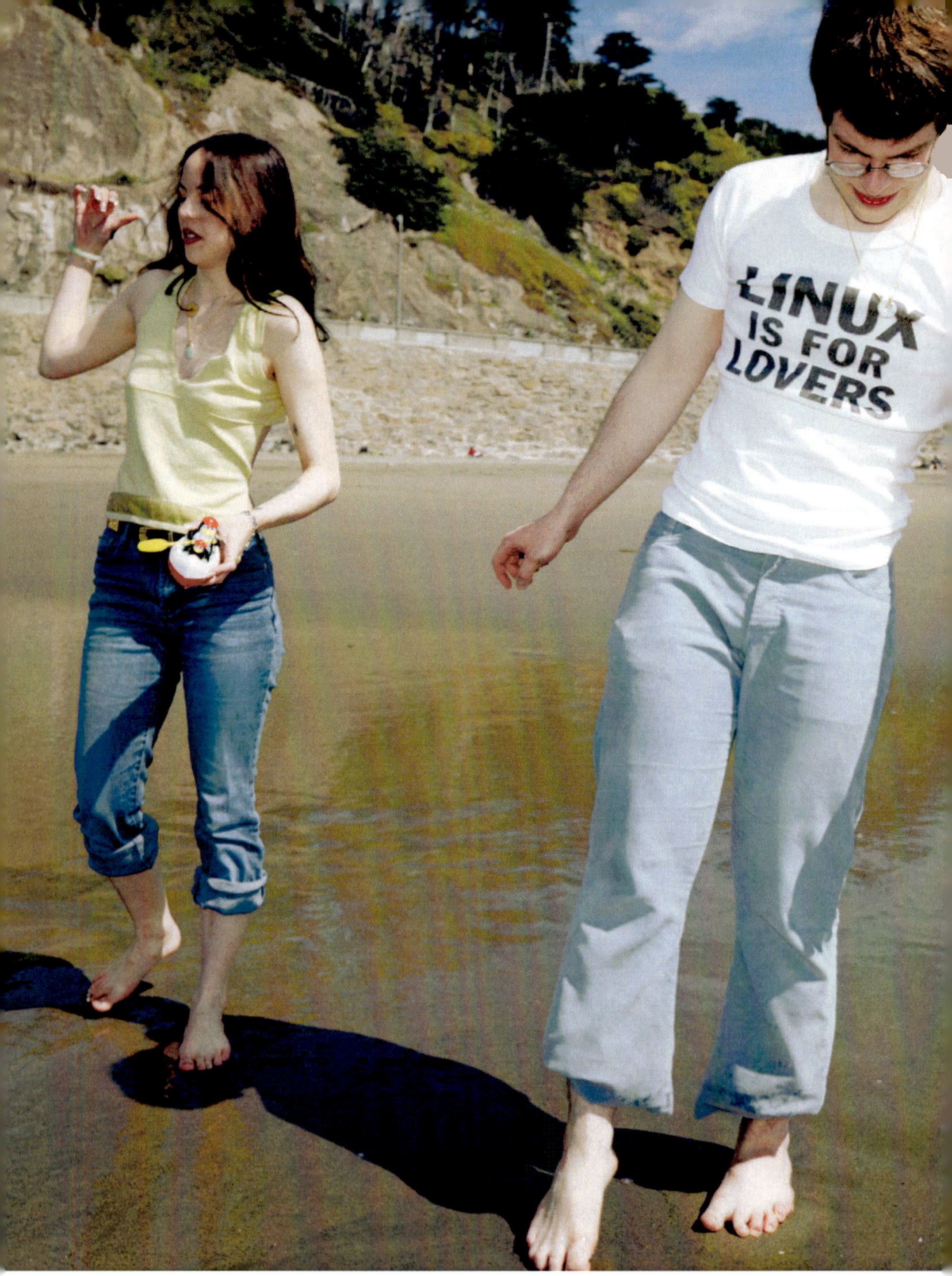

above: Jamie Robinson, photographs from an aborted IBM advertising campaign entitled 'Peace, Love, Linux', artist's project, Vol 1 #26, Summer/Autumn 2003
opposite: Angelo Rindone, *Maternita*, poster from the chainworkers' campaign which promotes the cult of San Precari, used as the cover image for the Precarious Reader, Vol 2 #0, Summer 2005

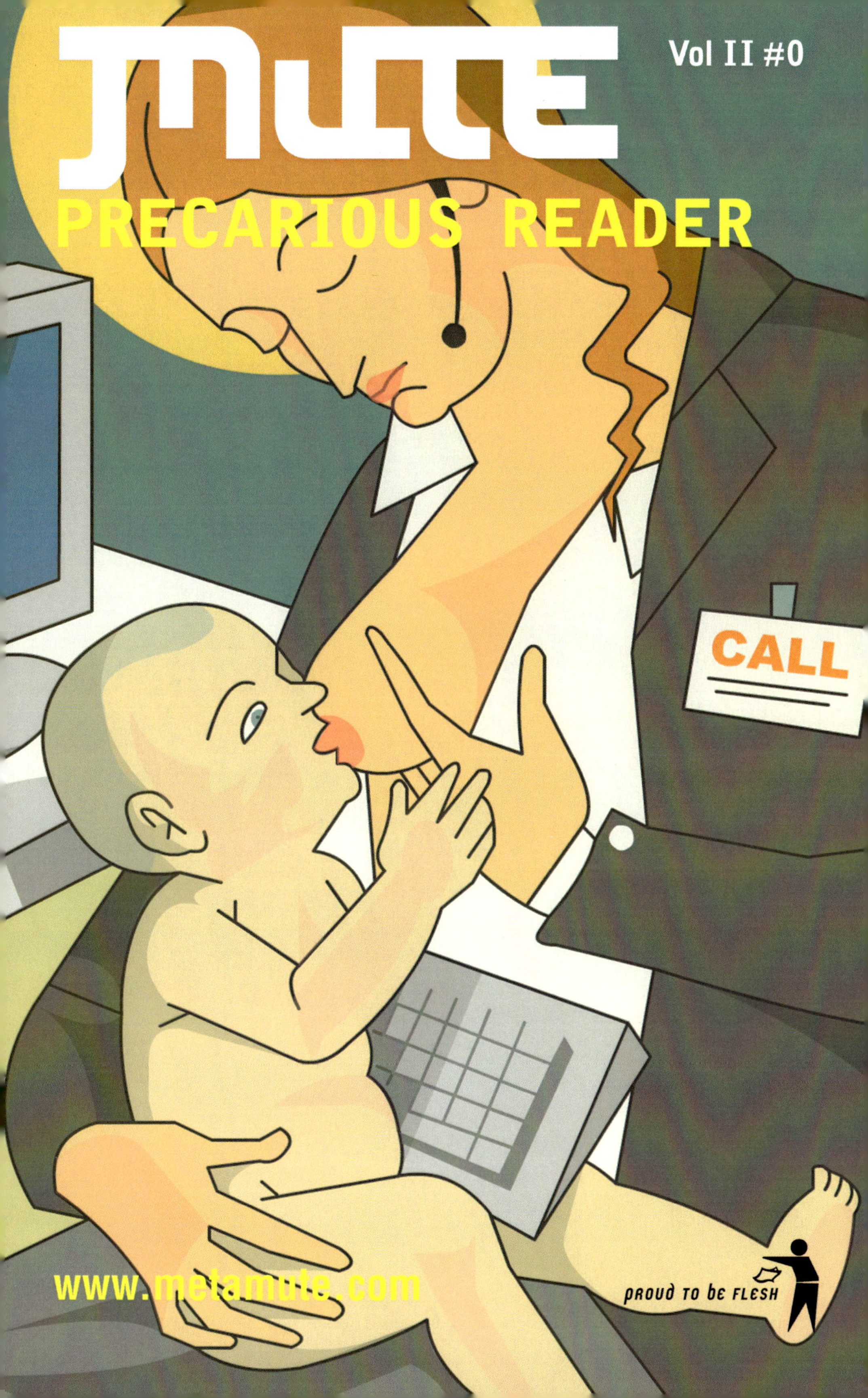
MUTE
Vol II #0
PRECARIOUS READER
CALL
www.metamute.com
proud to be flesh

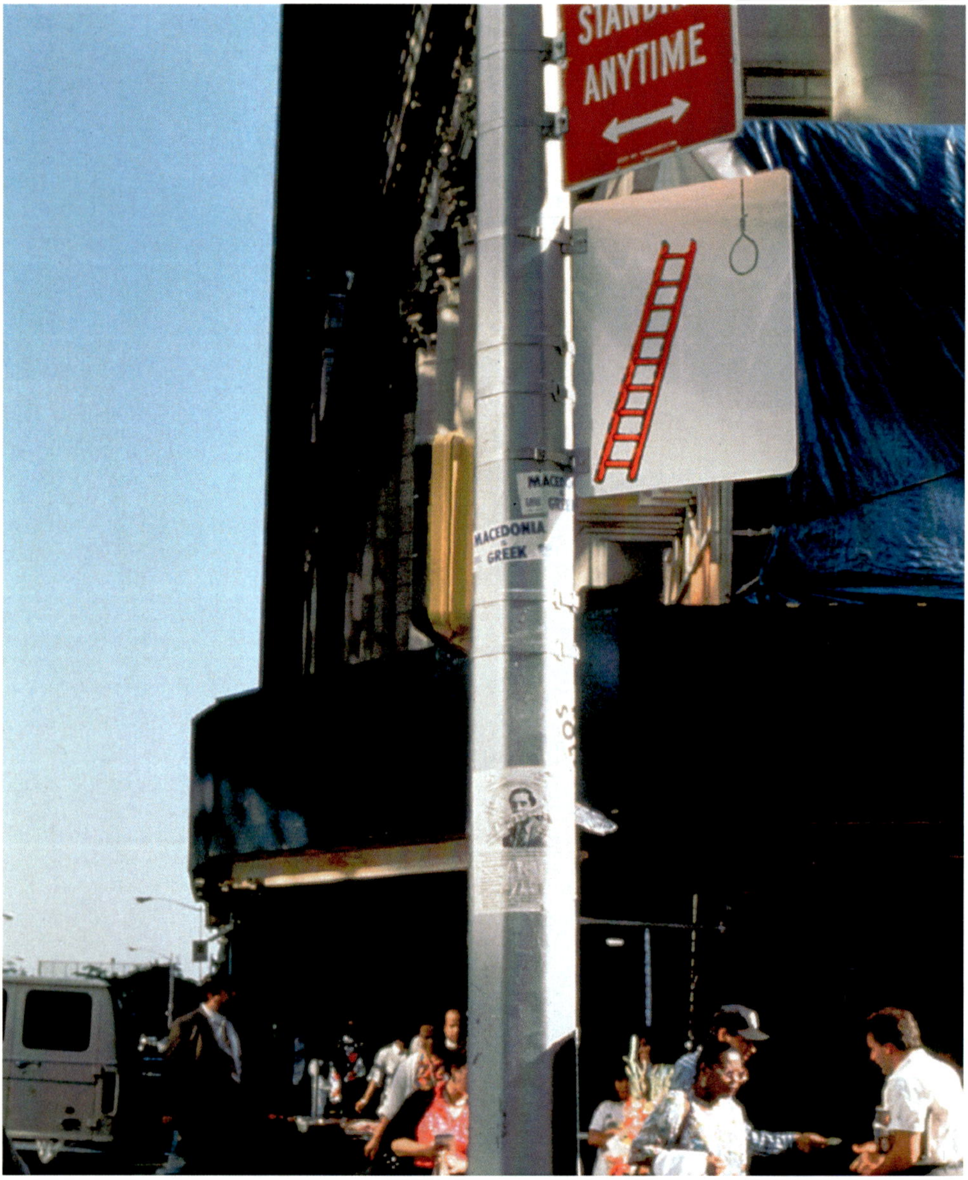

Stephen Duncomb, *Leisler's Rebellion*, 1992, REPOhistory, 'Lower Manhattan Sign Project', used to illustrate Gregory Sholette's 'Mysteries of the Creative Class, or I Have Seen The Enemy and They Is Us', Vol 1 #29, Winter/Spring 2005

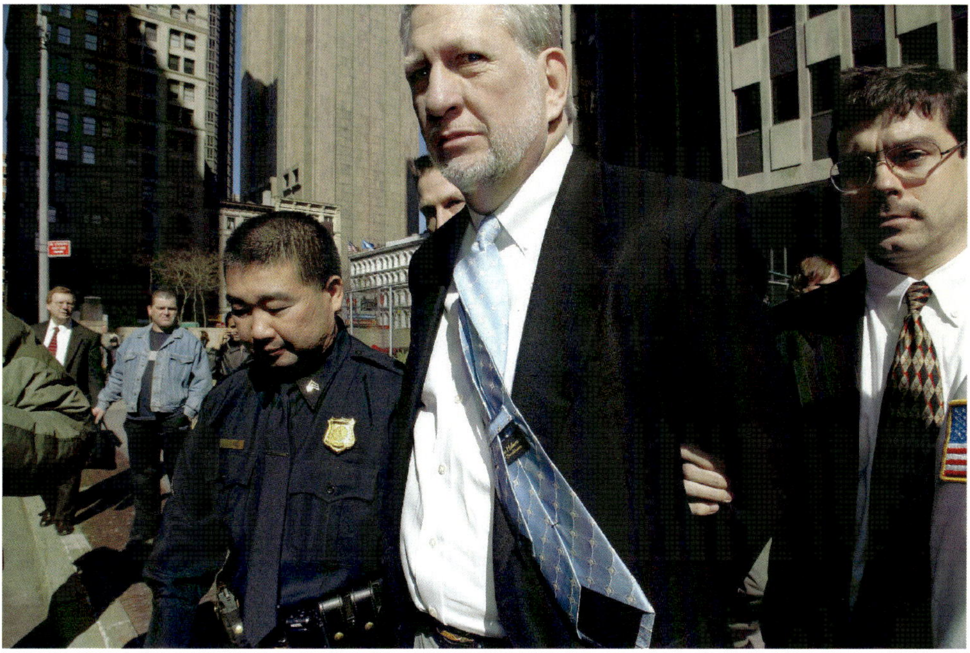

Former WorldCom CEO, Bernard Ebbers, in handcuffs on his way to court, photograph by Allan Tannenbaum, used to illustrate Anthony Davies' 'Basic Instinct', Vol 1 #29, Winter/Spring 2005

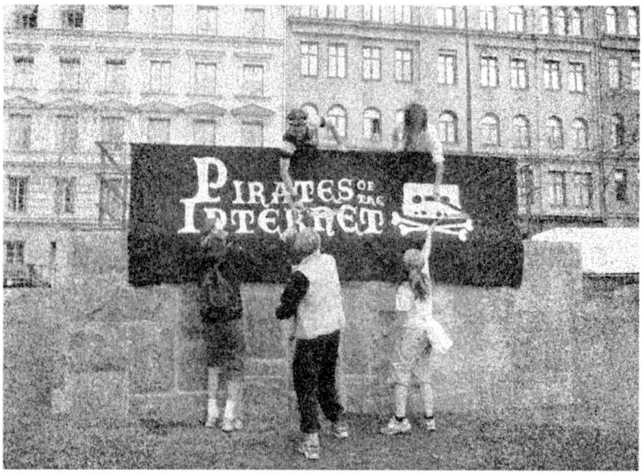

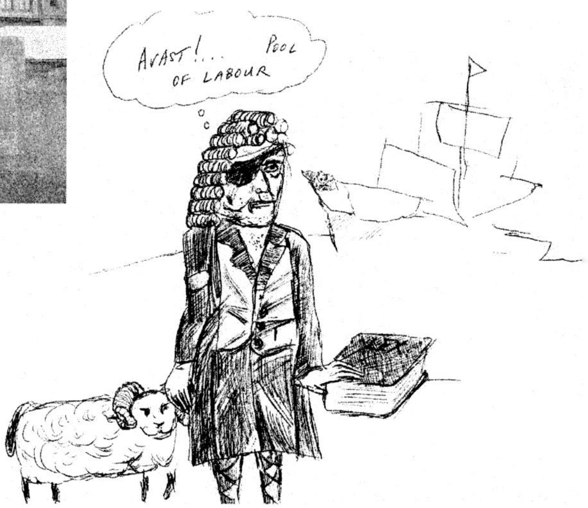

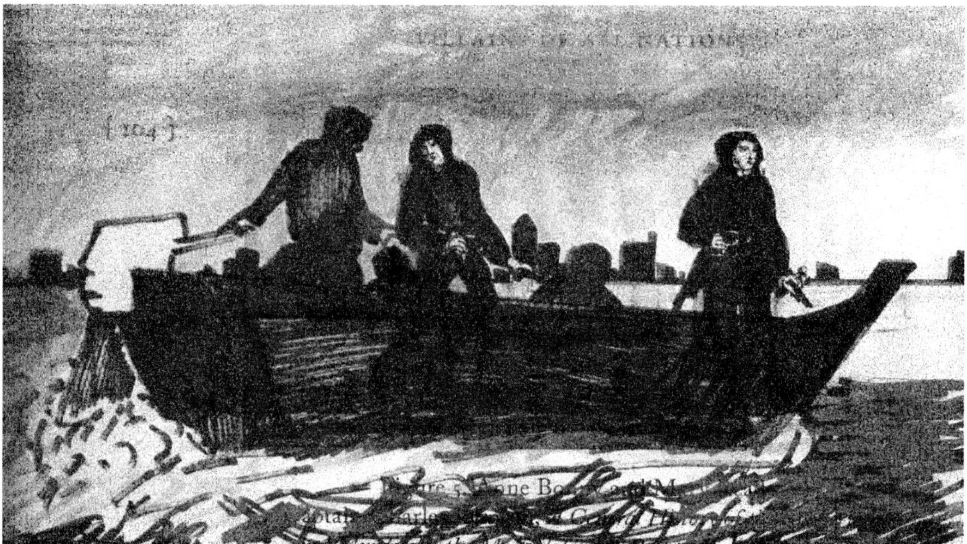

from top:
Pirates and filesharers demonstrating in Stockholm on Sunday 1 May 2005, courtesy of Piratbyran, used to illustrate 'Copy that Floppy!', Anthony Illes' interview with Palle Torsson, Vol 2 #1, Autumn/Winter 2005
Benedict Seymour, *Freedom, Equality and Bentham*, Vol 2 #1, Autumn/Winter 2005
Anja Kirschner, preparatory drawings for her film *Polly II: Plan for a Revolution in Docklands*, Vol 2 #1, Autumn/Winter 2005

MD: What I'm trying to make sense of, again, is the obvious disjuncture, to my mind, between the historical materialism of CAE's cogent analysis of the 'new geography of power relations' under post-industrial, global capitalism and the dream logic of CAE's call for a Bataillean 'nonrational economy of the perverse and the sacrificial'. That way lies the Foucauldian politics of the pleasure dungeon, in which S&M is somehow reconstituted as a radical political act: a shattering of the rational Western psyche in an engulfing 'animality' that challenges the ontological foundations of the Powers That Be.

It seems to me you're hoisted on the horns of the dilemma that polarised political radicals and psychedelic bohemians in the '60s. Radicalism's tradition had one of its greatest voices in Marx, whose oeuvre is a series of glosses on the theme: change the world! The main battalions of the counterculture – Leary, the Pranksters, the *Oracle* (a hippy newspaper) – were descended from Emerson, Thoreau, Rimbaud: change consciousness, change life! Doesn't this binary opposition return to haunt CAE?

CAE: 'Haunting' is the right word for this split. Every time CAE goes too far one way, we get a haunting feeling, and we come back the other way. Again, CAE doesn't see your proposed opposition as an either/or split; it's an and/both complementary pair. We support both ontological anarchy and epistemological anarchy. As Paul Feyerabend or Charles Fort argued, there is no theory that is not in heaps of critical trouble. All views, perceptions, myths, theories and explanations have their shortfalls and suffer within the parameters of experience, just as each has elements of explanatory power. Marx offered a tremendous critique of political economy; unfortunately, he forgot to factor in the nonrational elements of the social. As Max Weber argued, hyper-rationalised order can only end in human abuse on an institutional level, so is it any wonder that so many Marxist regimes took off on a totalitarian trajectory? On the other hand, Fourier offered beautiful insights into the nonrational activity of people. Unfortunately, he forgot that society cannot be created in a vacuum, so is it any wonder that every time Harmony was built, it was crushed from within and from without? The problem in both of these cases was a zealous dedication to an incomplete theory. The ideologue's desire for textual purity in the world is the problem.

Contrary to this type of fixed positioning, CAE prefers a more nomadic approach. The more ways of viewing the world, the better chance we have to make sense of all the situational variations we encounter in life. If we learned anything from the Frankfurt School (Freud and Marx – now *there* is an incompatibility!), it's that, more often than not, it is creative and constructive to embrace contradiction and incommensurability and refuse enslavement by rigid models, canonised texts and socially constructed facts.

MD: CAE's embrace of the political equivalent of chaos theory, with its emphasis on bottom-up, 'emergent' solutions rather than 'command-and-control' management – the growing belief that there's no way to 'organise [domination] out of existence', as you put it in *Electronic Civil Disturbance* – owe an obvious debt to Deleuze and Guattari. The latest issue of the academic journal, *The South Atlantic Quarterly*, wonders, in all seriousness, if ours will be remembered as the Deleuzean century, and I've heard the term 'digital Deleuzeans' applied to Sadie Plant, Manuel De Landa and other cultural theorists who eschew socialism and capitalism for what might be called the emerging, postmodern politics of nonlinear dynamics. What accounts for Deleuze's growing influence among wired intellectuals?

CAE: D&G recognised a very important continuum in politics. They understood that the order of the logos (to be simplistic, the state) has a much deeper nemesis than anti-logos. Anti-logos is where many political continuums end: there is the logic of the state, and the anti-logos turns it against the logos – militarised discipline against oppositional militarised discipline (the organised activist tradition). D&G lengthened the continuum by suggesting the power of nomos – an emergent, nonrational, nomadic power. Recent examples of eruptive nomos are Tiananmen Square or the LA Riots.

This notion always appealed to CAE; however, we disagreed with one key premise: that the logos should be rigidly associated with the state, and the nomos should be rigidly associated with the street. At the time D&G were writing their magnum opus, this association was correct, but by the mid-'80s, the situation had partially inverted. The streets were no longer a seething pool of potential resistance but, relative to the environment of the virtual class, a low-velocity sedentary structure. On the other hand, with the help of the revolution in communications and information technology, the corporate state reconfigured itself into a high-velocity nomadic vector. What D&G forgot is that just as there is an anti-logos, there is also an anti-nomos.

MD: Intriguingly, you sound a cautionary note in *The Electronic Disturbance* when you observe that 'decentralisation does not always favour resistant action; it can have a state function.' Should we be concerned about the ironic commonality between Deleuzean visions of better living through decentralisation and the '"out-of-control" business strategies for an emerging global economy built on networks' espoused in Kevin Kelly's *Out of Control: The Rise of Neo-Biological Civilisation*? Or is a Deleuzean politics of chaos and complexity the only workable alternative to the 19th century world views of capitalism and socialism, which are now hopelessly obsolete?

CAE: We sounded more than a cautionary note about nomadic power in both *TED* and *ECD*; it might be more accurate to call it a major alert. The rise of neo-Spencerian ideology (to call it Darwinistic is an insult to Darwin), with its delight in 'natural' forces working among the socially and economically 'fit' and 'unfit', in conjunction with the current revolution in biotechnology, has set us on an historical course aimed squarely at social catastrophe. (CAE goes deeper into this set of problems in our most recent book, *Flesh Machine.*) Writing in the '70s, D&G never saw this coming, as they were still focused on the more hopeful situations of May '68 and the early rumblings of the Autonomia movement.

The reason so many wired intellectuals and social thinkers in general like D&G is because they were among the first philosophers to offer a theory with open architecture. You can take what you need from this enormous slush pile of expandable ideas, transform them, re-route them, whatever. The D&G texts do not ask for fidelity, although some academics are trying to ruin them by insisting that they do. The idea that there are Deleuzeans, a Deleuzean school or a Deleuzean century is appalling. If such people are that deluded, they may as well claim to be Nietzscheans, too.

MD: Since we've spent much of this interview skirmishing in the no-fly zone between politics and aesthetics, I can't resist the boneheadedly obvious question: Is art an effective force for political change? What, at the end of the day, is the cultural fallout of John Heartfield's photomontages, or Leon Golub's paintings, or the punk collages of Dead Kennedys album cover artist Winston Smith, or CAE's symbolic disturbances for that matter?

CAE: CAE would not argue that art is a force of political change, but it's undoubtedly an important component in the process of resistance. Art prepares the ground for the introduction of new realities and visions; art can act as a catalyst for critical and imaginative thought; and art can act as a signpost of political identity and solidarity. Of course, these swords all cut both ways. Look at it from the other side: Why is so much attention given to expression management and representational management? Because socialisation by symbolic seduction and envelopment is preferable to socialisation by force. Symbolic control is much more orderly and far less expensive than militarised control (the court of last resort). Those who can crack, manipulate and recombine cultural codes have significant power, so long as they are adept at finding points of distribution (the real contestational ground in 'free speech' issues). We should also add that, in terms of the production of resistant representation, it's counterproductive to think of it in terms of one individual's body of work. You're right; no single work ever changed the world. It's the collective production that's important. I think we can all agree that we can look back and see a history of leftist resistance. The aggregate of representation that reveals this history is a sign of hope and perseverance that cannot be undervalued. From it, we know that, even though we have consistently gotten our collective butt kicked, there is a courage within the movement(s) that will never let us surrender.

Do As They Do, Not As They Do: etoy and the Art of Simulacral Warfare

Josephine Berry

Vol 1 #16, Spring 2000

Last 29 November, US online toy retailer, eToys, brought a suit against the European net art collective etoy, blocking them from using their own domain name [www.etoy.com] – registered two years before eToys even existed – in a clear-cut case of corporate might and spite, not to mention greed. The closeness of 'etoy.com' to the retailer's own URL, [www.etoys.com], argued every kiddy's favourite corporation, was confusing customers who also risked being exposed to pornographic and violent (a.k.a. European and arty) content. eToys leaned heavily on the family values card to secure a preliminary US court ruling in their favour. Not surprisingly, this action elicited torrents of vitriol from etoy fans and the Reclaim the Domain Name System lobby alike. Quite a lot more surprising, however, given the hotness of the DNS topic right now, was the professionalism and commitment demonstrated by Toywar – etoy's name for its resistance campaign and website Toywar.com – whose antics finally secured eToys' total climb-down as they watched their shares plunge by 70 percent from $67 to $20 a share. In what has been described as 'the Brent-Spar of e-commerce', on 25 January eToys dropped the case 'without prejudice' (i.e. withholding the option to resume proceedings again) and agreed to pay etoy's court costs of $40,000. There is no doubt that this has been a landmark victory in the crucial battle over domain names and an inspiringly unorthodox example of 'dispute resolution'.

But hold on, did I say 'professionalism' and 'commitment' just now? Wouldn't those words look more at home in a go-gettin' corporate presentation? Precisely the trick. Etoy was itself, as Douglas Rushkoff recently put it, intended 'both as a satire of the corporate value system and a barometer of the information space'. If power is corporate and global, argue etoy, then art should be, too. The etoy campaign is replete with both metaphors and strategies lifted straight out of the corporate world. Potential recruits are incited to 'HELP US PROTECT THE etoy.BRAND AND BECOME A SHAREHOLDER!' Partisan efforts are rewarded with loyalty points corresponding to 'etoy.SHARES' in the 'etoy.ART-BRAND'. In a press release, their spokesman, Zai, informs us that 'investors keep etoy alive. They invest into the future of internet art.' Indeed, US-based activist art group RTMark's decision to award etoy 'sabotage project funding' could effectively be seen in terms of a joint venture. Not only are individual art groups adopting the walk and talk of the corporate world but they're even corporatising amongst themselves, sharing resources and databases, and piggybacking on each other's brand value.

Could it be that etoy's use of shares and markets effectively extends the modernist game of turning the conditions of the artwork's making into the subject of the artwork itself (e.g. turning the canvas into the subject of the work) to the immaterial realm of financial markets? In other words, is the market really becoming more than just the subject of the art? Is it becoming subject and support (of the signifier) in one? Is an etoy.SHARE an actual share and its metaphor at the same time? Before 'speculating' on this any further, it should be mentioned that the role played by the Toywar in the free-fall of eToy's shares is greatly contested. The *FT*'s view is reassuringly prosaic, blaming eToy's humpty-dumpty antics on 'the cost of tripling its customer base over the Christmas holidays', amongst other things.

Etoy's own line on the status of their share system masquerades an equally neutralising and predictable language: that of art history. Commenting on the possible illegality (within the US legal system) of issuing 'etoy.SHARES', they neatly sidestep the whole modernist trajectory mentioned above. Insisting on the docility of the signified, they claim: we never sold a share to a person who did not know that this is an 'ART INVESTMENT' [...] according to international lawyers and advisors the word 'share' is not limited or registered for the use in financial markets! If artists can call art products 'landscape XY', 'naked body blabla' or 'the death' [...] we insist on the right to call our work etoy.SHARE [...] because value systems, stock markets and the surreal etoy.CORPORATION are our TOPICS!

So, if an etoy.SHARE is not literally a share, but can, nonetheless be bought, acquired and exchanged, what is it? If etoy is not really a corporation but is, at its own insistence, involved in effecting fluctuations in the market value of another company, its 'rival brand' so to speak, what is the artwork's relationship to its signified?

Surely, what art risks when pastiche tips over into market manipulations and legal victories is the loss of the very thing that distinguishes it from its satirical victim: its own autonomy. Perhaps this sounds like an apology for a discredited ideal of disinterested, or ineffectual, art, but it's hard not to feel that etoy's deployment of markets, albeit ludic and PC, isn't achieving a too perfect symmetry with its dark other.

Everything Must Go

Benedict Seymour

Vol 1 #16, Spring 2000

'Ironic mimesis is not critique, it is the mentality of a slave!' It may be hard to fit on a badge, but this was one of the more resonant slogans plastered across the walls of London's Institute of Contemporary Arts (ICA) in the dying months of the 20th century. Amid the slew of agit-prop stickers and corporate Newspeak that formed the CRASH! show's background hum of unrest, this testy aphorism hung in the air, needling at you and its surroundings. The phrase seemed to refer beyond the gallery, to the banal self-reflexivity of the media, cultural recycling, the 'anarchic' mummery of licensed fools like Chris Evans or Jim Carrey, of which the show's curators have written so harshly. But it also turned back on its immediate environment, drawing attention to the artists' own varied, but almost universal, reliance on modes of subversive appropriation.

The ICA obviously didn't feel as absolute about the psychic servitude involved in this strategy, declaring in the pre-show blurb: 'The artists in CRASH! mimic a range of activities and services, from trading, marketing, spin doctoring, genetic engineering, and advertising to spying and hairdressing.' Is there a margin for critical reflection in such techniques, or do the institutions and discourses imitated overwhelm the art? What modes should an effective critical art deploy? And is 'critique' a proper vocation for art, anyway? These were questions raised (but not necessarily resolved) by the show – and this precisely because of the curators' unusually vocal commitment to a kind of engaged, socially conscious art not much witnessed in the 'Cool Britannia' '90s.

Matt Worley and Scott King, already known for their self-published magazine [also titled *CRASH!*], billboard subversions and style mag rants, coordinated this gallery extension of their dissident media project, in collaboration with the ICA's Emma Dexter and Vivienne Gaskin. Having made clear their impatience with the false liberations of post-industrial capitalism – from 'flexible' working to corporatised leisure – they now had a proper gallery with a selection of artists, activists and theorists of their choosing with whom to explore the themes of 'Corporatism and Complicity' referenced in the exhibition's subtitle. Proclaiming that CRASH! would be 'both a reflection and a condemnation' of contemporary life, this was an unusually ambitious, confrontational approach which would take some living up to.

The curators stressed their intention to break with the self-indulgence and harebrained trivia of recent British art, and emphasised a commitment to ideas, politics and a less fetishistic conception of the artwork. Instead of decorative self-absorption and an obsession with 'identity', this would be non-commodified, performative and even artless art, with a design upon its viewers' minds as much as their senses/wallets. The artists were looking at some subjects already familiar from the work of their populist yBa forbears, 'real and even banal everyday concerns' being a hot ticket in the *arte povera* '90s, but their ambitions were larger, encompassing the topics of work and money, consumerism and dissent, globalisation and investment, democracy and the market and the interpenetration of all of these.

In the corporatism-and-complicity equation, the latter could have been a reference to the general state of culture *vis-à-vis* the market, or specifically that of art, but for sure it was also a self-dramatising acknowledgement of the show's own conditions of possibility. Colliding the neutral space of the office (Rachel Baker installed a temp agency for artists, complete with desk and waiting room, to put artists in touch with potential employers; Szuper Gallery engaged in online day trading near the entrance to the show) with the makeshift architecture of contemporary protest (Inventory erected a wigwam full of polemic and information – a centre of operations, not a piece of art), the show as a whole was more ambivalent than the CRASH! boys' rhetoric let on. If it lacked the wild energy of their punk rock heroes, preferring constructive dialogue and dissident focus grouping to riotous assembly (Kate Glazer hosted an ongoing discussion forum in the gallery and online called 'Thinktank/Mindpool'), the show did share punk's proto-Thatcherite brazenness about feeding from the hand it was biting. It seemed both unnerving and appropriate that sponsorship should come from the '90s masters of 'ironic' retro advertising, Diesel.

Of course, corporate patronage is not exactly unusual, but Matt Worley's noisy dissatisfaction with the 'Prada Meinhof' and the choice of this particular sponsor seemed to point up the ironies of art's compromised position. Who better, cynics might ask, to fund a simulacral recycling of '70s political and conceptualist gestures than the arch recyclers of '70s kitsch? The CRASH! catalogue is punctuated with updated Situationist squibs and, sometimes, clumsy *soixante-huit*-icisms ('Never work, Never Sleep', 'Burn It Down', 'London's Burning With Boredom Now'), just as Diesel clothing's influential ad campaigns deployed what you might call an 'ironic mimesis' of the mendacious, high consumerist rhetoric the Situationists more maliciously *détourned* ('Diesel: For Successful Living'). Diesel were surely aware of the kind of non-conformism they were trying to align themselves with, since their pitch relies on their target group's self-perception as 'different', sophisticated and un-duped. As Worley himself has written, vampiric capitalism recently moved on from recycled kitsch to the exhumation and (unselfconsciously) ironic mimesis of the signs of its erstwhile antithesis, from Che Guevara bars and terrorism on T-shirts to the e-commerce 'revolution' and the rehabilitation of Marx; the sign of capitalism's material triumph is also the index of its symbolic feebleness. The superficial or not-so-superficial similarity between sponsors, curators and artists, in relying on modes of pastiche and varieties of subversion, emphasised just how ambiguous the return to a critical art might be in the current climate, whatever the convictions of those involved.

Could CRASH! escape from its potential neutralisations and make a show that was more than a blank parody of political dissent? Perhaps, despite the curators' commitments, the artists weren't too worried. All shared a suspicion of art's once-vaunted claim to autonomy, and their often textual or performative 'pieces' tended to emphasise that art, business and other kinds of work exist in a continuum: Janice Kerbel gave us meticulously detailed plans for a bank job, as if taking the old conceptualist ideal of art as a (uncommodified) blueprint for a work to be executed by others to its logical, materialist conclusion; Matthieu Laurette's 'art' was the ongoing project of his subsistence, living, since 1996, on money-back products – an example of scrimping rebelliousness, whose margin of aesthetic 'freedom' must become as routine and time-consuming as any other job.

On the other hand, beyond the preliminary assumption of art's implication in everything else, there seemed to be important differences in orientation. The forms of simulation deployed by the artists – ranging from a direct (re)enactment of corporate work-leisure in the temple of art (Szuper Gallery's day trading activities, Rachel Baker's temp agency) through John Beagles and Graham Ramsay's didactic appropriation of the schoolroom wall chart, *Wat Tyler Wot Happened?* (presenting viewers with a neglected history of metropolitan protest), to Heath Bunting's (spoof ?) DIY kit for producing GM resistant weeds (*Natural Reality Superweed Kit 1.0*) – were as diverse in content and agenda as they were unified in strategy. Perhaps it was this dependence on second order mimesis – whether imitating corporate discourse or directly intervening in its processes – that heightened the show's homogeneity. Even when the general tone of the artists was polemical and combative, as with the Inventory group, the politicised discourse was freighted with self-consciousness. Their list of demands, scribbled across the slats of a Venetian blind that hung in the centre of a tent, was sincerely belligerent, but ruefully and comically self-cancelling: 'We Demand that Sweden be flatpacked and shipped to Kosovo!/We demand that artists… oh, forget it.' Acknowledging the incongruity of the gallery situation and the intransigence of their audience, even enemies of ironic mimesis could not sustain a rabble-rousing discourse without, well, irony. As Novalis wrote, despair is the most terribly witty state of all.

Where Szuper Gallery seemed to indulge a fascination with the abstraction of high finance stemming from a desire to probe the latter for possible points of weakness, Carey Young's video, *Everything You've Heard Is Wrong*, got even closer to its imitated object. The video showed a corporate-suited Young presenting an immaculate rendition of a business communication skills presentation at Speakers' Corner. As the straggle of passers-by and oration-lovers gathered and dispersed in the foreground, a fervent Muslim demagogue could be made out at the edge of the frame, creating an odd collision of sacred and secular modes in this anachronistic relic of the old public sphere. The passion and depth of the one would contrast wryly with the neutrality and self-reflexivity of the other. And yet, despite their ostensible disparity in form and content, both perhaps aspired to a perfected communion, and neither mode could have been foreseen by the Victorian burghers who inaugurated this space. A presentation on public speaking at Speakers' Corner? The world had swung from Chartism to flowcharts. The circularity of the performance made one think of the cancerously proliferating book business, and the post-literacy of its authors. The recursive loop of addressing an audience with a lecture about how to hold an audience's attention, and the lecture's title, which xeroxed corporate language but also turned it against itself, gave off a cool absurdism.

It might be tempting to read the performance as a parodic reflection on the frictionless, corporate ideal of 'communication', the reification of the richness of language by a base functionalism. Yet the deadpan mode, which was funny but not *that* funny, distinguished her schtick from straight satire. In addition, Young's own reported enthusiasm for developing the synergies between creative businesses and the business-like creatives who work for them mitigates against such an interpretation. Perhaps this was the 'ironic mimesis' condemned in the slogan, a habit (or 'slave mentality') of empty mockery adopted in order to sustain the banalisation of everyday life? (This is surely the logic of the 'subversive' current affairs comedy show, not so much an assault on the status quo as a device for coping with, and hence reproducing, it.) But, on the other hand, who said art had to issue in 'critique'? The ambiguity and complexity of connotation here seems to me more interested in a Keatsian 'being in uncertainty' than a rush to either polemic or comic relief. If some of the CRASH! artists had already identified the enemy and the field of combat in advance, Young's approach retained a ludic openness that should not be summarily written off as co-opted. Young's practice, reformist rather than revolutionary in tendency, may accept the parameters of the brave, new corporate world, but in its sensitivity to the implosion of previously distinct categories could be more useful than reheating old battle cries for gallery consumption. As Young has suggested, creativity and imagination, the intellectual and conceptual dexterity traditionally the preserve of the artist, have become fetishised values in the post-industrial workplace. Where the CRASH! curators recoil in horror from this reification of human potential, Young seems to play with the possibilities of 'personal development'. Taking the logic of the yBas' entrepreneurialism a step further, on closer inspection, the CRASH! show could have been heralding the next stage in art's subsumption under capitalism as much as calling for its revenge.

The ambiguities of Young's work contrast usefully with those of another video-documented performance: *We The People* by Beagles and Ramsay. At first sight similar to Young's work in its incongruous intervention in the public sphere, the video shows the artists attempting to make contact with secret service agents and presenting a provocatively vacuous petition to 10 Downing Street (it read simply 'We The People', as if commencing a list of demands then immediately giving up). Apart from the deliberate futility of these activities, the fact that the actors/artists had assumed the iconic appearance of *Taxi Driver*'s postmodern antihero, Travis Bickle, from the proto-punk Mohican and manic De Niro grin down to the army boots, upped the ludicrousness quotient. Again, the performance's futile non sequiturs seemed calculated to expose the hollowness of an institution, the alienation implicit in democratic representation, within a comic mode now hyper-familiar from postmodern British TV comedy (think of Adam and Joe, or the routinised assimilation of Chris Morris' innovations in the *11 O'Clock Show*). But the identification with the psychotic, vengeful figure of Bickle – the isolated, skewed crusader of a corrupt post-Vietnam polis – cut both ways, suggesting more meanings than the piece could organise. Lost in the labyrinth of implications, the sense of disenfranchisement and atomisation evoked by the original film returned as bathos. Here, the work didn't get beyond its mimesis of an already over-familiar, if ambivalent, signifier, leaving the world as dizzyingly cluttered with references and depleted signs of representation as it was found.

One could summarise the difference between the CRASH! show's artists less on the level of technique or address (since imitation was common to almost all) than in whether or not they hoped to wring a final refusal of the global situation out of the deadlock their work evoked: in the case of Beagles and Ramsay, Heath Bunting or the Inventory group, pushing for a more radical gesture, to which their art and theorising was a partial contribution, or, on the other hand, as with Young, accepting the indeterminacy of the postmodern condition and the apparent absence of alternatives, turning one's attention to improving conditions within these limits as a kind of expanded, executive aestheticism. But did any of the work on show give a taste of these potentials, a breath of the new, improved life latent in 'the banality of everyday life'? Between the latter-day Situationists – who consider art already superseded by activism and regard such gallery interventions as merely one weapon in the cultural terrorist's arsenal – and the business artists – following Warhol's trajectory out of the autonomous sphere of art and into the office – there seemed little distinction. Neither offered a compelling aesthetic jolt of alterity or opened up a sense of escape. Ultimately, the show's very dependence on the genres of corporatised and commodified culture made the latter's presence suffocating – the artists almost seemed to be hiding in the cloak of the adversary, afraid to strike out into anything so arrogantly deluded as a self-sufficient work.

Except for Mark Leckey, that is. The only piece in the show that was willing to sell out to the sensuous, whilst confidently registering seismic cultural shifts, was his video (not a document of an intervention this time but a deconstructed montage of documentary footage), *Fiorucci Made Me Hardcore*. Shut away behind black rubber curtains in a club-like darkness and projected across the length and depth of the room, it was a disorienting and heady shot of image after the dry texts that preceded it. Like guilty voyeurs, viewers could finally indulge their sick taste for sensory stimulation and narrative pleasure in this history of popular dance culture, from Northern Soul to Acid House. Faced with the conceptualist mirror of late capitalism, who could blame you for taking the traditional route and getting out of it by getting out of your head?

This was not, in fact, an 'escapist' film, however. The form was chronological but discontinuous, the significance of the changes in gesture, dress and musical style registered in the diverse source materials not explicated for the viewer but offered up for analysis. But it did feel like a release after the preceding dialectic of indifference. Perhaps art, which admittedly has been fetishised as a site of play, ambivalence and otherness, is nevertheless suffering not from too much luxuriant, escapist incertitude but too little. There is a danger that, following the lead of a newly humble and self-flagellant capitalism (which, after all, has borrowed its new clothes from earlier artistic and political 'creatives'), artists will feel obliged to downplay art's residual freedoms, hairshirting themselves into the same reflex of repentance that gives us reality TV ('we don't want to make the viewers feel they are less interesting or important than the stars – plus we're strapped for cash'). Meanwhile, beyond the confines of the gallery, the artists and activists had been upstaged by events in Seattle, an eruption of organised political opposition to corporate domination which made it all look suddenly rather academic. Ironic or what?

Branded to the Bone

Chris Darke

Vol 1 #17, Summer 2000

> The bourgeois scheme is that they wish to be disturbed from time to time, they like that, but then they envelop you, and that little bit is over, and they are ready for the next.
> Claes Oldenburg, 1961

> It shouldn't have been a shock, but it was.
> Chris Wilcha, 1999

March to the Royal Festival Hall to hear a recital by the tabla virtuoso, Zakir Husain. Projected above the stage was the logo of that evening's sponsor, the financial services corporation HSBC. Nothing unusual about that; corporate sponsorship is so much a feature of high profile cultural events that the HSBC logo appeared as much in keeping with the evening as the musician's arrangement of performance rug and flowers. But, as an envoy from the Indian Embassy took the stage, name-checked the musicians, then introduced a representative of HSBC, a murmur ran through the audience which soon strengthened into a hiss of disapproval that hung over the auditorium. When Mr. HSBC began the customary spiel, in which arts sponsorship is gently massaged away from being mistaken for a lucrative exercise in tax-loss philanthropy, the hissing became a *sotto voce* groan. By the time we were told about HSBC's long relationship with the Indian subcontinent and about how many corporations have come to recognise that they have duties 'beyond making a profit', a slow handclap had started up, as if to express a collective sentiment of 'Yeah, right'. Mr. HSBC then revealed he had a cheque to award to a worthy cause, which he proceeded to present to a representative of Unilever. A storm of hilarious derision broke over the unfortunate CEO, who retired from the podium having barely started his acceptance speech.

There was enough sheer ire in the air that night to suggest that, post-Seattle, even anti-corporate souls over here had tasted blood. In setting the stage for a performance of Indian devotional music with a soft-focus appeal to its colonial legacy, HSBC didn't simply generate an unexpected PR breakdown. Rather, it was a case of the public having little tolerance for such juxtapositions. The audience at the Festival Hall expressed its hostility as outsiders given the uncommon privilege of shouting down a mode of speech that has become a dominant form of public discourse. PR spin is a language in which everything is addressed as product and everyone appealed to as a consumer, and hostile rejection is a direct response to the saturation of the culture by this corporate vernacular. The vehemence with which this response was expressed requires that, in order to blunt it, the sharp men and women of corporate PR will have to wage a new, more concerted form of spin-warfare.

But what if an insider within the belly of promotional culture were to persistently train a camera on it, probe its etiquettes, crack open its contradictions and, with an almost naïve insistence, ask 'What the hell am I doing here?' In May 1993, a 22-year-old philosophy graduate, Christopher Wilcha, went to work for Columbia House, the mail-order wing of Columbia Records, and took a Hi-8 camera with him. Over the next two years, Wilcha gathered footage for a 70-minute tape, *The Target Shoots First.* Part video-diary, part counter-motivational training film, *Target* is that rare document – a sustained essay in corporate anthropology and a young Gen Xer's search for clarity in contradiction. It's a work of well-balanced details and analytical commentary, elucidating anecdotal video-vérité. Wilcha has a journalist's sense of the facts that matter, so we learn early on that Columbia House is (was – there's since been a merger) owned by Sony/Time Warner, that their combined revenue was $70 billion and that, as an employee, he'll 'have access to Sony and Time Warner's cafeterias'. He also has a filmmaker's eye for the resonance in simple visual details: over shots of the empty and anonymous corporate corridors of his 19th floor eyrie, his commentary remarks on 'the weird institutional déjà vu – the corporate workplace reminds me of high school.'

But, fundamentally, *Target* is an essay in the processes of assimilation – of the kid by the corporation, of the kid's music by the record company machine. 'How naïve is that?' could be the pomo(ronic) response to this précis of *Target*'s themes. But the filmmaker's no ingénue; he's more interested in discovering whether it's still even possible to be quizzical about the condition that Naomi Klein describes in her book, *No Logo,* as being 'branded to the bone'. If the anti-WTO demonstrations proved anything, it's that it's no longer enough just to raise an eyebrow and come over all resignedly mandarin about what the American journal of political satire, *The Baffler*, calls 'the business of culture in the new Gilded Age'. To engage with it requires that one engage with the culture of business.

Wilcha's time as Assistant Product Manager of Music Marketing at Columbia House coincided with two major developments in the music industry. First, there was the advent of 'grunge', with the major cross-over success of Nirvana's *Nevermind.* Second, there was the change from vinyl to CD. 'The '90s way of buying was to replace a vinyl collection completely,' Wilcha narrates. 'Record clubs were one of the ways to do this.' Columbia House was reaching a market of eight million subscribers a month, but, as Wilcha discovered, it was also ripping off its artists while reaping the dividends of sales and direct marketing. Artists would be paid reduced royalties and publishing rates on the sales of club CDs. These general, infrastructural facts of music marketing are brought into focus by Wilcha's own sense of cultural alignment with the alternative rock scene. With the release of Nirvana's *In Utero* album, he's put in charge of producing the magazine for Columbia House subscribers – the senior writer having resigned. The film's good on the power divisions between marketing types and 'creatives', the former working on the 19th floor, the latter subordinate on the 17th. Wilcha's boss tells him: 'This is a Gen X band. You can speak for them.' He duly writes the feature and finds himself 'confronted by the fact that my identity as a punk rock fan and my job as a Columbia House employee have finally collided'. In gathering material for the film, Wilcha explores this dialectic while trying to demarcate some independent space: 'For the past six months, taping has been a way of convincing myself that where I work isn't who I am.' But it's also a way of bringing those contradictions into the open and of expressing a by-no-means fashionable unease with the processes of appropriation and assimilation at play, if not reconciling the contradictions of his new-found corporate identity with his individual cultural identity.

Yet *Target* is itself a document not so much compromised as complicated by its very access to internal corporate processes. I asked Wilcha whether he was at all concerned that, in showing the film to management, he might realise that it could be the model of a new genre of media-savvy corporate training video? 'The first screening (in 1999) coincided with a corporate merger,' he told me. 'They [Columbia House] merged with CD Now, the giant online retailer, and the week of my New York screening was the week they were announcing the merger, so the screening was completely off the radar. Finally, in the weeks that followed, a bunch of upper management people, including the President, watched it. Some people disagreed with what I had to say. Others in management, comically enough, saw it as some kind of sociological study of a failed business experiment. They wanted to know how we could replicate that kind of consumer reaction on the web, instead of seeing it as an expression of how people felt about their jobs.'

As an 'essay film' – a hybrid genre of documentary observation and first-person intervention whose time has surely come around again – the strength of *Target* lies in the way it develops and explores its key theme of assimilation. Wilcha's team produced a pilot version of the club magazine, successfully delivering a model for niche-marketing 'alt.rock' as well as 'divulging club sales tactics, innovating the selection, sneaking in criticism – we put anything into the magazine we like.' At which point, corporate assimilation takes yet another turn. 'Management brings in an advertising agency who, for a fee, sell our idea back to the company. It shouldn't have been a shock, but it was,' Wilcha relates.

The Target Shoots First can be seen as taking its place alongside the interventions and critiques of writers such as Klein and journals like *The Baffler*. It's also of a part with, but at one remove from, the neo-Situationist, perceptual prankssterism of 'culture jamming'. As a form of semiotic subversion, 'culture jamming' covers a range of art-based activism. From Adbusters' satires on the values and techniques of advertising, through etoy's interventions into the stock market, exploring the porous boundaries between the business of art and the 'art' of business, to RTMark's overtly risky brand-sabotage activities, culture jamming measures – and in some senses seeks to redefine – avant-garde art strategies against the speed with which such strategies may be assimilated by their very corporate targets.

Wilcha, Klein and *The Baffler* represent a tendency that's slightly different from this pranksterism – one that's based on a necessary defensiveness in the face of a market without limits of reach or responsibility. The symptom of such defensiveness is to wrest back certain journalistic precepts – of investigation and independent critique – that should, by nature, be resistant to the glossy cant of marketing. Should be – but haven't proven to be so. As media convergence has demonstrated, editorial values can quickly become hostages to advertising fortunes.

The value of the insights that Wilcha brings to bear on the co-optation of 'alternative culture' is what really aligns *Target* with work by journalists such as Klein and *The Baffler*. Culture becomes the field in which capitalism stalks the ever-newer 'new', and *The Baffler* has made analysis of this phenomenon its forté, along with the detailed institutional analysis of American journalism and union activity. The collection of 'salvos' from *The Baffler* published as *Commodify Your Dissent* date from around the mid-'90s but remain relevant in their splendidly distempered take on corporate culture as it chases, in ever decreasing circles, after the spectacle of the counter-culture until, as predicted, pop eats itself. And business picks up the tab. In the tail-chasing flurry of hungry assimilation, culture became marketing and marketing culture. In his 1995 essay, 'Alternative to What?', Thomas Frank, co-founder of *The Baffler*, writes:

> There are few spectacles corporate America enjoys more than a good counterculture, complete with hairdos of defiance, dark complaints about the stifling 'mainstream', and expensive accessories of all kinds. So it was only a matter of months after the discovery of 'Generation X' that the culture industry sighted an all-new youth movement, whose new looks, new rock bands, and menacing new 'tude quickly became commercial shorthand for the rebel excitement associated with everything from Gen X ads and TV shows to the information revolution.

The fear, felt by both Wilcha and Frank, is that all 'deviant' cultures are so rapidly assimilated that it's increasingly difficult to out-manoeuvre the mainstream, and that corporate culture is frighteningly adept at absorbing its dissident voices. 'I think it's often very hard for Americans themselves to see what's going on,' admits Frank:

> One of the comments we keep getting from our readers' letters is that they didn't think that criticism like this still went on. We hear that all the time. In the US, the labour movement has really fallen off the cultural map. Thirty

> years ago, every newspaper in the country had a labour reporter. Now, the only ones that do are *The New York Times*, *The Wall Street Journal* and *The Chicago Tribune*. Organised labour has to be the wellspring of scepticism towards the corporate universe. When those people showed up in Seattle, and a lot of them were from unions, this astonished people; they thought unionism was over in America.

There is, inevitably, a generational issue here, a question of a shared cultural and political memory that corporate culture does its best to undermine and erase. Hence the accuracy in critiques of cultural 'dumbing down', where infantilisation of the public incubates precisely the willed, induced amnesia that makes a good, loyal consumer out of a former citizen with a cultural life and political allegiances. In this respect, Wilcha is smart to compare his absorption into the corporate world of work with that of his father, and understands that his is one of the (last?) generations with a sense of self that could still be located outside of the mall. 'What my father went to business school to study,' he narrates, 'I trained for simply by being a committed consumer.' In conversation, Wilcha told me:

> I'm 28 years old now, and for a lot of kids who are around 25 – they're labelled Generation Y – these concerns are invisible to them. If you're in a band now, it's no longer a question of selling out as far as having your music in advertising is concerned, it's part of the marketing plan! It's a given. Literally it's been in the space of a couple of years that there's been a whole change in consciousness about the relationship between art and commerce, with culture being used to prop up and sell things.

We've been here before. Maybe we've been nowhere else since the 1950s. The professional Jeremiahs of Wilcha's father's generations were Vance Packard, author of *The Hidden Persuaders*, and Consumer Rights supremo, Ralph Nader. Perhaps, between them, Wilcha, Frank, Klein and others of their growing number might restore and revitalise critique, satire and analysis to the vital work of cultural analysis that exists outside of academia's self-absorption. One that understands that 'culture' means more than the miasma produced by the multinational entertainment oligopoly where, in Don DeLillo's phrase, 'nothing happens until it's consumed'. Perhaps we're in for a new generation of characters (after all, in *Target*, Chris Wilcha is 'Son of Organisation Man') who haunt the corridors of corporate culture, with their hostility and confusion yet to be dulled and bought off. Or perhaps we'll just wake up one day, niched to within an inch of our lives.

Culture Clubs

Anthony Davies and Simon Ford

Vol 1 #18, Autumn 2000

Today, a new variety of club is emerging: a type of club dedicated to the networking of culturepreneurs and the business community. Much of this activity has been in line with organisational and structural shifts occurring in the corporate sector – principally, the shift from centralised, hierarchical structures to flat, networked forms of organisation. In this report, we look at how these networks and 'new' economies are being formed, accessed and utilised, where they converge and where they disperse.

In the late-1990s, the surge to merge culture with the economy was a key factor in London's bid to consolidate its position as the European centre of the global financial services industry. Culture was part of the marketing mix that, within the context of the European Union (EU), kept London ahead of its competitors, particularly Frankfurt.[1] This can be traced back to the UK's exit from the Exchange Rate Mechanism in 1992 and a range of economic initiatives aimed at attracting inward investment, or Foreign Direct Investment (FDI). During this period, the UK accounted for 40 percent of Japanese, US and Asian investment in the EU. 'Cool Britannia' may have been a media spectacle, but it was the need to attract FDI, combined with the coordinates of a new service-based economy, that underpinned London's spectacular emergence as the 'coolest city on the planet'. (This state of affairs could be about to change with the proposed link-up between Frankfurt's Deutsche Börse and the London Stock Exchange, i.e. the iX market, and the recent German tax reforms that will pave the way for a radical restructuring of its corporate landscape.[2] With higher international inward and portfolio investment and the combined iX market, Germany looks set to become the leading market destination for young companies, making Berlin's pitch to become the new cultural 'it location' look increasingly viable.)[3]

In London, it was the cultural requirements of the 'new' economy that resulted in the emergence of culture brokers – intermediaries who sold services and traded knowledge and culture to a variety of clients outside the gallery system, from advertising companies and property developers to restaurateurs and upmarket retail outlets. Job descriptions such as artist, curator, critic and gallerist no longer reflected the range of activities these individuals were engaged in. For culture brokers, art production was just one element that, along with the music, drug, fashion, design, club and political scenes, could be brought together,

1. George Graham, 'Overseas banks warned on London', and George Graham and Stephen Timewell, 'City confident of keeping status', *The Banker* supplement, *Financial Times*, 27 November 1997.
2. Doris Grass and Vincent Boland, 'Deutsche Börse board split on link up with the LSE', *Financial Times*, 13 July 2000 and Haig Simonian, 'German tax reforms set to aid investors', *Financial Times*, 15 July 2000.
3. Nicholas Powell, 'Avant-garde flock to Berlin', *Financial Times Weekend*, 3/4 October 1998.

mediated and repackaged in a range of formats, from exhibitions and websites to corporate parties and in-store merchandising.[4] At the same point, many companies were beginning to move away from sponsorship toward an integrated partnership or alliance strategy. This marked a further shift from the 'something for nothing', arm's-length philanthropic model to a 'something for something' contract, in which marketing departments perceived cultural (and often environmental) programming as an integral part of ethical marketing strategies (the so-called Total Role in Society).[5]

Along with these new developments, corporate strategists realised that, because of the emerging knowledge-based economy, a company or individual could be valued principally on 'intangible assets', e.g. intellectual capital and access to networks. This brought about a revolution in the corporate sector.[6] The underlying trend has been to develop flatter, more flexible and intelligent forms of organisation. This, in turn, has put pressure on companies to form alliances and break down inflexible departmental structures and initiate cross-departmental project teams (increasingly staffed by short-term or outsourced contract workers). Indeed, we have recently witnessed the birth of an alliance culture that collapses the distinctions (or boundaries) between companies, nation-states, governments, private individuals and even the protest movement, as we shall demonstrate later. This trend toward alliances and partnerships has resulted in what have been variously described as 'virtual' or 'boundary-less' organisations. It has also made it increasingly difficult to identify 'cores'; as companies loosen their physical structures through outsourcing, concerns have also been raised about the danger that core activities are disappearing, leaving fragile shells or 'hollow' organisations.[7]

A number of corporate organisations are currently gauging the potential of extending their networks into strategic alliances with other sectors, particularly the public sector.[8] This new alliance culture between the public and private sectors can be seen within the context of the UK government's drive to establish a Third Way in which 'public' is no longer equated solely with 'the state' but with a combination of public/private agencies. With the private sector leading the way, public institutions are undergoing an ideological and structural transformation to make themselves more compatible with corporate alliance programmes. Like their corporate partners, many cultural institutions now

4. For a fuller discussion of these developments, see Simon Ford and Anthony Davies, 'Art Futures', *Art Monthly*, no. 223, February 1999.
5. For a discussion of this concept see Andy Law, *Open Minds*, London: Orion Business, 1999; and Stephen Alburty, 'The Ad Agency to End All Ad Agencies', *Fast Company*, no. 6, December 1996.
6. The INNFORM research programme founds widespread initiatives in almost all new forms of corporate organisation during the period 1992–6. See Richard Whittington et al., 'New notions of organisational fit', *Financial Times*, 29 November 1999.
7. Centre for Research in Strategic Purchasing and Supply (CRISPS), *Returning to core or creating a hollow?*, Bath: Bath University, 1999.
8. See Capital Strategies, the city corporate finance house, 'Education News' at http://www.capitalstrategies.co.uk

perceive their role as 'hanging out with culture', interacting with and being part of it. In their drive to formalise informality, they provide what are essentially convergence zones for corporate and creative networks to interact, to overlap with one another and to form 'weak' ties. The prominence that events such as charity auctions, exhibition openings, talk programmes and award dinners have attained demonstrates how central face-to-face social interaction is to the functional capacity of these new alliances.

Some institutions go further. At London's Institute of Contemporary Arts (ICA), for example, a networking club for cultural entrepreneurs and, initially at least, educationalists, arts administrators, television executives and business consultants has been set up in conjunction with Goldsmith's College, the National Endowment for Science, Technology and the Arts (NESTA), Channel 4, the Arts Council and Cap Gemini.[9] The Club is coordinated by Andrew Chetty and Sarah Duke at the ICA, Andrew Warren at Cap Gemini and Alan Phillogene at the Centre for Cultural Studies at Goldsmith's College. It is an invitation-only monthly event that provides 'a networking base for its members' and promises to introduce them to agencies, from television companies to venture capitalists and private organisations who 'may wish to support and commission them'.

Through initiatives like The Club, the ICA aims to become the leading institutional home for cultural entrepreneurs and perceives its role as that of a facilitator and 'ideal forum for the cross-fertilisation of ideas, and support base for these enterprises'.[10] After the success of the first two meetings at the ICA, the third will reputedly take place at Channel 4 in September. Such nomadism indicates that The Club itself has no fixed base or home and can move to any location within the network. This makes identifying the core organisation difficult and, in line with the complex and often hidden alliances that characterise the new corporate landscape, raises serious questions about transparency, representation and accountability.

Given their foregrounding of The Club's 'development and growth' potential, its coordinators must be aware of the current sale talks surrounding First Tuesday, the market leader of match-making clubs for internet entrepreneurs and venture capitalists. With 100,000 members on its database and the claim to have raised $150 million in seed capital from its networking events, it is no surprise that its valuation at £33.5 million was principally based on access to its 'extensive database of the digital elite'.[11]

A varicty of means exist to finance these clubs. First Tuesday takes a 2 percent commission on deals, while other culture clubs generate capital through

9. Cap Gemini Ernst & Young is one of the world's largest management consultancy and computer services firms and has collaborated with the ICA on previous occasions, most notably Imaginaria '99. The ICA's definition of 'cultural entrepreneur' is derived from an earlier collaboration with Demos. See Charles Leadbeater and Kate Oakley, *The Independents*, London: Demos, November 1999.
10. Sarah Duke, The Club press release, 14 June 2000.
11. Caroline Daniel, 'First Tuesday in sale talks', *Financial Times*, 20 July 2000.

membership (The Fourth Room) or building the most 'influential list of contacts in the world' (Free Thinking). With the creative industries generating £60 billion a year (7 percent of national gross domestic product) and having been estimated to increase at a rate of 5 percent per year, it is no surprise that The Club is endorsed by both government agencies (NESTA) and private companies.

At this stage, it is difficult to locate the mutual bonds and orientation of The Club, but it is a good example of the emerging inter-organisational relationships that characterise the 'new' economy. With representatives from the corporate, state, media, educational and cultural sectors, it may also represent the initial stages of a corporatised future for UK cultural and educational institutions. This falls in line with the forthcoming Department of Trade and Industry (DTI) spending review, which aims to refocus its funds into promoting enterprise, small business and 'knowledge transfer', in order to 'concentrate on managing change rather than attempting to direct companies' activities'.[12]

In the education sector, 'knowledge transfer' translates into an £80 million fund (the University Innovation Fund) to establish consultancies that will mediate between universities and businesses. With the ICA and Goldsmith's College stepping up contact with Cap Gemini and providing a 'support base (and provider) for enterprise', the so-called revolutionary venture capital models proposed by companies like The Fourth Room come into the equation.

The Fourth Room was set up in 1998 – by Wendy Gordon, former Chairman of The Research Business International; Michael Wolff, founder of brand consultancy, Wolff Olins; and Piers Schmidt, former head of strategy at Interbrand Newell and Sorrell – as a hang-out zone and creative bolt-hole for corporate executives and other 'leading individuals'. It has variously been described as a business development club, a networking club and a strategic marketing consultancy which aims to take the strain out of networking and 'put together venture ideas and management teams and take them from the moment of thinking through to the patent or crystallised idea'.[13]

The £10,000 per annum membership fee includes use of the clubhouse in central London and access to 'focus groups comprising of [sic] "ordinary" people and teenagers who will act as sounding boards for new ideas'.[14] In addition to the clubhouse, members receive a weekly in-house publication and an opportunity to eavesdrop on 'emerging cultural trends and monitor changing patterns and beliefs'.[15] This is described by the company as a corporate early warning system. As with The Club at the ICA, very little information is publicly available, but we know that The Fourth Room is 'dazzlingly white, with high ceilings, long windows and white painted floorboards', and that members are encouraged to draw on the walls with coloured crayons to release

12. Kevin Brown, 'DTI allocated funds to boost enterprise', *Financial Times*, 17 July 2000.
13. Piers Schmidt, 'Me and My Partner: Michael Wolff and Piers Schmidt', *The Independent*, 7 April 1999.
14. Helen Jones, 'Help is at hand to make the right contacts', *Financial Times*, 12 February 1999.
15. The Fourth Room, *Invitation booklet*, London: The Fourth Room, 2000.

their creativity.[16] As Piers Schmidt claims, 'it's all about collaboration', and, to this end, the aim is to get CEOs mixing with eco-activists like Swampy to discuss environmental issues over breakfast.

The relationship between Cap Gemini and the ICA and Swampy's proposed breakfast with CEOs at The Fourth Room indicates that terms such as 'collaboration' can be utilised to mask a variety of vested interests. The recent shift in terminology regarding arts funding (i.e. away from 'sponsored by' toward 'in partnership with', 'in association with' and 'co-produced by') is also indicative of a new agenda based on alliances and an increased corporate decision-making role in cultural programming. A signal event in this diversification was the UK-based Association of Business Sponsorship of the Arts (ABSA) re-branding itself as Arts & Business (A&B), in the conviction that 'the arts are the new secret weapon of business success'. As a government-funded organisation, A&B have taken collaboration and alliance a step further through the Professional Development Programme and the NatWest Board Bank, which has placed 1,500 young executives on the boards of arts companies.[17]

The Creative Forum members at A&B, which include American Express Europe, Arthur Andersen and Interbrand Newell and Sorrell, are seen as the 'shock troops' in the involvement of arts in companies, and, as a result, A&B receive £5.05 million a year from the government to run the Pairing Scheme. The arts organisations, it is claimed, gain from the decision-making and entrepreneurial skills of the executives, while the executives gain valuable experience of creative processes through working with artists.

Other examples of recent collaborations follow an informal, networked and often hidden alliance-type arrangement between galleries, public institutions and corporations. An alliance-type project covered by this new lexicon is the Fig-1 website, club and project space, which aims to present 50 projects in 50 weeks. Founded by curator, Mark Francis, and gallerist, Jay Jopling, and financed by Bloomberg, the financial information company, the claim to be simultaneously 'in association with' Bloomberg and 'independent, non-profit [and] free from institutional and commercial obligations' seems curiously paradoxical.[18] Rather, it appears that Fig-1 operates as a (principally new media) satellite organisation for White Cube and as a cultural scratch-and-sniff site for Bloomberg.

We turn, finally, to a consideration of what might be termed 'political engagement'. In order to meet the challenge posed by these new alliances and networked global businesses, new forms of flexible and subversive organisation have emerged that can disperse and re-form anywhere, at any time.[19] These strategic movements also take into account the fact that company networks and

16. Sandra Deeble, 'Fourth Room opens the doors of perception', *Financial Times*, 30 December 1999.
17. See the Arts & Business website http://www.absa.org.uk and Antony Thorncroft, 'From a cosy warm glow to hot support', *Financial Times*, 6 September 1999.
18. See the website http://www.fig-1.com
19. See, for example, John Vidal, 'The World@War', *The Guardian*, Society Section, 19 January 2000.

hollow organisations actively solicit and harness counter discourses to service the illusion of dissent and dialogue.[20] In a networked culture, the topographical metaphor of 'inside' and 'outside' has become increasingly untenable. As all sectors loosen their physical structures, flatten out, form alliances and dispense with tangible centres, the oppositionality that has characterised previous forms of protest and resistance is finished as a useful model.

In the cultural sector (particularly the 'cutting edge' art world), with so many brokers acting as corporate-friendly conduits to an artificially constructed 'outside', 'marginal' and 'socially engaged' culture, it should come as no surprise that these oppositional metaphors, for some, are difficult to dispense with.[21] Yet, in contrast to such attitudes, more astute activists and agitators, who once spoke of critical distance, now recognise that their challenge lies in the forms and quality of access and connection. Fittingly, a useful new metaphor for this challenge comes from the world of digital systems. In a networked society, individuals and groups are constantly alternating between 'on' and 'off'. As a result, we can expect to see emerging new forms of 'engagement' which exercise border controls on networks, withhold, filter and restrict access to information and disable the 'eavesdropping' strategies and 'early warning systems' employed by business consultancies, corporations and public institutions.[22] The extent and nature of these forms is still to be determined and will be examined more closely at a later date. But it can already be asserted that informal networks have become extremely effective forms of counter-organisation in the sense that – just as with corporate alliances – it is extremely difficult to define their boundaries and identify who belongs to them. Informal networks are also replacing older political groups based on formal rules and fixed organisational structures and chains of command. The emergence of a decentralised, transnational, network-based protest movement represents a significant threat to those sectors that are slow in transforming themselves from local and centralised hierarchical bureaucracies into flat, networked organisations.

These developments are taking place against a backdrop of waning confidence and belief in the ability of governments to regulate the growing power of global corporations and their networks of influence. But, thanks to corporate restructuring and the access it provides to global networks, new forms of knowledge-based political engagement promise possibilities and scales of effect previously unimaginable.

20. See Philip Knight, 'A forum for improving globalisation', *Financial Times*, 1 August 2000 and Richard Tomkins, 'Global chief thinks locally (Douglas Daft is persuading protestors to drink cans of Coke, not smash them)', *Financial Times*, 1 August 2000.
21. See *Art Monthly*, no. 233, Editorial, February 2000: 'It is hard to resist the lure of direct action, particularly for those of us frustrated by the inexorable process of commodification of even the most critical art practices, and by the marginal position occupied by art in our society as a whole', and exhibitions: 'Unconvention', Centre for the Visual Arts in Cardiff, November 1999–January 2000, and 'CRASH!', Institute of Contemporary Arts, November 1999.
22. See Merlin Carpenter and Anthony Davies, 'The protest had already impacted on London in the form of its absence', from the catalogue *As a painter I call myself the estate of*, Secession, Vienna, 2000.

Wide Area Disturbance

Ricardo Dominguez Interviewed by Coco Fusco

Vol 1 #23, Spring 2002

Coco Fusco: Has there been a significant change in the focus of anti-globalisation activism in the aftermath of Genoa and the attack on the World Trade Center?

Ricardo Dominguez: No. Activists are still asking the same questions about neoliberalism, and they are still using the same tactics to disrupt the gatherings of the G8 and the IMF around the globe. Interaction between the NGOs and street activists is the same – one leverages the other. Everyone seems to agree that the violence of Genoa and September 11 should not derail the use of non-violent direct action. In addition, the same critiques of the anti-globalisation movement persist: that it lacks a coherent ideology, that it does not offer any workable solutions to top-down globalisation, that it disregards the last 50 years of extremely violent struggle against neoliberalism in the South. The South's political and social thought offers possible reforms that can really challenge the North's neoliberal agenda and which shouldn't be ignored. Many say that the cultural thought and political practices coming from Chiapas, Woomera, Porto Alegre and Kerala can displace the narcissism of activists in the North.

CF: But the activists in the North have to stop believing the media hype that represents them as the only protagonists of note in what is actually a global struggle against dehumanising policies and growing poverty. Activists in the Third World have been subject to harassment, surveillance, imprisonment, torture and even disappearance for decades without receiving much attention from the North. While it may appeal to the leftist activists and netizens in the North to promote the idea that, in a post 9/11 world, they have all been deemed 'the enemy' in the same way that the entire Arab world has been designated a target by the US military, this is simply not true. No hackers in the US have been singled out for investigation as a result of the passing of the Patriot Act – at least not yet. If we focus solely on what is happening to Americans and Europeans interested in social change and whether they are imperiled, we end up supporting the American position that posits 'our' victimisation as more significant than the rest of the world's.

RD: Another important issue is the strategic viability of an 'eventism'. The 'tourism' of city-hopping, from Seattle to Genoa, is becoming an empty spectacle of violent confrontations for the media and policy-makers, and the movement is being constrained by events organised by global power-brokers. Issues beyond protest are being forgotten. This type of eventism also dictates the distribution of information produced by net.activists working for Independent Media Centres and related websites. Perhaps it is time to turn toward another form of eventism in order to dismantle neoliberalism. The

Zapatistas, for example, convoke their own events rather than responding to those organised by others.

CF: Do you see a shift in the attitude of street activists and NGOs regarding their sense of the viability, or relevance, of hacktivism?

RD: Yes. In 1998, when Electronic Disturbance Theatre (EDT) launched FloodNet, very few activists or hackers saw any use for direct action online. Between 1999 and 2001, EDT and other proponents of hacktivism began to have a marginal presence at hacker and street activist conferences. *2600* [*The Hacker Quarterly*] is now calling for more panels on Independent Media Centres, street activism, hacking and hacktivism at their next event because net.activism was so well received at their last event. This is an important sign that activism may be moving more to the centre of hacking culture, which may have a chance to gain some much needed political depth.

CF: EDT has not carried out any FloodNet actions in support of the Zapatistas during the past year. What has been happening with the Zapatistas in recent months?

RD: EDT has refrained from any actions because the Zapatistas have not made an international call for direct action against the Fox government at this time. They have been in a time of deep silence (since the two-week march from Chiapas to Mexico City in March 2001), thinking about the next stage of actions against the Mexican government's development of the Puebla-Panama Plan. This entails building a 12-lane highway between Puebla, Mexico and Panama that cuts right through Zapatista lands. The Zapatistas are also pushing for changes to the Indigenous Bill of Rights that the Mexican government first accepted and then gutted of any social relevance. The Zapatista use of the internet as a voice multiplier and organisational tool since 1994 should be considered one of the most important activist gestures of the '90s – many see a direct connection between the Seattle actions and the Zapatista's call for the development of the International Network of Struggle and Resistance at the start of 1996.

CF: EDT does have another project in the works called 'Anchor for Witnessing'. How does it expand the purview of online political engagement?

RD: 'Anchors for Witnessing: Counter-Surveillance for Off-Grid Communities' is an attempt to take on the issue of surveillance which is now so important, not only as a mechanism of social control but also as the latest new growth market in the Guarded Society. In 1998, when the media started to ask EDT about new tactics the Zapatistas were developing, we said that they were constructing 'wireless video servers (Anchors)' to upload real-time netcast video of human rights abuses by paramilitary and the Mexican military. At the time, this was just an idea we thought of presenting as an intimidation strategy; now EDT is making this a reality. These wireless 'Anchors' will use the technologies developed by corporate and military communities in the First World to centralise control of indigenous lands. But we will be making them available to those who are usually the targets of surveillance so they can document the abuses to which they are regularly subjected. The speed of transmission helps to prevent governments, or other power structures, from succeeding in suppressing information.

CF: Unlike other well-known hacktivist groups, EDT's activities have been absorbed by the art world in general and the net art community in particular. Documentation of your actions has been included in numerous net art exhibitions and publications, and your work has been presented widely at theatre and performance conferences. Why do you think that your particular blend of HTML *détournment* and political critique of neoliberalism has been interpreted as 'art'?

RD: We consider our project to be an example of radical net art aesthetics. We see ourselves as artists and theorists. We also felt that our poetics, with its emphasis on simulation, transparency, mass agency and negative casting of the networks, allowed a complex social sculpture to emerge that was not part of the self-referential net art fetish of code *qua* code. FloodNet established a mode of telepresence that was bound to conditions of the social beyond the digital domain. For EDT, net art offers the possibility not only for a human story to become present for many by viewing the artwork, but also for a moment of political solidarity with a distant 'other' to emerge.

CF: In writing about your art in the past, I have stressed its relevance as conceptual sculpture in the tradition of working with negative space, and its connection with a Latin American tradition of infusing minimal strategies with political content.[1] For instance, in the way you convert the net art game of foregrounding 404 files (a status code which tells you that a requested page was not found) into an indictment of governmental negligence. It is equally important that your work politicises connectivity and interactivity by calling on its users to assume an ethical stance *vis-à-vis* a distant other. In this sense, the work undermines what I would call the telematic fantasy of net.culture; that is, the assumption that communicating across vast distances represents a radical gesture in and of itself. *Dolores from 10h to 22h* extends this experiment with another form of simulation (the docudrama), bringing a human story from the South into the net art context to focus on the audience's relationship to viewing

1. The experimentation with negative space in Western art is fundamental to the elaboration of foreground and background in painting and drawing, and to the development of sculpture that highlights how the space around a designated object defines the object even when that object is absent. This is not that different from our numerical system's inclusion of the concept of zero, a cypher that represents nothing and, in doing so, gives meaning to all other numbers. Gestalt psychology looks at the tendency to perceive form and pattern as figure against background. Constructivist, Naum Gabo, is usually credited with being the first sculptor to concentrate on negative space, having used voids to define shape with his *Head No. 2* (1916). Modernist, Michael Heizer, with his earthworks consisting of gouged trenches, and postmodernist, Rachel Whiteread, with her casting of negative spaces such as the inside of bathtubs and rooms and the spaces under chairs, are among the better known artists working in this vein. See Coco Fusco, 'The Unbearable Weightiness of Beings: Art in Mexico after NAFTA', *The Bodies That Were Not Ours and Other Writings*, London: Routledge and inIVA, 2001, pp. 186–201.

the political violence of everyday life in a *maquiladora*.[2] However, judging from the rather flip interventions in the chat room, it would seem that net art viewers show their 'better selves' more effectively when they are called upon to engage in simulated aggression against an Oedipalised power source (i.e. jamming a server) than when they are asked to reflect upon how their own attraction to net.spectacularity might interfere with their recognition of the grotesque inequities of the global economic order, and that their privileged position can be measured in relation to their voyeuristic pleasure. In *The Language of New Media*, Lev Manovich argues that the most successful couplings of simulation and real life action are the screens on fighter planes that assist the pilots engaged in warfare. I would argue that a politicised net art practice will have to push this relationship further, to stop us from seeing the virtual space of the internet as an absolute representation of reality, the database as the sum total of knowledge and the power of seeing as something to indulge in solely for voyeuristic or narcissistic pleasure.

RD: Yes, I agree that, right now, aggressive simulation plays better than self-reflection with regard to our relationship to the everyday abuse of workers in the South. Most of the work that falls between net art and net.activism tends to deal with the injection of the organic, as an act of disturbance rather than as an act of internal critique – be it Mongrel at the Tate, or EDT, or the Toywar. A project like *Dolores* points to another space that is now emerging.

CF: How does your extensive background in theatre, as an actor and director, affect your approach to activism, both on- and off-line? Does it explain your emphasis on conceiving of electronic civil disobedience as theatre?

RD: My background in classical theatre, agit-prop theatre and performance art – intermixed with my history of direct action on the streets, my involvement with Critical Art Ensemble and the powerful theatre of resistance that Zapatismo created – allowed EDT to stage a dramatic sociological event. Our event was bound to a story that lucidly illustrates the social implications of top-down globalisation. EDT was able to create an 'invisible theatre' that moved many different individuals and organisations to make visceral responses in the cold space of code. So, my history in the theatre of emotion allowed me to build with the other members of EDT an organic and poetic staging of the unbearable weight of beings saying, 'Ya Basta!' While EDT stresses that its performance involves a type of electronic civil disobedience, we do not say that it is the only form of electronic civil disobedience. Our gesture staged a simulation of a distributed denial of service – the outcome of mass agency and digital liminality.[3] We move among net.hacking, net.activism, net.performance, net art and those who have no net.link at all. The Zapatista FloodNet and the

2. Originally an Arabic term that entered colonial Mexico via Spain to signify the processing of foreign grains, it now refers to assembly plants to which foreign materials and parts are shipped and from which the finished product is returned to the original market. Those plants are located in free trade zones in Mexico and the Caribbean.

Zapatista Tribal Port Scan are radical aesthetic data gestures that disturb the ontology of the networks without being bound to the networks. These gestures also point to a future form of life in which mass mediated communication is not a fallen sphere of consumerism but a 'decisive space', such as the one that Latin American media theorist Martin Barbero writes about, where it may be possible to redefine the social agora and to construct global democracies from the grassroots up.

CF: While it is true that EDT was facilitated by the net art community, the very context of your emergence has shifted radically since 1998. Net.art has become part of the very museum and gallery world against which it once saw itself as a reaction. More and more, the net is used by 'new media artists' as a promotional vehicle for the sale of new media objects and/or live performances. The institutionalisation of net art has also entailed a certain containment of its political dimension. For example, it is documentation of your FloodNet actions that museums request for their online exhibitions, not the enactment of a hacktivist gesture. So far, the recognition of hacktivism has not led to more dialogue between artists and museums about how net art can actively engage in institutional critique from within the museum space. On the contrary, the net art currently being showcased by major museums is, for the most part, techno-formalist and devoid of content, or so abstruse as to be virtually unreadable as political gesture. What would you say is the future of the political within net art practice in light of how cultural institutions are responding to it?

RD: A great deal has changed in the net art world since 1997. Many museums are now deeply involved in framing net art for public consumption. You can certainly see a different RT than was presented at the Whitney Biennial in 2000, which presented work by RTMark.com and Fakeshop.com that was both political and performative. In 2002, the focus is on techno-formalist net artists who are working very hard to become an *objet d'art* and gain a foothold in the market. It is important, for those artists working within a critical performative matrix, not to be sidetracked by the latest techno-formalist fetish of museums or the gallery system. In the post-9/11 climate, it is more important than ever to push for aesthetic 'voices' that can bear witness to other worlds beyond the ideology of the War on Terrorism.

It is not clear whether institutions will take on the task of presenting political net art beyond simple documentation. This may start to happen if network_art_activism begins to establish stronger ties with the previous

3. On the internet, a distributed denial of service (DDoS) takes place when a system attacks a single target by overloading it with an automated repetition of a message. This action jams the server and causes denial of service for users of the targeted system. FloodNet, on the other hand, enabled a multiplicity of users to overload a system via the simultaneous, automated sending of messages from a range of sites. While DDoS does not require mass participation for effect, FloodNet acquires its force through collective engagement. For coverage of *Dolores from 10h to 22h*, see http://www.metamute.com/events/dolores.htm
FloodNet: http://www.thing.net/~rdom/ecd/floodnet.html
Electronic Disturbance Theatre: http://www.thing.net/~rdom/ecd/ecd.html

generations of artists who have faced the dismantling of the political in art – both in the North and the South – so that the very immature form which is net art can gain a sense of history about institutional critique, in order to develop both a deeper aesthetic and historical knowledge about what other artists have done before history was erased by the digital hype. I really don't see the possibility of cultural support for political net art works like EDT's Zapatista FloodNet any time soon. But, for projects like 'Anchors for Witnessing', yes, there is interest and support. For political art projects that are about distribution, yes; but for projects that 'disturb', no.

CF: So, as things now stand, institutions want to fund projects that narrow the digital divide, but not ones that subvert the formalist tendencies of net art from within?

RD: Yes, projects that follow the market's drive to plug everyone in will, I think, continue to gain more institutional presence and support. Those works which don't fold into the other end of the market's drive for formalist containment, or the pure presentation of code *qua* code, machines *qua* machines, like network_art_activism, will be left in the archives and will never be supported as a live performance.

CF: You have mentioned several times that in gatherings of hacktivists and anti-globalisation activists, many raise the question of how to bring the issues and activities of political artists and activists from the South, or the Third World, into the foreground more effectively. What do you propose as a means of making this happen?

RD: I don't know if there is only one way to do this. Each little gesture builds toward a large social effect, and we cannot expect one gesture to easily solve such a deep and intractable problem as the lack of presence of the voices from the South on the networks or in the anti-globalisation movement. But, I think we have a much better chance of having the issues and activities of artists from the Third World taken on by hacktivists, net.artists, autonomous networks and the 'movement' than we do from most other sectors in the North. As for suggestions for making this crossover happen, well, I think, in the next year you will see important email lists emerge that will attempt to create a more intercontinental understanding of political art and net art: lists that will question the institutionalisation of techno-formalism as the only type of net art of value, lists that THE THING will host and archive [http://bbs.thing.net]. Also, we will begin to see a deeper critique of the utopian politics on the right and left that only define themselves via the computer as a tool for political and cultural liberation. We will see more projects appearing on networks from regions and people that have been pushed Off-Grid for a very long time. For me, the answer right now is to build a hybrid media network that is somewhere between THE THING and Zapatismo, which means pushing further down the same road on which I started. But, this time, the work will be even more effective, distributed and disturbing than EDT's performance ever was – something to be wished for.

Bill Posters is Guilty: On the Cultural Logic of Ambient

Neil Mulholland

Vol 1 #25, Winter 2002

As a cultural practice, 'ambient' has long been associated with the music of Erik Satie, Claude Debussy, Karlheinz Stockhausen, John Cage and Holger Czukay. This line of association owes much to Brian Eno's *Ambient 1: Music For Airports* (1978), music that invites both active and passive consumption. Eno's ambient has been the raison d'être of numerous disciples, such as Air and Boards of Canada, producers of music aided and abetted by the crystalline, uninterrupted play of Compact Disk. This canon of ambient music has been documented in numerous books, notably Mark Prendergast's *The Ambient Century* (2000) and David Toop's *Ocean Of Sound* (2001). Although these particular histories are significant, by clutching to music they miss out on wider definitions and articulations of ambient. By the end of the '90s, ambient wasn't simply a record shop genre, it didn't necessarily share the Zen ancestry of neo-Dada, or the ethereal calm of Eno's wallpaper music, or the hard-headed structure of *musique concrète*; in some cases, it wasn't even audible. In the '90s, the meanings of ambient were radically transformed and contested in numerous ways. Ambient became as viral and ubiquitous as ambience, no longer merely a cultural strategy but a prevalent cultural logic.

In some spheres, ambient seemed to be (and predominantly remains) synonymous with the increasing popularity of ecology movements and 'alternative', non-Western thought in the rich, post-industrial West. The ethnographic, transcultural world beat music of '80s acts, such as Talking Heads and Dead Can Dance, sanctioned numerous global trance records in the '90s. These ranged from the cult tranceuroxpress, fashioned by Norway's Biosphere, to the popular Baka chants and African rhymes mixed by France's Deep Forest. Everyone from The Orb to the Art of Noise sampled and suckled on global beat. Global beat was a musical ideology that allowed 'nature' to be appropriated and reconstructed as a mirror of, and for, 'culture', with immeasurably varied levels of sophistication. Non-music, or ambient noise such as whale and forest sounds, was curiously juxtaposed with classical and world musics, principally Gregorian, Celtic, African and Bulgarian song. In the hands of primitivist acts such as Enya, all samples became ambient in the sense that they could be commercially ascribed to fashionable neocolonial and psycho-theological notions of the vernacular, the pastoral and the Edenic. As a vague audio representation of the global eco-politics, ambient music gained an authoritative hold amongst anyone who wanted to buy into New Age. Ambient was a polite, well-dressed native who might go unnoticed. It was therapeutic, domesticated and at peace with its surroundings, and hence a favourite of anyone who wanted to present themselves as 'political, but not in a barricades sense'. Ambient, in this sense, was a representation of politics, the simultaneous manifestation and exploitation of a burgeoning green economic sector. It was made for the '90s, a decade in which people increasingly expressed their political beliefs through what they consumed while concurrently being uncomfortable with consumerism.

As a form of politics by osmosis, ambient offered a paradoxical solution to this dilemma – the solution being a denial of closure. At its best, this was manifested in the infinite run-on groove of Aphex Twin's 'We Are the Music Makers' (1991) and the concrete pastoralism of his *Richard D. James Album* (1996). However, since it produced few memorable commercial singles, the legacy of ambient primitivism tended to be a futile search for the sublime, a road to nowhere that can never be exhausted by the market. The evocation of the authority of nature, found in lacklustre '90s chill-out techno, eternally reverberates in today's TV ads for nostalgic ambient CD compilations (and ubiquitous organic products). Nocturnal '90s Westerners sought supplementary 'nature', but they wanted it in the right place at the right time, preferably electronically generated in the back room of a sweaty industrial club. Now they can bung it on the Bang & Olufsen and align chakras at home. This is befitting of the duplicitous and incongruous politics of the rave movement in the early-'90s. Deeply narcissistic yet supposedly eco-friendly, demanding, like a subfusc Situationist, the right to party before the right to work, the passive nihilism of ambient techno is one source of our current ambient polity.

In the '90s, this particular brand of ambient practice coexisted with more comprehensive critiques of the environment that drew on rearticulations of spatial and temporal meaning found in postmodern critical social theory, anthropology and geography. These critiques drew attention to the ways in which environments are engendered, empowered and contested by subtle and palpable means. The intimacies of postmodern geographies, explored by figures such as Marc Augé, Anthony Vidler, Doreen Massey and Edward Soja, built upon earlier ambient texts such as Gaston Bachelard's *The Poetics of Space* (1969), Robert Harbison's *Eccentric Spaces* (1977) and Jacques Attali's *Noise: the Political Economy of Music* (1977). Augé's *Non-Places: An Introduction to the Anthropology of Supermodernity* (1990), quickly became the *Music for Airports* of the '90s. The main stumbling block for '90s artists concerned with intangible social spaces, sonic fly-posting and geopolitical contexts seems to be that too much capital was made in the '80s of the ambient arena of social theory by the neo-avant-garde, artists who had culturally bowdlerised and exemplified postmodernisms to death. Artists such as Barbara Kruger and Krzysztof Wodiczko had carefully fostered ethical engagement with the built environment, considering the city as a stage and script. Nevertheless, such artists lacked an important element of the '90s ambient aesthetic; morphologically, they tended to bellow rather than emphasise the timbrel virtues of the voice. Their well-manicured, big-budget, spectacular political art retained fewer supporters in the '90s, when Situationist writings found new audiences. Nineties artists could not naïvely seek to recover Situationist metaphysics, nor did they wish to be regarded as the inheritors of the 'genuine' political avant-garde; rather, they sought provisional respite from critical postmodernism's epistemological hole (the liar's paradox) and its exasperating moral courteousness.

Nineties artists re-examined ambient critiques of spatial temporality, remodelling maps and re-exploring 'alternative' psychologies of space from a perspective that was politically detached yet aesthetically absorbed by late avant-garde tactics. The Situationist industry of the late-'90s belatedly academicised and commercialised the anticipation and zeal that accompanied the rediscovery of (well-worn) counter-cultural tactics practiced by hooligan politicos in the late-'60s and early-'70s. Nevertheless, for a short time, replicating these strategies as style had its benefits, chiefly helping to mitigate (rather than repudiate) the stifling theoretical injunctions of critical postmodernism in favour of more playful and subtle approaches aimed at non-specialist audiences. Artist, Shepard Fairey, who began his viral 'Obey' giant propaganda in Rhode Island in 1989 as 'an experiment in phenomenology', now has volunteer operatives bombing around the globe, manufacturing dissent by generating desire for a product (the late wrestler Andre the Giant) that does not exist. In Glasgow, during its stint as Capital of Culture in 1990, such ambient approaches were particularly attractive to artists, such as Ross Sinclair, David Shrigley and Jonathan Monk, who spent that year re-narrating the city as an architectural uncanny, *détourning* posters (Monk's *Cancelled*) and transforming derelict public toilets into bars (Shrigley's *The Ship*). Given that it was produced during an economic recession, this ambiart had to differ from that produced by artists such as Kruger and Wodiczko; it was very cheap, simple (much of it was spontaneous), and effective (it spread by word of mouth). Crucially, given its lack of closure, such work was, like the run-on grooves of ambient techno, ethically nonchalant. At that cultural moment, it did not matter if artists produced such stunts, nor did it matter if anyone ever saw them; they were whispering campaigns with nothing to promote and nothing to lose. Unlike later ambient practices by their contemporaries – such as Adam Chodzko's *God Look Alike Contest* (1992–3) and Mark Wallinger's *A Real Work of Art* (1994) – this group of artists received no official art world acclaim for their quintessentially timbrel poeticisation of space.

In the '90s, postmodernist ideas of interrupting the equilibrium and continuity of temporal space by exploring ambient strategies were gradually disassociated from their traditional strongholds of academia, architecture and art. This gave certain sectors of ambient a renewed sense of energy and vigour and the political determination for action. Ambient politics were most tenaciously evident in the culture jamming of pop bands such as the Kopyright Liberation Front and Negativland, groups who did see themselves as inheritors of post-Situationist avant-gardism. KLF's *White Room* (1991) exploited the demand for chill out primitivist ambience to fund their inimitable anti-art agenda – a vitalising blend of hacking, pranks, plagiarism, disinformation, forgeries, nonsense, poetic terrorism, psuedoscience and sabotage. Internationally, self-trained culture jammers were quick to embrace virtual spaces and new media as globalised, level playing fields. Nevertheless, much jambient took place in the built environment as witty direct actions, and frequently exhibited ecological concerns. Vancouver Sodders, for example, rented out busy city car parking spaces for sunbathing on deckchairs.

In the '90s, billboard liberation projects, popular since the late-'70s, were corporatised by organisations such as Adbusters, who attempted to bankroll dissent. Conceptually and economically, Adbusters' glossy, anti-corporate corporate strategy was perfect for the '90s in the way that it presented opposition as both legitimate and aspirational. Many of its campaigns focused on global corporations that produced unhealthy products, such as fast food, tobacco and alcohol ('Absolut Nonsense'), or had bad employment rights records. Subvertisements such as 'Buy Nothing Day' and 'Turn off TV' were sanctimonious enough to appeal to the paternalism of liberal and puritan Americans alike, providing a privately financed, simulacral welfare state. Fighting fire with fire (a tactic exhausted by pop Situationists such as Malcolm McLaren in the early-'80s), Adbusters embodied the oxymoronic politics of ambient as much as Benetton's *Colors* magazine or Naomi Klein's *No Logo* – instrumentalist charity remixed.

The avant-garde ambientertainment pioneered by groups such as the KLF, meanwhile, gained momentum among media terrorists, such as Chris Morris, who took jamming to mass audiences in the UK with self-reflexive TV news spoofs, *The Day Today* (1994) and *Brass Eye* (1997). Morris satirised the consequentialism of '90s anti-corporate corporatism by fusing the concerns of ambient music and guerrilla politics to the point where both collapsed into style. The 'Animals' episode of *Brass Eye* negated '90s negation, giving the animal rights movement (or rather its representations) the same treatment as third-rate celebrities and lacklustre politicians. Morris' return to radio to produce the Radio One programme, *Blue Jam* (1998–9), marked a fitting epitaph to the decade. The programme impeccably travestied the ambient musical genre, mixing smooth jazz loops, ambient groove, trance, trip-hop, drum'n'bass, rock, techno, pop, dub and funk – overlaying them with the avant-argots of a dark comic mind.

By the mid-'90s, ambient was big business in both political and leisure terms. As business clients became increasingly worried about cost-effectiveness during the economic recession of the early-'90s, the latter half of the decade saw ambient forms of jamming become increasingly common in European advertising, mirroring the impact of the recession on artists working in the built environment. In Britain, ambient advertising, a fledgling sector in 1995 worth

£10 million, is expected to be worth £110 million by the end of 2002. Ambient strategies have varied enormously, ranging from guerrilla marketing stunts, viral emails and fly posting to targeted text messaging. Environmental art has been heavily sourced by guerrilla stunt-driven outfits such as Cunning Stunts, who famously projected naked TV presenter Gail Porter onto the Houses of Parliament to publicise men's magazine *FHM*. *The Independent* followed, creating its own news by projecting 'To Let' onto Parliament during the 1997 general election. Wodiczko's favoured form of intervention has long been used by culture jammers such as comedian Mark Thomas (who projected 007 onto the MI6 building in London). Due to the popularity of this tactic amongst ambient advertisers, this has since been made an offence (but commercial pranksters simply add the fines to their fees). Glocal community action has been exploited, and parodied, by groups such as Diabolical Liberties, who last year were responsible for the viral 'Save Our Local Takeaways' campaign fronted by former World's Strongest Man, Geoff Capes. Numerous chippies and kebab houses, as well as BBC Radio 4, *Loaded* and the local press, were scammed into promoting Snack Stop instant noodles, a new product from powdered baby milk connoisseurs, Nestlé. Jamming-style ad pranksters seek radical chic to attract further publicity; no product is taboo, no space secure from reification. This March, Acclaim Entertainment promoted the launch of *Shadowman 2* on PlayStation 2 by inviting bereaved relatives to allow ad placements on relatives' gravestones.

Toward the end of the '90s, commercials appeared practically everywhere, from gas silos and shaved heads to shroud wraps on scaffolding. Public spaces were highly sought after by ambient media groups who maintained the sites and sold site-specific solutions to their growing list of clients. In Britain, spaces were practically monopolised on petrol pumps (Alvern Forecourt Media), on sandwich bags and takeaway containers (Bag Media), on over 10 billion bus and train tickets (Ticketmedia and Madmedia's Radion scented bus tickets), toilets (CPA Washroom Advertising and Captive View's sensor equipped 'Viewrinals'), changing rooms (Fitting Exposure), free postcards (Boomerang Media), phone boxes (Phonesites), Vespas (SkootMedia), shopping trolleys (The Media Vehicle), milk bottles (Milk Media), the bottom of beer glasses (PintAds), dining tables (Tablemedia), park benches (Benchmark), the floors of car parks and train stations (Face-IT Media) and on plasma screens installed inside buses (Media Initiatives). Such ambient marketing sought to circumvent the brand-saturated world by increasingly targeting fragmented audiences directly. In the UK, In Your Space placed airline adverts on trucks travelling along congested motorways, and FCA wrote ads for holidays in Wales into the grime of white vans stuck in London commuter traffic. Captive and gender-specific spaces – such as toilets, changing rooms and particularly bars – appealed to clients interested in targeting customers when they are most susceptible to suggestion, such as when they are already consuming or when they're drunk. Science fiction currently plays a key role, with many ambicommerce strategists pre-empting dystopian fictions such as Steven Spielberg's *Minority Report. Blade Runner*-esque images can be projected into the air by a 3D imager developed by the Media Vehicle. Borrowing an idea from Ray Bradbury's *Fahrenheit 451*, Metrocom are currently preparing to run commercials inside dark London Underground tunnels, mounting light boxes onto the tunnel wall to produce flick-book style moving pictures.

The resources available to such organisations outstrip those available to the growing numbers seeking to reclaim public space from private hands. The will to regain the public canvas from ambient interlopers is not supported by the Third Way; rather, it is actively discouraged by PPP schemes. Politically, economically and organisationally, ambicommerce is seeking to gain the upper hand. To increase their list of blue-chip clients and to fend off growing complaints from the Advertising Standards Authority, four British companies within the sector have sought to regulate themselves, breaking from the Outdoor Advertising Association to form The Out of Home Media Association in May. A common code of practice for the ambient industry will not restrain rebel ambient companies which know that cheap, inventive guerrilla marketing will always be desirable. Ambient brandalism may be the new spam that jammers seek to police, but ambient creatives are well aware of the opposition's tactics, since what they practice is a logical outcome of edit culture and its critique. In addition to financial restraints, the ambient commercial proliferation opposed by jammers was spawned by an astute awareness of space created by young graduates' knowledge of postmodern geographies and semiotic critiques of advertising. Semiotic Solutions' disdain for market research in favour of semiotic analysis seems to confirm that ambient is a cultural Möbius strip. Ambient is lean-burning and sustainable; it will expand exponentially with its own critique.

Countdown to Zero, Count up to Now

The Artist Placement Group Interviewed by Josephine Berry and Pauline van Mourik Broekman

Vol 1 #25, Winter 2002

Josephine Berry: Could you describe the cultural context in which APG and its thinking came about?

John Latham: It's a quite complicated beginning. I was teaching at St. Martin's, and Barbara came up with this idea: Why don't we go into the factories? These were no-go areas at that moment – and I think she had contact with the Fluxus group. There were high tensions in the art world about having anything to do with organisations of the industrial-commercial kind. They wanted to use art as something prestigious.

Barbara Steveni: Might I come in there? John was in America at the time, and the Fluxus group came to stay in our house and they were going to do an exhibition in, I think it was called Gallery One – they wanted some material. And I said, I'll go to the outer circular road, to the industrial estate, and I'll pick up some material. So I went there, and I got lost in the industrial estate, and it was dead of night, but the factory was absolutely booming away, and I thought, 'Well, why aren't we here? Not to pick up buckets of plastic, but because there's a whole life that we don't touch. This is what people go on about – academics, artists, politicians – but they go nowhere near it.' That was where the idea got born, and, when John came back, I told him about it.

At that time, artist types like Stuart and Deborah Brisley, John, myself and others were doing events and happenings in the street – like Peter Kuttner's *Nodnol Lives*. Very much out of the gallery and into the street. Looking at a reaction against the object and its value for the market – so that was the sort of context out of which it came. As John was saying, the whole idea of fine artists having anything to do with commerce and stuff was, like, real dirty. But the idea of context, 'Context is Half the Work', which John coined, developed into a main APG/O+I axiom [APG became Organisation and Imagaination (O+I) in 1989] through to today, developed as a result of making approaches to industry.

JB: Were you interested in Russian Constructivism as an example of artists going into industrial situations and contexts? Was that known about in London at that time?

BS: It was known about, and especially John was much more into art history. I was into life experience. In fact, I had no schooling.

JL: At that time, I was oblivious of art history. I just did what I'd been touched off by as an art experience. It was like seeing something so intensely moving that I had to understand it. And I didn't bother about the art history. When people talked about Picasso I said, 'Well who's he?'

BS: And I became very interested, when going into the factories, in the social role of the people, the individuals in there and how they were connecting up to what they were doing. And what was it that the organisation was doing that they were in. And all that developed out of a real interest and questioning, which I guess now would be called research. I think they thought I was a sociologist since I'd remarked at British Leyland, for example, on the fact that women worked only in the trimming shops, but they couldn't be found in other parts of the factory. So my interest was in the role and the purpose of individuals, and their relation to the wider unit beyond, and John's was in what the language was doing.

JB: Was meshing your quite different sensibilities around APG a fairly natural progression? You're saying that you had this more hands-on, sociological approach, and John was interested in, you might say, more esoteric areas of physics and language.

JL: I want to answer that one. I was a brush painter, gone into what it was I'd been hit by. As a brush painter, it was a completely irrelevant thing to do to think about having anything to do with anything else, really. It was a closed little research establishment to put it in a friendly way – or a waste of time, to put it in another. But I met two scientists, C.C.L. Gregory and Anita Kohsen, who were crossing their disciplines, and who were very dedicated to finding what the difference was between physical and human animal behaviour. Now they'd gone into partnership and we got an introduction to meet them because they lived in the neighbourhood, and, as time went on, they suddenly paid a visit, and the professor of astronomy said, 'Would you like to do a mural for a party we're giving on Halloween night?' Now I've told this story before, but the long and the short of it is that I discovered that a spray gun is a very meaningful instrument for getting over what had happened in painting – which was a countdown to zero. A countdown to zero starts from complete confidence in spatial appearances and in the skill that you've got in the mid 19th century, say with Delacroix, to a complete rejection of the idea that the spatial appearance of the world is anything but an illusion. That life is an illusion. And it was emphasised by the discoveries from Max Planck in 1900, who came up with the idea of the discrete bit, that everything was made up of discrete events, basically. And you don't find an interval between the discrete events. And this was very important because scientists can't talk about event structure. Physicists refer to waves and particles in space-time.

Pauline van Mourik Broekman: And how did this relate to the spray gun?

JL: This is accounting for it after the event. There had been a blank, unmarked canvas exhibited as a work and what that meant was that all art is on a par with no action. That was a very high powered, challenging statement.

JB: Was that Rauschenberg?

JL: Yes. Well, he worked a lot with Cage, and Cage may have been responsible for the idea in the beginning – a zero sound concert – the same kind of thing.

But what was important was the blank white board, and taking the spray gun to register a history on it with discrete marks of an accretive process that had permanence. Once a point mark has gone down, it doesn't disappear. And an inference that I drew later on was that this is an insistently recurrent event that makes it seem permanent. And an insistently recurrent event is like a quantum unit of light: it doesn't have an interval between its discrete bits. I think you'll come to see that this is very important: What we regard as time is counting. Counting via caesium atoms, clocks, days, years. And very high frequencies in the Planck world give us new techniques. It goes down to something really beyond what we can either repeat or imagine. An initial Insistently Recurrent Event (IRE) is an oscillation between nothing – the blank canvas – and a point mark, and it translates as a proto-event universe.

JB: If you extrapolate from that, does that oscillation suggest the ever present and explosive possibility of transformation? If reality has to reaffirm itself in this insistently recurrent way, is that an instability?

JL: The most logical series is what I'm really talking about. What we have to do is get past this idea of the Big Bang having started out of nothing. Physics has come to a point where it's very practical. You can find out what happens with most things. But it's got a problem, which Stephen Hawking refers to about once every ten years. And that is an admission that – and he said it in so many words – we don't know where to begin. At one time it was, 'If we haven't solved it by the end of the century, we won't know where to begin.' And, at the end of the century, he said on CNN, 'Let the 20 years start now.' It was the admission that it's too big a problem and we don't know where to begin.

Well, the arts had proposed not that the world starts with a bang but that it starts from a prehistory of an event structure which has a non-extended starting line, equivalent to the score in music – that's to say, not heard as sound. A non-extended state doesn't show up in physics, it's not allowed. What you do find though, and one of the ideas that compensates for it, is called a vacuum. Now, vacuum is a spatial word; you can't have vacuum in no space, or it's a nonsense to talk about it. But they can talk about it happily because there's a quantum vacuum, which means the non-space in between the two extended states which form the positive side of the wave. The vacuum is a state nought – very easy to translate into artists' terms. If you go into the structure of a concert, you experience a clock time duration; a thing starts with a waving of a stick, say, and ends with another waving of a stick. This is in 'count' time, say, in the minutes between the start and the finish. The performance is an ordering of time-bases or frequencies, rhythms and pause lengths. With the score aspect of time, these make up the three components of three-dimensional time, which now constitute the dynamics of a musical performance. So there you've got a score which is timeless apparently, but it has such control over what goes on in time that you have an equivalent there for an atemporal, omnipresent coding. It's not a coding so much as a matrix of previous experience.

JB: Is that the Least Event for you?

JL: Can I say yes? The Least Event, in music, you could understand as somebody recognising that a sound was interesting and feeling the do-it-again impulse. The do-it-again impulse is equivalent to saying insistently recurrent. Those two ideas belong together, because what then happens is we'll do it again and then we'll do it differently. And if you can think of a proto-event, a universe in a state where there isn't anything, a total zero extension in space and time, if you can imagine that series in a non-extended context, and it then becomes a habit within that non-extended state, you find that there are performances which are enactments from a score which grow in complexity all the time.

Well, the event-structured world is what the artist naturally works in. We work in it, deriding all the common sense objections and adulations and all the blah-blahs that come in from the outside and which are totally irrelevant to what goes on that's exciting to do, say, on a wall. It's that interest, that kind of impulse which is important because it reveals the actual universe to people who are totally blown by the fact that, to quote Stephen Hawking, we don't know where to begin. They all seem to know what they ought to do next because they have a medium for how to exchange value. And it's flawed just the same as the verbal medium.

JB: You mean money?

JL: Language and money together.

PvMB: Sticking with the cultural context of the '60s, if you were engaged with this critique of objects and their role as vehicles of value in the art system, how did your critique of language relate to the fact that a lot of other artists were using language precisely as an agent of dematerialisation, as a questioning, philosophical method – all of which they thought could challenge the same system of value, objects and spatial relations?

JL: I think what was intensely interesting in the history of ideas is that people always thought in a dualistic way. They've always thought that things are things, but we are not things. We are inhabited by mysterious forces. The most recent quotee is Descartes, who set philosophy on the course of two worlds. There came a point in the early 20th century, in Cambridge, where you found Bertrand Russell cooperating in mathematical philosophy. And he got a communication from Vienna, from Wittgenstein, who as a young punter had said, 'How about this, is this any use, or is it total nonsense?' And Russell wrote back and said, 'No it's wonderful, come over and talk to us about it.' And the nugget of what Wittgenstein was on about was that they would talk through and discover an atomic proposition or perhaps a set of atomic propositions, which are basic and indestructible.

JB: For language you mean?

JL: For language and logic. It's an attempt to systematise language logic. If we actually go into what then happened – 1912, I think, was the initial date in a period where the idea of the *Tractatus* was being written – he argued the case of the atomic propositions and it got published at the end of World War I. Wittgenstein had to go and fight in the Austrian army. He then returned to Cambridge and found that he didn't get on with anybody except the economist Keynes. That was his last sort of friend there, and he disappeared to Norway and places. He was thoroughly frustrated when things didn't work for the atomic propositions.

Well, 1951 is the date that I quote, anyway, of the Cage and Rauschenberg zero action works. It's also the date of the posthumous publication of Wittgenstein's *Philosophical Investigations*, which says, at the beginning, that the idea of the atomic propositions must have been mistaken. I'll now go over the bits and bits, sorting out what we mean by and what are useful types of expression. And he's famous for the second. But he's famous for starting a movement in philosophy which then went into its opposite, into reverse. He was the trigger for a big effort to get, even with what physics had found out, at the indestructible basic unit which is still not there. It wasn't identified. We're still looking for a particle, still spending billions of pounds in crashing one particle against another in these circuits, looking for an initiating particle or state.

Well, the point for us is that, if you think in terms of event, you don't go into all that language and all those heavy equations about the behaviour of matter because we've found forms for visualising the event structure. It's represented on the back of my *Time-Base Roller* as a memory, like a piece of music, which has got all music behind it so it can go as far back as a proto-Universe, whereas one bit of an extended state has neither location nor interval. Two Least extended states together set up what we call time, the initial kind of extendedness. We then go to scientific people and they tend to say, 'Well, you've got to actually describe what space is,' and we talked to someone who was interested in the idea and he said, 'Well, you've got to account for space somehow.' And I had this argument out with David Park, a professor of astronomy or astrophysics. Anyway, he was in the Williamstown USA Observatory. He had written a paper called 'Are Space and Time Necessary?' and it turned up mysteriously on my desk and I was amazed, so I read it. And 'necessary' meant, in a philosophical sense, do we need to talk about them, are they structural?

JB: Good question.

JL: I wrote to him, saying, 'I've got this paper of yours and I'm sending you a photograph of the Roller that had been in the Tate.' The Tate hadn't bought it, but it got shown and photographed, so I could send him a good photograph. He wrote back saying, 'This is really extraordinary, I had no idea that an artist might be interested in what we're interested in.' And a certain amount of dialogue came about, and I said, 'Why is it that you physicists don't regard the event as parent of the particle?' The answer I got was, 'In principle, you're probably right, but, in all our equations, we have gravity; gravity occurs in all our mathematics, and we can't get gravity into events.' Now, in my forms, gravity shows up as the 'coming to an end' of a score being played out. The internal dynamic on the gravity scale is that all events tend to coincide at a zero or dimensionless point. In General Relativity, density of matter in space finally translates from zero space, zero time, infinite temperature into an infinitely rich score somewhere, like in a drawer.

JB: Could we make a transition to art more directly? You say that the '50s was a zero point in art – a kind of compression of all of art history into a non-gesture. I'm interested in how you see the conceptual artists' interest in language, a decade on from that point, in which they were trying to escape from the finality of the object. Was that a zero point in itself?

JL: Short answer is, no.

JB: Why not?

JL: The date of the spray gun paintings might have coincided with a lot of other activity. Obviously it did. See, the difference is between a mark that goes across the surface and one which hits it vertically as a point. The point mark is an extension of the zero action works and blows in a new question as to nature's tabula rasa, a non-extended state as active where the received idea is that any 'nothing' state has to be passive. Newton's claim *Ex nihilo nihil fit* is flawed. The answer to your question is that the zero point is not just neutrally zero in meaning. It is that a non-extended, but omnipresent, score is inherited from long generations of this universe and begins from an active component in the zero which corresponds to many parts of the culture, including both sciences and faiths.

For me personally, conceptual artists and their language-based solutions were chasing the wrong hare. And the real one was the problem that Wittgenstein had come across, and that philosophy had come across – that language was a flawed medium. It didn't do what it set out to do in the most serious instances. So, what had been known for all the previous centuries – the belief systems and sacred texts which had come out from the prophets – had all recognised not to try and be logical; take it from the inspired source.

JB: How did these ideas connect to your preoccupation with artists doing placements, and an engagement particularly with the state and industry? And why were you led to engage with the establishment as a means of siting art in a more socially engaged context, rather than creating something like an alternative space of action?

BS: I think that it was very exciting to come across contexts – I'm answering this instinctively now – which were very heavily peopled and very full with material, with ongoing processes and unfamiliar activities: a context which had great extensions out and which seemed to be touching possibilities which artists were only trivially touching before. They were very conditioned by, say, promotional desires like Pirelli's desk diaries, etc. The idea that there might be another role within these contexts which obviously have a vast influence on our lives made it seem intriguing in juxtaposition with the way we were coming out of the gallery, and those types of things. Also, the media at the time was expanding into new forms – sculpture became inflatable, video was coming up, film and performance. So it seemed like a heavily interesting context to engage with, and the idea that one might change what the engagement would be in those contexts and could then filter through into the society differently was instinctively felt, at the time, as being a very exciting thing to do. Where else might one go? Didn't think so much of setting up an alternative. That wasn't nearly so interesting as what one had stumbled into – this was an alternative. And the possibility that one could stumble into it, and that one could actually have some effect, change things – in both directions – sounds so hideously idealistic... It's a bit like, 'You can never change anybody, least of all your parents.'

JB: But it felt at the time that there was leeway for change?

BS: Yes, absolutely. When we had our first presentation as APG, the Industrial Negative Symposium which brought artists and industrialists together for the first time down at the Mermaid Theatre, and the Event Structure Research Group, Jeffrey Shaw, one of APG's founding artists, and Theo Botschuiver came over from Holland, Billy Klüver (really shocking speaker) – anyway, it had a lot of press. I remember the speaker from Esso petroleum saying, 'I'm glad to see that APG is not asking for support, but to make a contribution.' And, at another point, Gustav Metzger got up and said, 'I want to burn down your factories,' and the British Oxygen guy walked out...

I do feel that we were virtually responsible for opening up these 'new horizons', or this can of worms, that led to all this institutionalisation, both by government departments and corporations, of how the artist might be 'used'. It was the hijack of what we did as artists by the Arts Council that made it a can of worms. At that time, the context was very exciting and shifting for both sides. It was only by doing the industrial placements that we began to find out how art activity, or how as artists, an optimum association might be developed which complied with making an artwork in these contexts – so that both sides were getting something out of it. So, after the industrial placements, which were seen as kind of terrible by the majority of the art world for tangling with this 'dirt' so to speak, I was personally, and artists that we worked with, able to find out just what sort of exchange and engagement could be had in these situations. What we discovered was that we have to take great care to preserve the integrity of art's motivation *vis-à-vis* the commercial and political interests around. That's what the Incidental Person, or artist's, presence is there to contend with and to insist on. But I think it might have opened up a can or worms which is taking it in this institutionalised direction now.

PvMB: But don't you think this can of worms was the precise same thing that gave you a sense of excitement? Was that engagement with what you call more 'peopled' environments to do with their magnitude, their existing power? Did you think that, if you intervened in these places, you could adopt their existing power rather than seeking it in alternative communities?

BS: Well yes! I realise that this is a very hot question, and it demands a very hot answer. I know this question is levelled all the time, and it's a main focus for me right now in today's global 'money-worshipping societies', and I don't have an immediate soundbite.

JL: The difference between the industrial and the governmental department placements was where the interests lay. If the artists went into the sectional interests, the establishment, they were walking into a fireball. The chances are that it would make more trouble. But the non-sectional interests that a government department has are different; certainly in Britain, the civil service is supposed to be serving the people. It is an institutionalised body that tries to get the elected government to do certain things, but it's always seeking more info from our side. When we got to the civil service, we were under investigation by the research department, Whitehall's research station.

BS: I slightly disagree with what John said about industry, because I was seeing it – as I think were the artists who we were working with – as an engagement we had with individuals and a very important learning process; an exchange with large chunks of society that we'd had no engagement with. I still think of it as a conglomerate of individuals whose activities were impacting on society. And I think a lot was learnt about exchange and stuff. And yes, we went to government, which appeared to have less sectional interests at the time. In the language of today, they were also trying to manage change. At the time, the thinking might have been, 'We've got to have these outsiders in here to think differently.' We were the outsiders.

JB: Do you think that an understanding of an organisation as a conglomeration of individuals and activities also made you believe that if you could influence key individuals, you could influence an entire system in a certain way?

BS: I think that was rather a naïve motivation, but it did feel that that was happening. Especially when the guy from ICI left and became, as he put it, 'APG's first dropout' from the company. It brought up the whole question of success and failure again – for whom, the organisation, society, the artist? It was to do with the fact that here was a context previously untouched by the art process which appeared now to change – a shift in the mindset perhaps – however naïve it was. I still think that you do have to engage with all the forces that are powerful, in different ways, and that one is also powerful as an individual, that ideas are powerful. You had to get your hands dirty, and I still think you have to get your hands dirty. I think it's about responsibility.

JB: So what do you think about class interests and solidarity, then? How does an individual artist go into an industrial situation in which you have class conflict, a conflict of power between workers and capitalists, between workers and management, and operate between those two 'groups'?

BS: Well, very delicately, and ready to be spat out on all occasions. And that was one of the things that we tried to set up. How far could one go without being spat out? And, again, what would be a relevant activity. What is coming up enormously now is the question of 'socially engaged art'. What the hell is that? And how is the aesthetic talking, the actual power of the aesthetic, or the power of the process of engagement. This is being found out and demonstrated through the whole explosion of 'artists in residence' that is coming out of our ears now. But I haven't quite answered your class thing. I had a personal thing which was that, although I was obviously a nice middle class girl and everything, not going to school, I didn't have an identification like that. They were all people to me and I automatically asked the question at all moments. I was responsible for being me.

PvMB: Do you mean that, not having had an education, you didn't feel socially situated in a way?

BS: Yes, certainly, I've never felt socially situated. Because I wasn't brought up by my parents. I didn't go to school. Anyhow, APG and I have been very heavily attacked for going in there very naïvely and not thinking, not dealing with class. But the point is that I think that artists have a responsibility to the impact of their insights when in these various engagements – as did APG input.

PvMB: Why was the self-consistency of APG's identity, one might say the preservation of its unique identity, so important to affecting the wider aim of transforming the social role of the artist?

BS: Part of maintaining the uniqueness of APG/O+I is, perhaps, the opaqueness of its terminology – for instance, the 'Incidental Person'. The Incidental Person was a useful way of describing a new socially engaged artist, or a new socially engaged role for a person that has come from the art trajectory, that John dreamed up to distinguish it from the word 'artist' that we had to get away from because of all its baggage. (Incidentally, for the Industrial Negative Symposium, Stuart and John jointly wrote a paper on the disappearance of the artist). So, I feel that, in relation to your question about uniqueness, that terminology was very useful to begin to define a new role which had come out of first working in industry and then government. The term was linked to the methodology we tried to develop in order to gain the maximum possibilities for exchange and development and new ideas. You also asked whether our idea could to be taken on by anybody else. Yes, certainly – using the Incidental Person was, and is, a good way of identifying a change of role for the artist. So, I guess the term stands historically along with its method of engagement for those with the understanding to 'use' it.

JL: It is important to note that you could actually tangle with the money. The Incidental Person, and O+I's possessiveness, has to do with the responsibility one has to host bodies. Supposing that we got to the Department of Education, or whatever, if we gave them something really hot and they took it up, we wouldn't let them simply say they invented it. We wanted – and I put it down in *The Report of a Surveyor* – a way of assessing what the contribution was after a placement, after an association. Any good results needed insisting on. What has happened is that the Arts Council is composed of people who are supposed to maintain the status quo. And it's a total disaster because it means no artist is actively allowed in there. As Donald Macrae apparently said, 'Only the established may innovate. No innovator is established.' Basil Bernstein quotes it in his book.

JB: Was it also ever your intention to introduce really, truly incidental people into these positions? Without the qualification of the art academy and so on?

BS: Absolutely. It was to try and develop a completely new role, and therefore ask how it comes up through education. One of the things we are trying to do, possibly, with the London Institute is to see how the experience can be taken into education, how it can be taken on in a range of areas. This is a different role.

JL: As a self-funding body, O+I has got to be responsible for turning out the goods, and arguing the goods, against the opposition. So Incidental Persons as participants need to be well enough informed to cope with the job. Now, if they're not trained in art, they would be liable to be tripped up. That said, the empowerment which it ought to give to everybody is where anyone can come across very good insights. The most unexpected insights can come to the most improbable people, and, instead of being dismissed as being too improbable to talk to, as one is by the local bureaucracy or the arts bureaucracy, that should effect something like what Joseph Beuys was doing in his way. Joseph said that the Incidental Person is a YES solution.

JB: In effect, you might argue that today, in what is called the knowledge economy, or within creative industries, what is being assimilated into production is precisely the creative impulse, the virtuosity, the psychic or social experience that might previously have been left out of industrial technique. In a sense, you could argue that everyone has become an Incidental Person within the knowledge economy – at least potentially – but in the most debased way. But do you also see something hopeful in that condition in which administration and production now assimilate precisely the kind of imaginative, creative impulses that they formerly excluded?

BS: Well, yes, but it's being taken in this most appalling direction, where it's the money that determines things.

PvMB: In a funny way, maybe it brings up language and the event again? If we're saying what's being imported are language elements, or art-like language, to stimulate innovation, creativity, change, etc, maybe language can have a positive role if we insist on its greater precision. Specificity could be used to combat the lazy blurring of definitions of artistic activity and commercial production, and instead be made to really describe, not obscure, what people do.

BS: That's exactly what has to be done.

PvMB: Digital culture is suffused with the rhetoric of dematerialisation, time-based processes, social collaboration, interactivity and collective authorship – do you feel any affinity with it?

JL: Not if it reasserts the space-based mindset. Collaboration is not one of the words we would be defined by.

BS: Oh?! But social collaboration has to be something I personally believe in for O+I, provided it can be heard above the rhetoric and not commodified by digital culture.

JL: This issue is around (failed) space-based belief systems and a Time-and-Event means of representing the real world. The event-structured media are inclusive where the space-based are divisive.

London, 2002

Learning the Right Lessons

David Garcia

Metamute.org, January 2006

In 2005, the London-based artist/activist outfit, C6, published *DiY Survival*, a short book to coincide with their show, Sold Out.[1] In the intro, C6 declare their aim to 'produce a guide of tactical means for collective art making'. The result is an amalgam of bits and pieces, ranging from the serious and helpful through to the self-mocking and frankly trite. This material has been helpfully divided into three sections: DIY Theory, DIY How To and, finally, DIY Case Studies. Part of the book's patchiness might be the result of a decision to minimise editorial intervention. Whether there was any selection is not quite clear. The intro tells us that the contents are the result of an open call put out to a number of sympathetic internet mailing lists, but it is unclear whether there was any further editorial selection or intervention. We are simply told that they were 'immersed in a flood of responses' and 'decided that their task was to let chance take over'.

It is clear, from the outset, that this book addresses the area of practice which, a decade ago, some of us dubbed 'tactical media' – although C6 wisely avoid a term that has already become quasi-institutionalised. Nevertheless, most aspects of what could be described as tactical media are represented in this book.

The term was originally coined to identify and describe a movement which occupied a 'no man's land' on the borders of experimental media art, journalism and political activism, a zone that was, in part, made possible by the mass availability of a powerful and flexible new generation of media tools. This constellation of tools and disciplines was also accompanied by a distinctive set of rejections: of the positions of objectivity in journalism, of the discipline and instrumentalism in traditional political movements and, finally, of the mythic baggage and atavistic personality cults in the art world. This organised 'negativity', together with a love of fast, ephemeral, improvised collaborations, gave this culture its own distinctive spirit and style and helped to usher in new levels of unpredictability and volatility to both cultural politics and the wider media landscape. But this was long ago, and the practices have long since become a familiar part of the media diet. So the question arises as to whether or not C6's *DiY Survival* is taking us anywhere new. Whatever the answer, it should at least give us the opportunity to take stock and ask whether any parts of this kind of practice retain value or credibility in a world it helped to change.

The cover of *DiY Survival* is sharp and funny and immediately raises expectations. It is a clever simulation of an Airfix-style model-building kit,

1. Betti Marenko (Ed.), *DiY Survival*, London: C6, 2005. Available for download at http://c6.org/drupal/files/C6_DiY_Survival.pdf

featuring one of those ubiquitous plastic frames to which the components of model Apache helicopters, Sherman tanks and so forth were attached. But in this version, we find instead the miniature parts needed to construct today's media 'freedom fighter': camcorder, laptop, balaclava, graffiti spray can etc. Although the book's cover can compete for attention with anything on the magazine rack, once inside, we are transported back into a ghetto – the world of 1970s fanzines. There is even an ironic (I hope) nod to the punk godfathers of DIY culture, with endless images of safety pins appearing to hold the disparate bits of content together. Of course, it's all very knowing, displaying a desire to recuperate the fast and furious punk ethos using 21st century Print on Demand technology. The trouble is C6's *DiY Survival* suffers badly in comparison with the angry, high-octane visual flare of punk. It is not that this uniquely English sense of failure, madness and defiant hedonism has disappeared but that you'd be better off looking for it on the NeasdenControlCentre website or watching an episode of *Black Books* or even listening to Babyshambles.

But, if we are able to turn a blind eye (and it's difficult) to the style problems, there is some useful and informative stuff to be found, particularly in the DIY How To section, which includes the hacklab mini-manual for building Linux networks from cast-off terminals, and a piece with tips for creating a wireless node. But, all too often, the good stuff is undermined by cheesy, copout, self-mockery, such as the 'How to be a Citizen Reporter' photo-style guide or the risible cardboard cut out for 'Robot Buddies'. The accumulated effect does little more than suggest an enclosed micro-culture every bit as self-regarding as the white cube art it purports to undermine.

The Homeopathic Option

In the DIY Theory section, there are some valuable moments, but it would have been so much more accessible (or just readable) with a more active editorial presence. For instance, it is great to have some of the distinctive rhetorical style of Brazilian 'Midia Tactica' in Hernani Dimantas' piece 'Linkania – The Hyperconnected Multitude'. But the text's value is undermined by too many unexplained references, such as one to Globo, Brazil's near-monopolistic media giant. On the level of detail, this is a trivial complaint but, more importantly, without some clearer context, we lose a sense of the uniquely Brazilian 'cannibalistic' interpretation of media tactics.

Wisely, the book chooses to kick off with its most coherent and tightly argued essay: Marcus Verhagen's 'Of Avant Gardes and Tail Ends'. This piece is worth closer examination not least because it could be assembled into, if not exactly a DIY Survival manifesto, then at least an articulation of its core belief in art's sovereign role as subversive agent. For the most part, the text is a brief history of the gradual erosion of the avant-garde's subversive bite. Verhagen makes useful, but overly simplified, distinctions, such as his opposition between the 'critical' and the 'hermetic' avant-garde. One of his most telling points is to have identified the way in which art has relinquished any aspiration to depict utopias in anything but ironic form. 'The utopian imagery once conceived by Signac and Léger as force for social renewal', he writes, 'is now the preserve of Benetton and Disney. How often are utopian visions offered without irony in contemporary art?'

This is just one of the arguments Verhagen mobilises to insist that the critical art and media which orientate themselves to traditional fine art contexts are pointless since the real power now lies elsewhere. He describes the contemporary landscape thus: 'Hollywood film, the magazine advertisement, or hit single: these constitute a more powerful force than the concert hall or the museum, they more faithfully represent the dominant values of the day and are better suited to co-opting avant-gardist work; after all commoditisation is more effective than canonisation.'

In the last few paragraphs of the essay, Verhagen advocates deploying Fredric Jameson's 'homeopathic strategies', which seem to consist of a Foucault-like process of 'unmasking' power – a form of ideology critique carried out with images. It is hard to see how this differs from the approach which has become a familiar part of visual art's currency since the first wave of critical postmodernism of the 1970s and '80s, in which mass cultural phenomena are examined and reproduced to 'reveal their internal workings, their means and objectives'.

Verhagen goes on to claim that 'homeopathic works are more difficult for the mainstream culture to appropriate because they are already in some sense part of it'. This is all too true, but, far from representing the ultimate in subversion, such an approach results in producing mere epiphenomena of communicative capitalism not only tolerated but consumed by it with relish. It is not that cultural or information politics are not important, it is just that, outside of a broader context and strategy of meaningful confrontations, they are simply not enough.

In his final clarion call, Verhagen declares that 'the grand subversions of the nineteenth century are coming to seem almost quaint, homeopathic tactics are surely more effective'. I would argue that the direct opposite is the case. It is only when the ideology critiques of image (or code) are deployed as part of a more general strategy of direct action that things start to move. The case of the AIDS activist campaigning group ACT UP's use of visual tactics in the 1990s is a classic demonstration of how cultural politics can have real power.

Telestreets' Dilemma

The report on the Italian Telestreets movement by Slavina Feat (mysteriously placed in the DIY How To section) encapsulates the limitations of the book whilst at the same time pointing to an instructive example. The report is about the Italian micro-TV movement, Telestreets, and its sister organisation, New Global Vision, a collective of Italian hackers who have used BitTorrent to disseminate an archive of radical political video on the net whilst also helping Telestreets to distribute local content nationally.

Feat's report is another of *DiY Survival*'s missed opportunities. It goes no further than recycling the familiar Telestreets hype that has been doing the rounds for a couple of years. It fails to raise the questions that we need to ask about this movement. To begin with, what is the status of the network today? Is it growing or shrinking, or did it (as I suspect, but do not know) reach its high watermark nearly two years ago? Is Telestreets now in decline or, worse, in the process of fragmenting under the weight of its own internal contradictions? Surely, a book with a critical agenda must aspire to more than publicity puffs like this.

The Telestreets example is important because it embodies some of the starker choices for those involved in tactical media. These dilemmas were already visible in a Telestreets meeting, which took place in Senigallia in 2004. This meeting coincided with the moment that the infamous *Gasparri* law was being pushed through the Italian parliament. This law, named after the then minister of communication, allowed Berlusconi to consolidate his domination of the Italian mediascape.

Nothing defines the connection between media power and political power so well as the Berlusconi phenomenon and the passing of this bill. So, given the fact that this was a defining moment for Telestreets, the choice to hold the meeting in Senigallia, a small coastal resort, was surprising. Although there were good reasons for this choice, Franco Berardi (Bifo) led a number of dissenting voices in arguing that Telestreets had missed the boat and that they urgently needed to raise the stakes and focus their energies on mobilising resistance against the Berlusconi regime. By over-emphasising expressive, or artistic, interventions and micro-media at the expense of direct confrontation, Telestreets was slipping into irrelevance. Bifo ended his 'hair raising' speech by declaring, 'the last thing we should be doing is embracing our miserable marginality'.

The Old Split

This anecdote illuminates three interconnected tendencies that have emerged since the tactical media of the '90s. Firstly, there is a widespread rejection of the homeopathic and the micropolitical in favour of ambitions scaled-up to global proportions, coupled with a willingness to move beyond electronic and semiotic civil disobedience and to engage in direct action, to literally 'reclaim the streets'. This is almost entirely a result of the emergence of the powerful global anti-capitalist movement, which (from its perspective) has transformed tactical media into the Indymedia project. But there is also a third, less visible and more troubling, tendency – a tendency toward internal polarisation. This polarisation is based on a deep split which has opened up between many of the activists at the core of the new political movements and the artists or theorists who, whilst continuing to see themselves as radicals, retain a belief in the importance of cultural (and information) politics in any movement for social transformation. While I have little more than personal experience and anecdotal evidence to go on, it seems to me that there is a significant growth in suspicion and, frequently, outright hostility among activists over the presence of art and artists in 'the movement', particularly those whose work cannot be immediately instrumentalised by the new 'soldiers of the left'.

So, what is it that has changed since the '90s to give rise to these tendencies? To understand, we must cast our minds back to the peculiar historical conditions of that time. The early phase of tactical media re-injected a new energy into the flagging project of 'cultural politics'. It fused the radical and pragmatic info politics of the hackers with well-established practice-based critiques of representation. The resulting tactical media was also part of (and arguably compromised by) the wider internet and communications revolution of the '90s which, like the music of the 1960s, acted as a universal solvent, dissolving not only disciplinary boundaries but also the boundaries separating long-established political formations. The power some of us attributed to this new 'media politics' appeared to be borne out by the role that all forms of media seemed to have played in the collapse of the Soviet Empire. It seemed as though old-style, armed insurrection had been superseded by digital dissent and media revolutions. It was as if the Samizdat spirit, extended and intensified by the proliferation of do-it-yourself media, had rendered the centralised, statist tyrannies of the Soviet Union untenable. Some of us allowed ourselves to believe that it would only be a matter of time before the same forces would challenge our own tired and tarnished oligarchies. Furthermore, the speed and comparative bloodlessness of the Soviet collapse suggested that the transformations that were coming would not have to be achieved through violence or personal sacrifice. This would be the era of the painless 'win win' revolution in which change would occur simply through the hacker ethos of challenging the domains of forbidden knowledge. It came to be believed that top-down power had lost its edge. As late as 1999, in his Reith lecture, Anthony Giddens could still confidently assert that 'The information monopoly upon which the Soviet system was based had no future in an intrinsically open framework of global communications'.

Giddens and other Third Way social theorists were part of a wider movement that dreamed that the profound political differences dividing previous generations had been put on hold. This was made credible through the ubiquity of one of the dominant myths of the information age, a myth shared by activists and new media entrepreneurs alike – the myth that knowledge will set you free. This founding narrative of technoculture, visible from Ted Nelson's *Computer Lib* onward, recycles (in intensified form) the age-old proposition that knowledge and freedom are not only connected but may actually entail one another.

The fact that a belief in the necessary relationship between knowledge and freedom has gone largely unquestioned is based, in part, on the depth of its lineage; 'ancient stoics and most modern rationalists are at one with Christian teaching on this issue'. And 'ye shall know the truth and the truth shall make you free'. As Isaiah Berlin pointed out in 1968, 'This proposition is not self evidently true, if only on empirical grounds.' It is, he asserted, 'one of the least plausible beliefs ever entertained by profound and influential thinkers'.[2] In addition to being fallacious, the accompanying rhetoric of transparency, freedom, access, participation, and even creativity, has come to constitute the ideological foundation of 'communicative capitalism', transforming tactical media's homeopathic micropolitics into the experimental wing of the so-called creative industries and 'corroborating the temporal mode of post-Fordist capital: short-termism.'[3]

Neoliberalism's effective capture of the rhetoric of 'freedom' and 'creativity' has reopened an old faultline, which the first wave of tactical media did so much to bridge: the faultline dividing artists from political activists. The theorist and activist, Brian Holmes, described its origins as going (at least) as far back as the cultural politics of the 1960s. He describes a split 'between the traditional working-class concern for social justice and the New Left concern for individual emancipation and full recognition and expression of particular identities'. According to this account, corporate foundations and think tanks of the '80s and '90s have succeeded in inculcating market-orientated variations on earlier counter-cultural values, rendering the interventions of artists (including tactical media makers) profoundly, if unwittingly, de-politicising. Holmes goes on to describe (or assert, I am not quite sure which) a critique in which 'the narcissistic exploration of self, sexuality and identity become the leitmotif of bourgeois urban culture. Artistic freedom and artistic license have led, in effect, to the neoliberalisation of culture.'[4] The puritanical and authoritarian tone of this analysis is just a little unnerving. At the very least, this tendency could lead to a crass and oppressive philistinism and might signal far worse to come.

Bifo's plea, at the Senegallia meeting in 2004, for Telestreets (and, by extension, all artist/activists) to scale up our ambitions is increasingly being answered. There is a growing number of inspiring cases which we can point to: the Yes Men's achievement in securing global distribution in mainstream

2. Isaiah Berlin, 'From Hope and Fear Set Free', 1964. Reprinted in Isaiah Berlin, *Liberty*, Oxford: Oxford Scholarship Online Monographs, 2002, pp. 252–81.
3. Ned Rossiter and Geert Lovink, 'Dawn of the Organised Networks', http://www.nettime.org, 2005.
4. Brian Holmes, *The Scandal of the Word 'Class': A Review of David Harvey, A Brief History of Neoliberalism*, Oxford: Oxford University Press, 2005, http://www.nettime.org

cinemas, Yomango's high voltage contributions to the global protest movement and Witness.org's extensive inititiatives in which the provision of indigenous activists with DIY media for use in their campaigns is connected to the legal processes of human rights. These and many other interventions are pointing to a growing willingness to strategically globalise dissent. This process has been accompanied by an urge to relinquish the cult of 'ephemerality' – one of the shibboleths of tactical media. In place of hit-and-run guerrilla activism, the direct opposite is now required: 'duration'. It's time for longer-term commitments and deeper engagements with the people and organisations networked around contested issues.

One of the most extraordinary examples of these developments is Women on Waves, a Dutch Foundation initiated by Rebecca Gomperts, who studied medicine at the University of Amsterdam, specialising as an abortion doctor before going on to study visual arts at the Rietveld Academy and Sailing at the Enkhuizen Zeevaartschool (Nautical College). The most celebrated achievement of Women on Waves is the Abortion Boat, a large floating clinic that tactically exploits maritime law, anchoring just outside the 12-mile zones of countries where abortion is forbidden. On the Abortion Boat, women can be given information and terminations by a team of Dutch medical practitioners (including Dr. Gomperts) on Dutch 'territory'. Thus, women are actively assisted and local organisations are supported and inspired in their struggle to legalise abortion.

Along with the practical intervention of the Abortion Boat, Women on Waves also uses art and design as part of its global campaign for abortion rights. For instance, the *I had an Abortion* installation consists of vests on wire coat hangers printed with this statement in all European languages. On the website [womenonwaves.org], a diary can be found of a Brazilian woman relating her experiences of wearing one of these T-shirts. The continued validity of the modes of political address pioneered by tactical media are apparent in her account of how the message on these T-shirts was preferable to something like 'Legalise Abortion!' which might have read like earlier forms of agit-prop. These T-shirts function 'not,' she declares, 'to make myself a target. That was not the point; it was to give all those women without a face a support. As to say, don't worry, it's all right, you're all right.' This fulfils one of the prime directives of classical tactical media: unlike traditional agit-prop, it is designed to invite discourse.

The example of Women on Waves is a reminder that cultural politics, in its modern sense, was, in large part, a creation of the women's movement. Those who question its value would do well to remember that feminism also served to transform the lives and politics of many men who were taught (sometimes painfully) that they were failing to live out the democratic values they publicly espoused. The way in which 'culture' is central to feminism's demands is powerfully explored by Terry Eagleton in his valuable book, *After Theory*, which describes the centrality of 'the grammar' in which the demands of feminism were framed. 'Value, speech, image, experience and identity are here the very language of political struggle, as they are in all ethnic or sexual politics. Ways of feeling and forms of political representation are in the long run quite as crucial as child care provision or equal pay.'[5]

This expanded political language was articulated not by activists and writers alone but by many important women artists. Women artists were crucial in shifting the centre of gravity of the art world of the '60s and '70s from Greenberg's formalism to a new, expressive and subject-centred naturalism, which remains influential and important to this day. Whatever the ambiguities, impurities and problems, and there are plenty, we should not be tempted to relinquish the essential legacy of cultural politics.

DiY Survival is not alone in failing to face up to the dilemmas and choices that confront us. There is much in the realm of the activist/art scene that, like C6's book, uncritically replicates myths of the information age along with the twin obsessions of the ratings-driven news cycle – spectacle and immediacy. If C6's *DiY Survival* has achieved anything, it is a timely reminder of the need not only to move on and learn new lessons but also, crucially, to learn the right lessons.

5. Terry Eagleton, *After Theory*, London: Penguin, 2003.

Heavy Opera

Anthony Iles

Vol 2 #5, Spring/Summer 2007

A fountain of water from the river Walbrook shoots up above my head, drums are pounding, a sound system's bass rumbles. I hear cheers, but I can also hear the clatter of police shields and batons around the corner. Seven years after London's Carnival Against Capitalism, when protesters outside the LIFFE exchange broke a water mains, sending a 30-foot jet of water into the air, I am walking just half a mile north of the same spot. Now, I can hear the Thames rushing up the valley the Walbrook follows, bursting its banks, laying waste to tall glass-fronted buildings as some of the most expensive real estate in London collapses around me. I'm swept up in a sonically induced fantasy, driven by the tracks on my MP3 player. I am taking part in *And While London Burns*, an operatic guided walk written by John Jordan and James Marriott, set to music by Isa Suarez and produced by Platform, an arts, campaigning and research group committed to longer term, less partisan approaches to transforming the activities of the financial institutions and corporations with head offices in the Square Mile.[1]

John Jordan has played a role in both these participatory dramas, firstly as a member of Reclaim the Streets – one of the anti-capitalist groups that coordinated the Carnival Against Capitalism in June 1999 – and, this time around, as an artist commissioned by Platform. The walk is an attempt to dramatise the research Platform has conducted into climate change. James Marriott, its co-founder, explains, 'It's a way of dramatising and humanising these systems [the role of multinationals and financial systems in fuelling climate change]. It's over-dramatised like all opera, which is why we chose the medium.'[2]

The walk begins at One Poultry. At a Starbucks opposite the ruins of the Roman Temple of Mithras, our attention is drawn to the multinational's logo with its allusions to paganism and older gods. The audio tour's protagonist remembers that, before Starbucks went global, its logo (designed by Seattle hippy entrepreneurs after a 15th century print) bore nipples and 'a pair of provocatively spread fishtails'. The mermaid allegorises both allegiance to, and fear of, the sea. She is exotic and, like the valuable cargoes on which the City's wealth was originally founded, unattainable for those doing the shipping. The City is still resplendent with powerful iconography from the 18th and 19th centuries; pineapples and other exotic objects frequently appear as architectural ornaments advertising the City's plunder. Today, retail spaces and spaceship

1. Available for download at: http://www.andwhilelondonburns.com/download
2. Anna Minton, 'Down to a Fine Art', *The Guardian*, 10 January 2007.

architecture adorned with surveillance cameras predominate. At the Royal Exchange (now a luxury shopping mall), our protagonist remembers:

I used to work here in 1989, when it was the Futures Exchange [...] the place was a permanent carnival, traders in bright coloured jackets shouting and gesturing to each other – it couldn't be more different now.

The new City outwardly tells little about where it draws value from, and it is this occultation of money the walk confronts by whispering its secrets in your ear. As its website [www.platformlondon.org] explains: 'For over 20 years, PLATFORM has been bringing together environmentalists, artists, human rights campaigners, educationalists and community activists to create innovative projects driven by the need for social and environmental justice'.

Platform has gone some way beyond the statements required to declare oneself a corporate entity in the art world. Operating more like an NGO, Platform sought autonomy from the dependencies of art, eschewing support from established galleries or art spaces. Instead the group concentrates upon building relationships between environmentalists, artists and employees of the core financial and carbon-extracting institutions which, at the same time, are the objects of their research and criticism. Since art has taken a relational turn, Platform's dialogic practice has been somewhat vindicated and is gaining the interest of institutions with a commitment to engaging with 'public issues' outside the institutional safety zone.[3] The group has often employed organised walks, 'walking as a research tool, as a ritual, as performance, as intervention, as a political tool'.[4] Here, in the Square Mile that demarcated the original Roman settlement of Londinium, Platform taps the rich network of influence and accumulation they call the 'carbon web' – 'the web of institutions that extract oil and gas from the ground'.

Walking, I am accompanied by three voices or groups of voices. The protagonist, a disillusioned City worker, drifts, trying to throw off the pressure and hypocrisy of the City in an anguished monologue. The guide, a softly spoken, reassuring female voice, tells me when to cross, to 'be careful', 'look left and right at the lights', as well as offering information about BP, the financial groups and investors that support it (Morely, Deutsche Bank, Royal Bank of Scotland). The third voice is a chorus which echoes the protagonist's monologue and riffs eccentrically on it, singing 'They stole her nipples', 'look up, look up to the sky' and, in the Royal Exchange, chants: 'More, more and more, give us more money, give us more and more [...]'

The carefully guided walk sometimes becomes a gallop as I realise I have taken a wrong turn, or when the voices urge me to speed up. As I am led under

3. Ibid. This celebratory piece highlights a new movement of artists fusing post-conceptual art and environmental art under the aegis of the Royal Society of Arts, whose director, Matthew Taylor, was formerly head of the Prime Minister's policy unit. It would seem that relational aesthetics is rapidly emerging as the idiom by which artists speak to policy makers on behalf of the public.
4. Platform website, op. cit.

and through the City's architectural machines of accumulation, the opera emphasises its status as a principal node in processing the world's financial flows. Later, I am spun around Bank station and the Swiss Re tower as the chorus and music build to a crescendo, prefiguring a portentous end to the narrative and the walk.

The accompanying music first appears to me as corporate muzak, like the sound of distilled comfort and class played as one waits for the bank's outsourced operatives to process your phone call. Later, the strings dramatise my rush around the City while street noise blends in as I lurch across streams of commuters and traffic. Once I accept that my route is programmed, I find myself caught up in what feels like the soundtrack to a live video game, gleefully aware that no one else is conscious of my directed path.

And While London Burns is really an 'experience' – in the sense that a trip to Disneyland is. The walk deploys four dramatic elements: the narrative of personal crisis, the music, the information about the Earth's decline under capitalism and the sounds and sights of the City itself. As the slew of information about the Earth's rising temperature builds to a picture of crisis, the protagonist becomes more erratic; we supposedly take on the burden of his self-realisation as our own. But, then, our 'own' crisis over climate change's destructive potential is experienced as adventure.

And While London Burns shares this array of simple mechanisms for dramatising the impending apocalypse with two recent films, *Apocalypto* and *Children of Men*. The latter plays out anarchist fantasies of a biopolitical neofascist state in the UK, presenting us with: 'a world one generation from now that has fallen into anarchy on the heels of an infertility defect in the population [...] Set against a backdrop of London torn apart by violence and warring nationalistic sects, *Children of Men* follows disillusioned bureaucrat Theo (Clive Owen) as he becomes an unlikely champion of Earth's survival'.[5]

Mel Gibson's *Apocalypto* draws a clumsy comparison between the internal breakdown of Mayan civilisation prior to Cortez's conquest of their lands and the demise of the US as a global hegemon: 'Throughout history, precursors to the fall of a civilisation have always been the same [...] It was important for me to make that parallel because you see these cycles repeating themselves over and over again. People think that modern man is so enlightened but we're susceptible to the same forces – and we are also capable of the same heroism and transcendence.'[6]

As with *And While London Burns*, these films indulge a reactionary millenarianism, apparently appropriate to our times, characterised by anxiety over reproduction, environmental devastation, migration and wars over resources. Each locates a subjective response to 'objective conditions' in a male

5. *Children of Men* website, http://www.childrenofmen.net
6. Mel Gibson on *Apocalypto*, from the film website, http://apocalypto.movies.go.com

subject, and we see an awakening to the real conditions of the societies in which they live.

For *And While London Burns'* authors, one gets the feeling that it is something of a stretch of the imagination to place themselves in this character's shoes, that some under-estimation of the ignorant and complacent 'suit' is operating. The dynamic between the identification of the listener with this disaffected conservative and the more 'radical imagination' celebrated through historical references was, for me, unconvincing.

I struggle with the opera's construction of experience (the listener's as well as the conditions they 'objectively' face) as consensus reality without challenge. It seems that, after so long working at the margins of artistic practice, Platform have finally conceded to the monoform. There is no transcendental subject, no lone saviour of civilisation. Although *And While London Burns'* authors are the first to admit that they are self-consciously playing with clichés to dramatic effect, this walk is the very opposite of psychogeographic practice.[7] The work engenders the opposite of an active, critical subjectivity.

If there is a dialectic to be found in *And While London Burns*, it is that of flight vs. contestation. The audio guide points to the irony of the City as both a centre of research into the causes and effects of climate change (in particular Swiss Re, whose re-insurance business is predicated upon the mediation of threats to profitability) and the self-satisfied ignorance of continued irresponsible plunder. As the opera's story unravels, we are informed that the protagonist's partner, Lucy, has left to live 'Off-Grid'. This response to the threat of environmental devastation is the conceptual equivalent of self-organising nuclear bunker drills at the height of the Cold War – a duck and cover strategy, internalising the nuclear state's imperative that we be afraid, that we submit to pointless rituals in the face of death. At the opposite pole, the rich shoring up their wealth and access to unadulterated leisure and consumption in Dubai are playing a similar end-game with equally futile consequences. As if, in the context of a global emergency, anyone will be safe in either a low-impact woodland home with its own energy supply or a glass tower surrounded by the best defences petro-dollars can buy. Both visions indulge in the fantasy that, in the globalised world, there is some escape or autonomy, a form of denial which hopes to obscure all ties between that secure haven and the reality of ongoing surplus value extraction from a landless, illegalised, starving (sub-)humanity.

And While London Burns puts this contemporary meme of millennial conservatism to work in a locale that is synonymous with unsustainable economics, personal debt and risk-taking. The work chooses to reinforce

7. As one definition would have it, 'The theory of the combined use of arts and techniques for the integral construction of a milieu in dynamic relation with experiments in behaviour.' Situationist International, 'Preliminary Problems in Constructing a Situation', *Internationale Situationniste* #1, 1958. Reprinted in Ken Knabb, *Situationist International Anthology*, Bureau of Public Secrets, 2006 and available at http://www.bopsecrets.org/SI/1.situations.htm

the personalisation and internalisation of a crisis for which capitalism itself should be paying the costs. Its dramatisation of the Earth's climactic instability hinges on a predicted four-degree rise in temperature that we are now almost certain to reach, according to the IPCC's [Intergovernmental Panel on Climate Change] recent report. The facts relayed during the course of this walk tend to confirm these projections. I am not in a position to challenge these facts. Without even trying to challenge these facts, it is still possible to object to the terms in which the urgency of change is being framed. The injunction of climate change is literally 'change'; through crisis, capital is reorganising itself and this has immediate social impacts. What is being proposed is a series of small adjustments for capital and many dramatic shocks for us. There appears to be very little going on in terms of large projects to actually reverse this situation; instead, there is a confluence of self-righteous self-flagellation at a consumer level and government programmes to bully workers, small to medium-sized businesses and new home owners.

Platform has a background of deeper engagement with these issues and access to research that should allow it an analysis of the joined-up system of capitalist 'wealth creation' and its effect on the social environment. However, as UK and other governments worldwide absorb green and environmental discourse and re-spin it as command – to eat less, work more, pay extra for energy and waste – some engagement with this instrumentalisation of ecological threat would be useful, rather than continuing to pursue an alarmist politics fuelling the fires of eco-fascism in becoming.

From apocalyptic predictions of dramatic climate change down to fashion tips for the greening of lifestyles, we experience exactly the same 'terrorism of conformity that underlies all the publicity of modern capitalism'.[8] The trouble with this work, and almost all public discussion of climate, is that, rather than critically evaluating the role of this ecological threat as part of the ongoing deterioration of living standards dictated by capital in most of the world, there is a tendency to exaggerate the threat, to rationalise it as a natural fact, and thus to approve and provide training for the modification of behaviour urged by capitalism.

8. 'Geopolitics of Hibernation', *Situationist International* #7, 1962, Reprinted in Knabb, op. cit. and available at http://www.bopsecrets.org/SI/7.hibernation.htm

Chapter 7

Under the Net: the City and the Camp

> Today it is not the city but the camp that is the fundamental biopolitical paradigm.
> Giorgio Agamben

In the era of 'free trade' in commodities and the global flow of information, the control of people has never been stricter. It is in this sense that postmodernity's much hyped 'flows' are rigidly denied to the majority of the world – left to eek out an existence in shacks and sewage – which has partly inspired *Mute*'s methodology, and that of this chapter. But, of course, it is not just the distance between the lives of the world's underclass and this elite space of flows that we have analysed, but its proximity too. In other words, hyper-exploitation is not only to be found at the edges of the 'First World' but at its centres and, conversely, highly defended pools of privilege are threaded throughout the 'Third World'. The articles in this chapter plot the ways in which the global proletariat and sub-proletariat are reconfigured, moved around and deployed against one another in a ceaseless attempt to drive down the cost of labour power and extract surplus value. Keeping this as its focus, the chapter develops an integrated understanding of localised 'race riots', the crisis of multiculturalism, urban regeneration, global slum clearance and migration.

As Angela Mitropoulos argues, in her article on the race riots in Australia's Cronulla Beach (2005), wherever the social/wage contract risks breaking down, 'the figure of the foreigner is put to work'. The ostensible fairness and symmetry of this contract, she explains, cannot be achieved without a border, a beyond, a 'foreigner'. In order to be a citizen, it is necessary for there to be non-citizens; in order to maintain the 'fair' exchange of labour for wages amongst a working elite, the majority's toil goes unremunerated or is paid a rate below the cost of their own reproduction. In his article on Chinese migrant labour in the UK, John Barker further elaborates this pitting of the working class against itself. Using J.A. Hobson's discussion of the role of Chinese labour in his 1902 book, *Imperialism*, Barker exposes the historical necessity of cheap goods and cheap labour in placating the Western proletariat. A declining wage can be masked by the availability of cheap goods, while the import or use of cheap (Chinese) labour maintains a downward pressure on the wage generally. As a result, we see neo-slavery (of, say, gang-run cockle pickers at Morecambe Bay) underwriting the cheap goods sold to us in supermarkets.

The Melancholic Troglodytes pick up on this dynamic, calling it 'surreal subsumption' – the co-existence of 'real subsumption' (a phase of capitalist development in which all of life becomes subject to exchange value) and 'primitive accumulation' (a stage in the transition to capitalism in which value is accumulated through theft or looting). The growth of slums is one manifestation of this surreal subsumption, their presence in many emerging 'world cities' serving to highlight the contradictions of a system in which the production of place-branded yuppie and tourist destinations is threatened by the stubborn presence of the surplus humanity with whose cheap labour the cities are (re)built. Amita Baviskar's discussion of slum clearances in Delhi draws out the relationship between the cultural makeover of cities – in this case ahead of the Commonwealth Games Delhi will host in 2010 – and the working class blood-letting it entails. The London Particular's photo-text collage, 'Fear Death by Water', sharpens this analysis, focusing on the twin strategies of cultural regeneration and new forms of class-cleansing population management in Hackney.

As London Particular member and *Mute* editor, Benedict Seymour, notes here, and in his article 'Drowning by Numbers' – on the disaster-movie scale of gentrification in post-Katrina New Orleans – renewal is a euphemism for 'primitive accumulation'. While the value-producing industry of developed economies is gutted and production moved to wherever labour is cheapest, fictitious values are generated, partly through a series of commodity bubbles and partly through ever more complex financial instruments. The real estate bubble has played a crucial role in producing the fictitious values that obscure an underlying drop in wages. Gentrification, argues Seymour, works to inflate property prices and launch a 'holistic attack on the wage' through raising the cost of living and destroying the social resources which provide a means of support. In New Orleans, the disaster-propelled eviction of the black blue-collar majority and the influx of migrant, and often rightless, Latino labourers dispatched to rebuild the city, provides an extreme version of this ubiquitous process.

This example of capital's deployment of racial conflict gives further justification to Matthew Hyland's argument, made in his essay about the Bradford riots of 2001, that 'A "race riot" [...] is always a "class riot"'. Claims made by mainstream media over the apolitical nature of the riots between Asian and White British youths in a former British mill town, participate in a kind of psychologisation of racism which denies any consciousness of colonial history and the effects of globalised capitalism. This psychologisation and personalisation, Hyland argues, is behind the emptying of the original meaning of 'institutional racism' as the Black Panthers' term for the systemic racism of the state is increasingly deployed to describe an anomalous defect embodied in certain individuals.

It is against this portrayal of the dispossessed as somehow bereft of politics that Richard Pithouse frames his account of resistance in the slums of Durban, South Africa. Banishing the cliché of the 'global slum', he insists on the particularity of the culture, infrastructure and politics of every slum. Against the representation of slums as vacuums of social organising and bereft of politics, Pithouse wields the example of Abahlali baseMjondolo – the Durban shack dwellers' movement. This radically democratic organisation of shack dwellers combines thousands into a sustained fight against evictions and for basic amenities. It is not for the likes of Mike Davis or tenured leftists to accuse the global underclass of failing to fight global capitalism, argues Pithouse, when they are not fighting it on their own privileged terrain. To stand and fight where you are and over local pressures or depredations is always 'a struggle to subordinate the social aspects of state to society' and thereby weaken relations of local and global domination. The seemingly modest demand for the right not to be moved is one that unites struggles from the streets of Hackney to the slums of Durban; from this refusal to make way for the bulldozer of development come other refusals which hamper capital's ruthlessly instrumental deployment of people. This chapter banishes any idea that the managed movement of peoples is about anything else.

History Has Failed and Will Continue to Fail

Matthew Hyland

Vol 1 #21, Autumn 2001

Through April, May, June and July this year, large groups of young 'Asians' have sporadically, but efficiently, fought police (and a few sub-fascist white opportunists) in the streets of towns across the North of England. The inevitable outcry of reasonable opinion has come in a variety of styles, but it has also revealed a remarkable consensus. Community leaders, columnists, police chiefs and politicians each spoke, according to type, about mindless thuggery or a tragically misguided collective outburst, but all agreed that the rioters' behaviour was somehow irrational. No doubt this shared certainty across the presumed political spectrum tells us something about social spectatorship and bourgeois thinking. What it indicates more urgently, though, is just how rational the action of the 'violent minority' may have been.

Perhaps the single silliest aspect of the coverage has been commentators' laments that an almost understandable reaction to organised, racist provocation was subsequently 'turned against' the police, as if the cops were little more than unfortunate bystanders. Of course, this could hardly be further from the truth. In Oldham, for example, the police's response to an evening's violence and intimidation by a specially bussed-in National Front/Combat 18 gang was to turn up in riot gear, arrest Asian men and try to disperse a crowd of angry local residents. As Arun Kundnani points out in his important essay, 'From Oldham to Bradford: the Violence of the Violated' (to be published in October 2001 in the Institute of Race Relations' collection, *The Three Faces of British Racism*), the police weren't 'defending the rule of law'; they were acting as an invading army, and as such, they were driven off the streets – dogs, armoured vans and all. It would be too much to expect left-liberal journalists to recognise the police as part of a racist state apparatus – not just when 'unwitting prejudice' gets the better of them but *when they're doing their job properly* – but apparently it never even occurred to them that young Pakistanis and Bangladeshis in one of the poorest parts of the country might see things that way. These earnestly anti-fascist souls flatter the far-right groups extravagantly in imagining that all the fury of the revolt was the product of their sorry manoeuvring.

Oldham and Bradford, in particular, were notable for the rioters' practical effectiveness – holding territory, repeatedly driving back police attacks and avoiding large numbers of arrests – and also for the risks taken by those involved. These two aspects are obviously not unrelated, as the counter-example of the London May Day debacle shows. The self-styled anti-capitalists agonised for weeks before and after the non-event over the tension between material and symbolic politics, or what's effective physically and how it would be represented. In Burnley, Leeds, Stoke-On-Trent, Bradford and Oldham, this debate seems never to have been scheduled. Simply doing what was necessary to hold off the police meant abandoning hope of a 'fair hearing' from the BBC or *The Guardian.* Indifference to being slandered on TV as criminals, along with the resolution to deal with serious police violence, tends to come with the realisation that the machinery of political and media representation isn't an open forum for communication but a weapon used by the social subject enjoying access to it against those who don't. At this point, those for whom the arsenal is unavailable attempt, quite rationally, to destroy the physical conditions in which it's used. The complete failure of the most sympathetic media and mediators to guess at any of this confirms the wisdom of absconding from their skewed agora.

The current unprecedented distance between representation and social reality is especially evident in public discourse about 'racism'. Five or ten years ago, the word was barely heard in polite discussion. Now it's the subject of almost daily homilies from politicians and journalists. This new visibility, however, has come at the cost of something approaching a complete reversal of the term's meaning. The 'Stephen Lawrence Report', by reporting judge Sir William Macpherson of Cluny, was central to this process. Macpherson's report can be seen as symbolic of the whole process whereby the evil of 'racism' has become a ubiquitous feature of public discourse, while the term is drained of its social and historical meaning. A Home Office green paper explicitly tied the report to the notorious Asylum and Immigration Bill as the two faces of New Labour's 'anti-racist' policy. The report popularised the term 'institutional racism', first used in the 1960s by black student leader Stokely Carmichael and the Black Panthers to designate the systematically racist policies of a state apparatus. Macpherson, however, is at pains to emphasise that 'the contrary is true'. He redefines 'institutional racism' as a purely personal, psychological defect that happens to be shared by a large number of people. It's a question of unwitting bigotry in 'the words and actions of officers acting together', simple ignorance to be cured by hours of quasi-therapeutic training. This piece of semantic juggling actually makes it more difficult than before to publicly address the racism administered by institutions in their normal functioning, as the only language in which this could be done has been hijacked and turned to innocuous ends. The report's complete failure to deal with a non-psychological fact like the number of black deaths in police custody demonstrates this, as does a recent report on the Crown Prosecution Service (CPS) by lawyer Sylvia Denman. The CPS was found to be 'riddled' with institutional racism, meaning it often treats its own black and Asian staff unfairly. Yet the huge and systematic racial disparity in suspects' chances of being prosecuted (black and Asian defendants are four times as likely to have their cases thrown out of court, implying a roughly corresponding ratio of doubtful charges brought by the CPS) wasn't even mentioned.

Oldham may have witnessed, almost, the first practical fruit of Macpherson's psychologising zeal (I say 'almost' because in the last year or so we've already seen the law against 'racial hate crime' in action: a black man fined £150 in Ipswich Crown Court for supposedly calling some cops 'white trash', and protestors prosecuted under 'racial aggravation' laws for hurting American soldiers' feelings by burning a US flag). One of the judge's most important and strangest recommendations is that a 'racially motivated incident' be defined as 'any incident which is defined as racist by the victim or *any other person*' (emphasis added). Not surprisingly, police statistics on the apprehension of 'racist crime' have improved dramatically since the words' meaning was opened up for spontaneous redefinition by any passer-by or policeman, eliminating the tiresome notion that the perpetrator, or at least the victim, should be the judge of motivation. Thus, Oldham police felt quite at liberty to treat the beating of 76-year-old pensioner ('And war veteran!' screamed the quality press) Walter Chamberlain by Asian youths as 'racially motivated', despite the complete lack of any evidence to this effect and the insistence of the victim and his family that such was not the case. Before long, the BNP were marching around the town with pictures of Chamberlain's battered face on placards. The new in-definition of 'racist incident' also generated the infamous statistic purporting that '60 percent of racist attacks in Oldham are carried out by Asians against whites', first published by the *Oldham Evening Chronicle*, whose offices were shortly afterward consumed by the (real not symbolic) flames of Asian indignation.

The psychologisation of race and racism can be seen as part of a wider tendency in government policy, scientific practice and academic and media discourse. Increasingly, these apparatuses of representation seek to manage social problems through intensive and pre-emptive monitoring of individuals seen as presenting 'risks', rather than waiting to judge particular actions or sets of circumstances (as in a traditional criminal trial or benefit claim, for instance). 'Risk', in the form of criminality, 'anti-social' tendencies or personality disorder, is presumed to dwell as a quasi-pathological tendency within the individual. It's only a matter of time until certain people actually commit a crime or have a psychotic 'episode', so why shouldn't the state intervene before they do something? We've already seen 'Community Safety Orders' allowing judges to turn any future acts like spitting, pissing or loitering into serious criminal offences for specific individuals who haven't yet been convicted of anything. Compulsory drug tests for everyone arrested are already underway in Hackney and are coming soon to the rest of the country, as is a permanent DNA archive of potential criminals. David Blunkett's first proposals as Home Secretary (taken from the Halliday report on sentencing reform) include 'Acceptable Behaviour Contracts' for teenagers, police powers to impose curfews, compulsory work or drug treatment on unconvicted young people and provision for ten-year supervision orders after completion of sentences. The forthcoming and deeply sinister Mental Health Act (see 'Mad Pride', *Mute*, Vol 1 #20) is another part of the picture.

Any critique treating these moves toward personalised social control as a 'civil liberties issue' is totally inadequate. The new techniques are designed to contain the disruptive potential of that social class with the least to lose. Any doubt that racial minorities will be disproportionately affected should be dispelled by the first examples of the new thinking put into practice. A recent Lambeth police experiment called 'Operation Shutdown' saw 'prominent or development nominals' – people 'known' to be 'involved with crime', although they hadn't necessarily ever been convicted and weren't wanted for anything at the time – stopped in the street, surrounded and very publicly videotaped by vanloads of cops. The number of black nominals was as high as Lambeth's grotesque figures for regular stop-and-search would lead one to expect. Merseyside police, meanwhile, are pioneering the DNA archive scheme by taking non-consensual samples from anyone reported in connection with a 'racial incident'. In general, the rise of 'informal justice' – treatment of alleged criminality outside the courts – is disturbing. As the already-mentioned high rate of black and Asian acquittals shows, at least in some cases, the courts' slow examination of what has happened corrects the criminalisation of certain subjects based on who they are. The example that comes most easily to mind is that of Delroy Lindo: fitted up 20 times by Haringey cops over a couple of years, with the charges always thrown out in court.

Arun Kundnani observes that the recent rioting was 'ad hoc, improvised and haphazard' in contrast to the organised community self-defence seen in 1981, when the Asian Youth Movement burnt down a pub where fascists had gathered in Southhall, or when members of the Bradford United Youth Movement

were arrested for making petrol bombs in response to fascist attacks in the area. Certainly, it would be grotesque to twist the recognition that this was the desperate action 'of communities falling apart from within as well as from without [...] the violence of hopelessness' into a glib celebration of its spontaneity. Nonetheless, it may be that the widely deplored 'excess' or 'incoherence' of the riots as a 'response to racism' reveals a feeling among at least some participants that the target for their anger, the set of conditions to be destroyed, can't be reduced to a single enemy or injustice. The risible failure of 'community leaders' attempts at mediation reflects many young Asians' complete disdain for these state-funded patriarchs' claims to represent them. It may also suggest that what was sometimes claimed for the street battles of the 1960s (by the Situationists for the Watts Rebellion and, with flagrant disregard for what actually happened, by various romantics for May–June '68 in France) might apply here: that no particular concession from above would have sufficed to content the crowd, to send them home newly reconciled to their lot. The idea that the violence was 'excessive' and apolitical patronisingly presumes that young Asians don't know that, in their experience of poverty and racism, they're confronting an historical totality rather than an isolated problem that the present system could choose to solve or not. For instance, the fact that Pakistani and Bangladeshi communities across the Pennine Hills are among the poorest 1 percent of Britain's population is partially related to the economic need to send money back to families at 'home'. This situation is inseparable, in turn, from imperial Britain's destruction of the Indian textile industry and the establishment of the Lancashire and Yorkshire mill towns as prototypical Export Processing Zones, spinning cotton grown in Bengal – among other places – into cloth to be sold back at a profit to the empire. Eventually, Pakistani and Bangladeshi labour was brought in to do night shifts, disdained by the existing workforce, until, as Kundnani puts it, '[t]he work once done cheaply by Bangladeshi workers in the North of England could [...] be done even more cheaply by Bangladeshi workers in Bangladesh'. So cheaply, in fact, that their pitiful earnings have to be subsidised by relatives now in precarious service sector work or on the dole in England. Thus, in the everyday constriction of their lifeworld, the mill towns' Asian youth take on the weight of colonial history, as well as globalised capital's ability to generate wretched 'necessity'. Even if today's desperation might somehow be overcome within the present social horizon, there is a sense that the past cannot be rectified, only avenged. It's significant that the few young Asians interviewed in mainstream media after the riots spoke not only of their own obstructed futures but also, without distinguishing past from present, of what their parents' generation endured. 'If they could get good jobs here, why would they be driving cabs?' asked one.

The debate over whether race or class was the 'reason' for the conflict seems absolutely sterile in this context. As certain commentators never grow tired of observing, the white working class suffers, too, especially in de-industrialised Northern towns. The likelihood that the ultimate sources of everyone's misery might be the same, however, doesn't alter the reality that things are quantitatively worse for certain racial groups for reasons which may not be tangible in the eternal present of newspapers and TV, but which, with a little attention to history, are anything but mysterious. Ultimately, race and class are inseparable: racism is most real in the intensified application, to particular ethnic groups, of expropriation and control techniques used against the entire working class. Conversely, class is always lived in a racialised way: expropriation and control are experienced differently according to (plural, contestable) attributions of 'race'. 'Ethnic minorities' have no choice but to be aware of this, whereas, among white Europeans, only those peddling the absurd idea that life is worst for whites seem to acknowledge it. Most who have the luxury of being able to do so like to imagine, no less absurdly, that whiteness means racial neutrality. Once again, Oldham offers plenty of examples. The most recent available Home Office figures (1998) show the rate of unemployment in the town at 4.3 percent overall and 38 percent for Pakistanis and Bangladeshis. Housing statistics, meanwhile, record that 13 percent of homes in the area were 'statutorily unfit for human habitation', with another 28 percent 'in serious disrepair'. These privately owned ruins were concentrated in the largely Asian areas, also noted for high rates of household overcrowding. The situation was hardly accidental. Paul Harris and Martin Bright in *The Observer* ('Bitter Harvest from Decades of Division', 15 July 2001) recall that young men coming into Northern textile towns from South Asia in the 1950s were often kept out of council housing by a two-year residency condition operated by local authorities. Consequently, they moved into the most run-down areas with the cheapest rents, and '[a]s the first Asians moved in, the whites moved out. As more Asians followed, they were housed nearby, often because in their own Bangladeshi or Pakistani quarter they felt safer from attack from the whites'. Not surprisingly, given their economic vulnerability, many young Asians sought to buy their own property as an investment, with the result that they became owner-occupiers of small, dilapidated houses unwanted by whites, without the money for repairs or relocation. Although these phenomena were the subject of research by Pakistani sociologist, Badr Dahya, as early as the 1970s, little has changed in the meantime. In 1993, Oldham Borough Council was found guilty of running a segregationist housing policy, moving white residents into new suburban estates where Asians were often denied accommodation or faced harassment and violence if they did get in. Hence, they stayed in their damp, overcrowded terraced houses, 'a community penned in', as further white flight kept property prices low. Confinement of ethnic groups in single areas 'naturally' led to educational segregation; as a generation grew up unaccustomed to ethnic mixing, the limitation of Asians' mobility could be portrayed in local and national media as 'self-segregation', or even the deliberate creation of 'no-go areas' for whites.

A 'race riot', then, is always already a class riot, although that doesn't mean it makes no difference whether or not racial groups stereotyped as enemies are fighting side by side. This is said not to have been the case in the Northern towns (unlike Brixton in 1981, '85, '95 and 2001, or LA in 1992), but 'Asians vs. whites' is nonetheless a misleadingly vague way to characterise the sides involved in the fighting. The question of collective subjectivity needs to be looked at closely here. As the difference between its meanings in, say, Manchester, San Francisco and Moscow (or now and 2,000 years ago) suggests, 'Asian' is a concept with unstable boundaries, most often used for convenience by people who don't see it as referring to themselves. There's little reason to assume that many of the youths involved in the recent clashes would have thought of themselves primarily as 'Asian'. *Guardian* journalist, Faisal Bodi, has drawn attention to hostility between groups of Muslims in the Northern towns, not only between Pakistanis and Bangladeshis, divided by the war that separated East and West Pakistan and created the state of Bangladesh, but also among Pakistanis, between Pathans, Punjabis and Kashmiris living in separate clusters in the same towns. These forms of ethnic and linguistic isolation, which, as Kundnani notes, reinforce the power of community patriarchs within their own clans, have a lot to do with the identity politics in practice in the race relations system: money for ethnically exclusive centres and language support 'pouring into' the towns, chiefly benefiting 'people whose livelihood depends on being linguistic intermediaries between minority communities and local authorities', as Bodi points out. In these circumstances, competition between areas for funding further exacerbates tension by giving the (fairly accurate) impression that one ethnic sub-group's gain is another's loss.

Such is the institutional hegemony of identity politics and the moral authority of victimhood today that the BNP has adapted its rhetoric correspondingly, emphasising a 'need' to preserve the fragile cultural and biological identity of British whiteness. Disingenuously sidelining the questions of class and power in trying to present 'whiteness' as an ethnicity 'like any other', this discourse could be said to take the cultural studies separation of cultural self-identification from its material basis to its logical conclusion. A more pompously world-historical version of the same kind of thinking is offered by Horst Mahler, once of the Red Army Fraction and now spokesman for Germany's xenophobic New Democratic Party. In the '70s, he says, the New Left (and the RAF as its armed wing) were fighting for national self-determination for 'Third World' countries like Vietnam and Palestine. That, he insists, is just what the 'left-wing' NDP wants now: 'self-determination' for Germans in Germany, Turks in Turkey, etc. – as if Germany, Turkey et al. were timeless, natural entities.

Yet the violence in Oldham, Bradford and elsewhere clearly demonstrates what the politics of identity always fails to recognise: that material necessity leads the way, and (self-)representation may or may not confusedly follow. When confronted with the need to defend themselves and their space against aggression from police and fascists, Pathans, Punjabis, Kashmiris, Bangladeshis and others acted together with unquestionable effectiveness. Bodi points to ecumenical, cross-community Muslim projects in housing and youth work as potential roads out of identity ghettoes; multi-denominational street-fighting against uniformed and freelance racists can be seen as another. This is not to say that, in the course of the turmoil, the rioters consciously assumed a new, shared 'Asian' or 'black' subjectivity. But, even if each small group of friends and family had been concerned exclusively with its own narrow interests (and there is no reason to believe that this was so), all were obviously aware that their own interests, in the most immediate, concrete sense, could safely be pursued only through cooperation.

Nor should it be taken for granted that the nameless, provisional, collective subject that seemed to flicker into being in the riots, if only for a few hours at a time, existed solely in reaction to white racist aggression. Both the persistence of the violence over four months and such supposedly gratuitous, but in reality eloquent and political, acts as the destruction of a BMW showroom suggest that the young men wanted not only to defend their communities but also to assert their own power and autonomy, in however indeterminate and limited a way. Well-meaning commentaries that reduce displays of force to unruly forms of protest deny 'subaltern' subjects a capacity for independent action; even the most violent protest, conceived as such, engages in a dialogue initiated by the more powerful side. By contrast, the very failure of the mill town rebellion to specify political 'demands' from a recognisable subject position has, in a highly problematic way, made the young 'Asians'' self-assertion an unanswerable fact. Perhaps this un-identifiability of a subject which nonetheless refuses to be ignored, this conspicuous neglect to address or be addressed by the organs of representation, contributed to the horror in which leaders of local communities, national politics and public opinion were united.

Fear Death by Water: The Regeneration Siege in Central Hackney

Benedict Seymour and David Panos (The London Particular)

Vol 1 #26, Summer/Autumn 2003

The Hackney Creative Quarter

Welcome to HTH2, formerly Hackney Town Hall Square. A £70 million-plus project for the cultural renewal of central Hackney in London's East End, HTH2 is the heart of the area's new 'creative quarter'.

Home of artists and immigrants, Hackney is a traditionally working class area undergoing protracted gentrification. The nomination and production of a creative (a.k.a. cultural) quarter is intended to act as a regeneration incubator, attracting a new class of customer to this formerly despised part of the capital. HTH2 combines a music venue (The Ocean Centre), a library and new media complex (The Technology and Learning Centre, or TLC), rehabilitated public space (the square itself) and theatre, comedy and other live arts (the refurbished Hackney Empire). The whole project was funded through a private finance consortium including MACE, Roche, Tarmac Constructions and Schroder's Bank.

The Ocean, with its concert halls, production facilities and bar, enjoys a 150-year rent-free lease from Hackney Council, plus a £300,000 a year grant. The council, declared bankrupt in 2001, recently auctioned off a large share of its housing, nurseries, doctors' surgeries, playing fields, schools, youth clubs, libraries and swimming pools. Prices were very competitive, and developers picked up bargains in an area which has seen London's steepest increase in property values. Hackney Council continues to cut back on services and staff, but has no long-term means to remedy its structural under-funding at the hands of central government.

With a remit to deliver 'vibrancy' to the square and its environs, HTH2 displays all the stigmata of regenerated space. Aseptic, generic and surveilled, it's a vitrification of place (something socially produced and by definition volatile) into planned 'ambience'. Silting up the channel between the area's past and future, the square places heritage (the TLC now hosts Hackney Museum) next to learning and culture, domesticating them all.

The square is not the only part of Hackney's regeneration programme, however...

The Hackney Siege

The Hackney Siege was a £1 million project for the spatial sterilisation of the area adjacent to the Town Hall Square. Lasting 15 days, it deployed squads of paramilitary police around the clock and shut down several streets and a major road. Forty-three Hackney residents were trapped inside their homes, some without television, from Boxing Day 2002 until well after twelfth night. A further 200 residents were compulsorily displaced on the order of the authorities during the course of the project.

More than just a conventional siege, this was a pioneering partnership between police and residents which transformed a state of emergency into a new model for everyday life in the city. The Hackney Zone of Exception (HZoE) was another good example of what regeneration professionals call 'people-led regeneration'. At its heart lay the police's pre-emptive ambush of a local man, the so-called 'yardie gangster', Eli Hall (29). Suspected of possessing illegal firearms, Hall was pursued by an Armed Response Unit, whose response efficiently anticipated any action on the suspect's part. After taking shelter in his bedsit on Marvin Street, Mr. Hall and his hostage were successfully contained within the house while the police rationalised his services. After a few days without heating, electricity or light, the hostage fled and the tenant set fire to his own home in a desperate effort to warm the place up.

Drenched by police water jets and worn out by the protracted process of consultation, Mr. Hall was wounded in the mouth by a police bullet and later, it is alleged, shot himself in the head. Having declined the munificence of the state and obstructed attempts at dialogue, his lifeless body was removed from his home.

Liquid Regeneration, Social Desertification

The Town Hall Square's new amenities riff on the idea of revitalisation by water and fluidity: the Ocean music venue has an educational facility called Rising Tide and a bar called Aqua, the Technology and Learning Centre's internet terminals give local people (of fixed abode) a chance to surf in the space of flows, and the HTH2 online forum about developments in the square was created by a trans-disciplinary network called F-L-U-I-D.

Picking up on the latent seaside connotations, the architects, Gross Max, have proposed a boardwalk-style 'special pavement' for the square, an effort to bring an ambience of play and sociability to this stony slab of municipal space. But if the 'urban beach' semiotics don't convince, then the TLC's glass façade and networked heart at least embody the centrality of sand to the whole package. Silicon implants are intended to turn the frumpy old square into a nexus where desiccated flows intersect.

Beyond the cloying hydraulic rhetoric, the real effect of this flood of culture is a creeping desertification. The official sites of education and entertainment that promise to compensate for gentrification actually contribute to the social cleansing of the area. Flushing out undesirable elements, from the homeless to the hooded youth, the square's well-policed makeover begins with the economic, semiotic and physical dissuasion of the poor and ends by sucking in a flood of new consumers better able to afford and enjoy the rehabilitated space.

The Hackney Zone of Exception continued the square's fixation on fluidity, materialising the metaphor with displacements of its own. The HZoE 'decanted' the inhabitants of this promising residential area for a 15-day trial period and helped move key siege stakeholder, Eli Hall, to 'a better place'. As council housing stock is privatised or demolished, many other local people, in particular elderly tenants, have already been definitively relocated.

The siege was not just about moving people out of the area, though. Complementing the spatial sterilisation of the square already achieved by the PFI projects, the siege's police cordon delivered instant crime reduction through 'total restriction'; the ability to suspend local citizens' right to freedom of movement for an indefinite period renders all criminals, both potential and actual, equally immobile. No more flow for them.

While the HZoE was only a pilot, plans to apply the same 'urban quarantine' approach on a city-wide scale are already well under way. As part of the wider regeneration project known as the War on Terror, the government is planning to introduce total urban lockdown, with whole cities sealed off in the (non)event of a possible terror threat. The liquefaction of urbanism paradoxically coincides with the attempt to place entire cities under arrest.

> Today it is not the city but rather the camp that is the fundamental biopolitical paradigm of the west. [This] throws a sinister light on the models by which social sciences, sociology, urban studies, and architecture today are trying to conceive and organize the public space of the world's cities without any clear awareness that at their very centre lies the same bare life (even if it has been transformed and rendered apparently more human) that defined the biopolitics of the great totalitarian states of the twentieth century.
> Giorgio Agamben, *Homo Sacer: Sovereign Power and Bare Life*

Gesamtkunstwerk

> The integration of artwork helps to make Hackney Town Square something special. At present, a visual artist, composer and light artist are collaborating with the architects to make the square into a special experience of all the senses. *Light*, texture, *sound* and, if budget allows, specially designed *water jets* and mist machines may create a unique atmosphere to be enjoyed by all.
> Gross Max Architects

> We liked the idea of doing almost nothing, creating more of an open invitation rather than a prescribed script [...] nearly invisible, nearly inaudible.
> Alan Johnson and Max Rolgasky, Artists

Contemporary regeneration means 'doing almost nothing' with almost no cash: over £70 million for a flagship cluster of cultural 'capital projects', £1 million on a state-of-the-art siege, but only £6 million for the repair of social housing. The council subsidises the Ocean Centre in perpetuity, but does not extend the same largesse to their human tenants.

If we used to be 'voluntary prisoners of architecture' (Koolhaas), trapped in the grid of functionalist urbanism, today we are the involuntary prisoners of situationism. After the top-down prescriptions of modern planning, macroscopic and instrumental, this is a molecular and affective urbanism of infinite sensitivity. Regenerated space wants to pre-empt your emotions and aspirations, conform itself to your desires. At its best, it is a siege on the subject, an anticipatory retaliation against your capacity to dream. Regeneration is 'holistic', it is 'bottom up', it is 'about people' – all the old Situationist virtues, minus the disruptive necessity of extricating our desires from the apparatus of profit.

While regeneration concentrates on cheesily impersonating the finer things – mosaics and lavender lighting, interactive musical pavements – more humble desires are neglected. After the major surgery of functionalist urbanism – council housing, ring roads, schools, etc. – this is a new regime of urban *acupuncture*: re-channelling intangible flows, adjusting the social chakras – a micropolitics of soft control.

Scrupulously reversing the old 'mistake', regeneration creates its negative image to suit the unprecedented miserliness of contemporary capitalism. The turn toward emotion and inclusivity masks a turn away from building new homes and infrastructure. Not that music and books aren't essential, but for every showpiece TLC opened, ten existing libraries were shut down.

Aside from the big fiascos, the culture palaces that tend to self-destruct and the swimming pools too expensive for the majority to use, regeneration is a programme of subtraction: the systematic destruction of collective resources, privatisation of services and evacuation of social space.

He Do the Police in Different Voices

The Town Hall Square is also the virtual network of consultation forums in which the physical space is cradled, by which it is preceded and post-mortemised.

In today's regeneration, participation and engagement are compulsory; 'apathy' is not an option. The permanent and ever-proliferating condition of consultation defers the encounter with social conflict and economic inertia. Endless consultation may consume most of the cash or permanently postpone its expenditure, but perhaps this is the point. More importantly, for the network of agencies that constitute the micropolitical 'Regeneration State', consultation devolves responsibility – not power – onto the patients of the regime. Whatever regeneration does, it must be legitimate because they asked you for your input at every stage. If you don't like the end results, you only have yourself to blame. Then again, when the preferred outcome pre-structures the options, when the propaganda is deceitful and even majority decisions – if unfavourable to the government's core agenda – are repeatedly ignored, people's disengagement from the frenzy of dialogue is not only understandable, it may be politically essential.

If you take the comments on the online forums seriously, what 'the people' actually want is not sentient street furniture and emotional lamp posts but shelter: 'new houses for everyone and safe places for little ones', repairs to their homes and estates, a host of selfish and functionalist concerns. It's as if they'd never even heard of the Situationists.

Like the 'dialogue' with which the police successfully prosecuted Eli Hall during the siege-consultation, the apogee of the regeneration forum is the séance. The HTH2 online forum is a safely contained, post-festum complaint session without actual performative force. Desire is solicited then conspicuously displayed on screen in order that it be displaced. Speech is stimulated to dissimulate the imposition of policy on the people. 'Giving the community a voice' results in a deathly civic silence.

Hurry Up Please, It's Time

Aesthetically avant-garde, cultural regeneration goes one better than the current fashion for artistic re-enactments. In Summer 2002, the siege was pre-enacted in the Town Hall Square when police cordoned off the area after a public occupation of the town hall. Soon after the Ocean opened, the Samuel Pepys pub opposite was shut down. On the Pepys' last night, 300 of the pub's clientèle spilled out into the square. After some of the revellers broke into the town hall in protest against the pub's closure, the police came in to mop things up.

Like a collective rehearsal for the HZoE's open plan imprisonment of the area's occupants, the Pepys posse were surrounded by a fleet of cop vans, the town hall besieged and the street sealed off. This was not what participatory democracy is supposed to look like. The police outdid the Italian caribinieri in their brutal response to this unsolicited display of local desires.

Spatial reform sometimes requires the direct use of force. The new order violently imposes itself on the partisans of the old. The closure of the Pepys, haunt of local musicians, crustie anarchists, miscellaneous drinkers and other 'Anti-Social Behaviour Orders' (ASBOs) waiting to happen, marked the end of an era. No more free music, no more late night lock-ins. From Ocean on, you have to pay – doors close 11:30 p.m.

The Ocean sucks dance culture into the belly of the regeneration state. Bringing a source of semi-independent cultural production into a new physical proximity to the town hall, it attempts to integrate elements of the local scene. A sop to the 'ethnic minorities' and black club promoters, the Ocean allows greater control of a potentially disruptive culture. Meanwhile, with the demise of the Pepys, another organically occurring cultural scene is forced out.

Sacred Life

> Such tactics are expensive – the Hackney siege has so far cost around £500,000 – but the priority is to preserve life.
> Metropolitan Police

The 'sacredness of life' is the fundamental axiom of contemporary policing and contemporary regeneration alike. Eli Hall's police consultation partners had his and the community's best interest at heart when they cut off the electricity and gas to his temporary accommodation and turned the water jets on him. The same solicitude motivated the government when it cut off funds to the bankrupt Hackney Council and imposed austerity on the people of the borough.

> Culture in all its forms is fundamental to our health and development as individuals and as a society.
> Hackney Cultural Strategy

The sacredness of life is an injunction to prolong biological existence insofar as it is productive of profit. The North and South of the square represent the two extremes of the biopolitical continuum this implies. The TLC is biopower's deluxe wing, Eli's deathpad its servants' exit. The TLC's ontologically correct fusion of body (gym) and spirit (internet) mirrors the cops' fusion of dialogue and deadly force. Moralising the flesh and physically incarnating the law, the Paragon gym ('turning virtues into reality') serves the cult of bodily effectiveness (*Korperkultur*). The disabled are welcome, of course – that's why the council abolished their free transport.

> You'll never take me alive.
> Eli Hall

On one side of the square, the law is 'live life to the full', net-surfing and nautilus machines; on the other, life is living law (*lex animata*): The police now incarnate the law in their proper persons and directly exercise their sovereign decision over the patient's (dead) body with their ensemble of guns, megaphones and water jets. True to regeneration's 'devolved', 'bottom-up' management, the authorities can proudly point out that Mr. Hall was, of course, the architect of his own demise. That's what self-administration is all about.

Hobo ASBO Boho

> Artists have a transportable infrastructure [. . .]. They are a natural first group to come into an area which will then seed the bars and other support systems for the creative industries.
>
> Fred Manson, regeneration guru

One of the few remaining homeless in the Town Hall Square is the 'mobile man', an elderly gentleman with his own transportable infrastructure. With his survivalist hoard – gas ring, tea flask and carefully organised Tesco bag system – mobile man has become entirely 'responsible' for himself, a model of self-management.

As such, he is the prototype for the majority of Hackney's erstwhile citizens. Stripped of homes, rights and resources, the less affluent exist with the permanent possibility of demotion to refugee status. As welfare support is terminated, leaving only the hypertrophied police-culture function of the state, individuals are thrown back on their own improvised resources.

Like Baudelaire's Parisian ragpicker, mobile man is also the prototype of the artist in the regeneration state. Obsessed with the debris of collapsing systems of taste, today's *bohème* rehearses a pre-emptive impression of proletarianisation ('white trash') as a means of upward social mobility. *Per cacus ad astra.* The few become stars and the majority will be forced out of this new creative zone as they were previously forced out of nearby, now gentrified Shoreditch.

> [. . . T]he square should become a public forum, an outdoor living room for all the people of Hackney.
>
> Gross Max Architects

The mobile man, the precarious tenant and the artist are secretly aligned. If the square, or anywhere else in the fluid Hackney Zone of Exception, is ever going to approximate 'a public forum', it will be as a self-instituted focus for the silent majority's unwanted desires. Eli's isolated, last-ditch stand against the forces of regeneration must become collective, interconnected and expansive.

Eli's army will comprise all the ASBOs of the zone; all the refugees and *Untermenschen*, from the hooded youth to the tramps, the tenants associations and those artists not satisfied with just recycling the entropy of the area; anyone who, for their specific reasons, cannot but revolt against this systematic shutdown of urban space, against the siege mentality of the gated communities and 'affordable apartments' – a boundless, truly fluid and self-proliferating siege engine that spreads across the city like a plague.

Create Creative Clusters!

David Panos

Vol 1 #28, Summer/Autumn 2004

At the end of April 2004, the London Development Agency (LDA) launched its new Creative London programme, a ten-year 'action plan' aimed at 'nurturing' the creative industries in the capital. The LDA is one of nine regional bodies set up by New Labour to regenerate local economies and promote the interests of business. For them, 'creative industries' is an umbrella term that embraces everything from advertising, design, film, fashion, new media and architecture to opera, dance, music and art. The sector has been identified as the second biggest in London after finance, and it is seen as the most significant potential growth area in the capital's economy. Creative London draws on £500 million of public and private sector investment, rolling out a host of programmes such as the creation of venture capital funds for investment; promotional strategies for different trades such as design, fashion and film; legal advice on intellectual property rights, as well as projects to re-brand and promote events like the Notting Hill Carnival and London Fashion Week. Over the course of a decade, it aims to create 200,000 new jobs and increase the annual turnover of the 'creative industries' from £21 billion to £32 billion.

After the embarrassing 'Cool Britannia' posturing of the late-1990s and the *fin de siècle* hubris around the New Economy, the idea that creativity is the great economic hope for the capital is far from new, but the relative sophistication of some of the LDA's new plans to harness and 'grow' this sector is novel. Phenomena once considered marginal to the cycle of accumulation have become models for growth. Many of the strategies are designed to stimulate the overall 'creative' power of the capital, emphasising the importance of a 'diverse ecology of small businesses', 'individual artists' and 'hobbyists' to the development of the creative economy. Like so many 'regeneration' strategies, the emphasis is on tiny interventions to stimulate market forces rather than grand projects that might necessitate social spending.

One of the central initiatives of Creative London is the establishment of 'Creative Hubs' across the capital. Graham Hitchen, the LDA's Head of Creative Industries, describes the process of building Creative Hubs as 'identifying the areas where we think there is potential to really consolidate a cluster of activity that might have started to emerge and then dramatically growing that local economy through the creative business sector'. This pre-emptive strategy intervenes into the development of such clusters by giving advice, creating partnerships and outlining a 'clear plan for growth'. Hubs would be administered by partnerships of private bodies and arts or training organisations with a 'track record in identifying creative talent' and would form a cross-London network, sharing information and pooling strategies.

The precedents for these Creative Hubs can be seen in areas like Brick Lane and Shoreditch. It is a decade since they were colonised by artists, designers and small, new media businesses, turning run-down, old, industrial hinterlands into the most fashionable districts in London. At the time, local government and the regeneration industry were largely oblivious to this revalorisation process, but today it seems it has been turned into an operating model. One council regeneration worker commented that 'the LDA think that if they had been in control of what happened in Shoreditch it would have been bigger and happened faster', and LDA strategy documents are already making rather far-fetched predictions about areas in South London becoming the 'next Hoxton'. Other Creative Hubs are currently being proposed for areas as diverse as Deptford, Haringey, Ealing and Croydon.

The Creative Hub strategy promises to provide 'more opportunities for all Londoners', but Shoreditch's transformation into a cultural node and night-time economy has had little positive impact on the 'local' (working class) residents in the surrounding area. Its actual effect has been to escalate property prices out of the reach of all but a privileged minority and drive up the overall cost of living. Ironically, the LDA has also identified this tendency as a problem for business; according to its research, one of the biggest concerns for creative start-ups is the soaring rents in Central London. Creative London proposes to respond to this inflation by establishing a Creative Property Advice Service that negotiates with councils and developers to create rent caps and special leases that shield fledgling creative businesses from the very price hikes they stimulate. As the perceived 'productive' element in a local economy, the culture industry will get special privileges not meted out to less desirable inhabitants.

Creative London also builds on the existing tendencies to use artists as regenerating 'urban pioneers', attracting the upwardly mobile into formerly undesirable areas. One of the most innovative aspects of the programme is the creation of a Creative Space Agency to act as a broker between artists and landlords whose property is vacant. Artists will be offered empty space across London on a rent-free basis to mount temporary shows or performances. Initially starting with property owned by the LDA and local councils, the plan is to extend the scheme to the private sector once it has been demonstrated to landlords that artists can act as free security guards whilst simultaneously rehabilitating a fallow property and increasing its value.

Of course, smart developers have been using artists and performers as part of their marketing strategies for some time, offering empty schools or warehouses for shows and performances before they are converted into live/work pads for yuppies. The Creative Space Agency formalises ad hoc arrangements previously negotiated directly between artists and developers. Although it will undoubtedly make more space available, projects can be vetted, behaviour regulated and the process brought under centralised control. Under the guise of making more 'public space' available, the scheme puts more of the city back to work; and, by decreasing the number of empty buildings available, it can be seen as a pre-emptive strike against squatting and other unregulated activities. Buildings are being offered to artists strictly on a project by project basis – use as a headquarters or residence will be forbidden, and the LDA is already jumpy about the potential PR 'downside' of having to evict artists who decide to live for free. The Creative Space Agency makes clear the exceptional role of art in the new economy. It is notable that in a city full of vacant property, there has been no comparable scheme developed for 'uneconomic' sections of society like community groups or the homeless.

Graham Hitchen points out that 'the important thing about Creative London is that it is not led by an arts agency – we are an economic development agency saying this is economically important'. Whilst the intervention of the LDA into arts policy is no doubt significant, Hitchen perpetuates a false opposition between the supposedly hard-nosed world of economics and the 'disinterested' or indeterminate sphere of public arts. Arts agencies have increasingly been forced to justify their existence by proselytising culture's economic function, just as the theory that informs the LDA's economic policy has become increasingly fixated on unquantifiable notions such as the role of networks and creativity. The theoretical roots of the programme can be seen in the work of US theorists like Michel Porter and Richard Florida. Porter's ideas about business clusters emphasise the importance of institutional support, collaboration, inter-business networking and shared infrastructure over old-style free market cost cutting and relocation, whilst Florida's 'Creativity Index' cites factors like how many gay people or 'bohemians' live in a city as indicative of its long-term economic potential.

The increasingly influential, yet nebulous, discourse about nurturing creative clusters and creative hubs is a desperate measure to shore up the economies of Western cities against the onslaught of globalisation. As they lose their remaining manufacturing base, and more and more middle class service jobs migrate to Asia, many have been forced to re-brand as 'Cities of Ideas'. Provincial towns and ailing industrial quarters have little choice but to create the necessary conditions for an elite centre for 'innovation', wooing the 'creative classes' to rehabilitate their fortunes. Seen in this context, Creative London is far from being a manifesto for dynamism. Rather, it is a defensive strategy that seems unlikely to deliver much apart from increased precariousness for the majority of working Londoners.

The Incidental Collection: Stuart Brisley's Peterlee Project

Mark Crinson

Vol 1 #28, Summer/Autumn 2004

In 1976, the performance artist, Stuart Brisley, took up an artist's placement in Peterlee New Town. In retrospect, it appears an unlikely combination. On the one hand, there was Peterlee, then still in its Development Corporation phase but originally a 1940s vision of a 'miners' capital' in the East Durham coalfield. Its first architect/planner, the Russian émigré and modernist, Berthold Lubetkin, had proposed modernist blocks linked by screens to suggest the local terraced houses, with other civic buildings zoned and placed strategically to develop concentrically and emphasise the saucer of land. But Lubetkin famously retreated to pig farming, disillusioned and defeated by official hubris and inter-ministerial wrangling. Pragmatism ensued; the town that was eventually built is mostly indistinguishable from other pallid developments of the time. The memory of terraces was left behind in favour of suburban semis and detached houses; the slagheaps were out of sight, the houses no longer huddled as mining camps around the pithead but scattered among the spacious green areas of the New Town. A few new industries were attracted to take up the slack of the worked-out mine seams: first, potato crisps, clothing and building firms; then, more recently but never adequately, service industries and Japanese car companies. Denied the facilities that might make it a centripetal force, the town also lacks any embodiment of its relation to the area's past.

On the other hand, by 1976, Brisley had achieved notoriety as an English rival to the masculine performance aesthetics of American Chris Burden or the Viennese Actionists. Brisley had used his body in cathartic rituals, unpleasant tests of endurance and rigidly staged tableaux: sitting in a bath filled with rotting meat and cold water, refusing meals served to him for ten days before Christmas while watching the food decay on the table. Little suggests a sympathy between Brisley's practice and Peterlee. Yet, unlike his contemporaries, Brisley's performances used allegory to displace self-expression in preference of commentaries on consumption and concise figurations of the immanent effects of power. (After Peterlee, his performances often reflected on communal histories in the face of larger corporate or political imperatives, some even based on equivalents to the physical actions of mining.) There was a conversational dimension to the performances themselves: unrehearsed and flirting with failure, yet insistently dependent on the audience's presence.

The Peterlee work was set up by the Artist Placement Group (APG), of which Brisley had been a founding member in 1966. The usual brief for APG artists was to work as 'creative thinkers' in industrial or government contexts

(Esso, the DHSS, the Scottish Office or, as in Brisley's earlier placement, the Hille Furniture Company), always conceiving of the artist as an 'Incidental Person' interjected into the relations of production and administration. Brisley accepted that being an artist was useless to the people of Peterlee. Despite its early ideals, residents had not participated in the making of Peterlee and had little say in its final effects: they could not even choose the colour of their front doors. They needed more control over their environment and an active sense of its relation to the history and memory of the area. So Brisley set up community workshops (eventually vetoed by the Development Corporation) and began collecting photographs and interviews covering the period from 1900 to 1976.

Archival projects are often associated with moments of traumatic or epochal change, the sundering of communities from their pasts as larger imperatives of planning and economic change supervene. But if Brisley's project simply appears to populate a *tabula rasa* with a past made obsolete by development, then its pioneering aspect is missed. As oral history, for instance, it is placed somewhere between the History from Below movement of the 1960s and the academic respectability given to oral history in the late-1970s, with some acknowledged influence from the Hackney Writers' Group. It was essential that the artist be 'incidental' – that local people provide the images and do the interviews as active repositories of collective memory rather than as subjects of official 'history'. Brisley's project also challenged an assumption that was intrinsic to Peterlee's development and, indeed, to other artists' residencies in New Towns: the belief that either the New Town or the existing wider area (here, a close-knit group of mining villages) lacked culture and recreation, and that they needed supplementing, if not replacing, by imported cultural forms which would help generate community. This is apparent in the work of Peterlee's previous town artist, Victor Pasmore, who had been appointed as consultant to the town's planners in 1955, a sop to the loss of architectural vision that had gone with Lubetkin's resignation. Pasmore left behind a group of abstract houses similar in clustered pattern-making to his contemporary painting and intended to be experienced kinetically, but alien to the climate and community. There was also a pavilion that, judging from its recent use in an artwork by Jane and Louise Wilson and a display at the Architectural Association, is now regarded as Peterlee's monument to 'good modernism'.

The recent exhibition at the Vardy Gallery offers a chance to reassess Brisley's placement, even if it belongs to another era beyond the watershed of the 1984 Miners' Strike. The photographs of the area, collected by local people and re-photographed at the time, appear in the display all the same size, mounted and grouped by village. So, while they lose the specific contexts of their highly localised social uses as photographic objects, they gain representative value as standing for an organic locality: the village as anthropological place. Structured into the archive, therefore, *Kultur* is seen to resist *Wissenschaft*. The archive shows that there is no necessary contradiction between historical disclosure and the pleasures of nostalgia, just as it is possible to find a line between heroicising the voices of the past and seeing them as victims. Certainly, this past has plenty of strikes, mining disasters and tales of extreme physical duress; yet these are troubles that are part of a wider photographic commemoration. This greater experience constantly intersects with larger narratives: the visit of the King of Uganda in 1912, the General Strike, coronation parties, the opening of pithead baths. But the lost paradise, or industrial pastoral, of this photographic memory is a place, above all, of the collective – whether it be miners posing with lamps at their feet, children in streets, local operatic societies, colliery ragtime and marching bands, seaside revellers, female weightlifters, carnivals, leek shows and whippet clubs. Necessarily (almost) absent from the archive, then, is Peterlee itself.

Two issues arise from reconsidering the Peterlee Project. One is where the archive can go from here. Over the last 27 years, it has remained largely dormant in the local council offices. There must be some doubt about whether it can offer more than local or family history, although another collecting campaign might tackle the Miners' Strike and Peterlee's history, reactivating them in a dialogue with the present. The other issue is what is retrievable from a moment of art history sometimes derided as merely well-meaning ('Art for Whom?', 'Art For All'), and whose radical potential is either buried under successive strata of more spectacular commodified art or diluted by the artists' residencies that now accompany most regeneration strategies. The issues are linked in the meditations on collecting that ramify throughout Brisley's recent work. Here, the idea of 'collection' itself offers notions of accumulation, eccentric or systematic, as well as of regular removal of refuse – the entropy that might reduce prized specimens to abject dust, as well as the curative role assumed by those who act as custodians of collections. It may be from such ideas that the Peterlee Project can find its future as the Incidental Collection.

Cheap Chinese

John Barker

Vol 1 #29, Winter/Spring 2005

In June of 2000, 58 Chinese people died of mass suffocation in the container of a lorry that arrived on a ferry at Dover. They died trying to enter the UK illegally. The direct cause of these deaths was the blocking of the container's air vents by the driver, a Dutchman named Perry Wacker. He is the worst of criminals: a panicker lacking the basic nerve required and, in this case, cutting the air supply for fear of being caught. The reporting of the case by large sections of the British media was either downright callous or sympathetic in abstract terms only; the horror felt from putting ourselves in the shoes of those who died proved to be too much.

In early February 2004, 19 Chinese workers who had entered the UK illegally died by drowning on the dangerous shoreline of Morecambe Bay, Lancashire – sands rich in cockles. This time the reporting of what happened was more sympathetic. Once again, the direct cause of their deaths was the reckless and incompetent greed of those employing them. It was reported that one of those who died, Guo Binlong, made a call on his mobile phone to his wife in the village of Zelang near Fuqing City not long before he drowned. He said, 'Maybe I'm going to die. It's a tiny mistake by my boss. He should have called us back an hour ago.'

Heartbreaking, twice over, is the 'tiny mistake' – that that's how Guo Binlong saw it – and the futility of the call. All the reporting implied that none of the 19 could read English, or perhaps even speak it, and, therefore, would not have understood the sign up by the beach that said 'Fast rising tides and hidden channels. In emergency ring 999.' Perhaps if it had been read and understood, even as the danger became obvious, there would have been a reluctance to ring 999.

In another case involving a 40-year-old Chinese man, Zhang Guo Hua, who entered the UK illegally and who died in Hartlepool after working a 24-hour shift in a plastics 'feeder' factory for Samsung, it was in no one's interests, as the reporter David Leigh put it, to make a fuss – neither employers nor fellow workers. He was cremated without an inquest. And, for Guo Binlong, the mobile phone – one of the technological wonders of the present era of globalisation, which allowed a phone call from the darkness of Morecambe Bay, with the cold water rising, to a village in China – was useless to him. In contrast, a young female Londoner was happily saved from sinking mud on the shore of the Thames by using her phone.

The reporting of these deaths, though more sympathetic, quickly identified the ruthless and criminal gangmasters as being responsible. Though they have remained largely unnamed, the condemnation has been far stronger than in the case of Perry Wacker. The broadsheet papers talked of these gangsters using stolen four-wheel drives in the same horrified tones that they portray loan sharks, as if the billions made by the 'high street' banks belonged to a different moral universe. No, these gangsters were 'tough Scousers with torn jeans' and, mixed in with them, Triads and Snakeheads.

In the same period as these horrific deaths, two other types of Chinese people in the UK are becoming important to its economy: students and tourists. All the students pay full overseas fees of £10,000 and, in 2003, there were estimated to be 25,000 students, making £250 million for British universities – a fourfold increase in three years. In 2004, the estimate is of 35,000 students. The attraction to British universities is obvious. For the students, it offers the chance of a university education when places are so limited in China, and when a British degree is said to look particularly good on CVs. What is certain is that the British government is not seeking to reduce their numbers, even when some also work in the black economy to help pay their way.

In October 2003, it was reported that the EU was expected to approve a new visa regime that will give Chinese people easier access to Europe. Chinese tour groups are expected to be given 'approved destination status'. This almost automatic visa-granting would have a built-in safety clause, from the EU's point of view, in that Chinese tour operators would be heavily punished if any of their clients failed to return to China. This does not apply to the UK, which is outside the Schengen Agreement but is equally keen to receive the money generated by such tourism, which is not negligible. Since 1998, the number of Chinese overseas travellers has almost doubled to 16.6 million. That is only a fraction of its 1.3 billion population, but the prediction is for 100 million overseas travellers by 2020, making them the world's biggest travellers. The UK does not want to be left behind, but it is seeking watertight assurances from the Chinese government that it takes back any failed asylum seekers and issues new papers to those who deliberately destroy them, an issue the Blair government made much of after the Morecombe Bay horror.

These numbers, and prospective numbers, are another indication of the development of a middle class in China – middle class in its consumption possibilities, that is, or what might otherwise be called nouveau riche. A copycat nouveau riche was highlighted by the recent 'BMW case'. The wife of a rich property owner deliberately ran over the wife of a peasant, Liu Zhongxia, whose tractor she claimed had scratched a wing mirror on her BMW in Harbin, Heliongjiang province, the heart of North East China's rust-belt, mimicking the Long Island heiress who recently maimed a few people in similar fashion after a nightclub entry argument. The driver, Mrs. Su, who had also paid someone to take her driving test, was acquitted, as no witnesses dared to turn up. That such bad behaviour and the incomes and spending power that allow it, now exist is hardly surprising given the dynamic growth of its industrial economy. It can be argued that it is only through the policies of the nationalist Communist Party –

determined to allow in Western capital only on its own terms (however much that might be wishful thinking) – that this growth has taken place. It is equally the case that it results from the shift of so much industrial production to China from the First World to take advantage of a low-wage workforce, which is also producing this nouveau riche. The divisions of levels of income and possibilities in China are now so great that they might be called class divisions, and so obvious that the new Communist Party leadership of Hu Jintao and Wen Jiabao have referred to it and to the necessity of narrowing the gap between rich and poor. Beyond the never-ending campaign to root out the corruption of officials and their parasitic relation to the peasantry, this sounds like wishful thinking.

There are not going to be 1.3 billion Chinese in the 'middle class'-level consumer class. What would they be producing? Even in the 'First World' it is a bogus promise. In the case of China, with such an across-the-board global consumer class, the global environmental crisis would be obvious even to those who do not wish to see it. Instead, the situation as it is, and as it is developing, is eminently suitable to the global investor class and its transnational corporations and companies. As Oscar Romero puts it, with the ruthless clarity of 'Third World' analysts, what matters to them is that 'national markets become increasingly liberalised so that they can seek the thin strata with high income in the underdeveloped countries [...] [T]hey do not aim to sell to the entire population, it would be sufficient for 300 million in the upper-income brackets out of the total Chinese population to become their customers, though this may create a dangerous gap between the two Chinas.'[1] To manage this dangerous gap, what better than a highly sophisticated, one-party state which can maintain a low-wage industrial assembly class, itself privileged from an even larger and lower-waged rural class? Three hundred million is enough – it dwarfs the present US market.

Taken with similarly proportioned figures in India, this development is a godsend to the global investor class which, as the South East Asian 'financial crisis' showed, was faced with a problem of global overproduction. A financial analyst also trading in snappy one-liners, Ed Yardeni, talked of the world needing all the yuppies it can get. Looked at in this light, the Chinese one-party system may be the more reliable, given the stunning defeat of the BJP party in India in the recent election, a party which, as Arundhati Roy described so well in her essay about the Gujarat pogrom, had sought to manage the 'dangerous gap' with a mixture of neoliberalism and Hindu nationalism. However chimerical the promises of the Congress Party might be, the election did allow the poor at least to say 'No' to the gap and the way it was being managed.

The poor of Britain and Europe know the present importance of China in particular. Life would be that much harder without its prices: a pair of jeans for a fiver or toys for a quid. Its coming importance was highlighted 100 years ago

1. Oscar Romero, *The Myth of Development*, London: Zed Books, 2001.

in J.A. Hobson's *Imperialism*, a book unfairly famous only for having been used and misused by Lenin:

> China seems to offer a unique opportunity to the Western business man. A population [...] endowed with an extraordinary capacity of steady labour, with great intelligence and ingenuity, inured to a low standard of material comfort [...] Few Europeans even profess to know the Chinese [...] the only important fact upon which there is universal agreement is that the Chinese of all the 'lower races' are most adaptable to purposes of industrial exploitation, yielding the largest surplus product of labour in proportion to their cost of keep.

Western ignorance seems to have changed little: the Sinology department at Durham University is scheduled to close, and the UK government is to withdraw the small support it gave to those doing M.Phils in Chinese.

Hobson was in no position to anticipate a communist revolution or the developing class system of the present. He did, however, foresee those fears of this industrial development getting out of Western control, manifested in notions of the 'yellow peril' which crop up throughout the 20th century to cause havoc in the minds of the leftist American writers, Jack London and John dos Passos:

> It is at least conceivable that China might so turn the tables upon the Western industrial nations, and, either by adopting their capital and organisers or, as is more probable, by substituting her own, might flood their markets with her cheaper manufacturers, and refusing their imports in exchange might take her payment in liens upon their capital, reversing the earlier process of investment until she gradually obtained financial control over her quondam patrons and civilisers.

Such speculation belongs elsewhere; I don't know, for example, how much Chinese capital is invested in US Treasury bonds, but presumably it figures prominently in professional, militarised Western geopolitics. In such considerations, presumably, oil figures a great deal; China's 'industrial revolution' depends on it. Last year alone, its oil consumption rose by 10 percent, along with what *The Times* called, on 11 June 2004, the 'rampant demand' from not just China but India and Brazil, countries 'continuing to guzzle world supply'. Guzzle! It may well be that the spread of US military bases across the oil-producing world is a product of those considerations.

At the same time, Hobson raises another possibility that:

> the pressure of working class movements in politics and industry in the West can be met by a flood of China goods, so as to keep down wages [...I]t is conceivable that the powerful industrial and financial classes of the West, in order better to keep the economic and political mastery [...] may insist upon the free importation of yellow labour for domestic and industrial service in

> the West. This is a weapon which they hold in reserve, should they need to use it in order to keep the populace in safe subjection.

Hobson himself had seen the use of Chinese labour in the South African gold mines. While, to our ears, he sounds melodramatic and sweeping, his considerations nevertheless overlap with yet another round of the 'Immigration Debate'. The disparity between the freedom of mobility for capital and non-freedom for labour is mentioned, if at all, and then forgotten, as if these really do represent parallel worlds. Instead, the same yes-and-nos go round the carousel. Yes, we need some skilled workers; yes, we must rationally look at future demographics and who will be needed to do the work to pay our pensions; but at the same time, watch out for bogus refugees who are really economic migrants; watch out for the illegal immigrant, but not too hard.

After the death of three Kurdish workers on a level crossing on their way to pick spring onions in the East of England, it was suddenly discovered there were 2000 Chinese in King's Lynn, as if they had never been seen before. In King's Lynn! Their deaths were more sordid in the banality of the accident than the thriller-like narrative of Romanian ex-train workers fixing signals so that other migrants could leap onto the Eurostar at obscure spots. The reality of the immigration debate is also more sordid. While the Third World is raided for trained nurses, whose training was a cost to those countries, immigration fears are regularly rehearsed. The net result is that so many immigrants live in fear, and this fear is as functional to capitalist economies in the present era as it has been in the past. Migrant workers in Fortress Europe, and especially illegally-entered migrants, are far more likely to accept wages and conditions that are essential to its needs and which, in turn, have a knock-on effect on wages and working conditions generally. Racist politicians and professional opinionists have their own grisly agenda, but these are functional to capitalist economies and their household names. The focus of these opinionists on 'failed' asylum seekers who are not allowed to work and, more recently, on a 'flood' of Roma and other Eastern Europeans who can work legally as EU citizens, gives the game away. Their spotlight is not on King's Lynn, a national blind spot. 'Policies that claim to exclude undocumented workers,' says Stephen Castle, 'may often really be about allowing them through side doors and back doors so that they can be readily exploited.' Or, as he put it some 30 years ago, commenting on the repatriation demands of Enoch Powell and other racist politicians: 'Paradoxically their value for capital lies in their very failure to achieve their declared aims.'

Inside Fortress Europe – for the UK in particular, with its avowedly American-style deregulation – this process is all too visible. It is the dirty secret of the UK's economic success under New Labour. And they are proud of it, these shadow social democrats; the UK's official trade and investment website boasts of it.

> Total wage costs in the UK are among the lowest in Europe,' it says. 'In the UK employees are used to working hard for their employers. In 2001 the average hours worked a week was 45.1 for males and 40.7 for females. The EU average was 40.9 [...] UK law does not oblige employers to provide a written employment contract... Recruitment costs in the UK is [sic] low [...] The law governing conduct of employment agencies is less restrictive in the UK. The UK has the lowest corporation tax of any major industrialised country.

Recently, Jack Straw has 'defied Europe' as the papers would have it. In a speech to the CBI, he promised that the UK would insist that the charter of fundamental rights creates no 'new rights under national law, so as not to upset the balance of Britain's industrial relations policy'; that is, the one established by previous Conservative governments. In Britain, there is nowhere for the exploited to turn and almost no employer is prosecuted for using illegal migrants.

To the extent that media coverage of the horror of Morecambe Bay went beyond fingering tough, Scouse gangmasters in stolen four-wheel drives, it focused on the power of supermarkets in the agricultural sector and their relation to those who do the harvesting – a harvest which doesn't stop for a festival because the operation is non-stop, all year round. Migrant labour is up by 44 percent in the last seven years. Much of it is 'legal', via seasonal agricultural schemes, but, of the 3,000–5,000 'gangmasters' who organise this, at least 1,000 are illegal and give no protection to their workers. But, then, 'gangmasters' are, in effect, employment agencies, and these, as New Labour like to boast, are the least restricted in the EU.

Despite Morecambe and the ensuing hand-wringing, nothing has changed. In September 2003, the House of Commons Committee on the Environment, Health and Food, chaired by MP Michael Jack, found that the agencies supposed to deal with 'illegal gangmasters' were making no real impact and set out the changes that would be needed. In mid-May 2004, a report by the same committee declared that the government had no clearer picture of the situation, and that enforcement action had not increased. It concluded there had been 'no evidence of any change in the government's approach since last September. Indeed, in some respects, enforcement activity has diminished because of lack of resources.'

The beneficiaries of this, the 'household' names of Tesco, Sainsbury's and the rest, are all profiting from this underclass. Andrew Simms describes a situation in which 'Long chains of sub-contractors, commercial confidentiality and contractual obfuscation, allow household names to hide behind plausible denials [...W]e have evolved a system better at hiding, or distancing cause from effect'. This at a time when New Labour has never stopped talking of responsibilities in return for rights, exchange value-business. Those who died at Morecambe are believed to have moved on from King's Lynn, in all likelihood taking a drop in pay from the vegetable-picking rates of a market dominated by the 'high street' supermarkets.

The distancing of cause from consequence, the not-me-guv cry of the rich, the powerful and their portraitists, appear in all their colours in the *Teeside Evening Gazette*'s report on a fire at the Woo One factory in the Sovereign Business Park, Hartlepool, at the beginning of April this year. It mentioned the death of Zhang Guo Hua, but only to emphasise that there was no proof of a connection between the haemorrhage that killed him and his working conditions. He had, it reported, been through the usual kind of work: cutting salads for Tesco suppliers in Sussex, fish-processing in Scotland and packing flowers in Norfolk. Usual for whom?

The Queen had opened the nearby Samsung plant in 1996, which has a global turnover of $33 billion. When it opened, the local MP, Peter Mandelson, wrote an article in praise of the company, saying 'Some have the impression that the success of the tiger economies is based on sweatshop labour. This is a false picture.' The false picture is that sweatshop labour is exclusive to the 'tiger economies'. Zhang Guo Hua worked a 24-hour shift in Hartlepool. It was his decision, of course, one can hear the not-me-guv voice saying. Woo One, the company Zhang Guo Hua worked for, was a 'feeder' factory for Samsung, its practices its own, as Samsung would have it. Zhang Guo Hua spent his last 24 hours stamping the word SAMSUNG onto plastic casings either for microwave oven doors or computer monitors, on his feet throughout. When he collapsed and went to hospital, it was under another name. It was only when he was dead that a friend gave Zhang's real passport. So that, even though he was cremated without an inquest, it was in his own name.

An ex-worker at Woo One said that the minimum working week was 72 hours and the minimum shift 12 hours. Its managing director, Keith Boynton, agreed that English workers were not required to work these hours, but it wasn't him guv; the Chinese workers were *technically* employed by an outfit called Thames Oriental Manpower Management with offices in New Malden, Surrey, close to Samsung's corporate HQ. Thames Oriental Manpower Management – a name that could only have been dreamt up by its proprietor, Mr. Lin, not a tough Scouser in ripped jeans but a man who had been granted asylum by claiming – claiming that is – that he was a North Korean refugee. Mr. Boynton of Woo One said, 'What he (Mr. Lin) pays the workers is up to him.' Mr. Lin, it was reported, had also taken control from Woo One of the nearby, three-to-a-room set of dormitories and presumably, because he is now the villain, charged what he liked.

At this time, Samsung boasted of record UK factory profits through 'unit cost reduction'. To get some idea of the process by which this might happen, two pieces of Marx's structural economic analysis come to mind. For one thing, Marx had deconstructed the notion of productivity long before the era of productivity deals. The very notion is one which exactly distances cause from consequence or, rather, and all the more modern for that, muddies the cause. 'Productivity' smears together the productiveness of labour – that is, the improved technology which allows for greater production – intensity of labour – which is how hard people work per hour (and here much of the improved technology simply increases the intensity of labour) – and the length of the working day. These latter two factors are characteristic of 'primitive accumulation', and boy was that going on in Samsung's Hartlepool circus. Marx's misnamed Equalisation of Profit law describes the mechanism by which this works. The surplus, or profit, engendered by companies like Woo One does not all go to them; the size of Samsung, the concentration of capital involved and its power in relation to both its suppliers and marketing, mean that it takes the lion's share of what has truly been accumulated, in primitive fashion, by small, dependent suppliers. This is not some one-off phenomenon; one study shows Toyota having some 47,000 small firms working for it in a hierarchical structure, with most of those in the lowest layer passing the surpluses of 'primitive accumulation' up the chain to transnational corporations like Toyota which benefits from that mystery called 'value-added'.

When the story about Zhang Guo Hua emerged in *The Guardian*, on 13 January 2004, local MP, Peter Mandelson, said that he had 'written to Samsung about allegations made against Woo One in this tragic case'. The question is, then, did he ever receive a reply, because, two days later, Samsung announced (out of the blue, it was said) that it was closing the factory involved – the Wynyard in Billingham. It blamed the high level of wages in North East England and said it was relocating to Slovakia, where wages stood at £1 an hour. To which address did Mr. Mandelson write? Was it passed on by a Post Office redirection instruction? Has he received a reply? It seems unlikely, given that Samsung's decision can hardly have been spur of the moment, or that a meeting with Woo One would hardly have been a priority in the two days remaining. It transpired that Woo One had already started to make its own move in the direction of Slovakia, and indeed announced, some three weeks later, that it was to close its computer casings plant in Hartlepool. On the news of Samsung's departure, Mr. Mandelson, his letter still in the post somewhere, said that the price of their product had fallen worldwide, and that was 'the reason for its closure'. Prime Minister, Tony Blair, said he deeply regretted the loss of jobs involved, but that this was 'part of the world economy we live in'.

There is, of course, much truth in what he says, but there is a complacency to the same voice that says so much of our responsibilities, which grates. If wages in Slovakia are £1 an hour, in China they are likely to be 50 pence. Yet there is a need, felt in the 'First World', to maintain low-cost mass production within its own frontiers, even while its investor class shifts production to such countries. There is, for one thing, a structural limit to how many lawyers, journalists, IT specialists and bankers are required, even in the First World –

whatever might be said about education, education, education – while, at the same time, there is an increasing reluctance to cushion the circumstances of the excluded population. For another, at the psychic level, there is a fear of political economy – that if so much industrial production is shifted to different parts of Asia, it will somehow weaken the West, by being both a sign and symptom of lazy decadence. More specifically than notions of decadence, there is a need for cheap labour in the First World, within its own frontiers, 'for it means that the South cannot extract monopoly rents for its cheap labour and bad working conditions', as Robert Biel puts it. There are sweatshops in London and Los Angeles even while automatic looms are capable of weaving 760 metres of denim per minute. As Hobson suggested, and the irony stands out in neon, this First World, low-cost production requires migrant workers, workers made fearful by an unscrupulous media and political class.

Migrant workers are also essential to low-cost China and its 'economic miracle'. The numbers are hard to establish; 80 million is one estimate – 94 another – of recent migrants from the Chinese countryside, many of whom are also 'illegal'. Many Chinese cities require residency permits, while it is these 'peasants' who do the jobs that Beijingers, for example, won't do themselves. And, just like anywhere else – Albanians in Greece, for example – they are accused of being thieves and dirty, while also exerting a downward pressure on local wages. Should there be a shrinkage of economic growth at a global level, these Chinese migrant workers will be the first to lose their jobs. For one thing, 90 percent of them work without contracts, according to Li Jianfei, a law professor at the People's University. Even the state-run Trade Union estimates that they are owed over 100 million Yuan in back wages, but a campaign for repayment is for those with contracts only. Much of this is in the booming construction sector, where non-paying subcontractors blame large companies underpaying them, the Law of Equalisation of Profit in crude form.

In more classical form, this law is also inherent in the condition of the coal mining industry. China's increasing oil dependence is well known, but it is also the world's largest coal producer. Chinese companies are making sizeable profits on legal and illegal mining operations, but at prices to industry which mean the real rates of profit of the consuming industries, often foreign-financed, are even greater. Exerting more pressure on the industry and its highly exploited workforce is central government's demand for more output. At the same time, the industry has an appalling safety record; around 7,000 miners were killed in 2003. There are promises of more inspectorates and the closing of illegal mines, but, in the face of this 'energy crunch', this is likely to remain rhetorical. Safety investment is far less than the announced allocation. The grim reality is that with the retrenching of state-owned industries and the accompanying loss of benefits and pensions, the unemployed and the rural poor have entered the industry in huge numbers and are willing to work for cash in appalling and unsafe conditions, often assisting coal mine owners in avoiding safety procedures to ensure continued employment, as the *China Labour Bulletin* puts it. The death of one man in Hartlepool is hardly on the same scale, but the pressures for 'not making a fuss' are similar.

The wishful thinking of the new Communist Party leadership about reversing the dynamics of inequality looks like mere cynical rhetoric, since it doesn't prevent it from maintaining a hard line against any independent worker protests over pay and conditions. A strike over pay at the partly Taiwanese-financed Xinxiong Shoe Factory in Dongguan City in April of this year resulted in several arrests. The Ferro-Alloy strike in Liaoyang province, involving 1,600 workers, resulted in long prison sentences for Yao Fuxin and Xiao; meanwhile, the workers are still without retrenchment compensation. In Hubei province, six workers have been arrested and are awaiting trial on charges of 'disturbing social order' after a peaceful demonstration at the Tieshu factory; this after 15 months of peaceful campaigning to recover more than 200 million Yuan in back wages, redundancy payments, workers shares and other moneys owed them by the bankrupt factory's management.

Other workers from the Tieshu factory have been sentenced to terms of up to 21 months of 're-education through labour', a punishment which bypasses the criminal justice system. We do not know the extent of prison labour in China, but it too is a component holding down general wages and conditions. There is nothing to get smug about, as prison labour in the UK is being organised in a much more serious manner than before. The Woolworth's-type chain in the North of England, Wilkinson's, is highly dependent on it for its products. A recent piece in *The Economist* on 6 May 2004 goes further, saying 'Hard-working immigrants transform the prison system.' It describes how Wormwood Scrubs (where a regime of extreme and racist staff violence is still being investigated) is full of cocaine mules from South America, and how the prison runs production lines for airline headsets and aluminium windows. The best jobs, it says, pay £25–£40 a week 'depending on a prisoner's place on the ladder of privilege (as in all prisons, inmates are paid more for the same job if they behave themselves)'. It goes on to say that this 'is serious money for a third-worlder [...] so a steady stream of remittances flows from Wormwood Scrubs to poor countries.' A grotesque conclusion might be that the poor victims of Morecambe Bay would have been better off there.

After the effective, international demonstrations against the World Trade Organization in Seattle, the unity displayed there, which was most unsettling to the global investor class, was quickly confronted with the sneers of professional opinionists. The many American trade unionists present, they said, had no global consciousness, they were just there to protect their jobs. Their demands for basic standards and rights for workers in the poor world were just a subtle form of protectionism, protecting their privileges. It is true that the Clinton administration would do almost anything to secure free trade deals in American interests, and also that Third World voices have been raised to say that such demands for minimum standards and conditions are aimed at cutting off the only way in which they can develop economically – that is, with a monopoly on cheap labour – but it is reasonable to ask, in return, who and what these voices represent. The Third World is not some homogeneous space, and the class divisions in India and China are clear to see. Increasing inequality within countries, rich and poor, is a global reality.

It is such a reality which gives us a nominally social democratic and a nominally communist government both spurning any effective protection of workers. Instead, then, why not support those working for better wages, conditions and respect in China, for example, lawyers like Cho Li Tai and the Centre for Women's Law Studies and Legal Services at Beijing University, peasant activists like Li Changping and, most of all, those imprisoned for demanding basic rights. For this to mean anything in the UK, a start would be mounting support for the Private Members' Bill of MP Jim Sheridan, backed by the TGWU, for a thorough registration of 'gangmasters'. If this were to succeed, it would at least remove one pillar of the government's boast of its cheap labour and lightly regulated employment agencies and go a step beyond cursory hand-wringing, which was the extent of the response to the Morecambe tragedy. Six months later, in August, it was reported that rival 'gangs' of cockle-pickers had to be rescued from the same sands.

Disrespecting Multifundamentalism

Melancholic Troglodytes

Vol 2 #2, Spring 2006

Give respect, get respect!
British Government Action Plan

It is essential to understand, at the outset, that Tony Blair's latest moral crusade, based on returning respectability to cities and villages, is not a gimmick or a quick fix but part and parcel of a protracted attack on the working class. The aim of this text is twofold: first, to analyse the nature of this attack by showing the antagonism between bourgeois *respectability* and proletarian *respect* and, second, to demonstrate how this conflict is related to the demise of two of capital's most pernicious ideologies – religious *fundamentalism* and secular *multiculturalism*.

Perhaps understandably, some readers may baulk at our contention that the journalistic inanity known as (Eastern) fundamentalism and its flip side of (Western) multiculturalism are in crisis. After all, are we not subjected in the media to a daily barrage of mullah-morons, self-righteously preaching the finer points of Shari'a law? Do we, then, not have to endure the gormless, liberal multiculturalist paternalistically tut-tutting his *uncivilised* interlocutors? Has not Hamas secured a major parliamentary victory for fundamentalism in Palestine? Did not Hezbollah inflict a massive military defeat on Israel? Is not religion calling the shots in Iraq? Is there not sufficient evidence that the world has gone completely insane? Should we not adopt a bunker mentality and hide until this tempestuous madness has run its course? By tracing the vicissitudes of the notion of respect, we hope to offer a more nuanced – as well as optimistic – assessment of the current state of class struggle.

Is there no respect of place, persons, nor time, in you?
William Shakespeare, *Twelfth Night*

Class society has always made use of both ideology (Marx) and discursive practice (Foucault) in order to secure the status quo. These mechanisms of regulation have, in turn, relied on nodal values through which *respectability* has been policed. These nodal values exist in a chain of signification, and the study of their evolution can be instructive.

During what is lazily referred to as pre-modernity (more accurately slavery, serfdom, feudalism, etc.), the nodal value greasing the wheels of society was *honour*. The gladiator in ancient Rome, the crusader during the Middle Ages and the knight during feudalism accrued honour through a mixture of courage, skill and sacrifice. Their lower class counterparts – the slave, the serf and the peasant – remained in a permanent state of *shame*.[1] Only occasionally could a lower class person wipe away the shame associated with their social status and gain honour. This required a superhuman endeavour, and Spartacus stands as an archetypal example of such a move. Outside this cosy polarity between shame and honour, *respect* began to make a tentative appearance amongst the populace. Artisans and craftsmen who managed to monopolise certain trades began to be granted a grudging respect by the aristocratic elite.

From the 17th century onward, with the gradual advent of the formal phase of capitalist domination, *absolute* surplus value extraction became the norm in many industries. Exchange value was characterised by the regulation of punctuality, sexuality and discipline. The nodal value that became associated with this phase was *dignity*, which implied that identity is independent of birth, institutional roles and hierarchy. The Dutch national liberation movement of 1579–81, the English Revolution of 1640–60 and the French Revolution of 1789 represent a series of historical ruptures which transformed society's nodal value from honour to dignity.

To turn up at work punctually, to engage in the production process conscientiously, to look and sound orderly and to discharge one's sexual duties spartanly (in other words to be a *good citizen*) were characteristics of dignity. By default, remaining unemployed, dirty and promiscuous became a sign of undignified behaviour, punishable by poverty and stigmatisation. The English Ranters were an early victim of bourgeois indignation. Naturally, most radicals have been deeply suspicious of dignity. F. Palinorc has dismissed it as a shibboleth of bourgeois thought: '[Dignity is an] absurd, utopian cry under a system of total value domination, analogous to the battle cries of *democracy* and *liberty*.'[2] Later, we will attempt to show how the situation is somewhat more complicated, but for the time being, let us pursue the historical development of capital further.

Those societies that have negotiated the passage from formal to real domination have experienced a more flexible form of surplus value extraction and a greater disparity between the private and public spheres of human behaviour. Also in this phase, workers begin to enter the economy as consumers of leisure, and the bourgeoisie is keen to control leisure's 'moral misuse'. Dignity began to display its limitations and was gradually marginalised by a more sought-after nodal attribute – *authenticity*. This is an individualised attribute which encourages political engagement based on the notion of *identity*. The ability to be *oneself* in public now becomes an ideal only available to a handful of clowns, method actors and 'mad' individuals who require neither

1. The concept of honour implies that identity is essentially [...] linked to institutional roles', P.L. Berger et al., *The Homeless Mind*, London: Penguin Books, 1973, p. 84. Once pre-modern institutions gave way under the relentless march of capitalism, honour became embourgeoisfied and emptied of its substance. Cervantes' *Don Quixote* captures the demise of the knight-errant and his chivalric code magnificently.
2. F. Palinorc, *Annual Review of Critical Psychology*, 3, Manchester: Manchester Metropolitan University, 2003, p. 183.

dignity nor honour since they know no shame. The rest of us are reduced to purchasing tourist authenticity in far off, 'uncontaminated' lands in the form of Nicaraguan coffee, Turkish whirling dervishes and the occasional divine miracle.

This historical chain of signification (honour – dignity – authenticity) is roughly aligned with pre-capitalism, formal capital domination and real capital domination. However, this schematic association breaks down upon closer inspection. Raymond Williams, for instance, talks of three types of cultural artefacts: the *dominant*, the *residual* and the *emergent*.[3] All three usually coexist in any one period of development. For instance, the dominant cultural node in contemporary India is dignity, which corresponds to the formal phase of capital domination. But India is a complex society which also evolves around residual cultural artefacts, like honour, and emergent ones such as authenticity. Most Indians require a mixture of honour-dignity-authenticity for obtaining respectability; but, depending on their specific cultural-economic status, they prioritise this chain of signification differently. But, and here is the key question for us, what happens if you are a caste member who is denied access to this chain of signification? In other words, what if you are not considered a full citizen with a delineated set of rights and duties? How, then, do you seek self-worth and social status as a prelude to interaction with the rest of society?

> Unthinking respect for authority is the greatest enemy of truth.
> Albert Einstein

The proletariat has historically employed three main strategies for overcoming the problems cited above. These three strategies correspond to varying degrees of proletarian empowerment:

Re-accentuation of Respectability

This first strategy re-accentuates the meaning of nodal values when the proletariat does not feel strong enough to reject them (Bakhtin). For example, in the 1960s, US blacks defined dignity according to class markers. Bourgeois blacks, such as Martin Luther King, Jr, understood dignity to mean upright citizenship and demanded equal employment and educational opportunities. Under this scheme, black dignity was to be guaranteed by enlightened leaders and enshrined in the law. The law may not be able to police racist prejudice, but its admirers believe it is capable of changing discriminatory behaviour and that this, in time, might lead to cognitive alterations.

Other blacks, such as the Black Panthers, were also seeking reforms, although in their case extra-legal actions were used in order to pressurise legislatures. Black Panthers understood dignity as full citizenship, and since blacks were only considered three-fifths citizens, the strategy aimed to obtain

3. See Raymond Williams, 'Base and superstructure in Marxist cultural theory', *New Left Review*, 82, 1973.

the remaining two-fifths of rights denied them by the Constitution. Meanwhile, black welfarism would restore dignity to black lumpenproletarians left out of the circuits of capital accumulation.

Lastly, proletarian blacks had a simpler and more radical conception of dignity, which was shaped by their everyday confrontation with racism. Proletarian dignity confronted both racist *behaviour* (e.g. lynching and segregation) and racist *attitude* (i.e. discrimination in the shape of Jim Crow laws or personal prejudice). The stable dictionary 'meaning' of the term dignity remained the same, but the personal 'sense' in which it was employed had shifted dramatically (Vygotsky). Proletarian dignity, therefore, cannot simply be ignored or dismissed as bourgeois. It must be understood in its concrete context and as part of a dialectical supersession of all values.

It is essential to understand that proletarian demands for dignity – whether expressed by black American workers in the 1960s, Russian workers in 1905 or Palestinian workers crossing Israeli checkpoints – are not a static entity, for they can fast evolve in one of two directions: Dignity can either solidify into reactionary *pride* or evolve into *proletarian respect*. Examples of the former include the notion of black pride promoted by fascists such as Farrakhan's Nation of Islam, Ahmadinejad's Iranian brand of Strasserism or, perhaps even, the British National Party's opportunistic slogan of 'rights for whites'.[4] Examples of the latter include the solidarity amongst British black proletarians during the 1970s and 1980s centred on respect. A similar phenomenon was witnessed amongst Native Americans in the 1970s during their struggle for land and an end to poverty, or during the first Palestinian Intifada, when fighting both the Israeli army and Palestinian leaders simultaneously generated mutual respect within, and between, refugee camps.

Collective Rejection of Respectability

There are occasions when, due to strength or sheer desperation, we manage to go beyond mere re-accentuation of bourgeois respectability and a deep-seated rejection sets in. A minority faction within the anti-war movement in the run up to the War on Iraq achieved this in some measure (the rest, be they secularist or religious, remained within the bounds of bourgeois respectability). The honour and glory of war was rejected, sometimes through rational arguments and sometimes through collective laughter and irony; the dignity of anti-Saddam victims who were opportunistically paraded in the media was exposed as a propaganda ruse and nullified. The authenticity of evidence put before us to justify the war was also queried at every turn. Some further examples of rejection of respectability may concretise the point: during a one-minute silence

4. Whilst hating the Nation of Islam and the Iranian theocracy, the BNP is happy to learn strategy from them. The BNP's recent success in infiltrating the anti-Jerry Springer Opera campaign has prompted them to try to set up a church in Lincolnshire under the name of the Christian Council of Britain. The head of this new church is a 'reverend' Robert West, who believes that 'The mixing of races challenges the glory of god', http://www.ekklesia.co.uk/content/news_syndication/article_060316bnp.shtml

in a demo against the First Gulf War, bourgeois respectability was compromised when a group of radicals insisted on shouting, 'No War but the Class War'; at the beginning of the Second Gulf War, an American protestor whose husband was killed in Vietnam said, 'I learned the hard way there is no glory in a folded flag.' Similarly, a sizeable minority of Iranian proletarians have rejected the concept of martyrdom and warfare as a route to heaven, as is evident in the struggle against the burial of the 'unknown soldier' within university campus grounds. 'Queer carnivalesque' would be another instance where we have witnessed a break with heteronormative notions of sexual respectability, as well as gay/lesbian essentialism.

Proletarian resistance creates a gap between reality and official ideology. This gap has to be filled by rhetoric. The further decomposition of the art of rhetoric in the speeches of Bush, Blair, the Pope, Ahmadinejad and Bin Laden is itself an indication that the chain of signification is losing its shine everywhere. The first canon of classical rhetoric, as practised in ancient Greece, was 'invention'. With the demise of the Sophists, invention was eclipsed by one or more of the other divisions, namely 'arrangement', 'style', 'memory' and 'delivery'. Today's politicians have conveniently dispensed with memory and delivery, leaving arrangement and style as the only two vehicles for rhetorical discourse.

There are also moments of desperation which lead to a frontal assault on bourgeois respectability. Refugees and asylum seekers who are being forcefully removed have been known to go on hunger strike or strip to their underwear at airports as a final act of defiance against immigration authorities. Here, *respectability*, which works through raising the threshold of shame (Goffman), is subverted by the *grotesque collective body* (Bakhtin). Similarly, prison revolts undermine in a matter of hours the systematic work of chaplains, social workers and prison staff whose programme is to instil prisoners with etiquette and dignity.

Creation of New Concepts for Bypassing Respectability

When the balance of class forces is in our favour and we have the luxury of time and space, use value may temporarily eclipse exchange value. These preconditions not only make possible a rejection of bourgeois respectability but also foster proletarian respect. Moments of social rupture are usually preceded by a preponderance of mutual respect amongst the proletariat. This is not simply a case of positing our *morality* against theirs, as Trotsky would suggest. Rather, it is a case of rejecting exchange value and morality as the regulator of the private-public split in favour of a qualitatively different form of immeasurable value based on human need and solidarity. For instance, the term 'respect' finds its origins in Jamaica as part of the 'rude boy' slang subculture and is transported to Britain where it is picked up by the 'white' working class.

> Nothing is more despicable than respect based on fear.
> Albert Camus

So far, we have postulated that respect is foregrounded among those sections of the proletariat traditionally denied access to the rulers' chain of signification. We have also suggested that its appearance is a sign of proletarian strength, since it is generated from below.

Conversely, if proletarians today are not creating autonomous, organic concepts such as respect (strategy three), and if they are not effectively rejecting capital's nodal values (strategy two), and if re-accentuation of honour-dignity-authenticity (strategy one) is usurped by reactionaries and turned into pride, then it is logical to assume that capital is enjoying unprecedented hegemony over us.

Yet things are not as hopeless as they seem. In recent years, the two ideologies that have most effectively shackled proletarians worldwide have been *fundamentalism* and *multiculturalism*. Significantly, both emerged at times of massive structural crisis for capital. Fundamentalism (and we beg the reader's forgiveness for over-generalising here), whether in its early 20th century US manifestation or its late 20th century Middle Eastern variety, was suitable for overseeing the transition from formal to real capital domination. However, it failed in both arenas. At the risk of oversimplification, we could state that religious fundamentalism in both the US and the Middle East emerged partly as a response to the failures of modernism, and yet, instead of replacing the latter, it ended up forging an uneasy alliance with modernism (especially in places where fundamentalism gained power). In the US, it was military Keynesianism that ultimately completed the transition, and in the Middle East, a kitsch cocktail of military Keynesianism (in industry) is being employed in conjunction with neoliberalism (in finance and banking) and populism (in agriculture) to bring forth the real phase of capital domination.

Both fundamentalism and multiculturalism prefer winning the cultural battle in the domestic sphere prior to restructuring the production of values in the public sphere. However, whilst fundamentalism is proudly monologic, multiculturalism is *falsely* dialogic (Bakhtin). It pretends to take the addressee into account, respecting difference and heterogeneity. In truth, secular multiculturalism is as haughty as religious fundamentalism. It listens but does not hear. And now that its project of *integrating* the foreigner within has reached an impasse, it has left the Western bourgeoisie without a recognisable strategy for continued hegemony. The crisis of multiculturalism reflects the failures of both secularism and postmodernism. The so-called separation of the church from the state was always a mirage. Secularism took the hibernation of religiosity for its destruction and lulled itself into a false sense of security. Marx observed this bourgeois self-deception with uncanny clarity: '[E]ven when man proclaims himself an atheist through the mediation of the state [...] he still remains under the constraints of religion because he acknowledges his atheism only deviously, through a medium.'[5]

5. Karl Marx, 'On the Jewish Question', *Early Writings*, London: Penguin Books, 1984, p. 218.

What Marx is saying is that ideological atheism (or if you prefer, bourgeois humanistic atheism) is merely the negation of theism. The synthesis is something else which is yet to emerge. This 'something else' we have characterised as *proletarian atheism*, since it will be a product of everyday proletarian self-activity and not secular legislation or rationalistic discourse.

The slow-death agony of fundamentalism and multiculturalism has left bourgeois respectability devoid of efficacy. The slowness of this process and the absence of new proletarian values may have obscured this tendency, but the everyday stench of bourgeois values is becoming harder to ignore.

> We may not pay Satan reverence, for that would be indiscreet, but we can at least respect his talent.
> Mark Twain

Satan may be worthy of both reverence and respect, but the bourgeoisie has lost the plot.[6] In this final section, we will provide examples related to our masters' inability to maintain respectability over us.

Let us take the 'naming and shaming' campaign against paedophiles, initiated by *The News of the World* and taken up by the British government to tackle *disrespect.* Note that, whilst *The News of the World*'s crusade was (largely) against white working class men, the government's Anti-Social Behaviour Orders campaign is (largely) against children wrongdoers who, in the past, were not usually named for legal reasons. Shaming, as we have seen, is traced to pre-capitalism. Its modern, bourgeois version never possessed the impact it needed for controlling proletarian behaviour. Today, this inappropriate usage of shaming has the ironic effect of granting *disrespectful* children a badge of honour amongst their peers. One final irony is that 'naming and shaming' was a tactic used by the radical plebeian press in the 18th and 19th centuries against the ruling class. If an impropriety (usually of a sexual kind) amongst the rich and famous was discovered, the radical press would blackmail the culprit for a hefty sum. Once the ransom was paid, the next issue of the paper would carry a titillating account of the sordid affair anyway in order to undermine bourgeois respectability; *The News of the World*'s campaign seems an exact reversal of this original impetus.

Our next example is even more ominous for British capitalism. The inability of both the Labour and Tory parties to reanimate a sense of modern nationalism

6. You want to know how badly the stupid bastards have lost the plot? Get a load of this: Kevin Roberts is a high-ranking bureaucrat with Saatchi and Saatchi. Recently, he gave US Defense Intelligence Agencies a talk in which he argued 'brand America' is failing because it is a 'High Respect, Low Love' kind of product. In contrast, he argues, there are brands that have 'High Love, High Respect' quotients such as Harley Davidson, Apple and JFK! So the trick is to make 'brand America' more like Harley Davidson and Apple, and the rest of the world will fall in love with the USA. (See M. Grimshaw, 'Religion, Terror and the End of the Postmodern: Rethinking the Responses', *International Journal of Baudrillard Studies*, January 2006, Vol. 3, no. 1).

The conspiracy nut may interject here that the Sa'atchi (literally, clockmaker) brothers are originally from Iraq! Could theirs be a long-term Sufi strategy of undermining the efficacy of the US military 'intelligence' through subtle counter-productive spin? Are the Sa'atchi brothers Iraq's revenge on US colonisers?

has alienated a sizeable minority of the population who now voluntarily identify themselves as the 'other'. The *other* consists of two main camps: firstly, the alienated and atomised proletarians who attempt to regain their self-respect individually and, secondly, proud and self-righteous 'Muslims', 'Asians', 'country warriors' and 'white fascists'. Ex-Home Secretary, David Blunkett, and his faithful sidekick, Trevor Phillips, clumsily attempted to impose British values on people, only to expose this 'imagined community' (Benedict Anderson) for the sham it has always been. Gordon Brown's recent call for a 'British Day' indicates his thinking runs along similar lines. Their new citizenship deal is an American rewriting of the social contract: once British values have been sufficiently inculcated and citizens have been coached in public displays of patriotism, the liberal state will graciously shower them with *tolerance*.[7]

The fact that a once-secure sense of Britishness increasingly relies on ritualistic displays of patriotism is a sign of weakness not strength. Ironically, the state is relying on a colonial strategy for internal control at a time when that pernicious species of vultures known as 'community leaders' are no longer in charge of their constituencies because they have lost the respect of the proletariat. It is arguable whether this atavistic cadre of vote-hunters ever enjoyed any genuine *community* support. Meanwhile, vacuous old multi-culturalists are still harping about 'equal dignity under the law', 'recognition of difference' and the finer distinctions of 'integration' (which is good) and 'assimilation' (which is not). Multiculturalists are still in denial; they will need time to acknowledge the gravity of their defeat. Poor, pitiful hacks are still 'multi-ing' and 'hybrid-ing' our cultures in the hope of covering up the fact that an increasing number of us already feel *trans-cultural*.

One final example will suffice. The case of the Danish cartoons revealed cracks in both multiculturalism and fundamentalism. Danish capitalism demonstrated the thin line separating tolerance from intolerance when Danish racists were given the green light to provoke their Muslim counterparts. Over a number of months, Muslim hate-mongers were, in turn, given carte blanche by Saudi Arabia and Iran to whip certain sections of their constituencies into frenzy. Once a number of scores were settled and political points underlined, the furore died down as mysteriously as it had been initiated.[8] In the process, European multiculturalism exposed its inherent intolerance and the might of Islam shook with trepidation before a few second-rate cartoonists!

7. Regarding the generation of a British identity, it is worth noting that, outside the country, various agencies, such as embassies, train prospective refugees in British culture before accepting them. Perhaps myths about British identity are easier to fabricate at a distance – in Africa, the Middle East and the ex-colonies.
8. The comparison with Rushdie's *Satanic Verses* is instructive. Then, Khomeini's fatwa found an immediate and widespread echo, the reverberations of which are still with us today. The Danish cartoon controversy only managed a partial mobilisation of the Islamic *ummah* and even that needed months of preparation by 'flying mullahs'.

> They cannot take away our self-respect if we do not give it to them.
> Mahatma Ghandi

Official ideologies in the form of fundamentalism and multiculturalism have fought (old) proletarian values to a standstill. Community-generated respect has been marginalised in the process. Organisations such as George Galloway's Respect Party and New Labour's 'respect campaign', based on ASBOs, have discredited the very term; this much we grudgingly admit. But significantly, both religious and secular respectability have lost their momentum, partly due to individual and collective proletarian resistance and partly due to their own inherent contradictions. We are, therefore, in a face-off situation with the ruling class over values. Old monologic (exchange) values have been shunned and new dialogic (use) values are yet to emerge. Since proletarians from different parts of the globe will generate these new values from within different linguistic repertoires, our task is to make sure their commonalities are made recognisable to all. Meanwhile, we should remain vigilant against reanimated versions of bourgeois respectability and expose their anti-working class agendas before they have become embedded within culture.

Under the Beach the Barbed Wire

Angela Mitropoulos

Vol 2 #2, Spring 2006

If, for a certain imaginary, the beach has often evoked a realm of authenticity hidden under the concrete strata of urban development, capitalist spectacle and exploitation, the relentlessly iconised Australian beach has, in addition, been put to use as proof of egalitarian sentiment and vast democratic horizons. Here, the generic vista of the Western frontier is shorn of its embarrassing wars over land, the guns and forts lined up against the natives, and is redrawn as pre-economic, pre-political idyll. Never quite acknowledged as urban but, even so, presented as more urbane and civilised than rural, uncultivated or desert lands, the space of the beach is assumed to have shaken off the dissensions of politics and economics much as the figurative beachgoer is presumed to effortlessly shed clothing. Like Rousseau's state of nature, the mystical space-time of the beach operates as both a denial of the nation-state – the presupposition of the *contrat social* in its legal, political and, not least, economic senses – and its naturalisation. And these projections are never more pronounced than in postcolonial spaces such as Australia, where persistent anxieties about unruly savages mingle with dreams of being closer to nature.

Popcultists have long campaigned for 'the beach' to be recognised as Australia's eminent utopia. Some five years ago, Craig McGregor argued that the beach represents 'our yearning for a world different from the concrete pavement universe that most of us inhabit for most of our lives. The beach today represents escape, freedom, self-fulfilment, the Right Path. It represents the way our lives should be.' Similarly, John Fiske contended that the beach 'is the place where we go on holidays (Holy Days), a place and time that is neither home nor work, outside the profane normality'. It is, perhaps, not surprising that such homilies have become more pious just as coastal areas have become more developed, increasingly the scene of bloated property values, mortgage anxieties and a burgeoning tourist industry run mostly on precarious labour. Indeed, these hymns to 'the beach' are a crucial affective support in this political economy and these industries, and they leverage affection all the more fiercely when deployed as eulogies or calls to restoration. Therefore, it is in part *because* beachside suburbs do not provide for an indifferent repose – longed for as both fortress and refuge against difference – that they have become the scenes of overt violence, riot police and emergency 'lockdown' laws that seek to restore, by force, the order on which seaside utopics were assembled.

The enchantment of 'the beach' began in Australia in the late-1940s – which is to say, in the immediate post-World War II period, at the ideological high point of Fordism and the Keynesian settlement. That post-war accord between unions and employers took shape as a nationalist compact between descendants of the English upper classes and working class Irish. Persuaded by clerical anti-communism, promises of property and class mobility – in the form of the post-war housing ownership boom and university admissions – the latter were seduced into forgetting their genealogy as convicts deported from Britain under policies justified by their depiction as a separate 'race'. This particular racialisation was set aside with the post-war Anglo-Celtic compact, which is the precise meaning of the figure of the Aussie and its egalitarian ethos – which is also an *ethnos* – of the 'fair go'. Frozen in that de-historicised and dreamlike zone after colonisation had been accomplished and before the collapse of the 'White Australia' policy in the early-1970s, the ostensible peace and contracted civility of the emblematic beachside has always depended on violence and separation, borders and fencelines, property and expropriation.

In the final month of 2005 in Sydney, it was these contingencies that would be laid bare and, with recourse to emergency laws, reasserted as necessary for the restoration of what was deemed natural. It is not clear what the immediate inducement was. Lifeguards were assaulted, it is said, because they made racial slurs while attempting to stop people from playing football (soccer) on Cronulla beach and, in the ensuing fight, came off second best. Cricket and Australian Rules (i.e. Celtic) football are commonplace on beaches and elsewhere – soccer, on the other hand, is regarded as the 'wog' game. Moreover, lifeguards are drawn from local residents, and their role is just as much concerned with beach safety as it is with enforcing the bonds between property and propriety. Yet, on this occasion, their authority – derived as it is from a customary consensus over their iconic status – faltered. And so, this apocryphal confrontation over land use and the perceived failure of Aussie supremacy would converge with earlier tales in Sydney of 'organised ethnic gangs' rapes of Australian women' and fears of miscegenation (in which women's bodies are considered, above all, as racial property) to produce what, elsewhere, would be called a lynch mob.

As is more or less well known, around 5,000 people gathered in Cronulla in December to 'Take Our Beaches Back' or, as it was put less obliquely in other circulating leaflets and text messages, to 'bash wogs and Lebs'. Slogans such as 'ethnic cleansing' and 'Aussies fighting back' were prominent enough on placards, posters and scrawled on skin, given force with punch and kick. Draped in Australian flags and singing 'Waltzing Matilda', large parts of the crowd rampaged around the suburb beating anyone they assumed to be a 'wog' or a 'Leb', including one woman, whose parents migrated from Greece, and a Jewish man. Such is the populist version of racial profiling – officiated more recently by the phrase, 'of Middle Eastern appearance' – that has become standard in Sydney, at the time of a global biowar. It might be noted here that the women who were raped in the most prominent of recent cases in Sydney would not so easily have 'passed' as Australian in Cronulla that day, yet their attackers would not have been given such unprecedented sentences if they had not been identified in court and the media as a 'Lebanese gang' targeting

'Australian women'. Indeed, that migration officials have deported or interned over a hundred people whom they incorrectly assessed to be 'illegal non-citizens' – such as Vivian Solon, a permanent resident deported to a hospice in the Philippines from her hospital bed after being hit by a car – suggests that this moment in Cronulla was, despite all the denials, continuous with the normative inclination of public policy and the racialising demeanour of the rights-bestowing, and rights-denying, state.

Since the events at Cronulla, there have been numerous accounts from the commentariat, whose affective range is distinctly more elitist than anti-racist, demonstrating far more shock at the appearance of an unruly mob than the pogrom it enacted. But, contrary to that perspective, which can only elicit demands for the restoration of law and order, the vulgar calls to reclaim ownership were merely the coarse, volunteerist expression of, most notably, the Prime Minister's civic declarations of sovereignty ('We will decide who comes here and the circumstances under which they come'), the more than decade-long policy of the internment of undocumented migrants by successive governments and, more recently, a war that is legitimated on racist grounds. As border policing became central to the conduct of elections and government policy throughout this period, the border was bound to proliferate across social relations and spaces, and in circumstances both casual and administered. This is why the worst of the attacks occurred in the train station. That train takes people from Sydney's Central Railway Station to the nearest beach, and, given the composition of Sydney as a whole, this includes people from the suburb of Lakemba, which has a high proportion of migrants from the Middle East. Cronulla, for its part, is notable for being the most Anglo-Celtic of suburbs in Australia. The Prime Minister once described the area as 'a part of Sydney which has always represented to me what middle Australia is all about'. Responding to the events at Cronulla, he would quickly deny that it was racism at work, adding, 'I do not believe Australians are racist,' and going on to propose that those who did believe such a thing lacked a cheerful disposition.

Over the subsequent three nights, there were retaliations. Hundreds of cars were smashed, people were beaten and shops were destroyed, as Cronulla and surrounding beachside suburbs were made unsafe for those whose belonging there had never before been threatened. One of the calls to retaliate declared: 'Our parents came to this country and worked hard for their families. We helped build this country and now these racists want us out [...] Time to show these people stuck in the 1950s that times have changed. WE are the new Australia. They are just the white thieves who took land from the Aboriginals and their time is up.'

In the midst of this, the NSW [New South Wales] Police Commissioner remarked that the Cronulla rally to 'Take Our Beaches Back' was a 'legitimate protest'. It was, according to him, born of a 'frustration' with the failure of the police and the state to do their job, which is to say, to ensure the Australian border remained secure *within* Sydney. The Prime Minister insisted that the problem of 'ethnic gangs' – which he unequivocally denied those at Cronulla might be regarded as – should be left to 'policy', i.e. the state. On the third day of rioting, the NSW Premier announced emergency laws to give police, among other measures, the power to lock down those beachside suburbs under threat. This was, he declared, a 'war' and the state would 'not be found wanting in the use of force'. And so the task of the Cronulla pogrom was more smoothly accomplished by the police acting as border guards, refusing entry to the beaches to those who could not prove that they belonged there. The 'lockdown' laws, in summary, allow the state to remove entire suburbs from the ostensibly normal functioning of the law for periods of 48 hours. Among other things, and within the designated 'lockdown' zone, the laws remove the presumption of bail for riot and affray, allow for the area to be cordoned off to prevent vehicles and people from entering it, empower police to stop and search people and vehicles without warrant or the standard criterion of suspicion, and to seize cars and mobile phones for up to a week.

In some respects, this could be viewed as a sequel to the so-called 'anti-terror' laws, recast here as an explicit attempt to re-territorialise the 'moving mêlée' – as one journalist described those engaged in the retaliatory riots. Yet, just as the failures of border controls have prompted recourse to measures both militaristic and ferocious, they have also reanimated the search for 'social solutions'. If the culture industry and its disciples remain enthralled by a depoliticising understanding of 'the beach', there is no shortage of more conventional disciplinary approaches that, for instance, have found renewed impetus in psycho-sociological clichés: deviance, crises of masculinity, youth alcohol abuse and, most comically, 'ethnic gangs' – who listen to rap music and use mobile phones. All of these constructs do not simply deny the existence of racism; they practically deploy racism through the assumption that the problem is a failure of integration. In other words, they reiterate the classic sociological preoccupation with social or, more accurately, *national* cohesion. Here, having assumed the nation-state as a natural entity – often by obliquely rendering it as 'community' or 'society' – it is the appearance of divisions that are not expedient for, or normalised by, the very assembly of national unity which is registered as a problem to be solved. That such a perspective has been echoed by much of the left, in their calls for a renewal of multiculturalism as a response to recent events, should in no way surprise, given that much of the left continues to aim for representing the nation and *its* people. And, as it implicitly denounces both pogrom and retaliations alike as the cause or abetting of 'racial disharmony', this is ironically where the left discloses the affective pull of its overwhelmingly Australian identification – an identity which is assumed to bestow rights, universally and without exceptions, that are legitimated through racism.

What is remarkable, however, is the extent to which multiculturalism continues to be idealised as a way of managing the exercise of 'difference-in-unity' that the nation-state at certain moments requires, without, presumably, having to resort to either violence or criminalisation. Which is to say, it was precisely alongside the much-touted apex of multiculturalism as official state policy in the early-1990s that the policy of automatic and extrajudicial internment of undocumented boat arrivals was introduced. In that moment, internment camps sat comfortably alongside tributes to Australia's diverse cultural mosaic, just as the most recent regime of border controls around the world were ushered in along with the 'globalisation' of trade and finance. For, if multiculturalism was initially tendered as a better form of governance at the time of lengthy wildcat strikes by migrant workers in the early-1970s, this is because it offered an improved means of assimilating certain differences while criminalising those who did not align with the imperatives of national labour market formation. This is what the paradigmatic post-Fordist border has sought to realise: the filtering of antagonism into competition, difference into niche markets and the recapitulation of an ostensible consensus over the nation as household firm vying for position in the world market. And it is on these questions that the part of the left which retains some commitment to notions of class struggle has either been silent or expressed its bewilderment. Coming just days after the introduction of the 'Workchoices' policy (which principally seeks to restrict, if not entirely abolish, any remaining non-individuated work contracts), the inclination here has been to understand recent events as a distraction, much like racism and indeed sexism are routinely theorised as the diversions of an apparently otherwise unified class consciousness.

Yet there is no experience of labour in capitalism that occurs outside a relation to the border. This association does not arise simply because migration controls create legally sanctioned segmentations within and between labour markets that, in turn, condition or 'socialise' the labouring circumstances of both immigrant and citizen. Nor does it occur only because, for instance, it is possible to show that the recent tendencies toward temporary residency permits and so-called 'flexibilisation' were both responses, by employers and governments, to a similarly coincident and prior exodus from the Fordist factories and the 'Third World' in the 1970s. Nor is it solely due to the fact that jurisdictions, currencies and the hierarchical links between them are manifest in *every* pay packet – although this is so obvious and, therefore, naturalised that it often needs emphasising.

While all of these are crucial in illustrating the significance of the border to the labouring experience, they are not quite sufficient to explain the force of that relation, its acquiring a necessary disposition. To put this another way, the particular – which is to say, *capitalist* – nexus between labour and border comes about because the asymmetrical wage contract only acquires *the semblance of a contract* through the delineation of the figure of the foreigner. Put simply, without the foreigner, the notion and practice of the social (or wage) *contract* as a voluntary agreement between more or less symmetrical agents falls apart.

There are three aspects worth considering here, and certainly in more detail: the conversion of the chance encounter into naturalised 'origin', the transformation of imperatives into individual choice and the punctuated temporality of the contract which normatively distinguishes wage labour from slavery.

Firstly, capitalism acquires a 'law-like' character through the establishment of borders, whether those of nation-states or, more generally, enclosures. For, while Marx's 'discovery' of the surplus labour that lies behind the formally equivalent wage contract is more or less well known, it is the border that permits the chance historical 'encounter between the man with money and free labourers' to 'take hold' – as Marx noted and Althusser emphasised in his later writings.

Secondly, the contract functions as the conventional mark of capitalism's distinction from feudalism, asserting that individuals have the power to organise their lives *against* the pressures of inherited inequalities; if not strictly as a matter of *will*, then, at the very least, as performativity. The contract is a theory of agency and self-possession. It formally asserts indeterminacy (or freedom) by explaining and *rationalising* the substance of any given contract as the result of a concordant symmetry. Consider here the Australian Government's 'Workchoices' policy that aims to replace 'collective' wage rates and conditions in particular occupations with individual contracts; that is, it is an instrument which seeks to generalise the conditions of precariousness that have existed outside the perimeter of the post-war 'settlement' referred to earlier. Responding to charges that this amounted to the reintroduction of coercion, since refusing to sign an individual work contract would entail not having the means to live, the Prime Minister said 'Everyone who wants a job will have one.' For the Prime Minister, the existence of coercion does not refute the contractual nature of waged work; it merely obliges a reassertion of contract theory.

Let us, then, consider Rousseau's argument that the 'social compact' requires 'unanimous consent' – or, more specifically, that 'no one, under any pretext whatsoever, can make any man a subject without his consent'. While this is often read as a foundational democratic argument against slavery and involuntary submission, it is, more accurately, the democratic substitution of the figure of the 'born-slave' with that of the 'foreigner-by-choice'. In this way, the existence of submission (or slavery) is redefined as the consequence of an individual's choice to reside within borders in which they do not belong – and they do not belong because they do not agree to the contract. After positing the natural foundations of the nation-state in voluntary agreement in the *Social Contract*, Rousseau goes on to argue: 'If then there are opponents when the social compact is made, their opposition does not invalidate the contract, but merely prevents them from being included in it. They are foreigners among citizens. When the state is instituted, residence constitutes consent; to dwell within its territory is to submit to the Sovereign'.

Just as Rousseau's perfect circle of democratic despotism cannot do without the 'foreigner', there is no semblance of the wage, as wage *contract*, without the border. This is the contingency of a specifically democratic capitalism, relating as it does to a certain axiom of money as universal equivalent and seemingly competent measure of all things, while preserving all the ambiguities through which repression, inequality, slavery and, not least, surplus labour time are explained and stabilised. Given that there is no way in which someone might profit at the expense of another through an agreement which is symmetrical, as the wage contract is asserted to be, racism (and sexism, which is never far away) *prepares us for, distributes and rationalises asymmetry.* The contractarian braces the contingent world of capitalist exploitation by ascribing it to individual authorship. Where this risks destabilisation, either by dissent or in the undeniable presence of inequality where all are born equal, the figure of the foreigner is put into service in the guise of the unpatriotic, the unassimilable and those deemed to be, for reasons of biology or 'culture', incapable of signing a contract – the very capacity of individual authorship. It is the latter that most clearly emphasises the bond between exploitation and racism, between the surplus as understood by political economy and the extrinsic (the foreign) as conceived by demography.

Thirdly, while the punctuated duration of the wage contract customarily distinguishes wage labour from slavery, the 'normal working day' was always demographically and geopolitically rationed. Cronulla did not simply represent 'middle Australia' but also the 'normal working day'. Seen from outside this limited perspective, borders have long operated as a form of detainment, beyond which the conventional (and perhaps simply Fordist) delineation between the time of life and that of work is suspended. In this sense, the distribution of racism (and sexism) is also the distribution of a particular temporality. Yet today, the 'regular' tempo of work more closely approximates the temporality of slavery (and, not least, of housework) in that no firm distinction operates between the time of working and not working, or, better, in the sense that unpaid labour time is laid bare as the condition of capital and the linear time of progress comes to a standstill.

The question, then, is, as it always was perhaps, how unpaid labour (or exploitation) is distributed, as well as whether or not it is counted. The Cronulla pogrom was as much about space, belonging and property as it was about relative advantage: about who is counted and who is detained, who might be said to possess one's labour such that they might contract for its sale, and who might be said to be a slave. Here, one might note the ways in which certain migrants are *held up* at the border, airport and detention centre no less than the ways in which the *banlieues* have existed as a *de facto* space of internment. In this time of detainment, it is not labour (as something that might be disassociated and 'sold' by one's self) that is stolen but whole lives. It is not surprising, then, that the moving mêlée emerged here, as both description of a response to the

Cronulla pogrom as well as apparition of chaos. Neither discernible as individuals nor enumerated as collective, with an emphasis on motion that is as spatial as it is temporal (appearing as quickly as it disappears), the moving mêlée had a whirlwind temporality that provisionally cut through the time of detainment even while it failed to escape it.

Not surprising, either, that the 'lockdown' came into being here, as a reconfiguration of the mechanisms of detainment, and it did not take long for a 'lockdown' to be invoked a second time. On 1 January in the country town of Dubbo, after indigenous teenagers fought with police against their attempt to arrest suspected car thieves, the police (as with the lifeguards in Cronulla) came off second best and a lockdown was subsequently put into effect. Nevertheless, given the aim of halting movement through a shifting definition of lawlessness and a mobile decree of emergency zones, it needs to be emphasised that the form of the 'lockdown' predates the monumental pretext of 9/11. In a more direct sense, the 'lockdown' echoes the (offshore) internment camps and the excision of territories from the 'migration zone' that have characterised post-1992 Australian migration policies – a model that has since been explored by UK and other European governments. Moreover, much like the state of emergency declared in France after the riots of the *banlieues*, the suspension of the putatively normal functioning of the law duplicates the colonial encounter in a metropolitan context. For these reasons, it would be a mistake to construe resort to emergency laws, such as the 'lockdown', as a mark of the triumph of border policing or, more generally, as cause for pessimism. Such instances do not signal a decline in our fortunes so much as they suggest the potentiality of a world that has surmounted its division into 'First' and 'Second', openly struggling with and against all the senses in which 'our' fortunes are dependent upon the expropriation of 'others'.

Demolishing Delhi: World-Class City in the Making

Amita Baviskar

Vol 2 #3, Autumn 2006

Banuwal Nagar was a dense cluster of about 1,500 homes, a closely-built beehive of brick and cement dwellings on a small square of land in North West Delhi, India. Its residents were mostly masons, bricklayers and carpenters, labourers who came to the area in the early-1980s to build apartment blocks for middle class families and stayed on. Women found work cleaning and cooking in the more affluent homes around them. Over time, as residents invested their savings into improving their homes, Banuwal Nagar acquired the settled look of a poor, yet thriving, community. It had shops and businesses; people rented out the upper floors of their houses to tenants. There were taps, toilets and a neighbourhood temple. On the street in the afternoon, music blared from a radio, mechanics taking a break from repairing cycle-rickshaws smoked bidis and drank hot, sweet tea and children walked home from school. Many of the residents were members of the Nirman Mazdoor Panchayat Sangam (NMPS), a union of construction labourers, unusual for India where construction workers are largely unorganised.

In April 2006, Banuwal Nagar was demolished. There had been occasions in the past when eviction had been imminent, but, somehow, the threat had always passed. Local politicians had provided patronage and protection in exchange for votes, municipal officials could be persuaded to look the other way, the NMPS union would negotiate with the local administration, squatters could even approach the courts and secure a temporary stay against eviction. Not this time. Eight bulldozers were driven up to the colony and trucks arrived to take people away. With urgent haste, the residents of Banuwal Nagar tore down their own homes, trying to salvage as much as they could before the bulldozers razed everything to the ground. Iron rods, bricks, doors and window frames were dismantled. TV sets and sofas, pressure cookers and ceiling fans, were all bundled up and clouds of dust and the sound of hammers and chisels filled the air. There was no time for despair, no time for sorrow, only a desperate rush to escape whole, to get out before the bulldozers came in.

But where would people go? About two-thirds of homeowners could prove that they had been in Delhi before 1998. They were taken to Bawana, a desolate wasteland on the outskirts of the city designated as a resettlement site. In June's blazing heat, people sheltered beneath makeshift roofs, without electricity or water. Children wandered about aimlessly. Worst, for their parents, was the absence of work. There was no employment in Bawana, and their old jobs were a three-hour commute away, too costly for most people to afford. Without work, families ate into their savings as they waited to be allotted plots of 12.5 square metres. Those who needed money urgently sold their entitlement to property brokers, many of them moonlighting government officials. Once, they might have squatted somewhere else in Delhi. Now, the crackdown on squatters has made that option impossible. They will probably leave the city.

The remaining one-third of homeowners in Banuwal Nagar couldn't marshal the documentary evidence of eligibility. Their homes were demolished and they got nothing at all. Those who rented rooms in the neighbourhood were also left to fend for themselves. One can visit Bawana and meet the people who were resettled, but the rest simply melted away. No one seems to know where they went; they left no trace. What was once Banuwal Nagar is now the site of a shopping mall, with construction in full swing. Middle class people glance around approvingly as they drive past, just as they watched from their rooftops as the modest homes of workers were dismantled. The slum was a nuisance, they say. It was dirty, congested and dangerous. Now we'll have clean roads and a nice place to shop.

Banuwal Nagar, Yamuna Pushta, Vikaspuri – everyday another *jhuggi basti* (shanty settlement) in Delhi is demolished. Banuwal Nagar residents had it relatively easy; their union was able to intercede with the local administration and police and ensure that evictions occurred without physical violence. In other places, the police set fire to homes, beat up residents and prevented them from taking away their belongings before the fire and the bulldozers got to work. Young children have died in stampedes; adults have committed suicide from the shock and shame of losing everything they had. In 2000, more than 3 million people, a quarter of Delhi's population, lived in 1,160 *jhuggi bastis* scattered across town. In the last five years, about half of these have been demolished, and the same fate awaits the rest. The majority of those evicted have not been resettled. Even among those entitled to resettlement, there are many who have got nothing. The government says it has no more land to give, yet demolitions continue apace.

The question of land lies squarely at the centre of the demolition drive. For decades, much of Delhi's land was owned by the central government, which parcelled out chunks for planned development. The plans were fundamentally flawed, with a total mismatch between spatial allocations and projections of population and economic growth. There was virtually no planned, low-income housing, forcing poor workers and migrant labourers to squat on public lands. Ironically, it was Delhi's Master Plan that gave birth to its evil twin: the city of slums. The policy of resettling these squatter *bastis* into 'proper' colonies – proper only because they were legal and not because they had improved living conditions – was fitfully followed, and, over the years, most *bastis* acquired the patina of de facto legitimacy. Only during the Emergency (1975–7), when civil rights were suppressed by Indira Gandhi's government, was there a concerted attempt to clear the *bastis*. The democratic backlash to the Emergency's repressive regime meant that evictions were not politically feasible for the next two decades. However, while squatters were not forcibly evicted, they were not given secure tenure, either. Ubiquitous yet illegal, the ambiguity of squatters' status gave rise to a flourishing economy of votes, rents and bribes that exploited and maintained their vulnerability.

In 1990, economic liberalisation hit India. Centrally planned land management was replaced by the neoliberal mantra of public-private partnership. In the case of Delhi, this translated into the government selling land acquired for 'public purpose' to private developers. With huge profits to be made from commercial development, the real estate market is booming. The land that squatters occupy now commands a premium. These are the new enclosures: what were once unclaimed spaces, vacant plots of land along railway tracks and by the Yamuna river that were settled and made habitable by squatters, are now ripe for redevelopment. Liminal lands that the urban poor could live on have now been incorporated into the profit economy.

The Yamuna riverfront was the locale for some of the most vicious evictions in 2004 and again in 2006. Tens of thousands of families were forcibly removed, the bulldozers advancing at midday when most people were at work, leaving infants and young children at home. The cleared river embankment is now to be the object of a Thames-style makeover, with parks and promenades, shopping malls and sports stadiums, concert halls and corporate offices. The project finds favour with Delhi's upper classes who dream of living in a 'world-class' city modelled after Singapore and Shanghai. The river is filthy. As it flows through Delhi, all the fresh water is taken out for drinking and replaced with untreated sewage and industrial effluent. Efforts to clean up the Yamuna have mainly taken the form of removing the poor who live along its banks. The river remains filthy, a sluggish stream of sewage for most of the year. It is an unlikely site for world-class aspirations, yet this is where the facilities for the next Commonwealth Games in 2010 are being built.

For the visionaries of the world-class city, the Commonwealth Games are just the beginning. The Asian Games, and even the Olympics, may follow if Delhi is redeveloped as a tourist destination, a magnet for international conventions and sports events. However wildly optimistic these ambitions, and however shaky their foundations, they fit perfectly with the self-image of India's newly confident consuming classes. The chief beneficiaries of economic liberalisation, bourgeois citizens want a city that matches their aspirations for gracious living. The good life is embodied in Singapore-style, round-the-clock shopping and eating, in a climate-controlled and police-surveilled environment. This city-in-the-making has no place for the poor, regarded as the prime source of urban pollution and crime. Behind this economy of appearances lie mega-transfers of land and capital and labour; workers who make the city possible are banished out of sight. New, apartheid-style segregation is fast becoming the norm.

The apartheid analogy is no exaggeration. Spatial segregation is produced as much by policies that treat the poor as second class citizens as by the newly instituted market in real estate, which has driven housing out of their reach. The Supreme Court of India has taken the lead in the process of selective disenfranchisement. Judges have remarked that the poor have no right to housing; resettling a squatter is like rewarding a pickpocket. By ignoring the absence of low-income housing, the judiciary has criminalised the very presence of the poor in the city. Evictions are justified as being in the public interest, as if the public does not include the poor, and as if issues of shelter and livelihood are not public concerns. The courts have not only brushed aside representations from *basti* dwellers, they have also penalised government officials for failing to demolish fast enough. In early 2006, the courts widened the scope of judicial activism to target illegal commercial construction and violations of building codes in affluent residential neighbourhoods. But such was the outcry from all political parties that the government quickly passed a law to neutralise these court orders. However, the homes of the poor continue to be demolished while the government shrugs helplessly.

Despite their numbers, Delhi's poor don't make a dent in the city's politics. The absence of a collective identity or voice is, in part, the outcome of state strategies for regulating the poor. Having a cut-off date that determines who is eligible for resettlement is a highly effective technique for dividing the poor. Those who stand to gain a plot of land are loath to jeopardise their chances by resisting eviction. Tiny and distant though it is, this plot offers a secure foothold in the city. Those eligible for resettlement part ways from their neighbours and fellow residents, cleaving communities into two. Many squatters in Delhi are also disenfranchised by ethnic and religious discrimination. Migrants from the eastern states of Bihar and Bengal, Muslims in particular, are told to go back to where they came from. Racial profiling as part of the War on Terror has also become popular in Delhi. In the last decade, the spectre of Muslim terrorist infiltrators from Bangladesh has become a potent weapon to harass Bengali-speaking Muslim migrants in the city. Above all, sedentarist metaphysics are at work, such that all poor migrants are seen as forever people out of place; Delhi is being overrun by 'these people' – why don't they go back to where they belong? Apocalyptic visions of urban anarchy and collapse are ranged alongside dreams of gleaming towers, clean streets and fast moving cars. Utopia and dystopia merge to propose a future city in which the poor have no place.

Delhi, Mumbai, Kolkata and many other Indian cities figure prominently in what Mike Davis describes as a 'planet of slums'. Slum clearances may give India's capital the appearance of a 'clean and green Delhi', but environmental activism has simply shifted the problem elsewhere. The poor live under worse conditions, denied work and shelter, struggling against greater insecurity and uncertainty. Is Davis right? Has the late-capitalist triage of humanity already taken place? Even as demolitions go on around me, I believe that Davis might be wrong in this case. Bourgeois Delhi's dreams of urban cleansing are fragile; ultimately, they will collapse under the weight of their hubris. The city still needs the poor; it needs their labour, enterprise and ingenuity. The vegetable vendor and the rickshaw puller, the cook and the carpenter cannot be banished forever. If the urban centre is deprived of their presence, the centre itself will have to shift. The outskirts of Delhi, and the National Capital Region of which it is part, continue to witness phenomenal growth in the service economy and in sectors like construction. Older resettlement colonies already house thriving home-based industry. The city has grown to encompass these outlying areas so that they are no longer on the spatial, or social, periphery. This longer-term prospect offers little comfort to those who sleep hungry tonight because they couldn't find work. Yet, in their minds, the promise of cities as places to find freedom and prosperity persists. In those dreams lies hope.

Thinking Resistance in the Shanty Town

Richard Pithouse

Vol 2 #3, Autumn 2006

In 1961, Frantz Fanon, the great philosopher of African anti-colonialism, described the shack settlements that 'circle the towns tirelessly, hoping that one day or another they will be let in' as 'the gangrene eating into the heart of colonial domination'. He argued that 'this cohort of starving men, divorced from tribe and clan, constitutes one of the most spontaneously and radically revolutionary forces of a colonised people'. Colonial power tended to agree and often obliterated shanty towns, usually in the name of public health and safety, at times of heightened political tension.

But, by the late-1980s, the World Bank-backed, elite consensus was that shack settlements, now called 'informal settlements' rather than 'squatter camps', were opportunities for popular entrepreneurship rather than a threat to white settlers, state and capital. NGOs embedded in imperial power structures were deployed to teach the poor that they could only hope to help themselves via small businesses while the rich got on with big business. At the borders of the new gated theme parks in which the rich now worked, shopped, studied and entertained themselves, the armed enforcement of segregation, previously the work of the state, was carried out by private security.

There are now a billion people in the squatter settlements in the cities of the South. Many states, NGOs and their academic consultants have returned to the language that presents slums as a dirty, diseased, criminal and depraved threat to society. The UN actively supports 'slum clearance', and, in many countries, shack settlements are again under ruthless assault from the state. Lagos, Harare and Bombay are the names of places where men with guns and bulldozers come to turn neighbourhoods into rubble. The US military is planning to fight its next wars in the 'feral failed cities' of the South with technology that can sense body heat behind walls. Once no one can be hidden, soldiers can drive, or fire through, walls as if they weren't there. Agent Orange has been upgraded. Gillo Pontecorvo's great film, *The Battle of Algiers*, is used as a training tool at West Point. The lesson seems to be that this kind of battle, with its walls and alleys that block and bewilder outsiders and give refuge and opportunity to insiders, must be blown into history. The future should look more like Fallujah.

Leftist theories which seek one agent of global redemption are generally less interested in the shack settlement than the NGOs, UN or US military. Some Marxists continue to fetishise the political agency of the industrial working class and contemptuously dismiss shack dwellers as inevitably reactionary 'lumpens'. The form of very metropolitan leftism that heralds a coming global redemption by immaterial labourers is more patronising than contemptuous and concludes, in Michael Hardt and Antonio Negri's words, that '[t]o the extent that the poor are included in the process of social production [...] they are potentially part of the multitude'. Computer programmers in Seattle are automatically part of the multitude, but the global underclass can only gain this status to the extent that their 'biopolitical production' enters the lifeworld of those whose agency is taken for granted. The continuities with certain colonial modes of thought are clear.

But other metropolitan leftists are becoming more interested in the prospects for resistance in shanty towns. Mike Davis' first intervention, a 2004 *New Left Review* article, 'Planet of Slums', famously concluded that 'for the moment at least, Marx has yielded the historical stage to Mohammed and the Holy Ghost', and so 'the Left (is) still largely missing from the slum'. This was a little too glib. For a start, the left is not reducible to the genius of one theorist working from one time and place. And, as Davis wrote these words, militant battles were being fought in, and from, shack settlements in cities like Johannesburg, Caracas, Bombay, São Paulo and Port-au-Prince. Moreover, proposing a Manichean distinction between religion and political militancy is as ignorant as it is silly. Some of the partisans in these battles were religious; others were not. In many instances, these struggles were not, in themselves, religious but rooted their organising in social technologies developed in popular religious practices. Davis' pessimism derived, at least in part, from a fundamental methodological flaw. He failed to speak to the people waging these struggles or even to read the work produced from within these resistances, and often read his imperial sources – the UN, World Bank, donor agencies, anthropologists, etc. – as colleagues rather than enemies.

At around the same time as Davis wrote his 'Slums' paper, Slavoj Žižek, writing in the *London Review of Books*, argued that the explosive growth of the slum 'is perhaps the crucial geopolitical event of our times'. He concluded that we are confronted by:

> The rapid growth of a population outside the law, in terrible need of minimal forms of self organisation [...] One should resist the easy temptation to elevate and idealise slum-dwellers into a new revolutionary class. It is nonetheless surprising how far they conform to the old Marxist definition of the proletarian revolutionary subject: they are 'free' in the double meaning of the word, even more than the classical proletariat ('free' from all substantial ties; dwelling in a free space, outside the regulation of the state); they are a large collective, forcibly thrown into a situation where they have to invent some mode of being-together, and simultaneously deprived of support for their traditional ways of life [...] The new forms of social awareness that emerge from slum collectives will be the germ of the future [...]

Žižek, being Žižek, failed to ground his speculative (although tentative) optimism in any examination of the concrete. But it had the enormous merit of, at least in principle, taking thinking in the slum seriously.

As Alain Badiou explains, with typical precision, there can be no formula for mass militancy that holds across time and space:

> A political situation is always singular; it is never repeated. Therefore political writings – directives or commands – are justified inasmuch as they inscribe not a repetition but, on the contrary, the unrepeatable. When the content of a political statement is a repetition the statement is rhetorical and empty. It does not form part of thinking. On this basis one can distinguish between true political activists and politicians [...] True political activists think a singular situation; politicians do not think.

The billion actual shack dwellers live in actual homes in communities, in places with actual histories that collide with contemporary circumstances to produce actual presents. Many imperial technologies of domination do have a global range and do produce global consequences, but there can be no global theory of how they are lived, avoided and resisted. Even within the same parts of the same cities the material and political realities in neighbouring shack settlements can be hugely different. This is certainly the case in Durban, the South African port city, from which this article is written. There are 800,000 shack dwellers in Durban, but the settlements I know best are in a couple of square kilometres, in valleys, on river banks and against the municipal dump in the suburb of Clare Estate. In this small area, there are eight settlements with often strikingly different material conditions, modes of governance, relations to the party and state, histories of struggle, ethnic make-ups, degrees of risk of forced removal and so on. In the Lacey Road settlement, ruled by an armed former ANC soldier last elected many years ago, organising openly will quickly result in credible death threats. In the Kennedy Road settlement, there is a radically open and democratic political culture. Kennedy Road has a large vegetable garden, a hall and an office and some access to electricity. In the Foreman Road settlement, the shacks are packed far too densely for there to be any space for a garden, and there is no hall, office or meeting room and no access to electricity.

Although Davis notes the diversity within the shanty town in principle, in practice, his global account of 'the slum' produces a strange homogenisation. This is premised on a casual steamrolling of difference that necessarily produces, and is produced by, basic empirical errors. For instance, a passing comment on South Africa reveals that he does not understand the profound distinctions between housing in legal, state-built and serviced townships and illegal, squatter-built shacks in unserviced shack settlements. He casually asserts as some kind of rule that shack renters, not owners, will tend to be radical. No doubt this holds in some places, but it's far from a universal law of some science of the slum. In fact, most of the elected leadership in Abahlali baseMjondolo (the Durban shack dwellers' movement whose local militancy has, to paraphrase Fanon, made a decisive irruption into the national South African struggle) are owners, or the children or siblings of owners.

Robert Neuwirth's *Shadow Cities: A Billion Squatters, A New Urban World*, also published this year, is vastly more attentive to the actual circumstances and thinking of actual squatters. Neuwirth lacks Davis' gift for rhetorical flourish, but his methodology is radically superior to Davis' often insufficiently critical reliance on imperial research. Neuwirth lived in squatter settlements in Bombay, Istanbul, Rio and Nairobi. Once there, he took, as one simply has to when one is the ignorant outsider depending on others, the experience and intelligence of the people he met seriously. In Neuwirth's book, imperial power has a global reach, but there is no global slum. There are particular communities with particular histories and contemporary realities. The people that live in shanty towns emerge as people.

Some are militants in the MST or the PKK. Some just live for work or church or Saturday night at a club. In the Kiberia settlement in Nairobi, he lived with squatters in mud shacks. In the Sultanbeyli settlement in Istanbul, there is a 'seven-story squatter city hall, with an elevator and a fountain in the lobby'. Neuwirth also describes the very different policy and legal regimes against which squatters make their lives, the equally diverse modes of governance and organisation within squatter settlements and the varied forms and trajectories of a number of squatter movements.

Davis sees slums in explicitly Hobbesian terms. As he rushes to his apocalyptic conclusions, he pulls down numbers and quotes from a dazzling range of literature, and some of the research he cites points to general tendencies that are often of urgent importance. Parts of his account of the material conditions in the global slum illuminate important facets of places – like Kennedy Road, Jadhu Place and Foreman Road, which were the first strongholds of Abahlali baseMjondolo – as well as aspects of the broader situation people in these settlements confront. For example, Davis notes that major sports events often mean doom for squatters, and, here in Durban, the city has promised to 'clear the slums' – mostly via apartheid-style forced removal to rural ghettos – before the 2010 football World Cup is held in South Africa. It is possible to list the ways in which Davis' account of the global slum usefully illuminate local conditions: postcolonial elites have aggressively adapted racial zoning to class, and tend to withdraw to residential and commercial theme parks; the lack of toilets is a key women's issue; NGOs generally act to demobilise resistance; and many people do make their lives, sick and tired, on piles of shit, in endless queues for water, amidst the relentless struggle to wring a little money out of a hard, corrupt world. The brown death, diarrhoea, constantly drains the life force away, and there is the sporadic, but terrifyingly inevitable, threat of the red death – the fires that roar and dance through the night.

But, even when the material horror of settlements, built and rebuilt on shit after each fire, has some general truth, it isn't all that is true. It is also the case that, for many people, these settlements provide a treasured node of access to the city, with its prospects for work, educational, cultural, religious and sporting possibilities; they can be spaces for popular cosmopolitanism and cultural innovation, and everyday life is often characterised, more than anything else, by its ordinariness – people drinking tea, cooking supper, playing football, celebrating a child's birthday, doing school homework or attending choir practice. It is this ordinariness, and in certain instances hopefulness, that so firmly divorces purely tragic or apocalyptic accounts of slum life from even quite brief encounters with the lived reality of the shack settlement. Furthermore, insofar as general comments about such diverse places are useful, an adequate theory of the squatter settlement needs to get to grips with the fundamental ambiguity that often characterises life in these places.

On the one hand, the absence of the state often entails the material deprivation and suffering that comes from the absence of the basic state services (water, electricity, sanitation, refuse removal, etc.) required for a viable urban life. But the simultaneous absence of the state and traditional authority and proximity to the city can also enable a rare degree of political and cultural autonomy. This ambiguity is often a central feature of squatters' lives and struggles. A.W.C. Champion was the head of the famous African Industrial and Commercial Workers' Union (ICU) that helped to organise resistance against the atrocious material conditions in the huge Umkumbane settlement in Durban. Speaking in 1960, just after the state had destroyed the settlement and moved its residents to formal township houses outside of the city, he recalled Umkumbane not only as a bad memory of shit and fire but also as 'the place in Durban where families could breathe the air of freedom'.

Neuwirth is able to capture this ambiguous aspect of shack life. He doesn't shy away from the horror of the conditions in some settlements. Indeed, he begins with Tema, a resident of the Rocinha settlement in Rio, telling him that 'The Third World is a video game' and goes on to show why this statement matters. But, because he has lived in the places that he describes and has spoken to the people that he writes about, he is able to capture the ordinariness of the ordinary life of people and communities and the fact that there are, at times, certain attractions to slum life. He quotes Armstrong O'Brian, a resident of the Southland settlement in Nairobi, who says, 'This place is very addictive. It's a simple life, but no one is restricting you. Nobody is controlling you. Once you have stayed here, you cannot go back.' Perhaps it is rumours of this air of freedom, this lack of control, that fill the sail on Žižek's radical hopes for the slum.

The question of the possibilities for shanty town radicalism should not, as Davis and Žižek assume, automatically be posed toward the future. Around the world, there are long histories of shack dweller militancy. In Durban in June 1959, an organisation in the Umkumbane settlement called Women of Cato Manor led a militant charge against patriarchal relations within the settlement, against the moderate reformism of the elite nationalists in the ANC Women's

League and against the apartheid state. This event still stands as a potent challenge to most contemporary feminisms, and progressive social innovation has not always taken the form of direct confrontation with the state. It is interesting to note that, against the often highly racialised stereotypes of shack dwellers as naturally and inevitably deeply reactionary on questions of gender, institutionalised homosexual marriage was, in fact, pioneered in South Africa in the Umkumbane settlement in the early-1950s. But the cultural innovation from shanty towns has not only been for the subaltern; it has often become part of suburban life. Bob Marley wouldn't have become Bob Marley without Trench Town, and so much American music (Dylan, Springsteen, et al.) stems from a shack dweller – Woody Guthrie.

It also needs to be recognised that shanty towns are very often consequent to land invasions, and that services – especially water and electricity – are often illegally appropriated from the state. Fanon insisted that 'the shanty town is the consecration of the colonised's biological decision to invade the enemy citadel at all costs'. Yet, most of the writing produced by contemporary imperialism tends to take a tragic and naturalising form and presents squatters as being passively washed into shack settlements by the tides of history. Unfortunately, Davis generally fails to mark the insurgent militancy that often lies behind the formation, and ongoing survival, of the shack settlement. So, for example, his naturalising description of Soweto as 'having grown from a suburb to a satellite city' leaves out the history of the shack dwellers' movement, Sofasonke, which, in 1944, led more than 10,000 people to occupy the land that would later become Soweto. However, Neuwirth's book is very good at showing that the shanty town often has its origins in popular re-appropriation of land and that it often survives through battles to defend and extend those gains, and to appropriate state services.

No doubt human rights discourse takes on a concrete reality when one is being bombed in its name. But, when grasped as a tool by the militant poor, it invariably turns out to contain a strange emptiness. Hence the importance of Neuwirth's assertion of value in the fact that squatters are 'not seizing an abstract right, they are taking an actual place', while he sensibly avoids the mistake of assuming that popular re-appropriation is automatically about creating a democratic commons. If the necessity, or choice, of a move to the city renders rural life impossible or undesirable, and if the cosmopolitanism of so many shanty towns puts them at an unbridgeable remove from traditional modes of governance, there is no guarantee that the need to invent new social forms will result in progressive outcomes. Shiv Senna, the Hindu fascist movement that built its first base in the shanty towns of Bombay, is one of many instances of deeply reactionary responses to the need for social innovation. At a microlocal level, the authoritarianism and misogyny that characterises the governance of the Overcome Heights settlement, founded after a successful land invasion in Cape Town earlier this year, is another. As Neuwirth shows, choices are made, struggles are fought and outcomes vary. Many settlements are dominated by slum lords of various types, but this is not inevitable and does not justify Davis' Hobbesian pessimism about life in shack settlements. Communal ownership and democracy are also possible, and there are numerous concrete instances in which they occur.

Neuwirth wisely resists the temptation to produce a policy model for making things better, insisting that 'the legal instrument is not important. The political instrument is', and that '[a]ctual control, not legal control is key'. His solution is old fashioned people power – the 'messy, time consuming' praxis of organising. It is not a solution that sees squatters as a new proletariat, a messiah to redeem the whole world. It is a solution that sees squatters struggling to make their lives better. The point is not that the squatters must subordinate themselves to some external authority or provide the 'base' for some apparently grander, national or global struggle. Squatters should be asking the questions that matter to them and waging their fights on their terms.

This is as far as the popular literature takes us. But the experience and thinking of shack dwellers' movements, some of which will travel well and some of which will not, can take us further. In Durban, the experience of Abahlali baseMjondolo has shown that the will to fight has no necessary connection to the degree of material deprivation or material threat from state power. It is always a cultural and intellectual, rather than a biological, phenomenon. It therefore requires cultural and intellectual work to be produced and sustained. Spaces and practices, in which the courage and resilience to stay committed to this work can be nurtured, are essential. Drawing from the diverse lifeworlds that come together to make the settlements and the movement requires a hybridised new to be woven from the strands of the old. Formal meetings are necessary to enable the careful, collective reflection on experience that produces and develops the movement's ideas and principles. The music and meals and games and prayers and stories and funerals that weave togetherness are essential to sustain both a collective commitment to the movement's principles and a will to fight.

The Abahlali have also found that, even if there is a growing will to fight, no collective militancy is possible when settlements are not run democratically and autonomously. If they are dominated by party loyalists, the ragged remnants of a defeated aristocracy, slum lords or some combination thereof, this will have to be challenged. Often, lives will be at risk during the early moments of this challenge, but the power of local tyrants simply has to be broken. The best tactic is to use the strength of nearby democratic settlements, to ensure protection for the few courageous people who take the initiative to organise some sort of open display of a mass demand for democratisation. If a clear majority of people in a settlement come out to a meeting against the slum lords, and if the people who break the power of the local tyrants immediately act to make open and democratic meetings the real (rather than the performed) space of politics, then a radical politics becomes possible. Part of making a meeting democratic is declaring its resolute autonomy from state, party and civil society. Then, and only then, is it fully accountable to the people in whose name it is constituted. A movement must be ruthlessly principled about not working with settlements that are not democratic.

People fight constituted power to gain their share and to constitute counter-power. Choices have to be made and adhered to. Any conception of shanty town politics that sees the mere fact of insurgency into bourgeois space as necessarily progressive, in and of itself, risks complicity with microlocal relations of domination and, because local despotisms so often become aligned with larger forces of domination, complicity with these larger relations also. Despite the speculative optimism of certain Negrians, the fact of mere movement driven by mere desire for more life is not sufficient for a radical politics. A genuinely radical politics can only be built around an explicit, thought-out commitment to community, constructed around a political and material commons. The fundamental political principle must be that everybody matters. In each settlement, each person counts for one, and, in a broader movement, the people in each settlement count equally.

After a movement has become able to put tens of thousands on the streets, brought the state to heel and made it into *The New York Times*, swarms of middle class 'activists' will descend in the name of leftist solidarity. Some will be sincere, and alliances across class will be important for enabling access to certain kinds of resources, skills and networks. Sincere middle class solidarity will scrupulously subordinate itself to democratic processes and always work to put the benefits of its privilege in common. But, as Fanon warned, most of these 'activists' will 'try to regiment the masses according to a predetermined schema'. Usually, they will try to deliver the movement's mass to some other political project in which their careers or identities have an investment. This can be at the level of theory, in which case lies will be told in order that the movement can be claimed to confirm some theory with currency in the metropole. It can also be at the level of more material representation, in which case the movement's numbers will be claimed for some political project which has no mass support, but has donor funding or the approval of the metropolitan left, so attractive to local and visiting elites. Tellingly, these kinds of machinations tend to remain entirely uninterested in what ordinary people in the movement actually think, attempting instead to isolate and co-opt a couple of leaders to create an illusion of mass support – to turn genuine mass democratic movements into more easily malleable simulations of their formerly autonomous and insubordinate selves. Often, struggle tourists will get grants to leave the alternative youth cultures of the metropole for a few weeks to come and assert their personal revolutionary superiority over the poor by writing articles riddled with basic factual inaccuracies that condemn the movement as insufficiently revolutionary. Invariably, it will not occur to these people that it may be a good idea to ask the people in the movement – who are missing work, getting beaten, threatened with murder, shot at and arrested in the course of their struggle – what they think about their political choices. Old assumptions about who should do the thinking and judging in this world show no signs of withering away. Indeed, from the safety of the elite terrain, the middle class left will often openly express contempt for the people they want to regiment. At times, this is highly racialised, and this is no local perversion. In Davis' book, slums, and the people that make their lives in them, often appear as demonic.

People who share some of the terrain of the middle class left (access to email, positions in universities or NGOs, etc.), but who find casual contempt for the underclass to be problematic or who refuse to allow themselves to be used as bridges for attempts at co-option, will be excoriated on that terrain as divisive trouble makers. However, they will, as Fanon wrote, find 'a mantle of unimagined tenderness and vitality' in the settlements where politics is a serious project, where, in Alain Badiou's words, 'meetings, or proceedings, have as their natural content protocols of delegation and inquest whose discussion is no more convivial or superegotistical than that of two scientists involved in debating a very complex question'.

The middle class tendency to assume a right to lead usually expresses itself in overt and covert attempts to shift power away from the spaces in which the poor are strong. However, the people that constitute the movement will, in fact, know what the most pressing issues are, where resistance can press most effectively and how best to mobilise. A politics that cannot be understood and owned by everyone is poison – it will always demobilise and disempower, even if it knows more about the World Bank, the World Social Forum, Empire, Trotsky or some fashionable theory than the people who know about life and struggle in the settlements. The modes, language, jargon, concerns, times and places of a genuinely radical politics must be those in which the poor are powerful, not those in which they are silenced as they are named, directed and judged from without. Anyone wanting to offer solidarity must come to the places where the poor are powerful and work in the social modes within which the poor are powerful. On this terrain, respect must be earned, via sustained commitment, and cannot be bought. All resources and networks and skills brought here must be placed in common. There must be no personalised branding or appropriation of work done. The post-Seattle struggle tourists must be dealt with firmly when they call the inevitable disinterest in their assumed right to lead 'silencing' and try to present that as an important issue. Local donor-funded socialists must be dealt with equally firmly when they call people 'ignorant' for wanting to focus their struggle on the relations of domination that most immediately restrict their aspirations and which are within reach of their ability to organise a collective, and effective, fight-back. Democratic popular struggle is a school, and it will develop its range and reach as it progresses. But a permanently ongoing collective reflection on the lived experience of struggle is necessary for resistances to be able to sustain their mass character as they grow and develop. It is necessary to create opportunities for as many people as possible to keep talking and thinking in a set of linked intellectual spaces within the settlements. Progress comes from the quality of the work done in these spaces – not from a few people learning the jargon of the middle class left via NGO workshops held on the other side of the razor wire. This jargon will tend to be fundamentally disempowering because of its general indifference to the local relations of domination that usually present a movement with both its most immediate threats and its opportunities for an effective fight-back. Moreover, the accuracy and usefulness of its analysis will often be seriously compromised by its blindness to local relations of domination and how these connect to broader forces. People who represent the movement in the media, in negotiations and in various forums, must be elected, mandated, accountable and rotated. There must be no professionalisation of the struggle, as this produces a vulnerability to co-option from above. The state, parties, NGOs and the middle class left must be confronted with a hydra not a head. There needs to be a self-conscious development of what S'bu Zikode, chair of Abahlali baseMjondolo, calls 'a politics of the poor – a homemade politics that everyone can understand and find a home in'.

Some will say that none of this means that global capital is at risk. This is not entirely true – stronger squatters inevitably means weaker relations of local and global domination. Given that states are subordinate to imperialism and local elites, confrontation with the state is inevitable and necessary. Because some of the things that squatters need can only be provided by the state, the struggle cannot only be limited to driving the coercive aspects of the state away. There also has to be a fight to subordinate the social aspects of state to society, beginning with its most local manifestations and moving on from there. But, insofar as it is true that squatter struggles are unlikely to, as Davis would have it, immediately produce 'resistance to global capitalism', what right has someone like Davis to demand that the global underclass fight global capital when he himself does not have the courage to take its representatives on his terrain as enemies? He concludes his book with the image of squatters fighting the US military with car bombs while he, as his book keeps making clear, has cordial and collegial relations with academic consultants for imperialism. This is not untypical. How many leftist intellectuals will really fight on their own terrain? We must all, surely, assume the responsibility to make our stand where we are, rather than projecting that responsibility onto others. And, if we are going to enquire into the capacity of the global underclass to resist, we should, at the very least, do this via discussion with people in the movements of the poor rather than via entirely speculative, and profoundly objectifying, social science. This latter is a route to a leftist version of the World Bank's mass production of social science, which blames the poor for being poor by rendering poverty an ontological, rather than historical, condition.

The experience of Abahlali is that, for most squatters, the fight begins with these toilets, this land, this eviction, this fire, these taps, this slum lord, this politician, this broken promise, this developer, this school, this crèche, these police officers, this murder. Because the fight begins from a militant engagement with the local, its thinking immediately pits material force against material force – bodies, songs and stones against circling helicopters, tear gas and bullets. It is real from the beginning. And, if it remains a mass democratic project, permanently open to innovation from below, it will stay real. This is what the Abahlali call 'the politics of the strong poor'; this is why the Abahlali have marched under banners that declare them to be part of the 'University of Abahlali baseMjondolo'.

Drowning by Numbers: the Non-Reproduction of New Orleans

Benedict Seymour

Metamute.org, December 2006[1]

> They became amphibious, and lived, as an English writer says, half on land and half on water, and withal only half on both.
> Karl Marx[2]

The USA as 'Developing Society'

Hurricane Katrina created a great opportunity for looting. But, contra to racist fantasies of post-storm rape and pillage, the real thieves were not the black underclass but the neoliberal elite. The man-made disaster of the deluge provided the ideal excuse for New Orleans' (mostly) white ruling class to set in motion long-held plans for a new New Orleans, minus the (mostly) black working class.

The looting taking place in Louisiana's 'Gulf Opportunity Zone' today represents potentially the most brazen and large-scale act of gentrification yet seen in the already rampantly gentrified USA. The transfer of public assets into private ownership and the destruction of working class housing, services and social networks is a hallmark of neoliberalism, but, up until now, the process has rarely been as brutally or rapidly performed – at least not on US territory. As the corporate macro-looters favoured by George Bush's 'laboratory for conservative economic policies'[3] in Iraq – such as Halliburton, Blackwater and the Shaw Group – suck in state money to 'clean up' after the devastation, the belatedly evacuated survivors of the deluge are decanted into temporary accommodation across the States, displaced and struggling to stay afloat.

Like the supersized, disaster movie version of the 'normal' gentrification process already long under way in New Orleans, the state relief effort and planned reconstruction reveal renewal as a euphemism for 'primitive accumulation': the state-backed transfer of property into private hands as

1. Originally commissioned by *Greenpepper* magazine, this text was written in February 2006
2. Karl Marx, 'So-Called Primitive Accumulation', *Capital Vol. 1.*
3. Paul Krugman quoted in Mike Davis, 'The Predators of New Orleans', *Le Monde Diplomatique*, October 2005, http://mondediplo.com/2005/10/02katrina
4. Karl Marx, *Capital Vol. 1*, Chapter 8 reads: 'The so-called primitive accumulation, therefore, is nothing else than the historical process of divorcing the producer from the means of production. It appears as primitive, because it forms the pre-historic stage of capital and of the mode of production corresponding with it.' While this definition holds good, it is important to see that primitive accumulation is a misnomer if understood to mean an originary, and now historical, phase of accumulation. Primitive accumulation is an ongoing and permanent part of capitalism. Cf. Loren Goldner, 'The Remaking of the American Working Class, The Restructuring of Global Capital and the Recomposition of Class Terrain', 'Once Again, On Fictitious Capital: Further Reply to Aufheben and Other Critics', and also Retort, Afflicted Powers. Also Wikipedia: http://en.wikipedia.org/wiki/Primitive_accumulation

a source of fixed and variable capital, free land and devalorised labour.[4] In this case, as we will see, those being divorced from their means of production – or, better, from their means of social reproduction – are not only newly proletarianised workers but the post-industrial reserve army created by decades of economic stagnation and austerity in the USA.

As in regeneration and reconstruction programmes elsewhere, the looting of New Orleans and Louisiana is not limited to the privatisation and colonisation of formerly working class areas, the theft of land and (crumbling) infrastructure. This transfer of fixed capital is always accompanied by a 'holistic' attack on the price of labour power, which works from all angles to deprive workers of their former means of subsistence, raising the real cost of living and destroying means of support, while creating new revenue opportunities for capital.

In the case of New Orleans, the hurricane is being treated as God's gift to the neoliberal consensus, a one-off opportunity to speed up the whole process by rendering the post-Katrina working class evacuation permanent. Turbocharged by the state relief effort, the gradual process of gentrification, which had already emptied the tourist centre of New Orleans of its black population, is poised to claim the rest of the city.[5]

Members of New Orleans' black majority are effectively prohibited from returning to rebuild their homes and their lives through a combination of economic dissuasion, logistical failure and technical/legal impediments imposed by federal and local government. The legal obstacles range from petty, but effective, restrictions (for instance, to vote in the forthcoming New Orleans primary, which will decide the future shape of the city, you need official ID – if you lost your ID in the storm, too bad), to surprising technical omissions (no satellite voting facilities are being prepared for the displaced citizens of Nola, though these were provided for expat Iraqis across the USA during the elections in Iraq!).[6] As one academic commentator remarked, the devastated New Orleans is now akin to a 'developing society', and as such, a fit case for Jimmy Carter and his team.[7]

But it is the State's failure to provide temporary accommodation in the city so that New Orleans' displaced population of former renters and (large minority of black) home owners can return – whether employed or unemployed – which plays the biggest part in turning evacuation into permanent eviction. The

5. Naomi Klein, 'Let the People Rebuild New Orleans', *The Nation*, 26 September 2005: 'The Business Council's wish list is well-known: low wages, low taxes, more luxury condos and hotels. Before the flood, this highly profitable vision was already displacing thousands of poor African-Americans: While their music and culture was for sale in an increasingly corporatised French Quarter (where only 4.3 percent of residents are black), their housing developments were being torn down'.
6. Michael Collins, 'The Disenfranchisement Of Katrina's Survivors', 1 March 2006, special for *Scoop* Independent Media, http://www.scoop.co.nz/stories/HL0603/S00016.htm#4
7. Cain Burdeau, 'Frustration Dominates New Orleans Race', 3 March 2006, Associated Press: 'It's almost to the point that we need election observers,' said Gary Clark, a political science professor at Dillard University in New Orleans, 'The limits we have now are almost the same as in a developing society: an economic infrastructure that's been devastated and various factions trying to seize political control and influence.'

25,000 trailers promised by FEMA have failed to materialise, while the nimby middle class bridles at the suggestion their neighbourhoods should become trailer parks.[8]

Furthermore, Mayor Ray Nagin's commission for reconstruction has called for a four-month moratorium on rebuilding in devastated working class neighbourhoods like the lower Ninth Ward and New Orleans East.[9] The message is clear: If you can't rebuild, why return?

True to form for contemporary urban renewal projects, which like to combine coercion with a façade of 'direct democracy', the attempted theft of New Orleans is being presented as a consultation process. The city commission's scheme, drafted by Republican real estate development tycoon(!), Joseph Canizaro, solicits residents to offer a 'viable' plan for reconstruction. Given the disarray and dislocation of former residents, it is hard to imagine how a 'people's plan' would be enabled by this pseudo-participatory framework, even if the residents were allowed back in the city. The rhetoric of choice combined with the shotgun timetable ('Four months to decide!' trumpeted *The Times-Picayune* newspaper's headline), as in regeneration schemes elsewhere, renders the consultation a sham.[10] If big business alone is allowed to rebuild, and, if a 'viable' plan means a plan agreeable to big developers like Canizaro, working class former residents have even less likelihood of returning to the city.

Sinking Wages and the Second Hurricane

As in other gentrification zones, the post-Katrina restructuring of wages is as important as the looting of potentially revenue-generating land and the commercialisation of formerly domestic, public or community spaces.[11]

The immediate labour shortage created by the forced diaspora from New Orleans might have been expected to push up wages for those involved in the reconstruction programme. In fact, the state and employers eagerly exploited the situation to *cheapen* labour power, while making sure the black working class was obstructed from returning to benefit from the demand for workers. To be precise, the storm was used to create a new collective worker in the region – a new working class minus the minimal advantages enjoyed by the city's former

8. Glen Ford and Peter Gamble, 'Fighting the Theft of New Orleans – The Rhythm of Resistance', *The Black Commentator*, 19 January 2006, no. 167. See also Saundra Amrhein, 'Who's rebuilding New Orleans?', *St. Petersburg Times*, 23 October 2005: '"But FEMA estimates that 100,000 families in the region need temporary housing. But only 3,105 families have been placed in travel trailers and another 70 in mobile homes," McIntyre said, "The nearest trailer settlement to New Orleans is 80 miles away in Baker."'
9. Ford and Gamble, op. cit.
10. Ibid.
11. While none of this could be described as 'outside' capitalism, public housing and community services represented an area created by capital in which the state allocated a portion of total value via appropriations, i.e. taxes, to the reproduction of labour power as a means by which to lower the price of labour power as a whole through economies of scale. That it is today destroying these economies indicates a shift to a more absolute non-reproduction of labour power. For this argument regarding the devalorisation of labour power I am indebted to Loren Goldner's 'The Remaking of the American Working Class'.

inhabitants. Post-Katrina, Bush immediately suspended the Davis-Bacon act – which requires employers to pay 'prevailing local wages' – waived the requirement for contractors to provide employment eligibility forms completed by their workers (a deterrent to the employment of 'illegal' labour) and halted affirmative action programmes in the region.

Although these measures were later restored, employers correctly read this as a signal to drop wages and basic labour rights and to tap into available supplies of immigrant labour. Latino workers poured into Louisiana, in response to job ads they had seen in Houston and other South Western cities, only to be greeted by a familiar cocktail of racism and hyper-exploitation. Sleeping under bridges or in abandoned cars, paying a fortune to camp in tents in the city park or sharing overcrowded rooms, they work long hours for weeks at a time and are rewarded with $10 an hour – wages which too often are never even paid.[12] As Gary Younge observed, this is simply slave labour in its contemporary form – a return to the institution on which old New Orleans was founded.[13]

As well as universally lowering wage rates in the regressive new New Orleans, the influx of immigrant labour – 'largely unaware that tens of thousands of blue-collar evacuees who would relish these jobs are unable to return for lack of family housing and federal support'[14] – serves as yet another disincentive to the residents of old New Orleans to return. Pricing the black population out, state representatives like Ray Nagin and the neoliberal media have been as quick to promote 'artificially inflamed' racism and inter-class competition as they have been slow to provide housing and aid.

Using immigrant labour to begin the clean up effort was not only cheaper for the individual capitalists concerned; the deployment of Latino workers, inadequately trained and unprotected by the frail privileges of citizenship, contributes to the overall recomposition and devalorisation of labour power in New Orleans. Low wages for immigrants also means a further devalorisation of the labour power of New Orleans' displaced residents. In turn, their presence in cities such as Houston, to which they have been 'decanted', serves as a downward pressure on wages there. Swapping populations around to effect an overall cheapening – or destruction – of labour power, this is another example of disaster-catalysed primitive accumulation. Hyper-visible in New Orleans, but an endemic part of globalisation, the US already gets much of its labour power for free through similar spatial prestidigitations. The cost of reproducing the labour power of immigrant workers – many of them recently proletarianised, having come from regions not yet fully integrated into capitalist production – is borne by their societies of origin, not by the US. Their low-to-no-wage status in New Orleans means absolute surplus value for their employers through

12. Gary Younge, 'Hard Times in the Big Easy', *The Nation*, 13 March 2006.
13. Ibid. Also, Jonathan Tilove, 'Cleanup Relies on Day Labor of Latinos', *Times-Picayune*, 8 January 2006.
14. Mike Davis, 'Gentrifying Disaster – In New Orleans: Ethnic Cleansing, GOP-Style', *Mother Jones*, 25 October 2005.

non-reproduction of the most immediate kind, but this basic looting is always going on whether individual employers realise it or not.[15] Once again, we should see the looting of New Orleans as exemplary of capital's current modus operandi, not exceptional. As has been remarked before, the exception is the (neoliberal form of) rule.

The flipside of all this gutting of variable capital – that is, the lowering of the price of labour power below reproductive levels – is the gifting of the business elite with a reduced bill for the rapidly diminishing consumption fund of the region's working class.[16] Bush's offer to pick up the tab for almost all of the $200 billion of flood damage was not predicated on higher taxes on the rich. On the contrary, this steroidal version of Keynesian deficit spending would be combined, as Mike Davis puts it, with 'a dream-list of long-sought-after conservative social reforms', targeting the poor: 'school and housing vouchers', which effectively transfer the cost of services onto those they used to support; 'a central role for churches', turning relief into an opportunity for moralising absolute surplus value extraction; 'an urban homestead lottery', making it harder for most people to find housing while creating a few new members of Bush's 'ownership society'; and, finally, 'extensive tax breaks to businesses, the creation of a Gulf Opportunity Zone, and the suspension of annoying government regulations' which include suspending prevailing wages in construction and environmental regulations on offshore drilling.[17]

The state of emergency licenses any amount of deregulation. The apparatus which at least offered some protection to workers, while limiting corporate

15. For more on this, see Loren Goldner, 'The Remaking of the American Working Class, The Restructuring of Global Capital and the Recomposition of Class Terrain': 'Through the incorporation of this non-capitalist work force, whose reproduction costs are free for capital (not, of course, for the society of origin) the total capital can reduce the cost of the total worker.' To put it in non-Marxian terms, the workers who come to the US from 'developing countries' are, as the economists say, a 'free input'. The process of producing them as workers, as beings-for-capital in any and every sense – feeding, training and developing their bodies and minds, educating, socialising, acculturating them – is not paid for by US capitalists, it's a free gift they get when they employ the worker. This 'social reproduction' of the worker is looted wholesale, as, to a greater or lesser extent, are whole communities and the social ties that they foster. Mike Davis has noted this phenomenon in his book *Magic Urbanism: Latinos Reinvent the US Big City*. He cites the example of Randalls, a Houston grocery chain, which has recruited more than 1,000 workers from closely related villages in the Tontonicapan highlands of Guatemala. Housed in a cluster of low-rise, faux Georgian apartment houses, these proletarianised Mayans come with built-in cooperative powers US capital never had to pay to inculcate: 'US employers [...] have become skilled at exploiting "positive externalities" like free labour recruitment and superb workgroup discipline that arise from organised communal emigration.'
16. While the literal enslavement of workers is not, long-term, a sustainable option for capital – since the value measure (socially necessary labour time for the reproduction of capital) must remain in force even in its state of exception if capital is not to simply defraud and devalue itself – in the contemporary conditions of accumulation where productive activity floats – or drowns – in a sea of over-valued monetary claims on non-existent surplus value (a.k.a. fictitious capital), the reckoning for this looting can be deferred through the stupendous spirals of the credit system. Fictitious capital commands that further looting is performed in the attempt to make good these empty claims on value, yet an over-reliance on looting, since it destroys the productive base of surplus value and indeed the materialised capital that constitutes our life world, tends to diminish its own ability to expand surplus value.
17. Davis, 'The Predators of New Orleans', op. cit.

rapine within 'average' levels of depredation, was hurriedly dismantled in the aftermath of the storm. What was once upon a time accomplished in the name of a national myth of rebirth – like the general mobilisation and devaluation of the working class imposed in the guise of fascist palingenesis (or Rooseveltian New Deal) in the '30s – can now only be catalysed by artificially aggravated disaster. Furthermore, where, in the past, devalorisation was combined with a rising standard of living, a shorter work day, new infrastructure and new institutions for the reproduction of labour power (housing, hospitals, schools), here, the panic depreciation of labour power coincides with the non-replacement of the means of social reproduction:

'Public-housing and Section 8 residents recently protested that the agencies in charge of these housing complexes [including the Department of Housing and Urban Development] are using allegations of storm damage to these complexes as a pretext for expelling working-class African-Americans, in a very blatant attempt to co-opt our homes and sell them to developers to build high-priced housing'.[18]

Rather than rebuilding New Orleans and reproducing these state-owned assets for their erstwhile beneficiaries, the drive to cheapen labour power dictates the conversion of sites of reproduction into sites of revenue accumulation. This also applies in the private sector: Landlords, reacting to reports of soaring land values in dry areas, have begun evicting tenants en masse and renting properties out at higher rates.[19] Working class tenants still in their homes – or yet to return to them – are being 'flash gentrified' out to make way for non-productive workers who offer a better rate of return for landlords. Whereas US capital

18. Mike Davis, 'Gentrifying Disaster – In New Orleans: Ethnic Cleansing, GOP-Style', op. cit. It should be noted that, although the non-return of blacks has been explicitly called for as policy, the exclusion of the Asian and white working class is an unstated but de facto goal of the same process.
19. Loc. cit.
20. 'Non-productive' here is used in Marx's – not Adam Smith's – sense. Non-productive labour is labour judged from the perspective of capital's imperative of expanded accumulation. Productive labour is labour which adds to and reproduces (expands) the total surplus value (i.e. capital) accumulated by exploiting the waged labour of the working class. The nature of the things produced, and the context of production, determines whether or not an activity is productive. For example, the US' spiralling investment in military production is classically unproductive – however many workers are employed in this sector and however essential to maintaining US global hegemony its wars may be – because tanks, bombers, guns, etc. do not reproduce total capital embodied in use values of whatever kind, even when they are not directly employed in destroying use values produced by other capitals, as in Iraq for example. Indeed, the US as a whole, when one considers its total capital in the light of its total debt, must be reckoned unproductive – but this judgement is being made in the form of the ongoing devastation of people and things, evidenced in events such as the destruction of New Orleans, and will not be complete until a future financial-social crisis completes a thorough-going destruction of use and exchange values of the kind experienced in previous crashes and inter-imperialist wars.

The FIRE economy elite (Finance, Insurance, Real Estate) that will take over New Orleans clearly belongs to the unproductive class (Marx's 'faux frais' of production), whose salaries come out of capital's 'consumption fund'. Classically, while they may be necessary to superintending, or lubricating, the process of accumulation, this class, although waged or salaried, is not productive of surplus value but rather are paid out of surplus value accumulated elsewhere in the system. In fact, today, this class is chiefly useful for expanding the fictive claims on value of US capital, so even their traditional status as 'incidental operating expenses' is eclipsed. This class is unproductive as never before; they are 'incidental expenses' incurred in the process of formerly squeezed surplus value out of industrial workers in the process of production, now it squeezes the unemployed and/or shit-workers out of their homes to free up more property for (ultimately unproductive, fictitious) capitalisation.[20] As workers and their homes are devalorised and wages are forced below the level necessary to secure means of subsistence, capital takes its ill-gotten spoils and turns them into collateral. The neoliberal vision for New Orleans is not the replacement of public housing and other resources but the transfer of land and property into the hands of developers and big business, a shift from the reproduction of labour power to its displacement to make way for speculation and unproductive consumption: casinos, jazz theme parks and elite *Truman Show*-style pseudo-communities.[21]

The whole state 'relief' programme functions as a second hurricane (for similar reasons, the reconstruction in Indonesia is now known as 'the second tsunami'), sweeping away the remnants of the welfare system and looting infrastructure to prop up big business.[22] True to the principles of the Washington Consensus, in ensuring that all aid functions as means of command and a source of increased (debt leveraged) revenue, the US is imposing unprecedented demands for loan repayment upon local governments in affected states. How will local government meet this demand? No doubt through lower wages, further cuts in services and benefits (Bush's legislation 'proposes aid that would benefit less than one-quarter of those made jobless by Katrina') and a continuation of the mass redundancies with which the state rewarded many of its own employees in the wake of the deluge.[23]

drowning in debt and destroying social reproduction. Once the housing and related bubbles deflate, they are likely to join the rest of the US proletariat in a swamp of less genteel, unproductive activity.

To clarify, the displaced working class now forced out of New Orleans were themselves increasingly an unproductive class (again, in capital's terms), whether as beneficiaries of dwindling welfare payments or as workers in increasingly heavily leveraged US companies whose dwindling capital supports towering 'inverse pyramids' of debt. Productive activity, as the rise of China as the US' offshore production plant makes clear, is tendentially impossible within the territorial limits of the USA. What America increasingly dedicates itself to is the destruction of value – both exchange and use value, since both embody surplus value, the root of capitalist wealth and the source of its crisis. Only by uprooting and looting such workers can capital hope to squeeze a desperate last dose of absolute surplus value out of its moribund 'reserve army of labour'. Yet, once again, given the macro-logic of US capital's decline, these little hits of valorisation are immediately swallowed up in the vast nexus of debt, deferral and extorted tribute that is the international financial system. Here, US debts are turned into a powerful tool for the domination of its economic rivals and creditors. The financial elite are clearly more than willing to offer up New Orleans and its working class to the nebulous deity of unlimited liquidity to the point at which not having a productive industrial base becomes a truly insuperable problem.

21. As Mike Davis notes, the Clinton-era HOPE VI programme, which fetishised diversity through 'mixed use, mixed income' housing, was conceived as replacement housing for the poor, but ended up replacing the poor themselves. This is the model for housing, and the other forms of 'displacement through (non) replacement' in the new New Orleans.
22. Klein, op. cit.
23. Davis, op. cit: 'The powerful House Republican Study Group has vowed to support only relief measures that buttress the private sector and are offset by reductions in national social programs such as food stamps, student loans, and Medicaid.'

Atavistic Accumulation

It is, then, no exaggeration to describe the devastation and subsequent looting of New Orleans as an example of primitive accumulation. Capital's total wage bill is reduced through looting of the non-capitalist periphery, looting of unreproduced – but over-valued – infrastructure and looting of nature – the non-replacement of natural resources evidenced by the erosion of the bayous and, since the introduction of the Gulf Opportunity Zone, intensified by the lifting of government environmental regulations. On top of this, we have the fundamental reduction of the wage of the disaggregated and dispersed ex-residents of the city, plus the raft of cuts in services and benefits for those who remain or return.

This primitive accumulation is the bitter culmination of US capital's long-term strategy of devalorisation, analysed by Loren Goldner in his essay 'The Remaking of the American Working Class'. By the start of the 20th century, the very development of the productive forces had pushed capital toward crisis: '[T]he productive forces have reached a level where any technological innovation produces more (fictive) capitalist titles to the total surplus value than it adds to that surplus value. The capital relationship can no longer maintain itself; it must therefore destroy an important portion of labor power, or labor power must destroy it'.[24]

Rather than enabling the valorisation of capital, then, technological development actually undermines the value of its own previously produced commodities, and thus converts the value represented in commodities, money and credit already circulating into 'fictive' titles to value. Capital is, at its core, profoundly deflationary. To put it another way, as the development of technology itself accelerates the devalorisation of existing technology, the retroactive process of 'techno-depreciation', in which more efficient technologies render their precursors obsolete, effectively destroys their value as commodities, putting capital accumulation into crisis through its very own productivity.

Marx's formula, whereby constant capital tendentially increases at the expense of variable capital – i.e. value produced by labour embodied in technology increasingly predominates over value-producing labour – not only drives the global expansion of capital but also sees a recomposition of production (the 'real subsumption' of labour under capital, as Marx calls it). In the last 100 years, the tendency of its own productivity to undermine capital's ability to valorise itself has been offset by driving down the cost of labour, extending and intensifying the process of production and looting outside the wage relation proper. For the most developed capitalist nations, this meant a shift from absolute surplus value extraction, the extension of the working day and primitive accumulation in the colonies to Fordist and Taylorist intensification of

24. Goldner, op. cit.

production ('relative surplus value extraction') in the capitalist core. Through the cheapening of the means of subsistence afforded by mass production (i.e. cheaper food and clothing, domestic technologies, mass culture, etc.), a process assisted by the role of the welfare state in providing mass health care and education, the cost of labour-power (variable capital) as a percentage of value could be pushed down. This allows for the devalorisation of labour-power without (necessarily) the material destruction of the worker. As the other developed capitals one by one succumbed to stagnation and industrial decline, the US used its post-World War II supremacy to keep down the price of labour-power while pushing the myth of a permanent improvement in the condition of workers.

But, as Marx pointed out, the (relative, deceptive and far from universal) rise in workers' standard of living and real wages comes on the eve of crisis. Since the mid-'60s, with US industry devalued by its more productive competitors in Europe and Japan, the US 'strategy' has involved a shift from the Fordist/Taylorist intensive recomposition of labour power to the dismantling of industrial production altogether. This reconfiguration, then destruction, of productive industry cannot be understood apart from its relationship to the sphere of circulation, however. The US continues to exploit its hegemonic position as the holder of the world's reserve currency, the dollar, to counterbalance its decline as a 'real economy', through its ability to dictate global terms of trade. The domestic stagnation, then demise, of value extraction through productive industry (*viz.* the decades-long decline of the US auto industry, aerospace, metal working, textiles, mining, agriculture, etc.) is offset by a global programme of primitive accumulation through the dollar, through the system of international loans and the imposition of free trade and privatisation on defaulting nations by means of Structural Adjustment Programmes, of which the current neoliberal attack on New Orleans is a spectacular, disaster movie variation.

Having extended, and speeded up, the working day in the '70s, shut down factories and welfare programmes in the '80s and expanded the unproductive tertiary sector in the '90s, today the US is chopping away the residues of the mechanisms by which it recomposed the total worker, lowering the total wage by destroying means of production, reproduction and workers themselves. After devalorisation, that is, the destruction or 'non-reproduction of labour power' through (Fordist) recomposition, today we have the final stages of devalorisation through its post-Fordist decomposition. After the 'real subsumption' of the worker under capital, we have surreal subsumption: the return of absolute surplus value extraction in formerly relative surplus value-centred economies. Coupled with intensified labour, multiplied by primitive accumulation, capital now attempts the destruction of already reduced standards of living and expectations on the part of already ravaged communities of workers.

Thus, while it is true that what is happening in Louisiana is primitive accumulation on a grand scale, it is not the beginning of productive accumulation but its end – if not for the global economy, then at least for the USA's. If the enclosures of the 16th century saw the transformation of peasants into 'free and rightless proletarians', the 'new enclosures' of the last 30 years (to use *Midnight Notes*' term) have converted large sections of the proletariat into surplus humanity: A post-industrial reserve army of precarious labour that shows little chance of coming back into active service or, rather, has only the bottom end of the service sector – a range of opportunities from McJobs and neo-slavery to incarceration – into which it can be corralled. Turning its population into 'insurgents', as the refugees of Katrina were at one point dubbed, the state reproduces its citizens as foreigners, as its enemy, in order to decompose their political strength and destroy their economic value.

Unlike the enclosures at the origin of capitalism, which, though brutal, imposed the conditions for surplus value extraction on an expanding scale and created a new form of socialised labour (albeit in inverted and distorted form), the current period of enclosures, of which New Orleans is exemplary, represent the looting of land and labour power for the reproduction, on an expanding scale, not of value but of fictitious capital – paper claims on value. Like the originary enclosures, the current cycle creates the conditions for absolute surplus value extraction, but within the context of spiralling debt and an ocean of fictitious values. The reconstruction of New Orleans as a city of luxury housing, casinos and consumerism is hardly the creation of a new, productive dynamo. Today, primitive accumulation only makes good the absence of production rather than serving as its foundation. In capital's own terms, this is problematic and ultimately unsustainable.

Looting – that is the many forms of non-reproductive accumulation going on in contemporary capitalism – reproduces looting on an expanded scale. The non-reproduction of constant and variable capital not only creates surplus value but also non-reproduction on an expanded scale – the 'planet of slums' described by Mike Davis. Up to the point at which a crisis of illiquidity (or working class insurrection) arrests the global movement and expansion of fictitious capital, the US – and its creditors – is obliged to continue the game, continue the enclosures, despite the escalating cost of permanent war, destruction and non-development of use values.[25]

25. To get some idea, in non-Marxist terms, of what 'non-development of use values' means, consider the current ecological crisis. If the majority of scientists are correct and global warming is accelerating at a potentially devastating pace, this represents the absolute destruction of (potential and actual) use values, the acme of the ongoing devastation conducted in the form of wars and so on. Rather than organising a rational response to the crisis of global warming, e.g. creation of viable and more efficient fuel sources, etc, capital is busily prosecuting a campaign of austerity in the guise of enforced recycling, taxation and, if the Kyoto agreement were ever to be put into practice, the progressive limitation of carbon emissions at the cost of the world's poor. Rather than using our immense productive capacity to generate real alternatives to carbon-based fuel, the limit of contemporary imagination is a Malthusian throttling of real (i.e. non-capitalist) development. The conditions of capital accumulation make alternative energy 'unviable', applying a calculus which, at the global level, would sacrifice the combined use values of the planet to the dictates of exchange-value. In the meantime, the NGOs and 'green' businesses make a nice profit by retailing new forms of immiseration and social discipline.

The US failure to reproduce its working class, its industries and its cities may be ignored by those who still stand to benefit – at least in the short term – from the enormous accumulation of debt-backed credit flooding its housing and (other) speculative markets. But a country that lets a major city disappear into the sea for want of basic repairs and maintenance is clearly in trouble. Combined with the humiliation of its failed 'laboratory for conservative economic policies' in Iraq, the devastation of New Orleans should put a nail in the coffin of the myth of America's post-industrial renaissance. The decline of the 'real economy' in the US marks the end of primitive accumulation as a supporting player in capital's drama and its move to centre stage.

As the world's leading producer of disaster movies, the US should perhaps adopt a new national mascot. Instead of the bald eagle, David Cronenberg's human-fly would be more fitting. Seth Brundle, the renegade scientist who inadvertently fuses his genes with the despised household insect in an attempt to teleport himself across his dilapidated ex-industrial warehouse, takes the first signs of his decay in human terms as tokens of renewed life and vitality. Elated, he feels he is becoming an *Übermensch*, living, if not as the knowledge economy boosters had it, on air, then on pure sugar. But he ends up typing with deciduous digits, extremities and sensibility falling away to reveal the horrifying insect within.

A narrative of transformation can only conceal regression for so long, but, in the US, the denial seems structural. New Orleans' destruction has been seized upon by conservatives as an opportunity to build a plastinated jazz cadaver over the dead or displaced bodies of the city's black, working class population. The black working and middle class are already fighting back against this grotesque and brutal process, asserting their right to return and reconstruct the city on their own terms. But we should bear in mind the depth of the crisis the US is facing and, unlike some liberal critics who now hark back to the New Deal and call for a return to the 'real economy', we should recognise that the US is no longer capable of restoring capitalist 'productivity'. Similarly, the self-organised, unpaid efforts of private individuals to reconstruct the city in the vacuum created and enforced by the state's agencies, is in itself a form of non-reproduction and should not be fetishised as a purely autonomous activity. To put it in terms that even a productivist Maoist could understand, we can't survive by creating a new, cosier relationship with the capitalist insect. Nor should we be content to pioneer the latest forms of non-reproduction in our struggles against capital. Expanded social reproduction on capital's terms is no longer an option. Much more difficult, yet the only 'viable' choice is to kill the insect before it kills us.

Chapter 8

Reality Check: Class and Immaterial Labour

Mute could never be accused of remaining indifferent to the techno-utopian thinking of the mid-'90s. But, despite our enthusiasm for, and interest in, the digital explosion of the net, we always aimed to discredit those fantasies attached to 'immateriality', in which labour magically disappears from the production of value, and the materiality of life is somehow jettisoned. It is no accident that, for many years, our strap line was 'Proud to be Flesh'. *Mute* also partook of its own share of techno-utopianism. This tended to involve visions of virtuality's power to heal rifts of class, space, race and gender, largely through the power of disembodied global communication. But, compared to the IT-propelled wet dreams of neoliberal capitalists and state planners, entailing the mirage of a 'weightless economy' in which knowledge workers perform 'immaterial labour' to produce one 'long boom', those alternative visions for the network society seem almost sober. At the very least, they continued to deal with the reality of domination, even if the panacea of cyberspace was overly optimistic. Behind the seductive visions of the network society, indulged in by cyberfeminists and venture capitalist alike, however, lay greater transformations, wrought in no small part by the same technologies: The shift from the relatively even distribution of manufacturing across the globe to the West's rapid de-industrialisation and all that this implies – an opening up of markets, expansion of supply chains and the flexibilised deployment of labour that relies heavily on IT communication networks.

The articles in this chapter strive to define these new contours of labour and capital's 'post-Fordist' recomposition, while consistently trying to understand the possibilities produced for new forms of struggle. This search for a politics of resistance adequate to post-Fordist globalisation also involves, of course, much intra-left debate and disagreement. Most at issue, in the articles compiled here, are the claims made by Italian post-autonomist Marxists, such as Maurizio Lazzarato and Antonio Negri, for the radical possibilities inherent in capitalism's increased dependency on the creativity and 'affectivity' of the worker. Now that repetitive, mind-numbing work is performed increasingly by robots, the argument goes, creativity and affectivity is demanded of workers – a far less controllable means of production. The erosion of boundaries between life and work is also conceived of, by Negri et al., as an opportunity as much as an incursion into free time. The net result of this thinking is that labour time – the basis of value production – becomes impossible to measure and, if labour time is no longer the basis of value, then capitalism's underlying logic is rendered defunct. A further double-edged condition of post-Fordist labour is its precariousness, as short-term contracts, shift work and a lack of benefits and job security become the norm. This precariousness, or 'precarity', affects workers across sectors and classes and, for that reason, some argue, creates the possibility for new alliances. The artist, the call centre worker and the sex worker supposedly now share some of the same exploitative conditions, and possible grounds for struggle.

These articles move at speed through different theatres of production, describing them with great acuity and often humour. Arthur Kroker took one of the first stabs at defining the techno-cultural elite which he named the 'virtual class'. In his interview with Geert Lovink, he describes how 'the will to virtuality' has completed the commodity's illusory severance from its economic base, conjuring 'the pure aestheticisation of experience'. This is a fantasy entered into by the virtual class –which also tends towards 'liberal-fascism' – a class committed to opening up trading zones to commodity circulation, while living in fear of migrating workers. Their aim is, baldly, to 'suppress the working class' says Kroker. Simon Pope, in his hilarious recreation of the internal monologues of the mid-'90s, Shoreditch digerati, ventriloquises a male pubescent mindset fixated with brands, kit, virtual and commercial combat, personal security and making money without doing any work. Pope is careful to graft the 'weightless economy' to its hinterland of real production: 'Where Josh's dad's business was built on international trade in fossil fuels, Josh makes his wedge from the trade in cultural currency.'

In the ten or so years over which these articles were commissioned, however, there is a distinct shift in focus from the virtual class to its underclass. This underclass unites the shit work of 'knowledge workers' in the world's call centres, highly exploited and indebted university students, the underpaid cleaners of Europe's 'progressive' cultural institutions, the dislocated logistics workers, who supply the postmodern manufacturing industry with its array of components, and the illegal, domestic and agricultural workers, whose historical precariousness has been eclipsed by the new-found 'precarity' of once-secure workers. As Angela Mitropoulos reminds us, global precarity has always been the standard experience of work in capitalism. 'Fordism,' she writes, 'is an exception in capitalist history'.

As the certainties of progress associated with Fordism crumble, so, too, does the confidence of modernity and its culture. Anna Dezeuze explores artists' fascination with the precariousness of the global poor and their makeshift strategies of survival. The work of artists like Francis Alÿs and Marjetica Potrč mimics the 'inventiveness' of shack dwellers and the urban poor, finding in their outsiderhood a 'certain freedom'. In Potrč's view, 'the world we live in today is all about self-reliance, individual initiative and small scale projects' – something she clearly embraces. This resignation, on the part of liberals, to the postmodern impossibility of mass movements and revolutionary social change is the target of

Brian Ashton's article, 'The Factory Without Walls'. For Ashton, the Thatcherite defeat of the left and the smashing of union militancy during the 1980s has led to the mistaken idea that production has become so globalised, its workforce so scattered and sub-contracted, that co-ordinated action is all but impossible. Uttering the maxim 'know thine enemy', he advocates research into the structures of contemporary capitalism and its global supply chains. 'The mass worker hasn't been destroyed', he argues, 's/he has just been reconfigured'. By going global, he concludes, 'capitalism is creating the opportunity for global working class struggle.' If IT has been deployed by capitalism to recompose itself by disbanding and outsourcing the centres of proletarian production, then it can similarly be used to recombine this class again. But, what the class identity of this reconfigured mass worker actually is, on what basis struggles will be fought and what role the 'knowledge worker' will play in all of this is productively disputed here.

Data Trash: The Theory of the Virtual Class

Geert Lovink

Vol 1 #4, Spring 1996

Canadian media theorist, Arthur Kroker, is the author of *The Possessed Individual, Spasm* and *Hacking the Future.* In recent years, he and Marilouise Kroker have often been in Europe and made appearances at Virtual Futures, V-2, Eldorado/Antwerpen, etc. Recently, they have also been discovered in German-speaking countries. Both are noted for their compact jargon, which makes their message seem to drown somewhat in over-complex code. But *Data Trash: The Theory of the Virtual Class* (1994) changed all that.[1] The long trek through squashy discourses had not been in vain. Firmly rooted in European philosophy, without being submerged, Arthur Kroker has found his topic: the virtual class.

The ongoing worldwide commercialisation of the net has produced a new sector in economic, and hence social, categories. Kroker's virtual class appears to be remarkably aggressive and cynical and, as anyone can observe, has little to do with grassroots democracy or issues of public access. In today's exploding digital markets, it's about grabbing as much as you can. Now that he has been able to define the adversary in such clear terms, Kroker is understandably thriving. The critics in the media are outraged: Why such pessimism? Aren't the good intentions of the media pioneers there for all to see? The rapping Kroker is becoming a nuisance. Apparently, he is kicking where it hurts.

Kroker wrote *Data Trash* together with Michael Weinstein, a political philosopher, rap poet and photography critic for *The Chicago Tribune.* According to Kroker, he is also 'a Nietzschean underground man who thinks deeply about the United States.' Arthur and Michael met during the Vietnam years and have collaborated for the past 20 years on the *Canadian Journal for Political and Social Theory* (now the electronic magazine CTHEORY). *Data Trash* is hyper-topical, which is remarkable for such a slow medium as a book. It leaves manuals, introductions and speculations behind in favour of a pincer movement, telling the story of the rise of a new class while, at the same time, reflecting upon its consequences. This is a far cry from the usual activities of media theorists for whom the net is still more something of a rumour than a concrete experience.

I asked Kroker how it is that his book can be so topical and reflective at the same time. His response was: 'My body does a lot of travelling. I like to take deep plunges in San Francisco, spreading psychosis. I visit MIT and the Boston area, and I spend time in Europe as well, roaming between Grenoble and Munich, to understand the cybermatrices. And I spend a lot of time on the net.'

1. Arthur Kroker and Michael A. Weinstein, *Data Trash, the Theory of the Virtual Class,* New York: St. Martin's Press, 1994.

Data Trash was written on the net; the writers haven't seen each other face to face in five years. 'We experienced that there was a third person, the third mind, who wrote the book. The computer had come alive and *Data Trash* was the result.'

The cultural strategy followed in this book is called 'Hacking the Media'. 'We like the notion of over-identifying with the feared and desired object, to such a point of obsession that you begin to take a bath in its acid juices. You travel so deeply and quickly in cyberculture that you force it to do things it never wanted to. I try to live my philosophy through cyberculture.' For Michael Weinstein, too, it was an unique situation because he largely resists the glowing horizon of technoculture and does not live in the corporate capital of America. Instead, he dwells in the twilight zone of Chicago, which produces rough Midwestern thinkers who reflect on the howling winds of sacrificial violence and the decline of the American empire.

Why does this emerging class not have a class consciousness of its own?

AK: 'If it did, it would be doomed as the emergent class. *Data Trash* is on suicidal and passive nihilism, as the radical Nietzsche predicted it in his *Genealogy of Morals*. Virtual Reality (VR) means to us the humiliating reduction of human beings to servo mechanisms, or, as Heidegger would say, a standing reserve – the humiliation of the flesh as you are poked and proved and sucked by the harvesting machines of the virtual reality scanners.'

To Kroker and Weinstein, VR does not mean head-mounted scanners and data gloves. In their terminology, VR is a whole assemblage of experiences involving a traditional class consciousness, the spread of the ideology of technoculture and the hegemony of 'liberal fascism' and its swing back into 'retro fascism' as the political force behind the so-called 'Will to Virtuality'. *Data Trash* seems the purest consummation of Marxism, the severance of the commodity form from its economic base, into the notion of the pure aestheticisation of experience. Kroker explains: 'We talk about the recombinant commodity form, in an economy run by the biological logic of cloning, displacing and re-sequencing. Or virtualised exchange, the replacement of a consumer culture by the desire to simply disappear, from shopping to turning your body into a brand name sign.'

Now that the Berlin wall has crumbled and everyone has left Marxism, Kroker and Weinstein have gone back to Marx for a close reading of the transition of capitalism into the phase of pure commoditisation. Living in America is not a question of trying to catch up with the media. The body is always moving to the rhythm of the media itself. *Data Trash* begins with two fundamental rejections: the techno-utopian stance taken by Howard Rheingold in his book, *Virtual Communities* (not the same Rheingold after his HotWired experience), and Neil Postman's neoconservative position. On the other hand, it critiques all brands of technological determinism which state that we don't have choices; there are real contradictions and lots of fractures, even in the supposedly closed virtual class. For Kroker and Weinstein, the field of political contestation is wide open.

GL: But is this class in itself not already virtual, in the sense of being invisible, dispersed and without clearly formulated class interests?

AK: We have done our investigations in many countries to try to understand the different class fractions. How would the virtual class be actualised in France as opposed to America or Canada? In every case, it turns out to be this curious mixture of predatory capitalism and computer visionarism, but it strikes us that it is a coherent class with pretty straightforward ideological objectives: It has to suppress the working class. In North America, one should position it within the framework of the NAFTA agreements. It freezes the working class and lower middle class in place so that they cannot move easily over national borders. When the workers complain, then they bring in the mechanism of a disciplinary state: the punitive side of the virtual class.

It's commonplace rhetoric now: they have to stampede everybody on the information superhighway, and every businessman knows that, if you're not going on it soon, you are going to be eliminated, economically and historically. And this whole notion has been appropriated by the virtual class. But, at the same time, it is not a traditional class because it does not operate in the traditional logic of the political economy. The very notion of capitalism has already mutated, not really into technology but into virtuality. Our work is a prolegomenon to the study of the virtual class, about the coming to be of a much more sinister and demonic force and that's the 'Will to Virtuality', a deeply disturbing, nihilistic aspect of the culture in which we live. It's about this suicidal urge to feed human flesh into image processing machines, in such intensity, hyper acceleration and suicidal seductiveness that flesh appears humiliated before it.

In the end, you have to choose an existence as an 'honoured collaborator', in Whitehead's sense of technoculture, rather than not act at all. For a lot of thinkers, the position of the human species as honoured collaborator of technoculture is their idea of a modernist position, what I call 'technological emergentism'. The human species is being superseded by technology. All right, they say (the Shannons, McLuhans, et al.), but we can still be an honoured collaborator, we can probe around the world and we can have media extensions of man. The notion of exteriorisation is the possibility of discovering new religious epiphanies of technological experience. We reject that perspective. It is not about 'reaching out' but about 'reaching in'.

GL: How does the virtual class relate to neoliberalism?

AK: The political programme of the virtual class goes way beyond the Reagonomics and Thacherism of the '80s. The agenda of the corporate class is to remove all barriers for the transnational movement of products. The knowledge industry, which is computer-based, should also move freely and universally. The technocratic class is not so much conservative as liberal;

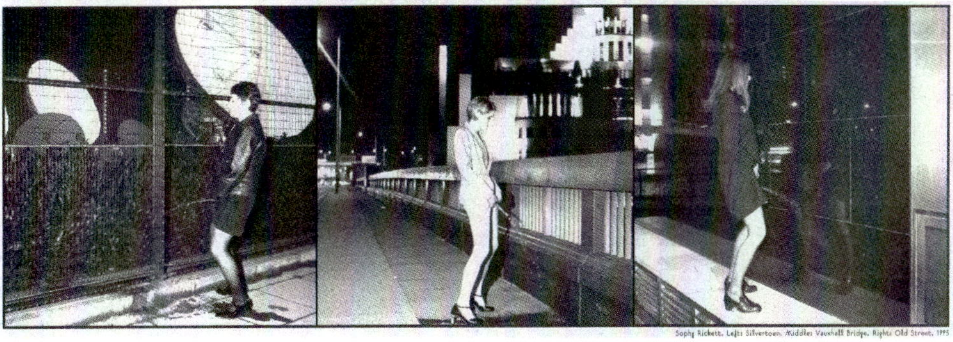

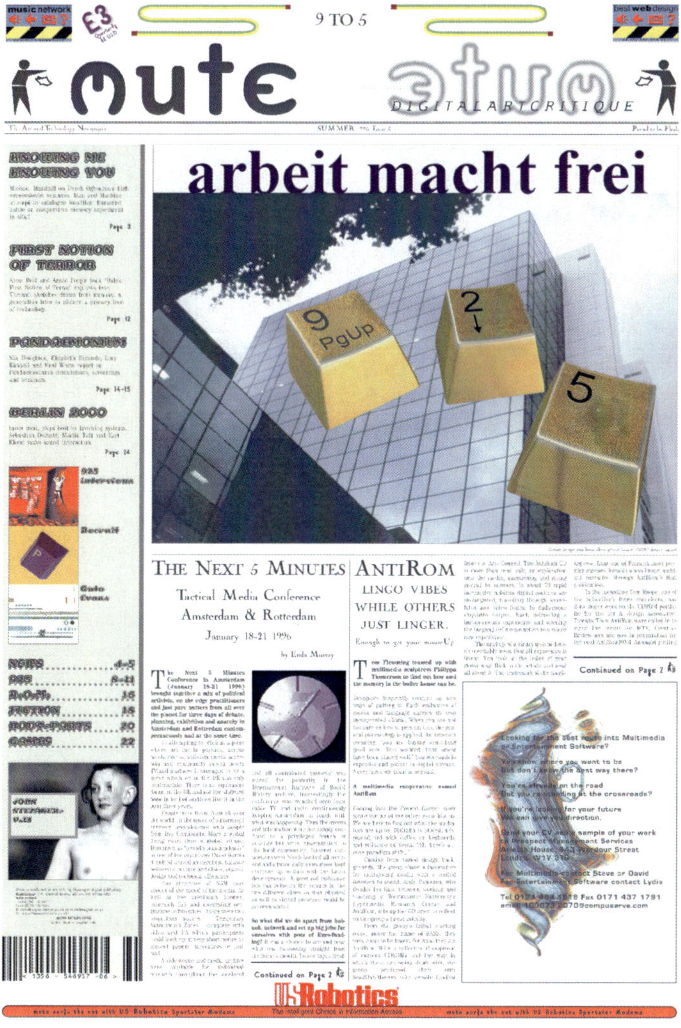

top: Sophy Rickett, from the series *Women Pissing*, used to illustrate Pauline van Mourik Broekman's review of the Stream exhibition, Vol 1 #4, Winter/Spring 1996
bottom: CORP death squad, *Arbeit Macht Frei*, cover image for the 9 to 5 issue, Vol 1 #5, Summer 1996

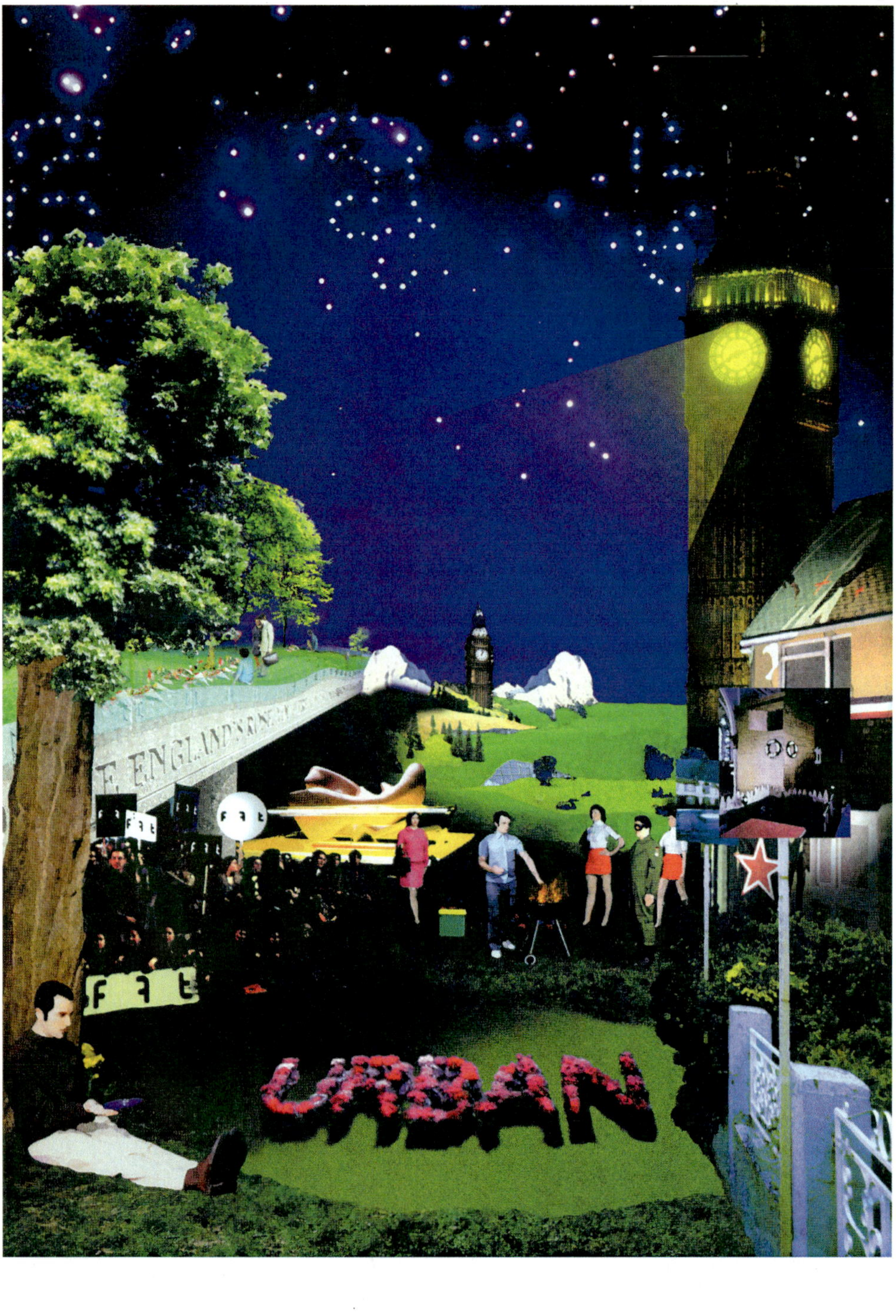

above: FAT, *FAT Park*, one of *Mute*'s first allocations of magazine space for interventions by other groups, Vol 1 #10, Summer 1998
opposite: Ammirati Puris Lintas, still from Rover 200 ad, used to illustrate Pauline van Mourik Broekman's piece on Cool Britannia, 'Signs of the Times@UK.plc', Vol 1 #10, Summer 1998

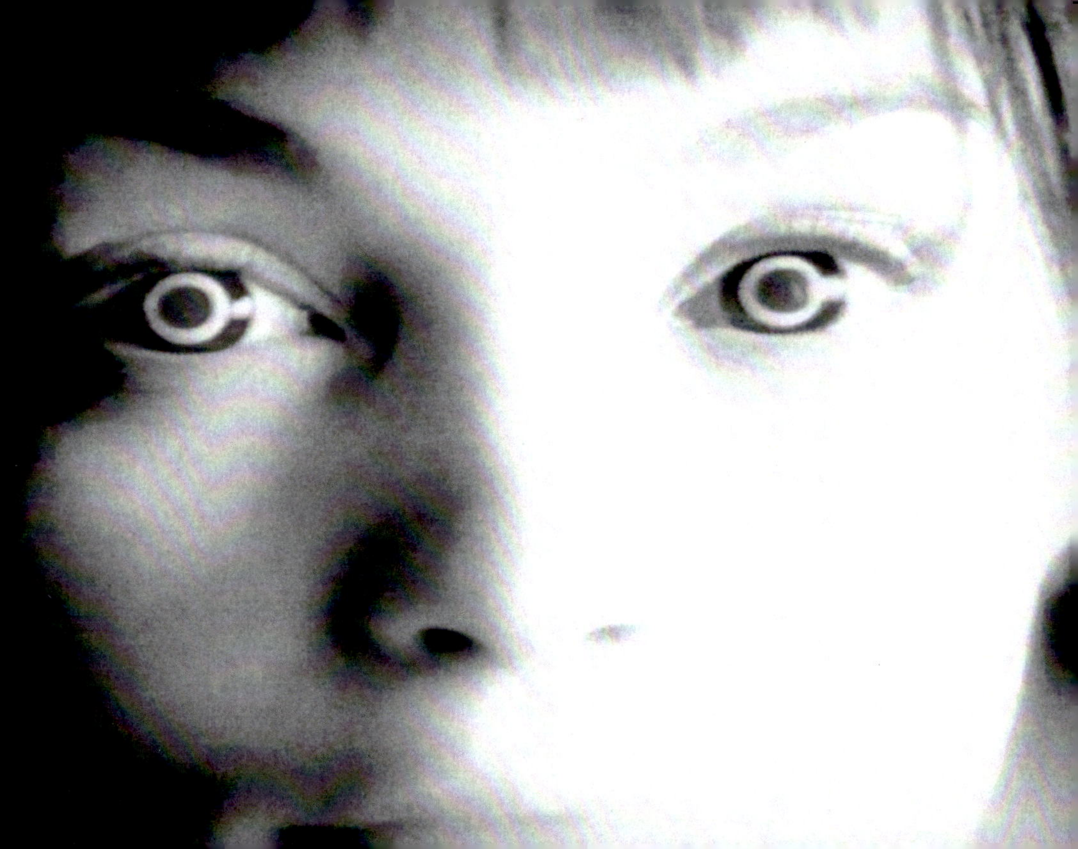

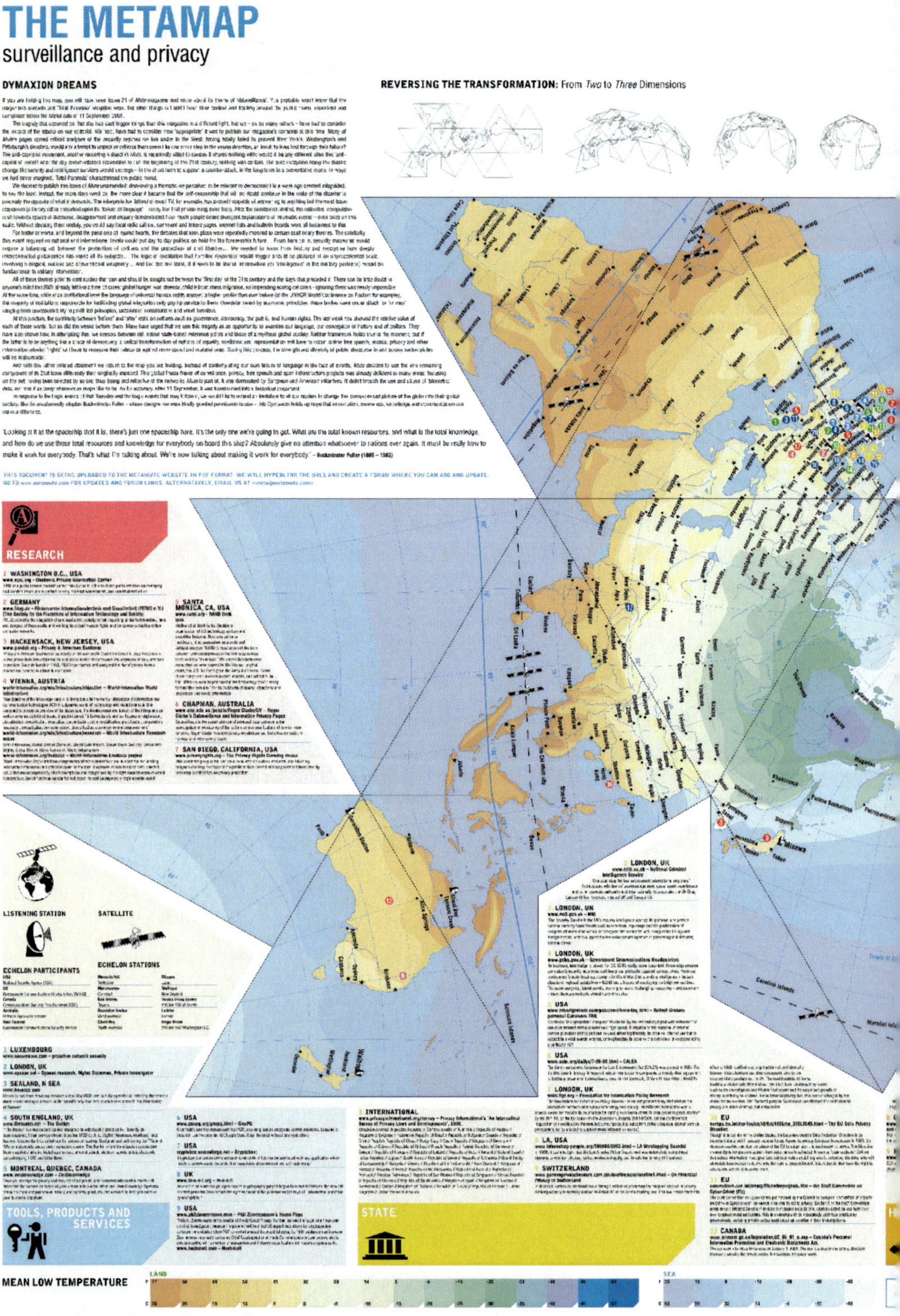

Mute, *The Metamap*, 2001, a map of global communications surveillance made for the Total Paranoia issue, Vol 1 #21, Autumn 2001

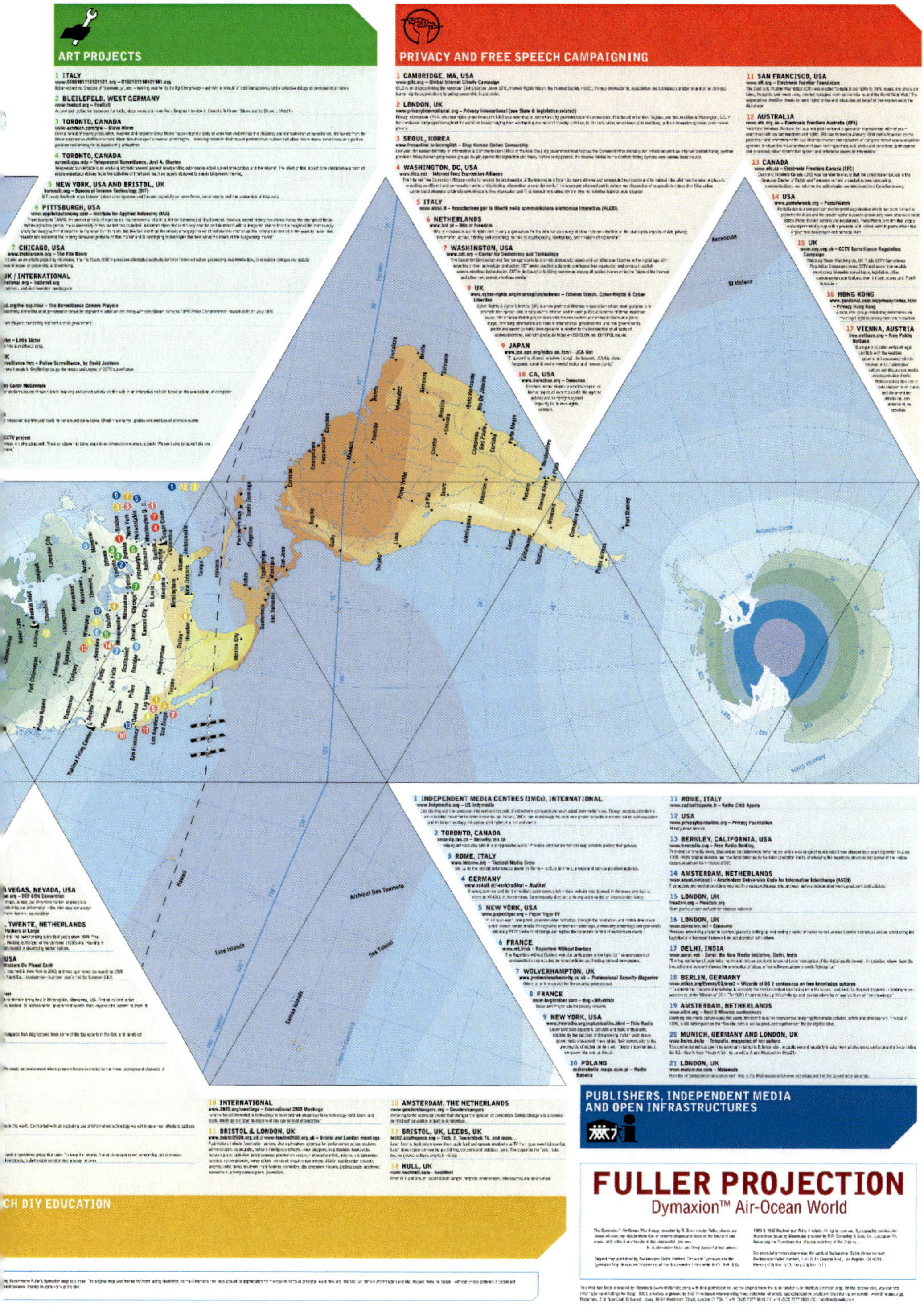

ART PROJECTS
PRIVACY AND FREE SPEECH CAMPAIGNING
PUBLISHERS, INDEPENDENT MEDIA AND OPEN INFRASTRUCTURES
CH DIY EDUCATION
FULLER PROJECTION
Dymaxion™ Air-Ocean World

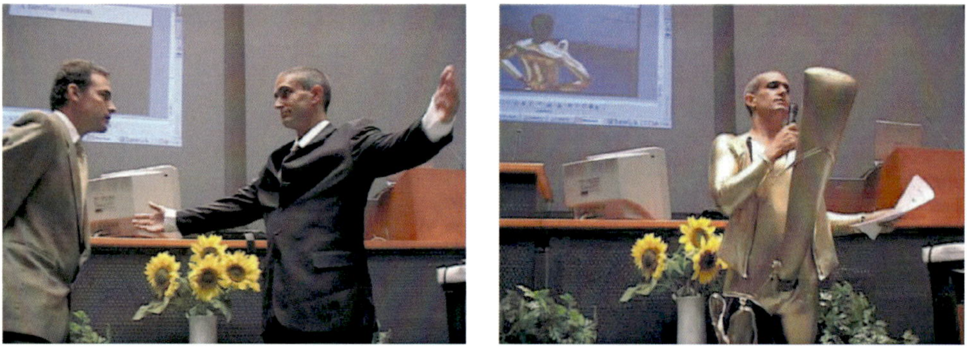

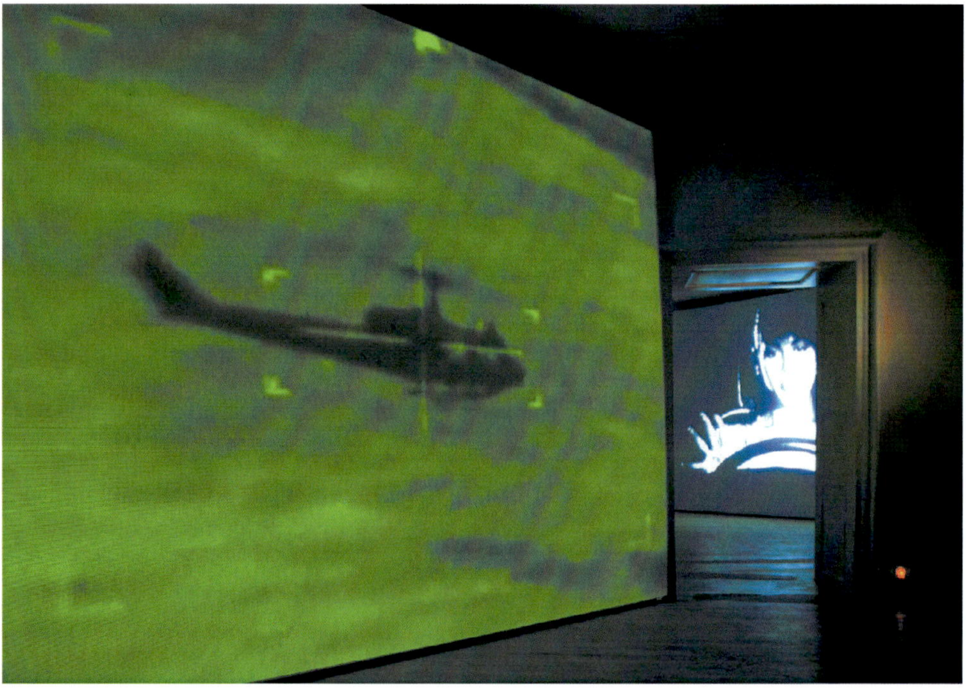

top: The Yes Men, *Employee Visualisation Appendage*, demonstrated at the Textiles of the Future event, Tampere, Finland, January 2001, used to illustrate Brian Holmes' 'Unleashing the Collective Phantoms', Vol 1 #24, Summer 2002
bottom: Jordan Crandall, *Drive*, 2000, installation view, Neue Galerie am Landesmuseum Joanneum, Graz, used to illustrate 'Unleashing the Collective Phantoms', Vol 1 #24, Summer 2002

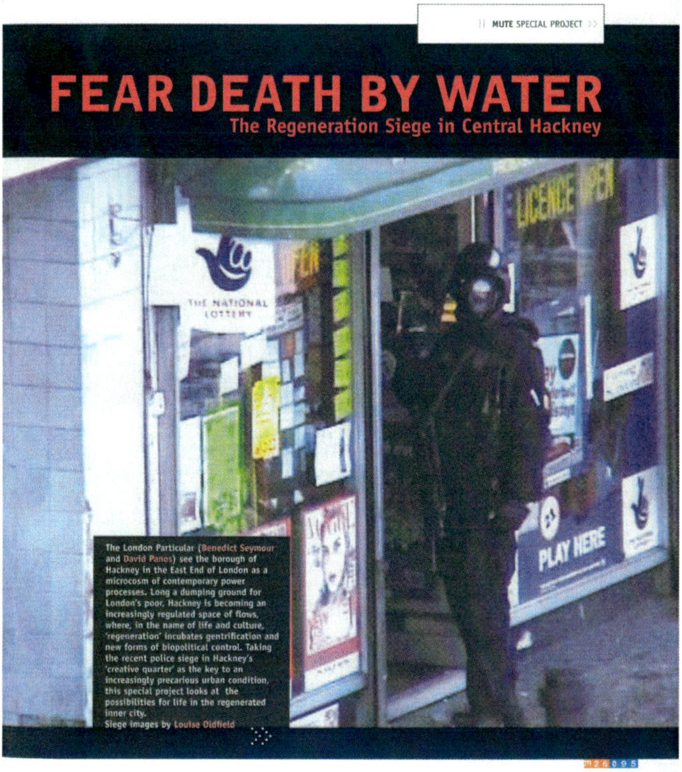

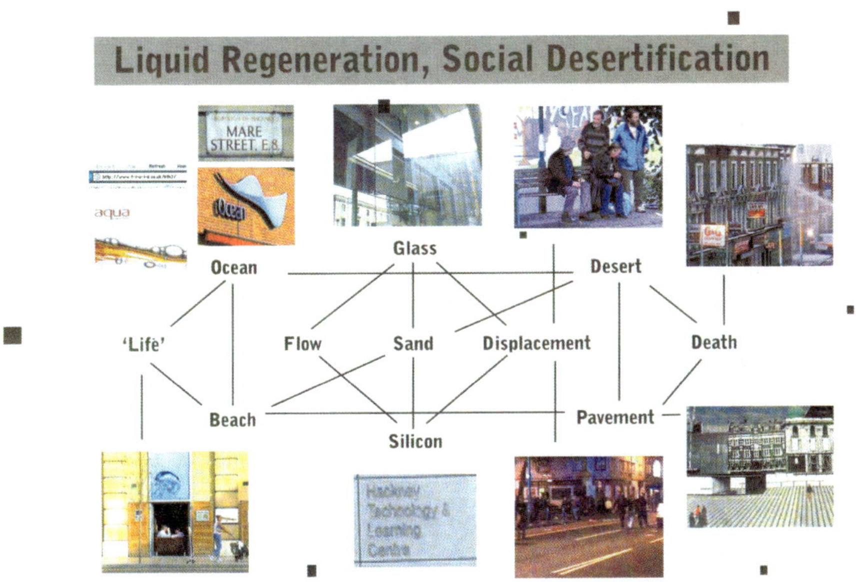

Louise Oldfield, used to illustrate The London Particular's 'Fear Death by Water', Vol 1 #26, Summer/Autumn 2003

subvert
the transcendental subject

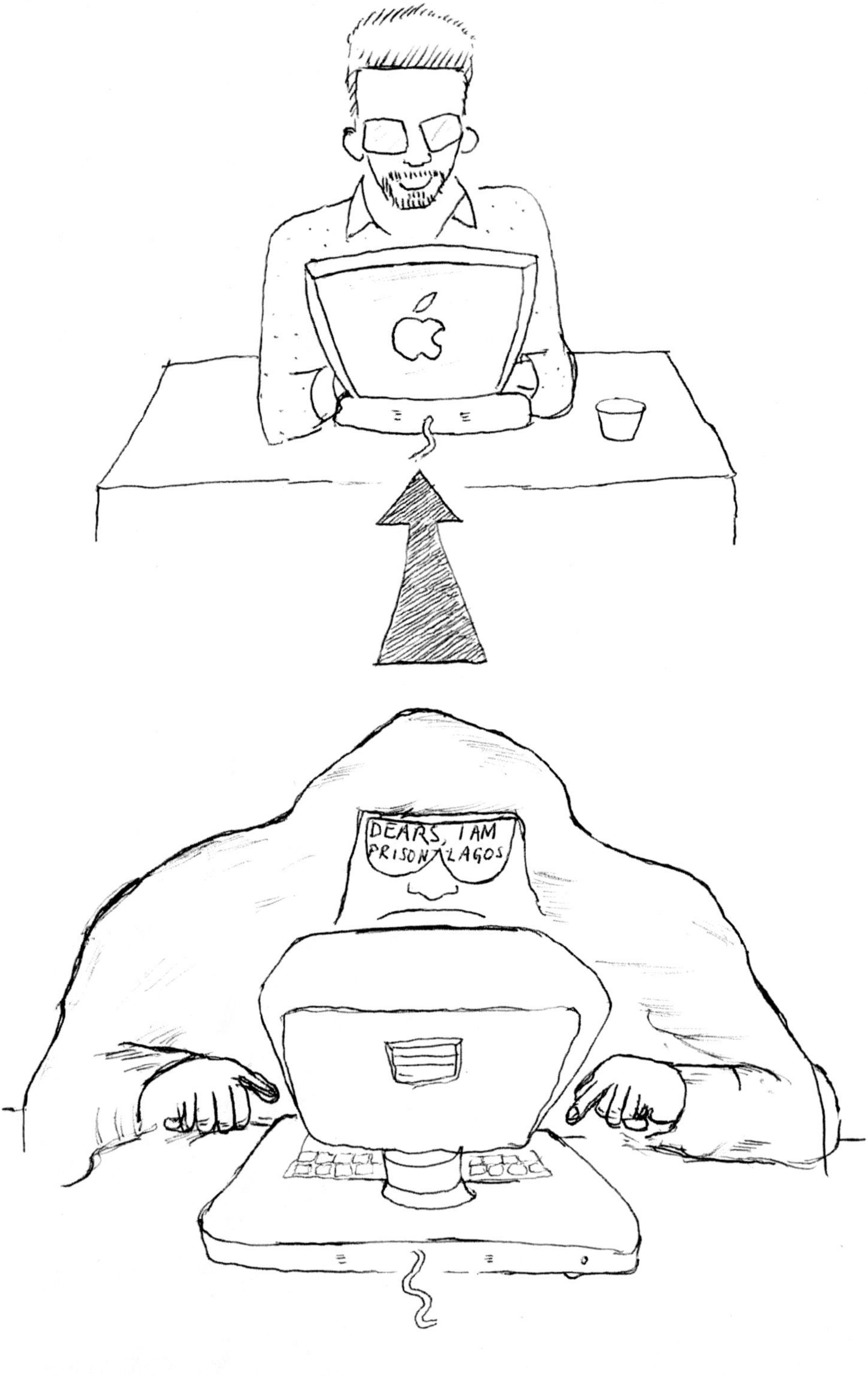

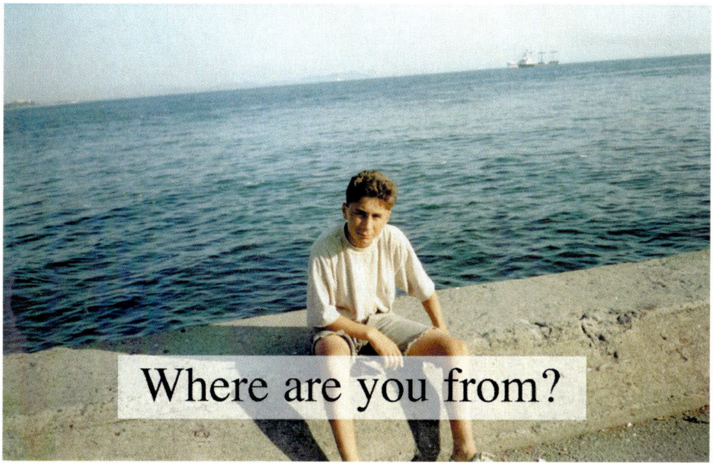

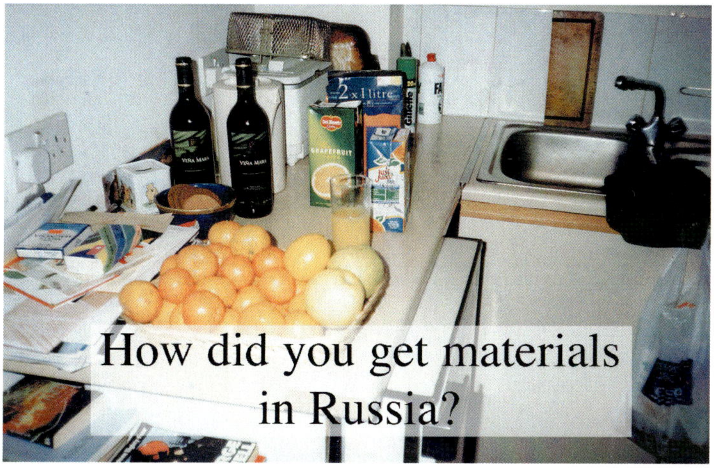

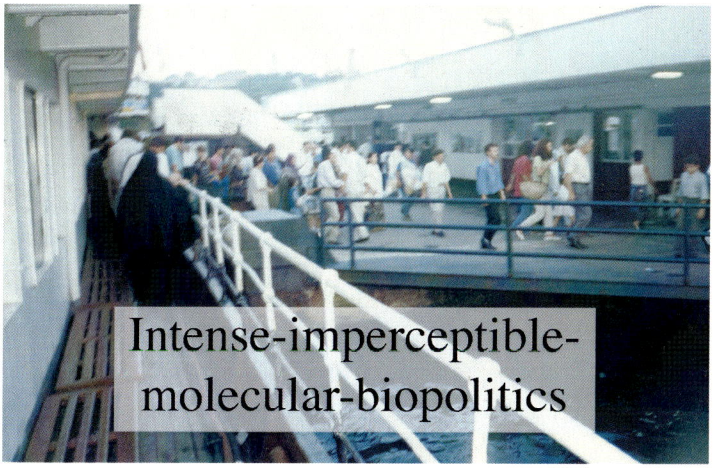

opposite: Benedict Seymour, *Subvert the Transcendental Subject*, used to illustrate Keston Sutherland's 'Junk Subjectivity', Vol 1 #28, Summer/Autumn 2004
above: Zeigam Azizov, images from *Migrasophia*, 2004, artist's project, Vol 1 #29, Winter/Spring 2005

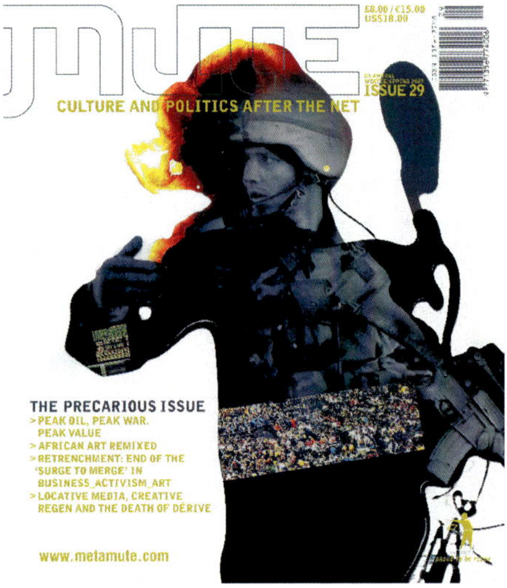

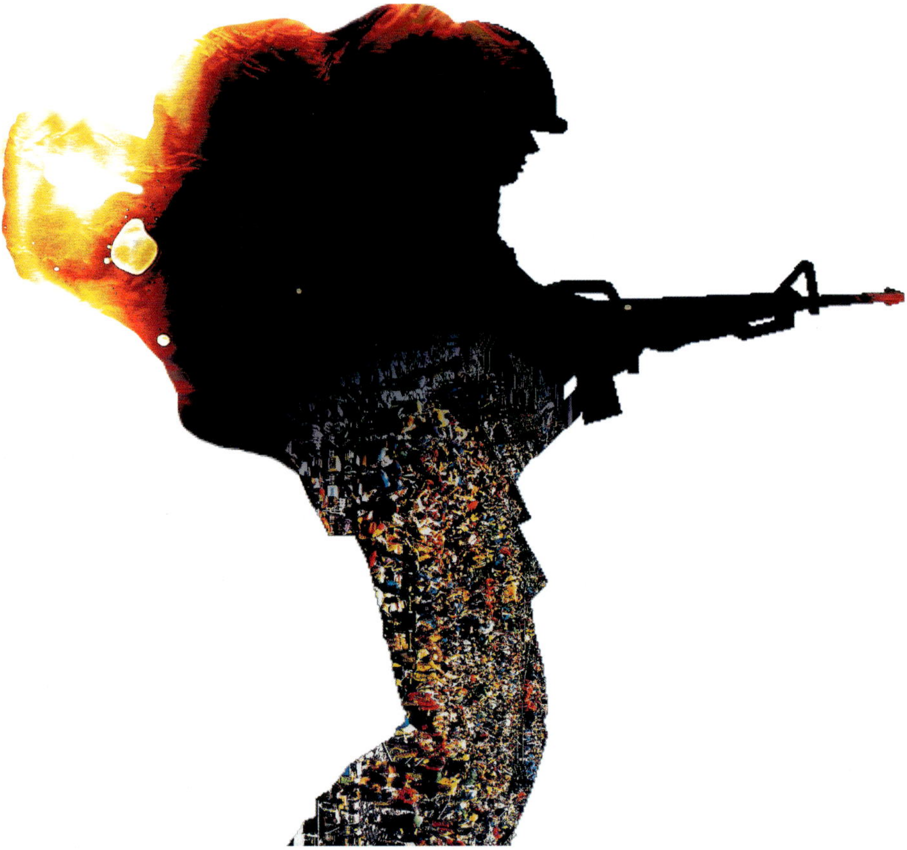

above: Simon Worthington and Richard Dawson, used to illustrate George Caffentzis' 'Peak Oil and National Security', and used as the cover image, Vol 1 #29, Winter/Spring 2005
opposite: Per Wizén, *Untitled (Carousel)*, cover image for the Underneath the Knowledge Commons issue, Vol 2 #1, Autumn/Winter 2005

MUTE

CULTURE AND POLITICS AFTER THE NET

Vol 2 #1
£5/ €7/ $6

UNDERNEATH THE KNOWLEDGE COMMONS

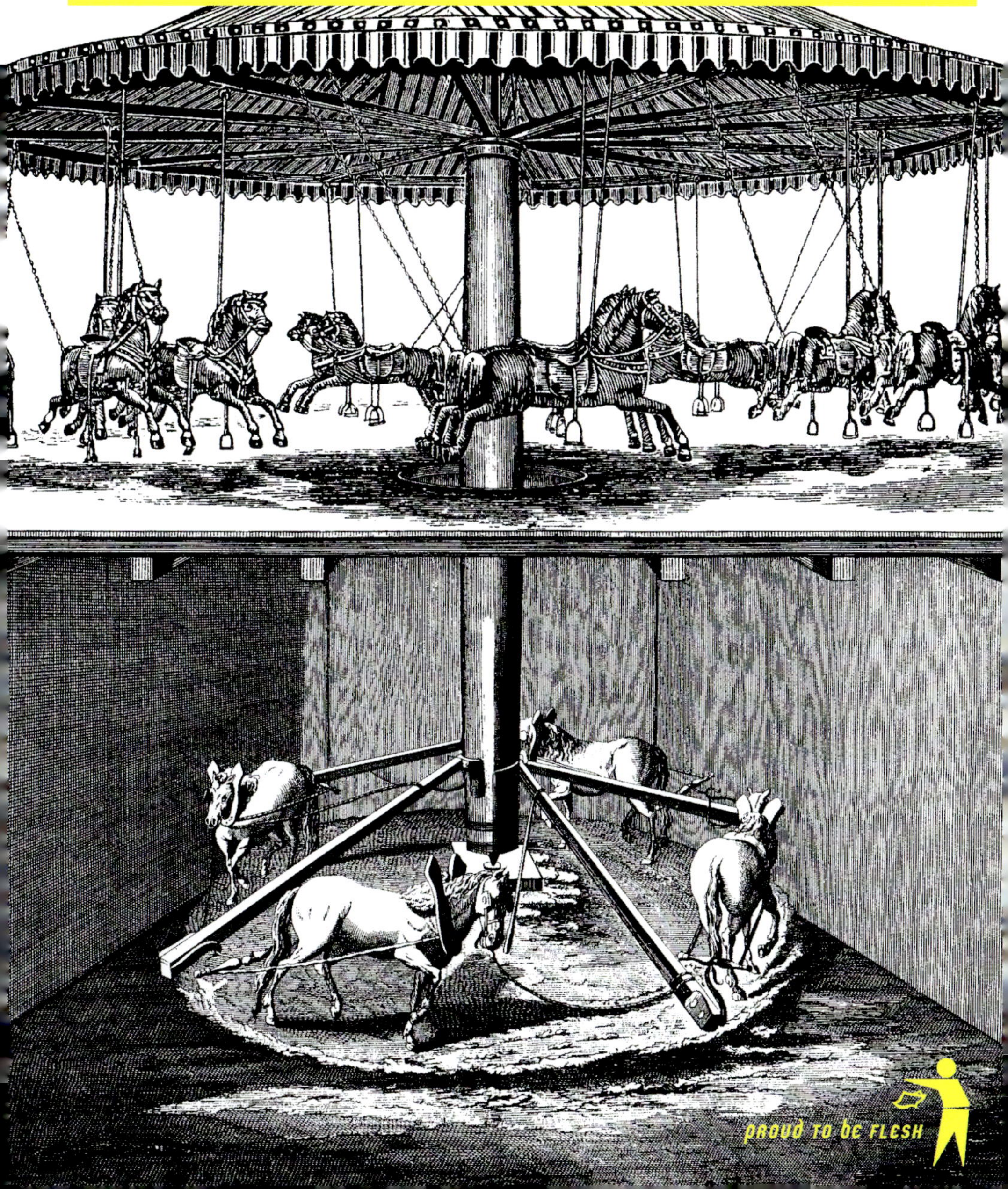

proud to be flesh

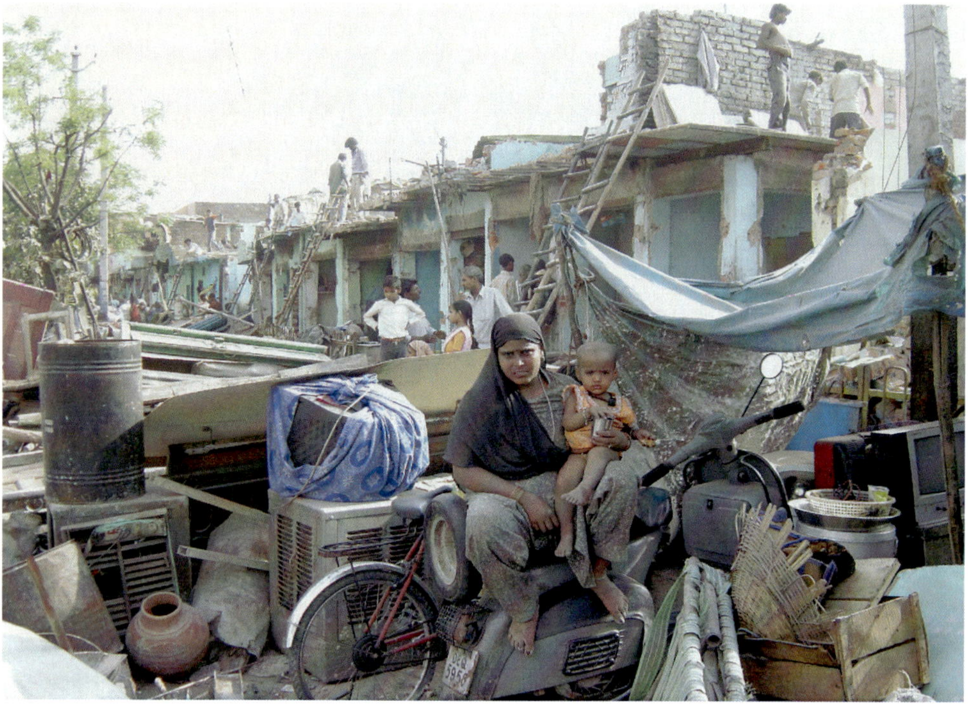

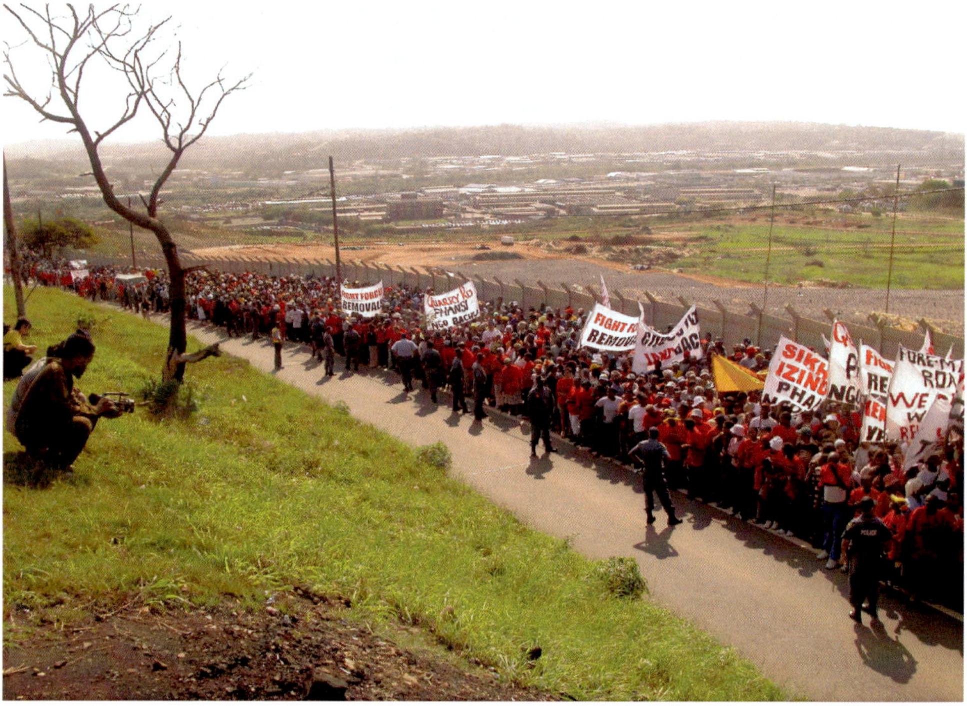

top: Amita Baviskar, Demolition of Banuwal Nagar, used to illustrate her 'Demolishing Delhi: World Class City in the Making', Vol 2 #3, Autumn 2006
bottom: Indymedia South Africa, March from the Kennedy Road Settlement, 2005, used to illustrate Richard Pithouse's 'Thinking Resistance in the Shanty Town', Vol 2 #3, Autumn 2006

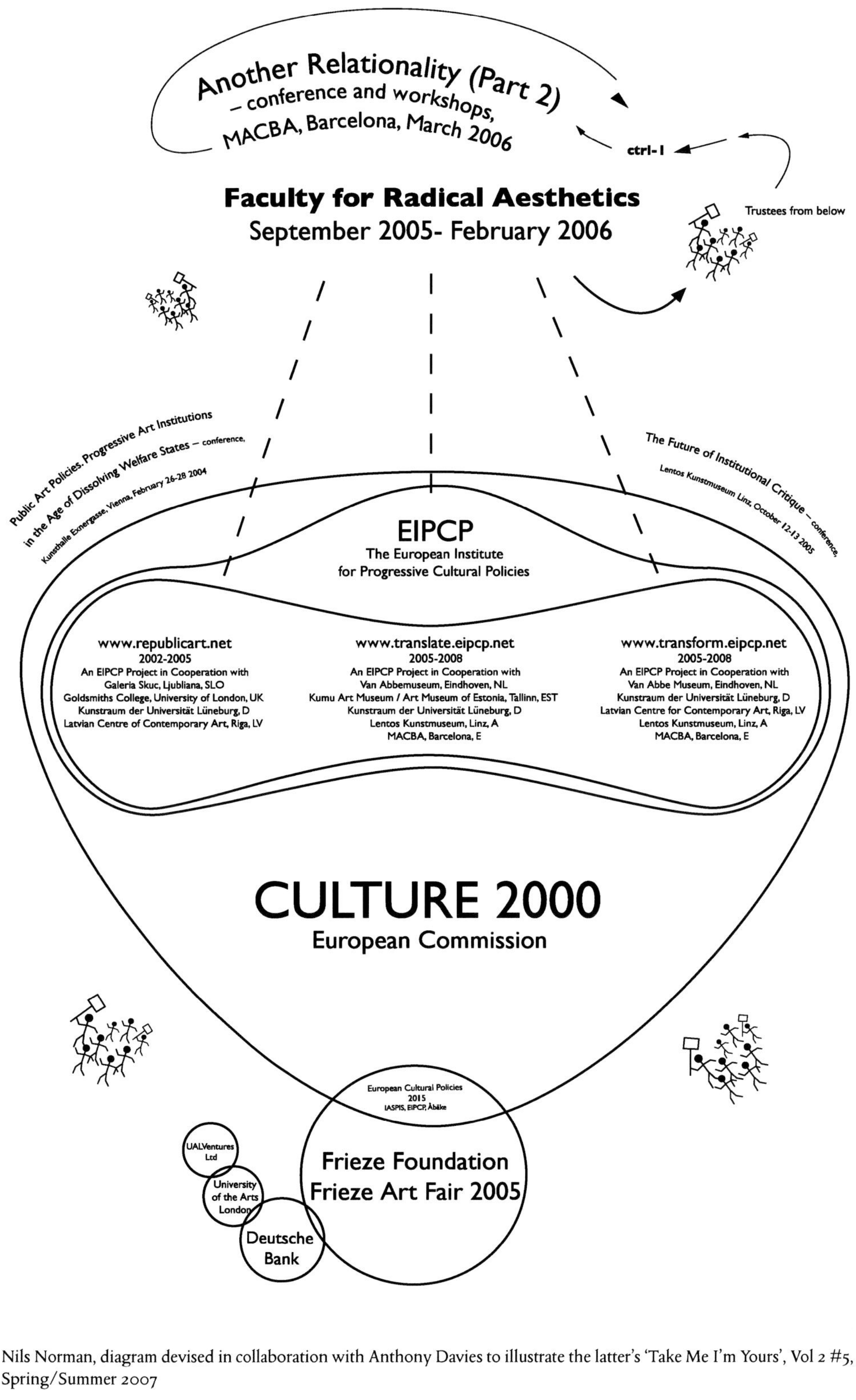

Nils Norman, diagram devised in collaboration with Anthony Davies to illustrate the latter's 'Take Me I'm Yours', Vol 2 #5, Spring/Summer 2007

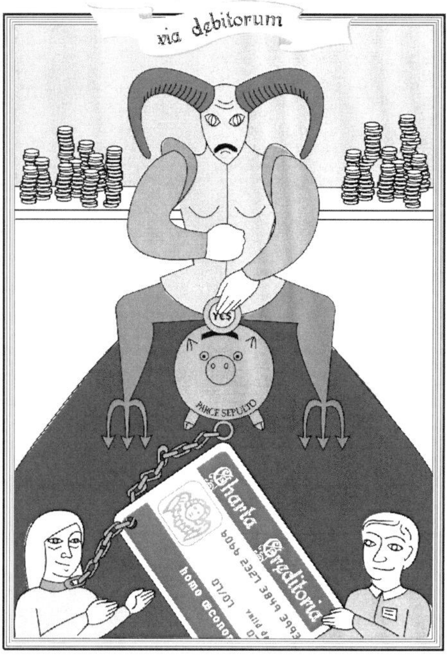

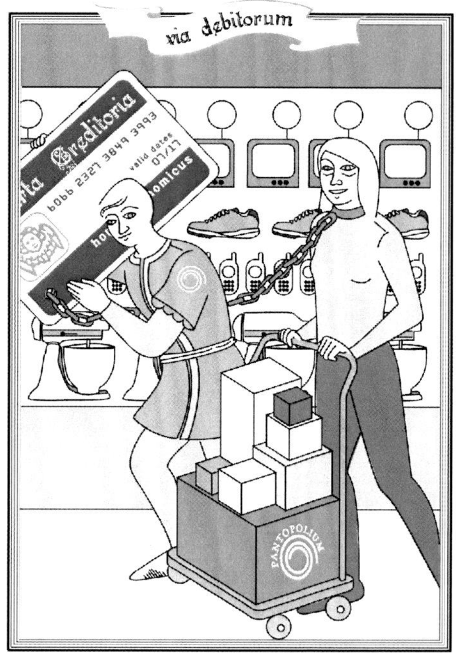

parce sepulto – spare who is buried

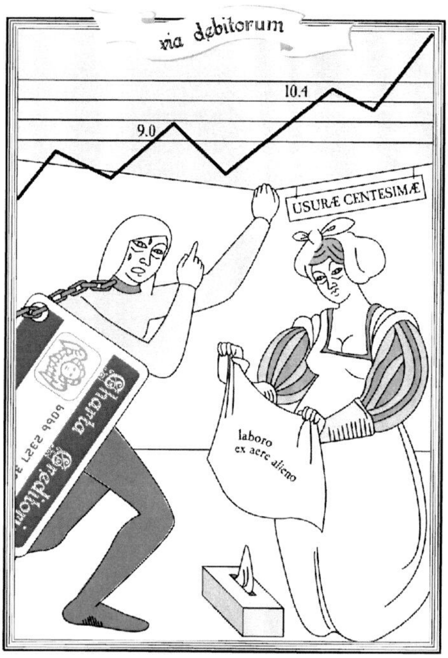

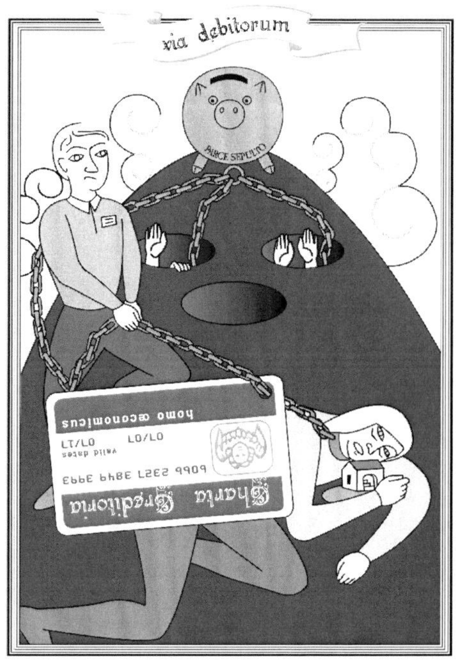

usurae centesimae – interest rate
laboro ex aere alieno – I'm oppressed with debt

Chiara Birattari and Zoe Romano, *Via Debitorum – Stations of the Debt*, used to illustrate Brett Neilson's 'The Magic of Debt, or Amortise This!', Vol 2 #6, Autumn 2007

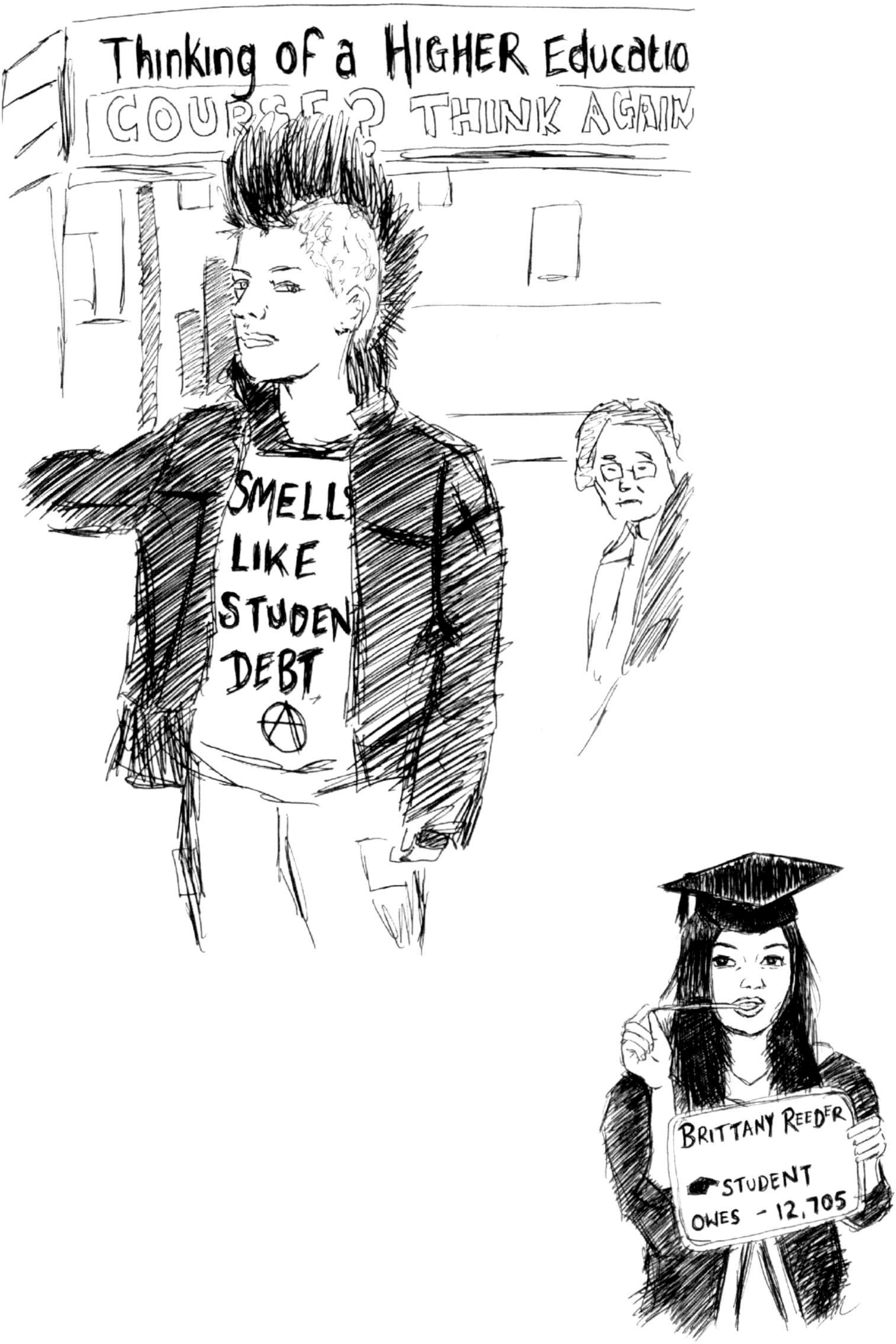

Esiri Erheriene-Esi, used to illustrate the Committee for Radical Diplomacy's 'Speculating on Student Debt', Vol 2 #6, Autumn 2007

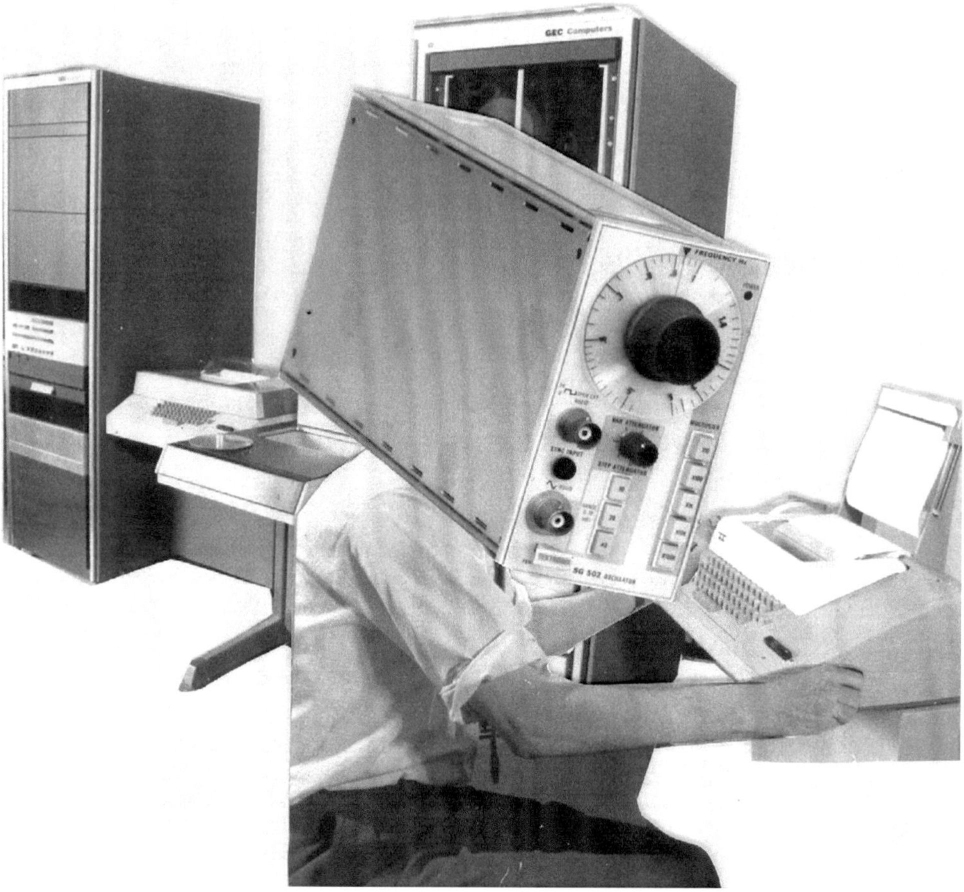

Pil and Galia Kollectiv, used to illustrate their 'Irony 2.0', Vol 2 #7, Spring 2008

it stands in opposition to national political forces that would obstruct pure transnationalism. President Bill Gates and President Bill Clinton have a common class ambition: to get everyone on the cybernet as fast as possible, through 'policies of facilitation'. Cyberspace promises better communication, greater interactivity, speed, a whole seductive rhetoric is on offer. Once everyone is on, there's going to be privatisation, what we call the 'politics of consolidation': shutting down the net in favour of commercial interest or pay in order to have your body accessed.'

GL: Yet, to outsiders, this virtual class doesn't appear to have an aggressive policy at all. Its daily work, writing software, seems to be pretty dull and harmless.

AK: A characteristic of the virtual class is that it is autistic. It's an absolute meltdown of human beings into these autistic, historically irresponsible positions with the sexuality of juvenile boys, being happy with machines. Shutting down the mental horizon while communicating at a global level and preaching disappearance. And, why not, because you've already disappeared yourself? But, as the guide at XEROX PARC said, 'Who needs the self anyway?' Privacy, for these people, has always been imposed on human beings by corporations; it's not something they claim they wanted. The XEROX PARC of the future is not about copying paper anymore but copying bodies into image processing machines. And who needs privacy in such a situation?

The other mental characteristic of the virtual class is that it is deeply authoritarian. It believes that virtuality equals the coming to be of a fully free human society. As CEOs of leading corporations used to say, 'adapt or you're toast', and they utter this with the total smugness of complacency itself. The other side of cyber-authoritarianism is the absolute outrage that grips them in the presence of opposition. Qualms about the emergence of the virtual class, or about the social consequences of technology, are met with either indifference or total outrage. Quite on the contrary, members of the virtual class see themselves as the missionaries of the human race itself, the avant-garde, in their terms, of the honourable collaboration with the telematic machines.

The virtual class has this aspect of seduction and then, on the other hand, the policy of consolidation, which is the present reality in which we live. It is a grim and severe and deeply fascistic class because it operates by means of the disciplinary state, imposing real austerity programmes in order to fund the research efforts benefiting itself. At the same time, it politically controls the working classes by severe taxation in order to make sure that people cannot be economically mobile and cannot accumulate capital in their own right. When it comes to Third World nations, they act in a classically fascistic way. They impose strict anti-emigration policies in the name of humanistic gestures. They shield their own local populaces from the influx of immigrants by creating a 'bunker state', by going for a 'Will to Purity'.

We're not dealing here with a 'Will to Power' or a 'Decline of the Western Society' but with a 'Recline of the West' and a 'Will to Virtuality'. The recliner is a new representative persona on the stage of world history. The recliner is best captured by the US TV series, *The Simpsons*, 'Just blame it on the guy who doesn't speak English, oh, he works for me.' Truly retro-fascistic ideas put into the mouth of cartoon characters. Bill Clinton is the perfect representative of the weak will, full of moral vacillations, yet authoritarian at the same time.'

GL: Still, you are not moving into a technophobic position, you use computers yourself and enjoy them. How can we make a distinction between the goals of this virtual class and opposite, alternative ways of using technologies?

AK: I have to be honest with myself, it's hard to think of life without computers. On the basis of real struggle and reflexion, I genuinely believe that these technologies do offer alternative possibilities from domination, towards certain forms of emancipation. *Data Trash* is also written as a manifesto for the coming to be of geek flesh, a realistic look at the world.

It would be interesting to look at the role of traditional political strategies in cyberspace itself. For example, the notion of 'Squatting the Media' is, for me, a fundamental point of media contestation and a theory in itself. Just as interesting would be the question of subversive forms of sexuality in cyberspace, like what the cyberfeminist group, VNS-Matrix, from Australia is doing: trying to make the stable science systems as unstable as possible to open up possibilities for ambiguity and paradox and for the reversal of reversionary mechanisms. That is done now through these playful, but deadly serious, interventions into the media-net itself, enriched with imagination. It attacks the system exactly in its own language and opens up possibilities for democratic consensus, without in any way being dogmatic.

'Squatting the Media' is, after all, politically significant, but it does not want to be explicit about it. When Karl Jaspers wrote *Man and the Modern Condition*, he said that the fundamental act of political rebellion today is the human being who refuses, who says no. It marks the end of any hegemonic ideological position and the beginning of politics again. 'Squatting the Media' represents a refusal and marks a return of morality into politics. It would be important to take practical examples of subversive intentions that operate deeply in cybernetic language itself, not outside of the media-net but inside it.'

The Futile Style of London

Simon Pope

Vol 1 #10, Summer 1998

This is London.

Josh

Precocious small boy steps, jetlagged, from Club Class. Inch-thick soles of Airwalk gleaming white as the black run at St. Anton. Droors-brand army surplus combat trousers and North Face puffa indicating an intention to do business on- and off-piste. Self-contained under hood and high-TOG breathable future fabric. Self-reliance velcroed tightly into place, an outward manifestation of the prep-school motto: 'You are alone. Trust no one.'

It's been a good year for Josh, what with his starting up Webcom.net. Dad would be proud. Those wild years at university seem distant. Saving trees (Dreads! What was he thinking of?) and sleeping with that girl whose dad was a NUM rep (Fatal mistake! Don't sleep with the enemy!). The one great thing about this business at this moment in time is that you can take what used to have cultural credence and sell it on to the world and his personal assistant. Slow it down, scratch it in that way that reminds other people of Bronx-bound trains and Futura 2000 graff. Put some loops over it, something with a big beat for stomping kids – kinda like early Beastie Boys. Add some titles in fake-fucked Courier, sim-printer-misfeeds and mid-frame, hair-in-the-gate film-stutter to deny all digital process and complete the whole Radical lo-fi feel.

And so Josh extends the business enterprise of his dad's generation into the '90s. Globe-trotting 007 execs dreaming of Suzie Wong extended by transnational gottabe Goldies dreaming of Jackie Chan flicks. Where Josh's dad's business was built on international trade in fossil fuels, Josh makes his wedge from the trade in cultural currency. It's high tide in the UK for pseudo-Japanese, infantilised graphics: flat colour, highly delineated, softly curved outlines (perfect for FreeHand and Illustrator), and moving in with Takishi was a stroke of genius for getting it real. A tap into the mainline of a totally obverse cultural resource. It's hard work fronting the business and trying to deal with a relationship which demands parity on every level. Maybe it's the single-sex school's fault, but too late to undo the conditioning. 'Some other cultures have just got it right; thousands of years of people knowing their place and still having the coolest gadgets.'

Justin

Justin, Josh's co-director, is the bread head. Justin used to be an account manager up West with one of the big noise, big budget agencies. Eight years living a one man yuppie revival in the pristine post-Lloyds white tower would have tipped a more scrupulous man over the edge. Walking monochrome corridors, scoping for black-clad door-whores for a moment's abrasion can seem futile, but leaving this cathedral dedicated to the power of spectacle would invoke an immediate 'access denied' in the four-star staff canteen. Each day necessitated more urgent solutions to the problem. How to squeeze into the half-lined, pleated and turned-up, two button, slim lapelled Agnès b? It was obvious that the countdown had begun. Ground zero approached fast, like a student out of the School of Hypermedia Research with an assignment to deliver and a liberty to take. Why not steal a few clients for yourself and make a go of it? Everyday could be casual Friday. Imagine: wearing post-rave leisurewear to WORK. Cool.

The two of them came together with the intention of first cajoling then melding a band of like-minded individualists into a 'design collective'. In vogue during the Summer of '96 and into the first half of '97, this notion that a loose association of college friends could turn into an international ad/PR/design agency for the kids appealed to everyone from TV post-production drones to fully indoctrinated Royal College post-graduates. Treat the office as a club, bedroom, chill-out and war zone and still make a healthy profit from the communication needs of the world's more obnoxious business ventures. The best of both worlds: the arrogance of the college leaver with financial rewards of the superannuated D&AD conformist.

For those who were stylistically disadvantaged by the '80s, a period of grace was declared in '97, when transition from besuited thirtysomething to crop-haired young Turk in only-available-in-New-York Nikes was made possible without anyone openly laughing in your face. The decision to move over to post-rave conformity had an unbearable inevitability about it, and the signs of final transformation, the Roni Size CD on repeat play in the studio, would be accompanied by the first self-reflective draw on some spliff AT WORK. Crossover achieved. Adolescence recovered.

Keeping the memories of this journey alive through to the other side is important. Not, as you may expect, so that the feeling of achievement might bolster an otherwise over-inflated ego but because clients love it. They troop into your studio (still unhappily besuited) and, faced with the haze of smoke and the background sounds of ambient darkside hardstep, feel like they've entered the den of iniquity that they always suspected lay behind every art student's bedroom door. This is somewhere they've never been before. Yes, they've had the holidays to Thailand, Phuket, Bali. OK, so they've visited friends in Hong Kong – and, since handover, Singapore; and they've watched *Trainspotting* and even read the book that time, but while they were at uni they couldn't get close. With eyes on an MBA at Yale and an internship with ANZ, there was no way that the risk was going to be worth it. So they're in their mid-30s and now they can actually BUY into this stuff.

'I've got the brains, you've got the looks. Let's make lots of money,' as one of Justin's favourite songs would have it. For brains they turned to Andy.

Andy

Andy is bright enough and could easily be several rungs up the ladder in the City, fixing Tokyo Marine's corporate intranet or holding the hand of floor traders as they try to comprehend the inanity of their everyday lives whilst squinting at the harsh pink and blue representations of Tiger economies crashing, HEY LOOK!, right there, on their screens. He knows his TCP from his IP, his NLMs from his AUTOEXEC.NCFs. Webcom.net would have a severely limited skillset had Andy not been delivered with a 2:1 after going full term at King's. Server-side back-end, UNIX-flavoured mindfuck gives most web designers instant impotence and an overweening self-doubt. Not good for business, let alone personal development. So all the black arts of CGI and increasingly Java are left to Andy. In most cultural and technological shifts, people like Andy aren't the public face of the industry. Now is no exception. They are in no way 'cool'. They like the same music as their older brothers and dress in whatever is on the floor and smells least like chip fat or the sweet, baked bean sweat of teen boys' bedrooms. When this cycle of boom and bust is long forgotten, Andy will still have his head down and know the worth of a good PING program. Enough of Andy.

Adam

Night time. Brewer Street. Soho. London. Rain on the narrow streets. Every surface appears as oil. Neon lights, peepshow pinks and reds fracture the taxi window. Hot ciabatta breath spills steam. Moist hearts onto dank glass. Adam drops his ennui-laden shoulders inside his Le Mans-inspired jacket and stares that blank Director's stare through fixed-focus eyes. In his dreams: the plastic grey rear seat, piped with red, takes a hint from last year's Helmut Lang and bucks the trend, preferring camel as the new black. Transformed by force of will into soft calfskin. Puckered and buttoned in tasteful restraint against the lard-arse behind the dry-clean-only Comme des Garçons poly mix stay-prest. A Saint, a double-Oh-seven. Black leather double breasted three-quarter length coat could conceal an Uzi. Could conceal the palmtop-remote-control-video-conference-web phone. A silent warrior-monk tooled up with yet-to-be-fulfilled potential.

Wardour Street. Soho. London. This Director's Cut commands a cross-fade, covetously, into the parallel world of film and video, where warp-driven, powder-fuelled lunches thrive on THAT tale of kilos of Colombian biked from pillar to post. Here's the potential to let your career fly like Tom Cruise in that Apple ad for *Mission Impossible* – through the loser-debris of misplaced zeal and missed Playstation R&D opportunities. Tumbling through 360 to avoid the rotor blade of JeansCorp-sanctioned Shockwave fun, whilst behind you, beneath you and all around, the flak ricochets from off of shattered website dreams. Feel the cold burn of inhaled ROM fumes – the exhaust of trashed graphics enthusiasts, blasted like so many particles, calculated and rendered in full 72 mil resolution by Silicon Graphics workstations. The beads of sweat form on Adam's artfully concealed but receding hairline, mirroring the grey rain as it slides asthmatically down the mildewed taxi window. Every journey home has been like this recently. A video tape plays and rewinds, caught in a frenzied loop, wearing his patience thin. Every drop-out amplified. Each iteration reinforcing the feeling that trust has been misplaced, that saving your best work for your highest profile client has not paid off. Art and Business. Like grape and grain. Start out on one. Don't finish on the other. And the aural signs are starting to show. The upspeak. Blurted out, too late for modification into much-respected Albarn mockney. Four long years from version three through six, slowly losing a grip on the point of it all. A time for change. Maybe reinvention is the only solution.

Notting Hill. London. Home. Flipping his last ten pence piece, the severed monarch's head floats, goading and mocking his situation. Only one thing left to do: just fucking phone Justin…

Unleashing the Collective Phantoms: Resistance to Networked Individualism

Brian Holmes

Vol 1 #24, Summer 2002

The classical function of the stock market is to provide resources for industrial development, through a speculative game that pays off later in the 'real economy'. But history is cunning, and the result of the dotcom boom may have been to free up vast amounts of private money for the development of a virtual public realm, where people can confront the major corporations on their home turf – that is to say, in transnational space. Huge amounts of infrastructure were installed throughout the world in the period from 1995 to 2000; now the oversupply crisis is accounted a disaster. An alternative history turns that equation upside down. The speculators of the late 20th century asked, 'Is there any limit to the profit we can make off the internet?' Today, a wilder speculation has arisen: 'Can we really make the networks useless for corporate capitalism?'

Unlike most people, I don't think the answer is primarily legal, or even technological. Instead it is cultural and artistic. It has everything to do with subjective capacities for resistance, and a history of resistance might suggest a different question: 'Can the expanding virtual class finally escape the domination of the flexible personality?'

Paradigm Shift

From Taylor and Ford to Stalin and de Gaulle, the adversary of the radical left in the 20th century was rationalising authority. Whether on the factory floor or in the military ranks that gave the orders, regimentation and the hierarchical pyramid supplied the images of authoritarian oppression. The difference between East and West was slim in that respect. The army muster and the assembly line set the pace of life on both sides of the Iron Curtain. The first to analyse this situation was the Frankfurt School.

The originality of the Frankfurt School was to combine Marx and Freud, to explore the industrial economy's masochistic libido. But to do so was not just to go beyond the pleasure principle. What the Frankfurt School studied from the 1930s onward was a new form of political-economic command that stretched its social fingers deep into the psyche. The liquidation of 19th century bourgeois individualism and the emergence of a central planning state, along with a totally mobilised factory society, were pursued on the subjective level by what they called the '*authoritarian personality*'. They understood this fascistic character structure as a 'new anthropological type'. Its traits were rigid conventionalism, submission, stereotypy, opposition to everything subjective, an exaggerated concern with sexual scandal, emphasis on power and the projection of unconscious impulses.

The Frankfurt School writers perfected their analysis of the authoritarian regimes in the 1940s and '50s while living in exile in the USA. There, they saw Prussian parade ground discipline transforming into the softer coercions of behaviourist psychology and the culture industry. We know the new forms of revolt that arose in the 1960s against those standardising forces: everything from Reichean group sex, burning draft cards and dollar bills to Provo events, Situationist drifting and LSD – what Marcuse called 'outbreaks of mass surrealism'. On a deeper level, there was an assertion of subjectivity, identity, sexuality, the personal as the political. A poetics of resistance helped to bring about the decline of regimentation, welfare state bureaucracies, mass-consumption models and factory discipline. But are we even aware how that decline helped shape today's political-economic system?

In response to the troubles of the 1960s and '70s, a new paradigm has arisen in the developed countries in the past 20 years, with a specific production regime, consumer ideology and social control mechanism, all integrated into a geopolitical order. For almost 20 years this development remained largely unconscious, unnameable. During that time, vanguard movements were obsolete, intellectuals were useless, artists were clowns, there was no alternative. Now the cracks are opening up everywhere. People are realising that the New World Order is not just oppressive at its edges, in the so-called developing countries. At the very heart of casual freelance culture, replete with PCs, mobile phones and general nomadism, the technology of control is continuously recreated. Winning the economic game today brings a high reward. You get to be the inventor of the 'flexible personality'.

Culture/Ideology

New paradigms are adopted because they work. Only in retrospect can we see them becoming modes of control. Flexibility was an extremely positive idea in California in the 1970s when the culture of microelectronics was invented. It was the polar opposite of the rigid 1950s: openness to others, embodied experience, self-expression, improvisation, refusal of hierarchies and discipline. These were the utopian days of Bucky Fuller, Gregory Bateson and the *Whole Earth Catalog*: no one would have dreamt that *Steps to an Ecology of Mind* could become a management tool. But the looser, more creative lifestyle did not just mean the emergence of a whole new range of products useful for stimulating consumption. In California, and ultimately in much of the developed world, the new culture seemed to promise a way out of the social conflicts that had stalled the Fordist industrial regimes.

Consider the way things looked to the Trilateral Commission in their 1975 report on *The Crisis of Democracy*. Not only were Third World countries using the powers of national liberation to demand higher prices for their resources while the US lost its war in Indochina; not only were the capital returns plunging while wildcat strikes multiplied and the big ecological standoffs began but, worst of all, the huge post-war investments into socialised education, conceived to meet the knowledge needs of the techno-economy, were backfiring and producing resistance to capitalism and bureaucracy, alternative values, demands for further benefits and socialisations. These new claims on the welfare state had to be added to the traditional demands of the working class – and then the crisis began. The Trilateral countries were becoming 'ungovernable', there was an 'excess of democracy'. The kind of systemic critique that the Frankfurt School had pioneered reached its height in the mid-1970s. From that point on, the authoritarian system had to start learning from the enemy within.

The transformation took a decade. The golden age of neo-management began in the mid-1980s, when unionised workers were replaced with robots and unskilled labour was sought overseas. Corporate operations and financial flows expanded beyond nations where regulation and redistribution were deemed excessive. The triple challenge for the managers was to keep tabs on a distant work force, to open up global marketing and distribution and, above all, to create a culture – or an ideology – that would entice significant amounts of younger people to run this new machine. The key word was 'flexibility'. The flexible system had to accept and divert the demands for autonomy, self-expression and meaning; it had to turn those very demands into a new mode of control. The magical answer turned out to be a communications device, a language-and-image transmitter: the networked personal computer. Now the computer was going to set you free.

Freedom has always been the great neoliberal watchword, from Hayek and the Chicago economists to the right-wing libertarians and the Cato Institute. Why not throw in the artists' and the dropouts' dreams, roving desire, semiotic proliferation, Deleuzoguattarian schizophrenic visions, multi-culti creativity? After all, the innovations were coming from there. The networked computer promised to place a whole new alchemy of cooperative production in the same kinds of global channels that were already working for the finance economy. Research and invention could happen directly within the circuits of production and distribution.

The laptop computer freed up individuals for physical and psychic mobility, and it could also be used as an instrument of control over distant labour. It miniaturised access to the remaining bureaucracy, while opening private channels into entertainment, media and the realms of 'fictitious' capital – the speculative economy that feeds off the dismantling of the public sphere. Best of all, it recoded every kind of cultural production as commodities, multimedia. Here was a mode of development that might solve, or at least gloss over, the full set of problems inherited from the 1960s, particularly the struggles around the welfare state. Small wonder that the governments and the corporations started actively promoting a myth of flexibility. The emerging 'virtual class' – including cultural producers, digital artisans, prosumers, what are now called 'immaterial labourers' – stumbled more or less blindly into it.

Guidance System

How does the culture/ideology work? War is popular these days, so let's take the military point of view. The weapon of choice during the Cold War was the inter-continental ballistic missile: a huge, never-used giant, endlessly deconstructed by the critiques of phallologocentrism. The New World Order takes off with a smaller, more practical device: the cruise missile. This kind of weapon gets constantly used, and not just on the battlefield. Since the heyday of Star Wars – both the Strategic Defence Initiative and the Lucas movie – the military-entertainment complex has become part of everyday experience.

'It seems that retailers will go to any length to capture customers', reads a 1997 article called 'Star Wars Turns on to Shoppers' (quoted by Sze Tsung Leong in *The Harvard Guide to Shopping*). 'Witness Safeway, which has recently used an artificial intelligence system from IBM called AIDA (artificial intelligence data architecture) – which was initially developed to detect and identify Russian missiles in space, but is now used [...] to analyse information on buying patterns with details of purchase from loyalty cards.' When consumer desire is 'turned on' and encouraged to proliferate, the ultimate control fantasy becomes that of tracking the flexible personality.

'Mass marketing, for all intents and purposes, is dead', writes business guru, Art Weinstein, in *Market Segmentation*. 'Precision target marketing [...] has taken over. By focusing on ever smaller yet profitable market segments, stronger company-customer relationships transpire. With technological products, users can practically invent markets for companies – customers become customisers.' When feedback devices are built directly into the distribution circuits, the sources of desire are directly available to corporate monitoring. So you can help perfect your own internal guidance system.

Until recently, such trends seemed comfortably ambiguous – just the irritating price for increased freedoms. But with security fever rising after 11 September, everything starts to look different. The incitement to perform and to find creative ways of deploying the new equipment reveals its hidden face, the fear of the excluded other, the imperative to ruthlessly extend and perfect the system. And the system really is threatened, not only by suicidal terrorism but by the collapse of the 'new economy', the growing protests against neoliberal globalisation, the revolution against the IMF in Argentina... The perfect solution is total mobilisation, the shift to a wartime footing. 11 September was a chance just waiting to be taken – the chance to consolidate the new paradigm on every level.

American artist, Jordan Crandall, has made the military compulsions of the networked system visible. His work began with the heritage of the 1970s: experimentation, cooperation, networked performance, adjustment to the presence of others in virtual space. But, in 1998, he hired a freelance military contractor to help him develop movement-predicting software, the algorithms of which show up as eerie green tracery around bodies in a video image. The subsequent exhibitions, Drive and Heat-Seeking, were fully-fledged explorations of the psychosexual relations of seeing and being seen through the new technologies in both their civilian and military uses.

Crandall recently published an article called 'Fingering the Trigger' on the nettime mailing list, which recounts the CIA's use of an unmanned, camera-and-missile-equipped Predator drone to fire upon a suspicious Afghani man who, it turns out, was probably just scavenging for metal. 'We align eye, viewfinder, and target in an act of aiming', Crandall writes:

> But we are aimed at, we are constituted in other acts of looking. These are analysis and control systems in which the body is situated [...] It sees us as a nexus of data, materiality, and behaviour, and uses a language of tracking, profiling, identifying, positioning and targeting [...] Within the circuitous visualisation networks that arise, one never knows which 'side' one is truly on, as seer switches to that which is seen; as targeter switches to that which is targeted.

Crandall thinks a new sexuality lodges in the body-machine-image complex – hence the image of the soldier man 'fingering the trigger'.

This work helps us to see what the easy money and pluralism of the Clinton years kept hidden: the outlines of a social pathology. It has an authoritarian cast – like everything that involves the military – but it does not produce unthinking, stereotyped behaviour of the kind we associate with fascism. What Crandall describes is an extremely intelligent process that, precisely by individualising – tracking, identifying, eliciting desire, channelling vision and expression – succeeds in binding the mobilised individual to a social whole. The new fascism discovers a complex, dynamic order for subjective difference, perspectival analysis, *jouissance*, even schizophrenic ecstasy. It integrates networked individualism.

Ghost in the Machine

Arthur Kroker had an inkling of these things. Almost a decade ago, he and Michael Weinstein wrote about the 'liberal fascism' of the 'virtual class': a technological elite, driven by possessive individualism, whose interests lay with the financial establishment, the military state and the big corporations. But, like all neo-Situationists in Baudrillard's wake, Kroker is obsessed by 'the recline of the West' and the hypnotic power of the digitised image: 'The virtual class is populated by would-be astronauts who never made it to the moon', reads a passage from *Data Trash*, 'They do not easily accept criticism of this new Apollo project for the body telematic.'

No doubt that was true in 1994, when the text was written, but the virtual realm has expanded vastly since then, and, with it, the space for critique. One major effort has been to describe the new mode of domination. Another is to create a poetics of resistance: *virtual class* relations, alongside the embodied ones that never disappeared.

Consider the Association of Autonomous Astronauts (AAA), founded in 1995 with a five-year mission to establish a planetary network to end the monopoly of corporations, governments and the military over travel in space. The AAA is a kind of multiple name, a freely invented identity. Forget about the moon, 'Reclaim the Stars' they said on 18 June 1999, during the Carnival Against Capitalism. The idea was not to create an art group but a social movement – a collective phantom acting on a global scale. 'Unlike a multiple name that is restricted to art practices, a collective phantom operates within the wider context of popular culture, and is used as a tool for class war', says an astronaut of the South London AAA in a text called 'Resisting Zombie Culture'.

One aspect of the project was infrastructural mapping, identifying the satellite hardware that links up the world communications network. But another was what Konrad Becker calls 'e-scape': 'Cracking the doors of the future means mastering multidimensional maps to open new exits and ports in hyperspace; it requires passports allowing voyages beyond normative global reality toward parallel cultures and invisible nations; supply depots for nomads on the roads taken by the revolutionary practice of aimless flight.' Ricardo Balli gives a further idea of what the galactic phantom might do: 'We are not interested in going into space to be a vanguard of the coming revolution: the AAA means to institute a science fiction of the present that can above all be an instrument of conflictuality and radical antagonism.'[1]

What does it all mean? The ideas sound fantastic, but the stakes are real: imagining a political subject *within* the virtual class and, therefore, *within* the economy of cultural production and intellectual property that had paralysed the poetics of resistance. Consider Luther Blissett, an obscure Jamaican football player traded from Britain to Italy, who fell short of stardom but became a proliferating signature, a multiple name, the 'author' of a book called *Mind Invaders: How to Fuck the Media*. Between tales of Ray Johnson and mail art, Blissett takes time out for some political-aesthetic theory:

> I could just say the multiple name is a shield against the established power's attempt to identify and individualise the enemy, a weapon in the hands of what Marx ironically called 'the worst half' of society. In *Spartacus* by Stanley Kubrick, all the slaves defeated and captured by Crassus declare

1. Both quotes are from 'Quitter la gravite', http://www.lyber-eclat.net/lyber/aaa/quitter_la_gravite.html

themselves to be Spartacus, like all the Zapatistas are Marcos and we are all Luther Blissetts. But I won't just say that, because the collective name has a fundamental valence, too, insofar as it aims to construct an open myth, elastic and re-definable in a network [...]

The 'open myth' of Luther Blissett is a game with personal identity, like the three-cornered football played by the AAA: a way to change the social rules so a group can start moving simultaneously in several directions. This 'fundamental valence' lies at the prehistory of the counter-globalisation movement. Just think of the way names like Ya Basta, Reclaim the Streets or Kein Mensch ist Illegal have spread across the world's social networks. One can see these names not as categories or identifiers but as catalysts, departure points, like the white overalls (*tute bianche*) worn initially in North Eastern Italy: 'The Tute Bianche are not a movement, they are an instrument conceived within a larger movement (the Social Centres) and placed at the disposal of a still larger movement (the global movement)', writes Wu Ming, in the French journal, *Multitudes*. This 'instrument' was invented in 1994, when the Northern League mayor of Milan, Formentini, ordered the eviction of a squatted centre and declared, 'From now on, squatters will be nothing more than ghosts wandering about in the city!' But then the white ghosts showed up in droves at the next demonstration, and a new possibility for collective action emerged: 'Everyone is free to wear a *tuta biancha*, as long as they respect the "style", even if they transform its modes of expression: pragmatic refusal of the violence/non-violence dichotomy; reference to *zapatismo*; break with the 20th century experience; embrace of the symbolic terrain of confrontation.'

Yet a strange thing happened, explains Wu Ming in another text: 'Some rhetorically opposed the white overall and the blue overall, and the former was used as a metaphor for post-Fordist labour – flexible, "precarious", temporary workers whom the bosses prevent from enjoying their rights and being represented by the unions.'[2] Between politics, class uncertainty and sheer word play, the Tute Bianche got into full swing. The technique of 'protected direct action' – allowing ludicrously padded protesters to face blows from the police – was a way to invade, not just the media screens but, above all, the minds of hundreds of thousands of other people. They converged in Genoa in July 2001 to open a real political debate in a country stifled by a neo-fascist consensus.

Another example of the effects created by a confusion of identities is the Yes Men, in their cameo or 'chameleo' appearances as representatives of the World Trade Organization. Here, we're talking about two artists whose names aren't hard to discover, but which makes the uncertainty over language no less interesting. To say 'yes' to neoliberal ideology can be devastatingly satirical, as when the self-elected WTO representative, Hank Hardy Unruh, displayed the logical fiction of the *Employee Visualisation Appendage*, a telematic

2. http://www.wumingfoundation.com/english/giap/giapdigest11.html

worker-surveillance device in the shape of a yard-long golden phallus. But what kind of satire is at work when Kein Mensch ist Illegal takes the neoliberal ideology seriously and declares all the world's borders open, for everybody? Like the fire-coloured masks worn by thousands at the Quebec City 'Summit of the Americas', today's networked protests have two faces: the laughter of open communication or the violence of a gagged mouth behind a chain link fence. Both faces are the truth of the contemporary political confrontation.

Voice and Exit

No doubt millions of the world's 'flexible' workers remain largely gagged – mute – with no voice and no hope of escaping. But, as use of the internet has increased and as people have seized its communicational power for both organisation and subversion, a metamorphosis has invaded the 'transnational public sphere', which formerly was only open to the corporations. The global e-scape remains virtual, but in the sense of Deleuze: virtuality as latency, as unmanifest reality, potential flight lines waiting to be taken.

The virtual class, in this sense, or the immaterial labourers – I've always preferred to say '*networkers*' – cannot stand in for the rest of the world's population. There is no universal subject, not even 'the individual', but an active indistinction of identity has begun to spread, like a new departure point. In a recent text, Paolo Virno locates the universal in *pre-individual* aesthetic and linguistic experience, in the impersonality of perception and circulating language. The chaotic dissension of public space then becomes the landscape not of defensive individualism but of evolving paths to *individuation*: 'Far from regressing', writes Virno, 'singularity is refined and reaches its peak in acting together, in the plurality of voices, in short, in the public sphere.'[3]

The kind of conflicts that began in the universities in the 1960s have crossed over into the global knowledge space, whose nature as a public domain in now intensely at issue. If the new voices and political confrontations should ultimately point to an exit from the flexible personality, and from liberal fascism, then there will have been no waste in the speculations of the late-1990s – whatever the multiple names of the investors.

3. http://multitudes.samizdat.net/spip.php?article65&var_recherche=Virno%20individuation

Recomposing the University

Marc Bousquet and Tiziana Terranova

Vol 1 #28, Summer/Autumn 2004

Far removed from the clichéd image of the 'ivory tower', today's universities have been opened up to the harsh realities of neoliberal economics: huge volumes of students, extreme levels of performance-geared management, casualisation of employment and the conversion of students into 'consumers'. In the name of democratisation and equality, the university has become a cross between a supermarket and a factory whose consumers are also its hyper-exploited labour force. Here, in an email exchange, Marc Bousquet and Tiziana Terranova – themselves employed in US and British universities respectively – describe the way the system works from the inside and look at the possibilities for getting out of it. Far from being a simple question of domination, they contend, the conditions of 'mass intellectuality' – also shared by many knowledge workers elsewhere in the 'social factory' – create enormous scope for new alliances and forms of resistance.

Tiziana Terranova: I think it would be good to start with the 'big picture' – that is, how the university is an open system opening onto the larger field of casualised and underpaid 'socialised labour power'. The latter is also often referred to as 'mass intellectuality' or even networked intelligence (an abstract quality of social labour power as it becomes increasingly informational and communicative). I have been thinking about it in terms of the opening up of disciplinary institutions as described by Deleuze in his essay on control societies. I would like to move from the idea that the university is some kind of ivory tower, or self-enclosed institution, whose current state and future concerns a minority of professionals, to the idea of the university as part of the 'diffuse factory' as described in autonomist work. I think that their description of a shift from a society where production takes place predominantly in the closed site of the factory to one where it is the whole of society that is turned into a factory – a productive site – is still very fitting politically. But, in fact, the debate seems to be stuck in the false opposition between the static, sheltered ivory tower and the dynamic, democratic market.

Marc Bousquet: You're right to call it a false opposition, since the university has never been a shelter from either commerce or politics. And yet the nostalgic idea of the university as a 'refuge' from social life is amazingly persistent, isn't it? The reality is very different. Especially in the US, where nearly 60 percent of high school graduates have some experience of 'higher ed', it should be obvious that the university is part of the social factory. The problem is that it's the wrong kind of factory.

TT: Maybe.

MB: Anyway, it seems that the ivory tower myth persists because it has so many useful functions. For intellectuals, as well as many artists and activists, the idea of the university as a refuge often gives them the feeling of Archimedes – as if it offered a stable fulcrum from which they can move the Earth itself. For others, the ivory tower image is a kind of smokescreen for the double-speak and structural transformations of neoliberalism, a chastity belt as the Bush-Thatcher-Clinton-Blair bloc leads it to market: 'the university is too much of an ivory tower – we have to make it practical' on the one hand, and on the other hand: 'because the university is so much of an ivory tower, we can trust that its profit-seeking will be benevolent'. It signifies all the way around the political clock. Really, 'ivory tower' is the classic ideologeme – practically un-dislodgeable from any point of view.

TT: So the university is no longer, simply, an ivory tower (although I am sure that even the ivory tower persists in pockets of isolated privilege, too), but it has not simply turned into a 'market' or 'supermarket' either – providing exciting new courses/services to discriminating student-customers in search of that elusive, perfect value-for-money combination. If anything, it is another site of implosion of the modern separation between consumption, production and reproduction.

MB: Yes, the sense of 'separate' circuits is quickly eroding. And 'supermarket', as opposed to 'market', is perfect. It goes beyond the nostalgia of the market-as-agora, or public sphere, to capture the sense of total commodification.

Once we see that the campus is seamlessly part of the whole (social and global) factory floor – in this sense an unprivileged location in a vast horizontal plane – it becomes an opportunity for the self-organisation of labour and, just as you say, reorganising the social relations of re/production. But, in my mind, that would mean giving up the fantasy of the fulcrum, of the ivory tower

model in which the university offers a 'safe space' to benevolent 'directors of the transformation', operating in a cloud-circled meta-plane for mental labourers. For the university to become a site of worker self-organisation and the reproduction of an oppositional mentality – much less the catalyst of a radicalised multitude or 'mass intellectuality' – it would mean operating in an unsafe manner.

TT: In your writings on US academic labour, you emphasise the increasing polarisation between tenured academics (of which many exercise mainly administrative/managerial functions as 'directors of transformation') and a large, casualised teaching force of graduate students and temporary workers.

MB: Tenured faculty schizophrenically experience themselves as both labour and management, a contradictory position reflected in US labour law. They also have another schizophrenia – that of seeking to produce, or direct, a cultural-material transformation while simultaneously serving capital (as reproductive labour) through the socialisation of a disciplined professional-managerial class.

Getting beyond either schizophrenia is a hazardous project that ultimately threatens the faculty's 'directorial' position. In the US, for instance, more than half of tenured faculty in public higher education are unionised. This is not impressive by European standards, but it's three times the average level of worker organisation in the US. I bring it up because – with a few exceptions – it has thus far been very much an old-style craft unionism, a labour aristocracy that preserves workplace hierarchy, and has been very much complicit in the perma-temping of the university workforce, preserving their own jobs while selling out the future. While those unions are moving slowly to address casualisation, the kind of dramatic change implicit in the notion of a mass intellectuality or even the smaller fraction of mental labourers off the campus, would really imply a reverse of the trajectory we usually imagine. So, not 'How can the university serve as a platform for changing society on behalf of the casualised?' but 'How can the casualised hijack the university in their own interest?'

This dictatorship of the flexible would not be a safe process for the tenured who imagine themselves as directors of transformation and safely above the fray.

TT: Yes, and this reversal need not necessarily concern only university staff, but it must somehow construct an immanent connection to the masses of students who are increasingly going through higher education.

MB: Yes, absolutely.

TT: I find what is happening in the UK with higher education very interesting from this point of view. As you might be aware, the UK system has been through a turbulent decade. In most areas, budgets have been cut back or frozen for a number of years, while student numbers have increased exponentially (for example, according to UCAS statistics, the number of accepted first year students has risen from 300,000 in 1996 to almost 370,000 in 2002 – an increase of 25 percent in just six years).

The UK higher education system has gone from being a manageable cottage industry, more or less autonomously run, with a moderate number of students living more or less well on a grant system, to something that in places really looks like mass higher education – without the grants and with a new system of fees. There is obviously much to be said about this process.

MB: More like the US model. Wide access, but fee-for-service. Though there was a period in which the largest US public systems – in New York and California – were both open-access and free (or nearly free) tuition.

TT: Many students are going into higher education because they think that they have no choice in terms of their future occupational opportunities, and they have been told that in spite of the massive debts that they will be likely to incur, higher education is, after all, a good investment in terms of future earnings. There is this weird conjuring trick where they are really 'sold' this image of themselves as customers in the university supermarket, while, for many of them, the reality is that they are working in supermarkets, hospitals and tempting in offices to pay for their maintenance while they are studying.

MB: Exactly right. Being a student is ideologically attached to the idea of 'leisure', when in reality it's increasingly visible as a way of being hyper-exploited as a temp worker.

TT: On top of all this work, they will also get a 'good' start in life by learning to live with debt and there will be a good deal of that in their future life. Thus, while they are addressed as customers, they appear to me to be, in many cases, very far away from the model of the spoiled student or the education customer. They are working twice as hard as their predecessors to support themselves through their studies; while working, they accumulate debts which they will have to work hard to pay back once they graduate, in an accumulation of interest rates that ranges from credit cards to personal loans to mortgages. There aren't really very many student-customers are there? It seems to me that it is production through and through.

What I wonder is what this mass of students is doing to higher education?

MB: You mean that they are changing the system by inhabiting it.

TT: Yes, I think that it is an exciting transformation and does not necessarily need to be interpreted as a 'dumbing down'. On the contrary, the entry of such a mass of students into higher education implies a political transformation in the role of the university – its reinvention, so to speak. The ways in which this transformation is being managed over here are totally predictable and unsurprising. On the one hand, there is a heightened level of top-down, managerial, informational control – an endless, centralised output of new guidelines, targets and initiatives which introduce post-industrial management into the old guild-like university system, which, in many cases, is pushing teaching staff workloads to extreme limits.

On the student side, although stratified, the UK system is still in a turbulent phase of growth, which means that 'new' and, for many, suspicious degrees (such as media studies) are over-recruiting, while older disciplines from mathematics to engineering are suffering. This lack of synchronicity between the degree market and the labour market is obviously a result of the interference of desire in what should be a 'rational' economic choice (thus undermining the notion of the rationality of the working class as an internal variable of capital, as Negri once put it). What seems to most concern the higher education managers, however, is not this lack of relation between the labour market and the degree market; they seem to be more concerned with preserving hierarchical differences between universities, degrees and, ultimately, social classes.

MB: So the massification of higher ed represents an opportunity for transformation (and I guess you mean to indicate a pretty wide field of possibility, not just for a tighter fit between study and labour markets). But management is responding aggressively to contain the opportunity?

TT: There is an attempt to restrain the turbulence and instability introduced by rising student numbers by engineering a differential system of value – one that would be able to clearly distinguish, for example, prestigious institutions (an Ivy League) from their less prestigious, but still reputable, peers (red brick universities), and from a bottom layer of vocationally-orientated, hands-on, working class, not-quite-universities (ex-polytechnics). This is why we are going from the 'star' system of evaluation (where different departments get a number of stars depending on performance at the research assessment exercise) to a 'league' system. Apparently, there were too many high ratings and not enough of a sense of 'value-difference'. A league system will thus be introduced, allowing a finely-graded hierarchisation of university degrees and research environments. The underlying idea is that 'excellence' can only be produced through a concentration of resources (including the best students) which goes against a great deal of what we know about 'knowledge ecologies', for example. An American colleague has suggested that here, too, the model is the United States where higher education has always been solidly stratified.

MB: Yes. More so every year.

TT: So, I wanted to ask you about your experience. In which ways have the discourse and technologies of managerialism and privatisation interacted with the ferocious educational hierarchies that we know are a feature of the US higher education system?

MB: That's a great question. There're at least two issues here – the ranking of campuses against each other, and the role of higher education as a system in reproducing the 'ferocious hierarchies' of class relations in the US and globally (which still remain largely invisible to the US population).

The increasingly finely grained ranking of campuses against each other is most important to the upper fractions of the professional-managerial class, for whom the ideology of the US as a 'classless meritocracy' remains partly viable (a fraction that includes most higher education faculties themselves, as well as media professionals, many lawyers, physicians, etc.). With the intensification of the ranking, the percentage of persons who feel that the 'meritocracy' is working appears to shrink. That realisation is probably a good thing, overall. For instance, the appearance of graduate employee union movements at Ivy League campuses over the past 20 years (Yale, Columbia, Penn, Brown, Cornell) reflects, in part, the collapsing viability of merit ideology, even while the 'rank' of schools against each other gains ever greater 'cultural capital'. The problem is that the 'cultural capital', while real, is relative. The rank of schools acquires more relative value because, overall, the 'cultural capital' disseminated by schooling has become scarcer in some way that it's important for us to try to understand.

TT: Do you see any consistent strategy or tactical manoeuvres through which such cultural capital is made scarce and then given a value?

MB: Well, the classic strategy of creating a 'surplus' of workers that has finally hit the American and European professional-managerial class, and the expansion of higher ed – not just internally, but globally – is a big part of that, isn't it? The US business papers have been full of panicky articles about the 'new' outsourcing 'crisis' of white-collar work (engineering, programming, design). It wasn't a 'crisis' when outsourcing referred only to manufacturing. The outsourcing of professional and managerial labour (even the reading of CAT scans performed in the US or UK by Indian physicians) puts a lot of pressure on the (formerly) national frames of higher-ed/cultural capitalism.

Equally important – as your great 'Free Labour' piece and Andrew Ross' 'The Mental Labour Problem' demonstrate – is the way that higher-ed creates opportunities for hyper-exploitation.[1] Don't you think that higher ed is a primary vector for the harnessing of affect, socialising bodies to the necessary technologies and creating the psychological desire to give mental/affective labour away for less than a wage?

TT: Well, this would be consistent with Louis Althusser's notion of education as 'Institutional State Apparatus' wouldn't it? And there is no doubt, as Foucault once put it, that the university still partially 'stands for the institutional apparatus through which society ensures its uneventful reproduction at the least cost to itself'. Sadie Plant used this quote to contest what she thinks is the 'Platonic' bias of many pedagogical approaches to higher education which contribute to making the university what Foucault said it was: the idea that knowledge is something that is 'recalled', ready-made from an original source, and then simply transmitted from mind to mind. This is really the uneventful reproduction of ready-made knowledges for the purposes of social reproduction.[2]

There is no doubt, that is, that the university is a site of reproduction of social knowledge and class stratifications. The range of courses and degrees now offered by higher education institutions means that, today, the university is producing nurses and doctors; managers and IT technicians; journalists, scientists, filmmakers, lawyers, artists, teachers and even waiters and the unemployed (yes, a degree does not always guarantee a 'middle class' job).

On the other hand, it is not simply reproducing classes and professions but also participating in a larger process of qualitative recomposition at a moment of crisis for post-Fordism in the mode of information, of which the outsourcing of white-collar work from the US is an example. Higher ed is not simply engaged in the production and reproduction of knowledges but also in that of an abstract social labour power which can be multiply deployed across a range of productive sites (from call centres to reality TV shows).

1. Tiziana Terranova, 'Free Labour: Producing Culture for the Digital Economy' and Andrew Ross, 'The Mental Labour Problem', *Social Text*, 63, Summer 2000, Vol. 18, no. 2.
2. Sadie Plant, 'The Virtual Complexity of Culture', *FutureNatural: nature/science/culture*, London: Routledge, 1996.

MB: Right.

TT: For me, a key moment of this process involves an engagement with managerial control. I would like to talk about your essay on managerialism in 'rhet-comp' [rhetoric and composition].[3]

MB: That piece just observes that the informationalising or perma-temping of academic labour is not a neutral condition with respect to the knowledge that the academy produces. We call this the problem of 'Tenured Bosses and Disposable Teachers'.

In rhet-comp, which is a sub-field of English language studies traditionally lower in status than literature and linguistics, more than 90 percent of the teaching is done by flex workers. (Flex workers deliver labour 'in the mode of information', as if they were data on the management desktop – easily called up by a keystroke, and then just as easily dropped in the trash.) Tenure is primarily reserved for persons who directly manage the temp workers, or who creatively theorise the work of supervised teaching. To a very real extent, the knowledge produced by the field is a knowledge for managers. Of course, not all the knowledge is about the work of management. Much of it is. But I think you could argue that even the field's knowledges on 'other questions' increasingly show the taint of the managerial worldview. There would have to be more research into that.

TT: So, the tendency is for a collapse of the academic and managerial function in the service of institutional and social reproduction?

MB: Yes, but the real change is that it's more than just reproduction. Academic managerialism is increasingly in the direct service of extracting surplus value from students as well as staff. The university is an accumulation machine; it employs students directly, and it farms cheap or donated student labour out to its 'corporate partners'.

The university's extraction of surplus value needs to be seen as an under-regulated, 'semi-formal' economy. For-profit universities accumulate investment capital. But 'non-profit' universities also accumulate in the form of buildings, grounds, libraries (fixed capital), and as investment capital in endowments. Accumulated resources, such as campus sports facilities, have to be understood, to a degree, as the collective property of the ruling class (as opposed to, say, the property of students). For instance, at my public research university, few students can afford to go to basketball games – local elites occupy all the seats.

As has been suggested elsewhere, especially by the players themselves, student athletes are unpaid workers contributing to campus and corporate accumulation.

TT: What seems to be at stake, then, is not simply the reproduction of a dominant ideology but also, more explicitly, the attempt to induce and/or

3. Marc Bousquet, Tony Scott, Leo Parascondola, (Eds.), *Tenured Bosses and Disposable Teachers: Writing Instruction in the Managed University*, Carbondale: Southern Illinois University Press, 2004.

capture (and contain and control) a biopolitical surplus value that exceeds social reproduction – a potential to induce social transformations and produce new forms of life.

What I am saying is that, even if many graduates are going to be disillusioned with the actual earnings and working conditions (or lack of) that they will have to face, it is difficult to know what this outsourced and redundant surplus of educated labour could turn into – how it is going to interact with the communication machine, for example. I think that the early phase of the 'free labour' bonanza (where many chose to perform work that they perceived as rewarding either for free or for very little money) is over. At least in Europe, I have noticed a great interest in the problem of the exploitation (and economic sustainability) of autonomous, 'creative' labour.

MB: I wish there was a similar interest in the US. It's definitely a question within managerial discourse, but still far less so in the mass of 'creative' labour. There is, of course, the graduate employee union movement, but there's almost nothing in the undergraduate population. The primary form of undergraduate labour activism remains the anti-sweatshop movement. It's very encouraging, of course. But it has real limits. It's not an activism that proceeds from the situation of the student as labour, but from the situation of the student as consumer. The problem of the undergraduate as labour – as you say, an element of production – is almost completely unexplored. I have had two students writing dissertations that partially speak to the topic, but there's really almost nothing on it. At least in the US, there's very little law and policy on the question as well. That's what I mean when I talk about the 'informal economy' of the informationalised university. The relations of production going on under the sign of 'student' or 'study' or 'youth' are desperately under-regulated. It's a question of hyper-exploitation.

There is a bit more work on the student as a future worker, especially as a mental labourer, but very little. It's not framed as a question of a reserve army, but rather as a question of 'extended youth', which young people are represented as 'choosing'. It's really a version of the Puritan discourse, where your social and economic positioning is read as a function of your moral state. The under-employed (with 'slack time') are so because they're morally slack and therefore require the benevolent intervention of work disciplines such as speed-up.

TT: Yes, the Protestant spirit is, at many levels, alive and well in managerial discourse. And maybe you have a point when you say that, from capital's viewpoint, it is simply a matter of building an informational reserve army of workers. On the other hand, we also need to ask what social needs and desires and what processes of subjectivation does this reserve army express – what values it is capable of creating?

The question is also that of a direct and active engagement with specific student populations and their relation to this socialised labour power at large.

This is why I have problems with a common, counter-hegemonic argument against tuition fees (the hegemonic argument being that 'we cannot afford mass higher education' or the 'many should not pay for the few' and that 'a degree is a financial investment for the future'). The counter-hegemonic argument, by contrast, says that, by making financial costs between different institutions variable, poorer students are kept away from the 'best' institutions; the argument is that tuition fees make social mobility across classes more difficult.

All of this is true, of course, but I think that it only captures a fraction of the huge depletion of resources that is perpetrated at the expense of a mass intellectuality. By making tuition fees variable, as you know well from the US, you also automatically make working conditions (and pay usually follows) dramatically different across different layers and sections of academic labour.

MB: You want to get beyond the liberal complaint about social mobility. It's a more fundamental question of equality?

TT: In a way. In another way, this notion of equality still identifies knowledge too much with access to a limited cultural capital – rather than the huge, diverse and mutating flux of specialised knowledges and transversal connections which is a trademark of social production in network societies. It is not only a matter that the best lecturers will tend to flow toward the institutions where working conditions are better (less students and admin, more money for research, access to international academic networks, etc.). It is mainly about how a large part of the living labour within the higher education system will be impeded – by higher workloads, scarce resources and tighter managerial control – from actively engaging and experimenting with the massification of socialised labour power. Such power does not express itself simply as a unified, or even fragmented, class but also as a constellation of singularities connected by communication machines and informational dynamics. All of this at a moment when organised labour is lagging behind (or is being easily accommodated by) the huge transformations induced by post-Fordism and globalisation.

MB: Going back to the question you raised about the role of living knowledge labour in transformation. I completely agree with you that the biopolitical potential is there in the lived experience of the student.

Their experience, especially of frustrated expectations, leaves them 'primed' and potentially volatile in all the ways you describe. After all, the huge role the US professional and managerial fraction plays in organising production globally has thus far created an oversized managerial fraction relative to the size of the state. And the oversized role of the US – also Europe and Japan, of course – in world consumption is related to the expectations associated with the labour of managing globally.

So, the frustration of those outsized expectations is volatile in ways we haven't totally explored. And yet, at the same time, there is a proportionately greater effort devoted to containing it.

TT: It's hard to know where it might go.

MB: The question of tuition brings me back to what you said before about the socialising function of education debt – about students being schooled by indebtedness. That is such an immense field for future research. Randy Martin has written about it in *The Financialisation of Daily Life*, in a great chapter about the politics of debt.[4] Debt is a way of making the relationship to dead labour more intimate than any possible relationship to living labour.

TT: Yes.

MB: There's something to be said about schooling, especially the university, and the whole system of cultural capitalism and shaping the relationship of living labour to dead labour. It would be great to think in more detail about what it means to understand 'cultural capital' as dead labour.

Anyway, what I really like about the questions you're posing is the way they insist that we return to the question of the relationship of mental labour to other forms of labour. Are knowledge workers a 'class' unto themselves? Or are they a class fraction? If the latter, are they, à la Bourdieu, the 'dominated fraction of the dominant class'? Or are they, à la Gramsci, the fraction of the working class that tends toward a traitorous alliance with the ruling class?

I tend to think that your work confirms the Gramscian position. I suppose that follows necessarily from the autonomist point of view.

TT: This is a really interesting question. Gramsci was a keen observer of 'civil society' – and he was very aware that the complex relation between social classes was an historical and dynamic relation of shifting alliances, with hegemony constituting a kind of 'moving equilibrium'. The space of civil society, however, is relatively solid, stratified and bounded. Classes enter relationships of alliance but are clearly distinguishable within the overall boundary of the nation-state and the dialectic between the dominant and the dominated.

MB: But, for you, it's more a question of reinventing the terms of the struggle itself?

TT: Autonomist work started with trade union-sponsored social research into the reasons for declining union membership. The result of that theoretical, empirical and political inquiry was a foregrounding of the alchemical dynamics of class composition. Union membership was declining because neither the structure of the union nor its culture could cope with a shifting class composition (such as an increasing number of young, male, unskilled immigrant workers and their refusal of the unionist work ethic). This was not simply a new contingent coming to join the old generation; this also implied a new set of social needs and desires which not only the union but also factory work, as such, could not satisfy. The figure of this first transformation was the 'mass worker' – undertaking unskilled, mass factory work that challenged the industrial production machine through the rigidity of its escalating demands and its simultaneous social mobility. The mass worker demanded, and caused,

4. Randy Martin, *The Financialisation of Daily Life*, Philadelphia: Temple University Press, 2002.

a reinvention of politics – rather than simply joining the class struggle as a new contingent would – it gave new impetus to the struggle for life time against the 'time-measure' of the wage/work relation. An implication is that class is not simply about the reproduction of dialectical domination, but it is also endowed with its own historicity – a kind of dynamic potential, a surplus of value that antagonistically produces new forms of life and demands new modes of political and cultural expression.

Which brings us to today's question. Should we read the expansion of higher education as, primarily, a desire of capital (for better trained, more manageable, stratified and hegemonised workers)? Or should we also read in this transformation the re-composition of class dynamics – a new production of values and forms of life which produce the basis for the reinvention of politics?

MB: Would it be waffling of me to say both are true? Just as the university is industrialised (albeit on a post-Fordist footing of perma-temped labour in the mode of information), it – like the factory – becomes the location of an oppositional agency. Students – in their new character as workers in the present rather than the future – will, in my view, eventually understand themselves as the agents of their own exploitation. In that moment, we'll understand the information university to have called forth its own gravediggers.

TT: Sure. And, as usual, we must be careful about not repeating the old mistake of thinking of the working class as existing in a state of 'unrealised consciousness' which needs to be awoken by an external agency. If we keep this in mind, the main question becomes, then, not so much to map different fractions of the dominant and dominated classes, and their relation to each other within the overall war of position, but to understand the shifting mode of class composition, its dynamics and the values that it produces (taking into account, for example, the heterogeneous axes of subjectivation linked to ethnicity, race, nationality, gender, sexuality and so on). The shift from the 'mass worker' to 'socialised labour power' (or a multi-skilled, fully socialised and abstract labour power), was, for the early Negri, a matter of achieving a new working class identity – one that was adequate to the increasing levels of abstraction and socialisation of labour. The old transcendent dialectic was replaced with an immanent one: class composition, capitalist re-structuration, class re-composition.[5] In other authors, such as Franco Berardi or Félix Guattari, however, the break with the dialectic is more radical. The emphasis is more on the heterogeneous production of subjectivity, which takes place at the level of material connections (crucially including desiring and technical machines, from the assembly line to media and computer networks).

Subjectivity and class are not simply modes of reproduction but also alchemical, microbiological and machinic factories of social transformation.

5. Antonio Negri, 'Archaeology and Project: The Mass Worker and the Social Worker', *Revolution Retrieved: Selected Writings on Marx, Keynes, Capitalist Crisis and New Social Subjects 1967–83*, London: Red Notes, 1988.

MB: I agree.

TT: We could maybe close by talking about the place of academic labour within the labour movement at large (including all those mutant forms of labour that the trade union movement cannot reach).

MB: The one thing I would say is that it couldn't be a privileged place. To give academic labour a vanguard position would be a disaster. A big part of the academic 'labour of reproduction' is the production, legitimation and policing of inequality. I think academic labour, including organised academic labour, needs to submit itself to the tutelage of more radical forms of labour self-organisation. More radical than the trade union movement, as you say. Mass intellectuality implies a revolutionary transformation in the academic consciousness, faculty especially.

That's why I place so much emphasis on thinking about students as already workers, not just future workers. They are less ossified, less committed to inequality, than the faculty. To a certain extent, they are also not invested in the labour aristocracy/bureaucracy of the trade unions. It would be crazy to call student life the perfect crucible for a movement to create greater equality, but the massification of higher-ed has made it more likely. This is not nostalgia for 1968; far from it. I think that the gigantic expansion of student experience, to the point where we have to see it as a modality of worker experience, creates opportunities so much larger than '68.

TT: I don't know about 'tutelage', but I would definitely be in favour of a greater effort to open up connections with other forms of labour on the basis of what academic labour shares with them (from the common plague of managerial command, and its attack on the time of life, to the common implication in the diffuse social factory). On the other hand, there is also a specific contribution that academic labour can provide. This specificity is part of its role as a key site in the production and reproduction of knowledges and forms of control (from policy-orientated social research to scientific patents and new technologies); in its contribution to the production of specific forms of labour directly implicated in the reproduction of the social (from doctors to computer scientists, from managers to artists and social workers); and also in its relation to a wider, abstract social labour power (informated, affective and communicational) which exceeds the disciplinary power of the work/wage relation. As you said, a big part of the university's work is still institutional – reproducing hierarchical differences and producing docile subjects – so, hacking the machine of social reproduction in higher-ed is bound to be complicated work. I doubt whether a successful engagement with this process would produce another 1968 – the latter was still a revolt against the institutions, while we know now that power operates in and through networks. But it will definitely be a challenging process to be part of – requiring commitment and imagination.

Call to Arms

Kolinko

Vol 1 #28, Summer/Autumn 2004

A Radical Enquiry

The *Hotlines* book describes a three-year process of enquiry into call centres, attempting to understand the situation there, workers' behaviour during, and against, work, conflicts and interventions – through leaflets and otherwise. In this enquiry, we saw ourselves as workers, participating in struggles and trying to support their development. We had a guiding principle: make clear to other workers, and ourselves, the actions that are already being carried out. Our goal was not to enlighten 'unreflective' workers, but to push beyond our own limited horizons.

We want to grasp the standpoint of the collective social worker, the effects of technological change, the impact of the social and international division of labour on everyday life, the experiences of other workers in their struggles and the power they develop through them. It's about breaking up the limited perspective which the isolating capitalist organisation of work imposes on us, blocking our own view of things.

Of course, our attempts to get an overview, to understand class conflicts and to throw our ideas into discussion – in other words, the ways and means we use for enquiries – demand a continuous debate. We used the *Hotlines* questionnaire mainly for reflecting our ideas and for starting discussions with other workers. Consequently, there was much it missed; it did not say much about struggles in other sectors, or about crisis, and nothing about war. Better leaflets would draw the lines between the events on the shop floor, or in the job centres, and the global transformations of capitalism – a means to encourage further discussion among workers by supplying information on other struggles. In the worst case, they won't read that stuff or know what to do with it; in the best case, they will use it during upcoming conflicts and start to disseminate their own experiences through leaflets or other media.

We do not believe in the supposed separation between workers and militants/activists, one lot with their crazy revolutionary ideas, the other only interested in more money and job security. While there may be thousands of examples of the 'individual worker' – individualism and competition while searching for a job, demands in collective bargaining situations, racism against newly emigrated workers – there are also many examples of the opposite: the doctor's receptionist who does not want to work in medical practices any more, even if she gets paid better, because she prefers being together with larger numbers of workers in a call centre; the casual worker who doesn't give a shit about money and security and goes surfing after four months of work.

Historically, there are many examples of workers acting against their economic interests – enjoying themselves by burning down their company, killing their boss and so on.

Enquiry is one method that can be used in order to understand this space between workers' behaviour, as labour power that wants to improve its conditions, and as the class that wants to put an end to exploitation. It can do this by dealing with real processes, contradictions and tensions. Workers already make enquiries; they are interested in the wages of their foremen, conflicts in other departments, the restructuring management has planned (sometimes even in the struggles of the landless in Brazil or the unemployed in Argentina). If they don't make such enquiries, they lose out, unprepared for the next conflict. In most cases, the division between those who are interested in what's going on and those who are not is not a division between so-called 'revolutionaries' and workers but between workers themselves.

For us, the issue of our exploitation corresponds directly with that of our struggle. We don't have to tell anyone that we/they are exploited; it's a collective effort to understand the social dimension and structure of how this exploitation is organised. We have no desire to be militants or activists, sacrificing ourselves for an historic mission, getting on everyone's nerves including our own. Rather, we make this choice: to deal with the situation collectively, rather than individually, whenever we have to sell our labour power or cope with the worsened conditions at job centres and the welfare office. For instance, we can decide together in which places of exploitation we want to earn our cash and, at the same time, participate collectively in conflicts. That way, our disgust for the capitalist daily routine, and our anger against the conditions and those who oppress and exploit us, can flow together into one common political project.

Enquiry is the condition, form and method of our attempts to understand the current struggle and to take part in it. Those who would still like to go into these questions in more detail from the perspective of our experiences should read the *Hotlines* book.

London Calling

I had heard a lot about call centres, day after day, for two years. I thought I knew what to expect.

The Company

One of the biggest market research companies in the world. They have offices, or call centres, in 36 countries, and big multinational and governmental clients. For example, the Australian General Union asked the company to conduct a survey about flexible work time. They should just have asked the company's workers – they knew all about it already.

The Call Centre

The call centre is in London, near London Bridge, on a side street facing a high, red brick wall with barbed wire on top. A group of young Spaniards and Italians stand in front of it, the Italians swearing about Berlusconi, the Spaniards smoking weed. Two doors, one pincode, and you are inside the 'postmodern chicken farm', as people call it. Packed little phone booths for hundreds of interviewers. Their job is market research – phoning people in France, Italy, Spain, Germany, the UK, Ireland, randomly selected by the computer. At the end of each row are the supervisors' desks.

The Conditions

The whole thing started with two days' unpaid training, basic brainwashing about market research, how to use the antique computer program and so on. The second day, a really nice guy from French Reunion Island came in ten minutes late and was sent home again, unpaid, but at least only half brainwashed. The stylish, gay Asian supervisor, who regularly handed out anti-globalisation information and was a very welcome guest at various call centre workers' parties, was able to justify giving him the sack.

After these two days, you can start working – if you get your shifts. You have to book them a week in advance, and, if there is no work, you won't get any. The management wanted to introduce a new shift scheme, with a top list of interviewers: whoever completes the most interviews, whoever has got the least 'idle time' and is the most punctual and obedient worker, can choose their shifts first. If you are a miserable worker, you'll get what's left over. Theoretically, you can book as many shifts as you want – of course, there are some legal restrictions, but they don't really count. I saw people working 12 hours a day, seven days a week, although that's a sad exception.

The Work

If you press 'y' after the computer asks you 'another interview?', it starts dialling random numbers. When you are lucky, you get connected to a fax machine or a modem and you can press '8', just to be asked the same question again. In between '8' and 'y' is the kingdom of idle time, but watch it – the king or queen of idle time gets into trouble. If you are connected to another human being, you have to start asking questions.

Most sensible people hang up after hearing the word 'market research'; all the others are usually very lonely, mentally unstable or just wrong in thinking they're doing you a favour. We do surveys about alcoholic drinks, fast food chains, mobile phone networks, DVD players and digital cameras, cars, petrol stations, post offices and more. We do it every day, 'til nine in the evening.

Imagine phoning a small Irish village on a Sunday night to ask about DVD players. At least you can hide behind your script. You are supposed to read it from the screen, word for word. How else could you possibly think of questions like 'Imagine Burger King is a person with its own personality. Would Burger King be introverted, bold, immature or warm-hearted?' The average interview takes about 20 minutes; on average you do three to four interviews in a four-hour shift, the fruit of 200–300 phone calls. Rumour has it that the company gets £70 for each interview.

The Workers

From all over the world, in their 20s, most of them 'creative' in one way or the other. It would be wrong to say that they are 'students', though most of them have been. You can talk about Guy Debord with a French female artist just back from Cuba, the drummer of an Italian anarchist hardcore band, a gay second generation Turkish boy from Cologne who is studying fashion design, a traditional Asian Muslim man from the East End, a girl from a village in the Alps with a population of 50 who just arrived in London – all in a four-hour shift. I've never worked in a place before where people were so critical and verbally able to dismiss their work, even capitalism, as such. But I have also hardly ever seen people accepting such mind-numbing work and patronising management behaviour. Because it's just a job for a while? Because they mainly did that kind of job after quitting school or university? Because of the week-to-week shift system? I still don't have a clue why.

The Supervision

There is one supervisor for 10–20 interviewers, monitoring the idle time, counting interviews and attempts, listening to what you say and how you say it. They come to your desk if you are not dialling for five minutes; they give you bad marks if you don't stick to the script. They walk around and tell you to put your book or newspaper back into your rucksack and to take the coffee back to the coffee machine, because hot drinks are not allowed. For an extra pound an hour and the privilege of not having to be on the phone, they wear themselves out.

The Sabotage

It starts with small things. Little drawings or scribbles in each phone booth. A lot of 'Leave your brain at the entrance' stuff. Someone is constantly stuffing the toilets with toilet rolls, so the management put out these notices: 'Whoever is putting paper down the toilets, please stop it. It is unnecessary, unhygienic and causes inconvenience for everybody.' The next day, people cross out the 'It', replacing it with 'Market Research', or the name of the most hated supervisor.

We started collective slam poetry, handing poem lines from neighbour to neighbour. Sometimes, we used the computer as well, pressing the right combination of codes to keep the computer dialling, assuming that there are only fax machines at the other end. But that's risky: the supervisor could be monitoring you. Sometimes, especially with lonely elderly people, we live out our social worker tendencies, talking about gardening and the new priest in the community, instead of fast food chains. Some Spanish guys developed a funny threesome, using the headset, passing the receiver on to the neighbour, so that the confused respondent talked to two interviewers. We faked the management instructions that are placed in every phone booth, calling for the return of the Idle Time King and mass orgies.

During Saturday shifts, there is a higher level of drug consumption. That's when most of the weird stuff happens. Receivers at the supervisors' desks glued to the phones, people pretending to be preachers or radio show presenters. But there was never a real collective action. Once, on a Saturday, 15 minutes before the end of a nine-hour shift, the supervisors circling to make sure we keep on dialling, some French girls suddenly started to cheer and applaud like crazy. All the pent-up energy broke loose and the whole call centre joined in, then packed their stuff and left five minutes early. We were never able to repeat that.

The End

In the end, after six months, I had my fair share of disciplinary meetings, but wanted to leave anyway. It was my first and last call centre job. I found interesting people there, situations of solidarity and flirtation, a real friend. In political terms, I am less sure. Perhaps the most radical act would have been to elect a shop steward or get rid of the zero-hour contracts and arbitrary management behaviour. But what for? To tie people even closer to this madness by offering proper contracts? By that measure, it would have become clear that we are workers with rights and our own interests. But why channel energy into producing formally correct working relations when there is all this disgust towards this kind of work, all this pent up creative anger?

What I missed here was a group of more experienced people, politically and job-wise, with whom to reflect on the situation. At first, I thought a leaflet, for example, about the new shift system, would be kind of 'external', so I just talked to my neighbours, made little drawings, like everyone did. But maybe something on paper, demanding a collective action and handed out to everyone, would have forced all of us to define a position. Who knows?

Precari-Us?

Angela Mitropoulos

Vol 1 #29, Winter/Spring 2005

Few could be unaware that an increasing proportion of the workforce is engaged in intermittent, or irregular, work. But I'd like to set aside, for the moment, the evidentiary weight and scope of those well-rehearsed findings that confirm beyond doubt the discovery and currency of precariousness, which render the axiomatic terrain upon which such facts are discovered beyond reproach. Instead, I would like to explore something of the grammar at work in these discussions. As a noun, 'precariousness' is both more unwieldy and indeterminate than most. If it is possible to say anything for certain about precariousness, it is that it teeters. This is to begin by emphasising some of the tensions that shadow much of the discussion about precarious labour. Some of those tensions can be located under various, provisional headings which bracket the oscillation between regulation and deregulation, organisation and dissemination, homogenous and concrete time, work and life.

There are notable instances of this: consider recent research commissioned by Australia's foremost trade union body, the ACTU, into what they call 'non-standard' forms of work. As reported, most of those surveyed said they would like 'more work'. It is not clear to what extent that answer was shaped by the research, i.e. by the ACTU's persistent arguments for a return to 'standard hours', re-regulation or their more general regard for Fordism as the golden age of social democracy and union organisation. 'Non-standard work' has mostly been viewed by unions as a threat, not only to working conditions but, principally, to the continuing existence of the unions themselves.

But what is clear is that the flight from 'standard hours' was not precipitated by employers but rather by workers seeking less time at work. This flight coincided with the first wave of exit from unions. What the Italian Workerists dubbed 'the refusal of work' in the late-1970s had its Anglophone counterpart in the figure of the 'slacker'. This predated the 'flexibilisation' of employment that took hold in the 1980s. The failure of this oppositional strategy nevertheless provoked what Andrew Ross has called the 'industrialisation of bohemia'. Given that capitalism persisted, the flight from Fordist regularity and full-time work can be said to have necessitated the innovation and extension of capitalist exploitation, in much the same way that gentrification has followed university students around suburbs and de-industrialising areas since the 1970s.

The search for a life outside work tended to boil down to an escape from the factory and its particular forms of discipline. And so, perhaps paradoxically, this flight triggered an indistinction between work and life commensurate with the movement of exploitation into newer areas. This is why the answer of 'more work' now presents itself so often as the horizon of an imaginable solution to the problem of impoverishment and financial instability – not more money or more life outside work, but more work.

Take the distinction between work time and leisure time. These categories become formalised with Fordism, its temporal rhythm measured out by the wage, clock and assembly line and distinguished by a proportionality and particular division of times, as in the eight-hour day and the five-day week. Here, leisure time bears a determined relationship to work as the trade-off for the mind-numbing tedium of the assembly line, rejuvenation and temporary respite from the mind-body split that linework enforces. Yet leisure time was, still, substantively a time of not-work.

By comparison, while the perpetually irregular work of post-Fordism might, though not necessarily, decrease the actual amount of time spent doing paid work, it nevertheless enjoins the post-Fordist worker to be continually available for such work, to regard life outside waged work as a time of preparation for, and readiness to, work. Schematically put, whereas Fordism sought to cretinise, to sever the brains of workers from their bodies so as to assign thought, knowledge, planning and control to management, post-Fordist capitalism might, by contrast, be characterised – in Foucault's terms – as the imprisonment of the body by the soul. Hence the utility of desire, knowledge and sociality in post-Fordism.

The long, Protestant history of assuming work as an ethical or moral imperative returns in the not always secular injunction to treat one's self as a commodity, both during and outside actual work time. One can always try to defer the ensuing panic and anxiety with pharmacology, as Franco Berardi argues. But something might also be said here about that other 'opiate', the parallel rise of an enterprising, evangelical Christianity, not to mention attempts to freeze contingency in communitarianism, of one variant or another. The precariousness of life – experienced all the more insistently because life depends on paid work – tends to close the etymological distance between prayer (*precor*) and the precarious (*precarius*).

Precarious Subjects

The term 'precarity' might have replaced 'precariousness' with the advantage of a prompt neologism, yet both continue to be burdened by a normative bias which seeks guarantees in terms that are often neither plausible nor desirable. Precariousness is mostly rendered in negative terms, as the imperative to move from irregularity to regularity, or from abnormality to normality. That normative burden is conspicuous in the grammatical development from adjective to noun: precarious to precariousness, condition to name.

Yet, capitalism is perpetually in crisis; capital is precarious, and normally so. Stability here has always entailed formalising relative advantages between workers, either displacing crises onto the less privileged, or deferring the effects of those crises through debt. Moreover, what becomes apparent in discussions on precariousness is that warranties are often sought, even by quite different approaches, in the juridical realm. The law becomes the secularised language of prayer against contingency. This assumes a distinction between law and economy that is certainly no longer, if it ever was, all that plausible. It is not clear, therefore, whether the motif of precariousness works simply to entice a desire for its opposite – security – regardless of whether this is presented as a return to a time in which security apparently reigned, or as a future newly immunised against precariousness.

There are nationalist denominations. Precarity (or *precarité*), in its current expression, emerged in French sociology, in attempts to grasp the convergence of struggles by unemployed and intermittent workers in the late-1990s. Most prominently, Bourdieu was among those who raised the issue of a diffuse *precarité* as an argument for the strengthening of the nation-state against this phenomenon, as well as the globalisation that was said to have produced it. In its far less nationalist versions, the discussion on precarity is marked – sometimes ambivalently and not always explicitly – by the presentation of a hoped-for means of resistance, if not revolution. A renewed focus on changing forms of class composition, or new subjectivities, may have brought with it an irreversible and overdue shift in perspective and vocabulary. But that shift has not in all cases disturbed the structural assumptions of an orthodox Marxism in the assertion of a newer, therefore more adequate, vanguard. Names confer identity as if positing an unconditional presupposition. Like all such assertions, it is not simply the declaration that one has discovered the path to a different future in an existing identity that remains questionable. More problematically, such declarations are invariably the expression and reproduction of a hierarchy of value in relation to others.

For instance, where Lenin's Party, defined as the figure of the 'revolutionary intellectual', paid homage to the mind-body split of Fordism and Taylorism (which cast others either as a 'mass' or, if actively oppositional, as 'counter-revolutionaries'), to what extent has the discussion on precarious labour avoided a similar duplication of segmentation and conformism? Or, to put the question in classical Marxist terms, to what extent can an identity which is immanent to capitalism (whether 'working class' or 'multitude') be expected to abolish capitalism and, therefore, its very existence and identity? Does a politics which takes subjectivity as both its question and answer reproduce a politics as the idealised image of such? Recourse to an Enlightenment subject is replete with the stratifications which presuppose it and ledgered according to its current values (or valuations), not least among these being the distinction between paid and unpaid labour.

Let me put this still another way: the discussion of the precarious conditions of 'creative labour' and the 'industrialisation of bohemia' tends to re-stage a manoeuvre found in Puccini's opera *La Bohème*. Here, a bunch of guys (a poet, philosopher, artist and musician) suffer for their art in their garret. But it is the character of Mimi – the seamstress who talks of fripperies rather than art – who furnishes Puccini and our creative heroes with the final tragedy with which to exalt that art as suffering and through opera. The figure of the artist (or 'creative labourer') may well circulate, in some instances, as the exemplary figure of the post-Fordist worker – precarious, immaterial and so on – but this requires a moment in which the precarious conditions of others are declared to be a result of their 'invisibility' or 'exclusion'.

For what might turn out to have been the briefest of political moments, the exemplary figure of precariousness was that of undocumented migrant workers – without citizenship, but nevertheless inside national economic space, and precarious in more senses than might be indicated by other uses of the word. And, far from arriving with the emergence of newer industries or subjectivities, precarious work has been a more or less constant feature of domestic work, retail, 'hospitality', agriculture, sex work and the building industry, as well as sharply inflecting the temporal and financial arrangements which come into play in the navigation of child-rearing and paid work for many women. But, rather than shaking assertions that the 'precariat' is a recent phenomenon, through the declaration that such work was previously 'invisible', the apprehension of migrant, 'Third World' and domestic labour seems to have become the pretext for calls for the reconstruction of the plane of visibility (of juridical recognition and mediation) and the eventual circulation and elevation of the cultural-artistic (and cognitive) worker as its paradigmatic expression. The strategy of exodus (of migration) has been translated into the thematics of inclusion, visibility and recognition.

On a global scale and in its privatised and/or unpaid versions, precarity is, and has always been, the standard experience of work in capitalism. When one has no other means to live than the ability to labour or – even more precariously because it privatises a relation of dependency – to reproduce and 'humanise' the labour publicly tendered by another, life becomes contingent on capital and therefore precarious.

The experience of regular, full-time, long-term employment which characterised the most visible, mediated aspects of Fordism is an exception in capitalist history. That presupposed vast amounts of unpaid domestic labour by women and hyper-exploited labour in the colonies. This labour also underpinned the smooth distinction between work and leisure for the Fordist factory worker. The enclosures and looting of what was once contained as the Third World and the affective, unpaid labour of women allowed for the consumerist, affective 'humanisation' – and protectionism – of what was always a small part of the Fordist working class: a comparably privileged worker who was nonetheless elevated to the exemplary protagonist of class struggle by way of vanguardist reckonings. Those reckonings tended to parallel the valuations of bodies by capital, as reflected in the wage. The 'lower end' of the (global) labour market and divisions of labour – impoverishment, destitution or a privatised precariousness – were accounted for as an inherent attribute of skin colour and sex, as natural. In many respects, then, what is registered as the recent rise of precarity is actually its discovery among those who had not expected it by virtue of the apparently inherent and eternal (perhaps biological) relation between the characteristics of their bodies and their possible monetary valuation – a sense of worth verified by the demarcations of the wage (paid and unpaid) and in the stratification of wage levels.

Biopolitical Arithmetic

To be sure, there are important reasons to continue a discussion of precarious labour and precarity, of how changes to work time become diffused as a disposition. Precarity is a particularly useful way to open a discussion on the no-longer-punctual dimensions of the encounter between worker and employer, and how this gives rise to a generalised indistinction between the labour market, self, relationships and life.

The more interesting aspect of this discussion is the connection made between the uncertainty of making a living and, therefore, the uncertainty of life that is thereby produced in its grimly mundane, as well as horrific, aspects: impoverishment as both persistent threat and circumstance, the 'War on Terror', the internment camps, 'humanitarian intervention' and so on. In this, the topic of biopolitics re-emerges with some urgency, or rather this urgency becomes more tangible for that privileged minority of workers (or 'professionals') who were previously unfamiliar with its full force. Impoverishment and war pronounce austere verdicts upon lives reckoned as interchangeable and therefore at risk of being declared superfluous. What does it means to insist here, against its capitalist calculations, on the 'value of life'?

This raises numerous questions – What are the intersections between economic and political-ethical values? Does value have a measure, a standard by which all values (lives) are calculated and related? – which are in turn transformed into organisational questions: How feasible is it to use precarity as a means for alliances or coalition-building without effacing the differences between Mimi and the Philosopher, or indeed reproducing the hierarchy between them? Is it in the best interests for the *maquiladora* worker to ally herself with the fashion designer? Such questions cannot be answered abstractly. But there are two, perhaps difficult and irresolvable, questions that might still be posed.

First, what are the specific modes of exploitation of particular kinds of work? If the exploitation and circulation of 'cognitive' or 'creative labour' consists, as Maurizio Lazzarato argues, in the injunction to 'be active, to communicate, to relate to others' and to 'become subjects', then how does this shape interactions with others, for better or worse? How does the fast food 'chainworker', who is compelled to be affective, compliant and routinised, not assume such a role in relation to a software-programming 'brainworker', whose habitual forms of exploitation oblige opinion, innovation and self-management? How is it possible for the latter to avoid assuming for themselves the specialised role of mediator – let alone preening themselves in the cognitariat's mirror as the subject, actor or 'activist' of politics – in this relationship? To what extent do the performative imperatives of artistic-cultural exploitation (visibility, recognition, authorship) foreclose the option of clandestineness which remains an imperative for the survival of many undocumented migrants and workers in the informal economy?

Secondly, why exactly is it important to search for a device by which to unify workers, however plurally that unity is configured? Leaving aside the question of particular struggles – say, along specific production chains – it is not all that clear what the benefits might be of insisting that precarity can function as this device for recomposing what was, in any case, the fictitious and highly contested unity of 'the working class'. To be sure, that figure is being challenged by that of 'the multitude', but what is the specific nature of this challenge?

Ellen Rooney once noted that pluralism is a deeper form of conformism; while it allows for a diversity of content, conflict over the formal procedures which govern interaction are off limits, as is the power of those in whose image and interest those rules of interaction are constituted. Often this arises because the procedures established for interaction and the presentation of any resulting 'unity' are so habitual that they recede beyond view. Those who raise problems with them, therefore, tend to be regarded as the sources of conflict if not the architects of a fatal disunity of the class. A familiar, if receding, example: Sexism is confined to being a 'women's issue', among a plurality of 'issues', but it cannot disrupt the form of politics.

What, then, is the arithmetic of biopolitics emerging from the destitution of its Fordist forms? If Fordist political forms consecrated segmentations that were said to inhere, naturally, in the difference of bodies, then what is post-Fordism's arithmetic? Post-Fordism dreams of the global community of 'human capital', where differences are either marketable or reckoned as impediments to the free flow of 'humanity' as – or rather, for – capital. In short, political pluralism is the idealised version of the post-Fordist market.

It might be useful here to specify that commodification does not consist in the acts of buying and selling, which obviously predate capitalism. Rather, commodification means the application of a universal standard of measure that relates and reduces qualitative differences – of bodies, actions, work – according to the abstract measure of money. Abstract equivalence, without its idyllic depictions, presupposes and produces hierarchy, exploitation and violence. Formally, which is to say juridically; neither poor nor rich are allowed to sleep under bridges.

What does it mean, then, to argue that the conditions of precarious workers might be served by a more adequate codification of rights? It does not, I think, mean that our conditions will improve or, rather, be guaranteed by such. Proposals for 'global citizenship' by Negri and Hardt are predated by the global reach of a militaristic humanitarianism that has already defined its meaning of the convergence between 'human rights' and supra-national force. Similarly, a 'basic income' has already been shown in the places it exists, such as Australia, to be contingent upon, and constitutive of, intermittent engagements with waged work, if not forced labour, as in work-for-the-dole schemes. The latter policy was applied to unemployed indigenous people before it became a recent measure against the unemployed generally. Basic incomes do not suspend the injunction to work often in low-paid, casual or informal jobs; they are deliberately confined to levels which provide for a bare life, but not for a livelihood. The introduction of work-for-the-dole schemes indicates that, where 'human capital' does not flow freely as such, policy (and pluralism) will resort to direct coercion, cancelling the formally voluntary contract of wage labour. The introduction of the work-for-the-dole scheme for indigenous people in Australia followed the collapse in their employment rates after the introduction of 'equal pay' laws. Their 'failure to circulate' was explained as an inherent, often biological attribute (chiefly as laziness), and, therefore, the resort to forced labour was rendered permissible by those politicians who most loudly proclaimed their commitment to multiculturalism and the reconciliation of indigenous and 'settler' Australians.

So, how might it be possible to disassociate the value of life from the values of capital? Or, with regard to the relation between a globalised nationalism and aspirations for supra-national arrangements, how might it be possible to sever the various daily struggles against precariousness from the enticements of a global security state? Rights are not something one possesses, even if many of us are reputed, by correlation, to possess our own labour in the form of an increasingly self-managed or self-employed exploitation. Rights, like power, are exercised in practice and by bodies. As juridical codes, they are both bestowed, and denied, by the state, at its discretion. There are no guarantees and there will always be a struggle to exercise particular rights, irrespective of whether or not they are codified in law. But, as a strategy, the path of rights means praying that the law or state might distribute rights, and entrusting it with the authority and force to deny them.

That said, precarity might well have us teetering. It might even do so evocatively, for better and often worse, praying for guarantees and, at times, shields that often turn out to be fortresses. But it is yet to dispense with, for all its normative expressions, a relationship to the adjective: to movement, however uncertain. 'Precarious' is as much a description of patterns of work time as it is the description, experience, hopes and fears of a faltering movement – in more senses than one, and possibly since encountering the limits of the anti-summit protests. This raises the risk of movements that become trapped in communitarian fears or in dreams of a final end to risk in the supposedly secure embrace of global juridical recognition. Yet it also makes clear that a different future, by definition, can only be constructed precariously, without firm grounds for doing so, without the measure of a general rule and with questions that should, often, shake us – particularly what 'us' might mean.

Reality Check: Are We Living in an Immaterial World?

Steve Wright

Vol 2 #1, Winter 2005

> A priest once came across a zen master and, seeking to embarrass him, challenged him as follows: 'Using neither sound nor silence, can you show me what is reality?'
>
> The zen master punched him in the face.[1]

Continued assertions that, today, we live in a knowledge economy or society raise many questions. In the next few pages, I want to discuss some aspects of these assertions, especially as they relate to the notion of 'immaterial labour'. This term has developed within the camp of thought that is commonly labelled 'postworkerist', of which the best known exponent is undoubtedly Antonio Negri. While its roots lie in that strand of post-war Italian Marxism known as *operaismo* (workerism), this milieu has rethought and reworked many of the precepts developed during the Italian New Left's heyday of 1968–78. If anything, it was the very defeat of the social subjects with which *operaismo* had identified – first and foremost, the so-called 'mass worker' engaged in the production of consumer durables through repetitive, 'semi-skilled labour' – that led Negri and others to insist that we had embarked upon a new age beyond modernity.[2]

According to this view of the world, amongst those with nothing to sell but their ability to work, a quite different kind of labour is currently either hegemonic or, at the very least, well on the way toward acquiring hegemony. Secondly, capital's growing dependence upon this different – *immaterial* – labour has serious implications for the process of self-expanding, abstract labour (value) that defines capital as a social relation. While Marx held that the 'socially-necessary labour-time' associated with production provided the means by which capital could measure the value of commodities (and so the mass of surplus value that it hoped to realise with their sale), Negri is of the opinion that, in a time of increasingly complex and skilled labour, and of a working day that more and more blurs the boundaries with (and ultimately colonises) the rest of our waking hours, value can no longer be calculated. As he put it a decade ago, in such circumstances the exploitation of labour continues, but 'outside any economic measure: its economic reality is fixed exclusively in political terms'.[3]

1. Thanks to Hobo for telling me this story. Thanks, too, to Angela Mitropoulos and Nate Holdren for their helpful suggestions with this piece. All mistakes my own, etc.
2. For the best introduction to post-workerism, see http://www.generation-online.org
3. Antonio Negri, 'Oltre la legge di valore', *DeriveApprodi 5–6*, Winter 1994.

This is pretty esoteric stuff, particularly the arguments over the measurability (or otherwise) of value. Should we care one way or the other? What I hope to show below is that, for all their apparent obscurity, these debates matter. This is because they raise questions as to how we understand our immediate context, including how we interpret the possibilities latent within contemporary class composition. Is one sector of class composition likely to set the pace and tone in struggles against capital, or should we, as *Midnight Notes* once suggested, look instead toward the emergence of 'strange loops [...] odd circuits and strange connections between and among various class sectors', as a necessary condition for moving beyond 'the present state of things'?

Unpacking Immaterial Labour

Maurizio Lazzarato's discussion of immaterial labour was perhaps the first extended treatment of the topic to appear in English. Part of an important anthology of Italian texts published in the mid-'90s, Lazzarato's work defined the term as 'labour that produces the informational and cultural content of the commodity'.[4] If the 'classic' forms of this labour were represented in fields like 'audiovisual production, advertising, fashion, the production of software, photography, cultural activities, and so forth', those who perform such work commonly found themselves in highly casualised, precarious and exploitative circumstances – as part of what, more recently and in certain Western European radical circles, has come to be called the 'precariat'.[5]

The Taylorist approach to production, that had confronted the mass worker, decreed that 'you are not paid to think'. With immaterial labour, Lazzarato argued, management's project was different. In fact, it was even more totalitarian than the earlier, rigid division between mental and manual labour (ideas and execution) because capitalism seeks even to involve the worker's personality within the production of value.[6]

At the same time, this managerial approach carried real risks for capital, Lazzarato believed, since capital's very existence was placed in the hands of a labour force called upon to exercise its creativity through collective endeavours. And, unlike a century ago, when a layer of skilled workers likewise stood at the centre of key industries, yet largely cut off from the unorganised 'masses', immaterial labour today cannot be understood as the distinctive attribute of one stratum within the workforce. Instead, skilled labour is present (if only in latent form) amongst broad sectors of the labour market, starting with the young.

Michael Hardt and Antonio Negri's *Empire* – a book that has come to stand (rightly or wrongly) as the centrepiece of post-workerist thought – built upon

4. Maurizio Lazzarato, 'Immaterial Labour', *Radical Thought in Italy: A Potential Politics*, Minneapolis: University of Minnesota Press, 1996, p. 133.
5. Ibid, p. 137.
6. Ibid, p. 136.

and modified Lazzarato's work. Accepting the premise that immaterial labour was now central to capital's survival (and, by extension, to projects that aimed at its extinction), Hardt and Negri identified three segments of immaterial labour:

a) the reshaped instances of industrial production which had embraced communication as their lifeblood;
b) the 'symbolic analysis and problem solving' undertaken by knowledge workers;
c) the affective labour found, above all, within the service sector.[7]

These experiences, it was conceded, could be quite disparate. Knowledge workers, for example, were divided between high-end practitioners with considerable control over their working conditions, while others were engaged in 'low-value and low-skill jobs of routine symbol manipulation'.[8] Nonetheless, a common thread existed between the three elements. As instances of service work, none of them produced a 'material or durable good'. Moreover, since the output was physically intangible as a discrete object, so the labour that produced it could be designated as immaterial.[9]

How can we make sense of such arguments? Doug Henwood, who praised *Empire* for the verve and optimism of its vision, was nonetheless moved to add:

> Hardt and Negri are often uncritical and credulous in the face of orthodox propaganda about globalization and immateriality [...] They assert that immaterial labour – service work, basically – now prevails over the old-fashioned material kind, but they don't cite any statistics: you'd never expect that far more Americans are truck drivers than are computer professionals. Nor would you have much of an inkling that three billion of us, half the earth's population, live in the rural Third World, where the major occupation remains tilling the soil.[10]

Nick Dyer-Witheford has likewise registered a number of concerns with Hardt and Negri's account of class composition.[11] To his mind, *Empire* glosses over the tensions between the three class fragments it identifies, while ultimately reading immaterial labour only through the lens of its high-end manifestations. And was all of this really as new as Hardt and Negri intimated? It's not as if 'affective labour', for instance, was anything but fundamental to social reproduction in the past, even if it did go unnoticed – because of its largely gendered composition, perhaps – in many social analyses.

7. Michael Hardt and Antonio Negri, *Empire*, Cambridge: Harvard University Press, 2000, p. 30.
8. Ibid, p. 292.
9. Ibid, p. 290.
10. Doug Henwood, *After the New Economy*, New York: New Press, 2003, pp. 184–5.
11. Nick Dyer-Witheford, 'Cyber-Negri: General Intellect and Immaterial Labour', *Resistance in Practice: The Philosophy of Antonio Negri*, London: Pluto Press, 2005, pp. 151–5.
12. Hardt and Negri, 2000, op. cit., p. 294.

Another issue concerns *Empire*'s insistence that 'the cooperative aspect of immaterial labour is not imposed or organised from the outside'.[12] Again, perhaps this is true for some high-end work. But does the obligation to ask, 'Do you want fries with that?' really represent a break with Fordist work regimes? Or might many of the McJobs that are prevalent in the lower depths of so-called immaterial production be better characterised as 'the Taylorised, deskilled descendants of earlier forms of office' and other service work?[13]

More recently, Hardt and Negri have attempted to address some of their critics in *Multitude*, the 2004 sequel to *Empire*. The first thing to note here is that, while immaterial labour remains a central pivot within the book's arguments, it is presented in a rather more cautious and qualified form than before. Indeed, Hardt and Negri are at pains to state that:

a) 'When we claim that immaterial labour is tending towards the hegemonic position we are not saying that most of the workers in the world today are producing primarily immaterial goods';
b) 'The labour involved in all immaterial production, we should emphasise, remains material – it involves our bodies and brains as all labour does. What is immaterial is its product.'[14]

Therefore, much like the ascendancy of the multitude itself, here the hegemony of immaterial labour as the reference point, or even vanguard, for 'most of the workers in the world today' is flagged as a tendency, albeit one that is inexorable. Toward the end of *Multitude*'s discussion of immaterial labour, Hardt and Negri insist upon what they call a 'reality check': '[W]hat evidence do we have to substantiate our claim of a hegemony of immaterial labour?'[15] It's the moment we've all been waiting for, and, unfortunately, the half a page discussion they proffer is something of a damp squib: an allusion to US Bureau of Statistics figures which indicate that service work is on the rise; the relocation of industrial production 'to subordinate parts of the world', said to signal the privileging of immaterial production at the heart of the Empire; the rising importance of 'immaterial forms of property' and, finally, the spread of network forms of organisation particular to immaterial labour.[16] Call me old fashioned, but something more than this is needed in a book of 400-plus pages dedicated to understanding their claims regarding the latest manifestation of the proletariat as a revolutionary subject.

Their reference to the growth in service sector activity is interesting for a number of reasons. Ursula Huws argues that the unrelenting rise in service work

13. Ursula Huws, *The Making of a Cybertariat*, New York: Monthly Review Press, 2003, p. 138.
14. Michael Hardt and Antonio Negri, *Multitude: War and Democracy in the Age of Empire*, New York: Penguin, 2004, p. 109.
15. Ibid, p. 114.
16. Ibid, p. 115.
17. Huws, op. cit., p. 130.

in the West might be cast in a different light if the domestic employment so common 100 years ago was factored into the equation.[17] Writing a decade earlier, Sergio Bologna suggested that certain forms of work only came to be designated as 'services' within national statistics *after* they had been outsourced; previously, when they had been performed 'in house', they had counted as 'manufacturing'.[18] Neither author is seeking to deny that important shifts have occurred within the global economy, starting with countries like Britain, Australia, Canada and the United States, yet they urge both caution in how we interpret the changes and advocate care in the categories used to explain them. Bologna – a collaborator of Negri's on a variety of political projects back in the 1960s and '70s – is particularly caustic about the notion of immaterial labour, labelling it a 'myth' that, more than anything else, obscures the lengthening of the working day.[19]

Goodbye to Value as Measure?

As stated earlier, one of the distinguishing features of post-workerism is the rejection of Marx's so-called 'law of value'. George Caffentzis reminds us that Marx himself rarely spoke of such a law, but there is also no doubt of his opinion that, under the rule of capital, the amount of labour time socially necessary to produce commodities ultimately determines their value.[20] In breaking with Marx in this regard, postworkerists draw some of their inspiration instead from a passage in the *Grundrisse* known as the 'Fragment on Machines'. This envisages a situation, in line with capital's perennial attempt to free itself from dependence upon labour, in which knowledge has become the lifeblood of fixed capital, and the direct input of labour to production is merely incidental. In these circumstances, Marx argues, capital effectively cuts the ground from under its own feet, for '[a]s soon as labour in the direct form has ceased to be the great well-spring of wealth, labour time ceases and must cease to be its measure, and hence exchange value [must cease to be the measure] of use value'.[21]

Negri, among others, has insisted for many years, and in a variety of ways, that capital has now reached this stage. Therefore, nothing but sheer domination keeps its rule in place: '[T]he logic of capital is no longer functional to development, but is simply a command for its own reproduction.'[22] In fact, a range of social commentators have evoked the 'Fragment on Machines' in recent times; apart from anything else, it has held a certain popularity amongst those (like reactionary futurologist Jeremy Rifkin) who tell us that we live in an increasingly

18. Sergio Bologna, 'Problematiche del lavoro autonomo in Italia (I)', *Altreragioni 1*, June 1992, pp. 20–1.
19. Ibid, pp. 22–4.
20. George Caffentzis, 'Immeasurable Value?: An Essay on Marx's Legacy', *The Commoner 10*, Spring–Summer 2005.
21. Karl Marx, *Grundrisse: Foundations of the Critique of Political Economy*, Hardmondsworth: Penguin, 1973, p. 705
22. Negri, 1994, op. cit., p. 28.
23. Marx, 1973, op. cit., p. 706.

work-free society. It's a pity, then, that few of these writers follow the logic of Marx's argument in the *Grundrisse* to its conclusions. For, while he indicates that capital does indeed seek 'to reduce labour time to a minimum', Marx also reminds us that capital is itself nothing other than accumulated labour time (abstract labour as value).[23] In other words, capital is obliged by its very nature, and for as long as we are stuck with it, to pose 'labour time [...] as sole measure and source of wealth.'

In its efforts to escape from labour, capital attempts a number of things that, each in their own way, fuel arguments that make labour time appear irrelevant as the measure of capital's development. Looked at more carefully, however, each can be seen in a somewhat different light. To begin with, capital tries as far as possible to externalise its labour costs: to take a banal example (although not so banal if you are a former bank employee), by encouraging online and teller machine banking and discouraging over-the-counter customer service. As for our own work regimes, many of us find ourselves bringing more and more work home (or on the train, or in the car). More and more of us also seem to be on standby, accessible through the net or by phone. Added together, such strategies (which, to add to the messiness of it all, may well intersect with our own individual aspirations for greater flexibility) go a long way towards explaining that blurring of the line between the 'work' and 'non work' components of our day that Hardt and Negri decry. On the other hand, they also cast that boundary in light other than that of the collapse of labour time as the measure of value, one in which – precisely because the quantity of labour time is crucial to capital's existence – as much labour as possible comes to be performed in its unpaid form.

Secondly, in seeking to decrease labour costs within individual organisations, capital also reshapes the process through which profits are distributed on a sectoral and global scale. In a number of essays over the past 15 years, Caffentzis has elaborated the idea, first outlined at some length in the third volume of *Capital*, that average rates of profit suck surplus value from labour-intensive sectors toward those with much greater investment in fixed capital:

> In order for there to be an average rate of profit throughout the capitalist system, branches of industry that employ very little labour but a lot of machinery must be able to have the right to call on the pool of value that high-labour, low-tech branches create. If there were no such branches or no such right, then the average rate of profit would be so low in the high-tech, low-labour industries that all investment would stop and the system would terminate. Consequently, 'new enclosures' in the countryside must accompany the rise of 'automatic processes' in industry, the computer requires the sweat shop, and the cyborg's existence is premised on the slave.[24]

24. George Caffentzis, 'Why Machines Cannot Create Value, Or Marx's Theory of Machines', *Cutting Edge: Technology, Information, Capitalism and Social Revolution*, London: Verso, 1997.

In this instance, if there *appears* to be no immediate correlation between the value of an individual commodity and the profit that it returns in the market, the answer may well be that there is none; the puzzle can only be solved by examining the sector as a whole, in a sweep that reaches far beyond the horizons of immaterial labour. Here, too, it's a matter of which parameters we choose to frame our enquiry.

Thirdly, and following on from the above, the division of labour in many organisations, industries and firms has reached the point where it is difficult – and probably pointless – to determine the contribution of an individual employee to the mass of commodities that they help to produce.[25] Again, this can foster the sense that the labour time involved in producing such commodities (whether tangible or not) is irrelevant to the value they contain. Marx, for his part, argued that the central question in making sense of all this was one of perspective:

> If we consider the aggregate *worker*, i.e. if we take all the members comprising the workshop together, then we see that their *combined activity* results materially in an *aggregate* product which is at the same time a *quantity of goods*. And here it is quite immaterial whether the job of a particular worker, who is merely a limb of this aggregate worker, is at a greater or smaller distance from the actual manual labour.[26]

In this regard, Huws' critique of notions of 'the weightless economy' deserves careful attention. Like Henwood in his fierce deconstruction of the 'new economy',[27] Huws draws our attention back not only to the massive infrastructure that underpins 'the knowledge economy' but also to 'the fact that real people with real bodies have contributed real time to the development of these "weightless" commodities'.[28] As for determining the contribution of human labour within the production of immaterial products, Huws argues that, while this might 'be difficult to model', that 'does not render the task impossible'. Or, in David Harvey's words, 'every day the personifications of capital – whether private or state – make judgements regarding value and its measure' in their efforts 'to reinforc[e] the connection between value and work'. He adds: 'Hardt and Negri may believe in the "impossibility of power's calculating and ordering production at a global level", but "power" hasn't stopped trying and the "impossibility" of its project derives directly from our own struggles against the reduction of life to measure.'[29]

25. David Harvey, 'All Labour is Productive and Unproductive', *The Commoner*, 10, Spring–Summer, 2005.
26. Karl Marx, 'Results of the Immediate Process of Production', *Capital Vol. I*, Hardmondsworth: Penguin, 1976; quoted by Harry Cleaver in *Reading Capital Politically*, Second Edition, Leeds: Anti/Theses, 2001.
27. Henwood, op. cit.
28. Huws, op. cit., pp. 142–3.
29. Harvey, op. cit., pp. 151–4.

Other Leads?

Not long ago, Dr. Woo pointed me to a presentation by Brian Holmes entitled 'Continental Drift, Or The Other Side of Neoliberal Globalisation'.[30] In large part, his talk is a reflection upon the arguments in Hardt and Negri's *Empire*, taking advantage of the hindsight provided by five years of events since the book's publication. For Holmes, many of the arguments advanced in *Empire* were important for challenging commonplace assumptions about how to make sense of the 'big picture' of global power relations, forcing a reconsideration of terms such as 'globalisation' and 'imperialism'. But, if the book helped in clearing away certain misconceptions, it has not been nearly so successful in supplanting them with more adequate ways of seeing.

'Continental Drift' addresses a host of issues, but Holmes makes three points which have great relevance to our current discussion. First, a privileged focus upon 'immaterial labour' is increasingly unsatisfactory for efforts to understand what is happening within contemporary class composition. Second, global events since the publication of *Empire* cast doubt upon the usefulness of seeing capital's domination as a smooth space that lacks centre(s). And, third, more attention has to be paid to the reasons why the world of finance has become such a crucial aspect of capital's rule in our time. Regarding the first point, Holmes offers some similar criticisms to those made by Dyer-Witheford. If the concept of immaterial labour is important for analysing certain kinds of work 'in the so-called tertiary or service sectors of the developed economies', talk of its hegemony can obscure not only 'the global division of labour', and thus 'the precise conditions under which people work and reproduce themselves', but also how 'they conceive their subordination and their possible agency, or their desires for change'. As for the second point, Holmes argues that global capitalism is better understood through the analysis of 'regional blocs' such as the European Union or the increasing engagement between China, Japan and South East Asia. Finally, he believes that a far better understanding is needed of the role of money – and of finance, above all – in capital's efforts to maintain its control at both the international and individual level (on this score, see also Loren Goldner's writings on fictitious capital).[31]

The richest explorations of regional blocs that I have encountered are those developed by 'world systems' analysts such as Immanuel Wallerstein, Giovanni Arrighi and Beverly Silver. Interestingly enough, their efforts to explain the emergence of a new cycle of global accumulation with its epicentre in Asia is intimately bound up with their attempt to understand why the expansion of money as capital has come so much to the fore over the past 30 years or so. For

30. Brian Holmes, 'Continental Drift, Or The Other Side of Neoliberal Globalization', 2005, http://info.interactivist.net/article.pl?sid=05/09/27/131214&mode=nocomment&tid=90
31. Loren Goldner, 'China In the Contemporary World Dynamic of Accumulation and Class Struggle', 2005, http://home.earthlink.net/~lrgoldner/china.html and Goldner, 'Fictitious Capital and the Transition out of Capitalism', 2005, http://home.earthlink.net/%7Elrgoldner/program.html

them, the predominance of financial expansion is symptomatic of a necessary phase in the cycle of accumulation, during which, as doubts mount about the profitability of production, industries are relocated, unemployed capital and labour pile up and 'a sharp acceleration of economic polarisation [occurs] both globally and within states'.[32] In recent times, Arrighi (who also penned one of the more considered reviews of *Empire*) has devoted much of his effort to understanding the waning fortunes of the US State and capital within this process,[33] while Silver has concentrated upon the prospects facing contemporary labour in an age of capital flight.[34] The work of these authors (much of which is on the net) is well worth a look, in part for the challenge it offers to a number of radical orthodoxies, and for the depth of analysis it brings to an account of the conflicts between, and within, the forces of labour and capital today.

There is still a great deal to unravel in the issues touched upon here. All the same, there are some useful leads as to where to go next. For example, the current centrality of money as capital, with all the peculiarities this entails, may offer another explanation for why it might appear that socially necessary labour time no longer has any bearing upon capital's existence as value in search of greater value. Speculative ventures – which have been rife in the past decade – seem to make money out of thin air. But, in actuality, they do nothing to increase the total pool of value generated by capital. At best, they redistribute what already exists. More uncertainly, they seek to sidestep the sphere of production and instead make money 'from betting on the future exploitation of labour'.[35] In the meantime, debt continues to balloon, from the micro scale of individual and family credit cards, to the macro level of public sector budgets and current account deficits. However ingeniously the burden of such debt is redistributed, the terms of the wager cannot be forestalled forever. When it is finally called in, things will become very interesting indeed. If nothing else, we may then find out at last whether or not, as Madonna sang,

> The boy with the cold hard cash
> Is always Mister Right, 'cause we are
> Living in a material world.

32. Immanuel Wallerstein, *The Decline of American Power*, New York: The New Press, 2003, p. 275.
33. Giovanni Arrighi, 'Hegemony Unravelling, Part 1', *New Left Review*, 32, March–April 2005.
34. Beverly Silver, *Forces of Labour*, Cambridge: Cambridge University Press, 2002.
35. Werner Bonefeld and John Holloway, 'Conclusion: Money and Class Struggle', *Global Capital, National State, and the Politics of Money*, New York: St. Martin's Press, 1995, pp. 213–4.

Thriving On Adversity: The Art of Precariousness

Anna Dezeuze

Vol 2 #3, Spring 2006

Walking around the immaculate spaces of the Guggenheim Museum in New York, I once came across a roughly built brick shelter, with two pillars and a roof, and a small shack with a large satellite dish. In an adjoining metal structure stood a single functioning toilet. In the reassuring bubble of an archetypical museum, the images of shanty town architecture and emergency refuges conjured by the basic components of this pared-down construction seemed very remote. The structure in front of me, I was informed by a wall-mounted text, corresponded to an existing type of core unit being built at the time in a far-away location: Kagiso, a suburb of Johannesburg. The artist, the Slovenian Marjetica Potrč, had just been awarded the 2000 Hugo Boss Prize.

Two years later, the Mexico-based, Belgian artist, Francis Alÿs, was short-listed for the same prize. His *Ambulantes (Pushing and Pulling)*, a slide series executed between 1992 and 2002, documents the astonishing range of street vendors, refuse collectors, deliverymen and salespeople walking around the streets of Mexico City, pushing and pulling loaded carts or wheeled stalls, and occasionally carrying loads on their heads.

Works such as Potrč's and Alÿs' point to a widespread interest, among artists and curators, in the precarious existence of shanty town dwellers and the millions of people across Third World cities whose mode of livelihood Mike Davis has described as 'informal survivalism'.[1] In order to address the apparent contradictions suggested by these works and by their appeal to official sponsors and institutions, I would like to sketch out some characteristic features of this trend and some of the problems it raises. Rather than providing a systematic overview, I will look in particular at the ways in which artists and curators have theorised this growing interest and explore a few of the perils and promises that precariousness holds for contemporary art today.

On Adversity We Thrive!

Potrč was one of the artists included in the exhibition, The Structure of Survival, at the 50th Venice Biennale in 2003. The Argentinean curator, Carlos Basualdo, chose to focus on the *favela*, or shanty town, as the guiding theme of an exhibition which featured more than 25 international artists. Basualdo's definition of the shanty towns as spaces of resistance, 'places in which original

1. Mike Davis, 'Planet of Slums: Urban Involution and the Informal Proletariat', *New Left Review*, 26, March–April 2004, p. 24.

forms of socialisation, alternative economies, and various forms of aesthetic agency are produced' has been echoed in other fields.[2] The philosopher, Slavoj Žižek, for example, believes that '[t]he new forms of social awareness that emerge from slum collectives will be the germs of the future and the best hope for a properly "free world"'.[3] Basualdo's ideas on this question developed more specifically from his engagement with the work of Brazilian artist, Hélio Oiticica, who, in 1967, coined the motto 'on adversity we thrive' (*'da adversidade vivemos'*).[4] For Oiticica, adversity was a condition of Third World countries, and should be the starting point for any Brazilian artist. Oiticica himself found inspiration for his work in the Brazilian popular culture of samba dancing and the shanty town architecture of the Rio favela of Mangueira.[5] In 2001, Basualdo appropriated Oiticica's motto as the title for an exhibition at the Musée d'Art Moderne de la Ville de Paris. Featured artists – among whom were Francis Alÿs as well as several who would subsequently figure in the Venice Biennale show – were discussed in terms of their experience of a Latin American reality characterised by 'constant precariousness' and 'adversity in tragically unstable socio-economic contexts'.[6]

If the critic, Guy Brett, described precariousness as a characteristic of Latin American art as early as 1989,[7] Basualdo's shows have contributed to the growing celebration of contemporary practices relating to issues of adversity and crisis. In our current, globalised world, as Basualdo has pointed out, crises operate beyond national boundaries and beyond distinctions between developing and developed countries.[8] Yet, rather than analyse the ways in which First World societies may be in a state of crisis, Basualdo, like many artists, has focused on the ongoing inventiveness of those who experience adversity first hand. The attraction of the precariousness of the 'developing world' for artists and curators seems to lie not in the situation of crisis itself as much as in the responses that it encourages. Potrč often speaks of the 'beauty' of slum architecture,[9] while Francis Alÿs marvels at the ways in which people in Mexico 'keep inventing themselves', like the man in his

2. Carlos Basualdo, 'On the Expression of the Crisis', *Dreams and Conflicts: The Dictatorship of the Viewer*, Venice: Biennale, 2003, p. 243.
3. Slavoj Žižek, 'Knee-Deep', *London Review of Books*, 26.17, 2 September 2004, p. 5, http://www.lrb.co.uk/v26/n17/print/zize01_.html
4. Oiticica used this motto in one of his works, a Parangolé cape, and included it in a manifesto-like text written on the occasion of the exhibition Nova Objetividade Brasileira at the Museum of Modern Art in Rio de Janeiro.
5. I have written about Oiticica's relationship to Brazilian popular culture in 'Tactile Dematerialisation, Sensory Politics: Hélio Oiticica's Parangolés', *Art Journal*, Summer 2004, Vol. 63, no. 2, pp. 58–71.
6. Carlos Basualdo, 'A propos de l'adversité', in *Da Adversidade Vivemos*, Paris: Musée d'Art Moderne de la Ville de Paris, 2001, p. 13.
7. Guy Brett, 'A Radical Leap', in *Art in Latin America, The Modern Era, 1820–1980*, London: Hayward Gallery, 1989, p. 255.
8. Carlos Basualdo, op. cit., pp. 243–4.
9. Marjetica Potrč, 'Urban, 2001', *Marjetica Potrč: Next Stop*, Kiosk, Moderna Galerija Ljubljana Museum of Art, 2003, p. 31.

neighbourhood who spends his day cleaning the gaps between the pavement flagstones with a bent wire.[10] The Turkish artist collective, Oda Projesi, who were included in The Structure of Survival, seem to summarise a widespread, if often implicit, belief when they explain that inhabitants of the prefabricated houses erected after the 1999 Adapazari earthquake 'construct these annexes by choosing the materials in accordance with their own conditions and needs, just like an artist or an architect'.[11] Similarly, both Alÿs and Potrč have celebrated the ways in which people occupy space in an unplanned fashion and erect shelters spontaneously. In 2003, Potrč exhibited a 'growing house' from a Caracas shanty town at the Palais de Tokyo in Paris. The 'iron wires sprouting from its rooftop', according to her, 'proclaim the vitality of the place.'[12] In 1994, Alÿs pieced together electoral posters declaring *viviendas por todos* (housing for all) in order to create a shelter-like structure fastened over a subway air duct in Mexico City. 'It was a direct comment on the state of local politics and at the same time an attempt to recreate these cells of squatters that I encountered everywhere in the city', he has explained.[13] Perhaps unsurprisingly, both Alÿs and Potrč come from an architectural background. Urban planning is their frame of reference, and their concerns with precariousness mirror the emerging attraction among architects to the hitherto unmapped slums of Third World cities.

The abandonment and neglect experienced by, to use Mike Davis' term, the 'informal proletariat' seems to be conceived by artists such as Alÿs and Potrč as a kind of freedom. In a 1990 essay, Guy Brett explained that, in Latin America, 'many grass-roots movements have appeared because of a complete loss of faith in the willingness or ability of governments to do anything about major problems'.[14] Many activists and non-governmental organisations in the West would recognise themselves in this description, and Latin American grassroots movements have been models for similar groupings elsewhere. For Potrč, there is a direct parallel between NGOs and shanty towns: both have been '[g]rowing without any control or planning' and both, according to the artist, embody our aspirations, dreams and ideals.[15]

In the catalogue for The Structure of Survival, Basualdo invited a group of Argentinean activists, Colectivo Situaciones, to write about responses to the devastating economic crisis in their country. Like many such groups, Colectivo Situaciones explain that their type of revolution differs from traditional 'modern emancipatory politics' in that they do not seek to gain state power. Instead, they are concerned with finding concrete means of self-sufficiently

10. 'La Cour des Miracles: Francis Alÿs in conversation with Corinne Diserens', *Francis Alÿs: Walking Distance from the Studio*, Wolfsburg: Kunstmuseum Wolfsburg, 2004, pp. 100–1.
11. Oda Projesi, 'Annex' on http://www.odaprojesi.com
12. Marjetica Potrč, 'In and out of Caracas', *Marjetica Potrč*, op. cit., p. 83.
13. 'La Cour des Miracles', op. cit., p. 109.
14. Guy Brett, 'Border Crossings', *Transcontinental: Nine Latin American Artists*, Birmingham: Ikon, 1990, p. 16.
15. Marjetica Potrč, 'Urban, 2001', *Marjetica Potrč*, op. cit., p. 31.

managing resources and of affirming common values of solidarity and sociability.[16] Similarly, Potrč believes that '[t]he world we live in today is all about self-reliance, individual initiative, and small-scale projects'.[17] This corresponds to a widespread belief that the utopias of the past, the grand narratives of 'emancipatory politics', remain forever unattainable. Potrč focuses on 'small gestures, not big ones',[18] while Alÿs, according to one critic, 'moves as an artist who has come to understand that the only thing left to do is to take small steps'.[19] Potrč does not wish to change anything; she claims she is interested in analysing, without judging, the 'facts of contemporary urban life'.[20] Alÿs, for his part, explains that Mexican society 'is a society that is governed by compromise' and that he has adopted compromise as the very modus operandi of his work.[21]

Neither Potrč nor Alÿs, however, perceive this resignation and compromise pessimistically. Like Colectivo Situaciones, they reject 'the idea that the omnipotence of market flows (with the wars that accompany them) leave no space for any struggles for liberation' and believe that it is 'possible that power and its opposition can coexist long term without eliminating one another'.[22] In this sense, their outlook brings to mind Michel de Certeau's analysis of everyday life as containing in itself the potential means through which to subvert the dominant order from within. 'Making do' – 'faire avec' – is, in fact, the title of a chapter in de Certeau's 1980 book entitled *The Practice of Everyday Life*. Alÿs' *Ambulantes* seem to embody de Certeau's idea that practitioners of everyday life constantly tinker 'within the dominant cultural economy in order to adapt it to their own interests and their own rules'.[23] On the one hand, Alÿs' photographs literally demonstrate practical tricks – such as how one can fit 14 cardboard boxes onto one small, hand-pulled cart. On the other hand, they point to the range of petty jobs that inhabitants of Third World countries have to keep inventing to survive and to find a useful function in a chaotic economy. As job precariousness has also become a concern for activist groups in First World countries – since 'jobs for life' are becoming a thing of the past – Alÿs' slide show immediately chimes with global struggles in the age of micropolitics.

16. Colectivo Situaciones, 'Through the Crisis and Beyond: Argentina', *Dreams and Conflicts: The Dictatorship of the Viewer*, Venice: Biennale, 2003, p. 245.
17. Marjetica Potrč, 'Back to Basics: Objects and Buildings', *Marjetica Potrč*, op. cit., p. 54.
18. Marjetica Potrč, 'Take Me to Shantytown', *Flash Art*, March–April 2001, p. 98.
19. Annelie Lütgens, 'Francis Alÿs and the Art of Walking', *Francis Alÿs: Walking Distance from the Studio*, Wolfsburg: Kunstmuseum Wolfsburg, 2004, p. 56.
20. 'Tracking the Urban Animal', *Circa*, Autumn 2001, no. 97, p. 29.
21. 'La Cour des Miracles', op. cit., p. 112.
22. Colectivo Situaciones, op. cit., p. 245.
23. Michel de Certeau, *The Practice of Everyday Life*, Berkeley and London: University of California Press, 1984, p. xiv.

Making Do

One of the problems with the discourse of precarity is the conflation of a wide variety of situations, ranging from the illegal immigrant working as a cleaner or the employee in a call centre, to the freelance web designer or the projectionist at the Cannes Film Festival.[24] It is precisely this kind of confusion that can occur when precariousness is used as a privileged theme in contemporary art. Within this conflation, the emphasis on precariousness runs the risk of erasing crucial differences at the same time as it tries to bring together a disparate group in order to promote a specific argument. Basualdo's Da Adversidade Vivemos and The Structure of Survival certainly included a wide range of practices under the umbrella of crisis and adversity. Fernanda Gomes' installations, which were included in both exhibitions, display a vocabulary of simple, sometimes fragile, everyday objects casually placed on the floor, hung or propped within an empty space. While these discrete and ephemeral arrangements evoke precariousness and instability, they seem far removed from the realities of everyday life in Latin American slums. Condemning Gomes' works for not having the same urgency as the works of some of her compatriots would be falling into the trap of asking them to conform to some kind of Latin American stereotype. Claiming that these works are about survival or that they propose a model for a new type of ethical art would suggest, however, that precariousness is in itself subversive.

This problematic slippage can be better understood when reading statements by artists such as Potrč or Alÿs who speak of their work in terms of the 'human condition'. Potrč justifies her placement of shanty town architecture as 'case-studies' in galleries by explaining that galleries are 'places where we think [about] the human condition',[25] whereas Alÿs claims he is 'trying to suggest this absolute acceptance of the "human condition"' by the people he sees struggling every day in his neighbourhood.[26] While the implications of Potrč's and Alÿs' works can indeed be extended from their locally specific origin to encompass wider reflections on human finitude and inventiveness in the face of death, the logic that inflects Basualdo's readings of Gomes' work operates in reverse; installations that suggest a general sense of instability, transience or fragility, he seems to suggest, must de facto be related to the particularly precarious social and economic conditions of living in Latin America. I believe that this logic is erroneous, and that these distinctions remain crucial. There are substantial variations among artists working in different countries, and, even within the same country, distinctions should be highlighted among social and ethnic groups, as well as successive generations of Latin American artists. Unlike Basualdo, I would like to emphasise the gap that separates Oiticica's 1960s oeuvre from some of the younger Brazilian artists,

24. For an overview of debates regarding job precarity, see 'Precarious Reader', *Mute*, Vol 2 #0, 2005.
25. Marjetica Potrč, 'Take Me to Shantytown', op. cit., p. 98.
26. 'La Cour des Miracles', op. cit., p. 83.

whose works betray the influence of the growing internationalisation of the art market. An instance of this shift can be seen in Alexandre da Cunha's work, which was included in The Structure of Survival. By displaying cheap objects (such as sleeping bags, raincoats and plastic brooms) to create shelter-like arrangements, da Cunha seems to me to be using conventional, trivial signifiers of precariousness in a way that aestheticises, rather than embodies or analyses, the nature of this condition. The creation of a 'slum chic' will no doubt find echoes in contemporary fashion and design trends. It is hard to find here even the slightest echoes of the existential precariousness hinted at by Gomes' ontological evocation of human finitude.

Where da Cunha seems to aestheticise the signifiers of precariousness, the Angolan artist, Antonio Ole, also included in The Structure of Survival, seems to be aestheticising precariousness itself. By arranging the found fragments of an impoverished architecture along the walls of the gallery in his *Township Wall*, Ole makes poverty look cheerful and picturesque. This points to a second major pitfall in the exploration of practices of 'making do' and thriving on adversity. This is a problem that Alÿs himself encountered when he was planning a film which sought to illustrate the virtue of *valemadrismo*, the Mexicans' 'capacity to accommodate oneself to *mala fortuna*, to bad luck, and even more, to actually turn one's misfortune into an advantage'.[27] This film was to tell the story of a dog called Negrito who lost a leg, but went on to develop a very successful juggling trick using the bone of its broken leg. Although Alÿs has not given the reasons why he abandoned this film, he admits that it was a 'somewhat romanticised account', and my guess is that he became wary of this, for celebrating *valemadrismo* can lead to an occlusion of the suffering itself, and perhaps even to a lapse back into a primitivising stereotype of the carefree, cheerful pauper who accepts his condition without protest. Calls such as David Aradeon's, reproduced in the catalogue for The Structure of Survival, to remember that inhabitants of Brazilian shanty towns are 'poor but vibrant, sensitive and creative', can easily slip into a confirmation of such romanticising stereotypes.[28]

Such problems, I would like to argue, take us back to the crux of precariousness and its existence at the junction of crises and reactions, of adversity and coping strategies. At the heart of this articulation lie two much broader issues. The first concerns the politics of the slums themselves. I mentioned earlier how Žižek has suggested that slum dwellers constitute the new proletariat, the agents of the next revolutionary challenge to capital. However, not everyone shares his optimism. Davis, for example, argues that, up until now, the dominant political force in the slums has been organised religion; survival rather than protest has

27. Ibid, p. 85.
28. David Aradeon, 'Are We Reading Our Shanty Towns Correctly?', *Dreams and Conflicts: The Dictatorship of the Viewer*, Venice: Biennale, 2003, p. 264.
29. Mike Davis, op. cit., pp. 28–34.

remained – perhaps unsurprisingly – the main agenda of this 'informal proletariat'.[29] Thus, the activity of 'making do' could, in itself, turn out to be more conservative than revolutionary, as millions of people struggle to make it through another day with little possibility of making organised and effective demands. In this sense, Alÿs' interest in the Mexicans' 'absolute acceptance' of their condition could be read as a call for passivity rather than action. In order to contradict this narrative and glimpse some potential change, it would be useful to further explore the grassroots model of micropolitics and the potential for change once the traditional revolutionary seizure of state power has been set aside in favour of 'self-reliance, individual initiative, and small-scale projects', to use Potrč's terms. Colectivo Situaciones, after all, still believe in a 'struggle for liberation'. The question remains whether, and how, the model of effective reaction, which they have substituted for the Marxist call for action, can ultimately lead to such liberation.

The second issue raised by the politics of 'making do' is the question of agency. George Yúdice has criticised de Certeau's notion of subversive tactics because they 'are wielded not only by workers but by the very same managers (and other elites) who reinforce the established order'.[30] In order to reveal the subversive potential of everyday life, it is necessary to 'distinguish among the practitioners of such tactics in terms of how the tactics enable them to survive and [to] challenge their oppressibility'.[31]

Toward a 'Coalition'?

In order to navigate these distinctions, I would like to finally turn to Žižek's definition of the slum dwellers of the world as the 'counter-class to the other newly emerging class, the so-called "symbolic class" (managers, journalists and PR people, academics, artists, etc.) which is also uprooted and perceives itself as universal'.[32] This definition, which effectively updates Marx's social analysis, seems to me to avoid the conflation of different kinds of precarious work in discourses about job security, while acknowledging a relationship that can be fruitful. Crucially, Žižek asks: 'Is this the new axis of class struggle, or is the "symbolic class" inherently split, so that one can make a wager on the coalition between the slum dwellers and the "progressive" part of the symbolic class?'[33] My contention here is that some artists can indeed occupy the 'progressive' place of a symbolic class trying to forge a coalition in the arena of art and discourse. If the celebration of 'making do' tactics can be recuperated by a conservative discourse of passivity and conformism, it can also, nevertheless, contain the seeds of a globalised discourse of protest, as long as the agents

30. George Yúdice, 'Marginality and the Ethics of Survival', *Social Text*, 1989, no. 21, p. 216.
31. Ibid, p. 217.
32. Slavoj Žižek, op. cit., p. 5.
33. Loc. cit.

of this coalition and their respective needs for empowerment are clearly distinguished. Once the utopias of the left have been set aside, the objective for many artists today is to find ways of bringing this coalition to light by eschewing the risks of voyeurism or romanticism. Potrč's rejection of 1980s social activism, as reinforcing the marginalisation of the homeless and the poor, is premised on a belief that artists need to move away from traditional models of critique in order to explore a model of the coalition based on empathy.[34] Alÿs' adoption of compromise as a guiding force for the redefinition of artistic practice offers a similarly empathetic model through which to relate to the subjects with whom he coexists in Mexico City. Other modes of coalition are being explored by contemporary artists, whether in traditional forms of documentary or activist reportage, or, for example, in the provocative alienation set up by Santiago Sierra's performances, which dramatise the radical differences between the informal proletariat and bourgeois art viewers.

Ultimately, the deep ambivalence that I experienced when I encountered Potrč's shelters in the white cube of the gallery points to the final, inevitable question for artists investigating precariousness: Can the rarefied conditions of display and reception in the contemporary art world really provide a platform for the exploration of political alternatives? Can art be a credible space in which to foreground this potentially revolutionary 'coalition between slum dwellers and the "progressive" part of the symbolic class'? How artists manage to articulate this coalition within the framework of the current art world, and to what effect, constitutes one of the most interesting questions of contemporary art. It also happens to be one of the more urgent questions for society at large – especially if we agree with Potrč that when '[y]ou lose sight of your dreams, you die'.[35]

34. 'Tracking the Urban Animal', op. cit., p. 29.
35. Marjetica Potrč, 'Urban, 2001', *Marjetica Potrč*, op. cit., p. 31.

The Factory Without Walls

Brian Ashton

Vol 2 #4, Winter 2006

Information Technology has enabled capital to coordinate the production of commodities like never before. It is a seeming contradiction: production is spread across the globe, parts are made here and there and moved thousands of kilometres to be assembled, but this process produces more commodities than ever before. Capital has renewed itself yet again, and, in the process, it has thrown the left into crisis. While the talk among intellectuals is of immaterial labour and precarity, capital is busy ironing out the kinks in its new system of production. At the same time, though, it is creating a communication system that enables workers to interact with each other across national borders and continents. Just about every worker is now an IT worker, and it is the potential that lies in this fact that poses the greatest threat to capital. It is not about immaterial or material labour. The intellectuals have got to stop creating hierarchies of labour, the mass worker and the social worker, the immaterial worker and the precariat. They would be better employed getting a proper understanding of how the supply chain – some capitalists call it the virtual enterprise – now works. Know thine enemy, as Sun Tzu said in *The Art of War.*

A team of researchers from the Cardiff Business School studied the chain of actions required to make a can of cola. The whole process, starting at a bauxite mine in Australia and ending with the can in somebody's refrigerator, took no less than 319 days. Of that time, only three hours were spent on manufacturing, the rest was spent on transport and storage. An advertisement for the shipping company, P&O Nedlloyd, claims that the journey of one single container can involve, literally, a hundred people. These range from the guy who loaded the container to the IT people, from the logistics planners to the dockers, from the haulage drivers to the warehouse workers, from the customs officer to the captain of the ship. This highlights time and labour. The control of these two factors is the major concern for those charged with the management of supply chains.

As the Cardiff Business School study highlights, logistics is a major factor in the supply chain. According to the Council of Logistics Management, logistics is 'the process of planning, implementing and controlling the efficient effective flow and storage of raw materials, process inventory, finished goods, extraction/production to the point of consumption'.

In the last 20 years, there has been a revolution in the world of logistics, a revolution that seems to have escaped the attention of the autonomous left. The cause of this upheaval was the application of technology to the globalisation of commodity production, or, as Marx put it in *Capital, Vol.1*:

> A radical change in the mode of production in one sphere of industry involves a similar change in other spheres. This happens at first in such branches of industry as are connected together by being separate phases of a process, and yet are isolated by the social division of labour, in such a way that each of them produces an independent commodity [...] But more especially, the revolution in the modes of production of industry and agriculture made necessary a revolution in the general conditions of the social process of production, i.e. in the means of communication and transport [...] The means of communication and transport were so utterly inadequate to the productive requirements of the manufacturing period, with its extended division of social labour, its concentration of the instruments of labour, and of the workmen and its colonial markets, that they became in fact revolutionised [...] And in the period of 'modern industry' the means of communication and transport handed down from the manufacturing period became impediments.

Autonomist Marxism sees the struggle of the working class as the driver of capitalist development. In the '70s, capital started to attack the concentrations of working class power that some have called the mass worker. It did this on three fronts: It started to break up the rigidities imposed on production by working class militancy using technology to de-skill the workers and reconfigure the factory layout; it started to relocate some productive capacity to smaller sites, subcontracting the work to other companies, and it used the state to impose crisis upon the working class. It was largely successful in its project and, as the '80s developed, defeat followed defeat for the working class. A political composition forged in battle was dismantled and discarded. It seems to this old car industry worker that it wasn't only capital that discarded us but that quite a number of communist intellectuals turned their backs on us, too. The consequence is that we now have a generation of anti-capitalists who don't know how to engage with the working class. Despite being surrounded by the class, they seem more interested in what goes on in the Mexican jungle, or prefer to go to Genoa and Seattle and give the state machine an opportunity to practice crowd control.

In the '60s and '70s, there was constant interaction between working class militants and the left emerging from the universities. This wasn't always positive, but where there was a synergy; theory and practice had some connection. We learned from each other and good work was produced. Here in Britain, work published by Solidarity and Big Flame is evidence of that. In Italy, Potere Operaio and Lotta Continua helped to develop an understanding of the strengths and weaknesses of capital's composition. Today, we may talk about a globalised production system, but how many of us can describe how it works? How does the can of cola get from A to Z? In the '70s, we knew how the factory and the transport systems worked, and in that knowledge lay our ability to combat capital. Today, it is certainly difficult to grasp exactly how things are made, but it is imperative that we gain deep knowledge of the processes of production and logistics, the supply chains of capital or, to put it another way, the factories without walls. Some capitalists see the supply chain as a virtual factory and want workers to relate to the supply chain rather than perceiving themselves as employees of the separate organisations that make up the chain.

Working class composition comes from struggle, but first capitalists have to bring the workers together and impose the discipline of production upon them. In the present period, we can only understand how that discipline is imposed if we take a global approach. The technical composition of capital is spread across the world, as are the workers in the commodity's supply chain. Discipline under such a system is imposed through the application of *kaizen* (continuous improvement) and just-in-time stock delivery, combined with the application of information technologies that police the workers' productivity.

This is reinforced by the change in how commodities are moved through the system. Capital has moved from a push to a pull economy; in other words, it is making things that are being demanded rather than making them to forecast demand. The motto of the pull economy could be, 'If it isn't sold, don't make another one.' The pull economy gives the big supermarket chains enormous power because they control the information that pulls a commodity through the supply chain. When you buy a tin of beans in ASDA, the information is sent out to all those along the chain in order for another tin of beans to be produced. Of course, millions of such pieces of information are flying through cyberspace every moment of the day. One of the results of the pull economy is an increase in precarious work: if demand is down, then workers are laid off. Companies have computer programs that calculate the number of workers needed to satisfy a given demand, drawing in extra workers from a pool of casual labour often supplied by employment agencies. And they increasingly outsource non core activities to service companies; this is one of the reasons for the mushrooming of the logistics industry in these last years. The automotive industry is moving to a pull economy model, and this is one of the main reasons autoworkers in the US are being battered at the moment.

If you spread your supply chains across the globe and reduce your stock levels to just-in-time, then you increase the importance of the logistical exercise in the completion of the cycle of accumulation. At the same time, you increase the possibility of effective working class struggle: When the truckers on the West coast of the US went on strike a year or so ago, they paralysed the supply chains of Wal-Mart and other chain store giants, sending waves of panic through many a boardroom. The importance of logistics cannot be over-estimated; try imagining the supply chain of any product without the logistical input. The globalisation of production has left many workers believing they can do nothing about it – when companies move production to China or India, they stand hypnotised by the lights on the capitalist juggernaut as it runs them over – but this apparent strength of multinational capital is, in fact, its weakness.

Historically, logistics workers have been carriers of radical thought and transporters of the news of working class struggles. They have, of course, been involved in many a battle themselves. In the last 20 years, many of those battles have been defensive – fighting to save jobs and maintain working conditions. The withdrawal of the state from the direct management of the logistics industry was the catalyst for a global attack that continues to this day. As the state withdrew, private capital stepped into the breech and attacked workforces throughout the industry. At the same time, these companies have been engaged in a frenzy of mergers and acquisitions that have resulted in the emergence of truly global organisations employing many thousands of workers.

Some idea of the size of these companies can be gleaned from two examples: United Parcel Services (UPS) and Deutsche Post (DP). UPS is a $33.5 billion company that operates in 200 countries and employs more than 340,000 workers. It provides transportation and freight logistics/distribution, international trade, financial services, financial mail facilities and consultancy services. It has grown by benefiting from the outsourcing processes that are common in industry and by acquiring other companies. It plays for big stakes; it bought the Fritz freight company for $450 million. DP is partly owned by the German government, which holds 41.6 percent of the shares. These will be sold to institutional investors over the next few years. DP runs the German postal service, owns DHL and last year, it bought the British registered company Exel. Exel was previously an acquisitive company; it had previously bought Tibbett & Britten, the seventh biggest logistics company in the world. This resulted in a company employing more than 103,000 people.

The Jaguar auto plant in Halewood on Merseyside can perhaps give us an idea of how a supply chain works and how logistics fit into the chain. Halewood was where Ford built the Escort, and where this proletarian worked for seven long years. It was regarded as the basket case of the Ford organisation, and the threat of closure was always hanging over it. Ford bought Jaguar and decided to manufacture Jags at Halewood while, at the same time, it decided to radically alter working practices in the plant. It brought in an American company called Senn-Delaney to change the mindset of the workforce, and it appears to have been successful because Halewood is now regarded as the best car plant in Europe. If such a company had been brought in during the '70s, their work would have been challenged by counter-information from the left.

When I worked in Halewood in the '70s, there were 14,000 of us employed on the site. Today Jaguar employs some 2,800 people, but this figure is deceptive because a sizeable chunk of the work has been hived off to suppliers which, in turn, pass some of the work on to smaller suppliers. In a supply chain, firms are categorised thus: Original Equipment Manufacturer (OEM), i.e. Jaguar; First Tier Supplier, i.e. Bosch; the smaller suppliers are called Second Tier, Third Tier, etc. Linking all these together are the logistics companies. At Halewood, UCI Logistics, a subsidiary of the Japanese company Nippon Yusen Kaisha (NYK), runs the logistical set-up. As lead logistics supplier, UCI is responsible for inbound logistics to Halewood as well as the internal logistics at the plant itself. In the Ford days, internal logistics would have been carried out by Ford workers. The inbound logistics service involves a supply chain operation and the collection of parts and sub-assemblies from suppliers around Europe, partly using their own fleet and partly using UCI Logistics-appointed partners. The internal logistics service involves offloading parts, movement of components to storage areas and making them available to the production lines without incurring line-side storage. It is also UCI's task to ensure that line-side stock never exceeds the two-hour volume Jaguar has stipulated. It is UCI workers who drive the forklift trucks that transfer material within the Halewood plant.

Let's look at the logistics of a particular product going into Halewood: the wheel and tyre assemblies. UCI moves 500,000 assemblies a year into Halewood. The contract includes both external logistics for the supply of alloy wheels from Italy to Pirelli's facility in the UK, and the delivery of completed assemblies to Halewood three times a day, together with the internal logistics at the Jaguar site. UCI chooses from 12 different types of assemblies on receiving automated instructions from Jaguar and delivers the product to the point of fit. The mass worker hasn't been destroyed, he or she has just been reconfigured.

Capital gets its power from the extraction of surplus value, and the supply chain is the factory without walls where this process takes place. In the past, socialists organised and agitated around the centres of commodity production – one thinks of the work done around Fiat's Mirafiori factory in Turin and Big Flame's efforts at Dagenham and Halewood – but is that sort of work going on today? If such agitation is to take place, it will have to be on a global scale. And the technology exists to do it. By going global with its supply chains, capital is creating the opportunity for global working class struggle. In order for such struggles to succeed, we need to know how the present composition of capital works. The craft worker and the mass worker knew how the system produced commodities in their day; we need to develop such knowledge today.

Take Me I'm Yours: Neoliberalising the Cultural Institution

Anthony Davies

Vol 2 #5, Spring/Summer 2007

Just prior to a workshop in which they had been invited to participate – as part of the conference, Another Relationality, at the Museu d'Art Contemporani de Barcelona (MACBA) – local activist collective, ctrl-i, issued a public declaration of withdrawal, accusing MACBA of complicity with the very neoliberal imperatives it purported to critique. On the surface at least, their statement – including the trenchant line, 'Talking about precariousness in the McBa is like taking a nutrition seminar at McDonald's' – had the hallmarks of a typical struggle against institutionalisation. But there was one key difference: ctrl-i is partly made up of temp workers formerly employed by the museum, and not, as might be expected, an unaligned or 'autonomous' body resisting co-optation. It was, moreover, their knowledge and critique of precarious labour conditions and cultural neoliberalisation in Barcelona that was to form the basis of their contribution. The collective had been born in direct response to an earlier MACBA event, El Precariat Social Rebel, at which, under the auspices of activist network, The Chainworkers, they spoke out against the museum's dubious employment practices and later gave up their jobs in circumstances that remain largely unclear.[1] While ctrl-i's unique status as temp workers and local activists may have prompted the invitation from MACBA, it also gave the group licence to dramatise Another Relationality's underlying themes in an emphatic act of withdrawal.[2]

To understand the context for this signal act of protest on the part of a group of culture sector workers, and to give a material basis to the discussions on institutionalisation currently taking place in publications such as *Art Monthly* and *Mute*, we first need to look at the uneven process of neoliberal restructuring as it courses its way through cultural and educational institutions.[3] According to Marxist geographer, David Harvey, neoliberalism's trademark rhetoric – that

1. Email correspondence with ctrl-i, August 2006. According to ctrl-i's account of their relations with the museum's temporary employment agency, Serveis Educatius Ciut'art, SL, some of those who had spoken out against the museum were removed from their contracted positions in the 'guided tour' programme and placed in other, less publicly engaged, roles. Within two months, all had left the museum. As temporary workers, none had recourse to claiming 'constructive' or unfair dismissal. In UK law, constructive dismissal is where an employee is moved to resign due to their employer's behaviour (and this can range from the interpersonal, harassment, etc. to the structural, where the nature or description of the job changes). See http://en.wikipedia.org/wiki/Constructive_dismissal For an online account of ctrl-i's relation to MACBA and their withdrawal letter, see http://www.metamute.org/en/node/7469 and i-manifest at http://sindominio.net/ctrl-i/invert_and_subvert.html
2. The invitation to ctrl-i to participate in the Another Relationality (Part 2) workshops was made by MACBA and Marcello Expósito on behalf of the now disbanded Faculty for Radical Aesthetics, an offshoot of the European Institute for Progressive Cultural Policies (EIPCP). See the call for applications at: https://lists.resist.ca/pipermail/aut-op-sy/2005-June/004311.html

human well-being is contingent on developing individual entrepreneurial freedoms, chiefly the freedom to operate in the market – should be contrasted with the unprecedented 'creative' destruction that accompanies neoliberal reform. In *A Brief History of Neoliberalism*, Harvey describes how this process results in an erosion of existing social relations, ways of life and thought, as the market gradually penetrates and puts to work the 'common sense' way that many of us live in, and engage with, the world. The state's role becomes principally that of ensuring the proper functioning of markets, setting up institutional frameworks which ultimately guarantee the 'maintenance, reconstitution and restoration of elite class power'. It is difficult to track these developments across different regional and national contexts, however, and this is exacerbated by the multi-faceted, hybrid and localised manner in which they unfold, another symptom/condition of the process Harvey terms 'uneven geographical development'.[4]

Where do state-funded cultural and educational institutions fit into all this? What role do they play? At a point at which many have been set to work by capital in ever more 'innovative' (read: commercialised) ways, a host of contradictions and antagonisms have surfaced. While some now openly promote the liberating capacity of new revenue streams linked to consultancy, outsourcing, business incubation and enterprise activities, others seek more tactical models of engagement, looking to new constituencies and standards of practice to offset the crisis of legitimation which opens up as institutions are subjected to neoliberal agendas.

An attempt to address some of these issues in the European cultural sector can be found in *European Cultural Policies 2015: A Report with Scenarios on the Future of Public Funding for Contemporary Art in Europe.*[5] This publication acted as the cornerstone of the International Artists' Studio Program in Sweden's (IASPIS) contribution to the Frieze Art Fair, 2005. Against the backdrop of an earlier rejected proposal to the Frieze Foundation, state-funded IASPIS decided to pursue a more general enquiry into the cultural and political questions opened up by their compromised participation in the fair, focusing specifically on its exemplary and problematic identity as a 'public-private partnership'.[6]

3. This article is based on a text originally commissioned by *Art Monthly*, in which debate on institutionalisation and so-called 'New Institutionalism' has been developed through Dave Beech's 'Institutionalisation For All' (March 2006, no. 294), Peter Suchin's 'On Institutionalisation' (April 2006, no. 295), Lisa Le Feuvre's 'The Institution Within' (June 2006, no. 297) and Jakob Jakobsen's 'Self-Institutionalisation' (July–Aug 2006, no. 298), as well as the conference Worlds Within Worlds: the Institutions of Art, July 2006 (http://www.artmonthly.co.uk/institutions.htm)
4. David Harvey, *A Brief History of Neoliberalism*, Oxford: Oxford University Press, 2005, pp. 87–119.
5. *European Cultural Policies 2015: A Report with Scenarios on the Future of Public Funding for Contemporary Art in Europe* was commissioned as part of Frieze Projects and distributed free of charge at the Frieze Art Fair in October 2005. The report is also available as a pdf file at http://www.iaspis.com and http://www.eipcp.net
6. Maria Lind, 'Introduction', *European Cultural Policies 2015*. The previous year, IASPIS had an artists-commission project proposal rejected by Frieze Foundation. The Foundation is supported by Arts Council England and the Culture 2000 programme. The 2005 Frieze Projects were commissioned in association with Cartier and supported by Arts & Business and Calouste Gulbenkian Foundation. See http://eipcp.net/policies/2015/lind/en

In collaboration with the European Institute for Progressive Cultural Policies (EIPCP) and London-based design group, Åbäke, IASPIS went on to commission reports from eight local experts on key social, political and economic determinants of cultural policy in seven regions across the EU. The reports integrated hypothetical scenarios of what the cultural landscape might look like in 2015, as well as introductions by IASPIS director, Maria Lind, and EIPCP director, Gerald Raunig. These latter two texts illustrate the grand ambitions of the project: to influence – and possibly reform – European cultural policy and to strengthen 'radical-reformist elements of the cultural-political discourse in Europe'.[7]

In spite of – or rather, because of – its political ambitions, *European Cultural Policies 2015*'s focus on the meshing of the state, its institutional apparatus and the market elides any significant debate on class power within art institutions themselves and across the commercial sectors with which they interact. This makes the underlying economic disparities and antagonisms associated with neoliberalism's specific mode of 'uneven development' impossible to gauge. It also obscures the interests of those whom the report's findings ultimately serve.

Along with the policy minutiae, however, we do get an insight into the inter-institutional faultlines opening up across Europe. The report's account of the breakdown of Frieze/IASPIS' earlier collaboration, and the subsequent soul-searching undertaken by IASPIS director, Maria Lind, and her colleagues, is symptomatic of such conflicts. 'Progressive' institutional voices – mostly those in the upper echelons (directors, key administrators and curators) – in conjunction with a new type of defector academic/activist 'communication consultant to the prince' look for new operational models to open up a critical engagement with the institution's complicity in cultural neoliberalisation.[8] Lind's introduction to *2015* registers IASPIS' discomfort regarding the 'collaboration' with Frieze, while the report itself atones by disclosing the financial details of the project. It's a characteristic deflective move. Frieze Art Fair's enthusiastic adoption of corporate values, dramatically high turnover and audience figures, together with the generally porous membrane separating its commercial and non commercial activities, become the anti-model of neoliberal institutional practice, the vanguard of the 'almost completely instrumentalised' cultural/art dystopia for which we are notionally all destined in 2015.

The *2015* report contrasts this nightmare vision of neoliberal cultural lockdown with a wet dream of agile, socially responsible and responsive trans-national infrastructures – something like EIPCP's ever-expanding network of

7. Gerald Raunig, 'Introduction', *European Cultural Policies 2015*, http://eipcp.net/policies/2015/raunig/en
8. Pierre Bourdieu and Loïc Wacquant have identified such consultants' role in granting a veneer of legitimacy to projects of the new state and business nobility. Their prototypical example was Anthony Giddens, British sociologist and ideological architect of the Third Way. See Pierre Bourdieu and Loïc Wacquant, 'Neoliberal Newspeak: Notes on the New Planetary Vulgate', *Radical Philosophy*, January 2001, no. 108, http://www.radicalphilosophy.com/default.asp?channel_id=2187&editorial_id=9956

'Co-organisers', 'Associated Partners', etc.[9] Behind its critical reflections on cultural policy, there lies a bid for future state funding. The report's not-so-tacit conclusion is that the European Commission should reconsider its priorities and shift monies away from the big players and richer member states (read: UK plc, Frieze and Co.) and over toward 'responsible actors' (read: IASPIS/EIPCP) and smaller, self-organising networks.

This goes some way to explaining the absence of any debate in the report on wage and labour relations within art institutions themselves. It also throws up other questions. For instance, given the EU's aim of promoting the transnational dissemination of culture as a catalyst for socio-economic development and social integration, and its funding of both Frieze and EIPCP, which of the two operational models delivered the most 'European Added Value'?[10] The introduction to *2015* threw up a series of binaries: IASPIS-EIPCP vs. Frieze Art Fair, public vs. public-private partnership, self-organised vs. instrumentalised, institutions as 'responsible actors' vs. institutions as mere 'facilitators'. However, these alternatives should not be read as divergent paths but as coexistent forms of neoliberalism, evolving at uneven rates and in different phases perhaps, but all moving in the same direction. Each leads toward the same future – one with a human face, the other without – as various institutional actors become the unacknowledged legislators of neoliberalism and work to pioneer a socially acceptable form of its hegemony.

This process sees a proliferation of transnational infrastructures connecting art institutions with self-organised (activist) networks. As a tendency, it can be tracked back at least as far as the earlier institutional incorporation of activist strategies in the late-1990s to early-2000s, with MACBA frequently being cited as one of the first institutions to spearhead this with their Direct Action as one of the Fine Arts workshop in 2000 and *Las Agencias* (The Agencies) in mid-2001.[11] However, the consolidation of left radical-reformist agendas and coalitions at the first European Social Forum in Florence in November 2002 provides the more obvious ideological blueprint for the type of 'critical' policy alternatives found in *2015*. Around this time, EIPCP also launched its 'Republicart Manifesto', setting the tone and operational parameters of a three-year, EU-funded programme of events, web essays and conferences. This hauled a range of micro-institutional programmes and discourses into its investigation of the 'development of interventionist and activist practices of public art'. The

9. They are listed in the 'cooperation' section of EIPCP's website and stand at around 50 organisations as of March 2007: http://eipcp.net/institute/cooperation/cooperation
10. 'European Added Value' is outlined in the 'Award Criteria' section of the European Commission, Culture 2000 Specifications document: http://ec.europa.eu/culture/eac/how_particip2000/pract_info/appel_2006_en.html
11. See Discordia exchange on progressive institutions: 'More Than One Shining Institution', http://www.discordia.us/scoop/story/2004/2/10/191433/396.html and Jorge Ribalta, 'Mediation and Construction of Publics: The MACBA Experience', April 2004, http://www.republicart.net/disc/institution/ribalta01_en.htm

manifesto also claimed to pose a corrective to the dialectical cul-de-sacs and 'revolutionary pathos' characterising '90s political art. It explicitly rejects 'reforming a form of state', but nevertheless lays out a road map that would later enable state-funded institutions to harness some of the provisional overlaps between their activities and those of social and political movements.[12]

EIPCP continues to function as the project leader in a transnational cartel of institutions and individuals, all of whom feed into its web portals, Republicart (2002–5), Transform (2005–8) and Translate (2005–), and back out to conferences, symposia, exhibitions and workshops. The network is now positioned at the institutional epicentre of a number of European cultural debates on progressive and radical-reformist cultural strategies.

The phrase 'progressive art institution', for example, can be tracked back to EIPCP and, as a generalised catch-all, has proven itself particularly adaptable to the kind of concerted effort the network makes to generate a coherent theoretical framework. This project starts to take shape in the run up to the 2004 conference Public Art Policies: Progressive Art Institutions in the Age of Dissolving Welfare States. An open discussion on web platform, Discordia, between the organisers, participants and other interested parties, offers an insight into some of the general confusion, disputes and problems associated with the term 'progressive'. According to EIPCP's Raunig, it should be read as 'Becoming' not 'Being' progressive: '[T]his becoming progressive happens between the two poles of movement (micropolitical actions, etc.) and institutions (political organisation, etc.). [T]he abstract negation of one of these two poles would lead directly into myths of freedom (which I also suspect behind notions like "open cultures" or "free networks", especially if in connection to the art field) or reformist reductions'.[13]

While key figures in the EIPCP network continue to promote various modes of 'non-dialectical' engagement, any claims to new forms of resistance and political action should be tested by their effect on the core of the (art) institutions in question. If they simply serve to insulate and insure these neoliberal cultural nodes against attacks on their legitimacy, or provide ideological cover for a process of economic restructuring, how 'progressive' are things becoming?

In addition to its pioneering approach to outsourcing, MACBA, according to its website, is economically supported by a foundation of 38 sponsoring members and 33 founding businesses, including multinational financial and consultancy services groups like Ernst and Young, Deloitte and scandal-hit Banco Bilbao Vizcaya Argentaria (BBVA).[14] As state-funded cultural and educational institutions pass through the eye of the neoliberal storm, it's hardly surprising that a conspicuous self-reflexivity about their inner contradictions

12. Republicart manifesto, September 2002, http://www.republicart.net/manifesto/manifesto_en.htm, and EIPCP 2002 intro, http://eipcp.net/institute/reflectionzone/eipcp2001/en
13. See Discordia, http://www.discordia.us/scoop/story/2004/2/10/191433/396.htm

has become the stock in trade of progressives and radical reformers alike, broadcasting consciousness of the problems, but holding their resolution in abeyance. With uneven rates of movement and development between states, regions and cities, the institutions in which these professionals work are now bogged down in an erratic process of 'catch up' as the state simultaneously withdraws public sector support and economically mobilises culture and education.

This can be seen in the plethora of strategies for public sector reform and outsourcing. On the one hand, new models of efficiency and standards of assessment are introduced; on the other, institutions are given the task of attracting inward investment, contributing to cultural tourism, urban regeneration and the creative industries. Cultural and educational institutions, then, are in the midst of various forms of neoliberal enclosure, and the concomitant restructuring is seen by competing individuals, networks and agencies as offering openings for a range of agendas seeking to gain purchase on institutional structures/bureaucracies. Referring to the market for higher education and universities, for example, academic, Ned Rossiter, has argued that 'just as NGOs and CSOs have filled the void created by the neoliberal state's evacuation from the social, so too must organised networks seize upon the institutional persona of the "external provider"'.[15]

At the other end of the scale, the many and varied external providers linked to finance capital are also busy at work. At the inaugural conference of the British Venture Capital Association in September 2006, for example, companies referred to a 'land grab' as they rushed to secure stakes in the future output of university departments.[16] This activity is mirrored in the University of the Arts London's (UAL) Innovation Centre and wholly owned subsidiary company, UALVentures – part of a dozen or so other schemes set up at UAL since 2002 to capitalise on staff and student enterprise initiatives, develop company spin-outs and build up IP portfolios.[17]

14. According to the MACBA website, the objective of the Foundation is to 'actively contribute to the creation and development of the Contemporary Art Museum through the growth of its permanent collection.' The MACBA Consortium on the other hand (which consists of two public administrations) contributes the resources to maintain the museum's basic functions. See MACBA Foundation http://www.macba.es/controller.php?p_action=show_page&pagina_id=24&inst_id=15175 and, for BBVA, see 'A Widening Probe in Spain', *BusinessWeek Magazine*, 22 April 2002.
15. Ned Rossiter, 'Organised Networks: Transdisciplinarity and New Institutional Forms', http://transform.eipcp.net/correspondence/1144943951
16. Jon Boone, 'University Spin-Outs Turn the Heads of Venture Capitalists', *Financial Times*, 28 September 2006. Venture capital firm Quester's commentary/report, 'Building University Spin-Outs: A VC's View on Three Key Ingredients to Success', October 2006, http://www.quester.co.uk/pdfs/Building_viable_university_spinouts.pdf
17. The University of the Arts, London is at the forefront of this debate in the UK, and in addition to the rapid growth of business incubators and enterprise initiatives, it has recently set up Creative Capital-World City. This state-funded initiative has been developed in conjunction with a number of London based 'partner' universities (including Kings College London, London Business School and the School of Oriental and African Studies) to open up key world markets for the UK Creative Industries. See: http://www.arts.ac.uk/docs/Creative_Capital_-_World_City.pdf and http://www.arts.ac.uk/business/about.htm

In response to this rapid proliferation of new enterprise zones in the cultural and educational sectors, some leading progressives advocate a rearguard challenge to neoliberalisation with the aid of what MACBA's head of public programmes, Jorge Ribalta, has called his 'trustees from below' (e.g. displaced, dispossessed and previously excluded constituencies).[18] With uncanny echoes of Blairite sociologist, Anthony Giddens', earlier totem, 'the state without enemies', these art institutions without enemies no longer recuperate resistance or institutionalise critique but claim to operate as its facilitators – partners in its very construction. And herein lies the principal contradiction: the content of the institution's discourse can be utterly inverted in the institutional form. While formally affirming the fight against precarious labour, for example, institutions continue to maintain high levels of labour insecurity among their workers. Ctrl-i's act of refusal brought this to wider attention, but it was already the subject of earlier critiques from activist network, The Chainworkers, at El Precariat Social Rebel (November 2003) and Spanish Indymedia activists at EuroMayDay Barcelona (2004). All these critiques actually occurred 'within' MACBA and, to varying degrees, at the behest of the museum itself (Indymedia Barcelona, for example, is said to have grown out of one of its workshops). MACBA not only 'commands' criticism but lays down the terms and conditions according to which it can take place. It does so by offering its facilities and expertise, by inviting the big international celebrity activists to further politicise their 'trustees' and by generally helping to integrate anti-capitalist and social movements into its programme. As Raunig puts it, 'a productive game emerges here in the relationship between activists and institution, which is neither limited to a co-optation of the political by the institution, nor to a simple redistribution of resources from the progressive art institution to the political actions.'[19]

For all the auto-critique conducted by institutional directors, curators and activists, for all the talk of transnational networks linking up radical reformist elements, this, then, begs the question: what tangible, 'progressive' change has occurred within art institutions? Or, indeed, for all those on temporary, fixed-term contracts in Spanish and other European (non-art) contexts?[20] Are we just looking at institutions looking at institutions looking at institutions, churning self-reflexivity as they oversee the creation of the EU's socially conscious variant of UK/US neoliberalism?

18. Jorge Ribalta, 'Mediation and Construction of Publics. The MACBA Experience', April 2004, http://www.republicart.net/disc/institution/ribalta01_en.htm
19. Gerald Raunig, 'The Double Criticism of parrhesia. Answering the Question "What is a Progressive (Art) Institution?"', http://www.republicart.net/disc/institution/raunig04_en.htm
20. Spain accounts for 31 percent of temporary workers in Europe and has more temp workers than Italy, the UK, Belgium and Sweden combined. See Sebastian Royo, 'The European Union and Economic Reforms: The case of Spain', http://www.realinstitutoelcano.org/documentos/243.asp An OECD survey from 2005 noted labour market segmentation between permanent workers protected by high severence payments and the growing army of temp workers with little employment stability as a 'harmful feature' affecting productivity growth. See http://www.oecd.org/document/10/0,2340,en_33873108_33873806_34585738_1_1_1_1,00.html

If two earlier phases of institutional critique broadly located in the '70s and '90s have been integrated into cycles of legitimation and further disabled by the ongoing privatisation of culture and education, should we take these more recent state-funded, institutionally led initiatives seriously as a 'third phase', as some have argued? Of all the interpretations put forward by EIPCP 'correspondents' and associates at the 2005 conference, The Future of Institutional Critique, and in the first issue of the web journal, *Transversal*, filmmaker Hito Steyerl's is perhaps the most plausible, though by no means unproblematic.[21] She notes the integration of cultural workers into the flexible, temporary and exploitative labour conditions ushered in by neoliberalisation, and claims that there is a 'need for institutions which could cater to the new needs and desires that this constituency will create'.

It's necessary here, when talking about needs, desires and constituencies, to acknowledge class struggle in these new enterprise zones/progressive art institutions and to maintain clear lines of antagonism in any proposed 'third phase' of institutional critique. As ctrl-i have shown, we could start by directly confronting in-house disparities and inequities and ask why radical reformers avoid debating ongoing, and often intensified, labour market segmentation (i.e. the differential between permanent and temporary workers) within their own 'exemplary' cultural and educational institutions. Why do those at the top of the institutional pile and their army of new consultants continue to promote self-reflexivity and claim to facilitate dissent, while acting as a buttress to elite class power? The question, then, is not so much about whether *2015*'s call for the EU 'to invest in long-term basic funding for transnational infrastructures' should be met (EIPCP's continued funding suggests that it has been, in their case), but about how, and to what extent, these infrastructures function in the service of capital.

21. Debates on a third 'phase' or 'wave' of institutional critique can be found in Simon Sheikh's 'Notes on Institutional Critique', Hito Steyerl's 'Institution of Critique' and Gerald Raunig's 'Instituent Practices: Fleeing, Instituting, Transforming'. All can be found at http://transform.eipcp.net/transversal/0106/raunig/en

Chapter 9

The Open Work

Finally you are no more than an imitation of an actor.
Friedrich Nietzsche

The most radical potential stored in the phenomenon of 'interactivity' must be the redistribution of creativity away from the author and toward the user, the group, the crowd, the social. The potential to reproduce, and recombine, information into new forms is the other function of the computer that carries this potential, undermining the auratic original and making it available for endless redeployment. Post-structuralism's critique of the author, 'his' reification and the concomitant eclipse of creativity's social nature, coincides, to a great extent, with the advent of (networked) computing – and its implied assault on the originality and exclusivity of cultural objects. John Cage turned the sound of an audience, waiting in silence for a performance to begin, into a piece of music only a decade before J.C.R. Licklider presented his concept of an 'Intergalactic Computer Network'. These distinct, and mutually disinterested, developments were, in fact, happening simultaneously, and would later become deeply entangled with one another. Largely through writing on music and sometimes on art, poetry and popular computing, this chapter follows these threads, to explore their knotty outcomes in '90s and '00s technoculture. Its writers ask how the 'open work' has fared, from its tender avant-garde beginnings to its reification in Web 2.0 and, debatably, its banalisation in relational aesthetics.

Flint Michigan, in his text 'Composing Ourselves', suggests that French music theorist, Jacques Attali's expanded concept of 'composition' is, in part, a reworking of Marx's idea of 'really free working, e.g. composition'. This formulation is key to many of these articles because it strives to articulate a kind of making/doing that is free from the alien demands of capital, the imperative to produce for value's sake. Attali's concept of 'composition' is something that exists beyond the 'rupture' of changing economic and technological conditions, to reveal 'the demand for the truly different system of organisation, a network within which a different kind of music and different social relations can arise'. Where Michigan takes issue with Attali is in his characterisation of this free working as 'A music produced by each individual for himself, for pleasure outside meaning, usage and exchange'. The connection between the socially transformative powers of music and creativity are somehow folded back into the confines of individual enjoyment, rendering Attali's concept paradoxical. Is it not incoherent to suggest that such ego-invested production challenges capitalism's systems of 'meaning, usage and exchange' when it leaves the sign-value of the author intact?

Keston Sutherland's lacerating account of the post-Soviet, poetic orthodoxy of the American L=A=N=G=U=A=G=E school – whose attacks on any 'subjective expressiveness' that can be 'identified with the psychic operations [...] of an 'Author' seems at first to clash with Michigan's dismissal of the composer-as-Author. But, Sutherland further unpacks his suspicion of this poetic school and its 'puritanical' refusal to allow the 'interpretative consumption' of expressiveness. For Sutherland, these poets' use of 'debris-syntax' and wilful deformation of language amounts to little more than a 'consumer revolt' against one of global capitalism's most vital tools – English. So, rather than this amounting to an anti-avant-gardist defence of the Author, Sutherland deems these gestures to be not radical enough, mere tokens of rejection in the face of the persistence of 'English-as-capitalism-logos' – a consumer revolt rather than something that redistributes the means/meaning of production.

Luc Ferrari's piece, *Presque Rien No. 1*, is discussed in Michigan's second text in this chapter. His simple recording of a Croatian fishing village in the early hours of the morning, writes Michigan, sets the composer 'alongside the listener'. The senses are freed from the responsibility to interpret authorial intention and left to an unfettered exploration of disembodied sounds, to engage in a 'desiring perception'. The freedom created by Ferrari's piece, which, at the same time, avoids *musique concrète's* subsequent naturalism, stands in antithesis to mid-'90s signature interactive artwork, *Osmose*, by Char Davies. In their discussion of the piece, the Bureau of Inverse Technology (BIT) describe how the viewer is strapped into VR goggles and heavy, breath-sensitive equipment and then 'released', for a strict 20 minutes, to navigate through a floaty VR 'mushspace'. Not only did the level of control and supervision surrounding the piece prevent any sense of voluntary exploration, but the supposed empowerment of the viewer was belied by *Osmose*'s 'morphine haze of compulsive serenity', its 'force-gentling'. The piece's declared 're-connection' of virtuality and 'wild nature' is nothing but an audio-visual pacifier, burying the truth of technology's relationship to 'nature' behind an insipid simulation.

In sharp distinction to this increasingly discredited genre of 'interactivity' – which finds its analogue in consultative politics' pre-emptive neutralisation of resistance – are the man-machine relations of Detroit techno. In his interview with techno legend, Jeff Mills, Hari Kunzru describes how 'Mills the DJ seems self-evidently a component of a human-machine assemblage, a system which includes crowd, PA, the whole apparatus of record production and the stylus cartridge [...]'. And, later, Mills relates how, when programming a sequence, he sometimes goes out and just lets it run for up to 24 hours: 'The machines fluctuate. Over time the sequence changes slightly. The machines mould themselves, giving their own character to a track.' If Ferrari's work set the composer alongside the listener, techno sets the composer and listener alongside the machine. The permutative power of computation, the warp of a specific machine, the impact of amplification and repetitive beats on a crowd, and the anti-naturalism of electronic sound are just some of the ways in which an 'alien' intelligence acts to disrupt the dyad of artist/viewer or composer/listener.

Of course, machinic propagation also has its down sides – something Paul Helliwell contemplates in his piece, 'Zombie Nation', in which he connects Web 2.0, relational aesthetics and the (commodity) crisis of the music industry. As he explains, music (and indeed capitalism) has started to resemble so-called relational aesthetics in the age of digital reproduction. He recounts how Attali joked at a record industry bash that, apart from gigs, in the age of free downloads, soon all that bands will be able to sell is the right to attend a rehearsal or go to dinner with them. As the music and other industries, such as publishing and software, lose control of the commodity, increasingly all that is left to sell are relations between people, in different spatial and temporal arrangements. The culture industry, argues Helliwell, is coming to operate increasingly like avant-garde culture. As relationality gets reified at one end of the scale, it is turned into a funding criterion for art production at the other. This attempt to ascribe to art a 'social function' spells doom, argues Helliwell, in step with Adorno, as its defining 'autonomy' is undermined.

By way of a coda to the debate, as well as the chapter, Howard Slater throws into relief the self-evidence of critiques of relational aesthetics by contemplating the work of little-known singer/musician Ghédalia Tazartès. The uniform formatting of social relations by social networking sites and the music industry depends on the uniformity of coherent subjects. By contrast, the music of Tazartès, developed in semi-obscurity over 25 years, acts as a 'taunt to unity' which outs the musician as an 'exposed "fake"'. His guttural voice, which moves across chimeras of identity and nationality, articulates the multiplicity of the self and the lie of identity. Such a refusal of identity reminds us of the distance that still exists between avant-gardist rejections of authorial self-hood, and the pseudo-relationality of the culture industry, with its dependence on stable identities, as it battles the crisis of digital abundance.

Dissimulations: The Illusion of Interactivity

Andy Cameron

Vol 1 #1, Spring 1995

The Interactive Story

[...] myth, legend, fable, tale, novella, epic, history, tragedy, drama, comedy, mime, painting, stained glass windows, cinema, comics, news items, conversation.[1] The form of the story permeates every aspect of our cultural life. History, politics, memories, even subjectivity, our sense of identity, are all representations in narrative form, signifiers chained together in temporal, spatial, and causal sequence. Narrative appears to be as universal and as old as language itself, and enjoys with language the status of a defining characteristic of humanity and its culture. A people without stories seems as absurd an idea as a people without language, (a people with language but no stories even stranger, for what use is language if not to tell stories?)

Over the past few years, there has been a tremendous investment in the idea of digital media, the use of computers, as a site of culture rather than just tools for business or science. This is partly due to a drive on the part of manufacturers to create new markets as price/performance ratios in digital technology improve, but, at the same time, there is a desire at work here, a fantasy which exceeds its technical and economic conditions. Implicit in the notion of digital media is the belief (read: desire) that digital computers and digital communications will provide a unified site for First World culture in the near future and that this new medium will offer distinct advances over existing media, above all by offering its audience interactivity.

Interactivity refers to the possibility of an audience actively participating in the control of an artwork or representation. For the purposes of this discussion, interactivity means the ability to intervene in a meaningful way within the representation itself, not to read it differently but to '(re)make' it differently. In its most fully realised form, that of the simulation, interactivity allows narrative situations to be described *in potentia* and then set into motion – a process through which model-building supersedes storytelling, and the 'what-if?' engine replaces narrative sequence.

There are those who see the replacement of narrative form by interactive simulation as political progress. Many who, in the 1960s and '70s, rejected the blandishments of mainstream narrative, the elision of its own means of production and the naturalisation of passive spectatorship, discern in interactive media an opportunity to go beyond the impasse of avant-garde structural

1. Roland Barthes, 'The Structural Analysis of Narrative', *Image, Music, Text*, London: Fontana. 1977.

materialist film practice. Similarly, in the rhetoric of neoliberal political thought, interactivity can be figured as a form of freedom, a liberation from the tyranny of authorship and from the servile passivity of reading.

This discussion is an attempt to speculate on the collision between a dominant cultural form – narrative – and the technology of interactivity. I will argue that there is a central contradiction within the idea of interactive narrative – that narrative form is fundamentally linear and non-interactive. The interactive story implies a form within which the position and authority of the narrator is dispersed among the readers, in which spectatorship and temporality are displaced, and in which the idea of cinema, or of literature, merges with that of the game, or of sport. Can an interactive construct, or a simulation, successfully adopt a narrative form?

Forking Paths and Synthetic Spaces

In his short story, 'The Garden of Forking Paths',[2] Borges imagines a novel in which the path of the story splits, where all things are conceivable, and all things take place. The author of this story-within-a-story is judged insane and commits suicide, and Borges' narrator is arrested and condemned to death – thus, the fate of the narrator and of the author in the interactive era is prefigured. It is not hard to see how the task of writing interactively might drive an author to insanity and suicide. To write not simply an account of what happened but a whole series of 'what-ifs' increases both the volume and complexity of an author's task exponentially. In addition, the situation is one in which the ability to develop the action in a particular direction is no longer the unique prerogative of an omnipotent author as his/her role is partly usurped by the reader.

How much interactivity does it take to make an interactive story? We don't know because we don't know what an interactive story is like, nor what it is for (more on this in a moment). It is true that the number and complexity of forking paths could be increased until the reader experiences a large degree of freedom and control within the text. The limits of this freedom are achieved within a constructed model that dispenses with the network of lines altogether, replacing it with a fictional space within which readers can turn left or right, look up or down, open a door, enter a room, at any time they choose – a spatio-temporal simulation which can generate a travelling point of view in real time, more commonly known as virtual reality or VR. In the VR model, although the reader/spectator enjoys seamless temporal and spatial liberty, the trade-off between interactivity and richness of content holds true. To date, VR has barely been able to dress the set, let alone cry 'action', or murmur 'once upon a time'. And there is another, simpler and deeper, problem. This is the question of ontology. The change from a linear model to a multi-linear or spatio-temporal (VR) model involves moving from one kind of representation, and one form of spectatorship, to another.

2. Jorge Luis Borges, 'The Garden of Forking Paths' (1944), *Fictions*, London: Penguin, 2000, pp. 75–86.

A Lonely Impulse of Delight

As he settled into the snug cockpit, he tried not to think about the obvious thing. Ahead of him, through the windscreen, he could see a long low hill. It was further away than it appeared to be, and much bigger. Yellow through the blue haze, the hill squatted on the plain, low and indolent and massive. He wanted to be over that hill and look beyond.

Before him stretched the grey runway, on the left a yellow haystack, on the right a white airfield building. All around him was the blue aeroplane.

Aficionados of the Hellcats flight simulator will recognise the landscape – an American airstrip on one of the Solomon Islands in the Pacific Ocean. The time is World War II. This is the prologue to an account of an experience of my own, flying a Hellcat on a mission against the Japanese Navy.

Hellcats is effectively a screen-and-mouse-based virtual reality system – second person VR – offering non-linear adventure stories. The reader – or should that be participant, or player – is free to move in any direction, at all times, as long as he or she never gets out of the plane. This cuts down the scope of the story significantly – it's like *Top Gun* with everything but the flight scenes cut out.

As a representation of the experience of Americans in the Pacific during World War II, Hellcats can be compared to *South Pacific* or *From Here to Eternity*. Yet, despite the similarities of place and time, Hellcats is a very different kind of representation. It represents one specific aspect of the experience of the war in the Pacific, but it is the experience of the machine, to misquote Stephen Heath, rather than the experience of the pilot. More precisely, it is the experience of the pilot insofar as he or she is an extension of the machine. Certain key attributes of narrative form are missing.[3] Narrative closure has to be fought for – if you crash your plane while taking off, the 'story' is short, insignificant and unsatisfying. It is up to the spectator to ensure that the action comes to a satisfying and meaningful end – closure is contingent on the moment of 'reading'. Temporal and spatial coherence are more or less complete, but strictly limited to the skies above the Solomon Islands. There is no specific enigma to be resolved, but a different kind of teleological imperative – that of a participant in a violent struggle. If we consider what Barthes has called the symbolic code – that code which accounts for the formal relationships created between terms within a text, the figurative patterning of antithesis, graduation, repetition etc. – we find it absent in Hellcats. The simulator does not signify in this way. Neither do we find much in the way of a referential or gnomic code – the code of shared cultural

3. Pam Cook (Ed.), *The Cinema Book*, London: British Film Institute, 1987, p. 212.
In *The Cinema Book*, Annette Kuhn gives this account of the formal attributes of classic cinematic narrative:
· Linearity of cause and effect within an overall trajectory of enigma-resolution.
· A high degree of narrative closure.
· A fictional world governed by spatial and temporal verisimilitude.
· Centrality of the narrative agency of psychologically-rounded characters.

knowledge about the world – nor the rich and diffuse code of connotations designated by Barthes as the code of *Semes*. The complex interplay of signs, Barthes' 'weaving of the voices' across different registers, the 'multivalence of the text' is lost, replaced with a wide band of sensory information referring to specific and schematic aspects of a situation – the proairetics of flight, the hermeneutics of battle.[4] However, although complex narrative codes are not hard-wired into the simulation, they are not altogether absent from it. The simulation is re-invested with narrative sense via the subjectivity of the participant – a personal, transient, and contingent narrative, unlegitimated by the external figure of the author.

Time

> I saw the movie last week. I want what happened in the movie last week to happen in the movie this week too; otherwise, what is life all about?[5]

A key distinction to be made between an interactive representation, like Hellcats, and narrative representations, like those of the cinema and literature, lies in the way that time is represented. Narrative refers to the past. Its temporal referent is once upon a time. The simulator, on the other hand, operates in the present. If, in a narrative, an event happened, in an interactive narrative, whether multi-linear or spatio-temporal, an event is happening, its time is now. This temporal shift has important consequences.

4. Roland Barthes, *S/Z*, Oxford: Blackwell, 1990.
In *S/Z*, Barthes outlines five codes of narrative. These are used to submit a short story by Balzac – 'Sarrasine' – to an extremely close textual analysis. Briefly the five codes are:
· The code of *Semes* – broad connotations within the text – femininity, age, etc.
· The Symbolic code – the code which structures the text in figurative patterns – antithesis, graduation, repetition etc. It is difficult to imagine this code within a non-linear, interactive structure – the pattern imposed by the author would be lost in the meanderings of the reader.
· The Cultural code – shared knowledge, common sense. See note on Hellcats above.
· The Hermeneutic code – the various (formal) terms 'by which an enigma can be distinguished, suggested, formulated, held in suspense and finally disclosed'. An interactive story might be organised principally in terms of the hermeneutic code, a cluster of clues surrounding a mystery could be organised logically yet non-sequentially. The hermeneutic code is goal-orientated, as are most games.
· The Proairetic code – the code of the actions, the code of the sequence. This code presents particular problems for non-linear interactive structures. A change in one part of the sequence will have the potential to change every subsequent action. The proairetic code embodies a relentless logic: if X is killed in scene 4 then X cannot be alive in scene 5.
To an extent, then, the proairetic code embodies something of the cultural codes, the code of knowledge. The proairetic code is the code of knowledge about time, and it is the certainties of this knowledge which interactivity appears to throw into question. There is a parallel between the interactive narrative and the electronic spreadsheet. The linear narrative is to the interactive narrative what the ledger is to the spreadsheet. Both interactive narrative and spreadsheet are 'what if?' engines. Both create the space for multiple parallel time. The best illustration of the problem of the proairetic code in interactive narrative is given by changing one of the numbers in a spreadsheet, doing a recalculate and watching the changes multiply and ripple across the whole sheet.
5. Woman outside the cinema in Woody Allen (Dir.) *The Purple Rose of Cairo*, 1984.

A linear narrative exercises a textual authority which is dispersed by interactivity. In a linear narrative, the reader submits to the prior authority of the text. Only the author has the power to make decisions about the storyline or point of view, and the invention of narrative sequence is his or her sole prerogative. The text is certain of itself; moreover, this certainty has a legitimising function. Hayden White writes:

> We cannot but be struck by the frequency with which narrativity, whether of the fictional or the factual sort, presupposes the existence of a legal system against or on behalf of which the typical agents of a narrative account militate. And this raises the suspicion that narrative in general, from the folktale to the novel, from the 'annals' to the fully realised history, has to do with the topics of law, legality, legitimacy or more generally 'authority'.[6]

Now this authority is expressed, and legitimacy conferred, at the moment of closure. By recounting what happened, an author is also closing off those things which didn't happen. A character picks up the phone rather than letting it ring, someone walks down the street and turns left instead of right. Closure, in this sense, is dispersed throughout the narrative. The events unfold as a pattern which progressively resolves itself into an image, each event integrating those which precede it into progressively higher levels of narrative sense. This process continues until the final closure at the end of the narrative, at which point the meaning of the story is revealed at last, and is revealed to have been immanent in all the events all along. Closure can be considered as a function of time, or, more precisely, of the way in which time is represented, whether as past and complete or present and ongoing.[7]

Aspect

In his standard work on aspect[8] the linguist, Bernard Comrie, distinguishes two forms of time reference in language – aspect and tense. Tense 'relates the time of the situation [...] to some other time, usually to the moment of speaking', whereas aspects are 'different ways of viewing the internal temporal constituency of a situation'. Where tense distinguishes between situations taking place in the past, present or future, aspect draws a distinction between the perfective – a situation viewed from the 'outside' as completed – and the imperfective – a situation viewed from the 'inside' as ongoing. The shift from narrative representation to interactive representation entails an aspectual shift

6. Hayden White, 'The Value of Narrativity in the Representation of Reality', *On Narrative*, Chicago: Chicago University Press, 1981, pp. 1–23.
7. Richon and Berger (Ed.), 'Fire and Ice', *Other Than Itself*, Manchester: Cornerhouse Publications, 1990. See Peter Wollen's discussion of the linguistic category of aspect and its effect on spectatorship and the categories of perfective and imperfective in Bernard Comrie's standard work, *Aspect*, Cambridge, Cambridge University Press, 1976.
8. Bernard Comrie, loc. cit.

like that from perfective to imperfective, from outside to inside the time of the situation being described.

Thus, aspect distinguishes between different ways of positioning the audience with respect to a situation. The perfective and imperfective aspect, and, by analogy, linear narrative and interactive simulations, correspond to two fundamentally different modes of spectatorship. An interactive simulation appears to designate the conditions for events rather than the events themselves. The interactive simulation sketches a web of possibilities and constitutes a system for producing story events in time – a story engine rather than a story.

It is in their respective modes of closure that we can locate the apparent disjuncture between the nature of interactivity and that of narrative. Thus, the moment the reader intervenes to change the story, perfective becomes imperfective, story time becomes real time, an account becomes an experience, the spectator or reader becomes a participant or player, and the narrative begins to resemble a game.

Games and Stories

In 'An Examination of the Works of Herbert Quain',[9] Borges invents an English multi-linear novelist of the 1930s. Less often referred to than 'The Garden of Forking Paths', this short story is no less remarkable for its dystopian vision of a banal and meretricious interactive literature – what Borges terms the 'regressive, ramified novel'. Borges prefigures the transformation of reading into playing when he makes Herbert Quain say of his second novel, *April March*, 'I lay claim in this novel [...] to the essential features of all games: symmetry, arbitrary rules, tedium.' Indeed, 'Quain was in the habit of arguing that readers were an already extinct species. "Every European," he reasoned "is a writer, potentially or in fact."'

Does something which is interactive have to be like a game? And, if so, does a game have to be as uninteresting as Borges suggests? Max Whitby[10] argues that the term 'interactive narrative' is an oxymoron – and believes that an interactive narrative can never be as satisfying as a traditional, linear story, because interactivity gets in the way:

Every successful form of communication involves protagonists, a set of conflicts and experiences, and, at the end, some sort of resolution so that the thing has a satisfying shape. Interaction largely destroys all that. By giving the audience control over the raw material, you give them precisely what they don't want; they don't want a load of bricks, they want a finished construction, a built house.

One form of interactive multimedia that does make sense is that of the game. Computer games are as spellbinding and absorbing as a good movie. However, what is going on in people's heads in a game is very different from what is going

9. Jorge Luis Borges, 'An Examination of the World of Herbert Quain' (1944), *Fictions*, op. cit., pp. 75–86.
10. Max Whitby heads the Multimedia Corporation, an offshoot of the BBC, which produces interactive titles in London.

on with a play or a novel. I don't want to say that one is better than the other, but you can obviously do things in films, plays and novels that you can't do in a game, and vice versa. Most of what is generally regarded as being interesting belongs to the world of cinema and theatre, and most of what we could regard as simply diverting or just a pastime belongs to the form of the game.

Value

So far, I have argued for a distinction between narrative and interactivity, or between stories and games, on the basis of the different way each represents time, leading on to differing modes of spectatorship. However, as Max Whitby points out, games and stories also have very different cultural values attached to them. The game is frivolous whereas narrative is serious.

There is a general assumption here that narrative representation – literature, history, cinema and so on – has a deep and lasting significance which the game lacks. In the end, Shakespeare or Proust or Pasolini seem to have more to offer than a game of football or Sonic. The game is outside of history, unworthy of serious remembrance. At the MIT multimedia conference in Dublin in 1993, a speaker bemoaned the fact that his son spent too much time playing computer games and not enough time reading books. Thinking of my own child, I found myself nodding in agreement. Yet, when a woman asked from the floor why reading a book was better than playing a computer game, he couldn't explain his assumption and neither could I. Two other speakers gave a fascinating account of an elastic movie. This was a multi-screen installation, constructed as part of a student workshop at MIT, which the spectator moved through and interacted with. The speakers called it an interactive media environment, an installation, a transformational space; fine art circumlocutions for the obvious term 'game' which they managed to avoid entirely throughout their paper. Then, they showed a video of their undergraduate students discussing the design of the project and the word 'game' cropped up over and over again. Finally, throughout the whole two-day conference on interactivity, discussion of console and TV computer games was almost entirely absent, in spite of the astounding commercial success of Nintendo and Sega in the youth market, in spite of CD-i, in spite of 3DO...

A Literary You-topia

If the repressed reading of interactivity is that of the game, the preferred readings are interactivity as liberation, and interactivity as postmodernism come true. In *S/Z*, Barthes describes two types of writing: readerly writing and writerly writing. What happens if we take the notion of the writerly at face value, innocently? What if we read excessively, irresponsibly, futuristically:

> The goal of literary work (of literature as work) is to make the reader no longer a consumer, but a producer of the text [...] The writerly text is

> a perpetual present, upon which no consequent language (which would inevitably make it past) can be superimposed; the writerly text is ourselves writing [. . .]
>
> In this ideal text, the networks are many and interact, without any of them being able to surpass the rest; this text is a galaxy of signifiers, not a structure of signifieds; it has no beginning; it is reversible; we gain access to it by several entrances, none of which can be authoritatively declared to be the main one; the codes it mobilizes extend as far as the eye can see [. . .][11]

In this excessive reading, the writerly becomes a fantasy of the multi-linear text, with Barthes, a kind of Nostradamus of literary theory, writerly writing the uncanny prophecy of an interactive literature come to pass. Indeed, a number of commentators have noted the way in which post-structuralist writing seems to anticipate the non-linearity of new technology. In *Hypertext – the Convergence of Contemporary Critical Theory and Technology*, George P. Landow suggests that the literary theories of structuralist and post-structuralist thinkers (especially Barthes and Derrida) find their embodiment in interactive, hypertextual forms made possible by new technology. Hypertextual and non-linear structures promise Barthes' writerly text, never far from the possibility of rewriting, multivocal, decentred, without boundaries, a text which can break free from the chains of closure, a text whose instability lies not in our postmodern apprehension of it but in its very condition of being. Hypertext, for Landow, is post-structuralism made flesh, transubstantiated – Foucault's *Death of the Author*, a corpse and a smoking gun, Derridean *débordement* actualised as hypertextual annotation [. . .][12] The problem with this kind of literal and utopian mapping of post-structuralist theory onto new technology is that it fails to acknowledge its own excessiveness. To literally and deterministically locate a set of complex, heterogeneous and ambiguous ideas about the social processes of reading within a specific technology seems to be missing the point. One might as well argue that the telephone system is post-structuralist. It is ironic that a set of theories which stress plurality and indeterminacy should be employed in the service of a reductive equivalence between very different types of object.

Instrumental stories

> Science has always been in conflict with narratives.
> Jean-François Lyotard[13]

11. Roland Barthes, *S/Z*, op. cit.
12. 'contemporary theory proposes and hypertext disposes; or, to be less theologically aphoristic, hypertext embodies many of the ideas and attitudes proposed by Barthes, Derrida and Foucault.' George P. Landow, *Hypertext*, Baltimore: Johns Hopkins University Press, 1992, p. 73.
13. Jean-François Lyotard, *The Postmodern Condition*, Manchester: Manchester University Press, 1986, p. xxiii.

We have seen how a putative theory of interactivity might oscillate between the preferred register of the postmodern (serious, plural, decentred and legitimated by the academy) and the frivolous register of the game (playful, ephemeral, banal and without value). A further approach is suggested in *The Postmodern Condition*, in which Lyotard outlines an opposition between narrative knowledge (convivial, traditional) and instrumental knowledge (cybernetic, scientific). The game can be considered as a cybernetic construct (a goal-directed system of control and feedback) and, as such, placed on the side of the instrumental, whereas narrative knowledge, argues Lyotard, is an older form – 'narration is the quintessential form of customary knowledge [...]' and 'what is transmitted through narrative is the pragmatic which establishes the social bond'. Legitimation and authority are immanent to narrative form and are established within and through the act of narration itself (see Hayden White quotation above). By contrast, authority and legitimation are extrinsic to the form of instrumental knowledge. In scientific discourse, legitimation must be fought for. Moreover, instrumental knowledge, according to Lyotard, is set apart from the language games that constitute the social bond. The analogous oppositions may be summed up thus:

INSTRUMENTAL KNOWLEDGE	NARRATIVE KNOWLEDGE
science	history
simulation	narrative
game	story
uncertain	legitimate
synchronic	diachronic

These oppositions sketch out the structural differences between two different kinds of representation, and two modes of spectatorship. It seems that the truth-effects of stories and games are very different. The question of legitimacy and certainty is central – the simulation remains a model which does not have the ability to auto-legitimate itself in the way an account does. Structured as it is around a core of what-if statements, the truth of a simulation or game can never be more than hypothetical.[14]

Conclusion

There are two potential endings for a discussion like this, either optimistic or pessimistic. Neither is sustainable. The 'interactivity is postmodern' school of thought sees interactive representation as a liberation from the repressive authority of traditional narrative form. There are echoes here of the avant-garde and anti-narrative movements in cinema and writing, which have their source in the utopian ferment of the '60s. Yet, the consequences of the opening up of closure – that interactivity will be 'commonplace, unlaborious, shallow, un-literary, heterodox'[15] – are more difficult to accept.

Others see the simulation as promising post-symbolic representation, bypassing the patriarchal distortions of perspective and the controlling point of view. According to this argument, an interactive simulation offers not the representation of objects but the representation of relations between objects within which the participant can select their own point of view. However, in characterising this as a shift from coded representation to experiential post-representation, what is glossed over is the coding and mediation involved in constructing the simulation in the first place. *Sim City*, the town planning simulation game, is just as much a cocktail of opinion, received wisdom and political ideology as any other doctrine of urban decay and renewal – it simply hides its politics more effectively.

Is this the end of the road for narrative, grand or otherwise? Are we to become a people without stories? Once again, the linguistic category of aspect provides a useful analogy here. We have seen how the shift from narrative to interactivity involves a shift from perfective to imperfective, from outside to inside the time of the events being described. Thus, narrative representation and interactive representation might be 'different ways of viewing the internal temporal constituency of a situation' as well as different forms of spectatorship.[16] As interactivity increases, so the spectator is thrown inside the representation to become a player.

At the heart of interactive representation, narrative reinstates itself through the subject, narrativising the experience, making sense of (simulated) events. If narrative is a technique for producing significance out of being, order out of contingency, then simulation can be seen as its inverse – a technique for producing being out of significance, of generating a simulation of contingency from first principles. Rather than a people without stories, interactivity offers the promise of a people within stories, and, rather than the end of narrative, an explosion of narrative within the simulator.

Like any other form of representation, interactivity is an illusion. It puts itself in the place of something that isn't there. What, then, might be the absent referent of interactivity? According to both neoliberals and techno-utopians, interactivity promises the spectator freedom and choice. It is precisely the absence of such freedom and choice that interactivity would appear to conceal.

14. For example, my five-year-old child enjoys crashing the aeroplane when he flies the simulator – it doesn't hurt him to crash the plane. However, when watching a television documentary about early USAF jet planes, which showed a plane cartwheeling and exploding in a fireball, he was upset because he felt he had seen someone die. The simulated crash and the account of a crash had, for him, a very different status.
15. Jorge Luis Borges, 'An Examination of the World of Herbert Quain', op. cit.
16. Holt's definition of aspect, quoted by Bernard Comrie, *Aspect*, op. cit., p. 3.

BIT on Osmose

The Bureau of Inverse Technology (BIT)

Vol 1 #3, Autumn 1995

> *Osmose* addresses our relation to the natural environment (i.e. wild nature) [sic] by using the medium of immersive virtual space to encourage gentle interaction and serenity – instead of violence and aggression – while offering an opportunity to experience a sense of profound re-connection between self and world.

BUREAU TESTIFIES: Oh please, Char. Whatever natural osmotic tendencies the piece *Osmose* was named for (this remains a blur), and claims resemblance to (who can really tell), the metaphor can best be used in explaining the story left out of all of the evangelical verbage around the piece – the osmotic relationship of technology leaking across a membrane of exclusion toward a greater concentration of money. NB osmosis in the biological sense (i.e. wild nature) is when water crosses a membrane toward concentration equilibrium: why dehydration results when you salt, sulphur or otherwise create an (ion) concentration gradient, why fresh water fish dehydrate in salt water and salt water fish balloon in fresh water. The simple equation *Osmose* suggests is to put money within the institutional membrane of the gallery and watch the technology flow to bloating. Concentration of technology toward money…

CharDavies is Visionary. Creator of *Osmose*, Director of Visual Research (and, incidentally, spouse of Company President) at software company giant SoftImage (incidentally a major sponsor of the work). The bulk of the velcro-zipped, matte-purple CharDavies/*Osmose* media kit, the prominence of the *Osmose* signage, the sheer mass of the hors d'oeuvres trays at the *Osmose* opening reception signal the presence of a not unassuming exhibit. 'Computer Animation Finds Niche in Museum', the *Montreal Gazette* of 25 August marvels.

CharDavies: 'One woman expressed it best: It made me feel like I was an angel.'

Osmose is precisely a 20-minute experience. The Immersant, assisted by two VR valets, assumes mediation of a strap-on breathing/balance interface vest and head-mounted stereoscopic display (strap-in time approx. five mins). Navigation enabled via in/exhale detectors and motion sensors on the subject's body; immersant point of view is beamed to vicarious sidecar audience in the dimmed room adjacent via stereoscopic video projection and disposable 3D glasses. A one-to-many transcendent experience. Immersions of less than 20 minutes are distinctly disallowed as they are insufficient to exert the lobal lull necessary for full impressionability. It is not enabled to subdivide the prescribed *Osmose*/BIT immersion time into two ten-minute VR QuickDips, the virtual valets are adamant; there henceforth develops a split bureau perception: intraBIT/extraBIT.

CharDavies: 'It's very important that this technology be used to express alternative world views. 3D computer graphics is a very powerful visualizing technology. It's not value free.'

IntraBIT: 'Immersed' in CharDaviesworld, feeling disorientated and absurd, one has to draw on whatever knowledge one has of the piece to try to make sense of it.

I would like to talk about the content of the piece: a blurry tree, a random selection of quotes from philosophers and thinkers that have little to do with each other, some more blur – that was clouds you are told by the man who has fixed you into the contraption, some bits of code that you guess have been used in the piece, but which, like the quotes, are disconnected and jumbled… the usermanualman at your side, while you are 'submerged' in the piece, explains that there are five layers, but you can't bend down too much because the proximity sensors between your back and the floor make the images go up (i.e. to make you feel like you are going down) and you go into a speedblurloop which is not what they want you to do. The voiceatyoursideman suggests gently that you can explore inside the leaf. Zooming in, you go into total greenblur – there is no detail except the occasional unantialiased jagged edge. I wonder at the brilliant interpretative insight of this artist to make the leaf green! The emptiness of the tree representation is a little difficult to take seriously, bereft as it is of any exploration of either the phenomenon of the tree or how it is taken to be meaningful – I can say nothing more. (But I will proffer two pieces by way of comparison that do detonate legible reactions. One piece – by rigo95: a one way road sign reauthored to read 'one tree' in twoword wit – demonstrates the tenuous appropriation and absurd relationship of tree in the immersive environment of the urban technology in which we live. Another piece, by Jeremijenko, is a symmetrical two-tree arrangement, hung in parody of architectural symmetry, one tree growing up and one growing down. The tree growth, ripped from and suspended amongst the 3D architecture, opens up a contemplative relationship through the slow growth and the actual phenomenon of the inverted tree, which turns its new shoots around to grow upright. Trees can be potent cultural icons for the artist if used with a trace of wit or imagination.)

But, to detect the Marshall McLuhanism overriding the sappy images *Osmose* renders… something about the means of production, the medium… why CharPainter is using the VR environment when it does nothing to three-dimensionalise the images, does nothing to bring them into the spaces of cultural exchange. These are flat images – they reperform painting, make it a reified production and do nothing to engage the public imagination. It is the equipment itself that engages, the spectacle of VR – that, unfortunately dearDavies, does not engage. So, 'immersed' in the CharDavies piece, feeling disorientated and absurd, one has to despair at the katemossthinness of the atmosphere.

ExtraBIT From the ante chamber in 3D blurscape, the meaninglessness of the immersed bureau agent's movements provide a patterned background to some disengaged reconstructions. It occurs to this bureau member to wonder exactly which worldview is being advanced by this, the Gentler-*Osmose*. Overtly constructed against models of military/scientific VR interactivity-by-domination, this simulation boldly reduces all possible experience to an exquisitely rendered, narrativeless digital swamp. This is the cut-less edge of the VR float tank – no hard surfaces, few distinguishable forms, no objectionably large objects, no scale adjustments, no social pressures, no disturbance. In superb isolation, the supplicant wafts amidst abstract amorphous elements, vague transitions and Kleenex-focus pastels, a morphine haze of compulsive serenity, the electronic mushspace. Anchorless, groundless, some might say pointless.

Short Sighted?

In her research to recreate a unity of self-interior and world-exterior 'eliminating the Cartesian duality between body and mind that has played a part in the shameless exploitation of nature by man', a catalysing process took place in the early-'80s when CharDavies removed her contact lenses and rediscovered space. This probably explains a lot.

Song of *Osmose*

The audio is a soothing aeroplane-embarkation mix for Spatialised Sound (i.e. moves when you do): elevated voice-synth music that imparts an approval of the human (CharDavies: 'Sound brings a lot of emotion to the piece'). It filters out the weight of a borrowed SGI, humming unobtrusively in the background somewhere like a quality digital refrigerator. An easily-overlooked piece of techno-trivia, this system runs quietly on a $1.4 million Onyx on loan from Silicon Graphics, a mainframe benevolence normally reserved for militarybusiness and gameviolence favours, which begs absent questions about why and what such a machine would, or even could, be doing if it weren't here… The soundtrack carries the emotional range of an imported flock wallpaper catalogue.

The intense vagueness of immersantworld is equalled, in degree only, by the rigorous precision of the *Osmose* operations infrastructure: it demands days-in-advance reservation (with a pronounced preference for press), security entry (appointment privilege is one hour prior to museum opening, requiring op-camera identity validation, armed guard cross-referenced approvalling, entry escort plastic nametag) and two contiguous VR pre-show valetmen making complex technical moves. Obscured in the intricate promotional encyclopaedia is a reference to the paper, signed on each embarkation, divesting *Osmose* of responsibility for any Immersant's personal/mechanical failing while under the influence of the art object.

CharDavies: 'The immersive experience encourages serene gentle and contemplative behaviour.'

It is force-gentling in a general, padded cellular team, the gathered witnesses to immersion, the public testimonials of overcome users: I'm a philosopher and it really is an altering experience, a cosmic consciousness type of embodiment, what I always thought would happen to me after I died. Now I'm not afraid.'

IntraBIT POSTSCRIPT: There is another performer who capitalises on the spectacle of technology to get outlandish attention, a little more honest and blatant in his tactics of exploding people rather than just dumbfounding them: the Unabomber. America's own vigilante anti-tech postal detonation master has been disturbingly successful in making himself heard. An audience out of reach of CharDavies, despite the money, despite her booked-out viewing sessions in the gallery. They both make the same conceptual slip, though – that somehow, in the complex fabric of contemporary society, one can extract the material conditions of existence (i.e. technology), and that we are all complicit in using, creating and understanding a certain solitude, devoid of, and different from, the social context, configured in the way we live and the technologies we use.

Perhaps Char could take her naïve naturenostalgia and contrived techno-blindness, her jungle of quotes, and marry Mr. Unabomber technodemoniser, pledge troth in concomitant deafness to the intricate social possibilities that cut through the machinery of capitalism and living, make little virtual bomb babies. Like the marriage of presleydaughter and michaeljackson…

But, back to Char, who, unfettered, makes a great story. Years ago, when she visited the bureau's own VR lab and was still one of the directors of SoftImage, she demonstrated the software and sung its praises. Struggling with a less capable rendering engine, a young bureau artist asked Char how to get access to this equipment for a project not having the requisite $30,000 for a licence

to buy SoftImage. Char turned to the starry-eyed aspirant and said bluntly, 'start your own software company'. Probably not bad advice to a young artist, many of whom still expect some sort of elite patronage and are never clued into the difficulties of maintaining a critical practice outside of the mainstream ideas of work. It does, however, seriously jeopardise the validity of cultural worker/visual artist as valuable social contributor. The imperative she presented in her answer [not so original] was that you buy yourself a cultural voice, or bomb yourself one. I don't know which of these options I find less appealing or more drastic; the latter, at least, involved some degree of imagination and technical expertise. Undermining her own value as artist, she has had to buy into the corporate idea and explore the immersive environment of commercialfrenzy.

GAMEOVER bureau of inverse technology.
intraBIT/extraBIT

Music is the Message

Jeff Mills Interviewed by Hari Kunzru

Vol 1 #11, Autumn 1998

A Hard City

Detroit has long been a landmark in the sonic imagination. After slavery, it became, like Chicago, one of the railheads of the black exodus Northward. The railroads acted as cultural arteries, transmitting people and musical forms from the deep South of New Orleans and the rural Mississippi Delta through the Midwest and into the bright, new urban world of the Great Lakes. In the process, the acoustic sound of Delta blues was exposed to the noise of industrial production lines, and mutated into the steam-train, factory-floor boogie of electric R&B. Basin Street Blues goes to Motor City Stomp. By the boomtime '60s, Detroit was synonymous with the hopeful three-minute soul-fictions of Motown, a label whose productivist ethic and mass market appeal was always an ironic mirror to the culture of Ford and General Motors that dominated the lives of its young, black public.

Motown people may have started out dancing in the streets, but, as the '70s wore on, they were gradually reduced to living just enough for the city. During the bleak Reagan years, Detroit seemed a dead zone, a symbol of the end of the old industrial order. But, by the start of the '90s, the decaying town, having absorbed the trauma of the oil crisis and world recession, had reinvented itself as the imaginary dark heart of a new global urban culture.

Detroit techno is the sound of the city. Not of city people but the city itself. The humans, if they are still alive at all, have been co-opted entirely by the urban machine, absorbed into its processes, their bodies disciplined by its unforgiving rhythms. It is no exaggeration to say that this style, with its bleak synthetic tones and hard four-four kick drums, has probably had more influence on what music sounds like around the world than any single genre since the blues.

Transmissions from the Future

Detroit's synthesis of funk-trance grooves and European disco-futurism was accomplished by a surprisingly small coterie of producers, who started their experiments in the mid-1980s. The stories of Cybotron, Model 500 and the transition from disco to electro-funk to techno have been well told elsewhere by writers like Matthew Collin (*Altered State*) and Kodwo Eshun (*More Brilliant than the Sun: Adventures in Sonic Fiction*). One of the pioneers was Jeff Mills, who, as producer and DJ, has seeded the sound from Durban to Tokyo and must bear no small responsibility for the fact that urbanites around the world now live in a media landscape in which stripped-down electronic beats soundtrack everything from their shopping trips to their drug experiences to their nights at home in front of the telly.

Mills is a quiet, bird-like man with a gaunt face and long fingers. When he deejays, he uses three decks, rarely playing a record for longer than a minute, and often opens all three channels at once, filtering the sound so one deck is playing a bassline, the second the middle and the third the lead. His involvement with his machines is so intense, so concentrated, that, as he darts from mixer to turntable, Mills the DJ seems self-evidently a component of a human-machine assemblage, a system which includes crowd, PA, the whole apparatus of record production and the stylus cartridge whose sensitivity he has turned up so it produces an angry, metallic treble buzz. It is unsurprising that, when Mills describes the experience of making music in a studio, he is preoccupied with the frustration he feels when 'the message' (for Mills music is always 'the message' or 'communication') is lost, or degraded, in transmission from mind to DAT.

'The producer has to transfer what he's thinking about to his hands and then to the machine,' he explains. 'The better the producer, the clearer the picture will be. It's a translation from my hands to the machine. And that's usually where it gets lost.' In a way this is a standard sentiment, a wish expressed by every artist since the Romantics began to lament the gap between inspiration and artefact, but Mills' wish for a closer symbiosis with his tools slides toward a desire for cyborgisation, for physical integration. 'What I hope,' he says, 'is for someone to create a sequencing program that relates from what you think to a keyboard or sound generator. A lot of ideas get lost because we can't make our machines do exactly what we thought about.'

To a mainstream musical culture, which is used to treating records as 'works', inviolate objects which contain some kind of artistic essence, Mills' conception of music must seem strange. 'After you make the record,' he says, 'you put the idea into the DJ's hands and it's up to the DJ to relay that message at the most opportune time or in the best way.' He seems to think of musical work as process, as information flow, opening up a channel between producer and dancer.

Mills' language of messages, communications and communiqués is part of the guiding theology of Detroit techno: the story of the informational circuit that runs from future to present, from the clear tomorrow of *Drexciyan* battlecruisers, UFOs ('you might see one fly…') and the rings of Saturn right the way back to the rotting streets of today. It is a circuit that channels energy through the body of the producer into his studio, energy that eventually exits via the PA and distributes itself over the dancefloor. Detroit itself is a satellite dish, collecting and amplifying the future-potential, sending it skittering over the rusting cars in the city streets…

Mills: 'For me, [my music is] about making people feel they're in a time ahead of this present time. Like if you're hearing someone speak in a language you don't understand, or you're in surroundings you've never seen before. It's about taking away your location, making the listener helpless.'

Unlike some other producers, Mills' future isn't a pure, chrome science-fiction dream. It's a *Verfremdungseffekt*, the disorientation of pure potential. The Detroit drum attack is just a kind of softening-up, forcing listeners to open themselves to the message.

From Bauhaus to… House

'I'm trying to show my idea of what life will be like in the 21st century. Technology is going to shape the way we think. For example, as things get more expensive, space will be rare. I can see that happening already in London. So technology will create spaces in other ways. Virtual spaces. Sound spaces.'

Detroit techno is architecture. That is why there is no narrative progression, no chord changes, no unfolding of themes, no counterpoint: sound spaces, not sound travelling through time. 'So few people understand that,' says Mills, talking about minimalism, 'how to just let it play…'

The cars and buildings have dematerialised in response to the pull of the future. 'We are almost out of the phase of the territorial,' says Mills. Detroit: the first portable city; its inhabitants virtualised it a long time ago. 'This is what a lot of people used to do in Detroit. We would create a track just for the ambience, just for the location where you live, and let it run throughout the day. This is not music you're eventually going to put on DAT and sell. It's just for living in.'

Machine Evolution

It's noticeable, when listening to Mills, that, although he thinks of his music in concrete terms (strings 'melt into the body' like 'turning a heater on'), sound often seems to be just signal for him, just a vehicle for the message. So, does this message have a content? The groundbreaking Detroit act, Underground Resistance, which Mills founded with Mike Banks, used to plaster their sleeves with manifesto-like language, preparing their audience for some undefined sonic revolution. So I wonder if 'the message' is political.

'Oh, no,' says Mills. 'It's abstract. It's what you're trying to say.' Well, that told me. Mills is totally unforthcoming about content or inspiration for the sounds on his records. There doesn't seem to be a clear aesthetic or social agenda, but he has some unusual organising principles. 'I think of a concept and maybe put it in some kind of colour scale,' he tells me at one point. 'I need a very clean feel with some amount of drama, so maybe I pick green. In my mind I have this idea of what green sounds like. Green is the frequencies which are much lower, not subsonic, but midrange.' Then he confusingly glosses this by saying, 'It's just like if you take a keyboard and start from white and go all the way to black.'

Mostly Mills talks about himself as the originator of the message, using the usual romantic vocabulary of the artist, the creator. But he is a creator with a peculiar relationship to his tools. 'Often I get half-way with a sequence and then just let it run. I'll go out, leave it running for up to twenty-four hours. The machines fluctuate. Over time, the sequence changes slightly. The machines mould themselves, giving their own character to a track. We did that a lot with UR. Sometimes we would let the sound run for days at a time. It would evolve into a very fixed state.'

Techno, self-evidently, is music of, and about, technology. Producers are intimate with their studio kit and the imagery of flight decks, control panels and instrumentation ('and now… I throw this switch') which has always peppered samples, and track titles sign their affinity with technicians of other kinds. Detroit – the imaginary site where an older generation of industrial machines is giving way to information machines, flows speeding up and dematerialising – is where human relationships to technology are being reconfigured.

Jeff Mills goes out to the cinema and leaves the machines to evolve their sequence in the studio, and, in doing so, makes perhaps the most eloquent commentary we have on a cultural shift in all kinds of production, artistic and otherwise. It's a tension which has long been felt in pop music, well expressed in the grumpy Indiekid T-shirt slogan from a few years ago: 'faceless techno bollocks'. (Elsewhere other T-shirts riposted 'fuck Britpop'). These days, the rock idol, Liam Agonistes, every inch the trad-artist, alone and romantically suffering onstage, is in mortal combat with something distributed, shifting (Mills is X102, UR, Axis…) and not altogether human. Sometimes Mills calls himself 'Purposemaker' and the listener finds the following (unattributed) statement on an inner sleeve: 'Only the consciousness of a purpose that is greater than any man can seed and fortify the souls of men.' It's too easy to identify the purposemaker as the artist and the power as God. In Detroit, the power that is greater than man, that is seeding and fertilising his soul, is inorganic, nameless, silicon-based.

Fear

'Sometimes, when I think of a rhythm,' says Mills, 'I think of a machine that is walking somewhere, some type of movement, and I try to vividly create that type of motion.' Robot tanks, assembly lines, colonising the imagination, articulated as hard drum tracks pounding the bodies of the dancers. Who is originating this rhythm? Us or them? Trace the process back. Which came first? Artist or machine? The idea of the machine in the mind of the artist? What placed the idea there? Infinite regress…

Detroit techno is also scary music, scary precisely because its unforgiving repetition reminds us of our immersion in remorseless, mechanised, computerised systems. Detroit fetishises this relationship: take drugs, jack your body to the rhythm of the machines – it's no different from what you do at the office every day. Perhaps you feel like a lab rat pressing a lever for doses of endorphins. At least, at 3 a.m. in a warehouse, as you come up on another pill, you know you're an honest lab rat.

This is everything we are supposed to forget about our lives. Aren't we expected to maintain the fiction that we are bounded, single and free? The fascination with Detroit lies in the way it links horror and a guilty, vertiginous pleasure. What would it feel like to give in, to stop worrying about your precious individual identity? To stop fighting, struggling, choosing and just get fucked up on the beat? In a culture driven by an ideology of individualism, which slyly encourages the subject to express its supposed uniqueness through hyper-regulated acts of consumption, surrendering the self is a complex act. Either it's a form of (underground) resistance, or a perverse celebration of one's slavery. Refusal of choice as the last valid revolutionary gesture? Or just another consumer suicide? Are you sure you want to shut down now?

Techno is invisible in America, perhaps because it reveals so much about the hollowness of American individualism. Yet it is not a closed statement, not a condemnation. For all the horror and darkness, the trapped feeling of so much of this music, there is still the voice of Jeff Mills, murmuring into my tape recorder: 'We're on the verge, something's coming, something's coming, something's coming…'

Free Improvisation Actuality

Ben Watson

Vol 1 #19, Spring 2001

Conventional thinking contrasts classical music to pop, assigning the technologies of score and recording to different epochs. Free improvisation doesn't credit the significance of such 'progress'; on the contrary, classical and pop are viewed as symptoms of an identical malaise. For Derek Bailey, Lol Coxhill and the hundred-odd international musicians who play free improvisation in public, recording is simply the technical apotheosis of the score. Following on from the radical critiques of classicism made by both free jazz and the 'indeterminate' compositions of the '60s, free improvisation focuses on a time-based art's most basic virtue: a cultivation of unpredictability as an end in itself. On the way, free improvisation is also an elegant answer to the accusations of recuperation and commodity-fetishism which Situationists, Art Strikers and Neoists hurl at visual artists. Here is an uncommodifiable art-happening that leaves no saleable residue, a poetry of modernist form that truly melts into air.

In 1919, Kurt Schwitters declared in *Der Sturm* that 'a perambulator wheel, wire-netting, string and cotton-wool are factors having equal rights with paint. The artist creates through the choice, distribution and metamorphosis of the materials.' Free improvisation is aural Dada: Any sound source – from traditional instruments played in outrageous ways to crisp packets, Pokémon watches or G3 PowerBooks – is permitted. Sampling and digital editing are ubiquitous, but subject to the judgement of the ultimate receiver: the distinctly analogue interface of airwaves and the human ear. Free improvisation, one of the few areas of cultural activity that adheres to Dada principles, comprises one of the most tenacious and vehement groupuscules in today's fractured music scene. Although improvisation is currently enjoying an Indian Summer – Sonic Youth are proselytisers, Tortoise are into it, Blast/Disobey puts its veterans in the limelight – it has weathered bop, prog, fusion, glam, punk, new romanticism, the Jazz Revival, minimalism, authentic, rave, lo-fi, the New Complexity and electronica without losing an (indeterminate) beat. It is fierce, angular, abstract. The timing is super-tight, closer to stand-up comedy than to the smudge and fuzz of post-rock or ambient. If you can't play, forget it. Its controversies, schisms and exclusions resemble those of revolutionary politics, claims to have 'broken out of the improv ghetto' by including such no-nos as tonality, regular rhythm or a hummable melody surface at regular intervals. But, far from accessing the energies of pop or funk, these invariably signal a failure of nerve, a lessening of tension, a lapse into feeble ingratiation.

It's not always great. Reputations burgeon, musicians coast. A recent complaint – voiced by Bailey, and also by bassist Simon Fell – is that you can predict the music on most improve-CDs by simply checking the names on the box. Musicians develop a personal 'sound', and people pay to hear it: What is deemed evidence of 'genius' is actually the reassurance of the already-known. So, the malign influence of the star system impacts on even these refusenik domains. However, there's probably no other scene in which musicians and listeners are more critical of these and other failings. Free improvisation: music for those who prefer the chill of actuality to the reliability of the concept.

Clubs
All Angels: (0)20 8348 9595
Cenophelle: (0)1932 571323
Flim-Flam: (0)20 8809 6891
Free Radicals: (0)20 7263 7265
Klinker: www.theklinker.freeserve.co.uk

Shop
Sound 323
323 Archway Road
London N6 5AA
sound323@aol.com

Radio
Infrequent

Print
Derek Bailey, *Improvisation: Its Nature and Practice in Music* (Da Capo Press)
Jeff Nuttall, *The Bald Soprano: A Portrait of Lol Coxhill* (Tak Tak Tak)
Ben Watson, *Derek Bailey and the Story of Free Improvisation* (Quartet)

Composing Ourselves

Flint Michigan

Vol 1 #21, Autumn 2001

As the author of one of the most provocative works of music theory, one that attempts to rescue music from the throes of its de-politicisation, Jacques Attali's recent reappearance in London fell a long way short of expectations. Going by the edited transcript of Attali's ICA talk in *Wire* magazine no. 129, Attali's ideas, first presented in his 1975 book, *Noise: The Political Economy of Music*, remain undeveloped and lacking in self-criticism. In many ways, his 'political economy of music' awaits its critique, for, as it stands, many of his more radical notions have been undermined by offers to manage cultural dissent, offers which have landed him work with the European Bank for Reconstruction and Development and which are reflected in the ambivalence of statements such as: 'Organising noises, creating differences in noises, is a way of demonstrating that violence can be transformed into a way of managing violence.'[1] Does his reappearance on the circuit, some 25 years after the book's publication, his failure to acknowledge the intellectual milieu that gave rise to his book (Baudrillard on the 'political economy of the sign' and Enzensberger's *Constituents of a Theory of the Media*, etc.) and the photos that adorn the *Wire* article not suggest that, once again, we are in the presence of a Public Intellectual? Is he yet another touting his 'discourse-object' to a public raised on the pacifying format of the seminar? One aspect of his book's appeal, as with Baudrillard's work, is his claim to have surpassed the political economy of Marx. Whilst such an endeavour is necessary for getting to grips with an acculturated capital, it is also more often used as a demonstration of intellectual might.

That said, Attali's key concept, that of 'composing', is itself surely a reworking of Marx's idea, buried in the *Grundrisse*, of 'really free working, e.g. composition'. This indebtedness to Marx may explain why Attali uses the term 'composing' when what he describes has always struck me as lying closer to 'improvising': 'Beyond the rupture of the economic conditions of music, composition is revealed as the demand for the truly different system of organisation, a network within which a different kind of music and different social relations can arise. A music produced by each individual for himself, for pleasure outside meaning, usage and exchange.'[2]

One of the difficulties with Public Intellectuals such as Attali is that, once they have theorised their 'beyond', they can't find the collective subjects to propel the social change that they apparently desire. But, whereas Baudrillard,

1. Jacques Attali, 'Ether Talk', *Wire*, no. 209, July 2001. Is this not another way of saying that music can be used to manage antagonism?
2. Jacques Attali, *Noise: The Political Economy Of Music* (1975), Manchester: Manchester University Press, 1985, p. 137.

in the early-'70s, urged 'symbolic transgression' as a counter to the enforced diversification of the working class, at least Attali has a more concrete notion of the antagonistic musician in mind – an idea of the musician pegged to the movement of economic history and its changing codes. But, as the quotation above testifies, his notion of 'composing' is seriously problematic. What does this 'individual pleasure' signify, what 'code' does it uphold? At one point in *Noise*, perhaps lost for words, Attali offers it up as 'egoistic enjoyment' and, with that, the dim outline of a collective subject seems to disappear from our view.

So, the radical potential of Attali's 'composing' – the bassline of which is the re-appropriation of our time and labour from the capitalist process of exchange-value – is negated by what Baudrillard calls the 'private individual as productive force' in which it is implicated. For me, this explains why Attali has difficulty developing 'composition' beyond those individualist dimensions which are of prime importance to the music industry, for 'pleasure outside meaning', which abandons the construction of new meaning, simply reaffirms the capitalist paradigm founded on the relation between the individual and pleasure. The exploration of this relation, which marks the subversive impact of improvisation, is also one that reaffirms music as a commodity, a reified relation that submerges the social relations improvising can bring to the fore. So, as a 'new' concept of political economy, 'composition', as Attali leaves it, becomes readily assimilable to the 'individualist productive force' of the music industry. As egoistic enjoyment, it can once more act as a sublimator of violence: 'We can explore these different forms of organisation [of music] much more easily, much more rapidly, than we can explore different ways of organising reality.'[3]

For 'composition' to work critically as an antagonistic practice, the 'network' of which Attali speaks needs to be something more than a simple homologue of the network of political economy already monitored by the music industry. For its social relation to be something more than an exchange of discourse-objects, maybe, with a nod to Attali, we should make a music without instruments, compose our own social relation and use the resultant music to 'explore different ways of organising reality'. The critique of Attali's political economy is a practice of collective subjects.

3. Loc. cit.

Concentrated Listening

Flint Michigan

Vol 1 #23, Spring 2002

Canon

Most of the early histories of electronic music take as their starting point two post-war institutions that pioneered experimental perception by means of music: the Groupe de Recherches Musicales (GRM), established in Paris in 1945, and the Cologne-based WDR radio studio. Both institutions were interested in moving away from the timbral restriction of orchestral instrumentation and, to varying degrees, from the reliance upon notation. Perceived as restrictions upon perception, these two parameters had already been subverted by those such as Edgar Varèse, with his use of percussive timbres and handwound sirens in *Ionisation* and, more presciently, in both his wish for sound to be studied scientifically and in his often thwarted plans to make electronic music. Both of these wishes were, to some degree, realised by GRM and WDR. The former, founded by Pierre Schaeffer, was the home of *musique concrète* – a movement that sought to explore the sonorous qualities of objects, to inventorise them and to compose using the resultant 'found sounds'. The latter, the home of *Electronische Musik*, substituted the pure pitches of electricity for conventional classical instruments. However, if GRM and WDR had succeeded in developing new timbres with which to intensify aural perception, the persistent virtuosity that Varèse sought to disassemble returned in WDR's attempts to perfect the mathematics of serialism, and the compositional accents which, with GRM, came to form the 'spine of narrative'.

Desiring Perception

From its early days of being a kind of counter-institution, the GRM and *musique concrète* quickly became a canonical alternative. Schaeffer's *À La Recherche d'une Musique Concrète* (1952) carried the sub-text that experimentation with sound could be reduced to a methodology. With the emphasis on studying sound objects and on sonorising narratives, the GRM provided a framework that could cushion the affectivity of sound; sound was harnessed to traditional artistic purposes and not to cultural dynamics that could help to change perception, make perception a conduit of desire. For Schaeffer, the musical object, when separated from its context, was to be used 'according to its familial relationships and the concordance of its characteristics'. The 'concentrated listening' that Schaeffer had hoped *musique concrète* would deepen had come to focus exclusively on the object, thus reducing the potentiality of aural perception to sound for sound's sake. Such restrictions served not only to reify musical practice under the auspices of a research programme but also to reinforce the authority of the composer to the detriment of the listener. In this light, 'concentrated listening' comes to imply a scholarly command rather than a mode of intensified listening that is more fitting to the fusion of desire and perception.

Almost Nothing

With the wider availability of recording equipment and studio technology, the institutional control of sound experimentation passed into less didactic hands. Those interested in the 'found sounds' associated with *musique concrète* came to reject the strict confines of the 'musical object' as they began to turn the microphone onto the social world around them, extending the notion of music beyond that of the dominant representation of the musical. In this way, *musique concrète* began to mutate into the field recording epitomised by Luc Ferrari's *Presque Rien No. 1*. Setting his microphone on the window ledge of a bedroom that overlooked the harbour of a Yugoslav fishing village, Ferrari proceeded to record the sounds in the early hours of the morning: 'I recorded those sounds which repeated everyday: the first fishermen passing by [...] Events determined by society.' The resultant piece, frowned upon by his colleagues at GRM, was in many ways an extension of Cage's *4′33″*; rather than remaining in the auditorium to demonstrate the loudness of 'silence' as Cage had done, Ferrari abandoned the legitimation of the institutional site at the same time as he abandoned his identity as 'composer' to become a meta-musician. In setting the 'composer' alongside the listener, *Presque Rien*, immerses both in the miniscule sounds of the social. Rather than maintaining desire and perception as mutually exclusive, rather than allowing compositional form to reify the passage of time, Ferrari offers up the informal and infinitesimal creativity of a 'situation'. As Gilles Deleuze puts it in *Cinema 2*: 'Between the reality of the setting and that of the action, it is no longer a motor extension which is established, but rather a dreamlike connection through the intermediary of the liberated sense organs.'

Second Nature

With the work of Chris Watson, the field recording came to represent the antithesis of the 'dreamlike connection'. Rather than mobilising desiring-perception by means of an undirected attentiveness, Watson's meticulous recordings of natural sounds not only direct perception to pre-existing representations, thus creating a 'sound realism', but they also take their legitimation from the concept of nature as authentic experience. Such a narrowing of focus for musical practice has the effect of severing desire from perception by drawing desire into registering the authenticity of the perceived rather than inveigling desire to alter perception. In this way, the senses are not 'liberated' to become 'theoreticians in their immediate praxis' (Marx), a dialectic of knowing and feeling, but become adjuncts to an inflation of the represented – an over-investment in that which is already perceptible. With Ultra-Red's project, *Second Nature*, based around the struggles of gay groups to maintain the open spaces of Griffiths Park in LA, *musique concrète* came to be inflected with political intent. From its opening sounds of outdoor love-making, we are witness to desire being an immediate component of the sounds themselves. These extend to the ambiences of the park and suggest that the social field that Ultra-Red are recording and altering is the site for diffuse desire; it is space itself that can be cathected, modified, made conducive to desire. Furthermore, as the title of their project suggests, there is a move away from the naturalistic use of an authentic nature and the positing of a 'second nature'. That the sounds are presented to the listener in microscopically altered form not only sensualises perception but also hints at the 'subtilised' perception of new desires and new drives. Such a second nature is played out in the way that Ultra-Red do not respect the naturalising authenticity of the 'field recording', but instead reveal that the natural is produced. Not only is protest made instinctual and homosexuality returned to nature, but the digital exploration of sound sources brings a fledgling politics of music to the fore. The binding of aesthetic form, the slavishness of canonical legitimation and the escalation of the represented are outflanked in favour of a pursuit of what it is now possible to perceive and alter. Schaeffer's 'concentrated listening' can thus become the sharing of 'micro-perception' between producer and listener, which, in its abandonment of notation and familiar timbres, is itself productive of a micropolitics of affective linkage – no longer is a divide maintained between composer and listener but both become meta-musicians: listeners as operators.

Free as the Air

Eddie Prévost

Vol 1 #23, Spring 2002

I'm sitting there on stage with my drum kit, barrel drum, cymbals, gong and bits and pieces. Beating and bowing. I'm listening to the other musicians. Then I hear a sound that is familiar yet wrong. I've heard it before, but it's out of phase, out of joint, displaced, dislocated. It's me but I'm not doing it. The phantom sampler has struck.

The conventional wisdom is that it is flattering to be copied. There was a time when copying was so difficult that one admired anyone who got near to the original. Now, anyone – with the right gear – can do it and you can hardly tell the difference. This is because there is no difference! The time frame can be so condensed (almost real time) that the copy can come out almost before the originator is aware of what they have done in the first place. The train seems to reach its destination before the engine has left the station!

All this can be slightly unnerving. A new relationship has developed in which there has been no negotiated social contract. I'm not so worried about any financial dropout by unlicensed use of my intellectual property. I can't make much money out of the sounds in the first place, so it seems churlish to object to anybody else trying. No, what bugs me is that 'I' am being selectively cannibalised, and it's behind my back (if you know what I mean?). Somehow my sounds, once they are made, are considered to be no longer part of me. They move beyond my control. They are deemed lost. Being lost means that they can be 'found' and used without a 'by your leave'. Recording a sound somehow confers, or transfers, its property status.

There was a good deal of mischievous humour attached to 'plunder phonics'. It took – mostly from commercially popular sources – existing recorded material, treating and incorporating it, in a subversive way, into another art medium. It poked fun at the pop artist who was being plundered. They were placed in a position of some cultural discomfort.

But, are sounds made 'free' by releasing them into the environment? Can a sampler claim to have 'found' this source material? Claiming that something has been found is no proof that it was lost or that its original owner has no continuing rights or responsibility as to what happens to it thereafter. So far samplers are assuming rights in the absence of any counter-claim. It feels like being mugged. It has been argued that such activity is justified as a response to the expropriation and mass exploitation by powerful capitalists. Unfortunately, a by-product of this action is to unconsciously recommend that it serves as a model for our relations with everyone. All people and their products become valid sources for unregulated and abusive expropriation.

Let me run this past you. I reckon that if someone, without my permission, can use my sounds, then they give me licence to intercept their sonic output. Is there not an implicit contract here? A mutuality? If anyone takes unasked, then surely the taker should be prepared for some kind of natural reciprocity. Yet can you imagine what would happen if I moved the speakers or turned the volume down on a fellow musician who was carrying out sampling? All hell would break loose. I would be infringing their rights of 'free' expression.

Junk Subjectivity

Keston Sutherland

Vol 1 #28, Summer 2004

Over the last 25 years, the phrase 'avant-garde poetics' has become synonymous with the banalisation of polemical language. A new orthodoxy has been scrivened into the so-called margin of aesthetics, a jargon of inauthenticity with its very own catalogue of abused nouns and outcast concepts, unvarying as the deep problems of capitalist existence that it serves to occlude. What are these nouns and concepts? *Dixit* jargon: They are the hangover of Romanticism. Sift through pretty much any article by Bruce Andrews and the familiar assortment of put-downs is there, icing the debris-syntax: We are against Content, The Obvious, The Smooth, 'the transitive ideal of communicating, the direct immediate broadcast [...] the Truth with a capital T [...] usual generic architecture of signification [...] continuities [...]' These phrases converge invariably on one principal target, the most loathsome because it is the manager of all the others. *Dixit* Andrews: 'Psychology-Centered Subjective Expressiveness on the part of the Author.' The self-proclaimed extremism of L=A=N=G=U=A=G=E poetics – the predominant US literary avant-garde – consists, roughly speaking, in this: It is the linguistic means of producing text material to which it ascribes the capacity of resisting the mechanisms of interpretive consumption that *homo consumer* falsely and proudly believes he owns. L=A=N=G=U=A=G=E poetry will not give its readers 'Subjective Expressiveness' that can be identified with the psychic operations (mood swings, etc.) of an 'Author'. It refuses to give them this Expressiveness because they take it the wrong way, i.e. as if it were propaganda or a latte, or because the state and billboards and TV use Expressiveness to sell dildos and wars, or because the mental operations of *homo consumer* herself cannot hit their peak freedom-rating until they are dis-aligned with the language most familiar to them – these and other reasons.

The dirty concept floating about in all these disjunctive anti-slogans and insurrectionary multi-implications is the concept of authority. The author is authority incarnate, or a special instance of authority, and whenever he uses language that signifies or in some way projects his authority, he is complicit in the general authoritative mystification of real life on which capitalism depends and of which capitalism is the beneficiary. Fortunately, however, it is quite possible to be a poet without being an author. All that needs to be done is for the poet to make sure that she rinses from her language all the soddenness of authoritative syntax, grammar, diction, argumentation and, of course, Psychology-Centred Subjective Expressiveness, and bingo! Suddenly we have a materialist poetry that smashes through the logic gates of the prison-house of language and pisses into the governor's Rolodex.

The new orthodoxy has become especially popular in the period since the collapse of the Berlin Wall and the victory of the US in the Cold War, partly because of the cautious and respectful attitudes toward L=A=N=G=U=A=G=E theory of those poets and critics writing in that period, who set out their own ideas about aesthetics and politics more or less in opposition to L=A=N=G=U=A=G=E theory. This same period has also seen an event unparalleled in the history of communication: The English language has become the final, indomitable and universal *lingua franca* of global capitalism. Possibly the internet has played a greater role in this obliteration of language difference than any other engine of propaganda and commerce (and their opposites). There in a millisecond, before the Syrian or Indonesian retina, is a vast hinterstate of English, all linked up and laid out in the tightest integration possible in the history of text production, creeping steadily across the world grid like an emancipated fungus. Capitalism benefits immensely from this outreach, and English *qua* capitalism-logos also benefits, becoming more dominant as it becomes more prolific. But, is English, as a medium for anti-capitalist communication, likewise invested with new potential as its enemy language becomes hugely more promiscuous? Are the possibilities for distorting and indicting the language of capitalism enlarged, along with the quantity of that language pumped into the market?

Over the past year, a ripple of interest slid through the mainstream media, concerning spam emails and the apparently poetic character of some of the language that shows up in them. The suggestion is always the same; as the BBC put it, 'lots of people are starting to find literary value hidden among the porn, penis patches, generic Viagra deals and mortgage offers'. This stuff is, of course, valueless in itself, the dark froth of the black market; but its victims, the passive recipients of unscrupulous Nigerian demands for bank account details and offensive invitations to look at cumshots, can find something magical in it all: Poetry. What makes this language good raw material for amateur poetising is its wrongness: frequently it is screwed-up English, a breach of conventional syntax and grammar, a funny rash of solecisms and mal-appropriated advert-talk. The offended Western consumer can laugh it all off in rhymes and verses, converting the gibberish of Dr. Arliru Ayodele or Chief Wale Adenuga into a piece of double-edged irony, poking fun simultaneously at the authors of the spam and, with a consciousness of being postmodern, at the idea of authors in general. Who would come up with this kind of language on their own? Clearly it couldn't be the expression of a native user of English; and so in English, it looks oddly mechanical, strikingly devoid of Truth with a capital T, absurdly incapable of living up to the transitive ideal of communicating. Fraudulent pleas for help from endangered Arabs are the misjudged replicas of Psychology-Centred Subjective Expressiveness, impossible to believe or care about, an irritation pure and simple. But, if the Western consumer pauses for a few seconds before deleting them, they can make hilarious reading; aren't they, in fact, avant-garde? Isn't their wrongness in fact strictly semiotic, strictly a matter of signification and its fragility, and is there any reason why it can't be taken for a sort of Brechtian alienation technique? And, thus, the excluded, fugitive bits of English-as-capitalism-logos are picked up and recycled to the credit (in stacks of symbolic capital) of their target consumers. A salutary poetics of consumer rights in the face of a barrage of unwanted commercial pressure.

The question for poets who care about the relation of aesthetics to politics is this: To what extent are our most militant theories of poetry underwritten by the Western ideology of consumer rights? Do the theories of interpretive freedom on offer in the avant-garde amount to a kind of ideological consumer watchdog? L=A=N=G=U=A=G=E poetry plainly does not constitute any kind of barrier against the use of English-as-capitalism-logos by corporations and governments, nor could it; transformations of syntax are superstructural phenomena and cannot be other than this. This is true of all poetry, not just L=A=N=G=U=A=G=E poetry. But is the mode of negation described by Bruce Andrews (and ascribed by him to his own work) anything more than the freedom to reject language commodities in the name of our rights as the consumers of those commodities, and to circulate pieces of disfigured language which, in the light of that ascription, can appear only as the tokens of our rejection?

The recycling of spam email into postmodern lyric is, from one angle, a symptom of this 'extremist' curtailment of negativity. The raw material comes from black-marketeers and fraudsters in countries the US bombs or enslaves through financial debt; it ends up reinforcing the orthodox aesthetic ideology of the US avant-garde. It is negated by means of a strictly ironic *détournement*, which amounts to positive inclusion in a dominant poetic culture whose creed is anti-author. The interface is violent and preposterous. What Western theoreticians of aesthetics are keen to be seen avoiding with sophisticated zeal – the rights of an author, authority for the English language in Western society – is almost certainly something that the African 'businessmen' sitting in front of their keyboards in their IMF colonies are highly anxious to take for themselves. Spam is not there to be re-ordered magically into poetry. It is evidence of the desire of people to cheat capitalism and to screw money out of gullible and greedy English-speakers. And, for anyone unconcerned with the consumer rights of Westerners and the para-political ideologies that make up their pedestal, that is poetry enough.

Zombie Nation

Paul Helliwell

Vol 2 #5, Spring 2007

> That which determines subjects as means of production and not as living purposes, increases with the proportion of machines to variable capital [...] its consummate organisation demands the coordination of people that are dead.
>
> Theodor Adorno, *Minima Moralia*

> I thought that beauty alone would satisfy. But the soul is gone. I can't bear those empty, staring eyes.
>
> Charles Beaumont in *White Zombie*[1]

> Too often people are happy drawing up an inventory of yesterday's concerns, the better to lament the fact of not getting an answer.
>
> Nicolas Bourriaud, *Relational Aesthetics*[2]

In my previous article for *Mute*, 'First Cut is the Deepest' (Vol 2 #4), I talked about a Panglossian enthusiasm for the social in art, courtesy of Nicolas Bourriaud's relational aesthetics. Described by Adorno as the means by which art expresses its own uncertainty, this enthusiasm for the social is not confined to art, but has become the motor of modern capitalism, one example of which is Web 2.0. For this reason, music is thrust centre stage, both as a means and a metaphor for unproblematic sociability and communication – from a mobile phone ad selling its music player by insisting 'there will be one song that will get you to phone home' to the opportunity to listen to music inspired by the abstract minimalism of Donald Judd at Tate Modern. In the same room as this event, we are moved along the curatorial timeline from Ad Reinhardt's stripped-down modernism (which Adorno would recognise) to the dawn of relational aesthetics, with the mirrored surfaces of Robert Morris incorporating you, the viewer, into the work. 'You' can also be seen in the mirrored cover of last year's Christmas issue of *Time* magazine, declared person of the year for your sterling unpaid work on Web 2.0. But sociability, even the kind produced by music, has never been unproblematic for power – as the essentially disciplinary nature of the discourses around the crowd and music reveal – at least until now. So, what do art, music and Web 2.0 have to say to each other and about us?

In commercial TV, wealth is circulated in two subsystems – one that produces the programmes and sells them to TV companies, and a second, wherein TV companies sell the viewers watching them to the advertisers. Web 2.0 dispenses

1. Edward Halperin, *White Zombie*, 1931, is out of copyright and downloadable for free at http://www.archive.org/detail/WhiteZombie
2. Nicolas Bourriaud, *Relational Aesthetics*, Dijon: Les Presses du Réel, 2002.

with the first subsystem; you provide the content for free, leaving only the second need to 'monetise eyeballs', in MySpace co-founder Chris DeWolfe's parlance. These eyeballs are doubly monetised because they also provide the basis for the stock market values of companies currently sucking in the dumb money (prior to rinsing it out). Several Wall Street finance houses encourage the reading of Charles MacKay's *Extraordinary Popular Delusions and the Madness of Crowds*, with its histories of Tulipomania and the South Sea Bubble, so that staff recognise the system is irrational and unstable.[3] It creates profits because it is irrational (as long as faith is high, the value remains high) and unstable (as soon as it goes, value collapses); it is a pyramid scheme (the smart money takes the difference and, later, the dumb money pays). If it were only the value of the work of Western 'creatives' being rinsed out (and more and more of the work of the West is in these unstable intangibles – brand, goodwill, design), it would not be such a tragedy, but capitalism is a global system.

This new sociability of Web 2.0, hosted on big corporate-owned servers, is the defeat of an arguably better working and more democratic ideal: peer-to-peer, strangled in its musical infancy by the not-so-invisible hand of copyright. Napster may be back from the dead and charging, but the music industry's worst nightmare – free music – is still on the prowl; its defeat is partial and temporary. In the long run, with digital copying and distribution effectively free, it is difficult to see how it can be otherwise. It is no surprise to find that MySpace is a direct response to peer-to-peer's 'defeat' and the changes a new format has brought about in the music industry. Indeed, it may be the prototype for further strategies of control for software, films, etc. Chris DeWolfe says the following:

> Tom [his MySpace co-founder] [... understands ...] what emerging musicians go through. He understands the frustration. I understood the macro trends of the music business. Labels were signing fewer acts, giving them less time to prove themselves and spending less money on marketing. We saw a need to develop a community for artists to get their music out to the masses [...] In the early days, there were a lot of bands signing up [...][4]

Deepening the work of Jacques Attali, Michael Chanan shows music as a constellation of antagonistic technologies, markets, commodities and services repeatedly pulled apart and remade by new technologies (from musical notation and printing to analogue recording and broadcasting). The combination of music software, peer-to-peer and MP3 (going beyond radio and cassette before it) threatened to unleash a world of free music by uniting the recording, promotion, distribution and consumption of music in one machine (the home

3. Chris DeWolfe and Tom Anderson', NataliePace.com, Vol. 3, Issue 1, 1 Jan 2006, http://www.i-sophia.com/newsletters/members/news.php?np=yes&issue=301/301&article=01.
Claire Bishop (Ed.), *Participation* (Documents of Contemporary Art), London: Whitechapel Art Gallery, 2006.
4. Natalie Pace, 'MySpace Conquers Google: Takes on World Exclusive Q&A with MySpace Co-founders.'

computer). This led to a fight between the large multinational electronics companies, producing the computers and MP3 players and their subdivisions marketing the recordings, owning the copyright or managing the artists. The record companies lost and are fighting a rearguard action. Unlike the vastly profitable days of CDs, when record companies could be subsidised with new money made by re-releasing old material in new formats, profits have fallen drastically and more bad news may be on the way.

As with many new technologies, the founders have not understood the transformation they are unleashing. Bands were actively recruited by MySpace as 'early adopters'; they chose it as a promotional tool (into the music industry), but they also claimed to want a more direct relationship with their fans outside of the record companies' control. By calling into question the economics of the music industry, MP3 has revealed the chronic dissatisfaction of artists, songwriters and producers – dissatisfaction of which they will soon be doubly free, when this relationship is all that bands have left to sell to their fans. The apparent defence of copyright by the music industry masks its relaxation – on MySpace, on YouTube. Paying for the right to make a copy is what makes music a commodity – fans demanded an extension of the right to make a copy as 'fair use' and they got it.

Recently, at MIDEM (the music licensing conference in Cannes), Attali joked that, other than playing gigs, soon all that bands will be able to sell is the right to attend a rehearsal or go to dinner with them. He was immediately handed a business card for a scheme enabling just that [www.artistshare.com], which promises the chance to '[Participate in] the one thing that cannot be downloaded [...] that the artist can hold on to [...] the creative process [sic].'[5]

The demand to pay for music is being resituated as active consumption – if you love your band, you'll pay. Ladies and gentlemen, welcome to the future of the music industry; it is, in its lack of anything material to sell, relational aesthetics, and the institution that will enable this is not the record companies or the art galleries but Web 2.0. The moral of the story is 'Be careful what you wish for.'

A fetish for 'liveness' pervades recorded music's last hours as a commodity, from the downsized, calculated naïveté and acoustic instrumentation of new folk and singer-songwriters to the live show – formerly an expensive means to advertise the CD, but now at their disposal the one means bands have with which to earn money. Music fans' habits have been conditioned by scarcity, the need to collect – what happens when this era is over? A whole industry has fossilised around this habit; it will take time to go whether it fights or not. The surplus of recorded sound on the computers of the world cannot be potlatched because to make a digital copy does not destroy the original or reduce its value. Music cannot even be given away because nothing is lost, it can only be shared

5. Jacques Attali, 'Ironie du Virtuel', *L'Express*, 21 January 2007, http://blogs.lexpress.fr/attali

in the weakest sense of the term. The CD is beginning to look like so much landfill and has already been pronounced dead by the departing head of EMI. Why even download anything when you can stream it? Recorded music is dematerialising beyond even the MP3 on your hard drive.

The relationship between music and art affects the light they throw on each other. Both have their origin in magic and in cults and have separated themselves (by becoming commodities and developing formal autonomy) to become the autonomous discourses that we currently know. During the 20th century, music, through recording, embraced reproduction and thus became mass culture, seemingly stripped of its autonomy – merely a commodity. Art defined itself in opposition, insisting on its aura, on its autonomy, its commodity nature hidden. At the same time, art, in denial of its commodity status, has tried to free itself from its autonomy, with its conceptual, performative and relational forms all leading to the generalised evaporation of the art object into the one-off happening (without presenting a barrier to the documentation being successfully commodified).

Recorded music is most often consumed asocially (via the CD played in privacy, the walkman, the MP3 player), but its logics of consumption continue to be social (the Top Ten, pirate radio shout-outs, the distorted MP3 on the phone on the bus). Web 2.0 is no different in its logics of consumption. It is awash with counters – Top Tens, customers who bought this also bought this, algorithms designed to predict what would appeal to you – a need to affirm some kind of community, to introduce the possibility of a chance encounter or a serendipitous discovery.

Žižek has written of the psychological dangers of blurring real and virtual identities, but perhaps another danger lies in online counters functioning as pecking orders. MySpace (a place for friends) just IS a giant popularity contest (Rank User – has no one seen *Carrie*?); this is the sole criterion and validation. Indeed, this extends to news stories about it which are nothing but 'so-and-so is becoming very popular'. The actual experience of MySpace is of slow uploading, fending off the advances of strangers with 970 friends (surely that's enough?), *Truman Show*-style viral advertising (this week I'm listening to…), kudos counters to help you fine-tune your product, but, above all, social anxiety (only five hits – I must persuade my friends to join). The fine line between this and vanity publishing risks the exposure of our ignoble motives. All this encourages self-reification with a Skinnerian thoroughness.

Social networking websites are experiments, like the relational art Jacques Rancière identifies as the invitation/encounter, the use that will be made of the site cannot be predicted. One of Bebo's founders compares the problem to inviting people to Welwyn Garden City – it's artificial so it won't grow unless it is 'seeded' and 'nurtured'. Almost all will emphasise that they don't want to be 'over-controlling', yet these are family malls – almost all ban pornography (before music, the motor of Web 1.0). Given the fink link on each photo – 'report inappropriate image' – it is a more controlled environment than any shopping mall. James Wales of Wikipedia likens its constitution to the unwritten one of Britain, evolving over time, and fellow developers insist they build what users ask for. What people 'ask for', even for themselves, is made over in the image of the commodity, and every click is marketing information.[6]

When Jaron Lanier calls Wikipedia and much of Web 2.0 'Digital Maoism', we know we are into a rerun of modernist disdain for the masses.[7] Lanier attempts to hook us by presenting himself as wronged by Wikipedia, which persists in describing him as a filmmaker when he has repudiated his Maya Deren phase and would prefer to be known for his term 'virtual reality'. He changes it, someone changes it back, as part of an 'edit war'; although he doesn't say as much, he's being 'cyber-bullied'. To my friends, however, Lanier is the man who beheaded Sony's robot cat at the ICA by picking it up by the scruff of the neck. This is Gombrowicz's 'interpersonal form', the extent to which we are created by others, which Bourriaud claims as the substrate of relational art. Despite this, Lanier is unhappy to be misrepresented and allowed no recourse, as was Gombrowicz. He is clear that the 'collective intelligence' harnessed by Web 2.0, the counters, the meta-searches compiling 'best-of' lists, just generates stupidity, that having large sites visited by everybody just generates traffic jams on the internet.

In comparison, cyber-theorist, John Brockman, is the Elias Canetti of this generation of crowd theorists, pointing out that crowds can (sometimes) be good. In *Here Comes Everybody*, the masses do not simply invade the net, they are also changed by the experience. But this is no more to the taste of the digerati (with their evolutionary systems, algorithms, positivism, signal processing metaphors and fetish for salons of 'smart' people) than it was to the 19th century intellectuals (ditto) at the birth of mass culture. John Carey, in his *The Intellectuals and The Masses: Pride and Prejudice Among the Literary Intelligentsia, 1880–1939*, points out in this steampunk version that the masses were symbolised by tinned food (a crowd metaphor that Canetti would recognise). This image recurs in the digital age as spam, with Monty Python's song echoing in the sound of senseless repetition clunking onto your hard drive. Indeed, like the fertile text of Gogol's *Dead Souls*, the new blogging tools enable the creation of fictitious people with fictitious opinions – splogs or blams. It seems that, no sooner has man created a new digital environment than it starts to be swamped like some re-run of the magic porridge pot (and, again, the moral of the story is 'Be careful what you wish for'). In digitally reproduced excess, even human opinion becomes toxic.

6. Ian Katz and Oliver Burkeman, 'The Web Revolutionaries – the Men and Women Who Reshaped the Net', *The Guardian*, Web 2.0 Special, 4 November 2006, http://www.guardian.co.uk/video/page/0,,1942132,00.html
7. Jaron Lanier, 'Digital Maoism: The Hazards of the New Online Collectivism', *Edge*, 30 May 2006, http://www.edge.org/3rd_culture/lanier06/lanier06_index.html

In his introduction to *The Intellectuals and the Masses*, Carey surveys modernist theories of the mass (José Ortega y Gasset, Friedrich Nietzsche and, more narrowly on crowds, Gustave Le Bon and Sigmund Freud) and finds them overwhelmingly hostile. So hostile, in fact, that he can only read Canetti's enthusiasm for the crowd as inconsistent rather than oppositional. For Canetti, the desire to become a crowd is something fundamental to humans (perhaps their species being) and is often achieved through music, from the symphony orchestra to the Maori's Haka war dance. Canetti's autobiography reveals two things that encouraged him to think about crowds 'as if they had a will of their own': One was being part of the mob that burnt down the Vienna Palace of Justice on 15 July 1927 (fire – another great crowd metaphor), the other was Pieter Bruegel's painting, *The Triumph of Death*, in which thousands of skeletons, formed into armies and churches more vital than the living, pull them over into death. This is where we first meet the modern crowd metaphor par excellence – the crowd of the dead, the legions of the damned, the humble zombie – and yet, until recently, they were a sluggish lot.

The term zombie entered the English language as a result of slavery, in Robert Southey's *History of Brazil*. William B. Seabrook's book, *The Magic Island*, a first-person account of Haitian voodoo rituals (like Maya Deren's much later *Divine Horsemen*), inspired *White Zombie* (1931), the first zombie movie. In this, we see a sugar plantation owned by Bela Lugosi and staffed by zombies. One of the shambling beasts falls into the grinding machinery and becomes at one with the product. This conjures anxiety about stolen labour on the part of both producer and consumer, embodied in what at once unites them and keeps them separate – the commodity. By 1968 and George Romero's *Night of the Living Dead*, filmed in de-industrialising Pittsburgh, their passivity was the passivity of the mass, non-violent resisters campaigning for civil rights. They lumbered because they were inevitable, the mass in human flesh to be sadistically destroyed, interested only in increasing the number of zombies – apocryphally by eating their victims' brains. By *Dawn of the Dead* (1978), their very existence is overproduction: 'When there's no more room in hell, the dead will walk the Earth' – zombies were the *proletarian dead proletarian shopping*. 'But why have they all come to the mall?' asks one of the living. 'I don't know [...] I guess it must have meant something to them in their lives.' For Web 2.0 users, like the human survivors in *Dawn* incarcerated by the zombie hordes in a shopping mall where everything is free, this anxiety of stolen labour can only increase (despite the muzak). Beneath the glossy, reflective surface of the commodity is putrefying zombie flesh – humanity is not superfluous in the age of globalised production, but only its 'creative' part is recognised (leading to its haunting by the latest in a long line of unquiet Marxist spectres).

From *White Zombie* onward, filmmakers unerringly return to music to suggest the lost echo of humanity (as if there were a song that could bring the dead back to life). The scene from which I quote in the epigraph of this article, like its equivalent scene in *Blade Runner*, is of a man and a woman at a piano. In *Day of the Dead*, a later Romero movie, the remnants of humanity are hidden underground trying to train the zombies to do useful work by means of conditioning, à la B.F. Skinner's fictional behaviourist utopia in *Walden Two*. The zombies are often left unattended, listening to classical music on their walkmans – one perks up and begins to sing along, but then loses the signal and is a zombie again.

Movie by movie, the zombies are getting more like us, or at least faster and smarter. In exile from Hollywood, zombie maestro, George Romero, is in Ontario filming a straight-to-DVD release with a hand-held DV camera – *Diary of the Dead*. Yes, there is a MySpace page, but the one prediction I'd make is that, by the end of the film, the zombies will be filming it (and posting it up like the cannibal happy slappers they are).

It is important to move our understanding of zombies out of ritual denunciation. There is pleasure in zombiedom and it lies in an infantilisation, in a Svejkian resistance, in an inability to respond fully to the social imperatives of advertising and shopping: a zombie's eyeball may be in or out, but it cannot be monetised. Indeed, there's even a variety of flashmob called a zombie walk. In the largest of these to date, on 29 October 2006, 894 participants gathered at the Monroeville Mall in Pittsburgh, one of the first big malls and the set of *Dawn of the Dead*. The flashmob, an activity originally intended to satirise crowd stupidity, has, in succumbing to its undoubted pleasures, become a critical practice.

I started in an art gallery so I'll finish there (they're getting to be popular places as the fetish for creativity spreads). In Windsor, Ontario, the locals are embarrassed that their town gallery is in the mall. They shouldn't be, for the art we now possess is entirely made over in the image of the commodity, the only model for cultural life we have left. And yet, as Adorno also argues, art's autonomy remains irrevocable. All efforts to restore art by giving it a social function – of which art is itself uncertain and by which it expresses its own uncertainty – are doomed. In the mid-1990s, at Bank's show *Zombie Golf*, plaster-cast zombies of the artists wandered round the exhibition space demanding brains. Dave Beech and John Roberts regarded them as simultaneously standing for the spectre of a repressed aesthetic ideology haunting art and its negation. Art may attempt to finish with it, but aesthetic autonomy has not finished with art.

For Adorno, art in its autonomy reveals its character as surplus labour, produced to meet no real need at all. What is good about art is that it is useless; it is exchange value without use value – it is an 'absolute commodity'. Thus, unlike any other commodity in capitalism, it does not pretend to be of any use and so reveals the excess of products and services around us as likewise useless. Many find this autonomy, or uselessness, deeply disturbing and wish to get rid of it and give art a use. They do not see this autonomy arising from art's heteronomy (as Adorno does) but as sealing off art within itself – hence art's embrace of non-art is regarded as more hopeful than it really is. For Adorno, the production of a work of art cannot be outside capitalism. Thus, it cannot be produced to meet true needs (as in an artisanal model of production), for no theory of true needs yet exists. Modern art became abstract because of the waning of experience under capitalism (commodification, the dialectic of Enlightenment) and cannot directly compensate for these losses. However, art is nothing if not historic material; it is not enough to abstractly negate relational aesthetics as a category and so wish it away – it must be dealt with on its own terms.

For Bourriaud, autonomy and sovereignty are simply 'yesterday's concerns' – they have been 'wound up'. Relational aesthetics claim to be heir to an irrationalist tradition (Dada, the Surrealists, the Situationist International) that resists instrumental rationality's occupation of the social – the dialectic of Enlightenment. That rationality is so successful it destroys all cultural practices constitutive of the human, reducing us all to zombiedom. For Bourriaud, in considering the place of artworks in the overall economic system, 'the work of art represents a social interstice', a place where the normal laws do not apply. Explicitly in resistance to this occupation, he posits an art that does not respond 'to the excess of commodities and signs but to a lack of connections' by 'performing small services in an attempt to restore the social bond.'

What about relational aesthetics? Can it actually do what it claims? Is it a critical practice, or merely an aesthetics and an art for the service economy?

Take the *State Britain* exhibit, which is poised on this precise point. Peace campaigner, Brian Haw's, Parliament Square protest began in June 2001 against the economic sanctions in Iraq. Parliament's Serious Organised Crime and Police Act banned unauthorised demonstrations within a kilometre of itself (ah, that evolving British constitution) and the majority of Haw's protest banners were removed by police on 23 May 2006. Mark Wallinger has recreated the demonstration in Tate Britain, bringing it back within the 1km radius. For Adorno, the police need not come (again) precisely because it is art and its autonomy remains irrevocable. Yet, in Adorno's work, perhaps, the heteronomy from which autonomy derives is a regulative concept, something in which he's not really interested. For Jacques Rancière, there are heterogeneous logics between the forms of art and the forms of non-art, between the two opposed politics of aesthetics: that art either becomes life by not being art (perhaps the political art of the banners themselves), or it does politics by explicitly not doing politics (perhaps the other art in Tate Britain). For critical art, the realignment of these logics between the art of politics and art, with neither side sacrificed, is achieved by this collage/juxtaposition. If *State Britain* did not cross the line into the 1km exclusion zone, this recreation of politics would be no more a critique of power than Fischli and Weiss' recreation of their own studio – only troubling to the extent that it is an uncanny double, a zombie. But, in crossing the 1km exclusion-zone line, the artwork may have been sacrificed to politics. And yet, even as it is denied or questioned, art's autonomy is being relied upon to create political meaning.[8]

The juxtaposition that is relational art itself has become problematic even to its supporters. Claire Bishop wants good works of art rather than feel good/do good works, to prevent sacrificing the aesthetic to the relational.[9] Conversely, Grant Kester seems to want this sacrifice; he wants out from under the aesthetic of art criticism.[10]

The founding of the Arts Council at 'an arms length' from government shows that there was a time when the autonomy of art was explicitly required. Yet, if Bishop and Kester agree on only one thing, it is that what the Arts Council requires of art now is 'social inclusion' and 'value for money' – a much more clearly instrumental role for art in delivering government policy – and that relational artists have become complicit in this, drawn in by the shrinkage of both real and discursive public space, by the deficit of politics. In its need to incorporate 'you the public' in the work, relational art makes itself useful by attacking the autonomy of the public, driving them into the arms of institutions for funding. Relational art sells its audience to power as crowd control. Kester's group, Littoral Arts, still thinks there is mileage in relational aesthetics through more collaboration, surrendering more to politics – to trade union funding, for instance – the people who sell you, 'the variable capital', to capital.

In her article, 'The Ethics of Aesthetics' (*Art Monthly*, March 2005), Sarah James critiques Bourriaud's thesis for 'its complicity with the dominant political status quo', and also notes a return of aesthetics as a concern of art. But is this return 'acquiescence to political entropy'? Or is it just a return to the demand that art produce something beautiful (for sale)? Art has been at war with its autonomy, but its status as absolute commodity (exchange value only) has gone unquestioned, and this contains its own dangers – that it may become the model for the rest of the economy. Just as art is heading out of relational aesthetics, it seems music and capital are piling in.

8. Dave Beech, 'Chill Out: Dave Beech On and Off the Politics of "young British art"', 1996, http://easyweb.easynet.co.uk/~giraffe/e/hard/text/beech.html and John Roberts, 'Home "Truths"', 1996, http://easyweb.easynet.co.uk/~giraffe/e/hard/text/roberts2.html
9. Claire Bishop, 'The Social Turn: Collaboration and its Discontents', *Artforum*, February 2006, http://www.artforum.com – but you'll have to register. Sadly, I can't get hold of Grant Kester's subsequent reply online. Jennifer Roche, 'Socially Engaged Art, Critics and Discontents: An Interview with Claire Bishop', 25 July 2006, http://www.communityarts.net/readingroom/archivefiles/2006/07/socially_engage.php Also see Leisurearts for a blog discussion of the debate between Bishop and Kester: http://leisurearts.blogspot.com/2006/05/grant-kester-artforum-claire-bishop.html
10. Grant Kester, 'Dialogical Aesthetics: A Critical Framework For Littoral Art', *Variant*, Issue 9, Winter 1999/2000, http://www.variant.randomstate.org/9texts/KesterSupplement.html

Guttural Cultural

Howard Slater

Vol 2 #5, Spring/Summer 2007

A box set that gathers together and reissues the three previous Ghédalia Tazartès releases on Alga Marghen, throwing in the usual bonus tracks, is par for the course in the music industry's ordinary sale of things. But that's where the similarities end. The form of the product may be pretty acceptable and collector-inducingly obsessive, but what's contained in it openly and, it could be chanced, unknowingly, defies categorisation. If you've not come across Tazartès before, you'll be in a majority, but, getting outside the mirror-scene a bit, your ears will become noisily whispered into by a minor voice. A voice so minor, yet layered, that it operates at the unpredictable level of molecular switchpoints; switchpoints of alterity without the border controls of introjected censorship. It's a voice that's been left alone for long enough (his first LP was released in 1979) to become a population of multiples, of 'vitality affects', but it's also a voice that wields, and is embedded in, a variety of machines.[1] From grimy electronic loops to mock opera, from world music to found sounds, from guttural sonorous inarticulacy to the lyrical flushes of Mallarmé and Daumal, from an improvisatory nonchalance to a textured choreographic plan, the 'music' that opens out here has taken 25 years to gain even this small level of exposure (Alga Marghen is hardly a label that people rush to Myspace to research!).

In eluding the taxonomy tax (a tax I feel I've tried to levy in even attempting to describe the music), Tazartès has been effectively seceding from all but a local popularity. At one level, his other recent CD releases have been issued by very small-run French labels – such as Demosaurus, Jardin Au Fou and Gazul – but the localness of Tazartès is there in the intimacy of risk across all his records: a kind of invitation to share in all the dislocation of impromptu passion. We are made congruent in listening to Tazartès as he actively works with the material of his 'self', with personified emotions made dissemblingly sonorous, putting us in mind of Nietzsche's shocking challenge to the identitarians: 'finally you are no more than an imitation of an actor'.[2] The centre, the locus, has been removed, diffused and subjected to a continual deferral of its stultifying and inhibiting taunt to unity. It is this focus for self-regard that, as he whines and whimpers like an exposed 'fake' or one at the limit-point of verbal expression, Tazartès implicitly maintains is the fiction. As controversial philosopher André Glucksman states on the sleeve notes to *Diasporas*, 'Ghédalia Tazartès

1. 'Vitality affects' is Daniel Stern's phrase. Daniel N. Stern, *The Present Moment in Psychotherapy and Everyday Life*, New York: Norton, 2004. For more on Guttural: http://en.wikipedia.org/wiki/Guttural
For David Fenech's interview with Ghédalia Tazartès (in French):
http://demosarurus.free.fr/demosaurus/ghedalia_Tazartes/ghedalia_tazartes_interview.htm
2. Friedrich Nietzsche, *Twilight Of The Idols*, London: Penguin, 1974.

is a nomad.' A much overused term should not detract from its accuracy when applied to this music: Tazartès not only wanders, *sui generis*, through the many musical categories and delimited locales that instill a self-affirming unity, he is lovingly in internal exile. Like a latter-day Rimbaud, he is an alchemist of the very local affects that he brings into voice and thereby discovers, affects that are both audibly inspired and reach out to a taped militant chant, a city square ambience, a tango refrain, a broken organ, a synthesised rhythm, his daughter gurgling or a massified cathedral bell.

This localness, this locale of a porous psyche in an admixtured place, is further contradicted with the overall sense of transports and movement we get when listening to these records. On *Diasporas*, the overall thematic seems to be the aping of a North African way of singing, which, these days, leads to all sorts of musings about cultural pillage rather than cultural inter-penetration. As there's very little biographical information on Tazartès, we can hardly know for sure whether he's of North African descent or whether he once worked at General Motors. But, this seems to be a decoy kind of response to a bogus question that leads back to the essentialisms and non-becomings of a cultural homogeneity, to a respecting of the boundaries and financially beneficial closed markets that are enforced by cultural commentators and treaty-makers alike. Tangiers is now in Paris via Istanbul. On *Diasporas*, in a track with the Ubu-esque title of '*La Vie et la Mort Legendaires du Spermatozoide de Humuch Lardy*' (The Life and Legendary Death of the Sperm of Humuch Lardy), we hear Tazartès singing to an accordion-like instrument, underpinned by a steady beat on a *djembe*. Yet, Tazartès changes his vocal style continually throughout the three minutes of this track, from vaguely Islamic to vaguely Jewish to vaguely Sioux Indian to vaguely feminine to explicitly cutting into the 'melody' by ha-hack-laughing like a temporarily mad man. The temptation would be to say, 'here in Tazartès, we have someone articulating what it is to be a species-being', or 'here, in Tazartès, we have the first pre-articulation (outside sci-fi) of the push to form a world government headed by conformed intellectuals'. Both responses would be undermined by the self-effacingness of this very idiosyncratic, self-exposed and disorientating 'music', a 'music' that the Musearecords website [www.musearecords.com] tells us began when Tazartès 'started to sing, at 12 years old, in the Bois de Vincennes, just for himself, after his grandmother died'. Grief is unlocalisable, as is the plurality of worlds that Tazartès presents: a 'redistribution of the sensible' (to adapt Rancière's phrase).[3]

Whether Tazartès assimilates or disseminates, comes together or openly unfolds, is not a choice we, as listeners, have to make. He does all these things. He is not national but differentiated and relational. Layering the bass timbre of his own voice into a chanted drone, adding a synthesised note, overdubbing a murmured refrain, goading himself into declamations of parodic or justifiable

3. Jacques Rancière, *The Politics of Aesthetics*, London: Continuum, 2006.

anger, he assembles sketches that have the impact of concertos. He multiplies himself into a contradiction of unedited tensions, colliding the disparate times of feeling with a minimum of respect paid to 'song structure' that makes Glucksman's description of him as 'an orchestra and pop group all in one person' entirely fitting. On 'Merci Stephane', Tazartès recites, body and soul, a poem by Mallarmé (in French) as a disco loop, complete with Chic-style rhythm guitar, slowly rises to the foreground of the track. We don't get the message as such – we get, more provocatively, the enigma. Akin at times to the later recordings of Luc Ferrari, who also did not shy away from the use of popular forms, Tazartès' use and magnification of the incidental, when coupled to his overdubs, summons up, as with Ferrari, a very real sense of 'temporal thickness': not just our experiencing of music but our experiencing in general can be polyphonic and polytemporal. The key to this 'thickness' may lie not only in the way that Tazartès can have us seemingly at the origins of language, with a totemic incantation being accompanied by a buzzing cellular network sound, but also in the way that this 'thickness' is intimately relayed across these 20-odd-year-old recordings by timbre, dirty timbre.

It's timbre that's outer-national. Timbre is the grain, the rasp, the fricative, the aural visceralisation of an unfurling emotion – a 'vitality affect'. It is fitting and fits with an attempted expression, not a well rehearsed one. When it's alloyed

to the incidental and the impromptu (for all Tazartès' tracks may be layered, but each layer comes across as being put down with no second takes), it amounts to a pre-articulation, an indication of a struggle, a none-too-easily-won means of expression, a means without precedent but not individual – singular instead; a group's pre-articulation: the group of the multiple self, dissolving the boundaries of the overly identified who want to win you over for lessness. So, in some ways, we are talking, thanks to Tazartès, of something more vital and communicative than language; for, across these tracks, there are words (in French) that many will not be able to understand. But this does not detract from our 'understanding'. Quite the opposite; it tempers our understanding with enigma and leads us to put trust in the 'unspoken' meaning of the timbre, be it of the voice or the variegated musical backing, applying to it a sincerity of intent and giving to us the image of an 'unthought known',[4] of something happening to the side of consciousness in a duct, a quiver. This is in stark contrast to a more recent and much acclaimed album by Scott Walker. Presented as a similarly heady mix of voice and unfamiliar musical backing, *The Drift* comes across as firmly implanted in the majoritorian culture of High Art Darke: a monotonal operatics with tracks as long as the last days of drum'n'bass. Here we can fully 'understand' the lyrics; they are a hermetic appeal to Englishness graduates. Maybe it'll be Ghedalia's gypsy-band, with their partially unwilled responses, that'll be visible on the horizon at the next Meltdown.

4. Daniel N. Stern, op. cit.

Audio Clip: *Une Éclipse Totale de Soleil*
Distorted drum box.
Bass blurs in a pumped semitune
Birds.
A child unspeaks.
Sings as if alone, straining to reach the high notes.
Another voice yodels to a repeated syllable.
Its throat becomes a cavernous auditorium.
Other voices rise, desperate and yearning.
Voices of ecstatic protest.
Voices of an affective class.
Notes from an oud or a one stringed violin enter.
Still the repeated syllable.
Is this the desert, a drawing room, an agora?
Some inviting schizo demos?
It's not a studio.
But the window is open:
birds again.
Pots and pans are struck nonchalantly as if trying to
keep to a rhythm or establish its semblance.
A high note held becomes sweet watery feedback.
Meanwhile Sioux surround the wagon train as
the strumming of a stringed box keeps pace.
A man's voice: gravelly and chkchkchking,
scrapes its own voice box for musical mucus,
hears its own gradial tones in a different part of
its disaggregating body.
Then, seamless of 'then', quick fire slightly agitated chatter.
Cha-cha drum box trills as the voice tries to keep pace
with desperate glottals not glossaries.
Tunes and rationality are trying to break through
as the beaten box sounds in a cave near to a bird cage.
A layering of electrifying groams give inspiration
to a distorting low-end organ as another
improvised punk-folk ditty unassumes itself into
the forefront of a newly compounding emotion.
Slower now the beat box, almost whistling with
cymbal hiss as another hand-assisted vocable wavers
repeatingly, its join of loop obvious and hiatus-rough.
The voice now sings risingly to crescendos as if unaccompanied,
as if alone and beckoning an audience years and years away.
No threat of external evaluation in this 'studio', this minaret,
this intensified polis, this afternoon.

Contributors

Saul Albert
Saul Albert misses his modem.

Irina Aristarkhova
Irina Aristarkhova writes on and lectures in cyberfeminism, new media aesthetics, and comparative feminist theory. Currently, she is Assistant Professor of Women's Studies and Visual Art at Pennsylvania State University.

Brian Ashton
Brian Ashton is an ex car-industry shop steward who developed an interest in the logistics industry while doing support work with the sacked Liverpool dockers in the mid-'90s. He is currently researching the global supply chains of the clothing industry.

Richard Barbrook
Richard Barbrook is a senior lecturer in the School of Social Sciences, Humanities and Languages at the University of Westminster. In the early-1980s, he was involved with pirate and community radio broadcasting. Helping to set up the multi-lingual Spectrum Radio station in London, he published extensively on radio issues during this period, much of which was published in his 1995 book, *Media Freedom*. In 2007, Barbrook published *Imaginary Futures*, a study of the political and ideological role of the prophecies of artificial intelligence and the information society which was selected as the winner of the 2008 Marshall McLuhan Award for Outstanding Book of the Year in the Field of Media Ecology. He is a trustee of Cybersalon and a founding member of Class Wargames.

John Barker
John Barker was born in London and still lives there. His prison memoir, *Bending the Bars*, is published by Christie Books. He indexes books professionally, and his short stories have appeared in anthologies, *Passport* magazine, *The Edinburgh Review*, and 3ammagazine.com

Will Barnes
Will Barnes is a long-time activist who lives in the United States. When asked for brief biographical information, he offered this response: 'I live in St. Paul, which is at the heart of the northern US plains economy. Hell, the Minneapolis-St. Paul environs is that economy. I work in the public sector. I'm a driver. I carry a union card.' Barnes has authored several works among which are a really large tome on the American Civil War, an historical analysis of Bolshevism and Stalinism prior to the last imperialist world war, and a critique of capitalist civilisation from the perspective of its revolutionary transformation. His most recent work is entitled *Nature, Capital, Communism*. All can be accessed at www.instcssc.org

Caroline Bassett
Caroline Bassett is Reader in Digital Media at the University of Sussex and writes widely on technology and cultural form. Amongst other things, she is author of *The Arc and the Machine* (Manchester: Manchester University Press, 2007). She is currently working on two projects: the history of anti-computing campaigns and the future of the semantic web.

Anustup Basu
Anustup Basu is an Assistant Professor at the University of Illinois at Urbana-Champaign. His essays on film, media, globalisation, and political sovereignty have appeared, or are forthcoming, in *boundary 2*, *Critical Quarterly*, *Postmodern Culture*, *Postscript*, *Mute* and the anthology *Global Bollywood: Travels of Hindi Song and Dance* (Minneapolis: University of Minnesota Press, 2008). Basu is currently completing a manu-script entitled *The Geo-televisual Aesthetic: Information, Capital, and Religiosity in Popular Hindi Cinema* (1991–2004) and guest editing a special issue of *South Asian Popular Culture* on new media ecologies. He was also the executive producer of *Herbert* (director: Suman Mukhopadhyay, 2005), which won the Indian National Award for Best Bengali Feature Film in 2005–6.

Amita Baviskar
Amita Baviskar is based at the Institute of Economic Growth in Delhi. Her research focuses on the cultural politics of the environment and development. Her first book, *In the Belly of the River: Tribal Conflicts over Development in the Narmada Valley*, discussed the struggle for survival by indigenous groups in central India against the building of a large dam. Her subsequent work further explores the themes of resource rights, subaltern resistance and cultural identity. She has edited *Waterlines: The Penguin Book of River Writings*, *Waterscapes: The Cultural Politics of a Natural Resource* and *Contested Grounds: Essays on Nature, Culture and Power*. She is currently writing about bourgeois environmentalism and spatial restructuring in the context of economic liberalisation in Delhi.

Franco Berardi (Bifo)
Franco Berardi is a writer, media theorist and media-activist. Founder of the magazine *A/traverso* (1975–81), he took part in the staff of Radio Alice, the first free radio station in Italy (1976–8). He was involved in

the Autonomia movement in Italy during the 1970s, then fled to Paris where he worked with Félix Guattari in the field of schizoanalysis. During the 1980s, he contributed to the magazines *Semiotexte* (New York), *Chimères* (Paris), *Metropoli* (Rome), *Musica 80* (Milano), *Derive approdi* (Roma) and *Multitudes* (Paris). He published *Mutazione e ciberpunk*, (Genova, 1993), *Cibernauti* (Roma, 1994), *Félix* (2001), *Il sapiente il mercante il guerriero* (2003), *Skizomedia* (2006) and *Generation postAlfa* (Tinta Limon, Buenos Aires). His book, *Félix*, has been republished by Palgrave McMillan (2009). Berardi is currently working on the project Bologna città libera and teaching at the Accademia di Belle Arti di Brera, Milano. He is co-founder of the rekombinant.org e-zine.

Josephine Berry Slater
Josephine Berry Slater is the editor of *Mute* magazine. She also teaches part-time at Goldsmiths on the Practices of the Culture Industry MA. Current research interests are the transformation of public and community arts within the context of urban regeneration, and the urban politics of neoliberalism.

Josephine Bosma
Josephine Bosma is a writer and critic. She started working in the field of new media art, making radio shows, documentaries and interviews about the topic for VPRO and Patapoe radio from 1993 to 1998. She has published interviews, reviews and texts about art and new media in various books, catalogues and magazines, both on- and off-line, since 1996. Her work mostly focuses on net art, sound art and net culture. She lives and works in Amsterdam.

Marc Bousquet
Marc Bousquet is the author of *How the University Works: Higher Education and the Low-Wage Nation* (New York: New York University, 2008). He blogs about culture, politics and higher education at the *Chronicle of Higher Education* group blog, *Brainstorm*, and *The Valve*.

Bureau of Inverse Technology
The Bureau of Inverse Technology (aka bit and sometimes BIT) is an organisation of artist-engineers whose stated aim is to be an 'information agency servicing the Information Age'. Bureau engineers, so-called BIT agents, are involved from design to deployment and documentation of radical products based on commercially available electronic entertainment components such as cameras, radios, networks, robots, sensors etc. The Bureau was founded in Melbourne in 1991 (though some accounts say 1992), and was incorporated with limited liability in the Cayman Islands in 1991 and subsequently re-incorporated in Delaware in 1997. Though its work has long been publicly available, the composition of the Bureau itself is shrouded in mystery, for some years cloaking its identity in anonymity. In 2004, the Bureau initiated a 'retreat from anonymity' when radio journalist and BIT co-founder, Kate Rich, took up a three-month Research Fellowship at Piet Zwart Institute for Media Design Research, Rotterdam.

Ted Byfield
Ted Byfield currently serves as Assistant Professor in the Communication Design and Technology Department of Parsons The New School for Design, New School University, and as a Visiting Fellow at Yale Law School's Information Society Project.

Andy Cameron
Andy Cameron created the Hypermedia Research Centre at the University of Westminster and went on to co-found the antirom design collective and Romandson Interactive Design studio in London in 1995 and 1999 respectively. In 2001, he was appointed visiting artist and, subsequently, creative director in interaction design at Fabrica, the Benetton research centre in the Veneto, North Italy. He has also produced a number of CD-roms and interactive installations for museums, commercial clients and art galleries. He co-curated and exhibited in I've Been Waiting for You at the Triad Gallery in Seoul as part of the Seoul Biennale, 2006. In the same year, he created Filmit, an innovative video sharing community for junior schools in the UK for OpenFuture and the Helen Hamlyn Trust in conjunction with Focus on Food and the Royal Horticultural Society. He continues to write about the politics and aesthetics of interactive and networked media.

Gregor Claude
Gregor Claude is based at Goldsmiths, University of London. His research interests include the cultural industries, digital media and social and cultural theory. The primary focus of his research has been the technology and politics of digital copyright.

Eileen Condon
Eileen Condon is a freelance researcher and author. She is presently compiling a report on the military build-up inside EU nation states, such as Italy.

Michael Corris
Michael Corris – an artist and a writer on art – holds professorships in art at the Art and Design Research Centre, Sheffield Hallam University and at the Newport School of Art, Media and Design, University of Wales. Recent publications include *Ad*

Reinhardt (London: Reaktion Books, 2008), a monograph on the work of David Diao (Beijing: TimeZone8 Books, 2005) and *Conceptual Art: Theory, Myth and Practice* (Cambridge and New York: Cambridge University Press, 2004).

Mark Crinson
Mark Crinson lectures in the History of Art at the University of Manchester. His most recent books are his edited volume *Urban Memory: History and Amnesia in the Modern City* (2005) and *Modern Architecture and the End of Empire* (2003). He is currently researching ideas about nostalgia and austerity and their relation to architecture in post-war Britain.

Chris Darke
Chris Darke is a writer and film critic whose work has appeared in *Film Comment, Sight and Sound, The Independent* and *Cahiers du cinema.* He is the author of *Light Readings: Film Criticism* and *Screen Arts*, a monograph on Jean-Luc Godard's *Alphaville* and is co-author of *Cannes: Inside the World's Premier Film Festival.*

Anthony Davies
Anthony Davies is a London based writer and organiser. He's published on art and economy in a range of magazines including *Mute, Art Monthly, Texte zur Kunst* and *Metropolis M.*

Mark Dery
Mark Dery (markdery@optonline.net) is a cultural critic. He is the author of *Escape Velocity: Cyberculture at the End of the Century* and *The Pyrotechnic Insanitarium: American Culture on the Brink.* His seminal essay, 'Culture Jamming: Hacking, Slashing, and Sniping in the Empire of Signs', popularised the guerrilla media activism known as 'culture jamming'; widely republished on the web, this text remains the definitive theorisation of this subcultural phenomenon. In *Flame Wars: The Discourse of Cyberculture*, an academic anthology he edited, Dery coined the term 'Afrofuturism' and kick-started academic interest in black technoculture in particular and cyberstudies in general. An independent scholar, he was the Chancellor's Distinguished Fellow at University College Irvine in January 2000 and was an assistant professor in the Department of Journalism at New York University from 2001 to 2009. He blogs at www.markdery.com and is at work on *Don Henley Must Die*, a book about the cultural psyche of Southern California.

Anna Dezeuze
Anna Dezeuze is a Postdoctoral Research Fellow in Art History and Visual Studies at the University of Manchester. As well as contributing to art magazines such as *Art Monthly*, she has published essays about a number of 1960s practices, including those of Fluxus and Hélio Oiticica, and co-edited (with Jo Applin and Julia Kelly) a special cluster on Assemblage/Bricolage for *Art Journal* (Spring 2008). Her edited volume, *The 'Do-it-Yourself Artwork': Participation from Fluxus to Relational Aesthetics* is forthcoming with Manchester University Press. She is currently working on a book project entitled *The 'Almost Nothing': Dematerialization and the Politics of Precariousness.*

María Fernández
María Fernández is Associate Professor of Art History at Cornell University. Her research interests include the history and theory of digital art, postcolonial studies, Latin American art and the intersections of these fields. Her work has been published in multiple journals and in several volumes including *The Companion of Contemporary Art since 1945* edited by Amelia Jones (Blackwell, 2006) and *At a Distance: Precursors to Art and Activism on the Internet* edited by Annmarie Chandler and Norie Neumark (MIT Press, 2005.) With Faith Wilding and Michelle Wright, she edited the anthology *Domain Errors: Cyberfeminist Practices* published by Autonomedia in 2002.

Simon Ford
Simon Ford is a freelance writer and art historian. He was previously Research Associate in Craft and Design and Curator of the Design Council Slide Collection at Manchester Metropolitan University and a curator at the Victoria and Albert Museum. He received his PhD in the History of Art from the Courtauld Institute of Art in 2000. He is the author of *Wreckers of Civilisation: The Story of COUM Transmissions and Throbbing Gristle* (1999) and *Hip Priest: The Story of Mark E. Smith and The Fall* (2003). His most recent book is *The Situationist International: A User's Guide* (2006).

Matthew Fuller
Matthew Fuller [http://spc.org/fuller] is author of *Behind the Blip, Essays on the Culture of Software* and *Media Ecologies, Materialist Energies in Art and Technoculture* and is editor of *Software Studies, a lexicon* amongst other titles. He works at the Centre for Cultural Studies at Goldsmiths.

Coco Fusco
Coco Fusco is a New York-based interdisciplinary artist and writer. She has performed, lectured, curated and exhibited around the world since 1988. Her performance and video works have been selected for numerous international biennials and festivals and she received a Herb Alpert Award in the Arts in 2003. Fusco is Chair of the Fine Arts Program

at Parsons The New School for Design. She is the author of *A Field Guide for Female Interrogators* (2008), *The Bodies That Were Not Ours and Other Writings* (2001) and *English is Broken Here: Notes on Cultural Fusion in the Americas* (1995). She is also the editor of *Only Skin Deep: Changing Visions of the American Self* (2003) and *Corpus Delecti: Performance Art of the Americas* (1999).

David Garcia
David Garcia co-founded Time Based Arts (Amsterdam) in 1983. He developed a series of international media arts events, including The Next 5 Minutes (1994–2003), and a series of international conferences and exhibitions on electronic communications and political culture. Since 2006, he has initiated (Un)common Ground, a rolling research programme investigating the new role of art and design as a catalyst for new forms of collaboration, where research consisted of structured expert meetings and publications. In 2007, he edited and contributed to the Book *(Un)common Ground: Creative Encounters Across Sectors and Disciplines.* Garcia is currently Dean of Chelsea College of Art and Design, London.

Andrew Goffey
Andrew Goffey is Senior Lecturer in Media, Culture and Communication in the Department of Media at Middlesex University. He has published widely on issues related to philosophy, science and culture. He is currently researching two books – one on the politics of software and one on the concept of experimentation.

Paul Helliwell
Paul Helliwell is mainly interested in the social function of art and music. His reading starts with Attali and Adorno and he has got as far as early Althusser. He became interested in this area as a result of his experiences playing guitar in the hugely unsuccessful (and justly forgotten) anarchist afro-punk band, Bush House. Now he makes acoustic folk music as horsemouth [www.myspace.com/horsemouthfolk]. He is active in the housing co-op movement. He works supporting deaf students in education. He is a big fan of zombies and the undead generally. He can be contacted at phelliwell2000@yahoo.co.uk

Brian Holmes
Brian Holmes is a cultural critic, living in Paris and Chicago. He recently published *Unleashing the Collective Phantoms: Essays in Reverse Imagineering* (New York: Autonomedia, 2008). He lectures widely and collaborates with the 16 Beaver group on the Continental Drift seminar. His text archive is at http://brianholmes.wordpress.com

Matthew Hyland
Matthew Hyland is a contributing editor of *Mute.*

Anthony Iles
Anthony Iles is a freelance writer and a contributing editor of *Mute.* He is co-author of a recent pamphlet on History from Below [www.caughtlearning.org/all_knees_and_elbows] and author of the self-published pamphlet entitled 'The Lower Lea Valley as Fun Palace and Creative Prison' [www.divshare.com/download/6016897-66f].

Jamie King
Jamie King is Director/Producer of the STEAL THIS FILM series [www.stealthisfilm.com] and founder of the VODO project for distributing and sustaining cultural productions via P2P [vodo.net]. Formerly an editor of *Mute,* his work for the last six years has centred on the social/political possibilities offered by new media communications. Jamie continues to consult on the application of digital networks to creativity and cultural production for a number of high-profile firms and organisations, including RSA and Channel 4 Television. In 2008, he was Keynote Speaker at the Creative Commons Conference in Sapporo and London Film Festival's Power To The Pixel strand. His academic and journalistic writings have been published internationally, including in *The Times, The Guardian* and *The Telegraph.* From 2004–7, Jamie was Lecturer/Senior Lecturer at Ravensbourne College of Media and Communications Masters Programme in Digital Media, UK.

Dmytri Kleiner
Dmytri Kleiner is a Berlin-based Canadian hacker and anarchist. Dmytri explores the intersections of art, technology and political economy with the telekommunisten collective [telekommunisten.net].

Hari Kunzru
Hari Kunzru has worked with *Mute* since 1995. He is the author of the novels *The Impressionist* (2002), *Transmission* (2004) and the short story collection, *Noise* (2005). In 2003, Granta named him one of its Best of Young British novelists. He is a member of the Executive Council of PEN. A selection of his writing and photography is online at [harikunzru.com/hari].

Peter Linebaugh
Peter Linebaugh is a scholar and historian. He wrote *The London Hanged* and, with Marcus Rediker, he wrote *The Many Headed Hydra.* Recently, he wrote *The Magna Carta Manifesto.* He's a child of the American Empire which he'd like abolished. Otherwise, he's a good family man.

Geert Lovink
Geert Lovink is a Dutch-Australian media theorist and internet critic. He studied political science in Amsterdam and received his PhD from the University of Melbourne. He has been involved in the cultural politics of the internet since the early-1990s. He is the co-founder of projects such as the Digital City, Nettime and Fibreculture. In 2002, MIT Press published two of his books, *Dark Fiber* and *Uncanny Networks*. Since then, other books appeared such as *My First Recession* (2003) and *The Principle of Notworking* (2005). In 2004, he moved from Brisbane to Amsterdam to found the Institute of Network Cultures. From there, he initiated research networks such as VideoVortex, Incommunicado, Urban Screens and MyCreativity. He is research professor at the School of Interactive Media (University of Applied Sciences) and associate professor in the new media programme at Media Studies, University of Amsterdam. In 2005–6, he was a fellow at the Berlin Institute for Advanced Study where he finished his third study on critical internet culture for Routledge, New York, entitled *Zero Comments*.

Suhail Malik
Suhail Malik is Critical Studies Course Leader for Postgraduate Fine Art in the Department of Art at Goldsmiths, where he is also Director of the Political Currency of Art Research Group. Malik has written catalogue essays for major exhibitions by the Chapman brothers, Nigel Cooke, Aya Ben Ron and Ian Monroe amongst others. He has also written on the market and critical conditions of contemporary art and current technical and political theory, and is currently working on a philosophy of American power.

Melancholic Troglodytes
Melancholic Troglodytes (meltrogs1@hotmail.com) is a collective of proletarians from different cultural backgrounds. We are involved in catering, painting and decorating and educational industries. We came to accept our inability to change things a long time ago. Our literature is read by very few and understood by fewer still. Nowadays we perform our 'revolutionary role' without much conviction. But we do have a bucket-list (a list of things we want to do before we kick the bucket). The bucket-list keeps us going!

Flint Michigan
Flint Michigan wrote for *Datacide* magazine from the mid-1990s onwards.

Angela Mitropoulos
Angela Mitropoulos writes on the intersections of border politics, labour and political philosophy. Some of her recent writings are 'Borders 2.0 – Future, Tense' (*Mute*) and 'The Materialisation of Race in Multiculture' (*darkmatter*). She is currently writing on the coincidence of financial and climatic crises in leveraging the appeal of an oikopolitics.

Ewan Morrison
Ewan Morrison is the author of the novels *Swung*, *Distance* and *Menage* (all Jonathan Cape) and the collection of short stories *The Last Book You Read and Other Stories*. He lives in Glasgow and writes a weekly column for *Scotland on Sunday* under the name Weegie Bored.

Neil Mulholland
Neil Mulholland [www.neilmulholland.co.uk] is a writer based in Scotland. He is Reader in Contemporary Art Theory and Director of the Centre of Visual and Cultural Studies at Edinburgh College of Art.

David Panos
David Panos is a filmmaker, musician and activist. His collaborative work with Benedict Seymour as The London Particular involves political and critical interventions in the process of urban regeneration in East London. He is the co-founder of the Difficult Fun record label and the bands Antifamily and Aufgehoben. Panos has also collaborated with artist filmmaker Anja Kirschner on a number of music and film-based projects.

Luciana Parisi
Dr Luciana Parisi (L.Parisi@gold.ac.uk) is the Convener of the Interactive Media MA at Goldsmiths, University of London. In 2004, she published *Abstract Sex: Philosophy, Biotechnology and the Mutations of Desire* (Continuum Press). Currently, she is writing a monograph on soft architecture and the metaphysics of computational culture.

Celia Pearce
Celia Pearce is a game designer, author, researcher, teacher, curator and artist, specialising in multi-player gaming and virtual worlds, independent, art and alternative game genres, as well as games and gender. She began designing interactive attractions and exhibitions in 1983 and has held academic appointments since 1998. She received her PhD in 2006 from SMARTLab Centre, then at Central Saint Martins College of Art and Design. She is currently Assistant Professor of Digital Media in the School of Literature, Communication and Culture at Georgia Tech, where she also directs the Experimental Game Lab and the Emergent Game Group. Her game designs include the award-winning virtual reality attraction, Virtual Adventures (for Iwerks and Evans & Sutherland) and the Purple

Moon Friendship Adventure Cards for Girls. She is the author or co-author of numerous papers and book chapters, as well as *The Interactive Book* (Macmillan, 1997). She has curated new media, virtual reality, and game exhibitions and is currently Festival Chair for IndieCade, an international independent games festival and showcase series. She is also a co-founder of the Ludica women's game collective. Her work can be found online at http://cpandfriends.com and her Georgia Tech research in multiplayer games and virtual worlds can be found at http://egg.lcc.gatech.edu

Richard Pithouse
Richard Pithouse lives in Durban, South Africa. He has worked as a factory worker, freelance journalist and academic and is currently an independent researcher and writer. He has been a member of Abahlali baseMjondolo since the movement was formed in 2005.

Eddie Prévost
Eddie Prévost was a co-founder, in 1965, of the seminal improvising ensemble, AMM (a group which has included formally and informally trained musicians e.g. John Tilbury, Lou Gare, Cornelius Cardew, Keith Rowe, Christian Wolff and Rohan de Saram). AMM has performed worldwide and has an extensive discography. Prévost has also worked with numerous free jazz and improvising musicians (e.g. Evan Parker, Marilyn Crispell, Paul Rutherford and Alexander von Schippenbach), with a number of younger musicians (e.g. Tom Chant and John Edwards who comprise Prévost's 'Touch' Trio) as well as with musicians from other cultures (most notably Yoshikazu Iwamoto). He has also performed in the techno-ambient field (GOD, Main, EAR) and plays the 'open-ended' compositions of Cardew, Wolff and Cage. In 1998, he made music for The Merce Cunningham Dance Company during their London season. His first solo CD, *Loci of Change*, was released by Matchless Recordings (MRCD32) late in 1996. This was followed by *Material Consequences* and a tam-tam solo CD entitled *Entelechy*. He occasionally lectures and writes about music. His books, *No Sound is Innocent* and *Minute Particulars*, were published by Copula in 1995 and 2004 respectively. In 2006, he edited *Cornelius Cardew: A Reader*. Since 1999, Prévost has convened a weekly improvisation workshop in London. So far, this has been attended by over 200 musicians representing over 20 different nationalities. From this workshop, many musical groups have emerged, with some of which Prévost also performs. For a fuller discography see www.matchlessrecordings.com.

Louis Rossetto
Louis Rossetto co-founded *Wired* magazine with Jane Metcalfe in 1993. Under the five years of his editorship, it won two National Magazine Awards for general excellence and one for design. *Wired* helped to invent the commercial web when it launched HotWired in 1994, the first site with original content and Fortune 500 advertising. Rossetto is currently CEO and Creative Director of craft chocolate manufacturer TCHO.

Andreas Rüthi
Andreas Rüthi's still life paintings in oil form a developing series. Usually containing a postcard of a work of art, their repetitive form builds into a kind of diary. Changing groupings of objects, mementoes and images – and their cast shadows – make a sequence which is always open to the possibility of change, through the surprises inherent in each individual painterly encounter. The paintings are made from observation, usually by fluorescent light, against a white background. Their references and associations show a wry humour, a dialogue with art history as with the nature of reproduction and repetition; but the logic of the procedure suggests a kinship with forms of abstraction, and with conceptual art in its classic concern with time.

Timothy Savage
Timothy Savage worked as a radical journalist and DJ at alternative radio stations in Ottawa and Montreal, Canada. He studied and taught film in New York, has travelled widely and likes to drink and dance at squat parties in London on occasion. Despite his fond attachment to unemployment, he has been teaching English to adult immigrants and refugees in London for the past seven years.

Benedict Seymour
Benedict Seymour is a writer and former deputy editor of *Mute*. He has written, and made films, about regeneration and gentrification with The London Particular [www.thelondonparticular.org], and makes music with his bands, Antifamily and Petit Mal [www.myspace.com/petitmalpetit mal, www.difficultfun.org]. He is currently working on a film about the financial crisis, with the working title *32 Short Films about Bernard Madoff*, and holds the position of Lecturer in Fine Art on the MFA at Goldsmiths, London.

Howard Slater
Howard Slater (howard.slater@googlemail.com) is a trainee counsellor and sometimes writer who lives in East London.

Keston Sutherland
Keston Sutherland lectures in English at the University of

Sussex. He is the editor of Barque Press and *QUID* and the author of numerous books of poetry, most recently *Neocosis* and *Hot White Andy*. A full list of his publications is available on his homepage at Sussex [sussex.ac.uk/english/profile176509.html].

Horacio Tarcus
Horacio Tarcus is an Argentine historian who obtained his doctorate in the National University of La Plata. He is a teacher and researcher at the University of Buenos Aires. He is the author of the following books: *El marxismo olvidado en la Argentina* (1996), *Mariátegui en la Argentina* (2002), *Diccionario biográfico de la izquierda argentina* (2007) and *Marx en la Argentina* (2007). In Buenos Aires in 1998, he founded the Centre of Documentation and Research of the Culture of the Left in Argentina, of which he is the director.

Tiziana Terranova
Tiziana Terranova teaches and researches the cultural politics of networks at the Università degli Studi 'L'Orientale' di Napoli after a very long bout of teaching and research in UK universities. She is the author of *Network Culture* (Pluto Press, 2004) and many other essays exploring the relation between science, technology, culture, politics and networks.

University of Openess
The University of Openess (UO) was a user-led facility of learning and research with its first campus at Limehouse Town Hall, London, and its first online presence at [http://uo.twenteenthcentury.com]. The UO ran a core curriculum and regular classes, and had several faculties which included the Faculty of Unix (which ran a free weekly class), the Faculty of Cartography (which staged the Cartographic Congress, May–June 2003), the Faculty of Physical Education (bi-weekly/ish urban exploration and training), the Faculty of Education (ran the Arted mailing list) and the Faculty of Collaborative Research (which kept a log of inter-faculty conflicts).

Pauline van Mourik Broekman
Pauline van Mourik Broekman is the co-publisher and co-founder of *Mute*, which she and Simon Worthington edited until 2004 and continue to work with as contributing editors. In addition to working on *Mute* projects, she has written and spoken widely on culture and technology, the politics of institution-building and publishing magazines in the 'digital era'. She also co-authored *Mute Magazine Graphic Design* (2008), a companion volume to *Proud to be Flesh*, published by Eight Books.

Ben Watson
In late 1986, sensing the coming data storm, Ben Watson took a course in COBOL, RPGII and Systems Analysis at Control Data Institute in Leeds. Over the next decade, work with Relational Databases and Structured Query Language on the Unix operating system (mostly accounts software) granted Watson an unclouded view of the economic imperatives behind 'open' systems. A contract to write a book about Frank Zappa saved him from a lifetime of IT drudgery. *Writing at The Wire* (1987–2005) provided an opportunity to develop a critique of cyberboosterism in the realm of music culture, culminating in the formation of The Esemplasm and the release of *Frankfurter Ahnung*, a manifesto for the anti-capitalist artist. He currently broadcasts on www.resonancefm.com (2pm Wednesdays). A selection of six years' weekly broadcasts may be sampled from www.archive.org/search.php?query=audio%20oesemplasm&sort=-publicdate. Watson lives in Somers Town, London, with Esther Leslie with whom he runs the website www.militantesthetix.co.uk

Simon Worthington
Simon Worthington is co-founder and co-publisher of *Mute*. He studied art at the Slade (London) and CalArts (Valencia, California). At *Mute*, he has developed a number of sister projects, including community wireless network YouAreHere, software platform OpenMute, European magazine network Magnet [magnet-ecp.org] and alternative computer/art fair Extreme Computing [www.xcom2002.com], a collaboration with e-bulletin NTK. He was also co-organiser of and contributor to the University of Openess (UO), London, where he co-founded the Faculty of Cartography [uo.twenteenthcentury.com/index.php/FacultyCartography]

Steve Wright
Steve Wright works in the Caulfield School of Information Technology at Monash University. He is the author of *Storming Heaven: Class Composition and Struggle in Italian Autonomist Marxism* (London: Pluto Press, 2002).

Brian Wyrick
Brian Wyrick (brian@pseudoscope.com) is an artist and web developer. He makes films with the artists' collective, Group 312 Films, in Chicago.

Soenke Zehle
Soenke Zehle teaches transcultural literary and media studies at Saarland University and the Saar Academy of Fine Arts [tmsp.org].

Index

S

Published by Mute Publishing
in association with Autonomedia

Mute Publishing
Unit 9, The Whitechapel Centre
85 Myrdle Street
London E1 1HQ
UK

www.metamute.org
mute@metamute.org
Tel: 44 (0)20 7377 6949
Fax: 44 (0)20 7377 9520

Autonomedia
PO Box 568, Williamsburgh Station
Brooklyn
NY 11211-0568
USA

www.autonomedia.org
info@autonomedia.org
Tel/Fax: 718-963-2603

ISBN: 978-1-906496-28-9

Editors, *Proud to be Flesh*:
Pauline van Mourik Broekman and Josephine Berry Slater with Michael Corris, Anthony Iles, Benedict Seymour and Simon Worthington

Managing Editor: Rebecca Gordon-Nesbitt
Design: Fraser Muggeridge studio
Proofreading: 100% Proof
Marketing: Lois Olmstead

Editors, contributing editors and section editors, *Mute* magazine, 1994–2009:
Josephine Berry Slater, John Paul Bichard, James Flint, Matthew Hyland, Daniel Jackson, Jamie King, Demetra Kotouza, Hari Kunzru, Suhail Malik, Tom McCarthy, Paul Miller, Pauline van Mourik Broekman, Melancholic Troglodytes, William Shoebridge, Tina Spear, Laura L. Sullivan, Stefan Szczelkun, Simon Worthington

Cover: Richard Dawson, *Meat*, 2009
richard@happyretouching.com

Mute gratefully acknowledges the support of Arts Council England and the British Academy